Joel McCrea's
Film and Television Co-Stars
Volume II
From I to Z

David Alan Williams

Dedication

This book is dedicated to Joel McCrea and his many fans…

Acknowledgements

All thanks must first go to our Lord and Savior Jesus Christ, for without Him all are lost.

Many thanks to everyone involved in getting this book completed. My sincere appreciation goes to the folks on the audiemurphy.com message board for suggesting Joel McCrea as the subject of the next book in this series.

To www.findagrave.com, www.westernclippings.com, RKO Radio Pictures, RKO Pathé Pictures, Samuel Goldwyn Company, Metro-Goldwyn-Mayer (MGM), Film Booking Offices of America (FBO), Cosmopolitan Productions, Paramount Pictures, Twentieth Century Fox Film Corporation, Walter Wanger Productions, Allied Artists Pictures, Mirisch Corporation, Four Star Productions, National Broadcasting Company (NBC), Howard Productions, Columbia Pictures Corporation, Universal Pictures, Universal International Pictures, Raymond Stross Productions, Enterprise Productions, United Artists, Warner Brothers, Bronco Films, Liberty Entertainment Inc, www.aveleyman.com, www.childstarlets.com, www.imdb.com, Wikipedia, for their information, photographs, and films of Joel McCrea.

Thanks also to www.createspace.com.

Thanks to Joel McCrea himself.

Thanks to TCM-Turner Classic Movies.

Thanks also to author Tony Thomas for *Riding the High Country* and *Joel McCrea: A Film History*, and author Robert Nott for *Last of the Cowboy Heroes: The Westerns of Randolph Scott, Joel McCrea, and Audie Murphy*.

Any costar omitted is not intentional and purely the fault of the author.

Contents

Also by

David Alan Williams

Audie Murphy's Films & Television Co-Stars From A to Z

Audrey Hepburn's Films & Television Co-Stars From A to Z

Veronica Lake's Films & Television Co-Stars From A to Z

Audie Murphy Movie Lobby Cards

Alan Ladd's Films & Television Co-Stars Volume I From A to K

Alan Ladd's Films & Television Co-Stars Volume II From L to Z

Let's Never Forget: On This Day in Audie Murphy's Life

Joel McCrea's Films & Television Co-Stars Volume I From A to H

Introduction

Joel Albert McCrea was born in South Pasadena, California November 5, 1905 and was an American actor whose career spanned 50 years and appearances in over ninety films.

He was the son of Thomas McCrea, who was an executive with the L.A. Gas & Electric Company. As a boy, he had a paper route, and delivered the *Los Angeles Times* to Cecil B. DeMille and other people in the film industry. He also had the opportunity to watch D. W. Griffith filming *Intolerance*, and was an extra in a serial starring Ruth Roland.

McCrea graduated from Hollywood High School and then Pomona College (class of 1928), where he had acted on stage and took courses in drama and public speaking, and appeared regularly at the Pasadena Playhouse, Even as a high school student, he was working as a stunt double and held horses for cowboy stars William S. Hart and Tom Mix. He worked as an extra, stunt man and bit player from 1927 to 1928, when he signed a contract with MGM, where he was cast in a major role in *The Jazz Age* (1929), and got his first leading role that same year, in *The Silver Horde*. He moved to RKO in 1930, where he established himself as a handsome leading man who was considered versatile enough to star in both dramas and comedies.

In the 1930s, McCrea starred in *Bird of Paradise* (1932), directed by King Vidor, causing controversy for his nude scenes with Dolores del Río. In RKO's *The Sport Parade* (1932), McCrea and William Gargan are friends on the Dartmouth football team, who are shown snapping towels at each other in the locker room, while other players are taking a shower. In 1932 he starred with Fay Wray in *The Most Dangerous Game* - which used some of the same jungle sets built for *King Kong* as well as cast members Wray and Robert Armstrong. It is a very suspenseful film worth watching over and over again. A particularly funny scene, which wasn't supposed to be, was when the ship wrecks at the beginning and a man gets dragged under water to be eaten by sharks, the man says as he is being pulled under, "Oh, It got me!" a gruesome scene at the end is when the bad guy gets eaten by his own pack of starving dogs.

In 1934, he made his first appearances with two leading ladies he would be paired with often: with Miriam Hopkins he made *The Richest Girl in the World*, the first of their five films together, and with Barbara Stanwyck he appeared in *Gambling Lady*, the first of their six films. Later in the decade, he was the first actor to play "Dr. Kildare", in the film *Internes Can't Take Money* (1937), and he starred in two large-scale Westerns, *Wells Fargo* (1937) with his wife Frances Dee, and Cecil B. DeMille's *Union Pacific* (1939).

McCrea reached the peak of his early career in the early 1940s, in such films as Alfred Hitchcock's *Foreign Correspondent* (1940), *The More the Merrier* (1943) directed by George Stevens, and two by Preston Sturges, *Sullivan's Travels* (1941) with Veronica Lake, and *The Palm Beach Story* (1942).

McCrea also starred in two William A. Wellman Westerns, *The Great Man's Lady* (1942), again with Stanwyck, and *Buffalo Bill* (1944), with character actor Edgar Buchanan and a young Maureen O'Hara. After the success of *The Virginian* in 1946, McCrea made Westerns exclusively for the rest of his career, like *Ramrod* (1947) again with Veronica Lake, with the exception of the British-made *Rough Shoot* (1953), also known as *Shoot First*.

Performing in Westerns was a return to what he had done earlier in his career, and McCrea enjoyed the genre. In a 1978 interview, he said:

"I liked doing comedies, but as I got older I was better suited to do Westerns. Because I think it becomes unattractive for an older fellow trying to look young, falling in love with attractive girls in those kinds of situations...Anyway, I always felt so much more comfortable in the Western. The minute I got a horse and a hat and a pair of boots on, I felt easier. I didn't feel like I was an actor anymore. I felt like I was the guy out there doing it."

In the early 1950s, McCrea starred as Jace Pearson on the fifty-two episode radio series Western procedural police drama, *Tales of the Texas Rangers*.

Some of his great westerns of the 1950s included *Stars in My Crown* (1950) which was an amazing film with him playing a preacher who backs down a mob of KKK with a Bible, *Saddle Tramp* (1950) with Wanda Hendrix, *Frenchie* (1950) was a retelling of Max Brand's *Destry Rides Again*, *Cattle Drive* (1951), *The San Francisco Story* (1952), *The Lone Hand* (1953), *Border River* (1954) with Yvonne DeCarlo, *Black Horse Canyon* (1954), as Wyatt Earp in *Wichita* (1955), *Stranger on Horseback* (1955) which was a story by Louis L'amour, as Sam Houston in *The First Texan* (1956), *Trooper Hook* (1957), a wonderful western from Louis L'amour *The Tall Stranger* (1957), *The Oklahoman* (1957), *Gunsight Ridge* (1957), *Fort Massacre* (1958) with Susan Cabot, *Cattle Empire* (1958), and as Bat Masterson in *Gunfight at Dodge City* (1959).

In 1959, Joel McCrea and his son Jody McCrea starred in the NBC-TV series *Wichita Town*, which lasted only one season.

A few years later, McCrea united with fellow veteran of Westerns Randolph Scott in *Ride the High Country* (1962), directed by Sam Peckinpah, which was to be his last feature film for several years. 1970 saw the release of two films: *Cry Blood, Apache*, again with his son Jody. McCrea made his last film appearance in 1976, in *Mustang Country* with Patrick Wayne and Robert Fuller. I talked with Robert Fuller numerous times over the last ten years and one of the things we talked about was how he was a big fan of Joel McCrea and was just in awe of him, had so much respect for him, and loved working with him.

In 1968, McCrea received a career achievement award from the L.A. Film Critics Association, and the following year he was inducted into the Western Performers Hall of Fame at the National Cowboy & Western Heritage Museum in Oklahoma City, Oklahoma. For his contribution to the motion picture industry, Joel McCrea has a star on the Hollywood Walk of Fame at 6901 Hollywood Blvd. and another star at 6241 Hollywood Blvd. for his contribution to radio.

McCrea married actress Frances Dee in 1933, after they met while filming *The Silver Cord*. The couple had three children, David, who became a rancher; Peter, who became a real estate developer; and Jody, who became an actor. Joel and Frances remained married until his death — spending 57 years together.

According to David Ragan's *Stars of the '30s*, the McCreas were prodigious savers, accumulating a large estate, which included working-ranch properties. Joel McCrea's work ethic was in part attributed to his Scottish heritage and it also may have stemmed from his friendship in the 1930s with fellow personality and sometime actor, Will Rogers. McCrea recounted that "the Oklahoma Sage" gave him a profound piece of advice: "Save half of what you make, and live on just the other half."

McCrea – who was an outdoorsman who had once listed his occupation as "rancher" and his hobby as "acting" – had begun buying property as early as 1933, when he purchased his first 1,000 acres in a then-unincorporated area of eastern Ventura County, California, which later became Thousand Oaks, California. This was the beginning of what became a 3,000-acre spread on which McCrea and his wife Frances lived, raised their children, and rode their horses.

By the end of the 1940s, McCrea was a multi-millionaire, as much from his real-estate dealings as from his movie stardom. In the late 1960s, he sold 1,200 acres of land to an oil company, on the condition that they would not drill within sight of his home.

The McCrea's ultimately donated several hundred acres of their personal property to the newly formed Conejo Valley YMCA for the city of Thousand Oaks, California. Today, the Conejo Valley YMCA is located in "Joel McCrea Park".

Joel McRea was the subject of an episode of Ralph Edwards' *This is Your Life* in 1972.

Joel McCrea made his final public appearance on October 3, 1990, at a fundraiser for Republican gubernatorial candidate Pete Wilson in Beverly Hills. He died less than three weeks later, on October 20, in Woodland Hills, California from pneumonia, at the age of 84.

The Joel McCrea ranch was listed on the National Register of Historic Places in 1997, with eight buildings and four contributing structures over 220 acres. The home has recently had its grand opening as a museum by Joel's grandson Wyatt McCrea.

Scarlet River and *The Hollywood Story* are not included, as he appeared as himself and did not act as a character.

Which co-star..............

1. Raised pineapples in Guatemala?
2. Was tried and acquitted for attempted murder at age nine?
3. Was a successful dentist?
4. Posed for the August 1984 issue of *Playboy* at age 55?
5. Worked as an animator at Disney Studios on such classics as Fantasia and Bambi?
6. Joined the army at age fourteen and served with the expedition that pursued Pancho Villa into Mexico?
7. Died after slipping and falling through a glass shower door in his home July 30, 1980, at age 66?
8. Changed his professional name to that of his characters' name in his first movie?
9. Was the basis that Looney Toons animator Chuck Jones based the character of Pepe le Pew, the romantic skunk, on his most well-known performance?
10. Worked for the Office of Strategic Services (OSS), the predecessor of the CIA?
11. Became the first African American to have a regular role on a nationwide radio program?
12. Held a master's degree in drama from the University of Iowa?
13. Was at the time noted as being the youngest stage director in America?
14. Graduated with an engineering degree from the California Polytechnic State University?
15. At the age of 14, he stowed away on a boat and came to America?
16. Was the first actor to portray Rex Stout's famous detective Nero Wolfe, starring in *Meet Nero Wolfe* (1936), the film based on the first novel in the series?
17. Was also the co-founder of the I Am An American Foundation?
18. Reputed to have been the first motion picture actor to have been recruited from the stage?
19. Was married to Torbert MacDonald, an eleven-term Massachusetts Congressman who was John F. Kennedy's roommate at Harvard University, and who remained a close friend and confidant throughout his life?
20. Was the 21st Lieutenant Governor of Nevada?
21. Was a 1928 Olympic silver medalist in the shot put?
22. Became a grandmother at age 39, similar to her co-star Elizabeth Taylor who became a grandmother at the same age (she and Taylor also shared a February 27 birthday, and each gave birth to one of their children on their birthdays)?
23. And her husband Frank Gilbert ran one of the first successful programs for breeding cheetahs in captivity?
24. Appears in more of the films on both the original and the tenth anniversary edition of the American Film Institute's 100 Years... 100 Movies lists than any other actor?
25. Last husband was the vaudeville actor Harry Fox for whom the foxtrot dance was named?
26. During the Irish War of Independence (1919–1922), was part of an IRA Active Service Unit as early as 1920, carrying out IRA directives? He fled with a bounty set on his head by the British, although he claimed only to have been a courier for guerrilla leader and tactician Michael Collins.
27. Accompanied by noted actor Gary Cooper, Phyllis was the first civilian woman to travel to the Pacific theater of war during World War II, on a USO tour?
28. Her eldest child was President John F. Kennedy's godson?
29. Outlasted every comedian on the Columbia payroll except The Three Stooges?
30. On her gravestone, just beneath her dates of birth and death, is written "Christian Actress"?
31. Career hit bottom in the 1950s, and he took work as a department-store Santa Claus to make ends meet?
32. With the help of his friend and actor Russell Hayden, Curtis helped develop Pioneertown, a western movie set location in Southern California that was used for many television and film westerns?
33. Lived in "The biggest house on the beach – the beach between San Diego and Vancouver"?
34. Likeness was drawn in caricature by Alex Gard for Sardi's, the New York City theater district restaurant. The picture is now part of the collection of the New York Public Library?
35. Had a street and a cow named after her by American Doughboys in France?
36. Was present at Disneyland on "Dedication Day" in 1955 and was asked by Walt Disney to christen the Mark Twain River Boat, which she did with a bottle filled with water from several major rivers across the United States?
37. On leaving school, became a salesman of bootleg whiskey to New York speakeasies and then joined a detective agency?

38. Ventures into real estate were particularly successful (at one point she owned four different major office buildings in Los Angeles, each of them named after her)?

39. Composed the lyrics to the Redskins fight song "Hail to the Redskins" which became one of the most famous football anthems.

40. Studied to be an opera singer and also had successes as an inventor? Among his innovations were the folding theatre-seat, the hand fire extinguisher, and greaseless potato chips.

41. In 1931, he took out insurance against premature aging that might be caused by his fright make-up?

42. As a child model, her image had appeared in so many different advertisements by the time she was nine years old that *Film Daily* called her "the most photographed child in America due to commercial posing?"

43. In 1952, he was hailed in Paris as that city's most influential American painter?

44. Was a light-heavyweight boxer and once went fourteen rounds with Jack Dempsey?

45. Died December 4, 1937 in Los Angeles, California after being hit by a limousine driven by a chauffeur working for Jack Warner?

46. Is credited with coining the name "The Blob" for the movie, which was originally titled "The Molten Meteor."

47. Was the first Hungarian actor to make a film in the United States?

48. Was the first woman president of a scheduled airline in the US?

49. In 1907, she was named "Most beautiful woman in America"?

50. Served in the United States Navy, having been the model for naval recruitment posters during World War II?

51. Was killed by a bull on the family farm?

52. In 1940, at age 78, she went to Hollywood, where she began her acting career and continued acting until she was 97?

53. Directed the first motion picture ever in Hollywood in 1909, entitled *Justified*?

54. Attended Cornell University, where he graduated with a degree in engineering, and after graduation he taught mathematics, including six years as an instructor at Cornell?

55. Wanted, at one point in his career, to play romantic leads instead of tough "heavies" and to that end, he sought to have plastic surgery performed on his broken nose? Executives at United Artists successfully obtained a restraining order against him from doing so, however.

56. While managing an apartment on September 16, 1957, the La Brea District Apartments, a disgruntled houseboy strangled her with the cord of her blue silk dressing gown?

57. Was on his way back to Britain from America in 1939 with the intention of joining the armed forces when the ship on which he was traveling was captured by Nazis and he spent five years in a German P.O.W.?

58. Father committed suicide in 1922 by jumping off the Brooklyn Bridge?

59. Took an unpaid position as consultant and coach to President Eisenhower, advising him on how to look his best in his television appearances before the nation? A pioneering media consultant, he had an office in the White House during this time.

60. Was orphaned at the age of four and partially raised in foster homes, but by 1944 had become the highest-paid woman in the United States?

To find the fascinating answers to these exciting trivia questions, simply read the book............

I hope you enjoy learning about these folks as much as I did.

DW

John Ince, also known as John E. Ince, was born August 29, 1878 and was an American stage and motion pictures actor, a film director, and the eldest brother of Thomas and Ralph Ince. A leading man from the early 1910s, he also directed and scripted several of his own vehicles. Concentrating almost exclusively on directing from 1915 through 1928, Ince returned before the cameras as a character actor in the early years of the talkies.

Some of his roles including *Hour of Reckoning* (1927), *Wild West Whoopee* (1931), *Destry Rides Again* (1932), *One Man's Journey* (1933) with Joel McCrea, *Gambling Lady* (1934) again with Joel McCrea, *Barbary Coast* (1935) a third with Joel McCrea, *Special Agent K-7* (1936), *Way Out West* (1937) with Laurel and Hardy, *Termites of 1938* (1938) with The Three Stooges, *Mr. Smith Goes to Washington* (1939), *Dude Cowboy* (1941), *A Scream in the Dark* (1943), *The Best Years of Our Lives* (1946), *That's My Gal* (1947), and *Gun Cargo* released in 1949.

He died April 10, 1947 at age 68 in Hollywood, Los Angeles, California.

Ralph Ince

Ralph Waldo Ince was born in Boston, Massachusetts January 16, 1887 and was an American pioneer film actor, director, and screenwriter whose career began near the dawn of the silent film era. Ralph Ince was the brother of film trailblazers John Ince and Thomas H. Ince.

He was the younger of three sons and a daughter raised by English immigrants, John and Emma Ince. Sometime after his birth Ince moved to Manhattan where his entire family was engaged in theater work; his father as a musical agent and mother, sister Bertha and brothers, John and Thomas as actors. Ralph Ince studied art with cartoonist Dan McCarthy and for a while worked as a newspaper cartoonist for the New York World and later magazine illustrator for the New York Mirror and The Evening Telegram. At times over his acting and directing career Ince would continue to contribute cartoons to popular magazines of the day. Early on in his career Ince, who had done some stage acting as a child, was a member of Richard Mansfield's stock company playing parts in *The College Widow* and *Ben Hur.*

Around 1906 Ince became an animator in the fledgling film industry working for Winsor McCay, but soon turned to acting and joined Vitagraph Studios where he became known for his portrayals of Abraham Lincoln in a series of one reel films. Ince began directing at Vitagraph around 1910 and was officially advanced to the director's chair in 1912, though he still continued to act in many of his films and throughout his career. Ince would go on to direct some 171 films between 1910 and 1937 and appear in approximately 110 films over nearly the same time period.

Ince married three times, first to Vitagraph player Lucille Lee Stewart, sister of actress Anita Stewart. Their fifteen-year marriage ended in 1925, two years after she had left him. The following year he married Lucille Mendez, a stage and screen actress. This union ended in 1932 after Mendez claimed Ince damaged her career by not allowing her to accept certain job offers. Ince's last wife was Helen Ruth Tigges, a native of Frazee, Minnesota. She was the mother of his only child born just months before his death at age 50.

Some of his film roles included *Not for Publication* (1927), *Wall Street* (1929), *Little Caesar* (1931), *The Lost Squadron* (1932) with Joel McCrea, *Men of America* (1932), *Blue Smoke* (1935), and *The Perfect Crime* (1937).

Ralph Ince died on April 10, 1937 when a car his wife was driving struck an iron standard near their residence in the Kensington district of London, England. The force of the impact, though not great, proved fatal to Ince when his head struck the dashboard. Helen Ince suffered cuts and bruises that required hospitalization. Ince and his wife had moved to Britain shortly after they had married in 1932 to continue his film work there.

14

Teddy Infuhr

Teddy Infuhr was born Theodore Edward Infuhr in St. Louis, Missouri November 9, 1936 and was an American child actor.

Teddy Infuhr, youngest of four, moved with his family to Los Angeles when he was three and was initially prodded into acting by his mother. A young student at the Rainbow Studios, he was spotted by a talent agent and booked the very first film he went out on with *The Tuttles of Tahiti* (1942) at the age of five. Throughout the rest of the 1940s he would find steady roles as mean-spirited tykes, trouble-makers or bullying types, never settling down to one specific studio.

A good portion of his work was noticeable yet he also appeared unbilled much of the time. Unable to move into the major child star leagues, he was cast in some of the biggest pictures Hollywood had to offer including *A Tree Grows in Brooklyn, Spellbound,* and *The Best Years of Our Lives.* One of his more oddball roles included the role of Gale Sondergaard's fly-catching nephew in *The Spider Woman.*

Ted found a recurring role in the "Rusty" canine adventure series, beginning with *The Return of Rusty* and finishing with *Rusty's Birthday.* He was also one of the bucolic brood in the Ma and Pa Kettle series that was introduced with the classic *The Egg and I.* He appeared more times in that series than any other of the regular child stars.

After the war, he had larger parts in *The Boy with Green Hair, Fighting Fools, West of El Dorado* and *Blondie's Hero* and appeared with Gene Autry a few times.

One of the few child actors that Natalie Wood's mother allowed her to socialize with on the set.

For his role in *The North Star,* Teddy had to shave his head bald. The embarrassed 7-year-old returned to school wearing a hat and refused to remove it to the dismay of his teachers until they found out the reason.

More of his roles included *Pardon My Sarong* (1942) with Abbott and Costello, *The Virginian* (1946) with Joel McCrea, *Phantom Valley* (1948), *Gene Autry and The Mounties* (1951), *The Cisco Kid* (1952), *The Abbott and Costello Show* (1953), and *Men of the Fighting Lady* (1954).

Unfortunately, he did not survive the transition from awkward adolescent to adult, ending his career unbilled as a troubled teen in *Blackboard Jungle* (1955). Luckily, Teddy played it smart, and found a vocation, graduating from chiropractic school in 1958. Long married to wife Rita, with whom he had two sons, he has had no qualms or regrets about leaving show business. Until his death in Thousand Oaks on May 12, 2007 at age 70, he attended nostalgia conventions.

Jack Ingram

Jack Ingram was born John Samuel Ingram in Frankfort, Illinois, November 15, 1902, and was an American film actor. He appeared in over 300 films between 1935 and 1966.

A WWI veteran who later studied law at the University of Texas, tough-looking Jack Ingram began his long show business career as a minstrel player and later reportedly toured with Mae West. He began turning up playing scruffy henchmen and assorted other B-Western villains in the mid-'30s and was later the featured heavy in *Columbia* serials.

Ingram would go on to appear in a total of 200 Westerns and approximately fifty serials in a career that later included appearances on many television programs. Many of his later films and almost all his television westerns, were filmed on Ingram's own 200-acre ranch on Mulholland Drive in the Santa Monica Mountains overlooking Woodland Hills, which he had purchased from Charles Chaplin in 1944 and which remains a wilderness today.

He first appeared in *Westward Ho* (1935), and then worked steadily in films like *Winds of the Wasteland* (1936), *Gunsmoke Ranch* (1937), *The Arizona Kid* (1939), *The Green Archer* (1940), *West of Texas* (1943), *Ghost Guns* (1944), *Superman* (1948), *Atom Man vs. Superman* (1950), Frenchie (1950) with Joel McCrea, *Lost in Alaska* (1952) with Abbott & Costello, *Man Without a Star* (1955), *Utah Blaine* (1957), and *A Big Hand for the Little Lady* (1966).

He also had roles in *The Kid From Texas* (1950), *Sierra* (1950), *The Cimarron Kid* (1952), and *Column South* (1953), all with Audie Murphy.

Some of his television appearances were in *The Range Rider* (1951-1953), *The Adventures of Kit Carson* (1951-1953), *The Lone Ranger* (1950-1953), *Hopalong Cassidy* (1954), *The Cisco Kid* (1950-1954), *Buffalo Bill, Jr.* (1955), and *Tales of Wells Fargo* (1958).

He died February 20, 1969, in Canoga Park, California of a heart attack. He is interred in the Oakwood Memorial Park Cemetery in Chatsworth, California.

Jean Inness

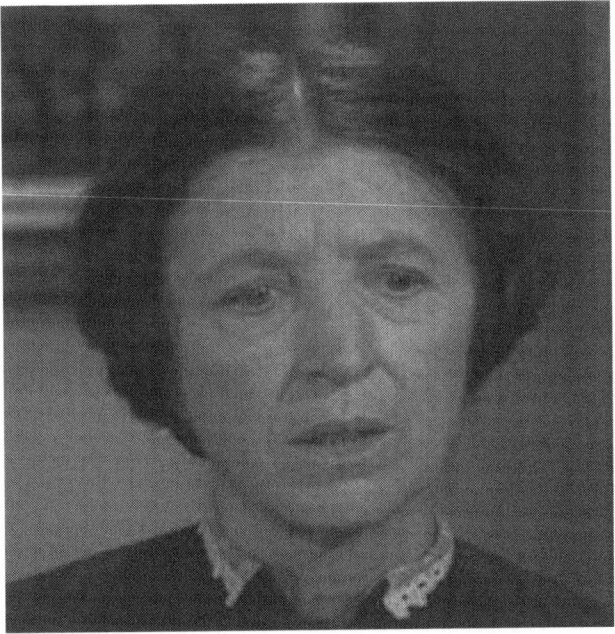

Jean Inness was born on December 18, 1900 in Cleveland, Ohio. She was an actress, known for *Edge of Doom* (1950), *The Story of Ruth* (1960), and *Dr. Kildare* (1961),

More of her roles included *Yankee Doodle Dandy* (1942), *The Gunfighter* (1950), *Space Patrol* (1954), *Friendly Persuasion* (1957), *Wichita Town* (1959) with Joel McCrea, *Twilight Zone* (1961), *Have Gun - Will Travel* (1962), *The Andy Griffith Show* (1965), *Rosemary's Baby* (1968), and *Love, American Style* (1971).

She was married to Victor Jory from December 23, 1928 until her death on December 27, 1978 at age 78 in Santa Monica, California.

Ellis Irving

Ellis Irving was born in Sydney, New South Wales, Australia January 6, 1902 and was a film actor who appeared in a number of British films.

Some of his roles included *The Bermondsey Kid* (1933), *The Black Mask* (1935), *Member of the Jury* (1937), *The Sea Hawk* (1940), *Strawberry Roan* (1944), *Green Fingers* (1947), *Pool of London* (1951), *Shoot First* (1953) with Joel McCrea, *Strictly Confidential* (1959), and *The Patriots* (1960).

He was married to the actress Sophie Stewart. He died March 27, 1983 at age 81 in Australia.

George Irving

George Henry Irving was born in New York City, New York October 5, 1874 and was an American film actor and director who made over 200 films from 1914 until his retirement in 1954.

Irving was initially an Actor-director, until he switched exclusively to acting in the mid 1920s and became a character actor until the later 1940s. He mostly played reputable and stern persons in films. He is best known for his roles as lawyer Peabody in *Bringing Up Baby* (1938) and as Robert Wentworth in *Coquette* (1929).

More of his roles included *Paid in Full* (1914), *Wanderer of the Wasteland* (1924), *Dance Hall* (1929), *Expensive Women* (1931), *Island of Lost Souls* (1932) with Alan Ladd, *Manhattan Melodrama* (1934), *The Outcasts of Poker Flat* (1937), *Sergeant York* (1941), *The Great Man's Lady* (1942) with Joel McCrea, *Son of Dracula* (1943), *Magic Town* (1947), and *Omnibus* (1954).

George Irving and his wife, Katherine Gilman, had two daughters, Katharine and Dorothy. He died from a heart attack in Hollywood in September 11, 1961, at age 86.

Victor Izay

Victor Izay was born on December 23, 1923 in Watertown, New York. He was an actor, known for *Billy Jack* (1971), *Employee of the Month* (2006), and *Wild Hogs* (2007).

He served as a sergeant during World War II in the Armored Corps, 486 Ordnance Evacuation Company (tank recovery unit). He was involved in the D-Day landing. After the war, he enrolled at Los Angeles City College, studying along drama alongside Victor French and Vic Tayback (the trio calling themselves 'The Three Vics')

Some of his roles included *The Westerner* (1960), *Ride the High Country* (1962) with Joel McCrea, *Dr. Sex* (1964), *The Astro-Zombies* (1968), *The D.A.* (1971), *Blood Orgy of the She-Devils* (1973), *Mannix* (1969-1974), *Gunsmoke* (1965-1974), *S.W.A.T.* (1975), *Future Cop* (1977), *T.J. Hooker* (1982), *Young Guns* (1988), *Brotherhood of the Gun* (1991), *Gunsmoke: The Long Ride* (1993), and *Assassin Emeritus* (2008).

He was married to Jo Roybal and Connie Izay. He died on January 20, 2014 in Glendora, California at age 90.

Jenie Jackson

Jenie Jackson was born on November 27, 1921 in California. She was an actress, known for *Ride the High Country* (1962) with Joel McCrea, *How Sweet It Is!* (1968), and *Imago* (1970).

Her other roles were *The Great Adventure* (1964), *The Lucy Show* (1965), *The Wild Wild West* (1966), *Winchester 73* (1967), *Justine* (1969), and *Hello, Dolly!* (1969).

She died on March 14, 1976 in Hollywood, California at age 54.

Selmer Jackson

Joel McCrea and Selmer Jackson in *Espionage Agent*

Selmer Jackson was born in Lake Mills, Iowa May 7, 1888 and was an American film actor. He appeared in nearly 400 films between 1921 and 1963.

More of his roles included *Thru Different Eyes* (1929), *Two Against the World* (1932), *The Richest Girl in the World* (1934) with Joel McCrea, *Revolt of the Zombies* (1936), *Charlie Chan at the Olympics* (1937), *The Law West of Tombstone* (1938), *Union Pacific* (1939), again with Joel McCrea, *Espionage Agent* (1939) a third with Joel McCrea, *Buck Privates* (1941), *It Ain't Hay* (1943), *The Time of Their Lives* (1946), *The Cobra Strikes* (1948), *Gunmen of Abilene* (1950), *Jack McCall, Desperado* (!953), *Annie Oakley* (1955), *Adventures of Superman* (1952-1956), *The Life and Legend of Wyatt Earp* (1956-1957), *Alfred Hitchcock Presents* (1958-1961), and *The Alfred Hitchcock Hour* (1963).

He died March 30, 1971 in Burbank, California from a heart attack at age 82.

Bud Jamison

Bud Jamison was born William Edward Jaimison in Vallejo, California February 15, 1895 and was an American film actor. He appeared in 492 films between 1915 and 1944.

Jamison joined the ranks of stage and vaudeville performers making movies in California. Jamison's husky build and willingness to participate in messy slapstick and rowdy action guaranteed him work in silent comedies. In 1915 he was a member of Charlie Chaplin's stock company at the Essanay studio. From there he moved to the Hal Roach studio, playing hot-tempered comic foils for Harold Lloyd, Snub Pollard, and Stan Laurel. In the 1920s he joined Universal Pictures' short-comedy contingent, and later worked in Mack Sennett comedies. In his earliest films Bud Jamison looked too young to be totally convincing in heavy makeup as a veteran policeman, detective, or authority figure. As the years progressed, he grew into these roles, and by the time sound movies arrived he was well established as a reliable character comedian.

Jamison had a superb tenor singing voice, and loved to sing when the cameras were not rolling. Talking pictures gave producers a chance to exploit his singing, and for the rest of his career he would occasionally be called upon to vocalize in films. A brief series of color travelogues, filmed in 1930, featured Bud Jamison and comic Jimmie Adams as "The Rolling Stones," two singing vagabonds seeing the country. Jamison would even be hired just for his singing, as in *Pot o' Gold* where he plays a vagrant who harmonizes in jail. He also sings "You'll Never Know Just What Tears Are" in The Three Stooges short, *A Ducking They Did Go* (1939)

For the most part Jamison continued to play cops, robbers, bosses, servants, and various professional men who clash with comedy stars. He appeared opposite Bing Crosby, W. C. Fields, and Andy Clyde in Sennett's talkies. Like other members of the two-reel-comedy community, he found work at various studios: Hal Roach (with Thelma Todd and ZaSu Pitts, and Charley Chase). Educational Pictures (with Buster Keaton), RKO Radio Pictures (with Clark & McCullough, Leon Errol, and Edgar Kennedy), and Columbia Pictures (with Keaton, Clyde, Chase, Harry Langdon, and the Three Stooges, among many others). Jamison is best known for his Columbia Stooge shorts. including their debut, *Woman Haters* (1934)(in which Jamison speaks in verse, as the head of the Woman Haters Club).

Moe Howard of the Stooges (who referred to Jamison as "Buddy Jamison") fondly recalled singing barbershop harmony with Charley Chase, actor Vernon Dent, and Jamison many times on movie sets.

Some of his many roles included *Mustaches and Bombs* (1915), *Lonesome Luke on Tin Can Alley* (1917), *Kicking the Germ Out of Germany* (1918), *Do You Love Your Wife?* (1919), *Loose Lions and Fast Lovers* (1920), *Brownie's Little Venus* (1921), *One Horse Town* (1922), *Monkeying Around* (1923), *Troubles of a Bride* (1924), *Two Lips in Holland* (1926), *Birthday Greetings* (1927), *His Unlucky Night* (1928), *He Trumped Her Ace* (1930), *The Pottsville Palooka* (1931), *Speed in the Gay Nineties* (1932), *Don't Play Bridge with Your Wife* (1933), *Dora's Dunking Doughnuts* (1933), *A Very Honorable Guy* (1934), *The Whole Town's Talking* (1935), *The Captain Hits the Ceiling* (1935), *All-American Toothache* (1936), *A Pain in the Pullman* (1936), *Come and Get It* (1936) with Joel McCrea, *Whoops, I'm an Indian!* (1936), *The Wrong Miss Wright* (1937), *Murder in Greenwich Village* (1937), *Violent Is the Word for Curly* (1938), *Blondie* (1938), *Three Little Sew and Sews* (1939), *A Plumbing We Will Go* (1940), *Captain Caution* (1940) with Alan Ladd, *The Monster and the Girl* (1941), *All the World's a Stooge* (1941), *Time Out for Rhythm* (1941), *Yankee Doodle Andy* (1941), *I'll Never Heil Again* (1941), *Wild Bill Hickok Rides* (1942), *You Can't Escape Forever* (1942), *Three Little Twirps* (1943), *Lost in a Harem* (1944) with Abbott and Costello, and *Incendiary Blonde* (1945).

Jamison suffered from diabetes during his later years. A devout Christian Scientist, he died on September 30, 1944 at age 49 after refusing treatment for kidney cancer.

He is buried in Inglewood Park Cemetery in Inglewood, California.

Lois January

Lois January was born Laura Lois January in McAllen, Texas October 5, 1913 and was an American actress who performed small roles in several B-movies during the 1930s.

Her first credited role was in 1933, in the film *UM-PA*. Her most famous role, however, although she never achieved name recognition, is probably as the Emerald City manicurist in *The Wizard of Oz* (1939) who sings to Dorothy that "we can make a dimpled smile out of a frown" and, later in the same film, as the woman holding a cat which causes Toto to jump out of the hot air balloon just before it departs leaving Dorothy apparently stranded.

January had many roles during her Hollywood career. During the 1930s she played in numerous westerns as the heroine, usually opposite Johnny Mack Brown, Bob Steele, Tim McCoy, and Bob Baker, among others. In 1935 she starred opposite Joel McCrea in *Splendor*, Reb Russell in *Arizona Badman*, and in 1936 she starred with Brown in *Rogue of the Range*, and alongside Tim McCoy in *Border Cabellero*. While on contract with Universal Pictures she continued to play heroine roles in westerns, and in 1937 she starred opposite Bob Baker in *Courage of the West*. The reissuing of the 1935 exploitation film *The Pace That Kills* (under the title *Cocaine Fiends*) would eventually lend January even more exposure, however limited.

Her career slowed in the way of starring roles by the mid-1940s, but she continued to act. In 1942 she was the "poster girl" for Chesterfield cigarettes. From 1960 through 1987 she played numerous small roles on television, to include roles on *My Three Sons* (1960-1971), *Bridget Loves Bernie* (1972), *Kolchak: The Night Stalker* (1974), and *Marcus Welby, M.D.* (1972-1976). Her last acting role was in 1987, on the television movie *Double Agent*. During the 1980s she attended several western film festivals.

She died in Los Angeles, California of Alzheimer's disease on August 7, 2006, at age 92.

Maurice Jara

Maurice Jara was born Saul R. Jara December 15, 1922, in Los Angeles County, California. He appeared in thirty-five films and television programs from 1950 to 1972. Some of his film roles were in movies such as *The Lawless* (1950), *Flying Leathernecks* (1951), *Tropic Zone* (1953), *Fighter Attack* (1953), *Drum Beat* (1954), *The First Texan* (1956) with Joel McCrea, *Walk the Proud Land* (1956), *Giant* (1956), *The Lone Ranger and the Lost City of Gold* (1958), and his last film *They Came to Cordura* (1959). He appeared in television programs like *Sky King* (1952), *Boston Blackie* (1953), *Ramar of the Jungle* (1954), *Adventures of Superman* (1955), *Broken Arrow* (1957), *Rawhide* (1959), *Lawman* (1960), *Ben Casey* (1963), *Marcus Welby, M.D.* (1970), and his last role in *Hec Ramsey* (1972).

He died July 23, 1995, age 72 in San Jacinto, California.

Claude Jarman, Jr.

Joel McCrea and Claude Jarman, Jr. in *The Outriders*

Claude Jarman, Jr. was born in Nashville, Tennessee born September 27, 1934 and is an American former child actor.

Jarman was ten years old and in the fifth grade in Nashville, Tennessee when he was discovered in a nationwide talent search by MGM Studios, and was cast as the lead actor in the film *The Yearling* (1946). His performance received glowing reviews and he was awarded with an Academy Juvenile Award as a result.

More of his early roles included *High Barbaree* (1947), *Roughshod* (1949), *The Outriders* (1950) Joel McCRea, *Rio Grande* (1950) with John Wayne, Hangman's Knot (1952) with Randolph Scott, and Fair Wind to Java (1953).

He continued his studies at the MGM studio school, but MGM was finding him increasingly difficult to cast, and by the time he reached his late teens his career was virtually over. Republic Studios cast him in a couple of B-movies, but discouraged, he moved back to Tennessee to finish high school.

Following coursework in pre-law at Vanderbilt University, Jarman appeared in Walt Disney's *The Great Locomotive Chase* (1956), which was his final movie. After that, he served three years in the U.S. Navy doing public relations work. He appeared in a couple other television roles such as *Wagon Train* (1959) and *The Best of the Post* (1960).

He returned to acting with a role on an episode of the television production *Centennial* (1978). Jarman was a special guest as a past award winner at both the 1998 and 2003 Academy Awards Ceremonies. Later, he moved to working behind the scenes, and had success as a producer and film festival executive producer, as well as serving as Director of Cultural Affairs for the city of San Francisco. He has seven children with three wives, including two daughters with his current wife Katherine.

Enid Jaynes

Enid Jaynes was born Enid Gay Yousen on August 12, 1935 in Nebraska. She is an actress, known for *The Rifleman* (1959-1962), *Geronimo* (1962), and *Brannigan* (1975).

More of her roles included *Wichita Town* (1960) with Joel McCrea, *Johnny Ringo* (1960), *Wanted: Dead or Alive* (1961), *Have Gun - Will Travel* (1963), *The Donna Reed Show* (1965), *The Big Valley* (!967), and *Cannon* (1974).

She was previously married to Sanford Shapero and Jules V. Levy.

Isabel Jeans

Isabel Jeans was born in London, England September 16, 1891 and was an English stage and film actress known for her roles in several Alfred Hitchcock films and her portrayal of Aunt Alicia in the 1958 musical film *Gigi*, among others. Jeans was the daughter of an art critic.

She planned to become a singer but began her career on the London stage in 1908 at age 15, at the invitation of Herbert Beerbohm Tree. An early Broadway appearance was in *The Man Who Married a Dumb Wife* in January 1915 and as Titania in *A Midsummer Night's Dream* in February 1915. She played Lady Mercia Merivale in the London musical hit *Kissing Time* (1919). She appeared in a production of James Elroy Flecker's *Hassan* at His Majesty's Theatre in London in 1923. Incidental music for the play was by Frederick Delius, and the ballet in the House-of-the-Moving Walls was created by Fokine. In 1924, she appeared in Ivor Novello's play *The Rat* at the Prince of Wales's Theatre in London. The following year, she was in Richard Brinsley Sheridan's play, *The Rivals* at the Lyric Theatre, Hammersmith, together with Claude Rains, his ex-wife Marie Hemingway, and his then-current wife, Beatrix Thomson.

She appeared in major roles in two Alfred Hitchcock silent films, *Downhill* (1927) and *Easy Virtue* (1928) and various other British films, before playing a number of grande dames in Hollywood films starting in 1937, such as *Youth Takes a Fling* (!938) with Joel McCrea, Hitchcock's *Suspicion* (1941), as well as in such films as *Banana Ridge* (1942), *Gigi* (1958). and *A Breath of Scandal* (1960).

Later stage roles included a revival of *The Happy Hypocrite* in London in 1936. Later Broadway roles were Crystal Wetherby in *The Man in Possession* in 1930 and Mrs. Emmeline Lucas in *Make Way for Lucia* in 1948. English productions included Anton Chekhov's plays, *The Seagull*, (1949 at the Lyric Theatre, London and then St. James's Theatre), Jean Anouilh's play, "Ardele" (1951 at the Vaudeville Theatre), Noël Coward's play, *The Vortex* (1952 at the Lyric Theatre in Hammersmith), T.S. Eliot's play, *The Confidential Clerk* (1953 at the Lyric Theatre), and William Congreve's play, *The Double Dealer* (1959 at the Old Vic Theatre, and other plays there that season, with Judi Dench). She also acted in West End productions of plays by Oscar Wilde, including *Lady Windermere's Fan* (1945 at the Haymarket Theatre, directed by Sir John Gielgud; and 1966 at the Phoenix Theatre (London)), *A Woman of No Importance* (1953 at the Savoy Theatre) and as Lady Bracknell in *The Importance of Being Earnest* (1968 at the Haymarket Theatre).

Jeans' brother Desmond was an actor and boxer, while her sister Ursula became a respected character actress and married the actor Roger Livesey.

She was married twice: first to the actor Claude Rains, from 1913 to 1918; and then to the barrister and playwright Gilbert Edward "Gilley" Wakefield, from 1920 until his death in 1963. She enjoyed horse racing and poker.

She died September 4, 1985 at age 93 in London, England.

Allen Jenkins

Joel McCrea and Allen Jenkins in *Dead End*

Allen Jenkins was born David Allen Curtis Jenkins in Staten Island, New York April 9, 1900 and was an American character actor who worked on stage, screen, and in television.

He studied at the American Academy of Dramatic Arts. In his first stage appearance, he danced next to James Cagney in a chorus line for an off-Broadway musical called *Pitter-Patter*, earning five dollars a week. He also appeared in Broadway plays between 1923 and 1962, including *The Front Page* (1928). His big break came when he replaced Spencer Tracy for three weeks in the Broadway play *The Last Mile*.

Jenkins was called to Hollywood by Darryl F. Zanuck and signed first to Paramount Pictures and shortly afterward to Warner Bros. His first role in films came in 1931, when he appeared as an ex-convict in the short *Straight and Narrow*. He had originated the character of Frankie Wells in the Broadway production of *Blessed Event* and reprised the role in its film adaptation, both in 1932. With the advent of talking pictures, he made a career out of playing comic henchmen, stooges, policemen, taxi drivers, and other 'tough guys' in numerous films of the 1930s and 1940s, especially for Warner Bros. Allen Jenkins was labeled the "greatest scene-stealer of the 1930s" by *The New York Times*.

Some more of his roles include *I Am a Fugitive from a Chain Gang* (1932), *The Mayor of Hell* (1933), *The Case of the Howling Dog* (1934), *Three Men on a Horse* (1936), *Dead End* (1937), *Destry Rides Again* (1939), *My Wife's an Angel* (1943), *Wonder Man* (1945), *Wild Harvest* (1947) with Alan Ladd, *Bodyhold* (1949), *The Abbott and Costello Show* (1953), *I Love Lucy* (1952-1953), *Hey, Jeannie!* (1956–1957), *Pillow Talk* (1959), he voiced the character of Officer Dibble on the Hanna-Barbera TV cartoon, *Top Cat* (1961–62), *The Red Skelton Show* (1954-1962), *It's a Mad, Mad, Mad, Mad World* (1963), *Robin and the 7 Hoods* (1964), *Batman* (1967), *Adam-12* (1971), *Bewitched* (1971-1972), and *Police Story* (1974).

Eleven days before his death, he made his final appearance, at the end of Billy Wilder's remake of *The Front Page* (1974).

He went public with his alcoholism and was the first actor to speak in the U.S. House of Representatives and the Senate about it. He helped start the first Alcoholics Anonymous programs in California prisons for women.

Jenkins, James Cagney, Pat O'Brien, and Frank McHugh were the original members of the so-called 'Irish Mafia'. He was the seventh member of the Screen Actors Guild.

He died of lung cancer early on the morning of July 20, 1974 at age 74.

Megs Jenkins

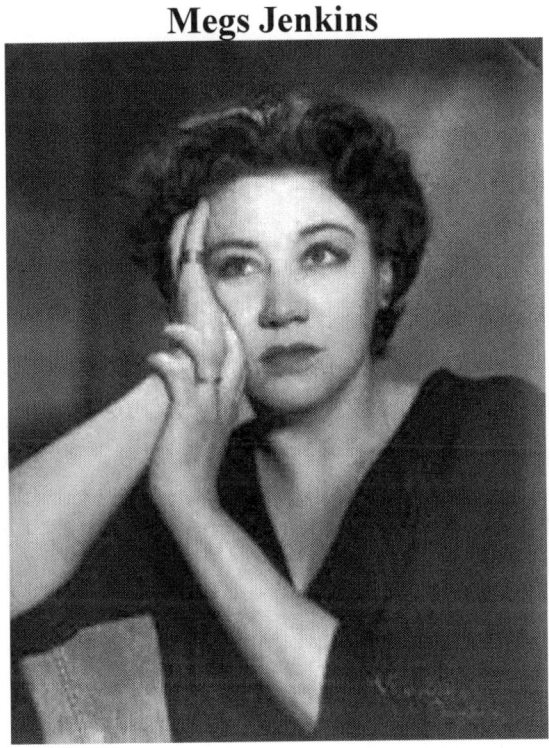

Muguette Mary "Megs" Jenkins was born in Birkenhead, Cheshire, England April 21, 1917 and was an English character actress who appeared in British films and television programs.

She was the daughter of a construction engineer. She originally trained to be a ballet dancer. Although born in England, she often played Welsh characters.

She made her first noticeable film debut in 1943 in *Millions Like Us* appearing as the main character's (Patricia Roc playing Celia Crowsonher) Welsh room-mate and confidante. She appeared in such classics as *Green for Danger* (1946), in which she turned out to be the twin sister of a Nazi collaborator, *The History of Mr. Polly* (1949), *Secret People* (1952) with Audrey Hepburn, *The Cruel Sea* (1953), *Shoot First* (1953) with Joel McCrea, *Indiscreet* (1958), *Murder Most Foul* (1964), *Bunny Lake Is Missing* (1965), and *Oliver!* (1968).

She played the housekeeper Mrs Grose in two adaptations of Henry James's *The Turn of the Screw*: the 1961 film *The Innocents*, and a 1974 TV adaptation.

Other roles included *David Copperfield* (1969), *The Befrienders* (1970-1972), *The Amorous Milkman* (1975), *Oh No, It's Selwyn Froggitt!* (1976-1977), *Worzel Gummidge* (1979-1980), *Young at Heart* (1980-1982), *A Woman of Substance* (1985), *Strike It Rich!* (1987), and *All Creatures Great and Small* (1990).

She died October 5, 1998 at age 81 in Suffolk, England.

Frank Jenks

Joel McCrea and Frank Jenks in *Youth Takes a Fling*

Frank Jenks was born in Des Moines, Iowa November 4, 1902 and was an acid-voiced American supporting actor of stage and films.

Jenks began in vaudeville and went on to a long career in movies and television, mostly in comedy. He was one of the more familiar faces and voices of the Hollywood Studio era. For almost ten years beginning in the early 1920s, Jenks was a song and dance man in vaudeville.

In 1933, when sound films had become the norm, and Broadway actors were moving to Hollywood in droves, Jenks's flat, sarcastic delivery landed him a film career. He was often cast as a sarcastic cabbie, reporter, cop, or soldier. Usually a supporting actor, Jenks did appear occasionally as a film lead for low-budget films for PRC. In the Cary Grant- Rosalind Russell classic, *His Girl Friday* (1940), Jenks had his most famous role, as the cynical newsman "Wilson."

More of his roles included *Broadway to Hollywood* (1933) with Moe and Curly Howard, *The Last Outlaw* (1936), *Love Is a Headache* (1938), *Youth Takes a Fling* (1938) with Joel McCrea, *You Can't Cheat an Honest Man* (1939), *Seven Miles from Alcatraz* (1942), *Rosie the Riveter* (1944), *Zombies on Broadway* (1945), *Kilroy Was Here* (1947), *Blondie's Hero* (1950), *Boston Blackie* (1951-1953), *Adventures of Wild Bill Hickok* (1953), *Adventures of Superman* (1952-1955), *Cheyenne* (1956), *The Amazing Colossal Man* (1957), *Wagon Train* (1960), *Perry Mason* (1958-1961), and *Room for One More* (1962).

He died May 13, 1962 at age 59 in Hollywood, California.

Hans Joby

Hans Joby was born in Kronstadt (Brasso), Austria-Hungary [now Brasov, Romania] (3 August 3, 1884 and was an Austrian film actor. He appeared in sixty-three films between 1920 and 1944. He was also billed as "Captain John Peters", and often played aristocratic Prussian-types, memorably in Laurel and Hardy's silent short *Double Whoopee* (1929) which also featured Jean Harlow.

Some of his other roles included *The Enemy* (1927) with Joel McCrea, *Hell's Angels* (1930) again with Jean Harlow, *Melody in Spring* (1934), *Special Agent K-7* (1936), *Hitler - Beast of Berlin* (1939), with Alan Ladd, *Bitter Sweet* (1940), *All Through the Night* (1941), *Spy Smasher* (1942).

He died April 30, 1943in Los Angeles, California.

Carmencita Johnson

Carmencita Johnson was born March 31, 1923 in Los Angeles, California. As a child, Carmencita Johnson acted the same year of her birth, and in the *Little Rascals* movie series. When she turned 20, she began to work as a synchronized swimmer in Esther Williams aquatic movies. Her resemblance to the actress Lana Turner also got her work as Turner's stand-in during the 1940's.

More of her roles included *The Courtship of Myles Standish* (1923), *The Shining Adventure* (1925), *The Trail of '98* (1928), *Frankenstein* (1931), *Mystery Mountain* (1934), *These Three* (1936) with Joel McCrea, *The Adventures of Tom Sawyer* (1938), *Reap the Wild Wind* (1942), *Hollow Triumph* (1948), and *A Place in the Sun* (1951).

Carmencita married in 1949, retiring from film work. She and her husband moved to Ojai, California, in 1961, where she became a tireless supporter of the arts. She helped form the Arts Advisory Board. She was selected Ojai Valley Woman of the Year in 1985, and was the longtime publicist for artist George Stuart.

She appeared in one more film *Irish Whiskey* in 1997.

She died September 26, 2000 at age 77 in Ventura, California.

Chubby Johnson

Chubby Johnson was born Charles Rutledge Johnson on August 13, 1903, in Terre Haute, Indiana. He made a living as a journalist and did not become a movie actor until he was in his 40s, making his debut in the Randolph Scott oater *Abilene Town* (1946) in support of Scott, Ann Dvorak and Edgar Buchanan.

He continued to practice his craft as a member of the press, serving as a radio announcer as well as pounding the keys as a columnist, until he was nearly 50. Chubby appeared in Errol Flynn's horse opera *Rocky Mountain* (1950) as part of an army of quirky character actors which included Guinn 'Big Boy' Williams and Slim Pickens. Chubby then quit the Fourth Estate for a Hollywood career.

When Republic Pictures sought a replacement for Eddy Waller to play sidekick to B-movie cowboy star Allan Lane in the *Rocky Lane* series, Chubby filled in for most of 1951-52. He also starred in the series *Sky King* (1951) as ranch foreman Jim Bell. The low-budget series, a spin-off from a five-year-old radio show in which individual episodes were made for approximately $9,000 each, ran on NBC from Sept 16, 1951, until Oct 26, 1952. The series was then picked up by ABC, which ran the same NBC episodes from November 8, 1952, until September 12, 1954. A season of new episodes was aired in 1955.

Chubby freelanced as a character actor after these stints on the boob tube, appearing in support of James Stewart in the Anthony Mann classic *Bend of the River* (1952), and in their *The Far Country* (1954), which also featured character actor par excellence Walter Brennan, the movies' first triple-Oscar threat. Chubby then went on to appear in support of Doris Day in *Calamity Jane* (1953), Audie Murphy in *Gunsmoke* (1953), Ronald Reagan in *Law and*

Order (1953), Barbara Stanwyck and Ronnie again in *Cattle Queen of Montana* (1954), *The First Texan* (1956) with Joel McCrea, and James Cagney in *Tribute to a Bad Man* (1956), one of the legend's rare forays into the western.

Other stars Chubby supported were Richard Chamberlain and Claude Rains in *Twilight of Honor* (1963), the 1963 courtroom drama that won the ill-fated Nick Adams a Best Supporting Actor Oscar nomination; James Garner in *Support Your Local Sheriff!* (1969); and Burt Reynolds in his audacious debut as a big-screen star as the eponymous *Sam Whiskey* (1969). He also appeared uncredited in the classic *High Noon* (1952).

After appearing as a regular in the short-lived series *Frontier Doctor* (1958), Chubby appeared as Concho on another TV western, *Temple Houston* (1963), which starred Jeffrey Hunter. He also guested on many other TV westerns, including *Bonanza* (1959), *Gunsmoke* (1955), and *The Rifleman* (1958).

Chubby continued to appear in films until 1969, with *Sam Whiskey* (1969) serving as the nightcap to his career. He died on Halloween Day 1974 from complications from a leg infection.

Kay Johnson

Catherine Townsend "Kay" Johnson was born in Mount Vernon, New York November 29, 1904 and was an American actress who performed on the stage and in Hollywood films.

Her father was architect Thomas R. Johnson, who worked in the firm of Cass Gilbert, the architect of several noteworthy buildings in New York City, including the Woolworth Building, the New York Customs House, and many library buildings. Kay, as she was known, resolved to become an actress after leaving boarding school in Ohio. Her mother reluctantly permitted her to take a course at the American Academy of Dramatic Arts.

Her first leading role was in a play called *Beggar on Horseback*, and her first stage work of note was in the production of Karel Čapek's play *R.U.R.* in Chicago. She moved to California after appearing in *The Little Accident* in Providence, Rhode Island. She was accompanied by her soon to-be-husband John Cromwell who worked as a director in Hollywood. They wed in October 1928.

Kay Johnson was signed to a contract with Metro-Goldwyn-Mayer by Cecil B. DeMille following a performance of the *The Silver Cord* at the Repertory Theater in Los Angeles, California. The play was produced by Simeon Gest

31

of the Figueroa Playhouse. Her film debut came in *Dynamite* (1929) with, written by Jeanie Macpherson and featuring Joel McCrea, Charles Bickford, and Conrad Nagel. Production was delayed while Johnson recovered from an appendectomy.

She went on to appear in *The Ship From Shanghai* (1930), *This Mad World* (1930), *Billy the Kid* (1930), *The Spoilers* (1930) with Gary Cooper and Betty Compson, DeMille's *Madam Satan* (1930), *Passion Flower* (1930), Capra's *American Madness* (1932), *Thirteen Women* (1932), *Of Human Bondage* (which starred Leslie Howard and Bette Davis), *Jalna* (1935) and *Mr. Lucky* (1943). Johnson was cast opposite Warner Baxter in a screen adaptation of *Such Men Are Dangerous* by Elinor Glyn. The story was adapted to the screen by Fox Film.

Johnson's film career continued until 1954 when her final appearance came in the British film *Jivaro* (also known as *Lost Treasure of the Amazon*).

Johnson was married to John Cromwell, an American film actor, director, and producer, from 1928 until their divorce in 1946. They had two sons, one of whom is actor James Cromwell of *Star Trek First Contact* (1996) as Zefram Cochran, the inventor of warp speed, and Stephen King's *The Green Mile* (1999), among countless other films and television roles since 1974.

Kay Johnson died November 17, 1975 from undisclosed causes at the age of 70 in Waterford, Connecticut.

Noble Johnson

Joel McCrea and Noble Johnson in The Most Dangerous Game

Noble Johnson was born in Marshall, Missouri April 18, 1881 and was an African-American actor and film producer.

Standing 6'2" at 215 pounds, his impressive physique and handsome features made him in demand as a character actor and bit player. In the silent era he assayed a wide variety of characters of different races in a plethora of films, primarily serials, westerns and adventure movies. While Johnson was cast as black in many films, he also played

Native American and Latino parts and "exotic" characters such as Arabians or even a devil in hell in *Dante's Inferno* (1924).

The old orthochromatic film stock of the early days was less discriminating about a person's color, as were black and white stocks in general, permitting some African-American actors a break, as their "color" was washed out or less obvious when photographed in black and white. As late as the early 1960s, there were very few African-American members of the Screen Actors Guild. Since there was a lack of opportunity for them as black performers, they were confined mostly to race films until the 1960s.

Noble was great friends with fellow actor Lon Chaney. They were schoolmates in Colorado.

Johnson was also an entrepreneur. In 1916, he founded his own studio to produce what would be called "race films", movies made for the African-American audience, which was ignored by the "mainstream" film industry. The Lincoln Motion Picture Company, in existence until 1921, was an all-black company, and the first to produce movies portraying African-Americans as real people instead of as racist caricatures (Johnson was followed into the race film business by Oscar Micheaux and others). Johnson, who served as president of the company and was its primary asset as a star actor, helped support the studio by acting in other companies' productions such as *20,000 Leagues Under the Sea* (1916), and investing his pay from those films in Lincoln.

Lincoln's first picture was *The Realization of a Negro's Ambition* (1916). For four years Johnson managed to keep Lincoln going through his commitment to African-American filmmaking. However, he reluctantly resigned as president in 1920, as he no longer could continue his double business life, maintaining a demanding career in Hollywood films while trying to run a studio.

In the 1920s Johnson was a very busy character actor, appearing in such top-notch silent films as The *Four Horsemen of the Apocalypse* (1921) with Rudolph Valentino, Cecil B. DeMille's original *The Ten Commandments* (1923), *The Thief of Bagdad* (1924), and *Dante's Inferno* (1924).

He made the transition to talkies, appearing in *The Mysterious Dr. Fu Manchu* (1929) as Li Po, in *Moby Dick* (1930) as Queequeg to John Barrymore's Captain Ahab, and in the Boris Karloff film *The Mummy* (1932) as "the Nubian". He was Ivan in *The Most Dangerous Game* (1932) with Joel McCrea. He was also the Native Chief on Skull Island in the classic *King Kong* (1933) (and its sequel *The Son of Kong*, 1933) and appeared in Frank Capra's classic *Lost Horizon* (1937) as one of the porters. One of his last films was John Ford's classic *She Wore a Yellow Ribbon* (1949), in which he played Native American Chief Red Shirt. He retired from the movie industry in 1950.

Johnson died of natural causes on January 9, 1978, in Yucaipa, California at age 96. He is buried in the Garden of Peace at Eternal Valley Memorial Park in Newhall, California.

Tor Johnson

Tor Johansson, better known by the stage name Tor Johnson, was born in Kalmar, Sweden, October 19, 1903 and was a Swedish professional wrestler (billed as The Super Swedish Angel) and actor.

Johnson was the son of Karl J. Johansson and Lovisa Petersson.

Johnson weighed 400 pounds at his heaviest. He had a full head of blond hair, but shaved it to maintain an imposing and villainous appearance in his wrestling and acting work. He began getting bit parts in films upon moving to California, usually as the strongman or weightlifter, as early as 1934. His film career ended in the early

1960s, after he appeared in a string of poorly-rated films. However, he continued to make appearances on television and made a number of commercials.

During his career as an actor, Johnson befriended director Edward D. Wood, Jr., who directed him in a number of films, including *Bride of the Monster* (1955) and *Plan 9 from Outer Space* (1959).

More of his roles included *Shadow of the Thin Man* (1941), *Ghost Catchers* (1944), *Lost in a Harem* (1944), *Behind Locked Doors* (1948), *Abbott and Costello in the Foreign Legion* (1950), *The San Francisco Story* (1952) with Joel McCrea, *Houdini* (1953), *Rocky Jones, Space Ranger* (1954), *The Unearthly* (1957), *Bonanza* (1960), *Shirley Temple's Storybook* (1961), and *Head* (1968).

He was very friendly to work with; actress Valda Hansen, who worked with Johnson in 1959's *Night of the Ghouls*, described him as "like a big sugar bun." During this period, Johnson appeared as a guest contestant on the quiz show *You Bet Your Life*, during which he showed the show's host Groucho Marx, his "scariest face". Marx ran off the stage in mock terror, then returned and pleaded: "Don't make that face again!"

On May 12, 1971, Johnson died from heart failure at age 67 at the San Fernando Valley Hospital in San Fernando, California. He was buried at the Eternal Valley Memorial Park in Newhall, California.

Johnson was portrayed by wrestler George "The Animal" Steele in Tim Burton's film *Ed Wood* (1994).

I. Stanford Jolley

I. Stanford Jolley and Joel McCrea in *Wichita Town*

Isaac Stanford Jolley, Sr., known as I. Stanford Jolley was born October 24, 1900, and was a prolific American character actor of film and television, primarily in western roles as cowboys, law-enforcement officers, or villains. Recognized by his slight build, narrow face, and pencil-thin moustache, Jolley appeared some five hundred times on the large or small screen.

Born in Morristown, New Jersey, Jolley toured as a child with his father's traveling circus and worked in vaudeville. He first performed on Broadway in 1924 opposite Charles Trowbridge in *Sweet Seventeen*. He also worked in radio until he performed his first uncredited part in the 1935 Bette Davis film, *Front Page Woman*. He appeared in twenty-five films for Republic Pictures between 1936 and 1954, but he was never under contract to the studio. According to his wife, he never earned more than $100 on any of his multiple film appearances.

34

In 1939, he played an uncredited part as a hotel clerk in *Mr. Wong in Chinatown*. Appearing in scores of films, mostly westerns, Jolley was cast in 1940 as Molotoff in *Chasing Trouble*, with other performers in the comedy/espionage film including western actors Milburn Stone and Tristram Coffin. In 1942, he was cast as Gil Harkness in the western *Outlaws of Boulder Pass*. In 1944, he was cast as Saladin in the swashbuckling "western" film set in the Middle East, *The Desert Hawk*, and as Bart Kern in the Tex Ritter film, *Gangsters of the Frontier*. In 1945, Jolley was cast as Marshal Mullins in *Springtime in Texas*, a 55-minute film about a crime boss, Pete Grant, played by Rex Lease, who controls the West Texas town of Pecos.

In 1946, Jolley portrayed Dr. Blackton in *The Crimson Ghost* and also did the voice of the undefined title character. That same year, he portrayed Sheriff Bill Armstrong in *Silver Range* and James Beeton in the western musical *Swing, Cowboy, Swing*. In 1948, Jolley was cast as the loan shark Rance Carson in *Tex Granger, Midnight Rider of the Plains*, with Robert Kellard in the title role. In 1949, Jolley appeared as Professor Bryant in *King of the Rocket Men*, again with Tristram Coffin. That same year, he was cast as Mark Simmons in *Trouble at Melody Mesa*, starring Brad King as a marshal. He also appeared as Toad Tyler in 1949s *Rimfire*. In 1950, Jolley was cast as J.B. "Dude" Dawson in the low-budgeted Republic Pictures film serial, *Desperadoes of the West*. In 1951, he was cast as Sam Fleming in *Oklahoma Justice*, with Johnny Mack Brown, with whom he had also appeared in *Silver Range*. That same year, Jolley appeared as Rocky in the western film, *Son of Belle Starr*, a drama about Starr's son, "The Kid" or Ed Reed, played by Keith Larsen, who attempts to lead an upright life despite his family background. In 1954, he played the stationmaster in Vermont in the Bing Crosby/Danny Kaye Christmas classic *White Christmas*. In 1956, Jolley appeared as Henry Longtree in the short film *I Killed Wild Bill Hickok*.

He had parts in *Sierra* (1950), *The Red Badge of Courage* (1951), *Tumbleweed* (1953), and *Posse From Hell* (1961) with Audie Murphy.

From 1950-1953, Jolley first appeared on television with six castings in different role in the syndicated series *The Lone Ranger* with Clayton Moore. He appeared twice in 1953 in another syndicated western series, *The Range Rider*. He guest starred as the henchman Walt, along with Clayton Moore and Darryl Hickman, in the 1954 episode "Annie Gets Her Man" of the syndicated Gail Davis and Brad Johnson western, *Annie Oakley*. He appeared as Sheriff Bascom in the 1954 episode "Black Bart" of the syndicated Jim Davis series, *Stories of the Century*.

In 1958, Jolley appeared on ABC's *Walt Disney Presents* in the role of Sheriff Adams in the episode "Law and Order, Incorporated", with Robert Loggia as Elfego Baca. His then 32-year-old son, Stan Jolley, was the art director of the segment. Others in the episode were former child actor Skip Homeier and Raymond Bailey, later the banker Milburn Drysdale of CBS's *The Beverly Hillbillies*.

He appeared with Alan Ladd in *One Foot in Hell* (1960) and Joel McCrea in *Wichita Town* (1960).

In 1965, he appeared as Enos Scoggins in "The Greatest Coward on Earth" of the Chuck Connors series, *Branded*. He had also appeared with Connors on ABC's *The Rifleman* in one of the last episodes of the series in 1963 in the role of Joe Fogner in "Hostages to Fortune" (1963). He appeared four times in 1956 in archival footage on the children's western *The Gabby Hayes Show*.

Jolley's last western roles were in 1976: as (1) a farmer in ABC's *The Macahans*, the pilot of James Arness's second western series, *How the West Was Won*, and as a (2) drunkard in the short-lived Tim Matheson and Kurt Russell series *The Quest*.

Jolley and his wife, Emily Mae or "Peggy" Jolley (1901–2003), had two children, the art director I. Stanford "Stan" Jolley, Jr. (born 1926), and the late Sandra Jolley Carson (1919–1986), the former wife of actor Forrest Tucker and the widow of actor Jack Carson. Sandra Jolley was originally an Earl Carroll showgirl. Jolley was hence the father-in-law of Tucker from 1940–1950 and of Carson from 1961 until Carson's death in 1963.

Jolley died December 7, 1978, of emphysema at the age of seventy-eight at the Motion Picture Country Hospital in Woodland Hills, California. His wife died in the same facility in 2003. The Jolleys are interred at Forest Lawn Memorial Park in the Hollywood Hills neighborhood of Los Angeles.

Pamela "Brooke" Tucker, offered this reflection of her grandfather: "The most important thing about my grandfather was that he was the antithesis of all the villains he portrayed. He was a gentleman and a gentle man. He was ALWAYS interested in what the other person had to say and when you met him, he made you feel as though you were very important and special. All of my friends growing up loved him.

Jolley's grave marker reads:

I. Stanford Jolley
Loving Husband And Father
1900-1978
A Gentle Man And As Jolly By Nature As He Was By Name
Loved By All and Especially His Family

Gordon Jones

Gordon Wynnivo Jones was born in Alden, Iowa April 5, 1911 and was an American character actor, a member of John Wayne's informal acting company best known for playing Lou Costello's TV nemesis "Mike the Cop" and appearing as The Green Hornet in the first of two movie serials based on that old-time radio program.

Jones had been a student athlete and star football guard ("Bull" Jones) at U.C.L.A., and had also played a few seasons of professional football. He started out playing small roles in Wesley Ruggles' and Ernest B. Schoedsack's *The Monkey's Paw* (1933) and Sidney Lanfield's *Red Salute* (1935). By 1937, he had moved on to a contract at RKO Radio Pictures. After *The Green Hornet* (1940) with Alan Ladd, Jones (who held a reserve commission in the army) was called into the service after filming his roles as "The Wreck" in *My Sister Eileen* (1942) and "Alabama Smith" in *Flying Tigers* (1943), a John Wayne vehicle that was one of the most popular action films of the war. This picture began Jones' twenty year onscreen association with Wayne, who was also a former football player from USC.

Jones remained associated with the service after the war, encouraging college students to consider the Reserve Officers Training Corps (ROTC). After resuming his acting career in the 1940s, Jones appeared in *Buffalo Bill* in 1944 and in prominent roles in the John Wayne features *Big Jim McLain* (1952) and *Island in the Sky* (1953).

By the end of the 1940s, Jones had aged into a beefier screen presence and into very physical character roles. He was no longer a leading man but he had developed a comic villain persona which meshed with the work of Bud Abbott and Lou Costello. Jones' association with the duo began in *The Wistful Widow of Wagon Gap* (1947) with the role of the film's heavy, Jake Frame, and continued through their television series *The Abbott and Costello Show* (1952-1953). Jones played "Mike the Cop", Costello's hulking, loud-voiced antagonist. The program was only produced for two seasons, but ensured continued recognition for Jones via frequent reruns and a 21st Century DVD release.

Jones also remained busy in films and on television throughout the 1950s, in pictures like Louis L'amour's *Treasure of Ruby Hills* (1955), *The Monster That Challenged the World* (1957), *The Perfect Furlough* (1958), and on TV series ranging from *The Life and Legend of Wyatt Earp* (1956), *Cheyenne* (1956), *The Adventures of Ozzie & Harriet* (1958-1959), *Laramie* (1959), *Richard Diamond, Private Detective* (1958-1959), *The Rifleman* (1959-1961), and *Have Gun - Will Travel* (1962).

Jones also appeared in two very successful Disney movies during the early '60s, *The Absent-Minded Professor* (1961) and *Son of Flubber* (1963). He played harried school coaches in both pictures. He also starred with Mitzi Green and Virginia Gibson in the short-lived TV sitcom *So This Is Hollywood* (1955).

Jones returned to the John Wayne stock company portraying Douglas, the bureaucrat antagonist to Wayne's G. W. McLintock in the Western comedy *McLintock!* (1963). Jones succumbed to a heart attack on June 12, 1963 at age 52, five months before the release of that movie.

Jones has a star on the Hollywood Walk of Fame on the West side of the 1600 block of Vine Street.

L.Q. Jones

L.Q. Jones and with the author in 2012

L.Q. Jones was born August 19, 1927, and is an American character actor and film director, known for his work in the films of Sam Peckinpah.

Jones was born Justus Ellis McQueen in Beaumont, Texas, the son of Jessie Paralee (née Stephens) and Justice Ellis McQueen, who was a railroad worker. He attended The University of Texas at Austin in late 1940s.

He made his film debut in 1955's *Battle Cry*, with Van Heflin, under his birth name. His character was named L.Q. Jones, and when it was suggested to him by film producers that he changed his screen name for future pictures, he decided that the name of his debut character would be a memorable one.

Jones appeared in numerous memorable films in the 1950s, 1960s, and 1970s. One notable early role was in *Santiago* (1956) with Alan Ladd, and *Love Me Tender* (1956) with Elvis.. He became a member of Sam Peckinpah's stock company of actors, appearing in his *Klondike* television series (1960–1961), *Ride the High Country* (1962) with Joel McCrea and Randolph Scott, *Major Dundee* (1965), *The Wild Bunch* (1969), *The Ballad of Cable Hogue* (1970), and *Pat Garrett and Billy The Kid* (1973).

He also appeared twice with Audie Murphy in *Showdown* (1963) and *Apache Rifles* (1964).

He was frequently cast alongside his close friend, Strother Martin, most memorably in *The Wild Bunch*. Jones also appeared in television, as recurring characters on such western programs as *Cheyenne* (1955), *Gunsmoke* (1955), *Laramie* (1959-1963), *Two Faces West* (1960–1961), and twenty-five times on *The Virginian* (1962) as ranch hand Andy Belden. He was cast once in the syndicated military drama *Men of Annapolis* (1958). He also appeared in *Voyagers!* (1983) with doomed actor Jon-Erik Hexum.

He directed, was the executive producer, and adapted the screenplay for *A Boy and His Dog* (1975), with Don Johnson and Jason Robards. Other films include *Men in War* (1957), *The Naked and the Dead* (1958), *Flaming Star* (1960), *Cimarron* (1960), *Hell Is for Heroes* (1962), *Hang 'Em High* (1968), *Stay Away, Joe* (1968), *Lone Wolf McQuade* (1983), *Casino* (1995), *The Edge* (1997), *The Mask of Zorro* (1998), and *A Prairie Home Companion* (2006).

He co-produced, co-starred, wrote, and cast Strother Martin again in the lead role of *The Brotherhood of Satan* (1971). He also wrote the novel, which he autographed a paperback copy to me when I met and talked with him about Audie Murphy at the Memphis Film Festival June 1, 2012, and he said "I Really liked Audie. He went through more things than most of us have ever thought of. Audie was a sweetheart".

He is currently attending western film festival gatherings for the fiftieth anniversary of *The Virginian*.

Marcia Mae Jones

Marcia Mae Jones was born in Los Angeles, California August 1, 1924 and was an American actress whose prolific career spanned forty-seven years.

Jones made her film debut at the age of two in the 1926 film *Mannequin*. She appeared in films such as *King of Jazz* (1930), *Street Scene* (1931), and *Night Nurse* (1931) before rising to child stardom in the 1930s with roles in *The Champ* (1931) and, alongside Shirley Temple in *Heidi* (1937) and *The Little Princess* (1939). She also starred in films such as *The Garden of Allah* (1936), *These Three* (1936) with Joel McCrea, and *The Adventures of Tom Sawyer (1938).*

Marcia Mae Jones blossomed into a wide-eyed, blonde, wholesome-looking teenager, and worked steadily in motion pictures through her late teens. She appeared in *First Love* (1939), in support of Deanna Durbin. In 1940 Monogram Pictures signed her to co-star with Jackie Moran in a few rustic romances; when this series lapsed, both Jones and Moran joined Monogram's popular action-comedy series starring Frankie Darro.

As a young adult she continued to work in motion pictures, notably in *Nine Girls* (1944) and *Arson, Inc.* (1948). Like many familiar faces of the 1940s, she appeared on numerous television programs. In 1951 she appeared as comic foil to Buster Keaton in Keaton's filmed TV series. She went on to work in such top-rated shows as *The Cisco Kid* (1951-1952), *The Adventures of Wild Bill Hickok* (1951), *Burns and Allen* (1955), *My Three Sons* (1964-1969), and *The Magician* (1973). Her last major role was in the Barbra Streisand film *The Way We Were* in 1973.

Jones was the youngest of four children born to actress Freda Jones. All three of her siblings, Margaret, Macon, and Marvin Jones, were also child actors.

She married and divorced on two occasions Robert Chic, as well as had two sons with him.   She died September 2, 2007 age 83 in Woodland Hills, Los Angeles, California.

Bobby Jordan

Robert "Bobby" Jordan was born in Harrison, New York April 1, 1923 and was an American actor, , most notable for being a member of the Dead End Kids, the East Side Kids, and the Bowery Boys.

Jordan was a talented toddler and by the time he was six years old, he could sing, tap dance and play the saxophone. At the age of four, he was working in an early film version of *A Christmas Carol*.

His mother took him to talent shows in and around Harrison, New York. He also modeled for newspaper and magazine advertisements, and appeared in short films and radio programs. In the late 1920s, his family moved to the upper west side of Manhattan. In 1929, he was cast as Charles Hildebrand in the 1929 Broadway play, *Street Scene*.

Though he was the youngest, Jordan was the first of the boys who made up the Dead End Kids to work in films, with a role in a 1933 Universal short. In 1935, he became one of the original Dead End Kids by winning the role of Angel in Sydney Kingsley's Broadway drama *Dead End*, about life in the slums of the east side New York City. The play was performed at the Belasco Theatre, and ran for three years with over 600 performances. He appeared for the first season and the beginning of the second, but left in mid-November 1936. He returned in time to join the others in 1937 in Hollywood, California, to make the movie version of the play, starring big names such as Humphrey Bogart, Joel McCrea, Sylvia Sidney, and Claire Trevor.

Following the making of *Dead End*, Jordan found himself "released" from his contract at Goldwyn, and subsequently appeared at Warner Brothers with the rest of the Dead End Kids. After one year, Warners released most of them, but kept Leo Gorcey and Jordan as solo performers. Jordan appeared (as "Douglas Fairbanks Rosenbloom") in Warner's Damon Runyon comedy *A Slight Case of Murder* (1938), and at Metro-Goldwyn-Mayer in *Young Tom Edison* (1940).

In 1940, Jordan appeared in the film *Military Academy* and accepted an offer from producer Sam Katzman to star in a new tough-kid series called "The East Side Kids." Leo Gorcey soon joined him, then Huntz Hall, and the trio continued to lead the series through 1943, when Jordan entered the United States Army during World War II as a foot soldier in the 97th Infantry Division. He was subsequently involved in an elevator accident that forced him to have surgery to remove his right kneecap.

When Jordan returned to films in 1945, he found that his former gang-mates Gorcey and Hall were obtaining the lion's share of both the content and the salary for the new *Bowery Boys* film series. Dissatisfied with his background status, he left the series after eight entries, and made only a few films thereafter.

On July 1, 1957, Jordan played Bob Ford, the assailant of Jesse James, in the Dale Robertson television series, *Tales of Wells Fargo*. The episode ends some two months before Ford assassinated James in the latter's residence in St. Joseph, Missouri. Hugh Beaumont appeared in the episode as Jesse James. His last performances was in a *Bonanza* episode, "The Many Faces of Gideon Blake."

In subsequent years, Jordan worked as a bartender, a bad choice for him considering his alcoholism. He worked to support his family as a door-to-door photograph salesman and as a roughneck for an oil driller.

In 1957, Jordan and his wife divorced. On August 25, 1965, he entered the Veterans Hospital in Sawtelle, California, for treatment of cirrhosis of the liver. He died a couple weeks later on September 10, 1965 at the age of 42. Of his former Dead End Kid and East Side Kid co-star, Leo Gorcey once observed, "Bobby Jordan must not have had a guardian angel."

Dorothy Jordan

Dorothy Jordan and Joel McCrea in *The Lost Squadron*

Dorothy Jordan in Clarksville, Tennessee, August 9, 1906 and was an American movie actress who had a short but successful career beginning in talking pictures in 1929.

Jordan studied at Southwestern University and the American Academy of Dramatic Arts. She performed in Broadway musicals, including *Garrick Gaieties*.

Jordan made her screen debut in the 1929 film *The Taming of the Shrew* and went on to make twenty-two more films in the next four years, including *Min and Bill* with Wallace Beery and Marie Dressler in 1930, *The Cabin in the Cotton* with Bette Davis in 1932, *The Lost Squadron* with Joel McCrea in 1932, and *One Man's Journey* also with Joel McCrea in 1933.

In 1933, Jordan left films and married filmmaker, screenwriter and later World War II U.S. Army Air Forces Colonel Merian C. Cooper, who co-wrote, produced, and directed the 1933 film *King Kong*. The couple had three children, a son and two daughters. In 1937, she came out of her leave and tested for the role of Melanie Hamilton in *Gone With The Wind*. Cooper was a good friend and frequent collaborator with Western director John Ford, forming Argosy Productions in 1947. It was for Argosy's *The Sun Shines Bright*, directed by Ford in 1953 that Jordan came out of retirement for a small role. She then appeared in a small role as the sister-in-law of John Wayne's character, Ethan Edwards, who seeks Jordan's daughter, played by Natalie Wood, in the epic 1956 Argosy film *The Searchers*. Jordan appeared once more, in a small role in the John Ford film *The Wings of Eagles* in 1957 before retiring.

Jordan and Cooper lived in Coronado, California and remained married until his death of cancer on April 21, 1973. Jordan died of congestive heart failure on December 7, 1988 at age 82 in Cedars-Sinai Medical Center in Los Angeles, California. Her body was cremated and her ashes are interred at the Chapel of the Pines Crematory in Los Angeles.

Victor Jory

Victor Jory was born in Dawson City, Yukon, November 23, 1902, and was a Canadian actor.

Jory was the boxing and wrestling champion of the Coast Guard during his military service, and he kept his burly physique. He toured with theater troupes and appeared on Broadway, before making his Hollywood debut in 1930 in the film *Renegades*.

He initially played romantic leads, but later was mostly cast as the villain. He made over 150 films and dozens of television episodes, as well as writing two plays. His long career in radio included starring in the series *Dangerously Yours*. He is most remembered for his role as Jonas Wilkerson, the brutal and opportunistic overseer, in *Gone with the Wind* and as Lamont Cranston, also known as 'The Shadow' in the 1942 serial film *The Shadow*.

From 1959-1961, he appeared with Patrick McVey in the syndicated television police drama, *Manhunt*. Jory played the lead role of Detective Lieutenant Howard Finucane. McVey was cast as police reporter Ben Andrews.

Some of his other roles include *Madame Du Barry* (1934), *A Midsummer Night's Dream* (1935), *Bulldog Drummond at Bay* (1937), *Dodge City* (1939), *The Light of Western Stars* (1940) with Alan Ladd, *Secrets of the Lone Wolf* (1941), *Hoppy Serves a Writ* (1943), *Bar 20* (1943), *South of St. Louis* (1949) with Joel McCrea, *The Cariboo Trail* (1950), *The Man from the Alamo* (1953), *Blackjack Ketchum, Desperado* (1956), *Wanted: Dead or Alive* (1959), *The Untouchables* (1962), *Cheyenne Autumn* (1964), *The Green Hornet* (1966), and *Mackenna's Gold* (1969).

He portrayed Judge Roy Bean in *A Time for Dying* (1969), Audie Murphy's last film. He had no scenes with Audie Murphy, but did have scenes with Audie's son Terry Murphy. As a matter of fact, he pronounced sentence on Terry Murphy for being a horse thief and had him hanged!

Some more of his roles were in *Mannix* (1969-1972), *Longstreet* (1971), *Papillon* (1973), *Kolchak: The Night Stalker* (1974), *The Rockford Files* (1978), *Devil Dog: The Hound of Hell* (1978), *Greatest Heroes of the Bible* (1978-1979), *Young Maverick* (1980), and his final film *Mountain Men* (1980).

He died in Santa Monica, California, February 12, 1982, and was cremated.

Eddie Kane

Eddie Kane was born in St. Louis, Missouri August 12, 1889 and was an American actor who appeared in over 250 productions from 1928 to 1959.

Some of his more famous films include *The Public Enemy* (1931), *The Mummy* (1932), *Mr. Deeds Goes to Town* (1936), *Mr. Smith Goes to Washington* (1939), *Meet John Doe* (1941), *Yankee Doodle Dandy* (1942), *It's a Wonderful Life* (1946), and *The Ten Commandments* (1956). Kane appeared in three Academy Award for Best Picture winners: *The Broadway Melody* (1929), *It Happened One Night* (1934) and *You Can't Take It with You* (1938).

His early career was in vaudeville as a member of the two-man team of Kane & Herman.

Some more of his roles included *Retribution* (1928), *Puttin' on the Ritz* (1930), *The Stolen Jools* (1931), *Once in a Lifetime* (1932) with Alan Ladd, *Once a Sinner* (1931) with Joel McCrea, *Autobuyography* (1934), *Pick a Star* (1937), *Something to Sing About* (1937), *Swiss Miss* (1938), *Sun Valley Serenade* (1941), *Tarzan's New York Adventure* (1942), *Man from Oklahoma* (1945), *Mexican Hayride* (1948), *Tombstone Territory* (1959), *The Life and Legend of Wyatt Earp* (1959Z), and *The Untouchables* (1959).

Kane retired after the 1950s and died of a heart attack at his home in Los Angeles in April 30, 1969 at age 79.

Boris Karloff

Boris Karloff was born William Henry Pratt at 36 Forest Hill Road, Honor Oak, London, England November 23, 1887 and was an English actor.

Karloff is best remembered for his roles in horror films and especially for his portrayal of Frankenstein's monster in *Frankenstein* (1931), *Bride of Frankenstein* (1935), and *Son of Frankenstein* (1939), which resulted in his immense popularity. His best-known non-horror role is as the Grinch, as well as the narrator, in the animated television special of Dr. Seuss's *How the Grinch Stole Christmas!* (1966). He also had a memorable role in the original *Scarface* (1932). For his contribution to film and television, Boris Karloff was awarded two stars on the Hollywood Walk of Fame.

His parents were Edward John Pratt, Jr. and Eliza Sarah Millard. His paternal grandparents were Edward John Pratt and Eliza Julia (Edwards) Pratt, a sister of Anna Leonowens (whose tales about life in the royal court of Siam [now Thailand] were the basis of the musical *The King and I*). The two sisters were of Anglo-Indian heritage.

Karloff grew up in Enfield. He was the youngest of nine children, and following his mother's death was brought up by his elder siblings. He later attended Enfield Grammar School before moving to Uppingham School and

Merchant Taylors' School, and went on to attend King's College London where he studied to go into the consular service. He dropped out in 1909 and worked as a farm laborer and did various odd jobs until he happened into acting. His brother, Sir John Thomas Pratt, became a distinguished British diplomat. Karloff was bow-legged, had a lisp, and stuttered as a young boy. He conquered his stutter, but not his lisp, which was noticeable all through his career.

In 1909, Pratt traveled to Canada and began appearing in stage shows throughout the country; and sometime later changed his professional name to "Boris Karloff". Some have theorized that he took the stage name from a mad scientist character in the novel *The Drums of Jeopardy* called "Boris Karlov". However, the novel was not published until 1920, at least eight years after Karloff had been using the name on stage and in silent films (Warner Oland played "Boris Karlov" in a movie version in 1931). Another possible influence was thought to be a character in the Edgar Rice Burroughs fantasy novel *H. R. H. The Rider* which features a "Prince Boris of Karlova", but as the novel was not published until 1915, the influence may be backward, that Burroughs saw Karloff in a play and adapted the name for the character. Karloff always claimed he chose the first name "Boris" because it sounded foreign and exotic, and that "Karloff" was a family name (from Карлов, a name found in several Slavic countries, including Russia, Ukraine, and Bulgaria). However, his daughter Sara Karloff publicly denied any knowledge of Slavic forebears, "Karloff" or otherwise. One reason for the name change was to prevent embarrassment to his family. Whether or not his brothers (all dignified members of the British foreign service) actually considered young William the "black sheep of the family" for having become an actor, Karloff himself apparently worried they did feel that way. He did not reunite with his family until he went back to Britain to make *The Ghoul* (1933), extremely worried that his siblings would disapprove of his new, macabre claim to world fame. Instead, his elder brothers jostled for position around their "baby" brother and happily posed for publicity photographs with him.

Karloff joined the Jeanne Russell Company in 1911 and performed in towns like Kamloops, British Columbia and Prince Albert, Saskatchewan. After the devastating tornado in Regina on June 30, 1912, Karloff and other performers helped with cleanup efforts. He later took a job as a railway baggage handler and joined the Harry St. Clair Co. that performed in Minot, North Dakota for a year in an opera house above a hardware store.

Due to the years of difficult manual labor that Karloff had had to perform in Canada and the U.S. to make ends meet whilst he was trying to establish his acting career, he was left with back problems from which he suffered for the rest of his life. Because of his health, he did not fight in World War I.

Once Karloff arrived in Hollywood, he made dozens of silent films, but work was sporadic, and he often had to take up manual labor such as digging ditches or delivering construction plaster to earn a living. A number of his early major roles were in film serials, such as *The Masked Rider* (1919), in Chapter 2 of which he can be glimpsed onscreen for the first time, *The Hope Diamond Mystery* (1920) and *King of the Wild* (1930). In these early roles he was often cast as an exotic Arabian or Indian villain. A key film which brought Karloff recognition was *The Criminal Code* (1931), a prison drama in which he reprised a dramatic part he had played on stage. Another significant role in the fall of 1931 saw Karloff play a key supporting part as an unethical newspaper reporter in *Five Star Final*, a film about tabloid journalism which was nominated for the Academy Award for Best Picture.

His role as Frankenstein's monster in *Frankenstein* (1931) made Karloff a star. The bulky costume with four inch platform boots made it an arduous role but the costume and torturously administered makeup produced the classic image. The costume was a job in itself for Karloff with the shoes weighing 11 pounds each. Universal Studios was quick to acquire ownership of the copyright to the makeup format for the Frankenstein monster that Jack P. Pierce had designed. A year later, Karloff played another iconic character, Imhotep in *The Mummy*. *The Old Dark House* (with Charles Laughton) and the starring role in *The Mask of Fu Manchu* quickly followed. These films all confirmed Karloff's new-found stardom.

The 5'11" brown-eyed Karloff played a wide variety of roles in other genres besides horror. He played Sheik Ali Ben Joseph in *Business and Pleasure* with Joel McCrea the same year he was memorably gunned down in a bowling alley in the 1932 film *Scarface*. He played a religious World War I soldier in the 1934 John Ford epic *The Lost Patrol*.

However, horror had become Karloff's primary genre, and he gave a string of lauded performances in 1930s Universal horror films, including several with Lugosi, his main rival as heir to Lon Chaney's status as the top horror film star. Karloff reprised the role of Frankenstein's monster in two other films, *Bride of Frankenstein* (1935) and *Son of Frankenstein* (1939), the latter also featuring Lugosi. Karloff revisited the Frankenstein mythos in several later films as well, taking the starring role of the villainous Dr. Niemann in *House of Frankenstein* (1944), in which the monster was played by Glenn Strange. He reprised the role of the "mad scientist" in 1958's *Frankenstein 1970* as Baron Victor von Frankenstein II, the grandson of the original creator. The finale reveals that the crippled Baron has given his own face (i. e., Karloff's) to the monster.

Karloff appeared at a celebrity baseball game as Frankenstein's monster in 1940, hitting a gag home run and making catcher Buster Keaton fall into an acrobatic dead faint as the monster stomped into home plate. Norman Z. McLeod filmed a sequence in *The Secret Life of Walter Mitty* with Karloff in the Frankenstein monster make-up, but it was deleted from the finished film. Karloff donned the make-up for the last time in 1962 for a Halloween episode of the TV series *Route 66,*.

While the long, creative partnership between Karloff and Bela Lugosi never led to a close friendship, it produced some of the actors' most revered and enduring productions, beginning with *The Black Cat* (1934). Follow-ups included *Gift of Gab* (1934), *The Raven* (1935), *The Invisible Ray* (1936), *Black Friday* (1940), *You'll Find Out* (also 1940), and *The Body Snatcher* (1945). During this period, he also starred with Basil Rathbone in *Tower of London* (1939) as the murderous henchman of King Richard III of England.

From 1945 to 1946, Karloff appeared in three films for RKO produced by Val Lewton: *Isle Of The Dead, The Body Snatcher,* and *Bedlam.* In a 1946 interview with Louis Berg of the *Los Angeles Times,* Karloff discussed his three-picture deal with RKO, his reasons for leaving Universal Pictures and working with producer Lewton. Karloff left Universal because he thought the Frankenstein franchise had run its course. The last installment in which he appeared—*House of Frankenstein*—was what he called a "'monster clambake,' with everything thrown in—Frankenstein, Dracula, a hunchback and a 'man-beast' that howled in the night. It was too much. Karloff thought it was ridiculous and said so." Berg continues, "Mr. Karloff has great love and respect for Mr. Lewton as the man who rescued him from the living dead and restored, so to speak, his soul."

He did not reprise the role of the monster in *Abbott and Costello meet Frankenstein* in 1948, as he thought it would be a farce and make fun of the character. After he saw the finished product he was pleased with the horror creatures playing it straight. He did appear with Bud and Lou with his name in the title the next year in *Abbott and Costello Meet the Killer, Boris Karloff* (1949).

During this period, Karloff was also a frequent guest on radio programs, whether it was starring in Arch Oboler's Chicago-based *Lights Out* productions (most notably the episode "Cat Wife") or spoofing his horror image with Fred Allen or Jack Benny. In 1949 he was the host and star of *Starring Boris Karloff,* a radio and television anthology series for the ABC broadcasting network.

An enthusiastic performer, he returned to the Broadway stage in the original production of *Arsenic and Old Lace* in 1941, in which he played a homicidal gangster enraged to be frequently mistaken for Karloff. Although Frank Capra cast Raymond Massey in the 1944 film, which was shot in 1941, while Karloff was still appearing in the role on Broadway, Karloff reprised the role on television with Tony Randall and Tom Bosley in a 1962 production on the *Hallmark Hall of Fame.* Somewhat less successful was his work in J. B. Priestley's play *The Linden Tree.* He also appeared as Captain Hook in the play *Peter Pan* with Jean Arthur. He was nominated for a Tony Award for his work opposite Julie Harris in *The Lark,* by the French playwright Jean Anouilh, about Joan of Arc, which was also reprised on *Hallmark Hall of Fame.*

In later years, Karloff hosted and acted in a number of television series, most notably *Thriller, Out Of This World,* and *The Veil,* but the last of these was never actually broadcast, and only came to light in the 1990s. In the 1960s, Karloff appeared in several films for American International Pictures, including *The Comedy of Terrors, The Raven,* and *The Terror,* the latter two directed by Roger Corman, and *Die, Monster, Die!* He also featured in Michael Reeves's second feature film, *The Sorcerers,* in 1966.

During the 1950s, Karloff appeared on British TV in the series *Colonel March of Scotland Yard,* in which he portrayed John Dickson Carr's fictional detective Colonel March, who was known for solving apparently impossible crimes.

Karloff, along with H. V. Kaltenborn, was a regular panelist on the NBC game show, *Who Said That?,* which aired between 1948 and 1955. Later, as a guest on NBC's *The Gisele MacKenzie Show,* Karloff sang "Those Were the Good Old Days" from *Damn Yankees,* while Gisele MacKenzie performed the solo, "Give Me the Simple Life". On *The Red Skelton Show,* Karloff guest starred along with horror actor Vincent Price in a parody of Frankenstein, with Red Skelton as "Klem Kadiddle Monster". In 1966, Karloff also appeared with Robert Vaughn and Stefanie Powers in the spy series *The Girl from U.N.C.L.E.,* in the episode "The Mother Muffin Affair". Karloff performed in drag as the titular character. That same year he also played an Indian Maharajah on the installment of the adventure series *The Wild Wild West* titled "The Night of the Golden Cobra". In 1967, he played an eccentric Spanish professor who believes himself to be Don Quixote in a whimsical episode of *I Spy* titled "Mainly on the Plains".

In the mid-1960s, Karloff gained a late-career surge of American popularity when he narrated the made-for-television animated film of Dr. Seuss' *How the Grinch Stole Christmas,* and also provided the voice of the Grinch, although the song "You're a Mean One, Mr. Grinch" was sung by the American voice actor Thurl Ravenscroft. The film was first broadcast on CBS-TV in 1966. Karloff later received a Grammy Award for "Best Recording For Children" after the story was released as a record. Because Ravenscroft (who never met Karloff in the course of their work on the show) was uncredited for his contribution to *How the Grinch Stole Christmas!*, his performance of the song was often mistakenly attributed to Karloff.

In 1968, Karloff starred in *Targets*, a film directed by Peter Bogdanovich, featuring two separate stories that converge into one. In one, a disturbed young man kills his family, and then embarks on a killing spree. In the other, a famous horror-movie actor contemplates then confirms his retirement, agreeing to one last appearance at a drive-in theatre. Karloff starred as the retired horror film actor, Byron Orlok, a thinly disguised version of Karloff himself; Orlok was facing an end of life crisis, which he resolved through a confrontation with the gunman at the drive-in theatre. It was Karloff's last film shot in the United States before his death in 1969.

In 1968 he played occult expert Prof. Marsh in a British film called *The Crimson Cult* (*Curse of the Crimson Altar*), which was the last of Karloff's film to be released during his lifetime.

Karloff ended his career by appearing in four low-budget Mexican horror films: *The Snake People, The Incredible Invasion, Fear Chamber,* and *House of Evil.* This was a package deal with Mexican producer Luis Enrique Vergara. Karloff's scenes were directed by Jack Hill and shot back to back in Los Angeles, California in the spring of 1968. The films were then completed in Mexico. All four were released posthumously, with the last, *The Incredible Invasion,* not released until 1971, two years after Karloff's death.

Cauldron of Blood, shot in Spain in 1967 and starring Karloff and Viveca Lindfors, was also released after Karloff's death.

While shooting his last films, Karloff had only one half of one lung and required oxygen between takes.

Karloff recorded the title role of Shakespeare's *Cymbeline* for the Shakespeare Recording Society (Caedmon Audio). The recording was originally released in 1962. A download of his performance is available from audible.com.

Karloff is also heard as the narrator of Sergei Prokofiev's *Peter and the Wolf* with the Vienna State Opera Orchestra under Mario Rossi. The performance from the LP era is still available as a CD.

Records Karloff made for the children's market included *Three Little Pigs and Other Fairy Stories, Tales of the Frightened* (volume 1 and 2), Rudyard Kipling's *Just So Stories* and, with Cyril Ritchard and Celeste Holm, *Mother Goose Nursery Rhymes*, and Lewis Carroll's *The Hunting of the Snark.*

He also edited several horror anthologies, commencing with *Tales of Terror* (Cleveland and NY: World Publishing Co, 1943)(compiled with the help of Edmond Speare). This wartime-published anthology went through at least five printings through Sept 1945. It has been reprinted recently (Orange NJ: Idea Men, 2007).

Karloff's name was also attached to *And the Darkness Falls* (Cleveland and NY: World Publishing Co, 1946); and *The Boris Karloff Horror Anthology* (London: Souvenir Press, 1965; simultaneous publication in Canada - Toronto: The Ryerson Press; US pbk reprint NY: Avon Books, 1965 retitled as *Boris Karloff's Favorite Horror Stories*; UK pbk reprints London: Corgi, 1969 and London: Everest, 1975, both under the original title), though it less clear whether Karloff himself actually edited these.

Tales of the Frightened (Belmont Books, 1963), though based on the recordings by Karloff of the same title, and featuring his image on the book cover, contained stories written entirely by Michael Avallone; the second volume, *Boris Karloff presents More Tales of the Frightened* contained stories authored entirely by Robert Lory. Both Avallone and Lory worked closely with Canadian editor and book packager Lyle Kenyon Engel, who also ghost-edited a horror story anthology for horror film star Basil Rathbone.

Although he is best known for playing many sinister characters on screen, Karloff was known in real life as a very kind gentleman who gave generously, especially to children's charities. Beginning in 1940, Karloff dressed up as Father Christmas every Christmas to hand out presents to physically disabled children in a Baltimore hospital.

Despite living and working in the United States for many years, Karloff never became a naturalized American citizen, and he never legally changed his name to "Boris Karloff." He signed official documents "William H. Pratt, a.k.a. Boris Karloff."

Karloff was a charter member of the Screen Actors Guild, and was especially outspoken regarding working conditions on sets that actors were expected to deal with in the mid-1930s, some of which were extremely hazardous. In 1931, Boris Karloff took out insurance against premature aging that might be caused by his fright make-up.

He married five times and had one child, daughter Sara Karloff, by his fourth wife. At the time of his daughter's birth Karloff was filming *Son of Frankenstein*, and reportedly rushed from the movie set to the hospital while still in full makeup.

Boris Karloff lived out his final years in England at his cottage, 'Roundabout,' in the Hampshire village of Bramshott. After a long battle with arthritis and emphysema, he contracted pneumonia, succumbing to it in King Edward VII Hospital, Midhurst, Sussex on February 2, 1969 at age 81. He was cremated, following a requested low-key service, at Guildford Crematorium, Godalming, Surrey, where he is commemorated by a plaque in the Garden of Remembrance. A memorial service was held at St Paul's, Covent Garden (the Actors' Church), London, where there is also a plaque.

However, even death could not put an immediate halt to Karloff's media career. Four Mexican films for which Karloff shot his scenes in Los Angeles in 1968 were released over a two-year period after he had died. They were dismissed, by critics and fans alike, as undistinguished efforts. Also, during the run of *Thriller*, Karloff lent his name and likeness to a comic book for Gold Key Comics based upon the series. After *Thriller* was cancelled, the comic was retitled *Boris Karloff's Tales of Mystery*. An illustrated likeness of Karloff continued to introduce each issue of this publication for nearly a decade after the real Karloff died; the comic lasted until the early 1980s. Starting in 2009, Dark Horse Comics started to reprint Tales of Mystery in a hard bound archive.

For his contribution to film and television, Boris Karloff was awarded two stars on the Hollywood Walk of Fame, at 1737 Vine Street for motion pictures, and 6664 Hollywood Boulevard for television.

Karloff was featured by the U.S. Postal Service as Frankenstein's Monster and the Mummy in its series "Classic Monster Movie Stamps" issued in September 1997.

Don Keefer

Donald "Don" H. Keefer was born August 18, 1916, and is a retired American actor known for the versatility of his roles. He was born in Highspire in Dauphin County near Harrisburg, Pennsylvania.

Keefer's first role was as Bernard in the 1951 film, *Death of a Salesman*, based on the Arthur Miller play. His longest-lasting roles were in ten episodes each of the CBS series, *Gunsmoke* (1957-1973), starring James Arness, and *Angel*, a 1960-1961 sitcom featuring French-American actress Annie Fargé.

More of his work includes roles in *Manhunt* (1952), *The Caine Mutiny* (1954), *Appointment with Adventure* (1955), *Away All Boats* (1956), *Hellcats of the Navy* (1957), *Richard Diamond, Private Detective* (1957), *Torpedo Run* (1958), *Wichita Town* (1959) with Joel McCrea, *Cash McCall* (1960), *Whispering Smith* (1961) with Audie Murphy, *Incident in an Alley* (1962), *Car 54, Where Are You?* (1964), *The Fugitive* (1964), *Twilight Zone* (1961-1964), *My Favorite Martian* (1964), *The Munsters* (1965), *The Loner* (1965), *The Russians Are Coming the Russians Are Coming* (1966), *Star Trek* (1968), *Butch Cassidy and the Sundance Kid* (1969), *The Grissom Gang* (1971), *Rod Serling's Night Gallery* (1972), *Walking Tall* (1973), *Attack on Terror: The FBI vs. the Ku Klux Klan* (1975), *Who Is the Black Dahlia?* (1975), *Baretta* (1975), *SWAT* (1975), *Starsky and Hutch* (1977), *The Incredible Hulk* (1977-1978), *The Scarlett O'Hara War* (1980), *Creepshow* (1982), *Highway to Heaven* (1986), *Lucy & Desi: Before the Laughter* (1991), *Lois & Clark: The New Adventures of Superman* (1996), and his last film to date *Liar Liar* (1997).

He died September 7, 2014 at age 98 in Sherman Oaks, California.

Ian Keith

Ian Keith was born Keith Ross in Boston, Massachusetts February 27, 1899 and was an American actor.

Ian Keith was a veteran character actor of the legitimate theater, and appeared in a variety of colorful roles in silent features of the 1920s. His stage training made him a natural choice for the new "talking pictures"; he played John Wilkes Booth in D. W. Griffith's first talkie, *Abraham Lincoln* (1930). Keith had a major role in director Raoul Walsh's 1930 western *The Big Trail*. In 1932, Cecil B. DeMille cast him in *The Sign of the Cross*. This established him as a dependable supporting player, and he went on to play dozens of roles—including Octavian (Augustus) in Cleopatra—in major and minor screen fare for the next three decades.

Ian Keith's tall frame (6' 2"), dark, handsome features (usually clean-shaven), and his resonant voice served him well. He became one of DeMille's favorites, appearing in many of the producer's epic films. He handled costume roles and modern-day professional types with equal aplomb. In the 1940s he became even busier, working primarily in "B" features and westerns and alternating between playing good guys (a chief of detectives in *The Payoff*, a friendly hypnotist in *Mr. Hex*, a blowhard politician in *She Gets Her Man*) and bad guys (a murder suspect in *The Chinese Cat*, a crooked lawyer in *Bowery Champs*, a swindler in *Singing on the Trail*). He appeared in a supporting role to Tyrone Power in *Nightmare Alley* (1947) as a former vaudevillian turned carnie who has succumbed to alcoholism. He also had a definite flair for comedy, and his florid portrayal of the comic-strip ham actor "Vitamin Flintheart" in *Dick Tracy vs. Cueball* was so amusing that he repeated the role in two more films.

More of his roles included *The Divine Lady* (1929) with Joel McCrea, *The Three Musketeers* (1935), *The Sea Hawk* (1940), *Wild Horse Stampede* (1943), and *Valley of the Zombies* (1946).

His authoritative stature also lent himself to tough-guy military roles, such as Admiral Burns in Ray Harryhausen's sci-fi epic, *It Came From Beneath the Sea* (1955).

He also appeared on many television episodes in the 1950s. In 1955, he was seen on screen in his only Shakespeare role, when he made a cameo appearance as the Ghost opposite Richard Burton's Hamlet in a sequence from the Edwin Booth biopic *Prince of Players*. Cecil B. DeMille brought him back to the big screen for *The Ten Commandments* (1956) as Ramses I.

Keith died on March 26, 1960, and was cremated in New York City at age 61.

Barry Kelley

Joel McCrea and Barry Kelley in *The Tall Stranger*

Barry Kelley was born in Chicago, Illinois August 19, 1908 and was an actor on Broadway in the 1930s and 1940s and in films during the 1940s, 1950s, and 1960s. The heavy-set actor created the role of Ike in *Oklahoma!* on Broadway.

In films, he often portrayed cops or judges in films, including *Boomerang* (his first film in 1947), *Knock on Any Door* (1949), *Ma and Pa Kettle* (1949), and *The Asphalt Jungle* (1950). The 6'4", 230-pound Chicago-born actor began acting on the stage in the 1930s. Kelley also appeared in dozens of television series. As in the movies, he usually was in westerns or crime dramas. Kelley had an uncredited role as a police chief in the 1964 Frank Sinatra musical *Robin and the Seven Hoods*.

More of his roles included *Fighting Man of the Plains* (1949), *Flying Leathernecks* (1951), *Law and Order* (1953), *The Lone Ranger* (1954), *Big Town* (1954-1956), *The Wings of Eagles* (1957), Louis L'amour's *The Tall Stranger* (1957) with Joel McCrea, *Buchanan Rides Alone* (1958), *Riverboat* (1959), *Wanted: Dead or Alive* (1960), *Laramie* (1962), *Cheyenne* (1959-1962), *The Fugitive* (1963), *The Munsters* (1964), *The Addams Family* (1964-1965), *Laredo* (1966), *Petticoat Junction* (1964-1968), *The Love Bug* (1968), and *The Extraordinary Seaman* (1969).

He died June 5, 1991 at the age of 82 in Woodland Hills, California.

Kitty Kelly

Kitty Kelly was born Sue O'Neil April 27, 1902 in New York City, New York and was an American stage and film character actress. She was best known as a member of the Ziegfeld Follies and her radio hosting with Columbia Broadcasting.

One of her best remembered roles is that of Lt. Ethel Armstrong in the 1943 *Paramount* wartime drama *So Proudly We Hail!* with Veronica Lake. However, she is probably more infamously remembered in the *Hal Roach Our Gang* comedy short *Beginner's Luck*, which was released by *M-G-M* in 1935. In that film, Kelly was cast as the pushy stage mother of *Spanky McFarland*. Thanks to his friends, she finds herself an unwitting victim, as well as a laughing stock, in the gang's attempt to sabotage and ruin Spanky's Shakespearean stage act in a talent competition.

Other roles throughout her career included *A Kiss in the Dark* (1925), *White Shoulders* (1931), *The Farmer Takes a Wife* (1935), *Geronimo* (1939), *All Women Have Secrets* (1939) again with Veronica Lake, *Hold Back the Dawn* (1941) again with Veronica Lake, *Lucky Jordan* (1942) with Alan Ladd, *Two Years Before the Mast* (1946) again with Alan Ladd, *Gunsight Ridge* (1957) with Joel McCrea, *Alfred Hitchcock Presents* (1958), *The Loretta Young Show* (1958-1961), *Dennis the Menace* (1961), *Bonanza* (1963), *Perry Mason* (1958-1965), *Get Smart* (1965), *Batman* (1966), *The F.B.I.* (1967), and *Firecreek* (1968).

She died June 29, 1968 at age 66 in Hollywood, California.

Nancy Kelly

Nancy Kelly and Joel McCrea in *He Married His Wife*

Nancy Kelly was born in Lowell, Massachusetts March 25, 1921 and was an American actress. A child actress and model, she was a repertory cast member of CBS Radio's *The March of Time* and became a movie leading lady in the late 1930s. She made thirty-six movies between 1926 and 1977, including portraying Tyrone Power's love interest in the classic *Jesse James* (1939), which also featured Henry Fonda, and playing opposite Spencer Tracy in *Stanley and Livingstone* later that same year. She had her greatest success in a character role, the suicidal mother in the *The Bad Seed*, receiving a Tony Award for the 1955 stage production and an Academy Award nomination for the 1956 film adaptation.

Nancy Kelly was born into a theatrical family. Her mother was silent film actress Nan Kelly, who coached her and managed her career. Her younger brother was actor Jack Kelly.

As a child model, her image had appeared in so many different advertisements by the time she was nine years old that *Film Daily* called her "the most photographed child in America due to commercial posing."

Kelly worked extensively in radio in her adolescent years. She played Dorothy Gale in a 1933 to 1934 radio show based on the *The Wonderful Wizard of Oz*. Kelly was the first ingénue on CBS Radio's *The March of Time* series, with a vocal versatility that made it possible for her to portray male parts as well as female. She also portrayed Eleanor Roosevelt.

As an adult, she was a leading lady in movies in the 1930s and 1940s, including director John Ford's *Submarine Patrol* (1938), *Frontier Marshal* (1939) with Randolph Scott as Wyatt Earp, the comedy *He Married His Wife* (1940) with Joel McCrea, *One Night in the Tropics* (1940) with Abbott and Costello, and *Tarzan's Desert Mystery* (1943) with Johnny Weismuller.

Kelly was subsequently a two-time winner of the Sarah Siddons Award for her work in Chicago theatre as well as a Tony Award winner for her performance in *The Bad Seed*, which she followed up by starring in the film version in 1956 and receiving a nomination for the Academy Award for Best Actress. She also starred on television, including leading roles in "The Storm" (1961) episode of *Thriller* and "The Lonely Hours" (1963) episode of *The Alfred Hitchcock Hour*. In 1957, Kelly was nominated at the 9th Primetime Emmy Awards Best Single Performance by an Actress for an Emmy Award for Best Single Performance by an Actress for TV episode "The Pilot" in *Studio One*.

Her last role was *Murder at the World Series* (1977).

Kelly's first husband was actor Edmond O'Brien. Her second was Fred Jackman, Jr. son of silent Hollywood cameraman and director Fred Jackman. Her third husband was theatre director Warren Caro. They had a daughter Kelly Caro in 1957.

She died January 2, 1995 at age 73 from complications of diabetes, Nancy Kelly was interred in the Westwood Village Memorial Park Cemetery in Los Angeles.

For her contribution to the motion picture industry, Nancy Kelly has a star on the Hollywood Walk of Fame at 7021 Hollywood Blvd.

Paul Kelly

Paul Michael Kelly was born August 9, 1899, and was an American child actor who later as an adult became a stage, film, and television actor.

Born in Brooklyn, New York, the ninth of ten children, Kelly began his career as a child actor at age seven and was appearing on the stage.

In 1911 Kelly began making silent films at age twelve with the Vitagraph Studios, which was based in Brooklyn, and where he was billed as *Master Paul Kelly*. His first was a short called *Jimmie's Job* (1911). Kelly was possibly the first male child actor to be given any starring roles in American films predating better known child stars such as Bobby Connelly and Jackie Coogan.

Kelly made his talking film debut in 1933's *Broadway Through a Keyhole*.
In the course of his long career, and relatively short life, it's estimated that Kelly worked on stage, screen, and television in over four hundred roles.

Later in his film career, as an adult, Kelly appeared in films mostly as a tough guy character actor in the 1930s, 1940s and 1950s, in such films as *Murder with Pictures* (1936), *Island in the Sky* (1938), *The Roaring Twenties* (1939), *The Howards of Virginia* (1940) with Alan Ladd, *Parachute Battalion* (1941), *Tarzan's New York Adventure* (1942), *Flying Tigers* (1942), *Fear in the Night* (1947), *Frenchie* (1950) with Joel McCrea, *The Painted Hills* (1951), *Gunsmoke* (1953) with Audie Murphy, *The Square Jungle* (1955), and his last film *Bailout at 43,000* (1957).

In 1948, Kelly won a Best Actor Tony Award his role in *Command Decision*. The award was shared with Henry Fonda for *Mister Roberts* and Basil Rathbone for *The Heiress*.

His career momentum was briefly halted with a two-year (1927–1929) forced hiatus when he served twenty-five months for manslaughter in California's San Quentin prison for the death of actor Ray Raymond, a few days after their fistfight.

Kelly later played the part of San Quentin Warden Clinton Duffy in the film *Duffy of San Quentin* (1954).

Raymond's widow, Dorothy MacKaye, later married Kelly. She was briefly imprisoned for being an accomplice in the killing; and, wrote about her experiences, titled, *Women in Prison*, that became a 1933 film, *Ladies They Talk About*, with Barbara Stanwyck.

He married a bit player he met on the set of *Flight Command* (1940), Claire Owen (née Zona Mardelle Zwicker), on January of 1941. She retired from acting, and went on to survive him.

He died of a heart attack in November 6, 1956, at age 57, after voting for Adlai Stevenson.

Tommy Kelly

Tommy Kelly was born April 6, 1925, in New York City, New York and is an American former child actor.

Tommy Kelly was the son of a fireman. He began his acting career at the age of twelve when he was selected to play the role of Tom Sawyer in the 1938 movie *The Adventures of Tom Sawyer*, an adaption of Mark Twains classic of the same name. Approximately 25,000 boys had auditioned for that role and it is said that famous producer David O. Selznick handpicked Kelly for the role. Despite Kelly reaching good reviews for his performance, the film was only a poor financial success. He also played the lead role in *Peck's Bad Boy with the Circus* later that year as Bill Peck.

In 1939, Tommy Kelly had a small but memorable part in *Gone with the Wind*, as the crying boy in a band in Atlanta, while the death lists are given out.

More of his roles included *They Shall Have Music* (1939) with Joel McCrea *Life Begins for Andy Hardy* (1941), *Mug Town* (1942), *The Beginning or the End* (1947), *He Walked by Night* (1948), *Battleground* (1949), and *The West Point Story* (1950). As he reached adulthood, his roles in movies were minor and he was often uncredited.

He appeared in The Magnificent Yankeein 1950, which turned out to be his last of nineteen films before retiring from his acting career.

As with many other stars, the war years found Tommy in the U.S. Army, where he served in the infantry, not the USO as did some other child stars; he fought in the European theater, participating in the critical campaign for the bridge at Remagen.

Tommy Kelly worked in Liberia as an administrator for the Peace Corps towards the end of the 1960s. He also held a teaching job in Washington D.C. in the 1980s. Ever conscious of the value of education, after obtaining a PhD under the G.I. Bill (his thesis focused, among other things, on the relative advantages of children who were educated in U.S. military dependent schools abroad, "Dr. Kelly" served as an International Relations Advisor, in the International Organization Affairs (IOA) unit of the Office of International Cooperation and Development (OICD) of the U.S. Department of Agriculture, where he prepared positions for the Office of the Secretary of Agriculture, with personal responsibility for OECD, and United States delegations to the governing boards of United Nations Organizations concerned with Food and Agriculture, a position he held until his retirement from Federal Service.

During that time he was an occasional guest of the American Film Institute (AFI), although he was generally reticent to discuss his years as an actor, after retiring from Hollywood at the age of 25. Tommy Kelly has been married to his wife Sue for over 60 years and has six children. He lives today in North Carolina.

Pert Kelton

Pert Kelton was born in Great Falls, Montana October 14, 1907 and was an American vaudeville, movie, radio, and television actress. She was the first actress who played Alice Kramden in *The Honeymooners* with Jackie Gleason and was a prominent comedic supporting film actress in the 1930s. She performed in a dozen Broadway productions between 1925 and 1968. However, her career was interrupted during the 1950s as a result of blacklisting.

Kelton was a young comedienne in A-list movies during the 1930s, often as the leading lady's wisecracking friend. She had a memorable turn in 1933 as dance hall singer "Trixie" in *The Bowery* alongside Wallace Beery, George Raft, Jackie Cooper, and Fay Wray. Directed by Raoul Walsh, the film depicts Steve Brodie, the first man to supposedly jump off the Brooklyn Bridge and live to brag about it. Kelton sings to a rowdily appreciative crowd in an energetic dive, using a curious New York accent to good comedic effect, with Beery and Raft arguing over her attentions afterward.

As the witty young Minnie in Gregory LaCava's pre-Code comedy *Bed of Roses* (1933), she plays a bawdy prostitute (along with Constance Bennett) fond of getting admiring men helplessly drunk before robbing them, at least until getting caught and tossed back into jail. Kelton has all the best lines, surprisingly wicked and amusing observations that would never be allowed in an American film after the Hollywood Production Code was adopted. The movie remains realistic in terms of the interactions of the characters and features an early turn by Joel McCrea as the leading man, a small boat skipper who pulls Bennett from the river after she dives to escape capture.

After her appearance in the film *Whispering Enemies* (1939), Kelton focused on radio, television and theatre. She did not return to the big screen until 1962, when she was cast as Mrs. Paroo in *The Music Man.*

During the 1940s, she was a familiar radio voice on such programs as *Easy Aces*, *It's Always Albert*, *The Stu Erwin Show* and the 1941 soap opera *We Are Always Young*. In 1949, she did the voices of five different characters on radio's *The Milton Berle Show*. She was also a regular cast member of *The Henry Morgan Show*. In the early 1950s, she played the tart maid in the Monty Woolley vehicle, *The Magnificent Montague.*

Kelton appeared in *Henry Morgan's Great Talent Hunt*, first aired January 26, 1951, hosted by Henry Morgan, and with Kaye Ballard, Art Carney, and Arnold Stang.

She was the original Alice Kramden in *The Honeymooners* comedy sketches on the DuMont Television Network's *Cavalcade of Stars*. These sketches formed the eventual basis for the 1955 CBS Television sitcom *The Honeymooners*. Jackie Gleason starred as her husband Ralph Kramden, and Art Carney as their upstairs neighbor Ed

Norton. Elaine Stritch played Trixie, the burlesque dancer wife of Norton, for one sketch before being replaced by Joyce Randolph.

Kelton appeared in the original sketches, generally running about ten to twenty minutes, shorter than the later one-season half-hour series and 1960s hour-long musical versions. However, she was abruptly dropped from her role as a result of blacklisting and was replaced by Audrey Meadows; rather than acknowledge that she was being blacklisted, her producers explained that her departure was based on alleged heart problems. In his book *The Forgotten Network*, David Weinstein says Kelton remained on *Cavalcade of Stars* through the final season of the series (1951-1952), and suggests that it may have been because Jackie Gleason had resisted attempts at having her dropped.

In the 1960s, Kelton was invited back to Gleason's CBS show to play Alice's mother in an episode of the hour-long musical version of *The Honeymooners* (also known as *The Color Honeymooners*), with Sheila MacRae as a fetching young Alice. By this time, the original age discrepancies were reversed, with Ralph married to a much younger Alice than himself. Gleason was one of several big names in entertainment determined to break the curse of the blacklist as many rejected the Red Scare of the 1950s as straight hysteria.

In 1963 Kelton appeared on *The Twilight Zone*, playing the overbearing mother of Robert Duvall in the episode "Miniature."

In her last years, she was strongly identified with Spic and Span because of her TV commercials for that product.

Kelton made her Broadway debut at age 17 in Jerome Kern's *Sunny*. She played "Magnolia" and sang a song of the same name.

Years later, she was twice nominated for Tony Awards: in 1960, as Best Supporting or Featured Actress (Musical) for Frank Loesser's *Greenwillow* and as Best Supporting or Featured Actress (Dramatic) for *Spofford* (1967–1968). However, her most memorable Broadway appearance was as the impatient Mrs. Paroo (the mother of Marian Paroo) in Meredith Willson's *The Music Man* (1957), which she reprised in the 1962 film adaptation; this has become the film role for which she is probably best remembered.

Pert Kelton was part owner of the Warner Kelton Hotel, built in the late 1920s, at 6326 Lexington Avenue, Los Angeles. The hotel catered to actors and musicians such as Cary Grant, Orry Kelly, and Rodgers and Hart. It had a small outdoor theatre at its rear, along with a wishing well that may have inspired the song "There's a Small Hotel" from the musical *On Your Toes* (1936). It also housed a speakeasy in the basement. A sign above the hotel entrance reads "Joyously Enter Here".

On October 30, 1968, Kelton died of heart disease at age 61 in Ridgewood, New Jersey.

Charles Kemper

Charles Kemper was born in Oklahoma September 6, 1900 and was an American stage-trained film character actor. The heavy-set film actor had memorable roles in films including *The Southerner* (1945), *Scarlet Street* (1945), *Gallant Journey* (1946), *The Shocking Miss Pilgrim* (1947), *Wagon Master* (1950), *Stars in My Crown* (1950) with Joel McCrea, and his last film role as Pop Daly in the film noir *On Dangerous Ground* (1951).

Kemper died May 12, 1950 at the age of 49 when he was involved in a car accident in Burbank, California.

Adam Kennedy

Adam Kennedy was born in Otterbein near Lafayette, Indiana March 10, 1922 and was an American actor, screenwriter, novelist, and painter, who starred as the Irish-American newspaper editor Dion Patrick in thirty-seven episodes during the first season, 1957–1958, of NBC's western television series, *The Californians*. Set in the San Francisco, California, of the 1850s, Patrick in the story line works with the vigilantes to restore order from the unrest created by the miners, the Forty-Niners.

Kennedy graduated from DePauw University in Greencastle, Indiana. He studied acting under Sanford Meisner at the Neighborhood Playhouse in Manhattan.

His first acting role, though uncredited was at the age of thirty-three as Yip Ryan, a United States Army pilot in the 1955 film, *The Court-Martial of Billy Mitchell*. The film also starred Gary Cooper as Billy Mitchell and Dayton Lummis as General Douglas MacArthur.

He appeared in the Louis L'amour western *The Tall Stranger* (1957) with Joel McCrea.

In 1956 and 1957, he appeared in three episodes of the religion anthology series, *Crossroads*: as Don in "God's Healing", as Ed Buckley in "Paratroop Padre", and as Art Jackson in the series finale, "Half Mile Down". During this same period of time, Kennedy was cast as Benton in the episode "In a Small Motel" on the *Chevron Hall of Stars* and in "Outpost" on the H.J. Heinz Company's *Studio 57*.

In 1957, he appeared in two syndicated series about the United States Navy: *Men of Annapolis* ("Mister Number Five") and *The Silent Service* ("The Spearfish Delivers"). That same year, he appeared in another anthology, CBS's *Dick Powell's Zane Grey Theater* as Adam Dempster in the episode "A Man on the Run".

Cast in *The Californians*, Kennedy appeared in such episodes as "Skeleton in the Closet", "Pipeline", "The Foundling", "Second Trial", "The Inner Circle", "The Golden Bride", "Murietta", "Shanghai Queen", "Bridal Bouquet", and "Golden Grapes", his final segment on the program aired on June 17, 1958. His co-stars were Sean McClory and Herbert Rudley.

Between 1955 and 1958, Kennedy appeared in four different roles in the CBS anthology series *Schlitz Playhouse of Stars*: as Charlie in "The Careless Cadet", as George in "Always the Best Man", as Johnnie in "The Blue Hotel", and as Steve Elliot in "The Trouble with Ruth". He appeared too in 1959 with Mary Astor, Suzanne Pleshette, and Inger Stevens in the episode "Dairy of a Nurse" of CBS's *Playhouse 90*.

He appeared twice on the half-hour version of CBS's *Gunsmoke*: as Andy Travis in "Kite's Reward" (1955) and as Bert Wells in "Gentleman's Disagreement" (1960). In 1962, he appeared as Sam Hagen in the episode "Stopover in Paradise" of another CBS western, *Frontier Circus*, starring Chill Wills. In 1965, he appeared as Brock Hayden in the NBC soap opera *The Doctors*. His final screen role was an uncredited part in the 1980 television movie, *Act of Love*, starring Ron Howard and Robert Foxworth and directed by Jud Taylor.

After his acting career ended, Kennedy adapted a novel into a screenplay for Stanley Kramer's 1977 film, *The Domino Principle*, which stars Gene Hackman as a convict who becomes an assassin. Kennedy wrote nine other screenplays, including *Raise the Titanic, The Dove* and *Barlow's Kingdom*. He penned twenty novels, including *The*

Killing Season (1967), *Maggie D.* (1973), *Just Like Humphrey Bogart* (1978), *The Fires of Summer* (1987) and *Somebody's Fool* (1993). Kennedy's oil paintings and watercolors have been displayed in the United States and Europe. In 1952, he was hailed in Paris as that city's most influential American painter.

Kennedy was married to the former Susan Adams. The couple had two sons, Regan Kennedy, living in New York City at the time of his father's death, and Jack Kennedy, then of Santa Barbara, California; a daughter, Anne Kennedy Stromsted of Norway, and a grandson. Kennedy died October 16, 1997 at the age of 75 of a heart attack at home in Kent in Litchfield County in western Connecticut.

Douglas Kennedy

Douglas Kennedy and Joel McCrea in *South of St. Louis*

Douglas Richards Kennedy was born in New York City September 14, 1915 and was an American supporting actor who appeared in more than 190 films between 1935 and 1973.

Kennedy was a character actor and occasional leading man in Hollywood. He attended Deerfield Academy in Deerfield, Massachusetts, and afterwards graduated from Amherst College in Amherst, Massachusetts. Making his debut in 1935, he played a significant number of supporting roles and was able to secure contract-player status, first at Paramount Pictures and later at Warner Brothers.

Some of those early roles included *'G' Men* (1935), *Those Were the Days!* (1940) with Alan Ladd, *The Great Mr. Nobody* (1941), and *Passage from Hong Kong* (1941).

His acting career was interrupted by World War II service as a major in the Signal Corps with the Office of Strategic Services and Army Intelligence. After that, he returned to films and played character roles, often western villains or territorial marshals, as well as isolated leads in low-budget pictures.

Roles after his service in WWII included *Nora Prentiss* (1947), *Johnny Belinda* (1948), *Ranger of Cherokee Strip* (1949), *South of St. Louis* (1949) with Joel McCrea, *Ma and Pa Kettle Go to Town* (1950), *The Texas Rangers* (1951), *Ride the Man Down* (1952), *Invaders from Mars, Hopalong Cassidy* (1954), *The High and the Mighty* (1954), *The Lone Ranger* (1950-1955), and *Dragnet* (1955-1956).

Kennedy is best remembered for his starring role in the syndicated series *Steve Donovan, Western Marshal* (1955-1956), with Eddy Waller as his sidekick, Rusty Lee.

More roles continued in *Last of the Badmen* (1957), *The Lone Ranger and the Lost City of Gold* (1958), *Wanted: Dead or Alive* (1958), *The Alligator People* (1959), *The Amazing Transparent Man* (1960), and *The Outer Limits* (1965).

Kennedy portrayed the sheriff, Fred Madden, in twenty-three epiosdes of ABC's *The Big Valley* (1965-1969), with Barbara Stanwyck. He appeared in *O'Hara, U.S. Treasury* (1972).

He made his last appearance in 1973 in three episodes of CBS's *Hawaii Five-O*, with Jack Lord.

Kennedy died August 10, 1973 of cancer at the age 57 in Honolulu, Hawaii, where he had been for the shooting of *Hawaii Five-O*. He is interred at National Memorial Cemetery of the Pacific in Honolulu.

Edgar Kennedy

Edgar Livingston Kennedy in Monterey County, California April 26, 1890 and was an American comedic film actor, known as "Slow Burn". A slow burn is an exasperated facial expression, performed very deliberately; Kennedy embellished this by rubbing his hand over his bald head and across his face, in an attempt to hold his temper. Kennedy is known for a small role as a lemonade vendor in the Marx Brothers film *Duck Soup*, as well as the many Hal Roach films he appeared in.

Kennedy was born to Canadian-born Neil Kennedy and Annie Quinn. He attended San Rafael High School before taking up boxing. He was a light-heavyweight and once went fourteen rounds with Jack Dempsey. After boxing, he worked as a singer in vaudeville, musical comedy and light opera.

Making his debut in 1911, Kennedy appeared in over 400 films, working with some of the biggest film comedians in the United States, including Roscoe Arbuckle, Charlie Chaplin, Laurel and Hardy, the Marx Brothers, Charley Chase, and the *Our Gang* series. He was also one of the original Keystone Kops.

Kennedy's burly frame originally suited him for villainous or threatening roles in silent pictures. By the 1920s Kennedy was working for producer Hal Roach, who kept the actor busy playing supporting roles in short comedies. Kennedy starred in one short, *A Pair of Tights* (1928), in which he plays a tightwad determined to spend as little as possible on a date. His antics with comedian Stuart Erwin are reminiscent of Roach's Laurel and Hardy comedies, produced concurrently. Roach also used Kennedy as a director on half a dozen two-reeler comedies.

In 1930, Edgar Kennedy was featured by RKO-Pathe in a pair of short-subject comedies, *Next Door Neighbors* and *Help Wanted, Female*. Kennedy's characterization of a short-tempered householder was so effective that RKO built a series around it. The "Average Man" comedies starred Kennedy as a blustery, stubborn guy determined to accomplish a household project or get ahead professionally, despite the meddling of his featherbrained wife (usually

Florence Lake), her freeloading brother (originally William Eugene, then Jack Rice) and his dubious mother-in-law (Dot Farley). Kennedy pioneered the kind of domestic situation comedy that later became familiar on television. Each installment would end with Edgar embarrassed, humbled or defeated, looking at the camera and doing his patented slow burn. *The Edgar Kennedy Series*, with its theme song "Chopsticks", became a standard part of the movie-going experience: Kennedy made six "Average Man" shorts a year for seventeen years.

Kennedy became so identified with frustration that practically every studio hired him to play hotheads. He often played dumb cops, detectives, and even a prison warden; sometimes he was a grouchy moving man, truck driver, or blue-collar workman. His character usually lost his temper at least once. In *Diplomaniacs*, Kennedy presides over an international tribunal, where Wheeler & Woolsey want to do something about world peace. "Well, ya can't do anything about it *here*", yells Kennedy, "this is a *peace conference!*" Kennedy, established as the poster boy for frustration, even starred in an instructional film titled *The Other Fellow*, in which loudmouthed roadhog Edgar always vents his anger on other drivers (each one played by Kennedy as well), little realizing that, to them, *he* is "the other fellow."

Perhaps his most unusual roles were as a puppeteer in the detective mystery *The Falcon Strikes Back* and as a philosophical bartender inspired to create exotic cocktails in Harold Lloyd's last film, *The Sin of Harold Diddlebock*. He also played comical detectives opposite two titans of acting: John Barrymore in *Twentieth Century* (1934) and Rex Harrison in *Unfaithfully Yours* (1948); in the latter, he tells conductor Harrison that "Nobody handles Handel like you handle Handel."

More of his roles included *Rockabye* (1932) with Joel McCrea, *Three Men on a Horse* (1936), *Charlie McCarthy, Detective* (1939), and *Crazy House* (1943).

Kennedy died of throat cancer at the Motion Picture Hospital, San Fernando Valley on November 9, 1948 at age 58. He was interred at the Holy Cross Cemetery, Culver City, Los Angeles County, California.

Jack Kenny

Jack Kenny was born John Kenny on November 16, 1886 in Chicago, Illinois. He was an actor, known for *Hidden Loot* (1925), *Northern Code* (1925), and *Beauty and Bullets* (1928).

More of his roles included *Come and Get It* (1936) with Joel McCrea, *The Lone Rider and the Bandit* (1942), *Captain Kidd* (1945), *The Wistful Widow of Wagon Gap* (1947) with Abbott and Costello, *South of St. Louis* (1949) again with Joel McCrea, *Comin' Round the Mountain* (1951) again with Bud and Lou, *Lost in Alaska* (1952) a third with Abbott and Costello, *Border River* (1954) a third with Joel McCrea, Louis L'amour's *Four Guns to the Border* (1954), *Wichita* (1955) a fourth with Joel McCrea, Louis L'amour's *Blackjack Ketchum, Desperado* (1956), *Gunfight at the O.K. Corral* (1957), *Wanted: Dead or Alive* (1958-1959), *North to Alaska* (1960), *Twilight Zone* (1960), *Ride the High Country* (1962) a fifth with Joel McCrea, and *Have Gun - Will Travel* (1960-1962).

He died on May 26, 1964 in Hollywood, California at age 77.

Dorothea Kent

Dorothea Kent and Joel McCrea in *Youth Takes a Fling*

Dorothea Kent was born in St. Joseph, Missouri June 21, 1916 and was an American film actress. She appeared in forty-two films between 1935 and 1948.

Some of her roles included *George White's Scandals* (1934), *Horses' Collars* (1935), *The Luckiest Girl in the World* (1936), *Some Blondes Are Dangerous* (1937), *Youth Takes a Fling* (1938) with Joel McCrea, *Million Dollar Legs* (1939), *Cross-Country Romance* (1940) with Alan Ladd, *King of the Cowboys* (1943), *Ten Cents a Dance* (1945), *The Missing Lady* (1946), *It Happened on Fifth Avenue* (1947), and *The Babe Ruth Story* (1948).

She died in August 23, 1990 from breast cancer at age 74. She was buried at the San Fernando Mission Cemetery; a final resting place designated for people who were of the Catholic faith.

Donald Kerr

Donald Kerr was born on August 5, 1891 in Eagle Grove, Iowa. He was an actor, known for *Four Daughters* (1938), *Flash Gordon's Trip to Mars* (1938), and *The Devil Bat* (1940).

He appeared in eight films with Abbott and Costello and ten episodes of their television show.

More of his roles included *Bombshell* (1933), *Annie Oakley* (1935), *Angels with Dirty Faces* (1938), *Primrose Path* (1940) with Joel McCrea, *The Unknown Guest* (1943), *The Naughty Nineties* (1945), *Little Giant* (1946), *Buck Privates Come Home* (1947), *Knock on Any Door* (1949), *Abbott and Costello Meet the Invisible Man* (1951), *The Abbott and Costello Show* (1953), *Abbott and Costello Go to Mars* (1953), *Abbott and Costello Meet Dr. Jekyll and Mr. Hyde* (1953), *Abbott and Costello Meet the Keystone Kops* (1955), *Abbott and Costello Meet the Mummy* (1955), *Jailhouse Rock* (1957), *Ride the High Country* (1962) again with Joel McCrea, *Petticoat Junction* (1964), and *John Goldfarb, Please Come Home!* (1965).

He died on January 25, 1977 in Los Angeles, California at age 85.

Frederick Kerr

Frederick Kerr was born Frederick Grinham Keen in London, England October 11, 1858 and was a British actor who appeared on stage in both London and New York and in British and American films; he also worked as a major theatrical manager in London.

As a youth just out of Cambridge, he went to New York City around 1880 and worked as a sketch artist, when sheer chance turned him into an actor. He was living in a boarding house on 7th Avenue, where a number of theatrical people also lived (among them, Henry Miller, who eventually became Kerr's manager). Osmond Tearle, an actor living there, heard from his own producer that an Englishman was needed for a production of *The School for Scandal*. Tearle recruited Frederick, who got the part in January 1882 (which is also likely the moment he took the stage name of Frederick Kerr). Kerr appeared in several more plays in New York City that year, but left for Britain to appear in a London play in December 1882. Over the next fifty years, he travelled back and forth across the Atlantic several times for theatrical work both in New York City and in London.

He appeared in nineteen films between 1916 and 1933. Some of those included *The Lady of Scandal* (1930), *Born to Love* (1931), *Beauty and the Boss* (1932), and *Lord of the Manor* (1933).

He is best known as old Baron Frankenstein in *Frankenstein* (1931). Due to Kerr's unexpected death May 3, 1933 at age 74 in London, England, the role of Baron Frankenstein was written out of the sequel *Bride of Frankenstein*, but is mentioned in various scenes.

J. M. Kerrigan

Joseph Michael Kerrigan was born in Dublin, Ireland December 16, 1884, better known as J. M. Kerrigan, was an Irish character actor.

He worked as a newspaper reporter until 1907 when he joined the famous Abbey Players. There he became a stalwart, appearing in plays by Lady Gregory, William Butler Yeats, and John Millington Synge (for whom he played the role of Shawn Keogh in *The Playboy of the Western World*.

His first screen appearance was in the silent film *Food of Love* in 1916. By the 1920s he was appearing on Broadway, often in plays by Shakespeare, Ibsen, and Sheridan.

He settled permanently in Hollywood in 1935, having been recruited along with several other Abbey performers, to appear in John Ford's *The Informer*. In that film and in Ford's *The Long Voyage Home* (1940), he plays similar roles, that of a leech who attaches himself to men until they run out of money.

Perhaps his best known role was in *The General Died at Dawn* (1936), where he plays a character actually named Leach, in which he steals scenes from Gary Cooper, Madeleine Carroll, and William Frawley. In it he plays a sinister little petty thief who, holding a gun on Cooper, says, "I may be fat, but I'm agile."

More of his early roles included *A Study in Scarlet* (1933), *Treasure Island* (1934), *Werewolf of London* (1935), *Barbary Coast* (1935) with Joel McCrea, *Little Orphan Annie* (1938), *Sorority House* (1939) with Veronica Lake, *The Wolf Man* (1941), *The Fighting Seabees* (1944), *Call Northside 777* (1948), *Fireside Theatre* (1952), *20000 Leagues Under the Sea* (1954), *The Fastest Gun Alive* (1956), *Wagon Train* (1959), *The Loretta Young Show* (1960), and *Lock Up* (1960).

One of his most recognizable minor roles in *Gone with the Wind* (1939), when he played John Gallegher, the seemly jovial mill owner who whips his convict labor in to "co-operation".

In 1946 Kerrigan broke into Broadway shows, playing the discombobulated leprechaun Jackeen J. O'Malley in the show "Barnaby and Mr. O'Malley", based on the Crockett Johnson comic strip.

Despite having small roles, Kerrigan has a "Star" on the Hollywood Walk of Fame at 6621 Hollywood Blvd.

He died in Hollywood, Los Angeles, California on April 29, 1964 at age 79.

Evelyn Keyes

Joel McCrea and Evelyn Keyes in *Shoot First*

Evelyn Louise Keyes was born in Port Arthur, Texas November 20, 1916 and was an American film actress. She is best known for her role as Suellen O'Hara in the 1939 film *Gone with the Wind*.

Evelyn Keyes was born to Omar Dow Keyes and Maude Ollive Keyes, the daughter of a Methodist minister. After Omar Keyes died when she was three years old, Keyes moved with her mother to Atlanta, Georgia, where they lived with her grandparents. As a teenager, Keyes took dancing lessons and performed for local clubs such as the Daughters of the Confederacy.

A chorus girl by age 18, Keyes was put under contract by Cecil B. DeMille. After a handful of B movies at Paramount Pictures, she landed her most notable role, that of Scarlett O'Hara's sister Suellen in *Gone with the Wind* (1939). That same year she appeared with Joel McCrea in *Union Pacific*.

Columbia Pictures signed her to a contract. In 1941, she played an ingénue in *Here Comes Mr. Jordan*. She spent most of the early 1940s playing leads in many of Columbia's B dramas and mysteries. She appeared as the female lead opposite Larry Parks in Columbia's blockbuster hit *The Jolson Story* (1946). She appeared in 1949 role as Kathy Flannigan in *Mrs. Mike*. She appeared again with Joel McCrea in *Shoot First* in 1953.Keyes' last major film role was a small part as Tom Ewell's vacationing wife in *The Seven Year Itch* (1955), which starred Marilyn

Monroe. Keyes officially retired in 1956, but continued to act, in such later roles in The Love Boat (1978), *A Return to Salem's Lot* (1987), *Wicked Stepmother* (1989), and *Murder, She Wrote* (1985-1993).

She was married to Barton Oliver Bainbridge Sr. from 1938 until his death from suicide in 1940. Later, she married and divorced director Charles Vidor (1943–1945), actor/director John Huston (July 1946 – February 1950), and bandleader Artie Shaw (1957–1985). Keyes said of her many relationships, "I always took up with the man of the moment and there were many such moments." While married to Huston, the couple adopted a Mexican child, Pablo, whom Huston had discovered while on the set of *The Treasure of the Sierra Madre*.

Her autobiography, *Scarlett O'Hara's Younger Sister: My Lively Life In and Out of Hollywood*, was published in 1977. Keyes expressed her opinion that *Mrs. Mike* was her best film. She also wrote of the personal cost she paid by having an abortion just before *Gone with the Wind* was to begin filming, as the experience left her unable to have children.

She died July 4, 2008 at age 91 in Montecito, California.

Terry Kilburn

Terry Kilburn was born in London, England November 25, 1926 and is an English-American former child actor. He is sometimes credited as Terence Kilburn or Terrance Kilburn.

Known for his innocent, dreamy, doe-eyed look, he achieved fame at the age of 11 portraying Tiny Tim in the 1938 Metro-Goldwyn-Mayer film version of *A Christmas Carol*, and also as four generations of the Colley family in *Goodbye, Mr. Chips* (1939). He also played leading roles in two Freddie Bartholomew films, *Lord Jeff* (1938) and *Swiss Family Robinson* (1940). He was featured in *They Shall Have Music* (1939) with Joel McCRea, and *The Adventures of Sherlock Holmes* (1939) with Basil Rathbone.

Kilburn had a small role in *National Velvet* (1944). In 1944, he also worked in *The Keys of the Kingdom*, starring Gregory Peck, but his scenes were cut. He had a small part in his last film, *Lolita* (1962).

From 1970–1994, Kilburn was artistic director of Oakland University's Meadow Brook Theatre in Rochester, Michigan. Meadow Brook Theatre is Michigan's only LORT theatre. It presents classic plays, comedies and musicals, and is known for its annual production of Dickens' *A Christmas Carol*, adapted by Kilburn's partner Charles Nolte.

Kilburn resides in Minneapolis, Minnesota. His partner of over fifty years, actor Charles Nolte, died in January 2010.

Victor Killian

Victor Arthur Kilian was born in Jersey City, New Jersey March 6, 1891 and was an American actor who was blacklisted by the Hollywood movie studio bosses in the 1950s.

Victor Kilian began his career in entertainment at the age of eighteen by joining a vaudeville company. In the mid-1920s he began to perform in Broadway plays and by the end of the decade had made his debut in motion pictures. For the next two decades he made a good living as a character actor in secondary or minor roles in films such as *The Adventures of Tom Sawyer* (1938). Frequently cast as a villain, while staging a fight scene with John Wayne for a 1942 film, Kilian suffered a serious injury that resulted in the loss of one eye.

More of his early roles included *Gentlemen of the Press* (1929), *The Wiser Sex* (1932), *Wrongorilla* (1933), *Adventure in Manhattan* (1936) with Joel McCrea, *Boys Town* (1938), *Only Angels Have Wings* (1939), *Virginia City* (1940), *Sergeant York* (1941), *This Gun for Hire* (1942) with Alan Ladd and Veronica Lake, *The Ox-Bow Incident* (1943), *Little Giant* (1946) with Abbott and Costello, *Colorado Territory* (1949) again with Joel McCrea, and *Stars in My Crown* (1950), yet again with Joel McCrea.

During the McCarthyism of the 1950s, Victor Kilian was blacklisted for his political beliefs but because the Actors' Equity Association refused to go along with the ban, Kilian was able to earn a living by returning to perform on stage. After Hollywood's blacklisting ended, he began doing guest roles on television series during the 1970s, such as *The Brady Bunch* (1970), *Planet of the Apes* (1974), *Gunsmoke* (1974), and *Kojak* (1975).

He is best known for his role as Grandpa Larkin (aka The Fernwood Flasher) in the television soap opera spoof *Mary Hartman, Mary Hartman* (1976).

Kilian's wife, Daisy Johnson, to whom he had been married for 46 years, died in 1961.

In the spring of 1979, Kilian appeared in an episode of TV's *All in the Family*, "The Return of Stephanie's Father", portraying a desk clerk in a seedy hotel. In the same episode fellow veteran Hollywood character actor Charles Wagenheim appeared as a 'bum' in the hotel's lobby. Just weeks before the episode aired, on March 6, 1979 (Kilian's birthday), the 83-year-old Wagenheim was bludgeoned to death in his Hollywood apartment after he was surprised coming home from grocery shopping during an act of robbery.

Five days later, on March 11, 1979, Victor Kilian, who lived alone in Hollywood just blocks from Wagenheim, was also beaten to death by burglars in his apartment.

On March 20, 1979, *All in the Family* posthumously aired the episode "The Return of Stephanie's Father," with Wagenheim's and Kilian's last screen performances.

Victor Kilian's cremated remains were scattered in the rose garden at Westwood Village Memorial Park Cemetery in Los Angeles.

Frank Killmond

Frank Killmond was born Francis Xavier Killmond on January 15, 1934 in Baltimore, Maryland. He was an actor, known for *Take a Giant Step* (1959), *Anatomy of a Psycho* (1961), and *General Hospital* (1963).

More of his roles included *A Nice Little Bank That Should Be Robbed* (1958), *Shotgun Slade* (1959), *Wichita Town* (1960) with Joel McCrea, *Psycho* (1960), *The Munsters* (1965), *My Three Sons* (1963-1970), *Cannon* (1975), *Wonder Woman* (1977), *Quincy M.E.* (1978), and *Lots of Luck* (1985).

He died on April 17, 1992 in Woodland Hills, Los Angeles, California at age 58.

Wright King

Thomas Wright Thornberg King was born January 11, 1923 in Okmulgee, Oklahoma. Wright was always interested in acting; after high school, he was studying to be an actor at the St. Louis School of Theatre. But when America entered WWII, Wright served in the Navy; he worked as a pharmacist's mate, stationed in the South Pacific. In 1946, after the war and an honorable discharge, Wright went to NYC, and under the G.I. Bill, he studied at the Actors Studio and the American Theatre Wing.

He had a successful career in numerous theatrical productions. In 1947, Wright was one of the first actors to work steadily in the new medium of live television.

He married June Ellen Roth in 1948. They had three sons: Wright Jr., Michael, and Meegan who grew up to be a fine actor.

Some of Wright's earliest TV appearances were on such series as *Captain Video and His Video Rangers* (1949), *The Ken Murray Show* (1950), and *Big Town* (1950-1951).

In 1949, Wright achieved recognition for his portrayal of the Collector in Elia Kazan's stage version of *A Streetcar Named Desire*. This led to a movie career when he reprised the role for the film version in 1951, acting alongside screen legends Vivien Leigh and Marlon Brando. Wright would have a long career in movies playing supporting characters.

Wright replaced Vaughn Taylor as Ernest P. Duckweather on the kiddie puppet show *Johnny Jupiter* when the series went from live TV to film, in 1953.

Other roles followed in such movies and shows as *The Bold and the Brave* (1956), *Stagecoach to Fury* (1956), *Maverick* (1957), *The Gunfight at Dodge City* (1959) with Joel McCrea, *Cast a Long Shadow* (1959) with Audie Murphy, *Outlaws* (1961), and five episodes of *Have Gun - Will Travel* (1957-1961).

Wright is best remembered by his fans for his two guest appearances on the original *Twilight Zone* (1961-1963) series. He played Paul Carson in the episode "Shadow Play," which raised the question: do we live in the real world and we have dreams at night, or is our reality just a dream? And he played Hecate in the episode "Of Late, I Think of Cliffordville," about a man going back in time to relive his youth.

Wright was most often seen on television in 1960 on the Steve McQueen western series *Wanted Dead or Alive*. After making two earlier guest appearances on it, he was seen in eleven other second-season episodes as Jason Nichols, a 'sidekick' to McQueen's bounty hunter Josh Randall.

More roles followed in *Voyage to the Bottom of the Sea* (1964), *King Rat* (1965), eight episodes of *Gunsmoke* (1955-1965), two episodes of *The Fugitive* (1964-1966), *Planet of the Apes* (1968) as Dr. Galen, and *Along Came a Spider* (1970),

Wright is remembered for playing Dr. Murger in the sci-fi film *Invasion of the Bee Girls* (1973), which was re-released in Drive-Ins years later under the title *Graveyard Tramps* (1983). This movie in which Wright King and William Smith fight off Anitra Ford and her swarm of sexually-driven Insect Women is a true cult classic.

He continued to get roles in *The Streets of San Francisco* (1973-1974), *McCloud* (1975), *The Macahans* (1976), *Helter Skelter* (1976), *Police Woman* (1977), three episodes as Jonathon in *Logan's Run* (1977-1978), *The Critical List* (1978), and *House Made of Dawn* (1987).

He is retired and living in Portland, Oregon.

Leonid Kinsky

Leonid Kinskey was born in St. Petersburg, Russia April 18, 1903 and was a movie and television actor who enjoyed a long career. Kinskey is best known for his role as Sascha in the film *Casablanca* (1942).

He fled the Russian Revolution and acted on stage in Europe and South America before arriving in New York City in 1921. He joined the road production of Al Jolson's musical *Wonder Bar*, before making his first film appearance, in the *Trouble in Paradise* (1932). His looks and accent helped him gain supporting roles in numerous movies, including *Duck Soup* (1933) and *Nothing Sacred* (1937), It is said that he was cast in his best-known role, Sascha in *Casablanca*, because he was a drinking buddy of star Humphrey Bogart.

More of his roles included *Hollywood Party* (1934), *Three Godfathers* (1936), *Three Blind Mice* (1938) with Joel McCrea, *Gildersleeve on Broadway* (1943), *The Great Sinner* (1949), *The Man with the Golden Arm* (1955), and *The Helen Morgan Story* (1957).

Kinskey continued to appear on television, well into the 1960s such as *Peter Gunn* (1959), *Have Gun - Will Travel* (1961-1962), *My Favorite Martian* (1964), the pilot episode of *Hogan's Heroes* (1965), *Perry Mason* (1966), *Batman* (1967), *Mayberry R.F.D.* (1970-1971), and *O'Hara, U.S. Treasury* (1971) with David Janssen.

Kinskey was married three times. His second wife was actress Iphigenie Castiglioni, to whom he remained married until her death in 1963. He was married to Tina York from 1983 to his death. He died September 8, 1998 of complications of a stroke in Fountain Hills, Arizona, at the age of 95.

Fuzzy Knight

John Forrest "Fuzzy" Knight was born in Fairmont, West Virginia May 9, 1901 and was an American film and television actor. He was also a singer, especially in his early career. He appeared in more than 180 films between 1929 and 1967, usually as a cowboy hero's comic sidekick.

Knight was the third child and son of James A. and Olive Knight, and attended nearby West Virginia University where he was a cheerleader and law student. He wrote a pep song, "Fight Mountaineers," which is still frequently used by the Mountaineer Marching Band ninety years later. He also wrote the melody for a WVU song entitled "To Thee Our Alma Mater," with words by fellow graduate David A. Christopher. He formed his own band in college and played drums, eventually leaving school to perform in vaudeville and in big bands such as Irving Aaronson's and George Olsen's.

Eventually his musical and comedy skills took him to New York, where he appeared in *Earl Carroll's Vanities* of 1927 and on Broadway in *Here's Howe* and *Ned Wayburn's Gambols*. He was billed under his nickname, Fuzzy (given him because of his peculiarly soft voice).

While touring with bands, Knight came to Hollywood and appeared in several musical short films for MGM and Paramount between 1929 and 1932. Mae West gave him his first notable film role in *She Done Him Wrong*, and he went on to play in hundreds of films over the next thirty years. By the 1940s, he was primarily playing in Western movies and was voted one of the Top Ten Money-Making Stars in Westerns in 1940.

More of his roles included *To the Last Man* (1933), *The Trail of the Lonesome Pine* (1936), *Union Pacific* (1939) with Joel McCrea, *Silver Bullet* (1942), *Riders of the Santa Fe* (1944), *The Egg and I* (1947), *Skipalong Rosenbloom* (1951), *Gold Raiders* (1951) with The Three Stooges, *Adventures of Wild Bill Hickok* (1955).

Knight became famous to a new generation when he co-starred as Buster Crabbe's sidekick on the 1955 TV series *Captain Gallant of the Foreign Legion*. In semi-retirement thereafter, Knight continued to make occasional appearances in films and TV shows through 1967.

He died February 23, 1976 at age 74 in his sleep at the Motion Picture Country House and Hospital in Woodland Hills, California, and was survived by his wife, actress Patricia Ryan (née Thelma de Long). He was buried in Valhalla Memorial Park Cemetery in Burbank, California. His unmarked grave is next to that of the grave of Slapsie Maxie Rosenbloom, Knight's two-time co-star, who died less than two weeks after Knight.

Susan Kohner

Susan Kohner was born Susanna Kohner in Los Angeles, November 11, 1936, and is an American actress.

She is the daughter of Mexican actress Lupita Tovar and film producer Paul Kohner, who was born in Bohemia. It was only natural for Susan to gravitate toward acting.

Her first role was in *To Hell and Back* (1955) with Audie Murphy. One more film in 1956, *The Last Wagon*, and one in 1957, *Trooper Hook*, brought her to the attention of producers in the movie industry.

She again played opposite Audie Murphy in the episode "The Flight" of the television program *Suspicion* (1957).

Susan made several films in 1959. The best of the lot was *Imitation of Life* (1959), a film starring Lana Turner and Sandra Dee. It was a dual story of Lana portraying a struggling actress and Susan as Sara Jane, struggling with the fact that although she appeared white, her mother was black. Susan's role as a young woman trying to cope in the white world while hiding the fact she was black was enough to win her an Academy Award nomination as Best Supporting Actress. Unfortunately, Susan lost out to Shelley Winters in *The Diary of Anne Frank* (1959). She did win the Golden Globe in the Best Supporting Actress categories.

Following her appearance in *Imitation of Life*, Kohner appeared in *All the Fine Young Cannibals* (1960), opposite Natalie Wood and Robert Wagner. She later had guest roles on episodic television including roles on *Hong Kong* (1961) and *Going My Way* (1963),

After appearing in *Freud* (1962), Susan left films for good with the exception of appearing in television programs like *Temple Houston* (1963), *Rawhide* (1964), and *Channing* (1964).

In 1964, Kohner married German novelist and fashion designer John Weitz, and retired from acting. Their children, Chris and Paul Weitz, are successful film directors in Hollywood, having helmed films such as *American Pie* (1999) and *About a Boy* (2002). Chris Weitz is best known for directing *New Moon* (2009) in *The Twilight Saga.*

On April 23, 2010, a new print of *Imitation of Life* was screened at the TCM Film Festival in Los Angeles, California. After the screeening, Kohner appeared on stage along with her costar Juanita Moore for a question-and-answer session hosted by TCM's Robert Osborne. Kohner and Moore received standing ovations.

Clarence Kolb

Clarence William Kolb was born in Cleveland, Ohio July 31, 1874 and was an American vaudeville performer and actor. He was the only child of second generation Austrian parents who owned a local meat company.

Kolb started out as one half of a vaudeville comedy team, Kolb and Dill, with Max Dill. They styled their act on the famous team Weber and Fields. In addition to their stage work, they appeared in a series of movie shorts and a feature length movie in 1917. Afterwards, Kolb made a return to vaudeville, and he only returned to the movies in the late 1930s.

He became famous for portraying the same type of character in many movies, namely a politician or businessman. He is best remembered for his role as the grumpy father in the multi-Academy Awards nominated hit comedy film *Merrily We Live* (1938), the corrupt mayor in the comedy *His Girl Friday* (1940), and as Mr. Honeywell in the television sitcom *My Little Margie* (1952).

More of his roles included *Wells Fargo* (1937) with Joel McCrea, *The Amazing Mr. Williams* (1939), *The Falcon in Danger* (1943), *The Hal Roach Comedy Carnival* (1947), *Adam's Rib* (1949), and *Shake, Rattle & Rock!* (1956).

Kolb played himself in his last movie appearance, *Man of a Thousand Faces* (1957), opposite Danny Beck (who played the late Max Dill).

Clarence Kolb died November 25, 1964 at age 90 from a stroke at the Orchard Gables Sanitarium at 1277 North Wilcox Avenue in Hollywood. He is interred in the Forest Lawn Memorial Park Cemetery in Glendale, California.

Henry Kolker

Joseph Henry Kolker was born November 13, 1874 in Berlin, Germany and was an American stage and film actor and director. He came to America at the age of five and his family settled in Quincy, Illinois. Kolker, like fellow actors Richard Bennett and Robert Warwick, had a substantial stage career behind him before entering silent films.

On stage he appeared opposite such leading ladies as Edith Wynne Matthison, Bertha Kalich, and Ruth Chatterton. Kolker is best remembered for his motion picture appearances and for appearing with Barbara Stanwyck in the ground-breaking Pre-Code film *Baby Face* (1933) as the elderly CEO of the company whom Stanwyck's character seduces. Another well remembered part is as Mr. Seton, father of Katharine Hepburn and Lew Ayres in the 1938 film *Holiday* directed by George Cukor.

Kolker entered films as an actor in 1915 and eventually ended up trying his hand at directing. Kolker's best known directorial effort is *Disraeli* (1921), starring George Arliss which is now a lost film with only one reel remaining.

More of his roles included *The Man Who Lived Twice* (1936), *Union Pacific* (1939) with Joel McCrea, *Sing for Your Supper* (1941), *Bluebeard* (1944), and *The Secret Life of Walter Mitty* (1947).

He died July 15, 1947 in Los Angeles, California at age 72.

Martin Kosleck

Martin Kosleck was born Nicolaie Yoshkin in Barkotzen in Pomerania, Germany March 24, 1904 and was a German film actor. Like many other German actors, he fled when the Nazis came to power. Inspired by his deep hatred of Adolf Hitler and the Nazis, Kosleck would make a career in Hollywood playing villainous Nazis in films. While in the United States, he would appear in more than 80 films and television shows in a 46-year span. His icy demeanor and piercing stare on screen made him a popular choice to play Nazi villains. He portrayed Joseph Goebbels, Adolf Hitler's propaganda minister, five times, and also appeared as an SS trooper and a concentration camp officer.

Kosleck was the son of a forester. His family was "German-Russian". He became interested in acting at an early age. He spent six years in the Max Reinhardt Dramatic School, particularly excelling in Shakespearian roles, and working in revues and musicals in Berlin.

At the age of 23, he appeared in his first film, a silent movie directed by Johannes Brandt called *Der Fahnenträger von Sedan*. Two years later he appeared in Lupo Pick's *Napoleon auf St. Helena*. Kosleck would appear in two more films in Germany in 1930; the science-fiction thriller *Alraune* (his first sound film) and *Die Singende Stadt*.

In the early 1930s, Hitler and the Nazi Party were growing in power. Kosleck spoke out against both and decided to leave Germany in 1931 for Britain. The following year, he arrived in New York and then traveled west to Hollywood. In 1933, when Hitler and the Nazi Party came to power, because of his opposition to the Nazis, Kosleck was placed on the Gestapolist of "undesirables".

He appeared in his first American film *Fashions of 1934* starring Bette Davis. However, he found little work in Hollywood, so he returned to New York and the stage. While Kosleck was acting in *The Merchant of Venice* on Broadway, Anatole Litvak invited him to Hollywood for a role in a Warner Brothers film. The highly controversial *Confessions of a Nazi Spy* (1939), starring Edward G. Robinson, Francis Lederer, Paul Lukas and George Sanders, was based on *The Nazi Spy Conspiracy in America*, a book by Leon Turron, an FBI agent who had uncovered the network of Nazi organizations throughout the United States. Kosleck, in a small role playing Nazi Propaganda Minister Joseph Goebbels, revealed a sinister streak of evil that would be sought after in wartime movies to come.

Many other German actors at the time resented being typecast as Nazis, Kosleck on the other hand reveled in it as a way to get back at the Nazis. He appeared in numerous anti-Nazi films of the early 1940s: *Nurse Edith Cavell, Espionage Agent* and *Foreign Correspondent* with Joel McCrea, *Underground, Berlin Correspondent, Bomber's Moon* and *Chetniks! The Fighting Guerrillas*. However, it was his impression of Goebbels that will remain in the memories of moviegoers, especially in Paramount's 1944 pseudo-documentary *The Hitler Gang*.

With the end of the Second World War, roles as Nazis declined. Kosleck then moved into B horror films, such as *The Frozen Ghost* and *The Mummy's Curse* (both starring Lon Chaney Jr., whom Kosleck disliked intensely), *House of Horrors* and *She-Wolf of London*, starring June Lockhart. *The House of Horrors* gave him his best-remembered role beyond Goebbels, as an insane sculptor, Marcel De Lange, who saves a monster from drowning and gets revenge by having the monster kill his critics.

With fewer film opportunities presenting themselves, Kosleck returned to New York City with his wife, the German-born actress Eleonore von Mendelssohn, a descendant of Moses Mendelssohn. Kosleck appeared on Broadway in *The Madwoman of Chaillot* in the late 1940s and early 1950s.

He would also appear on television as guests in episodes of numerous shows. In 1951, he appeared in the "I Lift Up My Lamp" episode of *Hallmark Hall of Fame*, a television anthology of plays and books. Throughout the 1950s and 1960s, he would appear in television episodes of *The Motorola Television Hour*, where he played Goebbels again, *Studio One, Thriller, The Rifleman, Voyage to the Bottom of the Sea, The Outer Limits, Get Smart, Batman* (playing Professor Avery Evans Charm), *The Man from U.N.C.L.E., The F.B.I., The Wild Wild West, Mission: Impossible* and *It Takes a Thief*.

In 1970, Kosleck played a Gestapo general in the television comedy *Hogan's Heroes*. He suffered from a heart attack in the 1970s, and thereafter worked only occasionally, mostly in television. During this time, he appeared in *Night Gallery, O'Hara, U.S. Treasury, Love, American Style, Banacek* and *Sanford and Son*. In 1980, he appeared in his last film, *The Man with Bogart's Face*.

Aside from acting, Kosleck was an accomplished painter who supported himself through his work as a portrait artist while waiting for a movie role. An impressionist-style portrait-painter, he painted both Bette Davis and Marlene Dietrich.

In 1951, his wife committed suicide. Kosleck died January 15, 1994 at age 89, following abdominal surgery, in a Santa Monica convalescent home.

Alma Kruger

Joel McCrea and Alma Kruger in *These Three*

Alma Kruger was born in Pittsburgh, Pennsylvania September 13, 1871 and was an American actress.

Kruger had a long career on stage before appearing in films. From 1907 to 1935, she featured in theatre plays on Broadway, mostly in Shakespearean plays such as *Hamlet* (as Gertrude),*Twelfth Night* (as Olivia), *Taming of the Shrew* (Widow), and *The Merchant of Venice* (Nerissa).

She appeared in her first film while in her sixties, *These Three* (1936) with Joel McCrea. She then proceeded to act in over forty films in the space of little more than a decade. Among her notable roles was Nurse Molly Byrd, the superintendent of nurses in the popular Dr. Kildare/Dr. Gillespie film series, appearing in all but the first two of the sixteen movies.

She portrayed Empress Maria Theresa of Austria in *Marie Antoinette* (1938) and the almost mother-in-law of Rosalind Russell's lead character in *His Girl Friday* (1940). In 1942, she appeared as the subversive society matron Henrietta Sutton in Alfred Hitchcock's *Saboteur* (1942). Kruger's last film appearance was in the film, *Forever Amber* (1947).

Alma Kruger died April 5, 1960 in Seattle, Washington from natural causes at age 88.

Patricia Laffan

Joel McCrea and Patricia Laffan in *Shoot First*

Patricia Laffan was born in Wandsworth, London, England March 19, 1919 and is an English actress. She is the daughter of Arthur Charles Laffan and Elvira Alice Vitali. Patricia was educated at Folkstone and at the Institut Français in London. At the Webber-Douglas Dramatic School, she studied for the stage.

Her first credited part was a minor role as Betty in *Caravan* (1946). The following year she was featured in the mystery film *Death in High Heels* (1947) with Don Stannard. In 1950, she appeared in the crime drama *Hangman's Wharf* as Rosa Warren. In the 1951 film *Quo Vadis*, she played Poppaea, the second wife of the Roman Emperor Nero. In *Escape Route* (1952), a crime thriller, she played Irma Brooks. She played Magda in *Shoot First* (1953) with Joel McCrea. She starred as the ruthless, PVC-clad alien Nyah in the *Devil Girl from Mars* (1955). The next year she had a supporting part as Miss Alice MacDonald in the mystery thriller *23 Paces to Baker Street* (1956). By the 1960s, she mainly appeared on television, in shows like *Anna Karenina* (1961), *BBC Sunday-Night Play* (1962-1963), *Maigret* (1963), and *Reluctant Bandit* (1965). She then retired from acting altogether.

In 2008, Laffan was interviewed for the British documentary *British B Movies: Truly, Madly, Cheaply*.

Veronica Lake

Veronica Lake and Joel McCrea in *Ramrod*

Veronica Lake was born Constance Frances Marie Ockelman in Brooklyn, New York November 14, 1922 and was an American film, stage, and television actress.

Lake won both popular and critical acclaim, most notably for her role in *Sullivan's Travels* and for her femme fatale roles in film noirs with Alan Ladd, during the 1940s. She was also well known for her peek-a-boo hairstyle. By the late 1940s however, Lake's career had begun to decline in part due to her struggles with mental illness and alcoholism. She made only one film in the 1950s but appeared in several guest-starring roles on television. She returned to the screen in 1966 with a role in the film *Footsteps in the Snow*, but the role failed to revitalize her career.

She released her memoirs, *Veronica: The Autobiography of Veronica Lake*, in 1970. She used the money she made from the book to finance a low-budget horror film *Flesh Feast*. It was her final onscreen role. Lake died in July 1973 from hepatitis and acute kidney injury at the age of 50.

Her father, Harry E. Ockelman, was of German-Danish descent and worked for an oil company aboard a ship. He died in an industrial explosion in Philadelphia in 1932. Lake's mother, Constance Charlotta (née Trimble; 1902–1992), of Irish descent, married Anthony Keane, a newspaper staff artist, also of Irish descent, in 1933, and Lake began using his surname.

The Keanes lived in Saranac Lake, New York where Lake went to St. Bernard's School for a time. She was sent to Villa Maria, an all-girls Catholic boarding school in Montreal, Canada, from which she was expelled. The Keane family later moved to Miami, Florida where Lake attended Miami High School, where she was known for her beauty. She had a troubled childhood and was diagnosed as schizophrenic, according to her mother.

In 1938, the Keanes moved to Beverly Hills where Constance Keene enrolled Lake in the Bliss-Hayden School of Acting. Her first appearance on screen was for RKO, playing a small role among several coeds in the 1939 film, *Sorority House*. Similar roles followed, including *All Women Have Secrets* and *Dancing Co-Ed*, both also in 1939. During the making of *Sorority House*, director John Farrow first noticed how her hair always covered her right eye, creating an air of mystery about her and enhancing her natural beauty. While still a teenager, Lake was introduced to the Paramount producer Arthur Hornblow, Jr. He changed her name to Veronica Lake because the surname suited her blue eyes.

RKO subsequently dropped her contract. A small role in the comedy *Forty Little Mothers* (1940) brought unexpected attention. In 1941 she was signed to a long-term contract with Paramount Pictures.

Lake's breakthrough role was in the 1941 war drama *I Wanted Wings*. The film was a major hit in which Lake played the second female lead. She also had starring roles in more popular movies, including *Sullivan's Travels* (1941) with Joel McCrea, *This Gun for Hire* (1942), *I Married a Witch* (1942), *The Glass Key* (1942), and *So Proudly We Hail!* (1943). René Clair, the director of *I Married a Witch*, said of Lake "She was a very gifted girl, but she didn't believe she was gifted."

For a short time during the early 1940s, Lake was considered one of the most reliable box office draws in Hollywood. At the peak of her popularity, she earned $4,500 a week. She also raised a reported $12 million in war bonds in various tours.

She became known for onscreen pairings with actor Alan Ladd. At first, the couple was teamed together merely out of physical necessity: Ladd was just 5 feet 5 inches tall and the only actress then on the Paramount lot short enough to pair with him was Lake, who stood just 4 feet 11 ½ inches. They made four films together.

A stray lock of her shoulder-length, blonde hair during a publicity photo shoot led to her iconic "peek-a-boo" hairstyle, which was widely imitated. During World War II, Lake changed her trademark image to encourage women working in war industry factories to adopt more practical, safer hairstyles, although doing so may have damaged her career.

Although popular with the public, Lake had a complex personality and acquired a reputation for being difficult to work with. Eddie Bracken, her co-star in *Star Spangled Rhythm* (in which Lake appeared in a musical number) was quoted as saying, "She was known as 'The Bitch' and she deserved the title."

Lake's career faltered with her unsympathetic role as Nazi spy Dora Bruckman in 1944's *The Hour Before the Dawn*. Scathing reviews of *The Hour Before the Dawn* included criticism of her unconvincing German accent. She had begun drinking more heavily during this period, and a growing number of people refused to work with her.

To boost her career, Paramount tried Lake in a series of comedies. Few were successful but she was in the popular thriller *The Blue Dahlia* (1946), in which she again co-starred with Alan Ladd. She then appeared with Joel McCrea in *Ramrod* in 1947. Paramount decided not to renew her contract in 1948 after another pairing with Ladd in *Saigon.* Looking back at her career years later, Lake remarked, "I never did cheesecake; I just used my hair."

After a single film for 20th Century Fox, *Slattery's Hurricane* in 1949, her career collapsed. By the end of 1951 she had appeared in one last film *Stronghold* (which she later described as "a dog"). Lake and her second husband, Andre De Toth, filed for bankruptcy that same year. The IRS later seized their home for unpaid taxes.

Lake then turned to television and stage work. In 1955 she collapsed in Detroit where she had been appearing on stage.

She earned her pilot's license in 1946 and later flew solo between Los Angeles and New York.

Lake's first marriage was to art director John S. Detlie, in 1940. They had a daughter, Elaine (born in 1941), and a son Anthony (born July 8, 1943). Anthony was born prematurely a week after Lake tripped and fell over a cable while filming. Anthony died on July 15, 1943. Lake and Detlie separated in August 1943 and divorced in December 1943.

She then married film director Andre De Toth in 1944 with whom she had a son, Andre Anthony Michael III (known as Michael De Toth), and a daughter, Diana (born October 1948). Days before Diana's birth, Lake's mother sued her for support payments. Lake and De Toth divorced in 1952.

In September 1955, she married songwriter Joseph Allan McCarthy. They were divorced in 1959. Lake's fourth and final marriage was to Royal Navy captain Robert Carleton-Munro in June 1972. They divorced after one year.

After her third divorce, Lake drifted between cheap hotels in New York City, and was arrested several times for public drunkenness and disorderly conduct. In 1962, a *New York Post* reporter found her working as a barmaid at the all-women's Martha Washington Hotel in Manhattan. The reporter's widely distributed story led to some television and stage appearances, most notably in the off-Broadway revival of the musical *Best Foot Forward*. (Her contract overlapped with the departing Liza Minnelli and the two briefly co-starred together.) In 1966, she had a brief stint as a TV hostess in Baltimore, Maryland, along with a largely ignored film role in *Footsteps In the Snow* (1966).

Her memoirs, *Veronica: The Autobiography of Veronica Lake*, were released in the United Kingdom in 1969, and in the United States the following year. In the book, Lake discusses her career, her failed marriages, her alcoholism, and her guilt over not spending enough time with her children. With the proceeds from her autobiography, she co-produced and starred in her final film, *Flesh Feast* (1970), a low-budget horror movie with a Nazi-myth storyline.

She then moved to Ipswich, England, where she met and married Royal Navy captain Robert Carleton-Munro, in June 1972. The marriage lasted just one year and Lake returned to the United States in June 1973. She went to the Virgin Islands to await her divorce decree when she fell ill.

Lake died on July 7, 1973 at the age of 50, of hepatitis and acute kidney injury in Burlington, Vermont's Fletcher Allen Hospital. Her son, Michael, claimed her body. Lake's memorial service was held at the Universal Chapel in New York City on July 11.

Her remains were cremated and, according to her wishes, her ashes were scattered off the coast of the Virgin Islands. In 2004, some of Lake's ashes were reportedly found in a New York antique store.

For her contribution to the motion picture industry, Veronica Lake has a star on the Hollywood Walk of Fame at 6918 Hollywood Boulevard.

Clips from her role in *The Glass Key* (1942 film) were integrated into the 1982 film *Dead Men Don't Wear Plaid*, as character Monica Stillpond.

Lake was one of the models for the animated character of Jessica Rabbit in the 1988 film *Who Framed Roger Rabbit*, especially for her hairstyle.

Jack Lambert

Jack Lambert was born in Yonkers, New York April 13, 1920 and was an American character actor who specialized in playing movie tough guys and heavies. He is best known for playing the psychotic cat-loving, iron-hooked Steve "the Claw" Michael in *Dick Tracy's Dilemma* (1947).

Following a spell on Broadway, Lambert moved to Hollywood and began working in films in 1942. He was a familiar figure in Westerns and crime dramas after World War II, in such movies as *Bomber's Moon* (1943), *The Canterville Ghost* (1944), *Abilene Town* (1946), *The Killers* (1946), *Belle Starr's Daughter* (1948), *Stars in My Crown* (1950) with Joel McCrea, *Bend of the River* (1952), *Kiss Me Deadly* (1955), *Vera Cruz* (1954), *Machine-Gun Kelly* (1958), *Alias Jesse James* (1959), *How the West Was Won* (1962), and *4 for Texas* (1963).

Lambert also appeared in many television series of the 1950s and 1960s, such as Rod Cameron's *State Trooper* (1957), *Richard Diamond, Private Detective* (1958), *Sugarfoot* (1959), *Have Gun - Will Travel* (1960), *Wagon Train* (1957-1963), *Get Smart* (1966), *Daniel Boone* (1966-1967), *Bonanza* (1960-1967), and *Gunsmoke* (1959-1970).

From 1959 to 1960, he was a regular cast member (as Joshua Walcek, sometimes called "Joshua MacGregor"), in twenty-three of the forty-two episodes of Darren McGavin's NBC western series, *Riverboat*.

He is often confused with Jack Lambert, a British character actor, as well as the former Pittsburgh Steelers linebackerJack Lambert.

He died February 18, 2002 at age 81 in Carmel, California.

Elsa Lanchester

Elsa Sullivan Lanchester was born in Lewisham, London October 28, 1902 and was an English character actress with a long career in theatre, film and television.

Lanchester studied dance as a child and after World War I began performing in theatre and cabaret, where she established her career over the following decade. She met the actor Charles Laughton in 1927, and they were married two years later. She began playing small roles in British films, including the role of Anne of Cleves with Laughton in *The Private Life of Henry VIII* (1933). His success in American films resulted in the couple moving to Hollywood, where Lanchester played small film roles.

Her role as the title character in *Bride of Frankenstein* (1935) brought her recognition. She played supporting roles through the 1940s and 1950s. She was nominated for the Academy Award for Best Supporting Actress for *Come to the Stable* (1949) and *Witness for the Prosecution* (1957), the last of twelve films in which she appeared with Laughton. Following Laughton's death in 1962, Lanchester resumed her career with appearances in such Disney films as *Mary Poppins* (1964), *That Darn Cat!* (1965) and *Blackbeard's Ghost* (1968). The horror film *Willard* (1971) was highly successful, and one of her last roles was in *Murder By Death* (1976).

Her parents, James "Shamus" Sullivan and Edith "Biddy" Lanchester, were considered Bohemian, and refused to legalize their union in any conventional way to satisfy the era's conservative society. They were both socialists, according to Lanchester's 1970 interview with Dick Cavett. Elsa's older brother, Waldo Sulivan Lanchester, born five years earlier, was a puppeteer, with his own *marionette* company based in Malvern and later in Stratford-upon-Avon.

Elsa studied dance in Paris under Isadora Duncan, whom she disliked. When the school was discontinued due to the start of World War I, she returned to Britain. At that point (she was about twelve years of age) she began teaching dance in the Isadora Duncan's style and, very enterprisingly, started to give classes to children in her South London district, through which she earned some welcome extra income for her household. At about this time, after the First World War, she started the Children's Theatre, and later the Cave of Harmony, a nightclub at which modern

78

plays and cabaret turns were performed. She revived old Victorian songs and ballads, many of which she retained for her performances in another revue entitled *Riverside Nights*. She became sufficiently famous for Columbia to invite her into the recording studio to make 78 rpm discs of four of the numbers she sang in these revues: "Please Sell No More Drink to My Father" and "He Didn't Oughter" were on one disc (recorded in 1926) and "Don't Tell My Mother I'm Living in Sin" and *The Ladies Bar* was on the other (recorded 1930).

Her cabaret and nightclub appearances led to more serious stage work and it was in a play by Arnold Bennett called *Mr Prohack* (1927) that Lanchester first met another member of the cast, Charles Laughton. They were married two years later and continued to act together from time to time, both on stage and screen. She played his daughter in the stage play *Payment Deferred* (1931) though not in the subsequent Hollywood film version. Lanchester and Laughton appeared in the Old Vic season of 1933–1934, playing Shakespeare, Chekov and Wilde, and in 1936 she was Peter Pan to Laughton's Captain Hook in J. M. Barrie's play at the London Palladium. Their last stage appearance together was in Jane Arden's *The Party* (1958) at the New Theatre, London.

Lanchester made her film debut in *The Scarlet Woman* (1925) and in 1928 appeared in three 'silent shorts' written for her by H.G. Wells and directed by Ivor Montagu (*Bluebottles*, *Daydreams* and *The Tonic*) in which Laughton made brief appearances. They also appeared together in a 1930 'film revue' entitled *Comets*, featuring British stage, musical and variety acts, in which they sang in duet 'The Ballad of Frankie and Johnnie.' Lanchester appeared in several other early British talkies, including *Potiphar's Wife* (1931), starring Laurence Olivier. She appeared opposite Laughton again in 1933 as a highly comical Anne of Cleves in *The Private Life of Henry VIII*. Laughton was by now making films in Hollywood so Lanchester joined him there, making minor appearances in *David Copperfield* (1935) and *Naughty Marietta* (1935). These and her appearances in British films helped her gain the title role in *Bride of Frankenstein* (1935). She and Laughton returned to Britain in 1936 to appear together again in *Rembrandt* and two years later in *Vessel of Wrath*, a.k.a. *The Beachcomber*.

They both returned to Hollywood in 1939 where he made *The Hunchback of Notre Dame* although Lanchester didn't appear in another film until *Ladies in Retirement* (1941). She and Laughton played husband and wife (their characters were named Charles and Elsa Smith) in *Tales of Manhattan* (1942) and they both appeared again in the all-star, mostly British cast of *Forever and a Day* (1943). She then received top billing in *Passport to Destiny* (1944) for the only time in her Hollywood films. In this, she played a cockney charlady who scrubs her way across occupied Europe in order to assassinate Hitler."

Lanchester played supporting roles in *The Spiral Staircase* and *The Razor's Edge* (both 1946) and also appeared in *The Bishop's Wife* the following year. She played a comical role in the 1948 thriller, *The Big Clock*, in which Laughton starred as a murderous, megalomaniac press tycoon. She had a substantial part as an artist specialising in nativity scenes in *Come to the Stable* for which she was nominated for a Best Supporting Actress Academy Award (1949).

During the late 1940s and 1950s she appeared in small but highly varied supporting roles in a number of films while simultaneously appearing on stage at the *Turnabout Theatre* in Hollywood. Here she performed her solo vaudeville act in conjunction with a marionette show, singing somewhat off-colour songs which she later recorded for a couple of LPs. Onscreen, she appeared alongside Danny Kaye in *The Inspector General* (1949), played a blackmailing landlady in *Mystery Street* (1950) and was Shelley Winters's travelling companion in the Western *Frenchie* (1950) with Joel McCrea. More supporting roles followed in the early 1950s, including a two-minute cameo as the Bearded Lady in *3 Ring Circus*, about to be shaved by Jerry Lewis. She then had another substantial part when she appeared again with her husband in the screen version of Agatha Christie's play *Witness for the Prosecution* (1957) for which both received Academy Award nominations - she for the second time as Best Supporting Actress, and Laughton, also for the second time, for Best Actor. Neither won. However, Lanchester did win the Golden Globe for Best Supporting Actress for the film.

Lanchester played a witch in *Bell, Book and Candle* (1958), and appeared in such classics as *Mary Poppins* (1964), *That Darn Cat!* (1965) and *Blackbeard's Ghost* (1968). She appeared on April 9, 1959, on NBC's *The Ford Show, Starring Tennessee Ernie Ford*. She performed in two episodes of NBC's *The Wonderful World of Disney*. Additionally, she had memorable guest roles in a classic *I Love Lucy* episode in 1956 and in episodes of NBC's *The Eleventh Hour* (1964) and *The Man From U.N.C.L.E.* (1965).

In the 1965–1966 television season she was a regular on John Forsythe's sitcom *The John Forsythe Show* on NBC in the role of Miss Culver, the principal of a private girls' academy in San Francisco. She continued television work into the early 1970s, appearing as a recurring character in *Nanny and the Professor*, starring Richard Long and Juliet Mills.

Lanchester continued to make occasional film appearances, singing a duet with Elvis Presley in *Easy Come, Easy Go* (1967) and playing the mother in the original version of *Willard* (1971).

She starred in the Rod Serling *Night Gallery* episode "Green Fingers" (1972) which was the scariest, most nightmare enducing episode of the series.

She was Jessica Marbles, a sleuth based on Agatha Christie's Jane Marple, in the 1976 murder mystery spoof, *Murder by Death*, and she made her last film in 1980 as Sophie in *Die Laughing*.

She released three LP albums in the 1950s. Two (referred to above) were entitled "Songs for a Shuttered Parlour" and "Songs for a Smoke-Filled Room" and were vaguely lewd and danced around their true purpose, such as the song about her husband's "clock" not working. Charles Laughton provided the spoken introductions to each number and even joined Elsa in the singing of "She Was Poor But She Was Honest". Her third LP was entitled "Cockney London", a selection of old London songs for which Laughton wrote the sleeve-notes.

In 1938 Lanchester published a book about her relationship with Laughton, *Charles Laughton and I*. In March 1983, Lanchester released an autobiography, entitled *Elsa Lanchester Herself*. In the book she alleges that she and Charles Laughton never had children because Laughton was homosexual. Maureen O'Hara, a friend and co-star of Laughton, denied this was the reason for the couple's childlessness. She claimed Laughton had told her that the reason he and his wife never had children was because of a botched abortion Lanchester had early in her career of performing burlesque. Lanchester admitted in her autobiography that she had had two abortions in her youth (one being Laughton's), but it is not clear if the second left her incapable of becoming pregnant again.

The two women did not like each other. Lanchester once said of O'Hara, "She looks as though butter wouldn't melt in her mouth, or anywhere else."

Not long after the release of her autobiography, Lanchester's health took a turn for the worse. Within thirty months, she suffered two strokes, becoming totally incapacitated and requiring constant care. She was confined to bed. In March 1986, the Motion Picture and Television Fund filed to become conservator of Lanchester and her estate which was valued at $900,000.

Elsa Lanchester died in Woodland Hills, California on December 26, 1986, at age 84, at the Motion Picture Hospital from bronchopneumonia. Her body was cremated on January 5, 1987, at the Chapel of the Pines in Los Angeles and her ashes scattered over the Pacific Ocean.

David Landau

David Landau was born David Magee March 9, 1879 in Philadelphia, Pennsylvania and was an American film actor who appeared on Broadway in twelve plays from 1919 to 1929 and in thirty-three films between 1931 and 1935.

Some of his roles included *I Take This Woman* (1931), *The Roadhouse Murder* (1932), *One Man's Journey* (1933) with Joel McCrea, and *Judge Priest* (1934).

He had a stroke in 1934 from which he never recovered. He died September 20, 1935 at age 56 in Hollywood, California. He is buried at Forest Lawn Memorial Park in Glendale, California.

Charles Lane

Charles Lane was born Charles Gerstle Levison in San Francisco, California January 26, 1905 and was an American character actor whose career spanned 64 years. Lane turned in his last performance at the age of 90. Lane appeared in many Frank Capra films, including *You Can't Take It With You* (1938), *Mr. Smith Goes to Washington* (1939), *Arsenic and Old Lace* (1944), and *It's a Wonderful Life* (1946). He was a favored supporting actor of Lucille Ball, who often used him as a no-nonsense authority figure and comedic foe of her scatterbrained TV character on her TV series *I Love Lucy*, *The Lucy-Desi Comedy Hour* and *The Lucy Show*. His first film of more than 250 movies was as a hotel clerk in *Smart Money* (1931) starring Edward G. Robinson and James Cagney.

Lane spent a short time as an insurance salesman before taking to the stage at the Pasadena Playhouse. Actor/director Irving Pichel first suggested that Lane go into acting in 1929, and four years later Lane was a founding member of the Screen Actors Guild. He became a favorite of director Frank Capra, who used him in several films; in *It's a Wonderful Life*, Lane played a seemingly hard-nosed rent collector for the miserly Henry Potter (Lionel Barrymore), who tried to explain to his employer that many of his tenants were moving out, taking advantage of affordable mortgages provided by the film's protagonist, George Bailey (James Stewart).

He also appeared in the 1949 film *Mighty Joe Young*, as one of the reporters cajoling Max O'Hara (Robert Armstrong) for information about the identity of "Mr. Joseph Young", the persona given featured billing on the front of the building, on opening night.

Among his many roles as a character actor, Lane landed the recurring role as newspaper editor Mr. Fosdick in the Peter Lawford sitcom *Dear Phoebe*, which aired on NBC in the 1954-1955 season. In that same season, Lane played the boss of the title character in June Havoc's NBC sitcom entitled *Willy*. He portrayed Emil Quincy in two episodes of the syndicated romantic comedy series, *How to Marry a Millionaire* (1957–1959), with Barbara Eden and Merry Anders. However, he is most widely remembered for his portrayal of J. Homer Bedloe on the television situation comedy *Petticoat Junction*. Bedloe was a mean-spirited railroad executive who periodically visited the Shady Rest Hotel while seeking justification to end train service of the Hooterville Cannonball, but he never succeeded in that objective. He guest starred

He was a good friend of Lucille Ball, and his specialty in playing scowling, beady-eyed, short tempered, no-nonsense professionals provided the perfect comic foil for Lucy's scatterbrained television character. He played several guest roles on *I Love Lucy*, most notably in the episode "Lucy Goes To the Hospital", where he is seated in the waiting room with Ricky while Lucy gives birth to their son. He also played the title role in the episode "The Business Manager", the casting director in "Lucy Tells The Truth. He also played the passport clerk in "Staten Island Ferry." Lane appeared twice in *The Lucy-Desi Comedy Hour*. He later had recurring roles as shopkeeper Mr. Finch on *Dennis the Menace* and during the first season (1962–63) of Ball's *The Lucy Show*, playing banker Mr. Barnsdahl. According to *The Lucy Book* by Geoffrey Fidelman, Lane was turfed because he had trouble reciting his lines correctly. However, Lane was in reality a placeholder for Lucy's original choice, Gale Gordon, who joined the program in 1963 as Mr. Mooney after he was free from other contractual obligations.

In 1963, Lane appeared in the mega-comedy *It's a Mad, Mad, Mad, Mad World*, playing the airport manager. His final acting role was at the age of 101 in 2006's *The Night Before Christmas*.

His last television appearance was at the age of 90, when he appeared in the 1995 Disney TV remake of its 1970 teen comedy *The Computer Wore Tennis Shoes*, with Kirk Cameron.

In 2005, the TV Land Awards paid tribute to Lane by celebrating his 100th birthday. Seated in a wheelchair in the audience, which had sung *Happy Birthday* to him, Lane was presented with his award by Haley Joel Osment and then announced "If you're interested, I'm still available [for work]!" The audience gave him a standing ovation.

Lane appeared in more than 250 films and hundreds of television shows and was uncredited in many of them. On his busiest days, Lane said he sometimes played more than one role, getting into costume and filming his two or three lines, then hurrying off to another set for a different costume and a different role. As for being typecast, Lane described it as "... a pain in the ass. You did something that was pretty good, and the picture was pretty good. But that pedigreed you into that type of part, which I thought was stupid and unfair, too. It didn't give me a chance, but it made the casting easier for the studio."

Lane's persona has been referenced in *The Simpsons*: on the audio commentary to the episode "Marge in Chains", its director Jim Reardon states that Lane's performance in *It's a Wonderful Life* inspired the character of the snide, humourless Blue-Haired Lawyer who appears in that and other episodes in the series.

More of his roles over his career included *The Road to Singapore* (1931), *Woman Wanted* (1935), *Internes Can't Take Money* (1937) with Joel McCrea, *Blondie* (1938), *Primrose Path* (1940) again with Joel McCrea, *Ellery Queen, Master Detective* (1940) with Alan Ladd, *Ride 'Em Cowboy* (1942) with Abbott and Costello, *The Great Man's Lady* (1942) a third with Joel McCrea, *Pardon My Sarong* (1942) again with Abbott and Costello, *The Boy with Green Hair* (1948), *The Affairs of Dobie Gillis* (1953), *God Is My Partner* (1957), *Richard Diamond, Private Detective* (1958), *The 30 Foot Bride of Candy Rock* (1959) with Lou Costello, *Twilight Zone* (1960), *The Carpetbaggers* (1964) again with Alan Ladd, *Get Smart* (1965), *The Munsters* (1966), *The Wild Wild West* (1967), *The Rookies* (1973), *Murphy's Romance* (1985), *Hunter* (1987), and *Dark Shadows* (1991).

He was, prior to his death, one of the last remaining survivors of the 1906 San Francisco Earthquake. In 1931, Lane married Ruth Covell and they remained together for 70 years until her death in 2002. They had a son named Tom and a daughter named Alice.

Despite his stern, hard-hearted demeanor in films and television, friends and acquaintances seem to unanimously describe Lane as a warm, funny, and kind person. On January 26, 2007, Lane celebrated his 102nd birthday. He continued to live in the Brentwood home he bought with Ruth (for $46,000 in 1964) until his death. In the end, his son Tom Lane, said he was talking with his father at 9 p.m. on the evening of Monday, July 9, 2007, "He was lying in bed with his eyes real wide open. Then he closed his eyes and stopped breathing." Charles Lane was 102. He died from Natural Causes. Lane was not the only person in his family to have a long life - his mother Alice died in her San Francisco home in 1973 aged 100.

Richard Lane

Richard "Dick" Lane was born in Rice Lake, Wisconsin May 28, 1899 and was an American television announcer and actor who made his mark broadcasting wrestling and roller derby shows on KTLA-TV, mainly from the Grand Olympic Auditorium in Los Angeles, California.

Early in life he developed talents for reciting poetry and doing various song-and-dance acts. By his teenage years, he was doing an "iron jaw" routine in circuses around Europe and worked as a drummer touring with a band in Australia. After the decline of vaudeville, Lane obtained extensive work in motion pictures and was best known at the time for playing Inspector John or William Faraday or Farraday (depending on the film) in all fourteen Boston Blackie Columbia Pictures features starring Chester Morris, starting with *Meet Boston Blackie* in 1941. During World War II, he appeared as emcee with USO troops entertaining G.I.s. His unit appeared at Fort MacArthur in September 1944. Lane also announced for the Jalopy Derby and Destruction Derby at Ascot Park, Gardena California.

More of his early film work included *Shop Talk* (1936), *The Outcasts of Poker Flat* (1937), *Crashing Hollywood* (1938), *Charlie Chan in Honolulu* (1938), *Union Pacific* (1939) with Joel McCrea, *The Amazing Mr. Williams* (1939), *The Bride Wore Crutches* (1940), *I Wanted Wings* (1941) with Veronica Lake, *Time Out for Rhythm* (1941) with the Three Stooges, *Riders of the Purple Sage* (1941), *Hellzapoppin'* (1941) with Shemp Howard, *Ride 'Em Cowboy* (1942) with Abbott and Costello, *A-Haunting We Will Go* (1942) with Laurel and Hardy, *Corvette K-225* (1943), *Bermuda Mystery* (1944), *Here Come the Co-eds* (1945) again with Abbott and Costello, and *The Bullfighters* (1945) again with Laurel and Hardy.

Due to his work at Paramount Pictures, Lane was able to obtain work at KTLA, which was owned by the studio at the time. When the station went commercial for the first time in 1947, Lane started work as a news presenter. One of the early highlights of his career was reporting on the first atomic explosion covered by a television newscast.

When KTLA agreed to broadcast wrestling matches from the Olympic Auditorium in 1946, Lane was hired to comment on the action. He started announcing for Roller Derby in 1951, and for Roller Games in the 1960s. His broadcasts featured such personalities as Gorgeous George, Mr. Moto, and Doc Grable. Contrary to popular opinion, it was Lane and not former ABC sports announcer Keith Jackson who coined the exclamatory expression "Whoa, Nellie!" when something "bad" happened in the ring or on the track. Lane was also the character "Leather Britches" on the Spade Cooley show on KTLA.

One of his wrestling calls was 'meat on the table' when one wrestler pretended to bite the ear of another wrestler. Another call familiar to viewers was "Wow, what action!" which invariably preceded a commercial break.

More of his acting roles continued with *Hit Parade of 1947* (1947), *The Creeper* (1948), *Mighty Joe Young* (1949), *The Admiral Was a Lady* (1950), *I Can Get It for You Wholesale* (1951), *Crossroads* (1956), *Leave It to Beaver* (1959), *Visit to a Small Planet* (1960), *The Killers* (1964), *Dear Brigitte* (1965), *The Munsters* (1965), *Kansas City Bomber* (1972) with Raquel Welch, *The Shaggy D.A.* (1976), and *The One and Only* (1978).

Lane died in Newport Beach, California on September 5, 1982 at age 83. In 1996, he was posthumously inducted into the Wrestling Observer Newsletter Hall of Fame.

John Larch

John Larch was born in Salem, Massachusetts October 4, 1914 and was an American film and television actor.

After his lead role in the radio serial *Captain Starr of Space* (1953–1954), John Larch entered films in 1954. He usually appeared in westerns and action films, including *Miracle of the White Stallions* as General George S. Patton Jr. (1963), *Collision Course: Truman vs. MacArthur* as General Omar Bradley (1976), replacing James Gregory as Mac in the Matt Helm movie *The Wrecking Crew* (1969) starring Dean Martin, Sharon Tate, and Elke Sommer.

Larch, an old friend of Clint Eastwood, appeared in Eastwood films, including *Dirty Harry* (1971) and *Play Misty for Me* (1971).

Larch also appeared in *Bitter Creek* (1954), *Dragnet* (1953-1954), *You Are There* (1953-1956), *Seven Men from Now* (1956), *The Restless Gun* (1957-1958), *Wanted: Dead or Alive* (1958), *Wichita Town* (1960) with Joel McCrea, *Gunsmoke* (1955-1961), *Laramie* (1960-1962), *How the West Was Won* (1962), *The Fugitive* (1964-1967), *The Virginian* (1962-1970), *O'Hara, U.S. Treasury* (1972), *Ellery Queen* (1975), *Charlie's Angels* (1977), *The Amityville Horror* (1979), *Vega$* (1979-1980), *The Dukes of Hazzard* (1981), *Airplane II: The Sequel* (1982), *Dynasty* (1982-1988), *War and Remembrance* (1989), and *Dallas* (1985-1990).

He is possibly most remembered as Anthony Fremont's father in *The Twilight Zone* 1961 episode "It's a Good Life". He also appeared in two other *The Twilight Zone* episodes, playing a psychiatrist in "Perchance to Dream" and the sheriff in "Dust".

He died October 16, 2005 at age 91 in Woodland Hills, Los Angeles, California.

Raymond Largay

Raymond J. Largay was born on March 7, 1886 in Oshkosh, Wisconsin. He was an actor, known for *Four Faces West* (1948) with Joel McCrea, *The Second Woman* (1950), and *April in Paris* (1952).

More of his roles included *Lilies of the Field* (1930), *Daredevils of the Red Circle* (1939), *The Hidden Eye* (1945), *The Razor's Edge* (1946), *Force of Evil* (1948), *Emergency Wedding* (1950), *The Lone Ranger* (1950-1952), *Jesse James vs. the Daltons* (1954), and *Lock Up* (1959-1960).

He was married to Sue Snee. He died on September 28, 1974 in Woodland Hills, Los Angeles, California,

Keith Larsen

Joel McCrea and Keith Larson in *Wichita*

Keith Larsen was born as Keith Eric Burt in Salt Lake City June 17, 1924 and was an American actor, screenwriter, director, and producer who starred in three short-lived television series between 1955 and 1961.

Keith Larsen was of Norwegian descent. During World War II, he served in the United States Navy. After the war he became involved in stage acting in Santa Monica, California.

Larsen was tapped by a talent scout to play a small uncredited role in 1951 movie *Operation Pacific*. In 1953, Larsen played the title role of Ed Reed, the Kid in the film *Son of Belle Starr*, in which his character tries to live an upright life despite the heritage of his two lawless parents, Belle Starr and Jim Reed.

More film roles included *Security Risk* (1954), *Wichita* (1955) with Joel McCrea, *Apache Warrior* (1957), *Women of the Prehistoric Planet* (1966), *The Omegans* (1968), *Night of the Witches* (1971), *The Trap on Cougar Mountain* (1972), *Run to the High Country* (1974), *Young and Free* (1979), and *Whitewater Sam* (1982).

Larsen's television weekly series included *The Hunter* (1954), *Brave Eagle* (1955), *Northwest Passage* (1958), and *The Aquanauts* (1960).

In the 1955–1956 television season, Larsen starred in the title role of the 26-week CBS western *Brave Eagle*. Keith Larsen starred as Brave Eagle, a peaceful young Cheyenne chief. The program was unusual in that it reflected the Native American viewpoint in the settlement of the American West. Larsen's principal co-stars were Kim Winona (1930–1978) as Morning Star, Anthony Numkena, a Hopi Indian then using the stage name Keena Nomkeena, as Keena, Brave Eagle's foster son, and Bert Wheeler (1895–1968) as Smokey Joe.

He guest starred in 1957 on three CBS programs, as Paul in the "Anitra Dellano Story" of *The Millionaire*, and in two anthologies, as Howard in "The Blackwell Story" on *Playhouse 90*, and as Eddie Seabord in the episode "Father and Son Night" on *General Electric Theater*, hosted by future U.S. President Ronald W. Reagan.

In the 1958–1959 season, Larsen starred in the M-G-M/NBC series *Northwest Passage*. the story of Major Robert Rogers, an American soldier in upstate New York during the French and Indian War. Buddy Ebsen co-starred as Sergeant Hunk Marriner and Don Burnett as Ensign Towne. In 1959, Larsen guest starred on the CBS series *Men into Space* in the role of Jim Nichols in the episode "Christmas on the Moon".

In 1960–1961, Larsen appeared as former Navy diver Drake Andrews in the CBS adventure series *The Aquanauts*, an Ivan Tors Production renamed in March 1961 as *Malibu Run*. His co-star was Jeremy Slate (1926–

2006). A sinus operation required Larsen to withdraw from the show, and he was replaced by Ron Ely as Mike Madison. The script line indicated that the character Andrews had rejoined the Navy.

After *The Aquanauts*, Larsen appeared as Jack Bennett in the 1961 episode "Blondes Prefer Gentlemen" of the ABC series *The Roaring Twenties*, with Donald May, Rex Reason, and Dorothy Provine. His other television roles, all in 1960, were as John Edwards in "The Hostage" episode of the ABC and syndicated western series, *Tombstone Territory*, as John Napier in "Nightmare Crossing" episode of NBC's *The Man and the Challenge*, and as the Indian, Blue Raven, in the episode "Seed of Hate" in NBC's western *Wichita Town* (1960) again with Joel McCrea.

Larsen was married three times. In 1953, he wed actress Susan Cummings. After their divorce, he married actress Vera Miles on July 16, 1960. He was married to Vera Miles until 1971. Their son, Erik Larsen, was born in April 1961. After Larsen and Miles divorced, he married Trang Thu Nguyen in 1983. The couple had one child. The marriage lasted until his death at age 82, in Santa Barbara, California December 13, 2006.

Harry Lauter

Herman Arthur "Harry" Lauter was born June 19, 1914, and was an American character actor originally from White Plains, New York. He came to be a familiar presence in low-budget films, serials (where he was often cast because of his facial resemblance to stuntman Tom Steele, who would double him), and television programs in the 1950s, though he only once really came close to stardom, as Clay Morgan, one of the leads in the series *Tales of the Texas Rangers*, which aired from 1955-1958. He starred in fifty-two episodes.

Lauter also made appearances on many television programs, particularly westerns: *The Gene Autry Show* (1950-1955) (sixteen episodes), *Annie Oakley* (1954-1957) (12 episodes), *The Lone Ranger* (1949-1956) and *The Range Rider* (eleven episodes each), *Gunsmoke* (1960-1968) and *Rawhide* (1959-1965) (ten episodes each), *Death Valley Days* (1953-1969) and *The Adventures of Ozzie and Harriet* (1956-1965) (seven episodes each), *Laramie* (1959-1963) and *Dick Powell's Zane Grey Theater* (1956-1959) (six episodes each), *The Virginian* and *State Trooper* (1957-1959) (five times each), and *Cheyenne* (1956-1962), *Bonanza* (1961-1962), and *Maverick* (1957-1961) (three episodes each).

Most of his career was spent as a serviceable second lead or heavy, though he continued to play bit parts in larger pictures, including an uncredited part as a plain-clothes policeman in the 1949 crime drama, *White Heat* which starred James Cagney and Edmond O'Brien. He also had an uncredited, unspoken role in the 1963 comedy *A Mad, Mad, Mad, Mad World* as a police dispatcher.

Other roles included *The Day the Earth Stood Still* (1951), *Hopalong Cassidy* (1953), *It Came from Beneath the Sea* (1955), *The Werewolf* (1956), *Richard Diamond, Private Detective* (1958), *The Gunfight at Dodge City* (1959) with Joel McCrea, *Wichita Town* (1959) also with Joel McCrea, *Posse from Hell* (1961) with Audie Murphy, *Showdown* (1963) again with Audie Murphy, *Gilligan's Island* (1965), *The Green Hornet* (1966), *Adam-12* (1970), and *Escape from the Planet of the Apes* (1971).

His last appearance was in 1979 as Marshal Charlie Benton in James Arness's *How the West Was Won*.

The son of an artist, he devoted much of his energy late in his life to his own painting and running an art gallery. He died October 30, 1990 in Ojai in Ventura County, California. His ashes were scattered into the Pacific Ocean.

Anderson Lawler

Joel McCrea and Anderson Lawler in *Girls About Town*

Anderson Lawler was born on May 5, 1902 in Russellville, Alabama. He was an actor and producer, known for *Half Marriage* (1929), *Girls About Town* (1931) with Joel McCrea, and *Ace of Aces* (1933).

More of his roles included *Born to Love* (1931) also with Joel McCrea, *The Cheyenne Kid* (1933), *The Man Who Reclaimed His Head* (1934), *The Return of Sophie Lang* (1936), *The Invisible Menace* (1938), and *Torchy Blane in Chinatown* (1939).

He died on April 6, 1959 in New York City, New York at age 56.

Marc Lawrence

Marc Lawrence was born Max Goldsmith in New York City, December 17, 1909, and was an American character actor who specialized in underworld types. He has also been credited as F. A. Foss, Marc Laurence, and Marc C. Lawrence.

He participated in plays in school, and then attended the City College of New York. In 1930, Lawrence befriended another young actor, John Garfield. The two appeared in a number of plays before Lawrence was given a film contract with Columbia Pictures. Lawrence appeared in films beginning in 1931. Lawrence's pock-marked complexion, brooding appearance and New York street-guy accent made him a natural for heavies, and he played scores of gangsters and mob bosses over the next six decades.

Later, Lawrence found himself under scrutiny for his political leanings. When called before the House Un-American Activities Committee, he admitted he had once been a member of the Communist Party. He was blacklisted and departed for Europe, where he continued to mak e films. Following the demise of the blacklist, he returned to America and resumed his position as a familiar and talented purveyor of gangland types.

Some of his films include *White Woman* (1933), *'G' Men* (1935), *Charlie Chan on Broadway* (1937), *The Lone Wolf Spy Hunt* (1939), *Charlie Chan at the Wax Museum* (1940), *The Shepherd of the Hills* (1941), *Hold That Ghost* (1941), *This Gun for Hire* (1942) with Alan Ladd and Veronica Lake, *The Ox-Bow Incident* (1943), *Hit the Ice* (1943), *Flame of Barbary Coast* (1945), *The Virginian* (1946) with Joel McCrea, *Key Largo* (1948), *Abbott and Costello in the Foreign Legion* (1950), *Helen of Troy* (1956), *Peter Gunn* (1959), *Richard Diamond, Private Detective* (1960), *Whispering Smith* (1961) with Audie Murphy, *Mister Ed* (1965), *Custer of the West* (1967), *King of Kong Island* (1968), *Diamonds Are Forever* (1971), *The Man with the Golden Gun* (1974), *Marathon Man* (1976), *Baretta* (1976), *The Dukes of Hazzard* (1979), *Super Fuzz* (1980), *Night Train to Terror* (1985), *The Big Easy* (1986), *Star Trek: The Next Generation* (1989), *From Dusk Till Dawn* (1996), *Star Trek: Deep Space Nine* (1999), *End of Days* (1999), and *The Shipping News* (2001).

His final film role was in *Looney Tunes Back in Action* (2003), appearing as an Acme Corporation vice president.

In 1991 Lawrence's autobiography was published entitled *Long Time No See: Confessions of a Hollywood Gangster*. Lawrence was also the subject of a novel, *The Beautiful and the Profane* published in 2002.

He married novelist and screenwriter Fanya Foss, with whom he had two children; she died on December 12, 1995. Lawrence died of heart failure on November 28, 2005, at the age of 95. He was buried at Westwood Memorial Park in Westwood, California. His son, Michael Lawrence, is a writer and artist based on the Greek island of Hydra, whose book, *My Voyage in Art*, details his meetings with several of his father's actor friends; while at UCLA he befriended the singer-songwriter James Douglas "Jim" Morrison. His daughter, actress Toni Lawrence, was once married to actor Billy Bob Thornton and starred in his film *Daddy's Girl* (1996).

Terry Lawrence

Joel McCrea and Terry Lawrence in *Trooper Hook*

Terry Lawrence was born on March 13, 1951 in Utah. He is an actor, known for his only role in *Trooper Hook* (1957) with Joel McCrea and Barbara Stanwyck.

Frank Lawton

Frank Lawton was born Frank Lawton Mokeley September 30, 1904, London, England and was an English actor. He was married to Evelyn Laye, with whom he acted several times including in *My Husband and I*.

His parents were stage players Daisy May Collier and Frank Mokeley (Frank Lawton (I)). His first major screen credit was *Young Woodley* (1930). He was best-known for his role as *David Copperfield* in the 1934 MGM film.

More of his roles included *The Skin Game* (1931), *Friday the Thirteenth* (1933), *The Invisible Ray* (1936), *The Secret Four* (1939), *Went the Day Well?* (1942), *The Winslow Boy* (1948), *Shoot First* (1953) with Joel McCrea, *The Rising of the Moon* (1957), *The Queen's Guards* (1961), and *The Human Jungle* (1963).

He died June 10, 1969, London, England at age 64.

Blanche Le Clair

Blanche Le Clair was born as Blanche Bishop in 1911 in New York City, New York. She was 16 when she got a contract with Paramount and went west in 1927. She was an actress, known for *A Trip Through the Paramount Studio* (1927), *Jealousy* (1929), and *Lightnin'* (1930) with Joel McCrea.

Her father designed and constructed the roller-coaster at the famous Palisades Park. He died on it in a famous accident at the time.

She died in 1964 in Long Island, New York at age 53.

Andrea Leeds

Joel McCrea and Andrea Leeds in *Youth Takes a Fling*

Andrea Leeds was born Antoinette Lees in Butte, Montana, August 14, 1914 and was an American film actress. A popular supporting player of the late 1930s, Leeds was nominated for an Academy Award for Best Supporting Actress for her performance in *Stage Door*(1937). She was progressing to leading roles, when she retired from acting following her marriage in 1939, and was later a successful horse breeder.

She began her film career in 1934 playing bit parts and using her given name. As Andrea Leeds she played her first substantial role in the film *Come and Get It* (1936) with Joel McCrea and achieved another success with her next film *It Could Happen to You* (1937).

As part of an ensemble cast that included Katharine Hepburn, Ginger Rogers, and Lucille Ball, Leeds was nominated for an Academy Award for Best Supporting Actress for her performance as an aspiring actress in *Stage Door* (1937). She read for the role of Melanie in *Gone with the Wind*, however the role was given to Olivia de Havilland.

Her wholesome quality led to her being cast in *The Goldwyn Follies* (1938) playing "Miss Humanity" – a woman considered by a jaded Hollywood executive to represent the ideal American woman. The film was not a success and received poor reviews.

She next appeared in two more films opposite Joel McCrea, *Youth Takes a Fling* (1938) and *They Shall Have Music* (1939), for the first time playing the lead female role. She continued to play the romantic female lead in an adventure film set in the 1906 Philippines, *The Real Glory*, opposite Gary Cooper and David Niven, and opposite Don Ameche in the first Technicolor biography of Stephen Foster, *Swanee River* (1939).

Her final film, *Earthbound* (1940), was a fantasy murder mystery in which Leeds' character solves the murder of her husband, aided by his ghost.

These films were relatively successful and Leeds remained a popular actress. In 1939 she married Robert Stewart Howard, son of California businessman and racehorse owner Charles S. Howard, and decided to leave films to devote herself to raising a family. Her father-in-law owned and raced Seabiscuit, and with her husband she became a successful horse owner/breeder.

The Howards also owned the Howard Manor in Palm Springs, a hotel originally built as the "Colonial House" by Las Vegas casino owner and Purple Gang member Al Wertheimer. (The hotel is now operated as the Colony Palms Hotel, and features the "Winner's Circle Suite" in honor of Seabuscuit and the Howards). After his death in 1962, Leeds ran a jewellery business. It was her only marriage, and produced two children, Robert Jr. and Leann, who died in 1971.

Andrea Leeds died on May 21, 1984 from cancer in Palm Springs, California, at age 69. A resident of the city for many years, a Golden Palm Star on the Palm Springs Walk of Stars was dedicated to her in 1994.

She was interred in Desert Memorial Park in Cathedral City, California.

Nelson Leigh

Nelson Leigh and Joel McCrea in *The First Texan*

Nelson Leigh was born Sydney Talbot Christie January 1, 1905 and was a prolific motion picture actor of the 1940s and 1950s. Leigh was a graduate of the University of Southern California, class of 1929.

Leigh made over 130 appearances in motion pictures of the era, mainly in supporting roles. Leigh tended to play authority figures such as military officers and clergymen, but also played roles varied as Jesus Christ in a Christian film *The Living Bible* (1952). He also played the Apostle Paul in the *Life of St. Paul* series and again in the *Acts of the Apostles* series. In 1954, he played a priest, Father Kerrigan, in the western film, *Jesse James v. the Daltons.*

He made many appearances in the Christian television anthology series, *This Is the Life* (1952-1967).

In 1949, he portrayed the Ghost of Christmas Past in a notoriously low-budgeted half-hour television version of Charles Dickens's *A Christmas Carol*, with Vincent Price as narrator and Taylor Holmes as Ebenezer Scrooge.

More of his roles included *Appointment in Berlin* (1943), *The Return of the Vampire* (1944), *The Bandit of Sherwood Forest* (1946), *Superman* (1948), *The Adventures of Sir Galahad* (1949), *The Lone Ranger* (1950), *Rogues of Sherwood Forest* (1950), *Hopalong Cassidy* (1952), *The Adventures of Kit Carson* (1951-1954), *Creature with the Atom Brain* (1955), *Sheena: Queen of the Jungle* (1955), *The First Texan* (1956) with Joel McCrea, *Gunfight at the O.K. Corral* (1957), *Operation Petticoat* (1959), *The Dark at the Top of the Stairs* (1960), *Perry Mason* (1959-1964), and *The Nickel Ride* (1974).

He died July 3, 1985 at age 80 in Hemet, California.

Nan Leslie

Nanette June Leslie, known as Nan Leslie or Nan Coppage was born June 4, 1926 and was an American actress of film and television. Her longest running role was as Martha McGivern in thirty-seven episodes of the first season from 1957 to 1958 of the NBC western television series, *The Californians*.

The daughter of Frank M. Leslie and the former Alma H. Turner, Leslie was a native of Los Angeles, California, where she attended University High School.

Leslie was cast opposite Sean McClory, as Jack McGivern, in *The Californians*, a fictional account of San Francisco during the California Gold Rush of the early 1850s. Richard Coogan starred in both seasons as Marshal Matthew Wayne. Other co-stars in the first season were Herbert Rudley as Sam Brennan and Adam Kennedy as newspaperman Dion Patrick. In the second season, Carole Mathews and Art Fleming, later the first host of the quiz program, *Jeopardy!*, joined the cast of the black-and-white half-hour series.

Prior to *The Californians*, Leslie was known for her roles in three 1947 films *The Woman on the Beach*, with Robert Ryan and Joan Bennett, and two productions based on Zane Grey western novels with Tim Holt in the starring role: *Under the Tonto Rim* and *Wild Horse Mesa*. For a time she was engaged to marry Holt.

Her acting career began with uncredited roles in twelve films, the first as Prudence in *Under Western Skies* (1945). Her first credited film role was as Jane Preston in the 1946 film *Sunset Pass* with co-star James Warren; the original *Sunset Pass*, a 1933 picture directed by Henry Hathaway, starred Kathleen Burke as Jane Preston, a young woman who seeks to rescue her brother from a life of crime. In March 1947, Leslie was among several actors and actresses attending the premieres in Kansas of *Trail Street*, an RKO Pictures release, with Randolph Scott in the role of Marshal Bat Masterson in the town of Liberal, Kansas.

Her first television guest-starring role came in 1949 on ABC's *The Lone Ranger*; by 1955, she had made eight guest-starring appearances on the landmark western series. From 1950 to 1955, she appeared in four episodes of CBS's *The Gene Autry Show*. Leslie was cast in two episodes of the NBC western series, *The Roy Rogers Show*; her first role being that of Bess Walton in "Jailbreak" (1951). Two years later, she was cast in the episode "Whirlwind Courtship" of the syndicated western anthology series, *Death Valley Days*, hosted by Stanley Andrews. In 1953, she also appeared as Jane Sawyer in "Arizona Troubleshooters" of another western series, *Hopalong Cassidy*. She was twice cast on the syndicated western series *The Range Rider*, as Joyce Lanyon in "Ambush in Coyote Canyon" (1952) and as Sue McCandles in "Saga of Silver Town" (1953). In 1954, she played Alias Annie in another syndicated western series, *Annie Oakley*, starring Gail Davis in a fictitious depiction of the markswoman Annie Oakley. She had met Davis c. 1945 at the RKO studios, and the two remained lifelong friends until Davis' death in 1997.

From 1953 to 1955, Leslie was cast in five episodes each of two other syndicated western series, *The Adventures of Kit Carson* and *The Cisco Kid*. In 1956, she appeared in three episodes of the ABC western series, *The Adventures of Rin Tin Tin*, twice as Joan Lambert in "Wagon Train" and "Fort Adventure". Her third role in that series was as Claire Corbin in "Rin Tin Tin and the Second Chance."

Leslie's other western roles included the part of Peggy in "White Man's Magic" (1957) of the ABC western series, *Broken Arrow*, as Nancy Barnett in "Three Graves" (1957) on *Dick Powell's Zane Grey Theater*, and as Beth McGarrett in "The Legend" (1959) of *Wanted: Dead or Alive*, with Steve McQueen. She was cast twice in 1958 and 1959, respectively, on the Peter Graves NBC children's western series, *Fury*, as Stella Lambert in "The Model Plane" and as Packy's mother in "The Pulling Contest". In 1959, she was also cast as Judy Travers in the episode "Treasure Trap" of another syndicated western series, *Shotgun Slade*, starring Scott Brady, and as Margaret Cook in "Day of Battle" of the NBC western series, *Wichita Town*, starring Joel McCrea.

Leslie also appeared in several drama series, including the 1954 role of Miss Oliver in the episode "High Stakes" of the series *The Public Defender*. In 1955, she appeared in "The Margaret Browning Story" of Don Fedderson's CBS anthology drama series, *The Millionaire*. She appeared as Laura Mattley in "The Antidote" of the NBC Cold War drama, *Behind Closed Doors*. She appeared three times on the CBS police drama, *The Lineup*, starring Warner Anderson and Tom Tully, and twice on the NBC police series, *M Squad*, starring Lee Marvin.

In 1957, she was cast as Muriel in "Death Defying Dozetti" of the series, *Circus Boy*. She portrayed a character Lydia in "Conscript" (1957) of the syndicated American Civil War drama series, *The Gray Ghost*, starring Tod Andrews as John Singleton Mosby. She played Barbara Lee Rickman in the 1957 episode, "The Fishing Trip" of the syndicated police drama, *Code 3*. In 1958, Leslie played Myrna O'Malley in "Short Haul" on the CBS crime drama, *Richard Diamond, Private Detective*, starring David Janssen. In this episode she was cast as the wife of Ted O'Malley, played by Sean McClory, Leslie's co-star from *The Californians*.

By 1960, Leslie's career began to wind down. She was cast twice on CBS's *Lassie*. In 1960, she played Amy Carson in "The Quick Noose" of the NBC western series, *Riverboat*, starring Darren McGavin. She played Midge Lewis in the 1960 episode, "The Big Blackout", of the NBC mystery series, *Thriller*, hosted by Boris Karloff. In 1961, she appeared as Jean Telford in "Flee Now, Pay Later" of Rod Cameron's syndicated detective series, *Coronado 9*, and as Josie in "Gladys Goes to College" on the CBS sitcom, *Pete and Gladys*, starring Harry Morgan and Cara Williams. He portrayed Beth Thomas in the 1961 episode "The Female Artillery" of *The Tall Man*. She appeared twice each on CBS's *The Jack Benny Program* and *Perry Mason*, starring Raymond Burr. In 1964, she was cast as Evelyn Waltham in "The Leper" episode of the Christian series, *This Is the Life*. Leslie played Ada Mayberry in the 1966 episode "Seminole Territory" on NBC's *Daniel Boone*, starring Fess Parker in the title role. Her last acting role was as Dorothy Vetry in the 1968 science fiction film, *The Bamboo Saucer*, starring Dan Duryea and John Ericson.

Leslie was twice married; her husbands were socialite Charles Pawley (1915-1975), to whom she was wed from 1949 until 1960, and Albert Jason Coppage (1920-1990), who was her spouse from 1968 until his death in San Juan Capistrano. She spent her later years in Mission Viejo, California. She died July 30, 2000 of pneumonia at age of 74 in San Juan Capistrano.

William Leslie

William Leslie was born on March 27, 1925 in Seagraves, Texas. He is an actor and writer, known for *Queen Bee* (1955), *The Horse Soldiers* (1959), and *Mutiny in Outer Space* (1965). He was in the Navy and played football and track at the University of Colorado.

More of his roles included *Scorching Fury* (1952), *Taza, Son of Cochise* (1954), *The White Squaw* (1956), *The Night the World Exploded* (1957), *Buchanan Rides Alone* (1958), *Wichita Town* (1960), *Hawaiian Eye* (1963), *Combat!* (1965), *I Spy* (1966), *Ironside* (1967), and as the narrator in *The Prosecutors: In Pursuit of Justice.*

George Lessey

George Lessey was born in Amherst, Massachusetts June 8, 1879 and was an American actor and director of the silent era. He appeared in 123 films between 1910 and 1946. He also directed seventy-six films between 1913 and 1922. Lessey also appeared in the original Broadway production of *Porgy and Bess* (1935) in one of the few white roles, that of the lawyer Mr. Archdale.

More of his roles included *Handcuffs or Kisses* (1921), *White Thunder* (1925), *Annapolis Salute* (1937), *Dr. Kildare's Strange Case* (1939), *Boom Town* (1940), *Men of Boys Town* (1941), *The Pride of the Yankees* (1942), *Pistol Packin' Mama* (1943), *Buffalo Bill* (1944) with Joel McCrea, *Eadie Was a Lady* (1945), and *The Missing Lady* (1946).

He died June 3, 1947 in Westbrook, Connecticut at age 67.

George J. Lewis

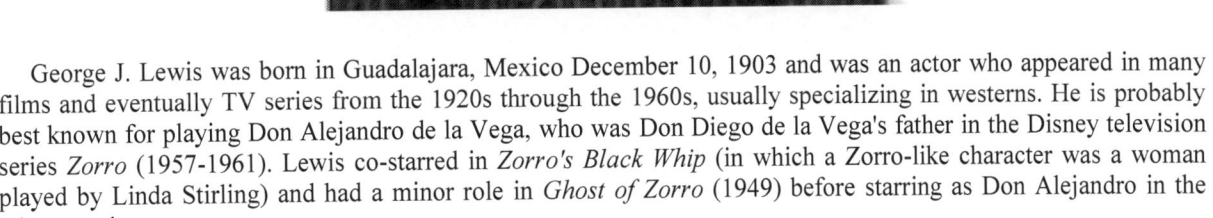

George J. Lewis was born in Guadalajara, Mexico December 10, 1903 and was an actor who appeared in many films and eventually TV series from the 1920s through the 1960s, usually specializing in westerns. He is probably best known for playing Don Alejandro de la Vega, who was Don Diego de la Vega's father in the Disney television series *Zorro* (1957-1961). Lewis co-starred in *Zorro's Black Whip* (in which a Zorro-like character was a woman played by Linda Stirling) and had a minor role in *Ghost of Zorro* (1949) before starring as Don Alejandro in the Disney series.

Lewis broke into films in the 1920s, and his handsome presence led to leading roles in a Universal Pictures short-subject series, *The Collegians*. The arrival of sound movies came as a blessing for Lewis, who was bilingual. He spoke English without any trace of accent, and could play character or dialect roles of practically any ethnicity. His language skills earned him leading roles in Spanish-dialogue features, produced by American studios for international release. He also played supporting roles in Educational Pictures shorts.

Most of George's screen work was in low-budget films, although he can be seen in a few major productions (in *Casablanca* he's an Arab peddler with a monkey). Some of his roles were sympathetic; he played the male leads in the 1944 serial *Zorro's Black Whip* and in the Vera Vague comedy shorts of the 1940s. Usually, George J. Lewis played villains in westerns and serials, chiefly at Republic Pictures. Cast as a sinister henchman, Lewis would carry out the villain's diabolical orders, setting death traps and ambushes week after week. The high point of Lewis's serial career was probably the 1945 Republic cliffhanger *Federal Operator 99*, in which he was the full-fledged villain of the piece, playing "Moonlight Sonata" on a piano while plotting crimes. Holding the heroine captive, the nonchalant Lewis asks the hero: "What will it be? Cash for me... or incineration for Miss Kingston?"

He appeared in Three Stooges films as Vernon Dent's knife-wielding conspirator in the Stooge short *Malice in the Palace* (1949), and its remake, *Rumpus in the Harem*. He was also featured with the Stooges (as George Lewis) in Hollywood's final two-reel comedy release, *Sappy Bull Fighters* (1959).

Many low-budget filmmakers scored successes in early television, and many familiar faces turned up in half-hour action fare. Lewis appeared in the first two episodes of *The Lone Ranger* which were "Enter the Lone Ranger" and "The Lone Ranger Fights On". He was a villain who helped betray a group of Texas Rangers and led them all into a deadly ambush, with the series star of course being the lone survivor. He played a Native American in an *Adventures of Superman* episode called "Test of a Warrior." Lewis continued to work in dozens of TV episodes including *Daniel Boone* until he retired in 1969.

He appeared in fourteen films with Alan Ladd, such as *Captain Carey, U.S.A.* (1950), *Branded* (1950), *Appointment with Danger* (1951), *Red Mountain* (1951), *The Iron Mistress* (1952), *Thunder in the East* (1952), *Desert Legion* (1953), *Shane* (1953), *Saskatchewan* (1954), *Drum Beat* (1954), *Hell on Frisco Bay* (1955), *Santiago* (1956), *The Big Land* (1957), and *Guns of the Timberland* (1960).

Some of his non-Alan Ladd roles included *Casablanca* (1942), *Captain America* (1944), *The Wistful Widow of Wagon Gap* (1947) with Abbott and Costello, *Abbott and Costello Meet the invisible Man* (1951), *Border River* (1954) with Joel McCrea, *The First Texan* (1956) again with Joel McCrea, *The Tall Stranger* (1957) a third with Joel McCrea, *Kid Galahad* (1962) with Elvis, *Get Smart* (1965), *Laredo* (1966), and *Family Affair* (1969).

Lewis died in Rancho Santa Fe, California of a stroke in December 8, 1995, two days before his 92nd birthday.

Mitchell Lewis

Mitchell Lewis was born in Syracuse, New York June 26, 1880 and was an American film actor whose career spanned both the silent and sound film eras. He appeared in more than 175 films between 1914 and 1956, although many of the roles in his later films were uncredited. During the silent era he played supporting roles, such as Sheihk Idrim in 1925's *Ben Hur*, but his career would have his roles diminish to small roles like the Captain of the Winkie Guards in *The Wizard of Oz* (1939).

More of his roles included *Tracked in the Snow Country* (1925), *Back to God's Country* (1927), *The Black Watch* (1929), *Never the Twain Shall Meet* (1931), *Business and Pleasure* (1932) with Joel McCrea, *The Count of Monte Cristo* (1934), *Mummy's Boys* (1936), *The Secret of Dr. Kildare* (1939), *Meet John Doe* (1941), *Rio Rita* (1942), *Lost in a Harem* (1944), *Courage of Lassie* (1946), *The Stratton Story* (1949), *Lone Star* (1952), *All the Brothers Were Valiant* (1953), and *Trial* (1955).

His last film was *The Fastest Gun Alive*, starring Glenn Ford and Broderick Crawford, which was released shortly before Lewis' death on August 24, 1956 at age 76 in Woodland Hills, Los Angeles, California.

Ralph Lewis

Ralph Percy Lewis was born in Englewood, Illinois October 8, 1872 and was an American actor of the silent era. He appeared in 160 films between 1912 and 1938. He was married to actress Vera Lewis.

Some of his roles included *The Million Dollar Handicap* (1925), *The False Alarm* (1926), *Casey Jones* (1927), *The Girl in the Glass Cage* (1929), *The Lost Squadron* (1932) with Joel McCrea, *Badge of Honor* (1934), *The Lost City* (1935), *The Accusing Finger* (1936), *West Bound Limited* (1937), and *The Buccaneer* released in 1938.

He died at age 65 on December 4, 1937 in Los Angeles, California after being hit by a limousine driven by a chauffeur working for Jack Warner.

Kay Linaker

Mary Katherine Linaker, known professionally as "Kay Linaker", "Kate Phillips", and "Kay Linaker-Phillips" was born in Pine Bluff, Arkansas July 13, 1913 and was an American actress and screenwriter, who appeared in many B movies during the 1930s and 1940s, most notably *Kitty Foyle* (1940). Linaker used her married name (Kay Phillips) as a screenwriter, notably for the cult movie hit *The Blob* (1958). She is credited with coining the name "The Blob" for the movie, which was originally titled "The Molten Meteor."

Linaker graduated from New York University and acted in supporting roles on Broadway before signing a film contract with Warner Bros.. She later taught in the film studies department at Keene State College in New Hampshire from 1980 to 2006.

More of her roles icnluded *The Murder of Dr. Harrigan* (1936), *Charlie Chan at Monte Carlo* (1937), *Young Mr. Lincoln* (1939), *Drums Along the Mohawk* (1939), *The Invisible Woman* (1940), *A Close Call for Ellery Queen* (1942), *The More the Merrier* (1943) with Joel McCrea, *Here Come the Waves* (1944), and *Bring on the Girls* (1945).

From the 1960s to her death April 18, 2008 at age 94 in Keene, New Hampshire, unbeknown to most, Mrs. Phillips dedicated much of her time supporting the children at Hampshire Country School in Rindge, New Hampshire. Mrs. Phillips volunteered countless hours over the many years as English teacher and drama coach at the very small private school for twice exceptional children whose alumni include Dr. Temple Grandin.

Eric Linden

Eric Linden was born in New York City September 15, 1909 and was a Swedish–American actor. He has a star on the Hollywood Walk of Fame.

Eric Linden was born to Phillip and Elvira (née Lundborg) Linden, both of Swedish descent. His father was a professional pianist and an actor on stage with the Theater Royal when he lived in Stockholm, Sweden. When Eric was six, Phillip Linden deserted his family in New York City. To help support his family, he sold newspapers on Tenth Avenue. Linden participated in school plays at DeWitt Clinton High School. After graduation, he worked his way through Columbia University.

The handsome Linden made his film debut during the Great Depression in RKO Radio Pictures' 1931 crime film, *Are These Our Children?*. He appeared in thirty-three films until 1941, mostly playing second leads. Other notable films included *Big City Blues* (1932), *The Silver Cord* (1933) with Joel McCrea, *Old Hutch* (1936), opposite Wallace Beery, *A Family Affair* (1937), and *The Good Old Soak* (1937). In 1939, Linden had a minor role as an amputee in *Gone with the Wind*.

However, his career petered out and he left Hollywood after his final film, *Criminals Within* (1943). Eric married late in life in 1955, age 46; he and wife Jo, an artist, settled in Laguna Beach, California and had three children: Karen, David, and Andrea. They divorced in 1977. In later years, he worked for the County of Orange in California.

Eric Linden died on July 14, 1994, in South Laguna Beach, California, at age 84.

Alfred Linder

Alfred Linder was born on June 27, 1902 in Karlsruhe, Germany. He was an actor, known for *The House on 92nd Street* (1945), *Guilty of Treason* (1950), and *The Invisible Boy* (1957).

More of his roles included *The Roaring Twenties* (1939), *The House on 92nd Street* (1945), *I Was a Male War Bride* (1949), *Les Miserables* (1952), *The Lone Wolf* (1954), *Adventures of Superman* (1954-1956), *Gunsmoke* (1956), and *Trooper Hook* (1957) with Joel McCrea.

He died on July 4, 1957 in Hollywood, California at age 55.

Orley Lindgren

Orley Lindgren was born on July 18, 1939 in Long Beach, California. He is an actor, known for *Young Man with a Horn* (1950), *Under My Skin* (1950), and *Red Planet Mars* (1952).

More of his roles included *Hitler's Children* (1943), *Anchors Aweigh* (1945), *The Great Lover* (1949), *Saddle Tramp* (1950) with Joel McCrea, *Adventures of Wild Bill Hickok* (1951), *Japanese War Bride* (1952), *Mister Scoutmaster* (1953), and as Young Andy Jackson in *Cavalcade of America* (1954).

Ivan Linow

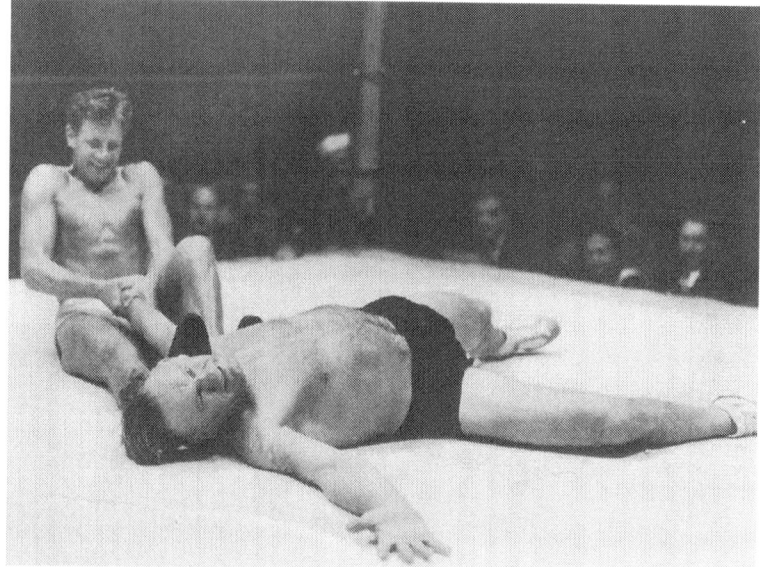

Joel McCrea and Ivan Linow in *The Sport Parade*

Ivan Linow was born in 1888 in Latvia as Janis Linaus. He was an actor, known for *The Red Dance* (1928), *The River* (1929), and *The Unholy Three* (1930).

More of his roles included *Fury* (1923), *Wages of Virtue* (1924), *The Crimson Flash* (1927), *Plastered in Paris* (1928), *The Silver Horde* (1930) with Joel McCrea, *Dumb Dicks* (1932), *The Sport Parade* (1932) again with Joel McCrea, *The Cat's-Paw* (1934), and *Another Face* (1935).

He died on November 21, 1940 in London, England at age 52.

Lucian Littlefield

Joel McCrea and Lucian Littlefield in *Wells Fargo*

Lucien Littlefield was born in San Antonio, Texas August 16, 1895 and was an American actor in the silent film era. He later made numerous cameo appearances on television series.

His role of the doctor in *The Cat and the Canary* (1927) is one of his more notable performances. He appeared with Laurel and Hardy, first as an eccentric professor in *Dirty Work*, and finally as a vet in their classic feature *Sons of the Desert*, both made in 1933. He also played Mary Pickford's father in *My Best Girl* in 1927.

Other roles include *Teeth* (1924), *Drag* (1929), *Skyway* (1933), *Wells Fargo* (1937) with Joel McCrea, *Those Were the Days!* (1940) with Alan Ladd, *The Great Man's Lady* (1942) again with Joel McCrea, *Scared Stiff* (1945), *Jinx Money* (1948), *The Abbott and Costello Show* (1953), *Lassie* (1955), *The Texan* (1959), and *This is the Life* (1961).

He died of natural causes in June 4, 1960 in Hollywood, Californiaat age 64, and was buried in Glendale's Forest Lawn Memorial Park Cemetery.

Norman Lloyd

Norman Nathan Lloyd was born in Jersey City, New Jersey November 8, 1914 and is an American actor, producer, and director with a career in entertainment spanning roughly eight decades. Lloyd has appeared in over sixty films and television shows. His prominent film roles include Fry in *Saboteur*, Bodalink in *Limelight*, Mr. Nolan in *Dead Poets Society* and Mr. Letterblair in *The Age of Innocence*. In the 1980s, he gained a new generation of fans for playing Dr. Daniel Auschlander, one of the starring roles on the groundbreaking medical drama *St. Elsewhere*.

His family was Jewish. He attended high school and college in New York City. He started his career as a song and dance child performer during the 1920s. He began his acting career in theater first at Eva Le Gallienne's Civic Repertory Theatre in New York, then joining the original company of the Orson Welles – John Houseman Mercury Theatre. Lloyd had a significant role with the first Mercury Theatre production as Cinna the poet, in Shakespeare's *Julius Caesar* (1937). The 1938 Broadway role in *Everywhere I Roam*, as Johnny Appleseed, was selected as one of the ten best Broadway performances of the year. Lloyd was also a featured radio actor, including as part of Orson Welles' Mercury Theater and later in Norman Corwin's *The Undecided Molecule*.

Lloyd met his wife, actress Peggy Craven, while they were co-starring in Elia Kazan's play *Crime*.

Lloyd came to Hollywood to play a Nazi spy in Alfred Hitchcock's *Saboteur* (1942), starting a long friendship and professional association with Hitchcock. After a few more villainous film roles, Lloyd also worked behind the camera as an assistant on Lewis Milestone's *Arch of Triumph* (1948). A friend of John Garfield, Lloyd appeared with him in *He Ran All the Way*, Garfield's last film before the Hollywood blacklist ended his film career.

A marginal victim of the blacklist, Lloyd was rescued professionally by Hitchcock, who had previously used the actor in *Saboteur* (1942) and *Spellbound* (1945). He also appeared in *The Unseen* (1945) with Joel McCrea. Hitchcock hired Lloyd as an associate producer and a director on his television series *Alfred Hitchcock Presents* in 1958. Previously, Lloyd was the director of the syndicated television series *The Adventures of Kit Carson* starring Bill Williams. Lloyd also directed the sponsored film *A Word to the Wives* (1955) with Marsha Hunt and Darren McGavin.

He continued directing and producing episodic television throughout the 1960s and 1970s. He took an unusual role in the *Night Gallery* (1972) episode "A Feast of Blood" as the bearer of a cursed brooch, which he inflicts upon a hapless woman, played by Sondra Locke, who had spurned his romantic advances. That same year he appeared with David Janssen in *O'Hara, U.S. Treasury*.

He appeared in *The Nude Bomb* (1980) which was a Don Adams *Get Smart* movie.

In the 1980s, Lloyd played Dr. Auschlander in the television drama *St. Elsewhere* over its six-season run (1982–1988). Originally scheduled for only four episodes, Lloyd became a regular for the remainder of the series. In addition to Ed Flanders and William Daniels, *St. Elsewhere* included a roster of relative unknowns, including Ed Begley, Jr., Denzel Washington, Stephen Furst, Eric Laneuville, David Morse, and Howie Mandel. Mandel, who played rowdy and unorthodox ER resident Dr. Wayne Fiscus, recalled that Lloyd "was very inspirational between scenes, always cheering up everybody, and always smiles when Norman Lloyd passed through!"

He appeared in *The Twilight Zone* (1986) revival show.

In 1989, he made his first film role in nearly a decade, playing Mr. Nolan, the authoritative headmaster of Welton Academy in *Dead Poets Society*. Initially, Lloyd was hesitant when asked to audition, because he thought the director and producers could judge whether or not he was right for the part by watching his acting on *St. Elsewhere*. Director Peter Weir was living in Australia and had not seen *St. Elsewhere*. Lloyd agreed to audition for him after winning his daily tennis match.

He appeared in *Star Trek: The Next Generation* (1993).

From 1998-2001 he played Dr. Isaac Mentnor in the UPN science fiction drama *Seven Days*.

He has played in various radio plays for Peggy Webber's California Artists Radio Theater and Yuri Rasovsky's Hollywood Theater of the Ear. His most recent film role was in *In Her Shoes* (2005). He is the subject of the documentary *Who Is Norman Lloyd?*, which premiered at the Sundance Film Festival on September 1, 2007.

In 2010, he guest starred in an episode of ABC's *Modern Family*. On December 5, 2010 he starred in a one-man show at the Colony Theatre, in Burbank, California, where he spoke of his career and answered questions from the audience, detailing his illustrious and singular path.

His wife of 75 years, Peggy, died on August 30, 2011, at the age of 98; the couple had two children, one of whom is the actress Josie Lloyd.

Lloyd's hobby is tennis, which he has practiced since the age of 8. He quipped in an interview "with the application and time I have devoted to it, I should have been a reigning World Champion".He has played against Charlie Chaplin, Joseph Cotten, and Spencer Tracy. Currently, in his late 90s, Lloyd still plays twice a week.

He has completed a role at age 99 as 'Older Robert' in *A Place for Heroes* set for a 2014 release.

Rollo Lloyd

Rollo Lloyd was born Rollo de Leon Lloyd on March 22, 1883 in Akron, Ohio. He was an actor and writer, known for *Midnight at Maxim's* (1915), *Barbary Coast* (1935) with Joel McCrea, and *The Devil-Doll* (1936).

More of his roles included *Laughter in Hell* (1933), *The Man Who Reclaimed His Head* (1934), *The Bride of Frankenstein* (1935), *Come and Get It* (1936) again with Joel McCrea, *Partners in Crime* (1937), and *Spawn of the North* (1938).

He died on July 24, 1938 in Los Angeles, California at age 55. According to the Los Angeles Times, director Tay Garnett and actor Frank McHugh secretly paid for Lloyd's funeral expenses.

Suzanne Lloyd

Suzanne Lloyd was born November 11, 1934 in Toronto and is a Canadian film and television actress. In addition to her film work, she was a frequent guest star on both British and American television, including *The Avengers* (1965), *Laramie* (1963), *Thriller* (1962), *Perry Mason* (1961), *Tales of Wells Fargo* (1961), *Walt Disney's Wonderful World of Color* (1961), and six episodes of *The Saint* (1964-1968).

Lloyd also had a recurring role as Raquel Toledano on the classic *Zorro* (1958-1961) television series.

Some of her other roles included *State Trooper* (1959), *The Bob Cummings Show* (1958-1959), *Alcoa Presents: One Step Beyond* (1959), *Wichita Town* (1960) with Joel McCrea, *Seven Ways from Sundown* (1960) with Audie Murphy, *Miami Undercover* (1961), *The Return of Mr. Moto* (1965), and *The Champagne Murders* (1967).

She moved overseas from the early 1960s until 1974, when she returned to the United States and made one more film *Mousey* (1974) before, surprisingly, retired from acting at the young age of forty.

She has appeared at autograph/memorabilia shows in California and on the east coast in recent years. She is best remembered for her role as the femme fatale "Maya the Catgirl" on the well-known *Twilight Zone* (1959) episode, "Perchance to Dream".

She attended the 2007 Twilight Zone Convention at the Hilton Hasbrouck Heights, Hasbrouck Heights, New Jersey, August 4-5, 2007.

Lloyd was married to record producer and composer Buddy Bregman from 1961 until their divorce in 1988. Their daughter, Tracey E. Bregman is an Emmy Award-winning actress.

Arthur Loft

Arthur Loft was born in Denver, Colorado as Hans Peter Loft May 25, 1897 and was an American film actor. He appeared in 224 films between 1932 and 1947.

Some of his credits included *Behind Jury Doors* (1932), *Stand Up and Cheer!* (1934), *Three Kids and a Queen* (1935), *The Lone Wolf Returns* (1935), *Don't Gamble with Love* (1936), *Ace Drummond* (1936), *Public Cowboy No. 1* (1937), *Who Killed Gail Preston?* (1938), *Down in 'Arkansaw'* (1938), *Hell's Kitchen* (1939), *Mr. Smith Goes to Washington* (1939), *The Roaring Twenties* (1939), *The Green Hornet* (1940) with Alan Ladd, *The Green Hornet Strikes Again!* (1940), *Hold Back the Dawn* (1941) with Veronica Lake, *They Died with Their Boots On* (1941), *Wild Bill Hickok Rides* (1942), *This Gun for Hire* (1942) with Alan Ladd and Veronica Lake, *The Glass Key* (1942) again with Alan Ladd and Veronica Lake, *Gildersleeve's Bad Day* (1943), *Buffalo Bill* (1944) with Joel McCrea, *Salty O'Rourke* (1945) a third with Alan Ladd, *The Naughty Nineties* (1945) with Abbott and Costello, *Two Years Before the Mast* (1946) a fourth with Alan Ladd, *The Virginian* (1946) again with Joel McCrea, *The Blue Dahlia* (1946) a fifth with Alan Ladd and fourth with Veronica Lake, *Till the End of Time* (1946), *Blondie Knows Best* (1946), and *Cigarette Girl* (1947).

He was married to Daisy Loft. He died January 1, 1947 in Los Angeles, California at age 49.

Ella Logan

Ella Logan was born as Georgina Allan in Glasgow, Scotland March 6, 1913 and was a Scottish-born actress and singer, who appeared on Broadway, recorded and had a nightclub career in the United States and internationally. She began performing under the name Ella Allan as a child.

She went on to become a band singer in music halls. At the age of 17 in 1930, she made her debut in the West End of London in *Darling! I Love You*. She toured Europe in the early 1930s. Logan eventually immigrated to the U.S. and began to sing at various clubs and to record jazz on the British Columbia label (part of EMI).

She then appeared in several Hollywood films, including *Flying Hostess* (1936), *Woman Chases Man* (1937) with Joel McCrea, *52nd Street* (1937), and *The Goldwyn Follies* (1938) with Alan Ladd. She appeared in several Broadway shows in the 1930s and early 1940s, but traveled to Europe and then Africa during World War II to entertain the troops. She also appeared on *The Ed Wynn Show* and *The Colgate Comedy Hour* in the 1940s and 1950s.

Logan returned to Broadway in 1947 starring as Sharon McLonergan in the original production of *Finian's Rainbow*, singing the show's most famous song, *How Are Things in Glocca Morra?*, among others. The production ran for 725 performances. She did not return to Broadway after that. In 1954, she was cast in a proposed animated film adaptation of *Finian's Rainbow* and re-recorded the score with Frank Sinatra. But the film was canceled, and the recordings were not released until the 2002 box set *Sinatra in Hollywood 1940-1964*. The original cast album was released in 1948, and was Capitol Records' first Original Cast album. She recorded the show's songs for a second time in 1954 for the LP *Ella Logan Sings Favorites from Finian's Rainbow,* accompanied by pianist George Greeley. It was released by Capitol Records in 1955. This was the second of her two solo albums.

In the 1950s, she became an international nightclub performer, appearing at such venues as the Copacabana and the Waldorf-Astoria in New York as well as in London and Paris. She also appeared on television. In May 1956, she appeared in London with Louis Armstrong and His All-Stars. In 1965 she was part of the cast of the infamous Broadway flop *Kelly*, until her role was cut during out of town tryouts. She continued to work occasionally in clubs, on television, and in theatrical stock productions, into the 1960s.

She was married to Fred Finklehoffe, a playwright and producer, from 1942 until the marriage dissolved in the mid 1950s. They had no children. Her niece is the actress/chanteuse Annie Ross (born as Annabelle McCauley Allan Short) and her nephews were Jimmy Logan, a Scottish TV star, and Allan Kemble, a Comedy Unicycle entertainer who was an international headline attraction on the continent and in world cabaret and stage venues.

Ella Logan died May 1, 1969 of cancer in Burlingame, California, at age 56.

Herbert Lom

Joel McCrea and Herbert Lom in *Rough Shoot*

Herbert Lom was born Herbert Karel Angelo Kuchačevič ze Schluderpacheru in Prague, Bohemia, Austria-Hungary [now Czech Republic] September 11, 1917 and was a Czech-born film and television actor who moved to the United Kingdom in 1939. In a career lasting more than 60 years he appeared in character roles, usually portraying villains early in his career and professional men in later years.

Lom's English was noted for a precise, elegant delivery. He is best known for his roles in *The Ladykillers* and *The Pink Panther* film series.

Lom was born to Karl Kuchačevič ze Schluderpacheru, and his spouse, the former Olga Gottlieb. Lom himself claimed that his family had been ennobled and the family title dated from 1601. Lom's film debut was in the Czech film *Žena pod křížem* ("A Woman Under Cross") (1937) followed by the *Boží mlýny* ("Mills of God")(1938). His early film appearances were mainly supporting roles, with the occasional top billing. At this time he also changed his impractically long surname to Lom ("a quarry" in Czech) because it was the shortest he found in a local phone book.

In January 1939, because of the threat of Nazi Germany occupying the rest of Czechoslovakia, Lom escaped to Britain. He made numerous appearances in British films throughout the 1940s, usually in villainous roles, although he later appeared in comedies as well. He managed to escape being typecast as a European heavy by securing a diverse range of castings, including as Napoleon Bonaparte in *The Young Mr. Pitt* (1942), and again in the 1956 version of *War and Peace* with Audrey Hepburn. He secured a seven-picture Hollywood contract after World War II but was unable to obtain an American visa for "political reasons". In a rare starring role, Lom played twin trapeze artists in *Dual Alibi* (1946).

Lom starred as the King of Siam in the original London production of Rodgers and Hammerstein's musical, *The King and I*. Opening at the Drury Lane Theatre on October 8, 1953, it ran for 926 performances. (His co-star who played Anna, Valerie Hobson, was by then married to the British politician John Profumo.) Lom can be heard on the cast recording. The same year he appeared with Joel McCrea in the film *Shoot First* aka *Rough Shoot*.

A few years later he appeared opposite Alec Guinness and Peter Sellers in *The Ladykillers* (1955), and with Robert Mitchum, Jack Lemmon, and Rita Hayworth in *Fire Down Below* (1957). He went on to more film success during the 1960s with a wide range of parts, starting with *Spartacus* (1960). Subsequent films in this period included *El Cid* (1961), *Mysterious Island* (also 1961), playing Captain Nemo, and Hammer Films' remake of *The Phantom of the Opera* (1962). Again in the leading role, the phantom's mask in this version was full face, which made casting an actor with a reputation for his vocal talents a sensible decision. "It was wonderful to play such a part, but I was disappointed with the picture", Lom says. "This version of the famous Gaston Leroux story dragged. The Phantom wasn't given enough to do, but at least I wasn't the villain, for a change. Michael Gough was the villain."

During this period, Lom starred in his only regular TV series, in the British drama, *The Human Jungle* (1963–64) as a Harley Street psychiatrist, over two seasons. In addition to *The Phantom of the Opera*, other low-budget horror films starring Lom included the witchhunting film *Mark of the Devil* (1970), which depicted torture scenes graphically. Reportedly, cinemas handed out sick bags to every patron at screenings of the film.

Lom was perhaps best known for his portrayal of Chief Inspector Charles Dreyfus, Inspector Clouseau's long-suffering superior in several of Blake Edwards's *Pink Panther* films. He also appeared in two different screen versions of the Agatha Christie novel *And Then There Were None*. In the 1975 version he played Dr. Armstrong, and later appeared in the 1989 version as General McKenzie.

Lom wrote two historical novels, one on the playwright Christopher Marlowe (*Enter a Spy: The Double Life of Christopher Marlowe*, 1971) and another on the French Revolution (*Dr. Guillotin: The Eccentric Exploits of an Early Scientist*, 1992). The film rights to the latter have been purchased but to date no film has been produced.

He died in his sleep on September 27, 2012 at the age of 95 in London, England.

Jack Lomas

Jack Lomas was born on March 23, 1911 in New York City, New York. He was an actor, known for *April in Paris* (1952), *Copper Sky* (1957), and *Cattle Empire* (1958) with Joel McCrea.

More of his roles included *We Who Are Young* (1940), *Nearly Eighteen* (1943), *It's a Wonderful Life* (1946), *The Luck of the Irish* (1948), *The Great Jewel Robber* (1950), *Million Dollar Mermaid* (1952), *Invasion U.S.A.* (1952) which was later remade in the 1980s with Chuck Norris, *Dragnet* (1953), *Seven Angry Men* (1955), *Somebody Up There Likes Me* (1956), *Adventures of Superman* (1957), *Maverick* (1958), and *Last Train from Gun Hill* (1959).

He died on May 12, 1959 in Los Angeles, California at age 48.

Montagu Love

Harry Montagu Love was born in Portsmouth, Hampshire March 15, 1877 and was an English screen, stage, and vaudeville actor.

Educated in Great Britain, Love began his career as an artist and military correspondent with his first important job as a London newspaper cartoonist. Love honed basic stage talents in London, and in 1913 sailed to the U.S. with a road-company production of Cyril Maude's *Grumpy.*

Usually Love was cast in heartless villain roles. In the 1920s, he played opposite Rudolph Valentino in *The Son of the Sheik,* opposite John Barrymore in *Don Juan,* and appeared with Lillian Gish in 1928's *The Wind.* He also portrayed 'Colonel Ibbetson' in *Forever* (1921), the silent film version of *Peter Ibbetson.* Love was one of the most successful villains in silent films.

He appeared with Joel McCRea in *The Divine Lady* (1929).

One of Love's first sound films was the part-talkie *The Mysterious Island* co-starring Lionel Barrymore. In 1937, he played Henry VIII in the first talking film version of Mark Twain's *The Prince and the Pauper,* with Errol Flynn. Love played the bigoted Bishop of the Black Canons in *The Adventures of Robin Hood* (1938), starring Flynn, too. However, he also played gruff authoritarian figures, such as Monsieur Cavaignac, who, contrary to history, demands the resignation of those responsible for the Dreyfus coverup, in *The Life of Emile Zola* (1937), as well as Don Alejandro de la Vega, whose son appears to be a fop but is actually Zorro, in the 1940 version of *The Mark of Zorro,* starring Tyrone Power.

In 1941, he played a doctor in *Shining Victory,* which also starred James Stephenson, Geraldine Fitzgerald and Donald Crisp. In 1939's *Gunga Din,* it is Montagu Love who reads the final stanza of Rudyard Kipling's original poem over the body of the slain Din.

Some more of his roles included *The Mystic Hour* (1933), *Lloyd's of London* (1936), *Rulers of the Sea* (1939) with Alan Ladd, *Sherlock Holmes and the Voice of Terror* (1942), and *Holy Matrimony* (1943).

His last film, *Devotion,* was released three years after his death at age 66 on May 17, 1943. He was interred at Chapel of the Pines Crematory.

Frank Lovejoy

Frank Lovejoy was born Frank Andrew Lovejoy, Jr. in the Bronx, New York March 28, 1912 and was an American actor in radio, film, and television. He is perhaps best remembered for appearing in the film noir *The Hitch-Hiker* (1953) and for starring in the radio drama *Night Beat.*

He grew up in New Jersey. His father, Frank Lovejoy, Sr., was a furniture salesman from Maine. His mother, Nora, was born in Massachusetts to Irish immigrant parents.

A successful radio actor, Lovejoy was heard on the 1930s crime drama series *Gang Busters*. Lovejoy was a narrator (during the first season) for the show *This Is Your FBI*. He played the title character on the syndicated *The Blue Beetle* during the 1940s, and starred in the later newspaper drama series *Night Beat* in the early 1950s and in episodes of *Suspense* in the late 1950s. He also starred as John Malone in *The Amazing Mr. Malone*.

In films of the 1940s and 1950s, Lovejoy mostly played supporting roles. Appearing in movies such as *Goodbye, My Fancy* (1951) with Joan Crawford, and *The Hitch-Hiker* (1953) directed by Ida Lupino, Lovejoy was effective playing the movie's everyman in extraordinary situations. He was in several war movies, notably Stanley Kramer's *Home of the Brave* (1949), *Breakthrough* (1950), Joseph H. Lewis' *Retreat, Hell!* (1952) which portrayed the United States Marine Corps' retreat from the Chosin Reservoir (aka the Changjin Reservoir) during the Korean War and as a Marine sergeant again in *Beachhead* (1954). In 1951, he had the title role in *I Was a Communist for the FBI* with co-stars Ron Hagerthy, Paul Picerni, and Philip Carey.

Lovejoy starred in two short-run TV series, *Man Against Crime* and *Meet McGraw*. Episodes of these two series have never been released commercially on DVD or VHS and never aired on reruns. *Meet McGraw* episodes were screened at the Mid-Atlantic Nostalgia Convention.

His television performances include the episode "The Hanging Judge" of Wichita Town (1960) with Joel McCrea, the episode "County General" (March 18, 1962) on the ABC series *Bus Stop* with Marilyn Maxwell in the role of Grace Sherwood. That same season, he appeared on the ABC crime drama *Target: The Corruptors!* about the efforts of a New York City reporter to expose organized crime.

Lovejoy was first married to Frances Williams (1901–1959), but divorced in the late 1930s. In 1940, Lovejoy married actress Joan Banks (1918–1998), with whom he had a son and a daughter.

On October 2, 1962, Frank Lovejoy died at age 50 of a heart attack in his sleep at his residence in New York City. His wife, Joan Banks, called for medical help after she was unable to wake him. The couple had been appearing in a New Jersey production of the Gore Vidal play *The Best Man*.

Paul Lukas

Paul Lukas and Joel McCrea in *Rockabye*

Paul Lukas was born Pál Lukács in Budapest, Austria-Hungary (now Hungary) May 26, 1891 and was an American actor. He won the Oscar for Best Actor for his performance in the film *Watch on the Rhine* (1943).

Lukas was born into a Jewish family, the son of Naria (née Zilahy) and Janos Lukacs, an advertising executive.

Lukas made his stage debut in Budapest in 1916 and his film debut in 1917. At first, he played elegant, smooth womanizers, but increasingly he became typecast as a villain. He had a successful stage and film career in Hungary, Germany and Austria, where he worked with Max Reinhardt. He arrived in Hollywood in 1927, and became a naturalized citizen of the United States in 1937.

He was busy in the 1930s, appearing in such films as the crime caper *Grumpy* (1930), the melodrama *Rockabye* (1932) with Joel McCrea, the comedy *Ladies in Love* (1936), and the drama *Dodsworth* (1936), and Alfred Hitchcock's *The Lady Vanishes* (1938),. He followed William Powell and Basil Rathbone portraying the series detective Philo Vance, a cosmopolitan New Yorker, once in *The Casino Murder Case* (1935).

His major film success came in *Watch on the Rhine* (1943), where he played a man working against the Nazis, a role he originated in the Broadway premiere of the play of the same name in 1941. His portrayal of Kurt Mueller, a German émigré with an American wife, played by Bette Davis, was universally lauded by critics. Brooks Atkinson of the *New York Times*, wrote, "As the enemy of fascism, Mr. Lukas' haggard, loving, resourceful determination becomes heroic by virtue of his sincerity and his superior abilities as an actor." He won the Academy Award for Best Actor for the role, winning out over luminary efforts as Humphrey Bogart in *Casablanca*, Gary Cooper in *For Whom the Bell Tolls*, Walter Pidgeonin *Madame Curie*, and Mickey Rooney in *The Human Comedy*. He also received the New York Film Critics Award for his performance.

Also in 1943, he guest starred as the eponymous character in an episode of the radio program *Suspense*, "Mr. Markham, Antique Dealer".Modern viewers also remember Lukas for his role as Professor Aronnax in Walt Disney's film version of Jules Verne's *20,000 Leagues Under the Sea* (1954). By that time, however, he was, at age 63, suffering from memory problems during the production, apparently leading him to lash out at cast and crew alike. Even friend Peter Lorre was not immune to the abuse.

In the 1940s, Lukas was a charter member of the Motion Picture Alliance for the Preservation of American Ideals, a conservative lobbying group opposed to possible Communist influence in Hollywood.

Lukas' film career picked up momentum in the 1960s with six films, including *Fun in Acapulco* with Elvis Presley in 1963 and *Lord Jim* with Peter O'Toole in 1965. His final film, *The Challenge*, was released in 1970.

The remainder of his career moved from Hollywood to the stage to television. His only singing role was as Cosmo Constantine in the original 1950 Broadway stage version of Irving Berlin's *Call Me Madam*, opposite Ethel Merman (although he is heard singing a song in the 1933 film *Little Women*, displaying a pleasant voice).

He died August 15, 1971 at age 80, in Tangier, Morocco, reportedly while searching for a place to spend his retirement years.

Lukas has a star on the Hollywood Walk of Fame at 6821 Hollywood Boulevard.

Nick Lukats

Nick Lukats was born on May 1, 1911 in Cleveland, Ohio. He was an actor and writer, known for *Waikiki Wedding* (1937), *Internes Can't Take Money* (1937) with Joel McCrea, and *Knute Rockne All American* (1940), for which he was a technical advisor for the film because he was a former Notre Dame football star.

More of his roles included *Navy Wife* (1935), *The Accusing Finger* (1936), *Murder Goes to College* (1937), *Rebellious Daughters* (1938), and *Navy Blues* (1941).

He died on January 6, 1979 in Barberton, Ohio at age 67.

Dayton Lummis

Dayton Lummis. Sr. was born in Summit, New Jersey August 8, 1903 and was an American actor of film and television who specialized in the genre of anthology and western series, often playing authority figures. From 1959-1960, he appeared as Marshal Andy Morrison in nine episodes of NBC's *Law of the Plainsman* western, with Michael Ansara and Robert Harland. In 1955, he portrayed General Douglas MacArthur in the film *The Court Martial of Billy Mitchell*.

Lummis studied theatre arts in Los Angeles at the Martha Oatman School. His first professional engagement, at the age of twenty-four, was with the Russell Stock Company in Redlands, California. He remained a regional actor until his Broadway debut in 1943.

Lummis was cast in his first screen role, a minor appearance, at the age of forty-two in the Burt Lancaster and Barbara Stanwyck film *Sorry, Wrong Number*. After a few other motion picture appearances, some uncredited, Lummis was cast as a police superintendent in the television series *Racket Squad* in the 1952 episode "The Strange Case of James Doyle" Hugh Beaumont, later the father, Ward Cleaver, on the sitcom *Leave It to Beaver*, narrated a third of the episodes of this series, which starred Reed Hadley as Captain John Braddock. That same year, Lummis appeared as Paul Clarkson in the episode "Where There's a Will" in the detective series *Mr. and Mrs. North*, starring Richard Denning. In 1954, he appeared as police Sergeant Jack Gotch in "The Big Trunk" episode of Jack Webb's *Dragnet*. In 1958, he appeared as Jonas Warman in the episode "The Healer" of NBC's *M Squad* crime drama, starring Lee Marvin.

Lummis appeared in numerous anthology series, including CBS's *Four Star Playhouse* anthology series. In 1955, he appeared twice on CBS's *Schlitz Playhouse of Stars*. Between 1954 and 1956 Lummis was cast in four separate roles on NBC's *The Loretta Young Show*. He appeared in the 1956 episode "Temptation" on CBS's *Lux Video Theatre*. In 1955, he portrayed an executive officer in the episode "Sky Pilot" of the CBS military anthology series, *Navy Log*. From 1953-1957, he was cast four times on the CBS anthology, *General Electric Theater*. He was cast as Colonel Duncan Smuthe in "The Tichborne Claimant" of the NBC series *the Joseph Cotten Show*, also known as *'On Trial*. In 1958, Lummis appeared on NBC's *Shirley Temple's Storybook* in the episode "The Nightingale". From 1956-1958, he appeared three times on CBS's *Alfred Hitchcock Presents* anthology. In 1958, he appeared twice CBS's *Playhouse 90*. In 1958 and 1959, he appeared on NBC's *Goodyear Theatre*.

Lummis was assigned his first western role as banker Jonathan Wilkins in the 1953 episode entitled "Trouble in Town" of *The Lone Ranger* series. Other western roles followed in 1956 as Stephen Austin in *The First Texan* with Joel McCrea, and 1957 as General Rogers on the syndicated series *The Adventures of Jim Bowie*, loosely based on the life of the Alamo defender Jim Bowie. Also in 1957, he appeared in the episode "The Fugitive" of another syndicated western, *Man Without a Gun*, starring Rex Reason and Mort Mills. That same year, he appeared as Jabez Lord in the episode "Hunter's Moon" of the NBC series *Buckskin* starring child actor Tommy Nolan. The nest year, he guest starred in "Excitement at Milltown" of Rod Cameron's syndicated *State Trooper*. He was cast as a Judge Randall in the 1959 episode "Gone But Not Forgotten" of the CBS series *Yancy Derringer*, starringJock Mahoney. In 1960, he appeared as Gideon Templeton in the episode "Path of the Eagle" of the NBC western series, *Riverboat*, starring Darren McGavin.

In 1960, Lummis was cast twice on the syndicated western series, *Death Valley Days*, first as Lew Wallace, governor of the New Mexico Territory and the author of the novel, *Ben Hur: A Tale of the Christ*, in the episode "Shadows on the Window".He then portrayed the character John De La Mar in "City of Widows."

In 1960, he appeared twice on Chuck Connors's ABC western *The Rifleman*. That same year, Lummis appeared twice on the syndicated *Death Valley Days*. In 1961, he played a judge in "Killer Without Cause" of the NBC series, *Laramie*. He appeared that same year in two Warner Brothers westerns on ABC: as Silas Rigsby in "Trouble at Sand Springs" of Will Hutchins's *Sugarfoot* and as Frank Collins, father of a wayward youth played by Richard Evans, in the episode "The Young Fugitives" of Clint Walker's *Cheyenne* His next western role was in the 1962 episode "The Ross Bennett Story" of NBC's *The Wide Country*, starring Earl Holliman and Andrew Prine.

In 1963, he was cast in *The Virginian*. Lummis starred in *Empire*, starring Richard Egan. In 1963, he was cast as Clayton Emory in episode "The Chooser of the Slain" of the short-lived Warner Brothers western series *The Dakotas*, starring Larry Ward and Chad Everett. Still another 1963 role was as Colonel Bob Grainger in "Fracas at Kiowa Flats" of the NBC series, *Temple Houston, starring Jeffrey Hunter.*

Lummis appeared three times in the NBC and ABC western, *Wagon Train*: as Major Barham in "the Martha Barham Story" (1959) with Ann Blyth in the title role, as T.J. Gingle in "The John Turnbull Story" (1962), with Henry Silva, and as the Reverend Philip Marshall in "The Myra Marshall Story" (1963), starring Suzanne Pleshette. He appeared four times on NBC's *Bonanza*: as Colonel Metcalfe in "Escape to Ponderosa" (1960), as attorney Hiram Wood in "the Secret" (1961), as Colonel Abel Chapin in "The Legacy" (1963), and as Judge O'Hara in "The Dilemma" (1965). The 1965 *Bonanza* appearance was Lummis' last western role for a full decade, when he appeared on February 3, 1975, as 71-year-old Mr. Holmby in the episode ""The Angry Land", one of the last episodes of CBS's longest-running western, *Gunsmoke*, starring James Arness. "The Angry Land" was the penultimate *Gunsmoke* appearance for Arness as well as Lummis's final screen role.

Lummis maintained a ranch in Malibu, California during his acting career. He was married to Dorothy L. Lummis (April 11, 1912—January 21, 1997), a Pennsylvania native who resided in Bryn Mawr in Delaware County at the time of her death. Lummis himself died March 23, 1988 at the age of 84 in Santa Monica in Los Angeles County, California. His son, Dayton Lummis, Jr. (born in 1936), of Santa Fe, New Mexico, is a former museum curator and author of numerous nonfiction works on the American West.

Pierce Lyden

Pierce W. Lyden was born in a sod house on a ranch near Hildreth in rural Franklin County, Nebraska, January 8, 1908 and was an American actor best known for his work in television and film Westerns.

Son of a horse buyer for the U.S. Army cavalry, he acquired as a youngster riding skills that later made it possible for him to do his own stunts as an actor in Hollywood westerns.

He attended the Naponee, Nebraska, High School, and acted in several plays there; he graduated from the University of Nebraska School of Music and Fine Arts in 1927 and later studied at the Emerson College of Oratory in Boston. Lyden supported himself in these early years by playing romantic leads in stock company productions in Lincoln and on the road; he appeared in a few Chautauqua presentations.

When talking movies eclipsed live theater presentations in small towns, Pierce Lyden went on to Hollywood in 1932. There he played villains' roles in B Western films, quickly becoming typecast as a "bad guy," specializing in fight scenes. He appeared in Saturday serials called cliffhangers as well as in feature films and television series. The number of his movie roles has been estimated at between 300 and 400 (actors who did not have major parts were not listed in film credits); he also appeared in about 150 episodes of *The Cisco Kid, Wild Bill Hickok, The Lone Ranger,* and other television series. He worked with the most famous Western movie actors, including Roy Rogers, Gene Autry, and Hopalong Cassidy. He was Photo Press Fan Poll "Villain of the Year" in 1944.

More of his roles included *Forgotten Girls* (1940), *King of Dodge City* (1941), *Daredevils of the West* (1943), *Bad Men of the Border* (1945), *Son of Zorro* (1947), *The Countess of Monte Cristo* (1948), *Atom Man vs. Superman* (1950), *Captain Video, Master of the Stratosphere* (1951), *The Great Adventures of Captain Kidd* (1953), *The Phantom from 10,000 Leagues* (1955), Louis L'amour's *Utah Blaine* (1957), Louis L'amour's *The Tall Stranger* (1957) with Joel McCrea, *Gunman's Walk* (1958), *The Slowest Gun in the West* (1960), and *Cheyenne* (1962).

In 1962, as the popularity of Westerns lessened, Lyden retired in Orange, California, where he had lived throughout his acting career. He wrote "Action Shots" about film personalities for the Orange County, California, *Register*, and the film industry magazine *Classic Images*; he published five books about his career and the making of films in his era. In his later years he was regularly invited to film festivals in the U.S. and abroad. Honors awarded him included membership in the Cowboy Hall of Fame and Heritage Foundation (1979) and the Golden Boot Award (1992). In 1989 Naponee, Nebraska, named a street for him and held a Pierce Lyden film festival; in 1997 he received Nebraska's Buffalo Bill Award. In 1996, a Golden Palm Star on the Palm Springs, California, Walk of Stars was dedicated to him.

Lyden died on October 10, 1998, at his California home at age 90. He was buried at Fairhaven Memorial Park in Santa Ana, California.

Dawn Lyn

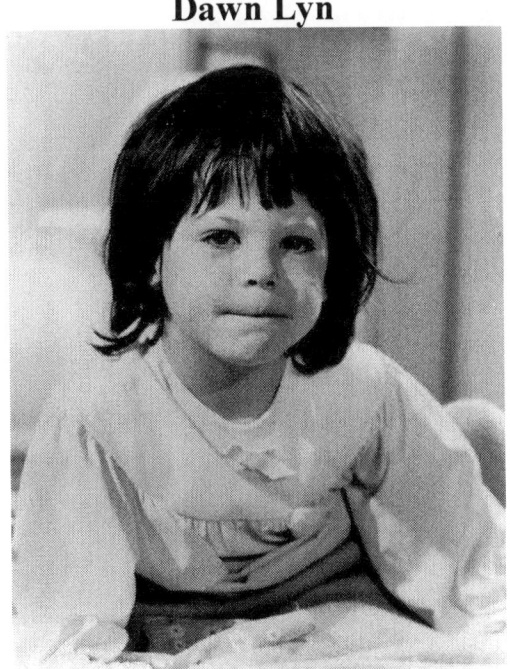

Dawn Lyn Nervik was born in Los Angeles, California January 11, 1963 and is an American actress best known for her role as Dodie Douglas during the last three seasons of the long-running CBS family comedy *My Three Sons* which ran from 1960–1972.

She first appeared as an American Indian child in the 1970 B-grade western *Cry Blood, Apache* with Joel and Jody McCrea.

In 1969, Lyn auditioned for the character Prudence Everett on the short-lived ABC series *Nanny and the Professor*, but when the pilot did not initially sell, she was released from her contract with ABC. ABC unsuccessfully sued to get Lyn for the part after she had already been cast for the role of the adopted daughter on *My Three Sons*.

In 1971 Lyn had a major role in the western *Shoot Out* as Gregory Peck's daughter. She also appeared in movies such as the *Walking Tall* trilogy. In 1973 Lyn auditioned for the role of Regan in *The Exorcist*, but was considered too young for the subject matter.

She had a recurring role as Reagan in the 1974 NBC series *Born Free* with Diana Muldaur and Gary Collins.

In 1974, Lyn appeared in the cult classic *Devil Times Five*, where Lyn's character Moe dumps a bucket of piranhas into a bathtub to creatively kill the character Lovely, played by Lyn's mother. (In *Cry Blood Apache*, the cowboy played by Lyn's father murdered the character played by her mother.)

She financially supported her mother and brother Leif Garrett from 1969 until around 1980 when her brother's fame eclipsed hers.

Lyn worked steadily in her youth on many popular series like *Gunsmoke* (1972-1973), *Adam 12* (1969-1974), *Harry O* (1974) with David Janssen, *Marcus Welby* (1970-1974), *Emergency!,*(1972-1976), and The Streets of San Francisco (1976), and Wonder Woman (1978).

Like many petite child actors, Lyn's 4'10" height began to work against, instead of for, her when in her teen years. She made a few appearances with Nickelodeon when the network revived the syndicated *My Three Sons* series; during a 1990 appearance in New York City for Nickelodeon, she was invited for an in-studio radio broadcast of *The Howard Stern Show* along with actress Erin Murphy (of *Bewitched* fame). Lyn and Murphy discussed international politics while egged on by Stern. It was Lyn's second appearance on Stern's program.

While living in Avalon on Catalina Island from 1997 to 2006, Lyn performed live voice acting with the Avalon Community Theater Radio Troupe. Actor Tony Dow sat in for an in-studio show and later appeared with Lyn at an island charity fundraiser along with his TV brother Jerry Mathers and TV mother Barbara Billingsley. ActorJohnny Whitaker, a childhood friend of Lyn's when *Family Affair* was being shot on the same studio lot as *My Three Sons*, joined her in a live broadcast of the troupe's satire of the film *Pearl Harbor*.

Dawn decided to branch out professionally, instead of concentrating on acting, and has done many things over the years. One of those includes co-owning a boutique on Pier 39 when she lived in San Francisco. People often ask her if she will act again; her answer is that while she has not actively pursued roles, that door is not closed.

Helen Lynd

Helen Lynd was born on January 18, 1902 in New Jersey. She was an actress, known for *Of Mice and Men* (1939), *The Strawberry Blonde* (1941), and *So Proudly We Hail!* (1943) with Veronica Lake.

Some of her other roles included *Success* (1931), *The Build-Up* (1933), *Hats Off* (1936), *Youth Takes a Fling* (1938) with Joel McCrea, *Road to Singapore* (1940), *The Great Man's Lady* (1942) again with Joel McCrea, *Moonlight in Havana* (1942), *When the Wife's Away* (1946), and her last film before retiring *Any Number Can Play* (1949).

She died on April 1, 1992 in Beverly Hills, California at age 90.

Diana Lynn

Diana Lynn was born Dolores Marie Loehr in Los Angeles, California, October 7, 1926 and was an actress. Lynn was considered a child prodigy because of her exceptional abilities as a pianist at an early age, and by the age of twelve was playing with the Los Angeles Junior Symphony Orchestra.

Dolores Loehr made her film debut playing the piano in *They Shall Have Music* (1939) with Joel McCrea, when it was decided that she had more potential than she had been allowed to show. Paramount Pictures changed her name to "Diana Lynn" and began casting her in films that allowed her to show her personality and developed her skills as an actress.

Her comedic scenes with Ginger Rogers in *The Major and the Minor* (1942), were well received, and in 1944 she scored an outstanding success in Preston Sturges' *The Miracle of Morgan's Creek* (1944). She appeared in two Henry Aldrich films, and played writer Emily Kimbrough in two films *Our Hearts Were Young and Gay* (1944) and *Our Hearts Were Growing Up* (1946) both co-starring Gail Russell.

She then appeared in *Texas, Brooklyn & Heaven* (1948) with Audie Murphy. After a few more films, she was cast in one of the year's biggest successes, the comedy *My Friend Irma* (1949) with Marie Wilson as Irma, and Dean Martin and Jerry Lewis in their film debuts. The group reprised their roles for the sequel *My Friend Irma Goes West* (1950). During the 1950s Lynn continued acting in films, and was the female lead in the much lampooned *Bedtime for Bonzo* (1951) opposite Ronald Reagan.

A marriage to John C. Lindsay ended in divorce in 1953. Lynn was then married in 1956 to Mortimer Hall, son of New York Post newspaper publisher Dorothy Schiff.

She acted frequently in television guest roles throughout the 1960s in such programs as *Checkmate* (1961), *Bus Stop* (1962), *The Doctors and the Nurses* (1964), *Burke's Law* (1964), *The Virginian* (1965), and *Company of Killers* (1971). By 1970, she had virtually retired from acting and had relocated to New York City, where she was running a travel agency. Paramount offered her a part in a new film, and after some consideration she accepted the offer and moved back to Los Angeles. Before filming started, she suffered a stroke and died nine days later December 18, 1971, at age 45. Lynn was interred at the Episcopal Church of the Heavenly Rest in New York City.

Diana Lynn has two stars on the Hollywood Walk of Fame: for motion pictures, at 1625 Vine Street, and for television, at 6350 Hollywood Boulevard.

Lynn was survived by her husband, and four young children. Her daughter Dolly Hall is a film producer.

Another daughter, Susan ... aka Daisy Hall, who bears a striking resemblance to her great-grandfather Jacob Schiff, is an alumna of the ultra-elite and highly-selective Emma Willard School for Girls in Troy, New York, and as an actress herself, has starred in numerous French- and lesser known American-produced films, during the 1980s, 1990s and 2000s.

Jeffrey Lynn

Jeffrey Lynn was born Ragnar Godfrey Lind in Auburn, Massachusetts February 16, 1909 and was an American actor. Lynn was a school teacher before he began his acting career. He came to Hollywood and made his film debut in *Out Where the Stars Begin* (1938). He achieved a notable success in 1938 appearing with the Lane Sisters in *Four Daughters*, and the popularity of the movie was so great that it was followed by three sequels, *Daughters Courageous* (1939), *Four Wives* (1939) and *Four Mothers* (1941) with Lynn reprising his role in each of them.

After the success of *Four Daughters*, Lynn was screen tested for the role of Ashley Wilkes in *Gone with the Wind* (1939). He was considered to be the front runner for the role, partly due to his physical resemblance to the character as written. Lynn was used extensively during the "Search for Scarlett" playing Ashley in the screen tests for many of the actresses who tried out for the part. David O. Selznick eventually cast the more experienced and popular Leslie Howard.

Instead, Lynn acted in *The Roaring Twenties* (1939), a gangster film that reunited him with *Four Daughters* star Priscilla Lane, as well as James Cagney and Humphrey Bogart. As one of a trio of friends, and the only one not to "go bad", Lynn won excellent reviews. The same year he appeared with Joel McCrea in *Espionage Agent.*

His success continued with such films as *The Fighting 69th* (1940) in which he portrayed poet-soldier Joyce Kilmer opposite Cagney, *It All Came True* (1940), *All This and Heaven Too* (1940) and *Million Dollar Baby* (1941). His movie career was interrupted by service during World War II and when he returned to the screen in 1948 he was not able to establish himself again. He was in the notably successful *A Letter to Three Wives* (1949) but his film career had stalled. Lynn starred in *Home Town Story* (1951) which featured Marilyn Monroe in a minor role. It was not until the 1960s that he achieved more successes with *Butterfield and 8* (1960) and *Tony Rome* (1967).

He began appearing in television, in such series as *Suspense* (1949-1953), *Robert Montgomery Presents* (1953-1955), *My Son Jeep* (1953)(with young Martin Huston), and *Lux Video Theatre* (1951-1953), specifically the episode "Thanks for a Lovely Evening" with Veronica Lake, during the early fifties.

He also made appearances on Broadway in the shows *Lo and Behold!* (1952), *Any Wednesday* (1966) and *Dinner at Eight* (1967).

Other roles continued in *The Edge of Night* (1956), *Lost Lagoon* (1958), *Ironside* (1969), *Barnaby Jones* (1973), *Simon & Simon* (1983), *Knots Landing* (1990), and *Midnight Caller* (1990).

A later notable appearance was in a guest role in *Murder, She Wrote* in 1987, a television sequel to the feature film *Strange Bargain* (1949), which reunited him with his original co-star, Martha Scott.

After his acting career went into decline, particularly in the 1950s, Lynn began working in real estate and from then his acting career was a secondary interest.

He died in Burbank, California November 24, 1995 at age 86 from natural causes. He was buried at Forest Lawn Memorial Park (Hollywood Hills)

Sharon Lynn

Sharon Lynn was born D'Auvergne Sharon Lindsay in Weatherford, Texas April 9, 1901 and was an American actress and singer. She began playing in silent films but enjoyed her biggest success in the early sound years of motion pictures before fading away in the mid 1930s. She is perhaps best known for portraying Lola Marcel, the villain in the Laurel and Hardy comedy feature *Way Out West* (1937).

More of her roles included *Curlytop* (1924), *The Cherokee Kid* (1927), *None But the Brave* (1928), *Sunnyside Up* (1929), *Lightnin'* (1930) with Joel McCrea, *Too Many Cooks* (1931), *The Big Broadcast* (1932), *Big Executive* (1933), *Go Into Your Dance* (1935), and *Thistledown* (1938).

She was married to Benjamin Glazer who died in 1956 and to John Sershen. She died May 26, 1963 in Hollywood at age 62.

Ian MacDonald

Ian MacDonald was born on June 28, 1914 in Great Falls, Montana and was an actor and producer, known for *High Noon* (1952), *Johnny Guitar* (1954), and *Apache* (1954).

Some of his other roles included *Madame Guillotine* (1933), *They Died with Their Boots On* (1941), *North of the Rockies* (1942), *The Strange Woman* (1946), *Ramrod* (1947) with Joel McCrea and Veronica Lake, *White Heat* (1949), *Colt .45* (1950), *The Texas Rangers* (1951), *The Savage* (1952), *The Lone Ranger* (1953), *Biff Baker, U.S.A.* (1953), *Timberjack* (1955), *Medic* (1956), *The Life and Legend of Wyatt Earp* (1957-1958), *Gunsmoke* (1958), *Riverboat* (1959), *Have Gun, Will Travel* (1959), *The Rebel* (1959-1960), and *The Man from Blackhawk* (1960).

He died on April 11, 1978 in Bozeman, Montana at age 63.

J. Farrell MacDonald

Joseph Farrell MacDonald was born in Waterbury, Connecticut June 6, 1875 and was an American character actor and director. He played supporting roles and occasional leads. MacDonald, who was sometimes billed as "John Farrell MacDonald", "J.F. McDonald" and "Joseph Farrell MacDonald" as well other variations, appeared as an actor in over 325 movies over a forty-one year career from 1911 to 1951, and directed forty-four silent films from 1912 to 1917.

MacDonald was the principal director of L. Frank Baum's Oz Film Manufacturing Company, and he can frequently be seen in the films of Frank Capra, Preston Sturges, and, especially, John Ford.

Early in his career, MacDonald was a singer in minstrel shows, and he toured the U.S. extensively for two years with stage productions. He made his first silent film in 1911, a dramatic short entitled *The Scarlett Letter* made by Carl Laemmle's Independent Moving Pictures Company (IMP), the forerunner of Universal Pictures,. He continued to act in numerous films each year from that time on, and by 1912 he was directing them as well. The first film he directed was *The Worth of a Man*, another dramatic short, again for IMP, and he was to direct forty-three more films until his last in 1917, *Over the Fence*, which he co-directed with Harold Lloyd. MacDonald had crossed paths with Lloyd several years earlier, when Lloyd was an extra and MacDonald had given him much-needed work – and he did the same with Hal Roach, both of whom appeared in small roles in *The Patchwork Girl of Oz*, which MacDonald directed in 1914. When Roach set up his own studio, with Lloyd as his principal attraction, he hired MacDonald to direct.

By 1918, MacDonald, who was to become one of the most beloved character men in Hollywood, had given up directing and was acting full-time, predominantly in Westerns and Irish comedies. He first worked under director John Ford in 1919's *A Fight for Love* and was to make three more with the director that same year. In all, Ford would use MacDonald on twenty-five films between 1919 and 1950, during the silent era notably in *The Iron Horse* (1924), *3 Bad Men* (1926), and *Riley the Cop* (1927).

With a voice that matched his personality, MacDonald made the transition to sound films easily, with no noticeable drop in his acting output – if anything, it went up. In 1931, for instance, MacDonald appeared in fourteen films – among them the first version of *The Maltese Falcon*, in which he played "Detective Tom Polhaus" – and in twenty-two of them in 1932. Although he played laborers, policemen, military men and priests, among many other characters, his roles were usually a cut above a "bit part": his characters usually had names, and he was most often credited for his performances. A highlight of this period was his performance as the hobo "Mr. Tramp" in *Our Little Girl* with Shirley Temple and Joel McCrea (1935).

In the 1940s, MacDonald was part of Preston Sturges' unofficial "stock company" of character actors, appearing in seven films written and directed by Sturges. His work on Sturges' films was generally uncredited, which was more often the case as his career went on – although the quality of his work was undiminished. He was notable in 1946 in John Ford's *My Darling Clementine* in which he played "Mac," the bartender in the town saloon. MacDonald also had an uncredited role in *It's a Wonderful Life* (1946); he played the owner of the tree which was damaged by George Bailey with his car.

More of his roles included *The Thirteenth Guest* (1932), *Romance in Manhattan* (1935), *Zenobia* (1939) with Oliver Hardy, *They Shall Have Music* (1939) again with Joel McCrea, *The Light of Western Stars* (1940) with Alan Ladd, *Sullivan's Travels* (1941) a third with Joel MCCrea, *The Palm Beach Story* (1942) number four with Joel McCrea, *The Great Moment* (1944) a fifth with Joel McCrea, *Behind Green Lights* (1946), *Whispering Smith* (1948) again with Alan Ladd, *The Range Rider* (1951), and *Superman and the Mole-Men* (1951).

MacDonald made his last film in 1951, a comedy called *Elopement*. He died in Hollywood on August 2, 1952 at the age of 77. He was married to actress Edith Bostwick until her death in 1943, and they had a daughter, Lorna. His grave is located at Chapel of the Pines Crematory.

Cactus Mack

Cactus Mack was born Taylor McPeters August 8, 1899 in Weed, New Mexico. A cousin of cowboy actors Rex Allen and Glenn Strange, Taylor Curtis McPeters was the oldest son born to John and Leona Byrd McPeters. He was the second of eleven children. Glenn Strange's mother was Leona's sister. Rex Allen was 21 years McPeters junior on his father's side. McPeters and Strange learned ranching in Coke, Texas, before their families moved to Willcox (Cochise County), Arizona.

McPeters married Etta Sarah Jessee on July 4, 1922 in Tombstone, Arizona. Cactus Mack was a talented musician. He played violin with Ray Whitley's "Six Bar Cowboys" and guitar with Fred Scott's "The Cimarron Cowboys".

He later played villain roles in many westerns, along with other character parts.

Some of his roles included *Riders of the Desert* (1932), *Custer's Last Stand* (1936), *The Law West of Tombstone* (1938), *Destry Rides Again* (1939), *Jesse James at Bay* (1941), *Red River Robin Hood* (1942), *Sheriff of Sundown* (1944), *The Virginian* (1946) with Joel McCrea, *Sheriff of Wichita* (1949), *Dallas* (1950), *Cattle Drive* (1951) again with Joel McCrea, *The Lawless Breed* (1953), *Duel at Apache Wells* (1957), *Rio Bravo* (1959), *Heller in Pink Tights* (1960), *Lawman* (1960-1961), and forty-eight episodes of *Gunsmoke* (1957-1961).

Injured during his final appearance on Gunsmoke, he required abdominal surgery in late 1961. As he was filming his closeups on location for *The Ugly American* with Marlon Brando, he died of a heart attack on April 17, 1962 in Hollywood, California at age 62.

Dorothy Mackaill

Joel McCrea and Dorothy Mackaill in *Once a Sinner*

Dorothy Mackaill was born in Hull, Yorkshire, England March 4, 1903 and was a British-American actress, most notably of the silent film era and into the early 1930s.

Mackaill lived with her father after her parents separated when she was eleven. She attended Thoresby Primary School. As a teenager, Mackaill ran away to London to pursue a stage career as an actress. After temporarily relocating to Paris, she met a Broadway stage choreographer who persuaded her to move to New York City where she became involved in the *Ziegfeld Follies* and befriended future motion picture actresses Marion Davies and Nita Naldi.

By 1920, Mackaill had begun making the transition from "Follies Girl" to film actress. That same year she appeared in her first film, the Wilfred Noy-directed mystery, *The Face at the Window*. Mackaill also appeared in several comedies of 1920 opposite actor Johnny Hines. In 1921 she appeared opposite Anna May Wong, Noah Beery, and Lon Chaney in the Marshall Neilan-directed drama *Bits of Life*. In the following years, Mackaill would appear opposite such popular actors as Richard Barthelmess, Rod La Rocque, Colleen Moore, John Barrymore, George O'Brien, Bebe Daniels, Milton Sills and Anna Q. Nilsson.

In 1924, Mackaill rose to leading lady status in the drama *The Man Who Came Back*, opposite rugged matinee idol George O'Brien. Her role of the nightclub chanteuse Marcelle catapulted Mackaill into a genuine Hollywood star and her career continued to flourish throughout the remainder of the 1920s. In early 1924 she starred in the western film, *The Mine with the Iron Door*, shot on location outside of Tucson, Arizona. That same year she was awarded the WAMPAS Baby Stars award by the Western Association of Motion Picture Advertisers in the United States, which honored thirteen young women each year who they believed to be on the threshold of movie stardom. Other notable recipients of the award that year were Clara Bow, Julanne Johnston and Lucille Ricksen.

Mackaill made a smooth transition to sound with the part-talkie *The Barker* (1928) and had success in talkies for the next couple of years. First National Pictures was acquired by Warner Brothers in September 1928, and her contract with First National was not renewed upon its expiration in 1931. Some of her roles that year of 1931 included *Once a Sinner* and *Kept Husbands* both with Joel McCrea.

Her most memorable role of this era was the 1932 Columbia Pictures release *Love Affair* with a young Humphrey Bogart as her leading man. She made several films for MGM, Paramount andColumbia before retiring in 1937 to care for her aging mother.

In 1955, Mackaill moved to Honolulu where she remained for the rest of her life. She had fallen in love with the islands while filming *His Captive Woman* in 1929. Mackaill lived at the luxurious Royal Hawaiian Hotel on the beach at Waikiki as a sort of celebrity in residence and enjoyed swimming in the ocean nearly every day. She occasionally came out of retirement to appear in roles for television, her first in an episode of Studio One in Hollywood (1953) and in two episodes of *Hawaii Five-O* in 1976 and 1980, which was filmed on location in Hawaii.

Mackaill was married three times. Her first marriage was to German film director Lothar Mendes, whom she married on November 17, 1926. They divorced in August 1928. On November 4, 1931, she married radio singer Neil Albert Miller. They divorced in February 1934. Her third and final marriage was to horticulturist Harold Patterson in June 1947. Mackaill filed for divorced in December 1948. She had no children from any of the marriages.

Mackaill died of kidney failure in Honolulu, Hawaii on August 12, 1990, at age 87. She was cremated and her ashes were scattered at sea off of Waikiki Beach.

Barry Macollum

Barry Macollum was born on April 6, 1889 in Ireland. He was an actor, known for *Beau Geste* (1939), *Revenge of the Zombies* (1943), and *The Trouble with Harry* (1955).

More of his roles included *Fury* (1923), *Internes Can't Take Money* (1937) with Joel McCrea, *Rulers of the Sea* (1939) with Alan Ladd, *It Ain't Hay* (1943) with Abbott and Costello, *Two Years Before the Mast* (1946) again with Alan Ladd, *Suspense* (1949-1951), *The Ten Commandments* (1956), *Going My Way* (1963), *Z Cars* (1965), and *The Girl from U.N.C.L.E.* (1967).

He died on February 22, 1971 in West Los Angeles, California at age 81.

Julian Madison

Julian Madison was born on November 23, 1907 in St. Paul, Minnesota. He was an actor, known for *It's a Gift* (1934), *Torture Ship* (1939), and *Secrets of a Model* (1940).

More of his roles included *Search for Beauty* (1934), *Private Worlds* (1935) with Joel McCrea, *The Feud Maker* (1938), *Death Rides the Range* (1939), and *Dick Tracy vs. Crime Inc.* (1941).

He died on September 29, 1972 in Los Angeles, California at age 64.

Noel Madison

Noel Madison was born in New York City, New York April 30, 1897 and was an American character actor in the 1930s and 1940s and appeared in seventy-five films, often as a gangster. He was the son of actor Maurice Moscovitch and his wife Rose. His father was a famous character actor, Maurice Moscovitch who sent his son abroad to study in Paris, Lausanne, and London. Upon returning to the U.S. following his stage debut in Great Britain, he began an active career on the American stage, specializing in highly sophisticated characters.

In 1930, he began appearing in films, most often in roles far different from the upper-class types he played on stage, mostly as gangsters and low-lifes.

Some of his roles included *Sinners' Holiday* (1930), *The Heart of New York* (1932), *The Girl from Missouri* (1934), *Woman Wanted* (1935) with Joel McCrea, *Our Relations* (1936), *The Man with 100 Faces* (1938), *Ellery Queen's Penthouse Mystery* (1941), *Miss V from Moscow* (1942), *Jitterbugs* (1943), and *The Gentleman from Nowhere* (1948).

In 1943, he mostly left films and returned full-time to the theatre, where he was active both as an actor and as a director.

He died January 6, 1975 at age 77 in Fort Lauderdale, Florida.

Marjorie Main

Marjorie Main was born Mary Tomlinson in Acton, Indiana February 24, 1890 and was an American character actress, best known as a Metro-Goldwyn-Mayer contract player and for her role as *Ma Kettle* in a series of ten *Ma and Pa Kettle* movies.

Main attended Franklin College in Franklin, Indiana, and adopted a stage name to avoid embarrassing her father, Samuel J. Tomlinson (married to Jennie L. McGaughey), who was a minister. She worked in vaudeville on the Chautauqua and Orpheum Circuits, and debuted on Broadway in 1916. Her first film was *A House Divided* in 1931.

Main began playing upper class dowagers, but was ultimately typecast in abrasive, domineering, salty roles, for which her distinctive voice was well suited. She repeated her stage role in *Dead End* in the 1937 film version with Joel McCrea, and was subsequently cast repeatedly as the mother of gangsters. She appeared again with Joel McCrea in *They Shall Have Music* (1939). She again transferred a strong stage performance, as a dude ranch operator in *The Women*, to film in 1939.

Main was signed to a Metro-Goldwyn-Mayer contract in 1940, and stayed with the studio until the mid-1950s. She made six films with Wallace Beery in the 1940s including *Barnacle Bill* (1941), *Jackass Mail* (1942), and *Bad Bascomb*(1946). She played Sonora Cassidy, the chief cook, in *The Harvey Girls* (1945). The director, George Sidney, says in the comments on the film that Miss Main was a "great lady" as well as a great actress who donated most of her paychecks over the years to the support of a school.

Perhaps her most famous role is that of "Ma Kettle", which she first played in *The Egg and I* in 1947 opposite Percy Kilbride as "Pa Kettle". She was nominated for an Academy Award for Best Actress in a Supporting Role for the part and portrayed the character in nine more Ma and Pa Kettle films. She played opposite Abbott and Costello in the western comedy *The Wistful Widow of Wagon Gap* (1947).

By the early 1950s, she had appeared in several MGM musicals, including, *Meet Me in St. Louis*, *The Belle of New York* and *It's a Big Country*. In 1954, Marjorie Main played her last roles for the studio; Mrs. Hittaway in *The*

Long, Long Trailer and Jane Dunstock in *Rose Marie*. In 1956, Main was well-received as The Widow Hudspeth in the hit film *Friendly Persuasion*.

In 1958, Main appeared twice as rugged frontierswoman Cassie Tanner in the episodes "The Cassie Tanner Story" and "The Sacramento Story" on NBC's western television series, *Wagon Train*. In the first segment, she joins the wagon train, casts her romantic interest on Ward Bond as Major Adams, and helps the train locate needed horses despite a Paiute threat. George Chandler guest stars as Cleveland McMasters in the first segment.

Main married Stanley LeFevre Krebs, who died in 1935. Despite her many claims of having had a happy marriage, Main's biographer Michelle Vogel quotes a late interview in which the actress related: "Dr. Krebs wasn't a very practical man. I didn't figure on having to run the show, I kinda tired of it after a few years. We pretty much went our own ways but we was still in the eyes of the law, man and wife".

In 1974, a year before her death, Main attended the Los Angeles premiere of the MGM documentary film *That's Entertainment*. It was her first public appearance since she retired from films in 1958. At the televised post-premiere party, she was greeted with cheers of enthusiasm and applause from the crowd of spectators. She died of lung cancer on April 10, 1975 at St. Vincent's Hospital in Los Angeles, where she had been admitted on April 3, at the age of 85. She is buried in Forest Lawn Memorial Park in the Hollywood Hills.

Dorothy Malone

Dorothy Malone and Joel McCrea in *South of St. Louis*

Dorothy Malone was born Dorothy Eloise Maloney in Chicago, Illinois January 30, 1925 and is an American actress. Her film career began in 1943, and in her early years she played small roles, mainly in B-movies. After a decade in films, she began to acquire a more glamorous image, particularly after her performance in *Written on the Wind* (1956), for which she won the Academy Award for Best Supporting Actress. Her film career reached its peak by the beginning of the 1960s, and she achieved later success with her television role as Constance MacKenzie on *Peyton Place* from 1964 to 1968. Less active in her later years, Malone returned to films in 1992 as the friend of Sharon Stone's character in *Basic Instinct*.

Her family moved to Dallas,Texas, where she worked as a child model and began acting in school plays at Ursuline Convent and Highland Park High School. While performing at Southern Methodist University, she was spotted by an RKO talent agent and was signed to a studio contract, making her film debut in 1943 in *The Falcon and the Co-Eds*.

Much of Malone's early career was spent in supporting roles in B-movies, many of them Westerns such as *South of St. Louis* and *Colorado Territory* both with Joel McCrea in 1949., although on occasion she played small but memorable roles, such as the brainy, lusty, bespectacled bookstore clerk in *The Big Sleep* (1946) with Humphrey Bogart, and the love interest of Dean Martin in the musical-comedy *Artists and Models*(1955).

By 1956, Malone transformed herself into a platinum blonde and shed her "good girl" image when she co-starred with Rock Hudson,Lauren Bacall, and Robert Stack in director Douglas Sirk's drama *Written on the Wind*. Her portrayal of the dipso-nymphomaniac daughter of a Texas oil baron won her the Academy Award for Best Supporting Actress. As a result, she was offered more substantial roles in such films as *Too Much, Too Soon*, where she portrayed Diana Barrymore, *Man of a Thousand Faces* (with James Cagney), and *Warlock* (with Henry Fonda and Richard Widmark). Additional screen credits include *The Tarnished Angels* (in which she reunited with former co-stars Hudson and Stack and director Sirk), *The Last Voyage* (with Stack) and *The Last Sunset* (with Hudson).

On New Years Day 1956, she appeared with John Ericson in the episode "Mutiny" of CBS's *Appointment with Adventure*. She guest-starred on NBC's 1958 1959 western series, *Cimarron City*.

During the 1963-1964 season, Malone guest starred on ABC's circus drama *The Greatest Show on Earth*, starring Jack Palance. From 1964-1968, she played the lead role of Constance MacKenzie on the ABC prime time serial *Peyton Place* except for a brief stretch where she was absent due to surgery. Lola Albright filled in until her return. In 1968, she was written out of the show after complaining that she was given little to do. Malone sued 20th Century-Fox for $1.6 million for breach of contract; it was settled out of court. She would later return to the role in the TV movies *Murder in Peyton Place* (1977) and *Peyton Place: The Next Generation* (1985). Malone had a featured role in the miniseries *Rich Man, Poor Man* (1976). In her last screen appearance, she played a mother convicted of murdering her family in *Basic Instinct* (1992) with Michael Douglas and Sharon Stone.

Dallas producers approached Malone to step into the role of Miss Ellie Ewing when Barbara Bel Geddes vacated the role in 1984. She declined.

Malone has been married and divorced three times and has two daughters, Mimi and Diane, from her first marriage to actor Jacques Bergerac. Her star in the Hollywood Walk of Fame is located at 1718 Vine. As of 2011, Malone is retired and living in Dallas,Texas.

Miles Mander

Miles Mander and Joel McCrea in *Primrose Path*

Miles Mander was born Lionel Henry Mander in Wolverhampton, Staffordshire, England May 14, 1888, (and sometimes credited as Luther Miles), was a well-known and versatile English character actor of the early Hollywood cinema, also a film director and producer, and a playwright and novelist.

Miles Mander was the second son of Theodore Mander, builder of Wightwick Manor, of the prominent Mander family, industrialists and public servants of Wolverhampton, Staffordshire, in the Midlands of England. He was the younger brother of Sir Geoffrey Mander, the Member of Parliament. He was educated at Harrow School, Middlesex (The Grove House 1901- Easter 1903); Loretto School, Musselburgh (east of Edinburgh) and McGill University, Montreal, Quebec, Canada. But he soon broke away from the predictable mold of business and philanthropy. He was an early aviator, a captain in the Royal Army Service Corps in World War I. He spent his twenties in New Zealand farming sheep, with his uncle, Martin Mander.

He achieved success as Sir Hugh Boycott in *The First Born* (1928) which he directed and acted in, and which was based on his own novel and play. He is better remembered for his character portrayals of oily villains, many of them English gentlemen or upper crust cads - such as Cardinal Richelieu in the musical film *The Three Musketeers* (1939), a spoof in which the Ritz Brothers played lackeys who substituted for the real Musketeers.

In his Hollywood debut, he had portrayed King Louis XIII in the much more serious 1935 version of that same Alexandre Dumas, père classic. Other famous film credits included *Wuthering Heights* (1939) with Laurence Olivier and Merle Oberon, in which he played Mr. Lockwood, the new tenant at the Grange, who is told the story of Cathy and Heathcliff. In the 1933 English version of G.W. Pabst's *Don Quixote*, he played the Duke who invites Don Quixote and Sancho Panza to his castle, and in the original *To Be or Not to Be* (1942), he was one of the two British officers to whom Robert Stack first reveals his suspicions about the treacherous Professor Siletsky (Stanley Ridges).

More of his roles included *Sherlock Holmes and the Missing Rembrandt* (1932), *Primrose Path* (1940) with Joel McCrea, *Captain Caution* (1940) with Alan Ladd, *They Met in Bombay* (1941) again with Alan Ladd, *The Return of the Vampire* (1944), and *The Imperfect Lady* (1947).

His first wife was an Indian princess, Princess Prativa Devi, the daughter of the Maharajah Nripendra Narayan of Cooch Behar. His brother Alan married her sister, Princess Sudhira. His second wife was Kathren ('Bunty') French, of Sydney, Australia, with whom he had a son, Theodore. He wrote a book of memoirs and advice to him, *To My Son—in Confidence* (1934).

He died February 8, 1946 suddenly of a heart attack at the Brown Derby restaurant in Los Angeles at age 57.

Rankin Mansfield

Rankin Mansfield was born on May 9, 1895 in Muscatine, Iowa. He is known for his work on *The Human Jungle* (1954), *Dial Red O* (1955), and *Badlands of Montana* (1957).

More of his roles included *How to Marry a Millionaire* (1953), *Dragnet* (1955), *The Oklahoman* (1957) with Joel McCrea, *Face of a Fugitive* (1959), *Tales of Wells Fargo* (1961-1962), and *The Manchurian Candidate* (1962).

He died on January 22, 1969 in Los Angeles, California at age 73.

Leona Maricle

Leona Maricle was born on December 23, 1905 in Wichita Falls, Texas. She was an actress, known for *Theodora Goes Wild* (1936), *Woman Chases Man* (1937) with Joel McCrea, and *Johnny Eager* (1941). She also had a long career on Broadway (1927 to 1965). She was in supporting roles in films with MGM, RKO and Columbia during the 1930's and 1940's.

More of her roles included *O'Shaughnessy's Boy* (1935), *Women of Glamour* (1937), *Beauty for the Asking* (1939), *Under Age* (1941), *My Pal Wolf* (1944), and *Without Reservations* (1946).

She died on March 25, 1988 in New York City, New York at age 82.

Marian Marsh

Joel McCrea and Marian Marsh in *The Sport Parade*

Marian Marsh was born Violet Ethelred Krauth in Trinidad, British West Indies (now Trinidad and Tobago October 17, 1913 and was an American film actress, and later, environmentalist.

He was the youngest of four children of a German chocolate manufacturer and his French-English wife.

Due to World War I, Violet's father moved his family to Boston, Massachusetts. By the time Violet was ten, the family had relocated to California where Violet's older sister, an actress who went by the name of Jean Fenwick, eventually landed a job as a contract player with FBO Studios.

Violet attended La Conte Junior High School and Hollywood High School. In 1928, Violet was approached by silent screen actress Nance O'Neil, who offered her speech and movement lessons. With sister Jean's help, Violet soon entered the movies. She secured a contract with Pathé where she was featured in many short subjects under the name Marilyn Morgan. She was seen in a small roles in Howard Hughes' classic *Hell's Angels* (1930) and Eddie Cantor's lavish Technicolor musical *Whoopee!* (1930). Not long afterwards, she was signed by Warner Bros. and her name was changed to Marian Marsh.

In 1931, Marsh landed one of her most important roles in *Svengali* opposite John Barrymore. Marsh was chosen by Barrymore, himself, for the role of "Trilby". Barrymore coached her performance throughout the picture's filming.*Svengali* was based on the 1894 novel *Trilby* written by George du Maurier. A popular play, likewise entitled *Trilby*, followed in 1895. In the film version, which Warner Bros. had retitled *Svengali*, Marsh plays the artists' model Trilby, who is transformed into a great opera star by the sinister hypnotist, Svengali. The word "Svengali'" has entered the English language, defining a person who, with sometimes evil intent, tries to persuade another to do what he desires.

Marsh was selected as one of the WAMPAS Baby Stars of 1931. And, with the critical praise and the audience's approval of *Svengali*, she continued in a string of successful films for Warner Bros. including *Five Star Final* (1931) with Edward G. Robinson, *The Mad Genius* (1931) with Barrymore, *The Road to Singapore* (1931) with William Powell, *Beauty and the Boss* (1932) with Warren William, and *Under 18* (1931)(again with William). She also appeared in *The Sport Parade* with Joel McCrea in 1932.

In 1932, in the midst of a grueling work schedule, Marsh left Warner Bros. and took several film offers in Europe which lasted until 1934. She enjoyed working in England and Germany, as well as vacationing several times in Paris. Back in the United States, she appeared as the heroine, Elnora, in a popular adaptation of the perennial favorite *A Girl of the Limberlost* (1934) which also starred Louise Dresser. Marsh had fondly admitted that this was her favorite film role. In 1935, Marsh signed a two-year pact with Columbia Pictures. During this time, she starred in such films as Josef von Sternberg's classic *Crime and Punishment* (1935) with Peter Lorre, *The Black Room* (1935) regarded as one of Boris Karloff's best horror films of the decade, and *The Man Who Lived Twice* (1936) with Ralph Bellamy. When her contract expired in 1936, Marsh once again freelanced; appearing steadily in movies for RKO Radio Pictures where she made *Saturday's Heroes* with Van Heflin, and for Paramount Pictures where she played a young woman caught up in a mystery in *The Great Gambini* (1937). She also appeared with comic Joe E. Brown in *When's Your Birthday?* (1937), and Richard Arlen in *Missing Daughters* (1939).

In the 1940s, Marsh played the wife in *Gentleman from Dixie* (1941) and, in her last screen appearance, Marsh portrayed the daughter in *House of Errors* (1942) which starred veteran silent film actor, Harry Langdon.

In the late 1950s, she appeared with John Forsythe in an episode of his TV series *Bachelor Father* and in an episode of the TV series *Schlitz Playhouse of Stars* before retiring in 1959.

On March 29, 1938, Marsh married a stockbroker named Albert Scott and had two children with him. After Scott's death, Marsh married Cliff Henderson, an aviation pioneer and entrepreneur and moved to Palm Desert, California, a town Henderson founded in the 1940s.

In the 1960s Marsh founded Desert Beautiful, a non-profit, all volunteer conservation organization to promote environmental and beautification programs. Cliff Henderson died in 1984 and Marsh remained in Palm Desert until her death November 9, 2006 at age 93. She is buried at Desert Memorial Park in Cathedral City, California.

Brenda Marshall

Brenda Marshall and Joel McCrea in *Espionage Agent*

Brenda Marshall was born Ardis Ankerson on the Island of Negros, Philippines September 29, 1915 and was an American film actress.

Ardis Ankerson attended Texas Woman's College for her freshman and sophomore years, 1934-1935. She was named the Freshman Class Beauty in 1934, chosen by modern dancer Ted Shawn

Marshall made her first film appearance in the 1939 *Espionage Agent*. The following year, she played the leading lady to Errol Flynn in *The Sea Hawk*. She starred opposite Joel McCrea in *Espionage Agent* (1939) and James Cagney in *Captains of the Clouds* (1942).

She had a popular success in *The Constant Nymph* (1943), but she virtually retired after this, appearing in only four more films. In one of these, she played scientist Nora Goodrich in the B picture cult classic *Strange Impersonation* (1946). Her last two film roles were *Whispering Smith* (1948) with Alan Ladd and *The Iroquois Trail* (1950).

In 1955, five years after her last film role, she made an appearance as herself (billed as Mrs. William Holden) in the fourth season episode of *I Love Lucy* entitled "The Fashion Show".

Brenda Marshall was her stage name but she refused to use the name off-camera and insisted that her friends call her by her real name. First married to actor Richard Huston Gaines (born July 23, 1904, in Oklahoma City, Oklahoma, died July 20, 1975, in North Hollywood, California) in 1936, they had one daughter, Virginia; the couple divorced in 1940. In 1941, Marshall married actor William Holden, who subsequently adopted Virginia Gaines (born November 17, 1937, New York City). Marshall and Holden had two additional children: Scott Porter Holden (born May 2, 1946, died January 21, 2005, of lung cancer in San Diego, California) and Peter Westfield Holden (born November 17, 1943). After several separations, Marshall and Holden were divorced in 1971.

Marshall died July 30, 1992 from throat cancer in Palm Springs, California, at the age of 76

Herbert Marshall

Joel McCrea and Herbert Marshall in *Foreign Correspondant*

Herbert Brough Falcon Marshall was born May 23, 1890 in London, England. Herbert Marshall had trained to become a certified accountant, but his interest turned to the stage. He lost a leg while serving in World War I and he was rehabilitated with a wooden leg. This did not stop him from making good his decision to make the stage as his vocation. He used a very deliberate square-shouldered and guided walk - largely unnoticeable - to cover up his disability. He spent twenty years in distinguished stage work in London before films.

He almost made the transition from stage directly to sound movies except for one silent film, *Mumsie* (1927), produced in Great Britain. His wonderful mellow, baritone British accent rolled out with a minimum of mouth movement and a nonchalant ease that stood out as unique. His rather blasé demeanor could take on various nuances - without overt emotion - to fit any role he played, whether sophisticated comedy or drama - and the accent fit just as well. He filled the range from romantic lead, with several sympathetic strangers thrown in, to dignified military officer to doctor to various degrees of villainy - his unemotional delivery meshing with the cold, impassive criminal character.

He was almost 40 when he appeared in his first picture in Hollywood, *The Letter* (1929), a worthwhile comparison (but for the primitive sound recording) with the more famous second version (*The Letter* (1940)) with Bette Davis. He was heavily in demand in the 1930s, sometimes in five or six pictures a year. Perhaps his best suave comedic role was in Trouble in Paradise (1932), the first non-musical sound comedy by producer/director Ernst Lubitsch - to some, Lubitsch's greatest film. That same year, Marshall did one of his most warmly human, romantic roles in the marvelously erotic *Blonde Venus* (1932), with the captivating Marlene Dietrich.

Through the 1940s, his roles were of a more character variety but substantial. He was deviously subtle as the pre-World War II peace leader actually working against peace for a veiled foreign power (Germany) in *Foreign Correspondent* (1940) with Joel McCrea. The film was one of Alfred Hitchcock 's earliest Hollywood films and, definitely, an under-rated adventure/thriller. Who could forget Marshall's small but standout performance as "Scott Chavez", who at the beginning of *Duel in the Sun* (1946) - with typical Marshall nonchalance - calmly shoots his cantina entertainer/Indian wife for her cheating ways?

By the 1950s, Marshall was doing fewer movies, but still a variety. His voice was perfect to lend credence to some early sci-fi classics like *Riders to the Stars* (1954) and *Gog* (1954) and the *The Fly* (1958). But he was also busy honing his considerable talent with various early-TV playhouse programs. He also fit comfortably into episodic TV including a rare five-episode run as a priest on *77 Sunset Strip* (1958). All told, Herbert Marshall graced nearly 100 movie and TV roles with an aplomb that remains a rich legacy.

He died January 22, 1966 at age 75 in Beverly Hills, Los Angeles, California.

Lewis Martin

Lewis Martin was born November 1, 1895 in San Francisco and was an American actor. He began his film and television career around 1950 in the Kraft Television Theatre. His first film was *The Blazing Sun* (1950).

He played bit parts in films like *War of the Worlds* (1953), *The Court Jester* (1955), and *Diary of a Madman*. He also appeared in many American TV-series around 1960, including four guest appearances on *Perry Mason* as Judge Libott.

More of his roles included *Cattle Drive* (1951) with Joel McCrea, *Houdini* (1953), *Hopalong Cassidy* (1954), *Sheena: Queen of the Jungle* (1955), *The George Burns and Gracie Allen Show* (1955-1958), *Shotgun Slade* (1960), *Perry Mason* (1960-1963), *Hazel* (1961-1965), and *Tarzan* (1967).

He died February 21, 1974 Los Angeles at age 74.

Tony Martin

Tony Martin was born Alvin Morris in San Francisco December 25, 1913 and was an American actor and singer who was married to performer Cyd Charisse for sixty years.

Martin was the son of Hattie (née Smith) and Edward Clarence Morris. His family was Jewish, and all of his grandparents had emigrated from Eastern Europe. He received a saxophone as a gift from his grandmother at the age of ten.

In his grammar school glee club, he became an instrumentalist and singer. He formed his first band, named "The Red Peppers", when he was at Oakland Technical High School, eventually joining the band of a local orchestra leader, Tom Gerun, as a reed instrument specialist, sitting alongside the future bandleader Woody Herman. He attended Saint Mary's College of California during the mid-1930s. After college, he left Gerun's band to go to Hollywood to try his luck in films. It was at that time that he adopted the stage name of Tony Martin. His *The Tony Martin Show*, a fifteen minute variety program, aired on NBC from 1954 to 1956 prior to the evening newscast. One of his guests was Dinah Shore, soon cast in her own hour-long NBC variety program.

He was a featured vocalist on the George Burns and Gracie Allen radio program. On the show Allen playfully flirted with Tony, often threatening to fire him. She'd say things like, "Oh, Tony, you look so tired, why don't you rest your lips on mine?"

In films, he was first cast in a number of bit parts, including a role as a sailor in the movie *Follow the Fleet* (1936), starring Fred Astaire and Ginger Rogers. Other roles that year included *Pigskin Parade* (1936) with Alan Ladd and *Banjo on My Knee* (1936) with Joel McCrea.

He eventually signed with 20th Century-Fox and then Metro-Goldwyn-Mayer in which he starred in a number of musicals. Between 1938 and 1942, he made a number of hit records for Decca. Martin was featured in the 1941 Marx Brothers film *The Big Store*, in which he played a singer and performed the now infamous (at least with Marx Brothers fans) *Tenement Symphony*, which was written by Hal Borne, who became his long-time musical director.

In World War II, he first joined the United States Navy, but as a result of rumors that he had gotten an officer's commission through bribery he left the navy and joined the United States Army Air Forces. As a corporal he was assigned to Capt. Glenn Miller's band, then was promoted to technical sergeant in the Air Transport Command and stationed in India, where Brig. Gen. William H. Tunner, commanding the Hump Airlift, put him to work as an entertainer, forming a troupe of amateur talent from the command and taking it around the various bases to perform. He eventually signed with Mercury Records, then a small independent run out of Chicago, Illinois. He cut twenty-five records in 1946 and 1947 for Mercury, including a 1946 recording of "To Each His Own" which became a million-seller. This prompted RCA Victor records to offer him a contract, which he signed in 1947 after satisfying his contract obligations to Mercury.

He appeared in film musicals in the 1940s and 1950s. His rendition of "Lover Come Back To Me" with Joan Weldon in *Deep in My Heart* - based on the music of Sigmund Romberg and starring José Ferrer - was one of the highlights of that film. He also starred as Gaylord Ravenal in the *Show Boat* segment from the 1946 film *Till the Clouds Roll By*.

In a seemingly unlikely pairing, Martin recorded for the Motown Records label in the mid-1960s, scoring a minor hit with the record "Talkin' To Your Picture." He was one of a number of more traditional vocalists signed to the label during the decade.

In 1937, he married Alice Faye, with whom he had appeared in several films. They divorced in 1941.

Martin remarried, to actress and dancer Cyd Charisse, in 1948. They remained married until her death in 2008. Martin adopted Charisse's son, Nicky, from her first marriage. They had one son together, Tony Martin, Jr. (August 28, 1950 – April 10, 2011), who predeceased his father.

Martin died on the evening of July 27, 2012, of natural causes. He was 98.

Louis Mason

Louis Mason was born on June 1, 1888 in Danville, Kentucky. He was an actor, known for *Spitfire* (1934), *The Return of Frank James* (1940), and *Whistling in Dixie* (1942).

More of his roles included *This Man Is Mine* (1934), *Pop Goes the Easel* (1935) with The Three Stooges, *Banjo on My Knee* (1936) with Joel McCrea, *They Shall Have Music* (1939) again with Joel McCrea, *Yankee Doodle Dandy* (1942), *God Is My Co-Pilot* (1945), *The Egg and I* (1947), *Adam's Rib* (1949), *Francis Covers the Big Town* (1953), and *A Star Is Born* (1954).

He died on November 12, 1959 in Los Angeles, California at age 71.

Paul Maxey

Paul Maxey March 15, 1907 in Wheaton, Illinois and was an American actor. Maxey played character roles in films from 1937, notably as the composer Victor Herbert in *Till the Clouds Roll By* (1946) and was in many TV shows from the 1950s onwards, notably in the role of Mayor John Peoples in the sitcom *The People's Choice* (1955–1958) and such other shows as *M Squad*, *Wagon Train*, *Dennis the Menace*, *The Untouchables* , *Perry Mason* and *Lassie*.

More of his roles included *They Won't Forget* (1937), *The Parson of Panamint* (1941), *Till the Clouds Roll By* (1946), *Ride the Pink Horse* (1947), *South of St. Louis* (1949) with Joel McCrea, *Abbott and Costello Meet the Invisible Man* (1951), *The Stranger Wore a Gun* (1953), *Miracle in the Rain* (1956), *Showdown at Boot Hill* (1958), *North to Alaska* (1960), and *Walk on the Wild Side* (1962).

He died June 3, 1963 at age 56 in Pasadena, California.

Edwin Maxwell

Edwin Maxwell in Dublin, Ireland February 9, 1886 and was an Irish character actor in Hollywood movies of the 1930s and 1940s, frequently cast as shady businessmen and shysters, though often ones with a dignified bearing.

From 1939 to 1942, Maxwell served as the dialogue director for the films of epic director Cecil B. DeMille. Maxwell is notable for appearing in four Academy Award-winning Best Pictures: *All Quiet on the Western Front* (1930), *Grand Hotel* (1932), *The Great Ziegfeld* (1936), and *You Can't Take It With You* (1938).

More of his roles included *The Gorilla* (1930), *Mystery of the Wax Museum* (1933), *Hollywood Party* (1934), *Come and Get It* (1936) with Joel McCrea, *The Shop Around the Corner* (1940), *The Great Moment* (1944) again with Joel McCrea, *The Walls of Jericho* (1948).

He died August 13, 1948 at age 62 in Falmouth, Massachusetts.

Kermit Maynard

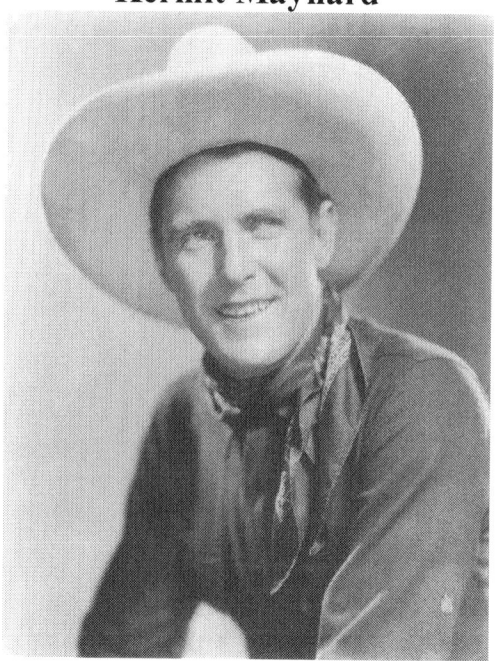

Kermit Maynard was born in Vevay, Indiana September 20, 1897 and was an American actor and stuntman. He appeared in 280 films between 1927 and 1962. He was a younger brother of actor Ken Maynard. He played college football as a lineman for the Indiana Hoosiers in the early 1920s.

More of his roles included *The Phantom of the West* (1931), *The Three Musketeers* (1933), *The Great Adventures of Wild Bill Hickok* (1938), *Bury Me Not on the Lone Prairie* (1941), *Buffalo Bill* (1944) with Joel McCrea, *Buffalo Bill Rides Again* (1947), *Mighty Joe Young* (1949), *The Lone Ranger* (1950), *It Came from Outer Space* (1953), *Wichita* (1955) again with Joel McCrea, *The First Texan* (1956) a third with Joel McCrea, *The Oklahoman* (1957) a fourth with Joel McCrea, *Wanted: Dead or Alive* (1958-1961), *Twilight Zone* (1961), *Laramie* (1959-1962), and *Gunsmoke* (1956-1963).

 He was was married to Edith Jessen from 1924 to 1971, (his death) and they had one child.

He died January 16, 1971 in North Hollywood, California, from a heart attack at age 73.

Virginia Mayo

Virginia Mayo and Joel McCrea in *Colorado Territory*

Virginia Mayo was born Virginia Clara Jones in St. Louis, Missouri November 30, 1920 and was an American vaudeville performer and film actress. Best known for a series of comedic films with Danny Kaye, Mayo was Warner Brothers biggest box office money maker in the late 1940s. She also co-starred in the 1946 Oscar-winning movie *The Best Years of Our Lives*.

She was the daughter of newspaper reporter Luke and wife Martha Henrietta (née Rautenstrauch) Jones. Her family had roots running back to the earliest days of St. Louis, including great-great-great grandfather Captain James Piggott, who founded East St. Louis, Illinois in 1797. Young Virginia's aunt operated an acting school in the St. Louis area, which she began attending at age six. She was also tutored by a series of dancing instructors engaged by her aunt.

Following her graduation from Soldan High School in 1937, Jones landed her first professional acting and dancing jobs at the St. Louis Municipal Opera and in an act with six other girls at the Hotel Jefferson. Impressed with her ability, her brother-in-law, vaudeville performer Andy Mayo, recruited her to appear in his act "The Mayo Brothers". Jones toured the American vaudeville circuit for three years serving as ringmaster and comedic foil for "Pansy the Horse" as the Mayo brothers performed in a horse suit. In 1941 Jones, now known by the stage name Virginia Mayo, got another career break as she appeared on Broadway with Eddie Cantor in *Banjo Eyes*.

In the early 1940s Virginia Mayo's talent and striking beauty came to the attention of movie mogul Samuel Goldwyn, who signed her to an acting contract with his company. One of her first films was the 1943 hit *Jack London*, which starred her future husband Michael O'Shea. Other roles soon followed as she became a popular actress who personified the dream girl or girl-next-door image in a series of films. A beneficiary of the Technicolor film process, it was said that audiences—particularly males—would flock to theaters just to see her blonde hair and classic looks on-screen. Her first starring role came in 1944 opposite comedian Bob Hope in *The Princess and the Pirate*. Remaining in the comedy genre, Mayo had several popular on-screen pairings with dancer-actor Danny Kaye, including *Wonder Man* (1945), *The Kid from Brooklyn* (1946), and *The Secret Life of Walter Mitty* (1947).

Going against previous stereotype, Mayo accepted the supporting role of unsympathetic gold-digger Marie Derry in William Wyler's drama *The Best Years of Our Lives* (1946). Her performance drew favorable reviews from critics as the film also became the highest-grossing film inside the United States since *Gone with the Wind*. At the zenith of her career, Mayo was seen as the quintessential voluptuous Hollywood beauty. It was said that she "looked like a pinup painting come to life". According to widely published reports from the late 1940s, the Sultan of Morocco declared her beauty to be "tangible proof of the existence of God." She would continue a series of dramatic performances in the late 1940s in films like *Smart Girls Don't Talk* (1948).

Virginia Mayo was a constant fixture in the movie theaters in 1949 as she co-starred in many movies all released that year. Among them were *Flaxy Martin*, opposite Joel McCrea in the western *Colorado Territory*, co-starred with future United States President Ronald Reagan in *The Girl from Jones Beach*, and with comedian Milton Berle in *Always Leave Them Laughing*. Mixing drama with comedy roles all year, Mayo received rave reviews for her performance alongside James Cagney and Edmond O'Brien in 1949's *White Heat* and received equally impressive reviews for her co-starring with George Raft in Roy Del Ruth's *Red Light* that same year. In a later interview Mayo admitted she was frightened by Cagney as the psychotic gunman in *White Heat* because he was so realistic.

At the beginning of the 1950s, Mayo scored success with the adventure film *The Flame and the Arrow* (1950) with Burt Lancaster. She co-starred again with James Cagney and a young Doris Day in *The West Point Story* (1950) (singing and dancing with Cagney) and appeared in the all-star cast of *Starlift* (1951). She starred opposite Dennis Morgan in David Butler's Technicolor musical, *Painting the Clouds with Sunshine* (1951) which was a moderate success. While Mayo appeared in several musicals, utilizing her training in dance, her voice was always dubbed.

During the rest of the 1950s, Mayo continued to appear in films with varying genres. She appeared with Alan Ladd in *The Iron Mistress* (1952). In 1953, she appeared in the comedy-drama-action film *South Sea Woman* with Burt Lancaster and Chuck Connors. She played Helena in Victor Saville's *The Silver Chalice* (1954) opposite Pier Angeli and Paul Newman in his film debut. Mayo co-starred with Rex Harrison and George Sanders in *King Richard and the Crusaders* (1954). Mayo played Cleopatra in the 1957 fantasy film *The Story of Mankind* with Vincent Price, Hedy Lamarr, Cesar Romero, Agnes Moorehead, and the Marx Brothers. Again with Alan Ladd in *The Big Land* in 1957. She appeared in the Louis L'amour western *The Tall Stranger* in 1957 with Joel McCrea again. Her last film of the decade was 1959's *Jet Over the Atlantic* with Guy Madison and George Raft.

By the 1960s, Mayo's film career had declined considerably although she continued to appear in films throughout the next several decades, with one of her last prominent roles being in *Fort Utah* (1967) with John Ireland. She was also one of the several stars to make a cameo appearance in the all-star box office bomb *Won Ton Ton, the Dog Who Saved Hollywood* (1976). Her final film appearance was in the 1997 film *The Man Next Door*. Later in life, Mayo appeared in stage and musical theater productions, often with her husband, Michael O'Shea (who co-starred in such stage productions as *Tunnel of Love*, *Fiorello*, and *George Washington Slept Here*).

Mayo also enjoyed notoriety as a television guest star in hit shows like *Night Gallery* (1971), *The Love Boat* (1986), *Remington Steele* (1984), *Murder, She Wrote* (1984), and a dozen episodes of the soap opera *Santa Barbara* (1984).

Virginia Mayo was one of the first to be awarded a star on the Hollywood Walk of Fame. Hers is located at 1751 Vine Street. In 1996 Mayo was honored by her hometown as she received a star on the St. Louis Walk of Fame.

She wed Michael O'Shea in 1947, and remained married to him until his death in 1973. The couple had one child, Mary Catherine O'Shea (born 1953). The family lived for several decades in Thousand Oaks, California. In later years she developed a passion for painting, and also occupied her time doting on her three grandsons. She converted to Roman Catholicism by way of Archbishop Fulton J. Sheen. A lifelong Republican, she endorsed Richard Nixon in 1968 and 1972 and longtime friend Ronald Reagan in 1980.

Virginia Mayo died of pneumonia and complications of congestive heart failure in Los Angeles, on January 17, 2005 at the age of 84. She is buried next to her husband in Pierce Brothers Valley Oaks Park in Westlake Village, California.

Clement McCallin

    Clement McCallin was born on March 6, 1913 in London, England. He was an actor, known for *The Wooing of Anne Hathaway* (1938), *Good Friday* (1950), and *The Rossiter Case* (1951).

    More of his roles included *The Swiss Family Robinson* (1939), *The Queen of Spades* (1949), *Cry, the Beloved Country* (1951), *Shoot First* (1953) with Joel McCrea, *The Plane Makers* (1963-1964), *Happy Deathday* (1968), and *Sykes* (1976).

    He was married to Brenda Bruce and Phillippa Anne Gurney. He died on August 7, 1977 in London, England at age 64.

Kevin McCarthy

Kevin McCarthy and Joel McCrea in *Stranger on Horseback*

Kevin McCarthy was born in Seattle, Washington February 15, 1914 and was an American stage, film, and television actor who appeared in over two hundred television and film roles, including the lead role in 1956 horror science fiction film *Invasion of the Body Snatchers*. For his role in the film version of *Death of a Salesman* (1951), he was nominated for an Academy Award for Best Supporting Actor and won a Golden Globe Award for New Star of the Year - Actor.

McCarthy was the son of Martha Therese (née Preston) and Roy Winfield McCarthy, McCarthy's father was descended from a wealthy Irish American family based in Minnesota. His mother was born in Washington state to a Protestant father and a Jewish mother. He was the brother of author Mary McCarthy, and a distant cousin of former U.S. senator and presidential candidate Eugene J. McCarthy of Minnesota. His parents both died in the 1918 flu pandemic, and the four children went to live with relatives in Minneapolis. After five years of near-Dickensian mistreatment, described in Mary McCarthy's memoirs, the children were separated: Mary moved in with their maternal grandparents, and Kevin and his younger brothers were cared for by relatives in Minneapolis. McCarthy graduated in 1932 from Campion High School in Prairie du Chien, Wisconsin, then attended the University of Minnesota, where he appeared in his first play *Henry IV, Part 1*, and discovered a love of acting.

During his service in World War II in the United States Army Air Corps, in addition to his acting career, McCarthy appeared in a number of training films. At least one of these films (covering the Boeing B-17), has been distributed on DVD.

McCarthy enjoyed a long and distinguished career as a character actor. Some of his roles included *Death of a Salesman* (1951), *Drive a Crooked Road* (1954), *The Gambler from Natchez* (1954), *Stranger on Horseback* (1955) with Joel McCrea, and *An Annapolis Story* (1955).

He had starring roles in his career; in particular the science fiction film classic *Invasion of the Body Snatchers* (1956). On television, he had roles in two short-lived series: *The Survivors* (1969) with Lana Turner; and NBC's *Flamingo Road* (1980–1982) as Claude Weldon, father of Morgan Fairchild character.

McCarthy appeared with Alexis Smith in the NBC anthology series, *The Joseph Cotten Show* in the episode "We Who Love Her" (1956). He was cast in an episode of the religion anthology series, *Crossroads*. McCarthy appeared in the 1959 episode "The Wall Between" of CBS's *The DuPont Show with June Allyson*. He guest starred in an episode of CBS's *The Twilight Zone* entitled "Long Live Walter Jameson" (1960), as the title character. He also appeared in the movie remake *Twilight Zone: The Movie* in 1983.

McCarthy made two appearances in *The Rifleman*, portraying Mark Twain in "The Shattered Idol" (episode 120), original Air Date: 12/4/1961, and Winslow Quince in "Suspicion" (episode 157), original Air Date: 1/14/1963.

In 1963, McCarthy appeared in the ABC medical drama *Breaking Point* in the episode entitled "Fire and Ice". He guest starred in the ABC drama *Going My Way*, about the Roman Catholic priesthood in New York City. He was cast as well in a 1964 episode of James Franciscus's NBC education drama, *Mr. Novak*. In 1966, he appeared in the episode "Wife Killer" of the ABC adventure series *The Fugitive*. In 1967, he guest starred in the episode "Never Chase a Rainbow" of NBC's western series, *The Road West* starring Barry Sullivan.

In 1968, he guest starred on *Hawaii Five-O* in the episode "Full Fathom Five" as the chief antagonist, Victor Reese. *The Wild Wild West* (CBS) Season 4 (1968-69). His turn as Maj. Gen Kroll in "The Night of the Doomsday Formula" made one of the best villains of the series. In 1971, he guest starred in the "Conqueror's Gold" episode of *Bearcats!* which starred Rod Taylor with whom McCarthy had appeared in the films *A Gathering of Eagles, Hotel* (1967 film) and The Hell With Heroes.

In 1977, he and Clu Gulager, previously cast with Barry Sullivan on NBC's *The Tall Man*, appeared in the episode "The Army Deserter" of the NBC western series, *The Oregon Trail*, with Rod Taylor. In 1985, McCarthy guest-starred in a fourth Season episode of The A-Team called "Members Only".

McCarthy appeared as Judge Crandall in *The Midnight Hour*, a 1985 comedy/horror television movie.

McCarthy was one of three actors (with Dick Miller and Robert Picardo) often cast by director Joe Dante. McCarthy's most notable role in Dante's films was in 1987 as the prime antagonist, Victor Scrimshaw, in *Innerspace*.

In 1989, he played television station owner R.J. Fletcher in Weird Al Yankovic's cult classic *UHF*. Yankovic noted that "Kevin McCarthy was terrific. We had set him up to be this really rotten bad guy; but every time the director said, 'CUT!,' McCarthy would burst out laughing."

In 1996 he played Gordon Fitzpatrick in *The Pandora Directive*, an FMV adventure game starring Tex Murphy.

In 2007 McCarthy appeared as himself in the Anthony Hopkins film *Slipstream*. The film made references to the film, *Invasion of the Body Snatchers*.

On October 24, 2009, McCarthy was honored at the Fort Lauderdale International Film Festival in Florida.

His last role in a feature-length movie was as The Grand Inquisitor in the sci-fi musical comedy The Ghastly Love of Johnny X released in 2012.

McCarthy was married to Augusta Dabney, with whom he had three children, from 1941 until their divorce in 1961. In 1979, he married Kate Crane, who survived him. The couple had two children.

From 1942, McCarthy had a close friendship with actor Montgomery Clift. McCarthy and Clift were cast in a play together, Ramon Naya's *Mexican Mural*. The two, along with McCarthy's wife Augusta Dabney, became the best of friends. They socialized together and acted together in several projects. The two collaborated on a screenplay for a film adaptation of the Tennessee Williams/Donald Windham play *You Touched Me!*, but the project never came to fruition.

McCarthy died of pneumonia on September 11, 2010 at the age of 96 in Hyannis, Massachusetts.

Muriel McCormac

Muriel McCormac was born on September 17, 1918 in Los Angeles, California. She was an actress, known for *Sparrows* (1926), *The Skyrocket* (1926), and *Dynamite* (1929) with Joel McCrea.

More of her roles included *Miracles of the Jungle* (1921), *The Man Who Won* (1923), *Discontented Husbands* (1924), *The King of Kings* (1927), and *The Red Dance* (1928).

She died on September 12, 2000 in Los Angeles at age 81.

Jody McCrea

Jody McCrea and Joel McCrea in *Wichita Town*

Joel Dee McCrea, known as Jody McCrea was born September 6, 1934 and was an American film and television actor; son of veteran film actors Joel McCrea and Frances Dee. He was married to Dusty Ironwing McCrea from 1976, until her death in 1996. He is survived by the stepchildren he raised, Jaquet Ironwing and David Ironwing.

Jody McCrea served in the United States Army, Special Services. He later briefly hosted *Country Style, USA*, an Army-produced recruiting television program filmed in Nashville, Tennessee, featuring various country entertainers. He acted with his father in *Wichita* (1955), *The First Texan* (1956), *Trooper Hook* (1957), *Gunsight Ridge* (1959), on the 1959–1960 television series *Wichita Town*, and *Cry Blood, Apache* (1970) which he also produced.

He went on to star in films (mainly westerns), including the World War I drama *Lafayette Escadrille* (1958), *The Broken Land* (1962)(with Jack Nicholson), *Law of the Lawless* (1964).

He was most notable for his comedic role as dumb-minded "Deadhead" ("Bonehead") in the *Beach Party* (1963) and subsequent films made by American International Pictures. Other beach movies in which he has appeared include *Operation Bikini* (1963), *Pajama Party* (1964), *Muscle Beach Party* (1964), *Bikini Beach* (1964), *Beach Blanket Bingo* (1965), and *How to Stuff a Wild Bikini* (1965).

When cast in the beach pictures, McCrea realized his comedic potential. When first offered the role of "Deadhead", for example, he was quoted at the time as saying that he "wasn't sure what the character would become". McCrea felt that the audience enjoyed Deadhead as they felt superior to him.

McCrea was an avid body builder, and the only actor appearing in the American International Pictures beach movies who could actually surf.

He made several television appearances, including *Wagon Train, Vacation Playhouse*, and *The Greatest Show on Earth*. He played Lieutenant Brannin, a cocky cavalry officer based loosely on George Armstrong Custer, in Sam Peckinpah's *Major Dundee* (1965), but his scene was deleted from the final cut.

In the early 1960s, Jody made an amusing appearance on the popular TV show *I've Got a Secret* as part of a group of entertainers related to famous Hollywood personalities.

He recorded a 45 rpm single in 1964 for Canjo Records to coincide with the film *Bikini Beach* (Side A: "Chicken Surfer"/Side B: "Looney Gooney Bird")

Although he occasionally acted in community theater, McCrea retired from acting in 1970 after his final film *Cry Blood, Apache*. He did appear in one more film called *Lady Street Fighter* (1985).

He became a rancher in Roswell, New Mexico, where he died in April 4, 2009 of a heart attack at age 74.

In June of 2009 country/western singer/actor Johnny Western was the celebrity guest at Audie Murphy Days in Greenville, Texas. He told me Jody McCrea was in negotiations to get *Wichita Town* released on DVD, but with his death was unsure if that would ever happen.

Etta McDaniel

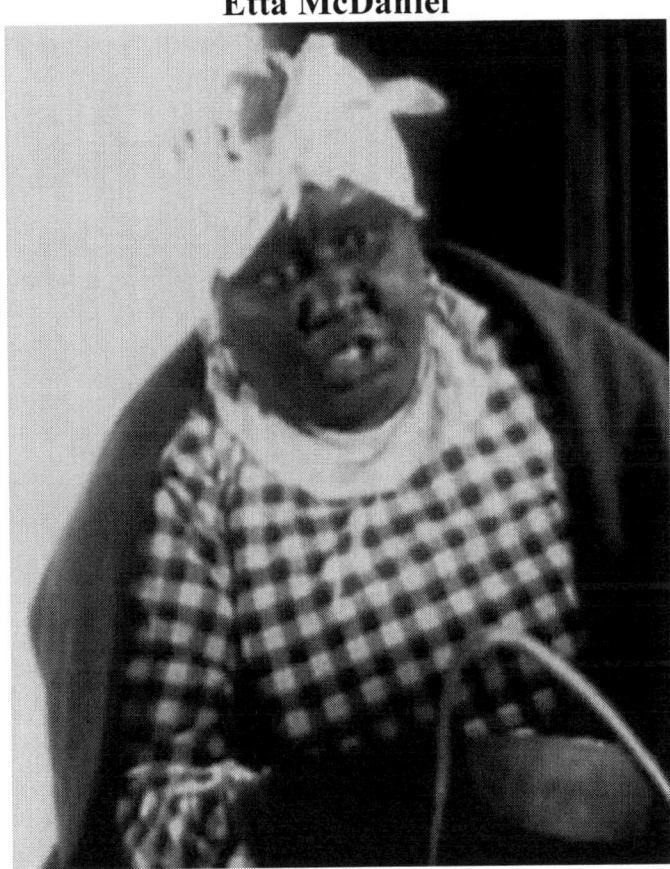

Etta McDaniel was born in Wichita, Kansas December 1, 1890 and was an African American actress who appeared in over sixty films between 1933 and 1946. She was the sister of actor Sam McDaniel and actress and Academy Award winner Hattie McDaniel.

She began her entertainment career as a member of minstrel shows with several others of her family.

Etta McDaniel's film début was in the 1933 *King Kong*, as the native woman who saves her baby from the approaching monster. She then became a supporting actor or extra, frequently in uncredited roles, performing as maids and nannies.

More of her roles included *The Invisible Ray* (1936), *Stella Dallas* (1937), *Chicken Wagon Family* (1939), *The Great Man's Lady* (1942) with Joel McCrea, *Son of Dracula* (1943), and *The Thin Man Goes Home* (1945).

She died January 13, 1946 at age 55 in Los Angeles, California.

Francis McDonald

Francis McDonald was born in Bowling Green, Kentucky August 22, 1891 and was an American actor whose career spanned fifty-two years.

Some of his roles included *Carmen* (1913), *The Devil at His Elbow* (1916), *The Kentucky Colonel* (1920), *My Lady of Whims* (1925), *The Carnation Kid* (1929), *Texas Buddies* (1932), *Operator 13* (1934), *The Prisoner of Shark Island* (1936), *The Last Train from Madrid* (1937) with Alan Ladd, *Union Pacific* (1939) with Joel McCrea, *Captain Caution* (1940) again with Alan Ladd, *One Night in the Tropics* (1940) with Abbott and Costello, *Bar 20* (1943), *Corpus Christi Bandits* (1945), *Black Bart* (1948), *Samson and Delilah* (1949), *Red Mountain* (1951), *Hopalong Cassidy* (1952), *The Cisco Kid* (1953), *Adventures of Superman* (1955), *The Ten Commandments* (1956), *Fort Massacre* (1958) again with Joel McCrea, *Wichita Town* (1960) also with Joel McCrea, *Perry Mason* (1957-1964), and *The Great Race* (1965).

He died September 18, 1968 at age 77 in Hollywood, California.

George McDonald

Joel McDonald and George McDonald in *Four Faces West*

George McDonald was a child actor, known for *Child of Divorce* (1946), *Four Faces West* (1948), and *Cover Up* (1949).

More of his roles included *Behind Green Lights* (1946), *The Egg and I* (1947), *Fighting Father Dunne* (1948), *Ma and Pa Kettle* (1949), *Mighty Joe Young* (1949), *The Good Humor Man* (1950), *Too Young to Kiss* (1951), and *The Pride of St. Louis* (1952).

He died on May 2, 1984.

Frank McGlynn

Frank McGlynn, Sr. was born in San Francisco October 26, 1866 and was an American stage and film actor who found success later in life playing Abraham Lincoln.

McGlynn was the eldest of two daughters and a son raised by Frank and Mary McGlynn. His father was second generation Irish from New York who supported his family as a carpenter and later working in real estate. McGlynn's mother was born in Australia of Irish parents who brought her to America at about the time of the California Gold Rush.

Originally McGlynn studied to be a lawyer. He received his law degree from the University of California, Hastings College of the Law and was admitted to the bar in 1894. By 1896 though, he was appearing on stage at the Casino Theatre performing in *The Gold Bug*, a burlesque musical comedy written by Glen MacDonough with music from Victor Herbert.

Later that year McGlynn toured in a road production of *Under the Red Robe*, a story based on the Stanley Weyman novel that was adapted for the stage by Edward Everett Rose. Over the following two decades McGlynn played mostly supporting roles with stock companies and in early silent films.

McGlynn's big break came in 1919, when at the age of fifty-three, the six –foot, four-inch actor was given the opportunity to play the lead in John Drinkwater's play *Abraham Lincoln*. The play had a run of 193 performances at the Cort Theatre in New York and played on the road for well over two years. In 1924, McGlynn appeared in a two-reel short film made by Lee DeForest and J. Searle Dawley in DeForest's Phonofilm sound-on-film process, in an excerpt of the play.

McGlynn went on to play in seven Broadway plays; his last as Johnnie, in *Frankie and Johnnie* at the Theatre Republic in 1930. McGlynn's 1919 performance as Lincoln also rejuvenated his film career which lasted into the late 1940s. He portrayed Lincoln in ten films.

More of his roles included *Abraham Lincoln* (1924), *The Jazz Cinderella* (1930), *Huckleberry Finn* (1931), *Employees' Entrance* (1933), *Captain Blood* (1935), *These Three* (1936) with Joel McCrea, *Wells Fargo* (1937) again with Joel McCrea, *The Lone Ranger* (1938), *Sergeant York* (1941), *Delinquent Daughters* (1944), and *Hollywood Barn Dance* (1947).

McGlynn died at the age of 84 on May 18, 1951 at his daughter's residence in Newburg, New York. He was survived by three daughters, Helen, Virginia Rose, Mary Rose, and a son, Rev. Thomas McGlynn. His wife, Rose (née Sheridan) McGlynn and son Frank, Jr. (also an actor), preceded him in death. He is interred in Glendale's Forest Lawn Memorial Park Cemetery.

Malcolm McGregor

Malcolm McGregor was born in Newark, New Jersey October 13, 1892 and was an American actor of the silent era.

McGregor appeared in fifty-five films between 1922 and 1936. A cross between Wallace Reid, Rudolph Valentino and the earlier Harrison Ford, McGregor, with slick-back hair, starred as the young whaling captain in a film version of Ben Ames Williams' *All the Brothers Were Valiant* (1923), perhaps the highlight of a busy career that mostly found the handsome, clean-cut actor supporting such glamorous female stars as Corinne Griffith, Florence Vidor, and Evelyn Brent. Like so many of his contemporaries, McGregor's career quickly waned after the changeover to sound and he was reduced to playing second fiddle to Bela Lugosi in the Mascot serial *The Whispering Shadow* (1932).

More of his roles included *You Can't Get Away with It* (1924), *The Vanishing American* (1925), *Matinee Ladies* (1927), *Freedom of the Press* (1928) with Joel McCrea, *Murder Will Out* (1930), *The Whispering Shadow* (1933), *China Seas* (1935), and *Undersea Kingdom* (1936).

McGregor retired after playing a gangster in a low-budget screen version of radio's *Special Agent K-7* (1936). McGregor died April 29, 1945 at age 52 from burns suffered in an accident in his Hollywood home.

Tom McGuire

Tom McGuire was born in Lancashire, England September 1, 1873 and was an English film actor. He appeared in 160 films between 1919 and 1949.some of his roles included *Captain Blood* (1924), *Pleasure Before Business* (1927), *Lights of New York* (1928), *The Beast of the City* (1932), *Palooka* (1934), *Woman Wanted* (1935) with Joel McCrea, *One Mile from Heaven* (1937), Heaven with a Barbed Wire Fence (1939), *Look Who's Laughing* (1941), *The Great Moment* (1944) again with Joel McCrea, *The Secret Life of Walter Mitty* (1947), *The Beautiful Blonde from Bashful Bend* (1949), and *Goodbye, My Fancy* (1951).

He died May 6, 1954 in Hollywood, California at age 80.

John McIntire

Joel McCrea and John McIntire in *The Gunfight at Dodge City*

John McIntire was born June 27, 1907, and was an American character actor. The craggy-faced film actor was born in Spokane in eastern Washington State but reared in Montana, having grown up around ranchers and cowboys, an experience that would later inspire his performances in dozens of Westerns.

A graduate of USC, McIntire began acting in radio and on stage, before embarking on a lengthy film and TV career as a character actor. He was already forty when he made his big-screen debut in 1947, but went on to appear in some sixty-five films, often playing police chiefs, judges, crazy coots and western characters. His films include the film noir classic *The Asphalt Jungle* (1950), the 1960 Hitchcock thriller *Psycho* and the 1960 drama *Elmer Gantry*, but some of his more memorable roles were in westerns such as the acclaimed *Winchester '73* (1950) and *The Far Country* (1955), both with James Stewart, and *The Tin Star*, with Henry Fonda (1957). He also played a judge in *Rooster Cogburn* (1975), the sequel to *True Grit* featuring John Wayne and Katharine Hepburn. His final film role was in *Turner & Hooch* (1989).

In the mid-1950s, McIntire moved into television, appearing in anthology series, sitcoms and dramas, including a regular role on ABC's *Naked City* (1958-1959), before his character was killed off. Though McIntire had never had the lead role in a film, television provided him with his most prominent and long-running role when in 1961 he replaced the late Ward Bond in the popular NBC-ABC series *Wagon Train*, playing trail master Chris Hale in more than 150 episodes between 1961 and 1965. His co-stars were Robert Horton, Robert Fuller, Denny Scott Miller, Terry Wilson, Frank McGrath, and Michael Burns.

He appeared as the boxing manager in *World in my Corner* (1956) with Audie Murphy as the boxer, and he played the veteran Texas Ranger training the title character, played by Audie Murphy, how to be a Ranger in *Seven Ways from Sundown* (1960).

He appeared with Joel McCrea in *Saddle Tramp* (1950), *Stranger on Horseback* (1955), *The Gunfight at Dodge City* (1950), and two episodes of *Wichita Town* (1959-1960).

McIntire subsequently replaced actors Lee J. Cobb and Charles Bickford on NBC's *The Virginian* in 1967, playing Bickford's character's brother. Prior to his *Wagon Train* role, he guest starred as William Palmer in the series finale, "The Most Dangerous Gentleman", of the short-lived 1960 NBC western *Overland Trail*, starring William Bendix and Doug McClure, his subsequent co-star on *The Virginian*.

McIntire married actress Jeanette Nolan, in 1935, and they had two children together, one of whom was the actor Tim McIntire (1944–1986) who starred in the 1978 film *American Hot Wax*. McIntire and Nolan both figured in *Psycho*; he played a sheriff, while she voiced some of the "mother" lines. McIntire worked more closely with Nolan in the 1977 Disney animated film *The Rescuers*, in which he voiced the cat Rufus and she the muskrat Ellie Mae. Four years later, the couple worked on another Disney film, *The Fox and the Hound*, with McIntire as the voice of Mr. Digger, a badger, and Nolan as the voice of Widow Tweed.

John McIntire died from emphysema and lung cancer in Pasadena, California, January 30, 1991. In addition to his wife Jeanette Nolan he was also survived by his daughter Holly McIntire. His son Tim McIntire preceded him in death in 1986 from heart problems.

Leila McIntyre

Leila McIntyre was born on December 20, 1882 in New York City, New York. She was an actress, known for *Swell People* (1930), *Reckless Decision* (1933), and *The Prisoner of Shark Island* (1936).

More of his roles included *Hurricane* (1929), *Private Worlds* (1935) with Joel McCrea, *Pick a Star* (1937), *Zenobia* (1939), *Wintertime* (1943), and *The Hoodlum Saint* (1946).

She was married to John Hyams. She died on January 9, 1953 in West Los Angeles, California at age 70.

Burr McIntosh

William Burr McIntosh was born in Wellsville, Ohio August 21, 1862 and had an eclectic career. He was known, at different points in his life, to be a lecturer, photographer, film studio owner, silent film actor, author, publisher of *Burr McIntosh Monthly*, reporter and a pioneer in the early film and radio business.

He was the son of William Ambrose and Minerva McIntosh. His father was the president of a public utility, New York and Cleveland Gas Coal Company, and a member of the South Fork Fishing and Hunting Club. The club's activities were blamed (but the members were not held legally responsible) for the failure of the South Fork Dam, which caused the Johnstown Flood in 1889 that resulted in the loss of over 2,200 lives in Johnstown, Pennsylvania. His sister Nancy McIntosh, an operatic soprano, was the protege, adopted daughter and heiress to the estate and royalties of W. S. Gilbert of Gilbert and Sullivan.

McIntosh graduated from Lafayette College in 1884, where he became a member of the Sigma Chi fraternity.

He began as a stage actor and then moved into silent films. His most enduring role was Squire Bartlett, who banished the character played by Lillian Gish from his home and into the cold Maine winter in D.W. Griffith's classic film, *Way Down East* (1920). Miss Gish described McIntosh as a gentle giant, "always apologizing for having to treat me so cruelly...".

He appeared in fifty-three films between 1914 and 1934.some more of those films included *Camille of the Barbary Coast* (1925), *The Golden Stallion* (1927), *The Rogue Song* (1930), *A Private Scandal* (1931), *Hallelujah I'm a Bum* (1933), and *The Richest Girl in the World* (1934) with Joel McCrea.

He died April 28, 1942 in Hollywood, California from a heart attack at age 79.

Edward McNamara

Edward McNamara and Joel McCrea in *The Palm Beach Story*

Edward James McNamara was born in Paterson, New Jersey August 13, 1884 and was a Broadway and Hollywood actor.

He sang while a police officer in Paterson, New Jersey. His Broadway career started in 1926, and his Hollywood career started in 1929.

Some of his films included *Lucky in Love* (1929), *I Am a Fugitive from a Chain Gang* (1932), *Great Guy* (1936), *Kitty Foyle* (1940), *The Palm Beach Story* (1942) with Joel McCrea, and (1943).

He died November 10, 1944 at age 60 in Boston, Massachusetts shortly after filming *Arsenic and Old Lace*.

Jack McNaughton

Jack Augustus McNaughton was born on December 22, 1905 in Mitcham, Surrey, England. He was an actor, known for *I Became a Criminal* (1947), *The Man in the White Suit* (1951), and *The Detective* (1954).

More of his roles included *Brass Monkey* (1948), *The Taming of Dorothy* (1950), *Shoot First* (1953) with Joel McCrea, *Private's Progress* (1956), *Tread Softly Stranger* (1958), *The Flesh and the Fiends* (1960), and *Coronation Street* (1963).

He died on February 22, 1990 in Cambridgeshire, England at age 84.

Robert McWade

Robert McWade was born in Buffalo, New York January 25, 1872 and was an American stage and film actor. From 1903-1927, he appeared in at least thirty-eight Broadway productions, his last being *The Devil In The Cheese*, with Bela Lugosi and Fredric March.

McWade also appeared in eighty-three films between 1924 and 1938, some of those credits included *The Sins of the Children* (1930), *Kept Husbands* (1931) with Joel McCrea, *Girls About Town* (1931) again with Joel McCrea, *42nd Street* with Dick Powell and Ruby Keeler (1933), *Straight from the Heart* (1935), and *Gold Is Where You Find It* (1938).

His father was notable stage actor Robert McWade, Sr. (1835-1913) and his older brother was character actor Edward McWade.

He died January 19, 1938 in Culver City, California at age 65.

148

Donald Meek

Donald Meek was born in Glasgow, Scotland July 14, 1878 and was a Scottish American character actor. He first worked as a stage actor and later became a film actor. Before becoming an actor, he fought in the Spanish–American War and contracted yellow fever which caused him to lose his hair. He was cast as timid, worrisome characters in many of his films, and is perhaps best known for his roles as Mr. Poppins in Frank Capra's *You Can't Take It With You* (1938) and as whisky salesman Samuel Peacock in John Ford's *Stagecoach* (1939).

From 1931 through 1932 Meek was featured as criminologist Dr. Crabtree, in a series of twelve Warner Brothers two-reel short subjects written by S. S. Van Dine.

More of his roles included *Six Cylinder Love* (1923), *The Love Kiss* (1930), *Murder in the Pullman* (1932), *Murder at the Vanities* (1934) with Alan Ladd, *Mark of the Vampire* (1935), *Barbary Coast* (1935) with Joel McCrea, *The Adventures of Tom Sawyer* (1938), *Little Miss Broadway* (1938), *My Little Chickadee* (1940), *Air Raid Wardens* (1943) with Laurel and Hardy, *State Fair* (1945), *The Hal Roach Comedy Carnival* (1947), and *Magic Town* (1947).

Donald Meek died on Monday, November 18, 1946 in Los Angeles, California at age 68, and was interred in the Fairmount Mausoleum in Denver, Colorado's Fairmount Cemetery. A prolific film actor in over 100 Hollywood movies during its Golden Age, he received a posthumous star on the Hollywood Walk of Fame.

George Meeker

George Meeker was born in Brooklyn, New York March 5, 1904 and was an American character movie and Broadway actor who became more of a legend off-camera than on. Meeker made several movies such as *Crime, Inc.* (1945), and *Thief in the Dark* (1928), and played an uncredited part in *All Through the Night* (1941).

More of his roles included *Chicken a La King* (1928), *Blessed Event* (1932), *Chance at Heaven* (1933) with Joel McCrea, *The Richest Girl in the World* (1934) again with Joel McCrea, *Tarzan's Revenge* (1938), *High Sierra* (1941), *Yankee Doodle Dandy* (1942), *Black Market Babies* (1945), *The Invisible Monster* (1950), and *Racket Squad* (1951).

Meeker has a star on the Hollywood Walk of Fame. He died August 19, 1984 at age 80 in Carpenteria, California.

George Melford

George H. Melford was born George Henry Knauff in Rochester, New York February 19, 1877 and was an American stage and film actor, director, producer, and screenwriter.

He was son of German immigrant Henrietta Knauff (the name Melford was an adopted stage name). George Knauff Melford had four sisters: Mary Knauff (Mrs. Godfrey Willis Wainwright); Henrietta Knauff; Alice Irene Knauff (Mrs. Edmond Francois Bernoudy) all of Los Angeles, and Mrs. Frederick Kells/Keils of Ottawa, Canada. Melford graduated from McGill University in Montreal, Canada.

He was an accomplished stage actor working in Cincinnati, Ohio, before joining the Kalem Company motion picture studio in New York City in 1909. Hired by director Sidney Olcott for character actor roles, in the fall of 1910 he was sent to work with a film crew on the West Coast. In 1911, with Robert Vignola, he co-directed Ruth Roland in his first short film, *Arizona Bill* based on a script he had written. From there Melford went on to direct another thirty films for Kalem Studios until 1915, when he was hired by Jesse L. Lasky to direct feature-length films for Lasky's Feature Play Company. That same year Melford became one of the founding members of the Motion Picture Directors Association.

In 1916 Melford directed *To Have and to Hold*, a film based on the Mary Johnston novel that had been the bestselling novel in the United States for 1900. In 1921 he directed what is probably his most famous silent film *The Sheik*, starring Rudolph Valentino.

Melford remained with Lasky's company for ten years, and then joined Universal Pictures, where he directed his first talkie in 1929. The following year he co-directed four Spanish language films including the acclaimed Spanish version of *Dracula*. Melford filmed it simultaneously with the English version on the same sets at night using a different cast and crew. Somewhat of a controversy has arisen about this film. Some sources say that Melford was assigned the job because he could speak Spanish, but other sources claim that Melford could not speak a word of Spanish and had to use a translator to communicate with the actors. The issue was cleared up when actress Lupita Tovar—who was in the film—said in an interview on the 75th anniversary DVD of the film that Melford in fact did not speak Spanish and had to use a translator.

His last major work as a director came in 1937 when he and Harry L. Fraser co-directed Columbia Pictures' first serial, a fifteen episode, five-hour-long adventure film titled *Jungle Menace* starring Frank Buck.

Some of his acting roles included *Ambush* (1939), *My Little Chickadee* (1940), *Lone Star Ranger* (1942), *The Dancing Masters* (1943), *The Great Moment* (1944) with Joel McCrea, *The Big Noise* (1944), *The Shocking Miss Pilgrim* (1947), *The Beautiful Blonde from Bashful Bend* (1949), *Cripple Creek* (1952), and *The Ten Commandments* (1956).

At age 60 the workaholic Melford needed to slow down and decided to give up the stressful job of directing to take on simple character actor roles. However, in 1946 Harry Fraser convinced him to co-direct *Jungle Terror*, a feature-length sequel to their successful *Jungle Menace* serial. Melford loved the film business, and although financially independent, he never stopped working. Having directed more than 140 films, he continued to work in small character roles. In the 1940s he was part of Preston Sturges' unofficial "stock company" of character actors, appearing in six films written and directed by Sturges.

He appeared in his last film in 1960 at the age of 83, dying in Hollywood on April 25, 1961, of heart failure. He is interred in Valhalla Memorial Park Cemetery in North Hollywood, Los Angeles, California.

Beryl Mercer

Beryl Mercer was born in Surrey, England August 13, 1876 and was a Spanish-born American-based actress of stage and screen.

Her father was Edward Sheppard Mercer, said to be Spanish despite his name, and her mother was the actress Beryl Montague. She became a child actor, making her debut on August 14, 1886 at the Theatre Royal, Yarmouth, when she was four. She returned to the stage when she was ten. In London she appeared in *The Darling of the Gods* and the production by Oscar Asche of *A Midsummer Night's Dream*. In 1906 she appeared as a Kaffir slave in the West End play *The Shulamite*. She traveled with this play to the USA, where she received good reviews.

Mercer was best known as a film actress for her motherly roles. She regularly appeared as a grandmother or cook or maid in some high profile films. She appeared in more than fifty films between 1916 and 1939 but her career was at a peak in the 1930s when she regularly starred in between five and ten films a year.

In 1933 Mercer appeared in *Cavalcade*, as a cook, and the following year made appearances in *Jane Eyre* (1934), *The Little Minister* (1934), and *The Richest Girl in the World* (1934) with Joel McCrea. She was in two talkie versions of *Three Live Ghosts*, one in 1929 and the other in 1935. In 1939, she appeared in *The Little Princess* as Queen Victoria.

She was married to Maitland Paisley early in her life. Her only other marriage was much later in the late 1920s briefly to actor Holmes Herbert. She had one child, Joan Mercer, later Bitting, born on September 16, 1917.

Mercer died in Santa Monica, California in July 28, 1939 at age 62, following surgery for an undisclosed ailment.

Gertrude Messinger

Gertrude Dolores Messinger was born in Spokane, Washington April 28, 1911 and was an American actress.

Gertrude Messinger, sometimes spelled Gertrude Messenger and also known as Gertie Messinger, was a B-moviefilm actress of the 1930s through the 1950s. She began acting early, playing child roles in silent films as early as 1917, when she had a role in the film *Babes in the Woods*.

During the 1930s her career took off, with her often starring alongside Bob Steele, Lane Chandler, and Harry Carey. Her earliest starring roles were in 1932, when she starred opposite Bob Steele in *Riders of the Desert*, and opposite Lane Chandler in *Lawless Valley*. For the remainder of the 1930s she was fairly active in films. In 1934 she starred in arguably her biggest movie, with a part in the film *Anne of Green Gables*, with the starring role being played by actressDawn O'Day. Her most active year was 1935, when she starred in nine films, most notably *The Fighting Pilot* with Richard Talmadge and *Wagon Trail* opposite Harry Carey.

More of her roles included *The Jazz Age* (1929) with Joel McCrea, *Riders of the Desert* (1932), *Rustler's Paradise* (1935), *Our Relations* (1936), *Zenobia* (1939), *Syncopation* (1942), *Samson and Delilah* (1949), *Sunset Blvd.* (1950), and *The Greatest Show on Earth* (1952).

She was married, briefly, to stuntman Dave Sharpe in the late 1930s. She would later marry cameraman Schuyler Sanford, who would eventually win an Oscar for his work on the film *Around the World in 80 Days*. Her career slowed considerably in the 1940s, but she continued to act through the 1950s, mostly in uncredited roles. She starred in a total of 52 films in her career, eleven of which were westerns, for which she would be best known. She died of congestive heart failure on November 8, 1995 at age 84 in Woodland Hills, Los Angeles, California.

Emile Meyer

Emile Meyer was born in New Orleans, Louisiana, August 18, 1910, and was an American actor usually known for tough, aggressive, authoritative characters in Hollywood films from the 1950s era, mostly in westerns or thrillers. He provided such noteworthy performances as Ryker in *Shane* (1953), as Father Dupree in *Paths of Glory* (1957) and the corrupt cop in *Sweet Smell of Success* (1957).

Other roles included *The People Against O'Hara* (1951), *Carbine Williams* (1952), *Stories of the Century* (1954), *Drums Across the River* (1954) with Audie Murphy, *Stranger on Horseback* (1955) with Joel McCrea, *The Adventures of Ozzie & Harriet* (1958), *Good Day for a Hanging* (1959), *Wichita Town* (1960) again with Joel McCrea, *Taggart* (1964), *My Favorite Martian* (1965), *A Time for Dying* (1969) again with Audie Murphy, *Bonanza* (1970-1972), and *Macon County Line* (1974).

His final film role was in *The Legend of Frank Woods* (1977).

He died March 19, 1987, at age 76 in Covington, Louisiana, from Alzheimer's disease.

Torben Meyer

Torben Emil Meyer was born in Copenhagen, Denmark December 1, 1884 and was a Danish character actor who appeared in over 190 films in a fifty-five year career.

Meyer began his career as a stage actor in Denmark. He appeared in his first silent movie, *Vor tids dame* in 1912 and made twenty more before making *Don Quixote* in 1926. This movie achieved considerable international stature, and Meyer followed the migration of leading European actors to Hollywood the following year. His first American role was as a spy in the silent movie *The Man Who Laughs* starring Conrad Veidt in 1928. Meyer arrived just when the transition to sound was in progress. In contrast to many other European-born actors, his thick accent became an asset for him. He appeared uncredited in numerous movies throughout the 1930s and 1940s, almost always cast as a German.

In 1930, Meyer received a small part in a Michael Curtiz film *A Soldier's Plaything*, and in 1932, Meyer appeared in two Swedish language American films, *Trådlöst och kärleksfullt* and *Halvvägs till Himlen*. Later that year, he had a small part in *Murders in the Rue Morgue*, based on the Edgar Allan Poe short story which starring Bela Lugosi.

Meyer had small parts as waiters in five different movies during 1932; in German émigré director Ernst Lubitsch's film *Broken Lullaby* starring Lionel Barrymore, in George Cukor's *What Price Hollywood?*, where he plays a waiter in the famous Hollywood restaurant 'The Brown Derby', in *Downstairs* starring Paul Lukas, in Mervyn LeRoy's *Big City Blues* starring Joan Blondell and in *The Match King*. Also that year, he had a small part in *The Animal Kingdom* starring Leslie Howard.

Next Meyer went from waiter to butler in a number of films in the 1930s; *The Crime of the Century* (1933), John Ford's *The World Moves On* (1934), *Preview Murder Mystery* (1936) starring Reginald Denny, *Piccadilly Jim* (1936) and *The First Hundred Years* (1938) both starring Robert Montgomery, and *The King and the Chorus Girl* (1937) starring Joan Blondell.

In 1935, Meyer was strangled by Boris Karloff's Frankenstein in James Whale's *Bride of Frankenstein*. Two years later, in 1937, Meyer had a number of bit parts; as a servant in *Tovarich* starring Claudette Colbert, Charles Boyer and Basil Rathbone, as Raymond Massey's servant in *The Prisoner of Zenda* starring Ronald Colman in the title role and as Tyrone Power's chauffeur in Sonja Henie's *Thin Ice*. In 1938 Meyer played a German Police Prefect in a Simon Templar movie, *The Saint in New York*, and the following year, he played a doorman in *Topper Takes a*

Trip starring Roland Young and Billie Burke. In 1939, Meyer had a bit part in Warner Bros. anti-Nazi movie *Nurse Edith Cavell* starring Anna Neagle.

In 1940, Meyer had a small role in *Dr. Ehrlich's Magic Bullet* starring Edward G. Robinson, Ruth Gordon and Otto Kruger, and later that year, featured in the Charlie Chaplin movie, *The Great Dictator*. He also appeared that year in *Four Sons* starring Don Ameche. He is seen in the beginning of the movie as a farmer driving a hay wagon from Nazi Germany into Czechoslovakia and then gives Don Ameche's character a ride home. Later that year, he got to play 'Mr. Schmidt' in Preston Sturges' *Christmas in July*, his first film with the writer-director. Meyer become part of Sturges' unofficial "stock company" of character actors, appearing in every American film written and directed by Sturges with the exception of *The Great McGinty*. He appeared as a 'doctor' in *Sullivan's Travels* (1941) with Joel McCrea and Veronica Lake. Evidently as a private joke, Sturges nearly always cast Meyer as a character named "Schultz", with conspicuous exceptions as playing Dr. Kluck in *The Palm Beach Story* in 1942, again with Joel McCrea.

In 1942, at age 57, Meyer acted in one scene in the anti-Nazi movie *Berlin Correspondent* with Dana Andrews, playing a restaurant manager who is harassing Virginia Gilmore for her ration card. Next he had a small part as a Dutch banker in *Casablanca* who is seated at a baccarat table. His female friend (played by Trude Berliner) wants to have a drink with Rick but is told no by Carl, the headwaiter (S.Z. Sakall). Meyer is annoyed by this rebuff telling Carl, "Perhaps if you told him I ran the second largest banking house in Amsterdam." He is informed that it wouldn't impress Rick, "the leading banker in Amsterdam is now the pastry chef in our kitchen" and "his father is the bellboy!"

In 1943, Meyer played a waiter again in RKO's spy thriller *Journey into Fear* starring Joseph Cotten, Dolores del Río, and Orson Welles. Next, he portrayed a gypsy in *Frankenstein Meets the Wolf Man* starring Bela Lugosi and Lon Chaney Jr. in the title roles. This was followed with a bit role in Warner Brothers' war drama *Edge of Darkness*, starring Errol Flynn and Ann Sheridan, where he plays a clerk for Kaspar Torgerson (Charles Dingle) in a Norwegian cannery. Next he played Gottwald in the spy drama *They Came to Blow Up America* starring George Sanders and Ward Bond.

The following year, Meyer, wearing a beard and mustache, played a sympathetic Swiss Red Cross representative named Karl Kappel in the 20th Century Fox, *The Purple Heart*, a war drama of captured US army air force pilots from the Doolittle Raid over Tokyo put on trial in Japan, starring Dana Andrews and Richard Conte. After this, he played Dr. Dahlmeyer in *The Great Moment* starring Joel McCrea. Next he played Emil Rameau's butler in the musical *Greenwich Village* starring Carmen Miranda and Don Ameche. Meyer received a bit part as a hotel manager in *Once Upon a Time* starring Cary Grant. In *Hotel Berlin* in 1945, which starred Helmut Dantine and Peter Lorre, Meyer plays a barber named Franz. Later that year he was a town official in the Fred Astaire musical *Yolanda and the Thief*.

After World War II, Meyer continued to receive roles. In 1946, he played a Count in the Bob Hope comedy *Monsieur Beaucaire*. The following year, he received a small part in *Millie's Daughter*. Later that year, Meyer who once played a lowly waiter in the famed Los Angeles restaurant 'The Brown Derby' back in 1932, now gets to play the head waiter there in *Variety Girl* which had cameos from literally dozens of Hollywood stars. In 1949, he portrayed doctors in two movies; he had a small part as Doctor Shultz in the comedy *The Beautiful Blonde from Bashful Bend* starring Betty Grable and a larger one as Doctor Hans Heinrich in the Bowery Boys film *Hold That Baby!* Later that year, Meyer played a captain of an ocean liner in the Bob Hope comedy *The Great Lover*.

In 1951, Meyer played Donovan in *Grounds for Marriage* starring Van Johnson. Later that year, he got a part as an auto mechanic in *Come Fill the Cup* starring James Cagney. The next year, Meyer played the mayor of a small French town during World War I in the John Ford drama *What Price Glory?*. Later in 1952, Meyer was a station master in *The Merry Widow* starring Lana Turner. The next year, Meyer appeared in the musical *Call Me Madam* starring Ethel Merman and Donald O'Connor. Next he portrayed another waiter in the Dean Martin and Jerry Lewis comedy *The Caddy*, and appeared as a chef in another Martin and Lewis comedy the following year, *Living It Up*.

Meyer appeared in the Bob Hope comedy *Casanova's Big Night* which also starred Joan Fontaine and John Carradine in 1954, his fourth Bob Hope movie. Next, he got to play cards again, as he did in *Casablanca*, in *Deep in My Heart* starring José Ferrer and Merle Oberon. Meyer was out catching butterflies in the Michael Curtiz comedy *We're No Angels* starring Humphrey Bogart, Aldo Ray, and Peter Ustinov. He played a scribe in the John Wayne film *The Conqueror* in 1956, and later he played a French waiter in the musical *Anything Goes* starring Bing Crosby and Donald O'Connor.

Meyer portrayed 'Gaston' in the sci-fly classic *The Fly* starring Vincent Price in 1958. Next he played Alex, the headwaiter at the Harmonica Club in *The Matchmaker* starring Shirley Booth, Anthony Perkins and Shirley MacLaine. The following year, he had the role of Hugo in *The Earth is Mine* starring Rock Hudson and Claude Rains, and in 1960 he appeared in the Elvis Presley movie *G.I. Blues*.

154

In the 1950s and 60s, Meyer made some guest appearances on TV shows such as *I Love Lucy* (1956), *Voyage to the Bottom of the Sea* (1964), and *I Dream of Jeannie* (1966),

In 1961, at the age of 76, he got his best role in the classic *Judgment at Nuremberg* starring Spencer Tracy, Burt Lancaster, Richard Widmark, Marlene Dietrich, Maximilian Schell, Judy Garland, and Montgomery Clift, playing the guilt-ridden "Werner Lampe", one of the ex-Nazi judges on trial whose inability to explain his actions is one of the most powerful moments. Two years later, in 1963, he had a small uncredited role in what would be the last movie of his career, *A New Kind of Love*.

Meyer died on May 22, 1975 of bronchial pneumonia in Hollywood, California at the age of 90. He was cremated and his ashes are in the Chapel of the Pines Crematory in Los Angeles.

Robert Middleton

Robert Middleton, was born Samuel G. Messer, May 13, 1911, in Cincinnati, Ohio and was an American film and television actor known for his large size and beetle-like brow. With a deep, booming voice, Middleton trained for a musical career at the Cincinnati Conservatory of Music and Carnegie Tech in Pittsburgh, Pennsylvania. He worked steadily as a radio announcer and actor.

One of his early works was as the narrator of the educational film "Duck and Cover". After appearing on the Broadway stage and live television, Middleton began appearing in films in 1954. He's also remembered on television as the boss Mr. Marshall on *The Jackie Gleason Show* (1953) and in film opposite Humphrey Bogart in *The Desperate Hours* (1955), Gary Cooper in *Friendly Persuasion* (1956), Richard Egan and Elvis Presley in *Love Me Tender* (1956), Dorothy Malone and Robert Stack in *The Tarnished Angels* (1958), and Dean Martin in *Career* (1959).

Middleton appeared in many television programs in the 1950s, 1960s, and 1970s including *Appointment with Adventure* (1955), *Alfred Hitchcock Presents* (1956-1957), *The Real McCoys* (1959), *Wichita Town* (1960) with Joel McCrea, *The Untouchables* (1960-1961), *Perry Mason* (1963), *Burke's Law* (1965-1966), *Get Smart* (1970), *Mission: Impossible* (1972), *Mannix* (1973), and *Hunter* (1977).

Other significant film roles include *The Court Jester* (1956) as a grim and determined knight who jousts with Danny Kaye in the famous "pellet with the poison" sequence, and as a sinister politician in *The Lincoln Conspiracy* (1977).

Betwixt and between were an array of brutish mountain daddies, corrupt, cigar-chomping town bosses and lynch mob leaders, such as *The Silver Chalice* (1954), *The Proud Ones* (1956), *Day of the Bad Man* (1958), *Hell Bent for Leather* (1960) with Audie Murphy, *Cattle King* (1963), *A Big Hand for the Little Lady* (1966), and *The Cheyenne Social Club* (1970).

Middleton died June 14, 1977, of congestive heart failure in Hollywood at the age of 66.

Michael T. Mikler

Michael T. Mikler was born Michael Theodore Mikler on August 13, 1933 in Slavia, Florida. He was an actor and assistant director, known for *Ice Station Zebra* (1968), *Westworld* (1973), and *Pat Garrett & Billy the Kid* (1973).

More of his roles included *Johnny Ringo* (1960), *Ride the High Country* (!962) with Joel McCrea, *Gunsmoke* (1960-1963), *The Outer Limits* (1963-1964), *12 O'Clock High* (1966), *The Fugitive* (1967), *Mission: Impossible* (1969), and *Alias Smith and Jones* (1971).

He died on June 23, 2008 in Los Angeles, California at age 74.

Victor Millan

Victor Millan was born Joseph Brown August 1, 1920, and was an American actor, academic, and former Dean of the theatre arts department at Santa Monica College in Santa Monica, California.

He served as a sergeant in the United States Army Air Corps during World War II. During the war, Millan was stationed in China, India, and Burma.

He enrolled at the University of California, Los Angeles (UCLA) following the end of World War II. Millan earned both his bachelor's degree and his master's degree in theatre arts from UCLA.

He had over eighty separate television and film credits, in addition to his theater work. Some of his earliest roles included the 1952 film, *The Ring*, which was directed by Kurt Neumann, *Drum Beat* (1954) with Alan Ladd, as well as *Walk the Proud Land* (1956) with Audie Murphy, *Touch of Evil* (1958), and *The FBI Story* (1959).

Other roles over the years included *Giant* (1956), *Wichita Town* (1959) with Joel McCrea, *Wanted: Dead or Alive* (1960), *The Fugitive* (1966), *The Big Valley* (1968-1969), *Cannon* (1971-1972), *Marcus Welby, M.D.* (1974-1975), *How the West Was Won* (1979), *Knight Rider* (1982), *Scarface* (1983), and *The Ed Begley, Jr. Show* (1989).

He taught theatre arts at Santa Monica College for his entire academic teaching career. He served as the Dean of the theatre arts department at the college for over 25 years.

Victor Millan died at his home in Santa Monica, California, on April 3, 2009, at the age of 88.

Vera Miles

Joel McCrea and Vera Miles in *Wichita*

Vera Miles was born Vera June Ralston in Boise City, Oklahoma August 23, 1930 and is an American actress who worked closely with Alfred Hitchcock, most notably as Lila Crane in the classic masterpiece *Psycho*, reprising the role in the 1983 sequel, *Psycho II*. Her other popular films include *The Wrong Man, The Searchers, Follow Me Boys!* and *The Man Who Shot Liberty Valance*.

Miles was born to Thomas and Burnice (née Wyrick) Ralston. She had three elder siblings. She grew up first in Pratt, Kansas, and later lived in Wichita, where she worked nights as a Western Union operator-typist and graduated from Wichita North High School in 1947. She was crowned Miss Kansas in 1948 and was the third runner-up in the Miss America contest. When she appeared as a contestant on the April 4, 1951, edition of the Groucho Marx quiz show *You Bet Your Life* described as "a beauty contest winner", Marx asked her about some of the titles she held. She replied, "I was first Miss Chamber of Commerce and then Miss Wichita and then Miss Kansas and Miss Texas Grapefruit and recently I've been chosen Miss New Maid Margarine and I had the honor to represent Kansas in the Miss America pageant."

Miles moved to Los Angeles in 1950, and landed small roles in films and television, including a minor role as a chorus girl in *Two Tickets to Broadway* (1951), a musical starring Janet Leigh, with whom Miles co-starred nine years later in the classic Alfred Hitchcock film *Psycho*. Miles eventually was put under contract at various studios. She once recalled, "I was dropped by the best studios in town."

More of her early roles included *When Willie Comes Marching Home* (1950), *The Beast from 20,000 Fathoms* (1953), *The Charge at Feather River* (1953), and *Wichita* (1955) with Joel McCrea.

While under contract to Warner Brothers, Miles was cast in *Tarzan's Hidden Jungle* (released in 1955) as Tarzan's love interest. During filming she married her *Tarzan* co-star, Gordon Scott; they divorced in 1959. Director John Ford chose Miles to star as Jeffrey Hunter's love interest in *The Searchers* (1956), starring John Wayne. That same year, she co-starred in *23 Paces to Baker Street* with Van Johnson. In 1957, she began a five-year personal contract with Alfred Hitchcock, and was widely publicized as the director's potential successor to Grace Kelly.

Miles' new mentor directed her in the role of Ralph Meeker's emotionally troubled new bride in "Revenge", the pilot episode of his television series *Alfred Hitchcock Presents*. Suitably impressed, Hitchcock directed her on the big screen alongside Henry Fonda, who played a musician falsely accused of a crime, in *The Wrong Man* (1956). *New York Times* film critic Bosley Crowther singled out Miles' performance, writing that she "does convey a poignantly pitiful sense of fear of the appalling situation into which they have been cast". Hitchcock undertook to reinvent his new star through grooming and wardrobe supervised by Oscar-winning costume designer Edith Head.

Production delays and her pregnancy cost Miles the leading role opposite James Stewart in *Vertigo* (1958), the project Hitchcock designed as a showcase for his new star (the role which eventually went to Kim Novak). When asked several years later about Miles by director François Truffaut for the book *Hitchcock/Truffaut*, Hitchcock explained their professional falling-out this way: "She became pregnant just before the part that was going to turn her into a star. After that, I lost interest. I couldn't get the rhythm going with her again." Miles reflected, "Over the span of years, he's had one type of woman in his films, Ingrid Bergman, Grace Kelly and so on. Before that, it was Madeleine Carroll. I'm not their type and never have been. I tried to please him, but I couldn't. They are all sexy women, but mine is an entirely different approach".

Despite their differences, Hitchcock cast Miles in what is arguably the role for which she is most remembered, that of Lila Crane in *Psycho*. She was cast in 1962 and 1965 episodes of *The Alfred Hitchcock Hour*. In 1962 she worked with John Ford again on *The Man Who Shot Liberty Valance*.

Miles was featured in many popular television shows. On February 26, 1960, she starred in the episode "Mirror Image" of the classic CBS television series, *The Twilight Zone* with Martin Milner. Miles guest starred on the Darren McGavin NBC western series, *Riverboat*.

On October 4, 1960, Miles appeared in the episode "Three Rode West" of NBC's *Laramie* western series in the role of Annie Andrews, a young woman who is seeking a husband and ends up being terrorized by outlaw Frank Skinner, played by Myron Healey.

In 1963, she co-starred in the first episode of ABC's *The Fugitive* titled "Fear in a Desert City" with David Janssen. In 1964 she co-starred in an episode of *The Outer Limits*, "Forms of Things Unknown" (broadcast May 4, 1964), along with David McCallum, Sir Cedric Hardwicke, Scott Marlowe and Barbara Rush.

In 1965 Miles portrayed Sister Gervaise in the episode, "There's a Penguin in My Garden", of *Mr. Novak*, a series starring James Franciscus as an idealistic Los Angeles high school teacher. She also played a supporting role in several episodes of the CBS television series *My Three Sons*, starring Fred MacMurray. In 1966 Miles co-starred with MacMurray in the Walt Disney film *Follow Me, Boys!*. In 1968 she starred opposite former co-star John Wayne in *Hellfighters*; scenes where she had played John Wayne's character's wife in *The Green Berets* were cut by Warner Bros. who wanted more action in the film. She played a cosmetics queen who commits murder in "Lovely but Lethal", a 1973 episode of NBC's *Columbo*. She made an appearance in an episode called the "Adventure of the Two-faced Woman" on the short-lived crime mystery series *Ellery Queen*. In 1983, two decades after she appeared in *Psycho*, Miles reprised the role of Lila Crane for *Psycho II*. Throughout the 1980s until her retirement in 1995, Miles continued to work in both television and film.

Some of those later roles included *The Love Boat* (1982-1984), *Alfred Hitchcock Presents* (1985), *Hotel* (1984-1987), *Murder, She Wrote* (1985-1991), and *Separate Lives* (1995).

Miles has been married three times. Her first husband was Bob Miles. They were married from 1948 until 1954, and had two daughters, Debra and Kelley. Her second husband was Gordon Scott. They were married from 1954 until 1959, and had one son, Michael. Her third husband was actor Keith Larsen. They were married from 1960 until 1971, and had one son, Erik.

Miles currently resides in California, refusing to grant interviews or make public appearances. Her grandson, actor Jordan Essoe, however, met with actress Jessica Biel in 2012 in preparation for Biel's portrayal of Miles in the film *Hitchcock*.

John Milford

John Milford was born in Johnstown, New York, September 7, 1929, and was an American actor in theatre, television, and films, playing scores of roles, often as a western villain.

Milford studied Civil Engineering at Union College but chose to pursue his first love, acting.

After making his film debut in *Marty* in 1955, Milford went on to act in dozens of film and TV roles, especially in *The Ten Commandments* (1956), *Face of a Fugitive* (1959), *Wichita Town* (1960) with Joel McCrea, *The Rifleman* (1959-1962), *Gunfight at Comanche Creek* (1963) with Audie Murphy, *The Fugitive* (1963-1966), *Get Smart* (1966), *Support Your Local Sheriff!* (1969), *The Bold Ones: The Lawyers* (1969-1972), *Planet of the Apes* (1974), *The Six Million Dollar Man* (1975-1978), *The Amazing Spider-Man* (1979), *Enos* (1980-1981), *Policewoman Centerfold* (1983), *T.J. Hooker* (1986), *Freddy's Nightmares* (1990), *The X-Files* (1995), *Melrose Place* (1997), and *Chicken Soup for the Soul* (2000).

In 1965 Milford had a recurring role as Cole Younger in the TV series *The Legend Of Jesse James*.

Throughout his career Milford continued to work in the theatre. He founded the Chamber Theatre at 3759 Cahuenga Blvd, pioneering Equity Waiver productions in Los Angeles, and helped launched the careers of actors such as Richard Chamberlain and Vic Morrow.

Milford's *Los Angeles Times* obituary credits him with using his engineering background to help create the original design for the Hollywood Walk Of Fame.

Milford died of skin cancer August 23, 2000. He was survived by his wife, TV producer Susan Graw, and two sons.

Ray Milland

Ray Milland was born Alfred Reginald Jones in Neath, Wales January 3, 1905 and was a Welsh actor and director. His screen career ran from 1929 to 1985, and he is best remembered for his Academy Award winning portrayal of an alcoholic writer in *The Lost Weekend* (1945), a sophisticated leading man opposite a corrupt John Wayne in *Reap the Wild Wind* (1942), the murder-plotting husband in *Dial M for Murder* (1954), and as Oliver Barrett III in *Love Story* (1970).

He was the son of Elizabeth Annie (née Truscott) and Alfred Jones. In the 1911 census the family were living at 66 Coronation Road, Mount Pleasant, Tonna, Neath, Wales. Of his parents, Milland wrote in his 1974 autobiography *Wide-Eyed in Babylon*, "My father was not a cruel or harsh man. Just a very quiet one. I think he was an incurable romantic and consequently a little afraid of his emotions and perhaps ashamed of them... he had been a young hussar in the Boer War and had been present at the relief of Mafeking. He never held long conversations with anyone, except perhaps with me, possibly because I was the only other male in our family. The household consisted of my mother, a rather flighty and coquettish woman much concerned with propriety and what the neighbors thought."

He was educated independently before attending King's College School in Cardiff. He worked at his uncle's horse-breeding farm before leaving home at the age of 21.

Before becoming an actor, Milland served in the Household Cavalry. An expert shot, he became a member of his company's rifle team, winning many prestigious competitions, including the Bisley Match in England. While stationed in London, Milland met dancer Margot St. Leger, and through her was introduced to American actress Estelle Brody. Brody queried Milland's commitment to an army career, which led to Milland buying himself out of the forces in 1928.

He left the army to follow a career in acting and appeared as an extra in several British productions before getting his first major role in *The Flying Scotsman*. This led to a nine month contract with MGM and he moved to the United States where he appeared as a stock actor. After being released by MGM he was picked up by Paramount, who used Milland in a range of lesser speaking parts, normally as an English character. He was loaned out to Universal in 1936 for a film called *Three Smart Girls*, and its success saw Milland given a lead role in *The Jungle Princess* alongside new starlet Dorothy Lamour. The movie was a big success and catapulted both to stardom. Milland remained with Paramount for almost twenty years, and as well as his Oscar winning role in *The Lost Weekend*, he is remembered for the films *The Major and the Minor (1942), The Big Clock (1948)*, and *The Thief (1952)*, the last of which saw him nominated for a Golden Globe. After leaving Paramount he began directing and ended his career moving into television.

Milland, who was at one time Paramount Pictures highest paid actor, co-starred alongside many of the most popular actresses of the time including Gene Tierney, Grace Kelly, Lana Turner, Marlene Dietrich, Ginger Rogers, Jane Wyman, Loretta Young, and Veronica Lake.

His first appearance on film was as an uncredited extra on the Arnold Bennett film *Piccadilly* (1929). After some unproductive extra work, which never reached the screen, he took on the agent Frank Zeitlin on the recommendation of fellow fledgling actor Jack Raine. It was his reputed prowess as a marksman that earned him work as an extra at the British International Pictures studio on Arthur Robison's 1929 production of *The Informer*. While he was working on *The Informer* he was asked to test for a production being shot on a neighboring stage. Milland made a good impression on director Castleton Knight and was hired for his first acting role as Jim Edwards, in *The Flying Scotsman*. Milland, in his autobiography, recalls that it was on this film that it was suggested he adopt a stage name; and chose Milland from the *Mill lands* area of his Welsh home town of Neath.

Believing that his acting was poor, and that he had won his film roles through his looks alone, Milland decided to gain some stage work to improve his art. After hearing that club owner Bobby Page was financing a touring company, Milland approached him in hope of work. He was given the role of second lead, in a production of Sam Shipman and Max Marcin's *The Woman in Room 13*. Despite being released from the play after five weeks, Milland felt that he had gained valuable acting experience.

In between stage work, Milland was approached by MGM vice-president Robert Rubin, who had seen the film *The Flying Scotsman*. MGM offered Milland a nine-month contract, based in Hollywood, and he accepted, leaving the United Kingdom in August 1930. MGM started Milland out as a 'stock' player, selecting him for small speaking parts in mainstream productions.

Milland's first introduction to a Hollywood film resulted in a humiliating scene on the set of *Son of India*, when the movie's director Jacques Feyder berated Milland's acting in front of the entire crew. Despite this setback, the studio executives talked Milland into staying in Hollywood and in 1930 he appeared in his first US film *Passion Flower*. Over the next two years Milland appeared in minor parts for MGM, as well as a few films loaned out to Warner Brothers, often uncredited. His largest role during this period was as Charles Laughton's nephew in *Payment Deferred* (1932).

While in this first period working in the United States, Milland met Muriel Frances Weber, who he always called "Mal", a student at University of Southern California. Within eight months of first meeting, the two were married on September 30, 1932 at the Riverside Mission Inn. The couple had a son, Daniel, and a daughter, Victoria (adopted).

Shortly after *Payment Deferred*, Milland found himself out of work when MGM dropped their option to renew his contract. He spent five months in the US attempting to find further acting work, but after little success, and a strained relationship with his father-in-law, he decided to head back to England hoping that two years spent in Hollywood would lead to roles in British films. Milland cashed in his contracted first-class return ticket to Britain and found an alternative cheaper way back home. Muriel remained in the States to finish her studies, and Milland found temporary accommodation in Earl's Court in London.

Milland found life in England difficult with little regular work, though he finally found parts in two British films, *This is the Life* (1933) and *Orders is Orders* (1934). Neither were breakthrough roles. Then, in 1933, Roosevelt's reforms to the American banking sector led to a temporary weakness in the dollar allowing Milland to afford a return to the United States. He returned to California, and found a small apartment on Sunset Boulevard, promising Muriel that he would buy a home once he was financially stable. With little prospect of finding acting work, Milland took on menial jobs including working in a bookie's. He decided to find regular employment and through connections made in his time in England, he was offered the role of an assistant manager of a Shell gas station on Sunset and Clark. On his return from his successful Shell interview he passed by the gates of Paramount Pictures, where he was approached by casting director Joe Egli. Paramount was filming a George Raft picture *Bolero*, but an injury to an English actor had left the studio looking for an urgent replacement. Egli offered Milland a two week contract, at ten times the salary the assistant job would pay. Milland took the acting role.

After completing *Bolero*, Milland was offered a five-week guarantee by Benjamin Glazer to work on an upcoming screwball comedy starring Bing Crosby and Carole Lombard entitled *We're Not Dressing* (1934). During filming he appeared in a scene with George Burns and Gracie Allen, which Milland recalls as falling into an "ad-libbed shambles", which he felt was better than the original script. The film's director Norman Taurog was so impressed that he rang the chief production executive and suggested that Milland be placed on a long term contact. After a short meeting, Milland was offered a seven year deal with Paramount. The contract gave Milland a secure income and he and Muriel moved into an apartment on Fountain.

During his first contract with Paramount, Milland was used as part of the speaking cast, but never as a top of the bill actor. Then in 1936 he was contacted by Joe Pasternak who was looking for an 'English' actor for the lead in his new picture, *Three Smart Girls*. Although Pasternak worked for Universal Studios, Paramount had agreed to loan Milland out for the film. On returning to Paramount after *Three Smart Girls* was wrapped, Milland was again cast in bit-part roles. He was then used as a test actor to find a new starlet for *The Jungle Princess*. When the studio chose Dorothy Lamour for the lead, Milland wrote in his autobiography that Lamour was confused to find that he was not to be her male lead and she requested Milland to be her co-star. Paramount was not keen, but when *Three Smart Girls* was released to rave reviews they gave Milland the role.

The Jungle Princess was a huge success, launching Lamour's career and leading to two further films in the same genre, *Her Jungle Love* and *Tropic Holiday*, both released in 1938, starring the same actors but in different roles. During this period Milland was loaned out to Universal for one more feature, *Next Time We Love* (1936) with James Stewart and Margaret Sullavan. By the end of 1936, Milland was now being considered for leading roles, and Paramount rewrote his contract, resulting in the tripling of his salary.

After returning from a break in Europe, Milland was cast as Captain Hugh "Bulldog" Drummond in *Bulldog Drummond Escapes* (1937). This was followed by another lead role in *Gilded Lily*, directed by Wesley Ruggles who had started Milland out in *Bolero*. A heavy work load followed with Milland completing *Ebb Tide* for Paramount and a couple of loan-outs to Universal and Columbia Pictures. These were followed by *Hotel Imperial* (1939) in which Milland suffered a near-fatal accident on the set. One scene called for him to lead a cavalry charge through a small village. An accomplished horseman, Milland insisted upon doing this scene himself. As he was making a scripted jump on the horse, his saddle came loose, sending him flying straight into a pile of broken masonry. Milland awoke in the hospital where he remained for a week with a badly damaged left hand, a three inch gash to his head and concussion. Milland completed 1939 with an appearance as John Geste in *Beau Geste* alongside Gary Cooper and Robert Preston and *Everything Happens at Night* with Sonja Henie.

According to Milland, 1939 also resulted in an a second injury to his left hand. As well as horse riding Milland enjoyed piloting aircraft and in his early career would loan out single-seater planes. As a contracted starring actor Paramount had insisted he give up this hobby. Instead Milland took up woodworking and outfitted a machine shop at the back of his newly built house. While operating a circular blade, he slipped, catching one of his hands on the saw. The injury resulted in Milland losing a part of his thumb and severely damaging his tendons. Milland believed that the injury left him with only 50% usage of his hand, but within weeks of the incident he flew to England to star in *French Without Tears*. By the time he returned to America, War was declared in Europe. The year finished with the news that Muriel was pregnant with their son Daniel.

In 1940 Milland appeared in a selection of romantic comedies and dramas alongside some of the leading ladies of the time, including *Irene* opposite Anna Neagle, *Arise, My Love* with Claudette Colbert and *Untamed* with Patricia Morison. When the United States entered the Second World War, Milland tried to enlist in the U.S. Army Air Forces, but was rejected because of his impaired left hand. He worked as a civilian flight instructor for the Army, and toured with a United Service Organisation (USO) South Pacific troupe in 1944.

As the Second World War continued, Milland found himself now appearing in more action orientated pictures. He starred as a wannabe pilot in 1941's *I Wanted Wings* with Veronica Lake, Brian Donlevy, and William Holden. He appeared again with Veronica Lake in *Sullivan's Travels* (1941) also starring Joel McCrea. This was followed by Cecil B. DeMille's *Reap the Wild Wind* (1942) alongside John Wayne. During the filming Milland's character was to have curly hair. Milland's hair was naturally straight, so the studio used hot curling irons on his hair to achieve the effect. Milland felt that it was this procedure that caused him to go prematurely bald, forcing him to go from leading man to supporting player earlier than he would have wished.

1943 saw Milland appear in the all-star musical *Star Spangled Rhythm*, in which he appeared as himself singing "If Men Played Cards as Women Do" alongside Fred MacMurray, Franchot Tone, and Lynne Overman. He also made an appearance in the collaborative drama *Forever and a Day*. In 1944 he appeared in the supernatural film *The Uninvited* and the Fritz Lang film noir production *Ministry of Fear*.

The pinnacle of Milland's career and acknowledgment of his serious dramatic abilities came in 1945 when he starred in *The Lost Weekend*. Milland recalled how after returning from an emcee engagement in Peru, he found a book delivered to his home, with a note from Paramount's head of production Buddy DeSylva, which read "Read it. Study it. You're going to play it." Milland found the book unsettling and felt that its subject matter, that of an alcoholic writer, challenging and alien to him. He was also concerned that it would require 'serious acting' something that he believed he had not undertaken to that point in his career. The film was to be produced by Charles Brackett and directed by Billy Wilder, the two men also collaborating to write the screenplay. Milland had already worked with both men, having starred in the 1942 comedy *The Major and the Minor*, and he was excited by their involvement.

Milland's first concern with taking on the role of Don Birnam in *The Lost Weekend* was that he might overact and look amateurish. After a shambolic attempt to act parts of the script while actually drunk Milland quickly realized that he needed to understand alcoholism. After the cast and crew had arrived on location in New York, Milland was allowed to spend a night in a psychiatric ward of Bellevue Hospital where the patients were suffering from alcoholism and delirium tremens. He found the experience extremely disturbing and left at three in the morning. Milland lost eight pounds for the role and spoke with the book's author Charles R. Jackson to gain insight into the illness. After the external shots in New York were complete, in which hidden cameras were used to capture Milland walking the streets, the crew returned to Hollywood. Milland found the set work far more challenging, knowing that the close-ups would give his acting no place to hide. Between the strain of acting and the morbidity of the subject Milland's home life deteriorated and he left for a period of two weeks. When the shoot was over, he and Muriel left for a vacation in Canada.

Returning to filming, Milland was assigned to a historical drama called *Kitty* (1945). This was followed by a romantic caper *The Well-Groomed Bride* (1946) opposite Olivia de Havilland. Many of the crew members on *The Well-Groomed Bride* had also worked on *The Lost Weekend*, and Milland recalled an encounter with a sound mixer who told him he had seen a rough cut of *Weekend* and that not only was Milland a sure nomination for an Academy Award, but he thought he would win. Milland had not considered himself worthy of an award but over the next few months he thought of little else, and was desperate to be nominated. After the first preview, reaction was mixed with Brackett stating that they had produced "something really worthwhile". Milland found the feedback to his role congratulatory but hushed, leading him to feel the film would bomb as a piece of cinema and would be seen as a social document. When the film was released in New York the studio was shocked by the critical reception. Milland was lauded and he not only won that year's Academy Award for Best Actor but also the Cannes Film Festival Award for Best Actor, the National Board of Review Award for Best Actor and the New York Film Critics Circle Award for Best Actor. He was the first Welsh actor to win an Oscar and when he collected the award from Ingrid Bergman he gave one of the shortest acceptance speeches of any Oscar winner. His performance was so convincing that Milland was beleaguered for years by rumors that he actually was an alcoholic. The actor claimed he was not.

Milland's success in *The Lost Weekend* resulted in his contract being rewritten and he became Paramount's highest salaried actor. When the film was premiered across Europe, Milland was sent to attend each opening. When he appeared in Cardiff, the largest city in Wales, he was given the key to the city.

He continued in his role as lead man after his Oscar win, and stayed contracted to Paramount until the early 1950s. In the late 1940s he appeared opposite Marlene Dietrich in *Golden Earrings* (1947) and Teresa Wright in *The Trouble with Women*. During the same period he starred in four John Farrow pictures, *California* (1947), *The Big Clock* (1948), *Alias Nick Beal* (1949), and *Copper Canyon*. He also worked with George Cukor who directed him in *A Life of Her Own* (1950) alongside Lana Turner.

In 1951, he gave a strong performance in *Close to My Heart*, starring with Gene Tierney as a couple trying to adopt a child. Also that year he was directed by Jacques Tourneur in *Circle of Danger*, set in the United Kingdom; it was the only time he filmed in his home country of Wales. The next year he appeared in *The Thief* in a role with no dialogue, for which he was nominated for a Golden Globe. In 1954, he starred opposite Grace Kelly and Robert Cummings in Alfred Hitchcock's only 3D movie, *Dial M for Murder*. Although never admitted by either, rumors were rife at the time that Kelly and Milland were engaged in an affair, fuelled by notorious gossip columnist Hedda Hopper.

After leaving Paramount Milland concentrated on directing. His first, a 1955 Western entitled *A Man Alone* centered on the aftermath of a stagecoach robbery. This was followed by *Lisbon* (1956); a crime drama starring Maureen O'Hara and Claude Rains. Both films were distributed by Republic Pictures.

Due to his experience as a film director, he achieved much success directing for television. He also made many television appearances. He starred from 1953–1955 with Phyllis Avery and Lloyd Corrigan in the CBS sitcom *Meet Mr. McNutley* in the role of a college English and later drama professor at fictitious Lynnhaven College. The program was renamed in its second season as *The Ray Milland Show*. From 1959–1960, Milland starred in the CBS detective series *Markham*, but the program failed to capture an audience even though it followed the hit western *Gunsmoke*.

In 1966 Milland took the lead in the Broadway play *Hostile Witness* directed by Reginald Denham. The play ran from February until July of that year, and in 1968 he reprised his role of Simon Crawford, Q.C. in a film of the same title, which he also directed.

He made few films in the early 1960s but of those he appeared in, three have become cult classics. He appeared in two Roger Corman pictures; the first was *The Premature Burial* (1962) - the third of Corman's 'Poe Cycle'. He followed this as Dr. Xavier in *X: The Man with the X-Ray Eyes* (1963). The third of these cult favorites was his self-directed, apocalyptic sci-fi drama *Panic in Year Zero!* (1962).

He returned as a film character actor in the late 1960s and the 1970s, notably in the cult classic *Daughter of the Mind* (1969), in which he was reunited with Gene Tierney, and in the role of Oliver Barrett III, in both *Love Story* (1970) and its sequel *Oliver's Story* (1978).

In the late 1960s, Milland hosted rebroadcasts of certain episodes of the syndicated Western anthology series, *Death Valley Days* under the title *Trails West*; the series' original host had been Ronald Reagan. He also turned in an appearance as a hand surgeon in the *Night Gallery* (1971) episode "The Hand of Borgus Weems."

Late roles included *Frogs* (1972), and *The Thing with Two Heads* (1972) a particularly weird and memorable film where his head was taken off his body and put on Rosie Greers body, becoming the title character, which actually gave me nightmares as a child.

More roles included *Columbo* (1971-1972), *Terror in the Wax Museum* (1973), *Escape to Witch Mountain* (1975), *Rich Man, Poor Man* (1976), *Rich Man, Poor Man - Book II* (1976), *Mayday at 40,000 Feet!* (1976), *The Hardy Boys/Nancy Drew Mysteries* (1978), *Battlestar Galactica* (1978), *Fantasy Island* (1978), *The Love Boat* (1979), *Charlie's Angels* (1980), *Hart to Hart* (1982-1983), *Sherlock Holmes and the Masks of Death* (1984), *The Sea Serpent* (1984), and *The Gold Key* (1985).

Milland was married to Muriel Frances Weber, from 1932 until his death, in 1986. They had a son, Daniel (b.1940) and an adopted daughter, Victoria.

He had a tattoo on his upper right arm of a skull with a snake curled up on top of it with the tail of the snake sticking out through one of the eyes. The tattoo can be seen for a brief moment in the movie *Her Jungle Love* (1938).

Milland's son, Daniel Milland, appeared in several minor acting roles in the 1960s. He died in March 1981, at the age of 41, in an apparent suicide. An AK-47 was found next to him on his bed and he had a wound to his head.

He died of lung cancer in Torrance, California on March 10, 1986, at age 81. He was survived by his wife, the former Muriel Weber, and his daughter.

Ivan Miller

Joel McCrea and Ivan Miller in *Woman Wanted*

Ivan Robert Miller was born on November 13, 1888 in York, Nebraska. He was an actor, known for *Charlie Chan's Secret* (1936), *Man from Music Mountain* (1938), and *Jesse James at Bay* (1941).

More of his roles included *Woman Wanted* (1935) with Joel McCrea, *Born Reckless* (1937), *Geronimo* (1939), *Man Made Monster* (1941), *Ride 'Em Cowboy* (1942), *G-men vs. the Black Dragon* (1943), and *An American Romance* (1944).

He died on September 27, 1967 in Los Angeles County, California at age 78.

John 'Skins' Miller

John 'Skins' Miller was born on November 6, 1890 in Philadelphia, Pennsylvania. He is known for his work on *The Time of Your Life* (1948), *Criss Cross* (1949), and *The Men* (1950).

More of his roles included *The Purchase Price* (1932), *Transatlantic Merry-Go-Round* (1934), *Internes Can't Take Money* (1937) with Joel McCrea, *Something to Sing About* (1937), *The Texas Rangers Ride Again* (1940), *Yankee Doodle Dandy* (1942), *Lost in a Harem* (1944), *Belle Starr's Daughter* (1948), *Riding High* (1950), and *Just This Once* (1952).

He died on July 15, 1956 in Los Angeles, California at age 65.

Mort Mills

Mort Mills was born January 11, 1919, and was an American film and television actor who had roles in over 200 movies and television episodes. He was often the town lawman or the local bad guy in many popular westerns of the 1950s and 1960s.

From 1957-1959 he had a recurring co-starring role as Marshal Frank Tallman in *Man Without a Gun*. Other recurring roles were as Sergeant Ben Landro in the *Perry Mason* (1960-1965) series and Sheriff Fred Madden in *The Big Valley* (1965-1966). In 1958, he guest starred as a particularly greedy bounty hunter who clashes with Steve McQueen's character of Josh Randall in the CBS western series, *Wanted: Dead or Alive*.

Though Mills did much television work, he also found regular work in motion pictures. He played the highway patrolman who pursues Marion Crane (Janet Leigh) in Alfred Hitchcock's classic thriller *Psycho* (1960). A few years later, he worked again with Hitchcock, playing a spy in East Germany under the cover of being a farmer in *Torn Curtain* (1966). Mills also appeared with Charlton Heston in Orson Welles's *Touch of Evil* (1958).

In 1955, he appeared as Samuel Mason on ABC's Disneyland miniseries *Davy Crockett*, starring Fess Parker. From 1957-1959, Mills co-starred with Rex Reason in the syndicated western series *Man Without a Gun*. He portrayed Marshal Frank Tillman. Reason played his friend, Adam MacLean, editor of the Yellowstone Sentinel newspaper. Mills was a regular as police Lieutenant Bob Malone in Howard Duff's NBC-Four Star Television series, *Dante* (1960–1961), set at a San Francisco, California, nightclub called "Dante's Inferno".

Other roles over the years included *Biff Baker, U.S.A.* (1952), *Hopalong Cassidy* (1953), *Rocky Jones, Space Ranger* (1954), *To Hell and Back* (1955) with Audie Murphy, *Tension at Table Rock* (1956), *The Iron Sheriff* (1957), *Ride a Crooked Trail* (1958) again with Audie Murphy, *Wichita Town* (1959) with Joel McCrea, *Twenty Plus Two* (1961), *Gunfight at Comanche Creek* (1963) a third appearance with Audie Murphy, *The Quick Gun* (1964) a fourth time with Audie Murphy, *Bullet for a Badman* (1964) his fifth and final appearance with Audie Murphy, *The Fugitive* (1963-1965), *The Green Hornet* (1966), *Adam-12* (1971), *Alias Smith and Jones* (1972), and *The Streets of San Francisco* (1973).

He showed his comedic side in the 1965 Three Stooges film *The Outlaws Is Coming* when he played Trigger Mortis. This is my favorite role of Mort Mills.

He died June 6, 1993, at age 74 in Ventura, California.

Nika Mina

Joel McCrea and Nika Mina in *Mustang Country*

Nika Mina is an actor, known for his only role as Nika in *Mustang Country* (1976) with Joel McCrea.

Miroslava

Miroslava and Joel McCrea in *Stranger on Horseback*

Miroslava was born Miroslava Šternová in Prague, Czechoslovakia (now the Czech Republic) February 26, 1925 and was a Mexican film actress who appeared in thirty two films.

Miroslava moved to Mexico as a child with her adoptive parents in the late 1930s, seeking to escape war in their native country. After winning a national beauty contest, Miroslava began to study acting. She appeared in a few Hollywood and Mexican films.

Some of her roles included *Five Faces of Woman* (1947), *Adventures of Casanova* (1948), *The Love Nest* (1950), *Streetwalker* (1951), *Two Faces Have the Destiny* (1952), *The Magnificent Beast* (1953), and *Stranger on Horseback* (1955) with Joel McCrea.

She was offered a role in *Ensayo de un crimen* (*Rehearsal for a Crime*) in 1955, directed by Luis Buñuel. Soon after the final wrap of the film, Miroslava committed suicide by overdosing on sleeping pills March 9, 1955 at age 30 in Mexico City, Distrito Federal, Mexico. Her body was found lying outstretched over her bed; she had a portrait of bullfighter Luis Miguel Dominguín in one hand. Her friends stated her suicide was due to unrequited love for Dominguín, who had recently married Italian actress Lucia Bosé. Bosè would go on to star in Buñuel's next movie, *Cela s'appelle l'aurore* (1956).

The Mexican and Hollywood star Katy Jurado claimed to be one of the first people to find the body of Miroslava after her tragic suicide. According to Katy, the picture that Miroslava had between her hands, was Cantinflas, but the artistic manager Fanny Schatz, exchanged the photo to that of the Spanish bullfighter Luis Miguel Dominguín.

In his 1983 autobiography, *Mon dernier soupir* ("My Last Breath"), Buñuel recalls the irony of Miroslava's cremation following her suicide, when compared to a scene in *Ensayo de un crimen*, her last film, in which the protagonist cremates a wax reproduction of Stern's character. Her life is the subject of a short story by Guadalupe Loaeza, which was adapted by Alejandro Pelayo for his 1992 Mexican film called *Miroslava*, starring Arielle Dombasle.

Ewing Mitchell

Ewing Young Mitchell was born in South Carolina December 29, 1910 and was an American character actor of film and television best known for his role as Sheriff Mitch Hargrove in twenty-six episodes between 1956 and 1959 of the aviation adventure series with a western theme, *Sky King*. He also played Sheriff Powers on another western series, *The Adventures of Champion*.

Mitchell appeared and sang baritone on Broadway during the 1930s. He made his television debut at the age of 40 on January 1, 1951, in the syndicated western series, *The Range Rider*. On that series through January 1, 1953, he made ten other appearances, mostly as a law-enforcement officer, the genre in which he specialized. He was also cast in 1951 as a waiter in the episode "Bad Man of Brisco" of another syndicated western series, *The Adventures of Kit Carson*. He appeared in that same series twice in 1952, both times as a marshal, in the episodes "Trouble in Tuscarora" and "Golden Trap". He was cast in April 1952 in the episode "The Case of the Cold Neck" of the CBS crime drama *Racket Squad*, starring Reed Hadley. In 1953, he appeared as Mr. Collins in the episode "Defense Plant Security" of the syndicated Cold War drama, *I Led Three Lives*. He also had roles in several films, mostly uncredited, before and after those particular television appearances.

Ewing was cast in seven episodes each of *The Gene Autry Show* (1951-1953) and Gene Autry's related *The Adventures of Champion* (1955-1956). He appeared four times on *The Roy Rogers Show* and on the syndicated *The Adventures of Wild Bill Hickok*, with Guy Madison and Andy Devine, and *Buffalo Bill, Jr.*, starring Dick Jones. On May 20, 1955, he played Adam Greer in the first-season episode "Farewell to Fort Apache" of *The Adventures of Rin Tin Tin*.

In 1956, he was cast in an episode of the CBS fantasy drama, *The Millionaire*, in the episode "The Jane Carr Story", with Angie Dickinson in the lead guest-starring role. He appeared twice in 1956 as Preacher Homer Wilkins in the CBS western series, *The Adventures of Jim Bowie*, starring Scott Forbes in the title role. In 1956, he played a Confederate colonel in the episode "Enemies" of Ronald W. Reagan's CBS anthology series, *General Electric Theater*.

His other appearances, mostly on westerns, include *Sugarfoot*, *Tales of the Texas Rangers*, *Tales of Wells Fargo*, *The Lone Ranger*, *Annie Oakley*, and *The Life and Legend of Wyatt Earp*.

He played a sheriff in the Joel McCrea 1954 western film, *Black Horse Canyon* and appeared again with Joel McCrea in *The Gunfight at Dodge City* (1959).

In 1958, he was cast as Fred Gerlock in "The Red Flannel Shirt" of the syndicated anthology series, *Death Valley Days*, hosted by Stanley Andrews. That same year, he made two appearances on John Payne's NBC western, *The Restless Gun*, as Dawson in "Gratitude" and as Sheriff Frank Kemper in "Bonner's Squaw".

It was *Sky King*, a contemporary western which originated on radio, with which Mitchell was most identified. He played the sheriff of fictional Grover County, Arizona. The series starred Kirby Grant as rancher Sky King who spent more time in his plane, the *Songbird*, than riding his horse. Gloria Winters played Sky King's niece, Penny, and early in its run Ron Hagerthy was cast as the nephew, Clipper King. The series filmed seventy-two total episodes.

Mitchell was one of the Silver Riders, expert equestrians who appeared in parades throughout the American Southwest. In his later years, Mitchell managed several ranches that he owned in Southern California.

He died in September 3, 1988 at the age of 77 of a stroke caused by a fall from a ladder in La Jolla in San Diego County, California, where he had resided.

Grant Mitchell

Grant Mitchell was born John Grant Mitchell, Jr. in Columbus, Ohio June 17, 1874 and was an American stage actor on Broadway and character actor in many Hollywood films of the 1930s and 1940s. He appeared on Broadway from 1902 to 1939 and appeared in more than 125 films between 1930 and 1948.

Mitchell was the only son of American Civil War general John G. Mitchell. His paternal grandmother, Fanny Arabella Hayes was the sister of President Rutherford B. Hayes. Like his father, he became an attorney, graduating from the Harvard Law School. However by his mid-to-late 20s, he tired of his legal practice and turned a long term dream into a reality by becoming an actor on Broadway. He played lead roles in plays such as *It Pays to Advertise*, *The Whole Town's Talking*, *The Champion*, and *The Baby Cyclone*.

Grant Mitchell was a brother of the Delta Kappa Epsilon fraternity (Phi chapter).

In film he initially made an appearance in 1916 and one or two other silents amidst his extensive theatre work but Mitchell's screen career really took off with the advent of sound.

Most of his appearances were in B films of the 1930s and 1940s, but he made many notable appearances in high profile films such as *A Midsummer Night's Dream* (1935; Epheus), *Mr. Smith Goes to Washington* (1939, Senator MacPherson), *The Man Who Came to Dinner* (1942, Mr. Stanley), and *Arsenic and Old Lace* (1944, a Reverend).

More of his roles over his career included *20,000 Years in Sing Sing* (1932), *Shadows of Sing Sing* (1933), *365 Nights in Hollywood* (1934), *The Garden Murder Case* (1936), *The Devil Is a Sissy* (1936), *Hollywood Hotel* (1937), *Youth Takes a Fling* (1938) with Joel McCrea, *Hell's Kitchen* (1939), *The Grapes of Wrath* (1940), *Larceny, Inc.* (1942), *And Now Tomorrow* (1944) with Alan Ladd, *Bring on the Girls* (1945) with Veronica Lake, *Blondie's Holiday* (1947), *Blondie's Anniversary* (1947), and *Who Killed Doc Robbin* (1948).

He died a bachelor at age 82 in Los Angeles, California May 1, 1957.

James Mitchell

James Mitchell was born on Leap Day, 1920 in Sacramento, California and was an American actor and dancer. Although he is best known to television audiences as Palmer Cortlandt on the soap opera *All My Children* (1979–2010), theatre and dance historians remember him as one of Agnes de Mille's leading dancers. Mitchell's skill at combining dance and acting was considered something of a novelty; in 1959, the critic Olga Maynard singled him out as "an important example of the new dancer-actor-singer in American ballet", pointing to his interpretive abilities and "masculine" technique.

His parents immigrated from England to Northern California, where they operated a fruit farm in Turlock. In 1923, Mitchell's mother, Edith, left his father and returned to England with Mitchell's brother and sister; she and Mitchell had no further contact. Unable to run a farm while single-handedly raising his remaining son, Mitchell's father fostered him out for several years to vaudevillians Gene and Katherine King. After Mitchell's mother died, however, his father remarried and brought both of his sons, but not his daughter, back to Turlock. At age seventeen, Mitchell left Turlock for Los Angeles, where he remained close to the Kings.

While studying drama at Los Angeles City College, Mitchell was introduced to modern dance at the school of the famed teacher and choreographer, Lester Horton. After receiving his associate's degree, he joined Horton's company, where he remained for nearly four years. While working with Horton, he became a close friend of dancer Bella Lewitzky; in the 1970s, he became President of the Board of Directors of her Dance Foundation, and afterwards remained a "major longtime [...] supporter" of hers. In 1944, Horton took Mitchell to New York with him to form a new dance company, but the venture abruptly collapsed.

As it happened, the failure of Horton's company was a significant turning point in Mitchell's career: while struggling to find either acting or dancing roles in New York, he successfully auditioned for Agnes de Mille, who was choreographing her first musical since *Oklahoma!*. Mitchell, who did not study ballet until he was in his mid-twenties, was at a loss when faced with de Mille's ballet combination. Much later, describing his approach to the audition, he said, "Well, I really hadn't too much familiarity with that but I threw myself across the floor and about the third or fourth pass, Agnes cried 'Stop' and summoned me over and said 'Where on earth did you get your dance training?'". De Mille nevertheless offered him the dual position of principal dancer and assistant choreographer. Given the option between touring with Helen Hayes and dancing for de Mille, he chose de Mille.

Bloomer Girl (1944) began an important artistic partnership with de Mille that lasted from 1944 to 1969 and spanned theater, film, television, and concert dance. De Mille's biographer, Carol Easton, describes him as the "quintessential male de Mille dancer" and de Mille's "closest confidant" in her artistic life. In one of her autobiographical volumes, de Mille herself said of Mitchell that he had "probably the strongest arms in the business, and the adagio style developed by him and his partners has become since a valued addition to ballet vocabulary." When, nearly thirty years later, an interviewer asked Mitchell to respond to de Mille's comments, he offered a more modest assessment of his career: "I was primarily an actor [...] and I think what Agnes was referring to was my acting and regard for the woman I was partnering. Because in the end I really was a partner. When I look at today's dancers, or I look at the great dance films, such as *Seven Brides for Seven Brothers*-I couldn't do any of that! I know I was a dancer, but I didn't have the technique. At most I was an actor-dancer."

Mitchell worked consistently on stage in both musicals and straight dramas until the late 1970s, including numerous regional theatre roles across the country. His other significant credits include Broadway appearances in *Carousel*, *First Impressions*, and *The Deputy*; off-Broadway appearances in *Winkelberg*, *The Threepenny Opera*, *Livin' the Life*, and *The Father*; *L'Histoire du Soldat* at New York City Opera; and national tours of *The Rainmaker* (with future *All My Children* co-star Frances Heflin), *The King and I*, *Funny Girl*, and *The Threepenny Opera*.

A character based on Mitchell appears in Anderson Ferrell's biographical dance play, *Dance/Speak: The Life of Agnes De Mille*, which debuted at New York Theatre Ballet in 2009.

As a film performer, Mitchell had only moderate success. In the early 1940s, he did both chorus dancing and extra work in a number of minor musicals and westerns. On the strength of his award-winning performance in *Brigadoon*, he was scouted by producer Michael Curtiz and signed to a contract at Warner Brothers. Curtiz initially intended to put Mitchell in a picture with Doris Day that never materialized. After several months, Mitchell eventually made two films for Warner Brothers, including Raoul Walsh's *Colorado Territory* (1949) with Joel McCrea, before following Curtiz to Metro-Goldwyn-Mayer. At MGM, he played supporting roles in six films between 1949–1955, most notably Anthony Mann's *Border Incident*, Jacques Tourneur's *Stars in My Crown* (1950) again with Joel McCrea, and Vincente Minnelli's critically lauded *The Band Wagon*, where he played the unsympathetic role of choreographer Paul Byrd — an experience he loathed so much that he refused to see the film— but he did not work for the studio again after appearing in the infamously over-budgeted flop *The Prodigal* (1955).

Mitchell's film career ended abruptly after he starred in Hal R. Makelim's Western *The Peacemaker* (1956), the only time he was ever billed above the title, as he played the lead, gunfighter Terrall Butler. After that, it took over two decades before he made his next and what proved to be his final appearance on the big screen, *The Turning Point* (1977). He also co-starred with Thelma "Tad" Tadlock in the famous sponsored film *A Touch of Magic* presented by General Motors at the 1961 Motorama.

Besides performing, Mitchell occasionally worked as a director and choreographer, particularly in the late 1960s and 1970s. He staged musicals at the Paper Mill Playhouse, the Mark Taper Forum, and The Muny, among other theatres. In 1956, he and Katherine Litz co-staged *The Enchanted* for American Ballet Theatre.

On television, Mitchell was considerably more active, especially in the late 1950s and early 1960s. In addition to working regularly as a dancer, he played dramatic roles in a number of television films and prime-time series, as well as in the anthologies that were once so popular, such as Play of the Week, Gruen Guild Playhouse, and Armstrong Circle Theatre. In 1964, he took his first contract role on a soap opera in *The Edge of Night*, as the corrupt Captain Lloyd Griffin. In 1966, he appeared in an episode of the espionage drama *Blue Light*. This was followed by a role in the entire run of the soap opera *Where the Heart Is* (1969–1973), in which he played the male lead, Julian Hathaway.

However, after *Mack & Mabel* flopped in 1974, Mitchell's performing career nearly ended altogether. He earned a BA from Empire State College and an MFA from Goddard College in order to teach full-time at the college level, and taught movement for actors at Juilliard, Yale University, and Drake University. After a few years of almost no work – although he was a guest star on *Lou Grant* and *Charlie's Angels* in the late 1970s, he once summed up the 1970s as "I cried and did a lot of gardening"; he was hired in 1979 for his best-known role, self-made millionaire Palmer Cortlandt on ABC's long-running soap opera *All My Children*. Initially hired for only one year, he remained on contract through 2009. His final appearance as a contract player was September 19, 2008, although his retirement was not made official until September 30, 2009. On January 4, 2010, he appeared briefly on the 40th anniversary celebration. He died a few weeks later January 22, 2010 in Los Angeles, California at the age of 89 from chronic obstructive pulmonary disease complicated by pneumonia. The show aired a tribute to Mitchell on April 20, 2010, stating that Palmer Cortlandt had suffered a heart attack during the previous night. The episode aired scenes and memories from the show and cast covering the near thirty years of Palmer's life in Pine Valley.

Mitchell's partner of thirty-nine years was the Oscar-award-winning costume designer Albert Wolsky.

Laurie Mitchell

Laurie Mitchell was born July 14, 1928, in New York City and raised in the East Bronx. She moved with her family to California while in her teens.

Acting school led to stage roles and then to movie assignments, beginning with *20,000 Leagues Under the Sea* (1954). More roles followed like *The Man Behind the Badge* (1955), *Girls in Prison* (1956), *Adventures of Superman* (1957), *The Oklahoman* (1957) with Joel McCrea, *Attack of the Puppet People* (1958), *Queen of Outer Space* (1958), *Some Like It Hot* (1959), *Richard Diamond, Private Detective* (1958-1959), *Wanted: Dead or Alive* (1959), *Hell Bent for Leather* (1960) with Audie Murphy, *Hawaiian Eye* (1961), *That Touch of Mink* (1962), *Gunfight at Comanche Creek* (1963) again with Audie Murphy, *The Addams Family* (1965), *Laredo* (1966), *Ironside* (1967), *Hogan's Heroes* (1968), *The Virginian* (1966-1969), and *The Bold Ones: The New Doctors* (1971).

Long-retired and now the wife of a medical salesman, she has recently been "rediscovered" by her fans and has begun making the celebrity expo and autograph show rounds.

Rhea Mitchell

Rhea Mitchell was born in Portland, Oregon December 10, 1890 and was an American film actress who began her career during the silent film era. She earned the name of "the little stunt girl" because of her willingness to attempt thrilling scenes in motion pictures.

Mitchell began her career in 1909 playing in the Baker Theater Stock Company in her hometown of Portland, Oregon. She followed with a season in the Orpheum Circuit and a run at the Alcazar Theater in San Francisco. Mitchell made her film debut in 1912 with the New York Motion Picture Corporation and would eventually appear in over 100 films during her career. She appeared a number of times with Western star William S. Hart playing a leading role in those films. In 1916 she played in *The Brink* with Forrest Winant and Arthur Maude.

After 1917, her roles became smaller and she appeared in a handful of films through the mid-1930s and in several bit parts during the early 1950s which often went uncredited.

More of her roles included *Good Women* (1921), *The Other Kind of Love* (1924), *Danger Patrol* (1928), *Whom the Gods Destroy* (1934), *The Ship That Died* (1938), *Harrigan's Kid* (1943), *The Romance of Rosy Ridge* (1947), *Stars in My Crown* (1950) with Joel McCrea, and *The Member of the Wedding* (1952).

After her retirement from films, Mitchell managed a large apartment house in Los Angeles. While managing a second apartment September 16, 1957, the La Brea District Apartments, a disgruntled houseboy named Sonnie Hartford, Jr., strangled her with the cord of her blue silk dressing gown. She was 66. She is buried at Hollywood Forever Cemetery in Los Angeles.

Steve Mitchell

Steve Mitchell was born on December 15, 1926 in New York City, New York. He was an actor and assistant director, known for *The Big Combo* (1955), *The Killing* (1956), and *Seven Men from Now* (1956).

More of his roles included *The Adventures of Ellery Queen* (1951) episode "The Twilight Zone", *The Beast from 20,000 Fathoms* (1953), *Alfred Hitchcock Presents* (1956), *Gunsight Ridge* (1957) with Joel McCrea, *The Texan* (1958-1960), *A Gathering of Eagles* (1963), *Hondo* (1967), *Adam-12* (1968-1970), *Wonder Woman* (1974), *The Next Step Beyond* (1978), *C.H.O.M.P.S.* (1979), and *Treasure Hunt* (2003).

He died on January 23, 2007 in Los Angeles County, California at age 80.

Thomas Mitchell

Joel McCrea and Thomas Mitchell in *Buffalo Bill*

Thomas Mitchell was born to Irish immigrants in Elizabeth, New Jersey, July 11, 1892, and was an American actor, playwright, and screenwriter.

Among his most famous roles in a long career are those of Gerald O'Hara, the father of Scarlett O'Hara in *Gone with the Wind* (1939), the drunken Doc Boone in John Ford's *Stagecoach* (1939), *Joan of Paris* (1942) with Alan Ladd, and Uncle Billy in *It's a Wonderful Life* (1946).

Mitchell was the first person to win an Oscar, an Emmy, and a Tony Award. Nominated twice for an Oscar, first for *The Hurricane* (1938), he won the Best Supporting Actor award for *Stagecoach* (1939); later, he would be nominated three times for an Emmy. He was nominated twice, in 1952 and 1953, for his role in the medical drama *The Doctor*, winning the Lead Actor Drama award in 1953. Nominated again in 1955, for an appearance on a weekly anthology series, he did not win. Mitchell won the Tony for Best Actor in a Musical, in 1953, for his role as Dr Downer in the musical comedy *Hazel Flagg,* based on the 1937 Paramount comedy film *Nothing Sacred,* rounding out the Triple Crown of acting awards.

He came from a family of journalists and civic leaders. Both his father and brother were newspaper reporters (his nephew, James P. Mitchell, later served as Dwight Eisenhower's Secretary of Labor). Like them, the younger Mitchell also became a newspaper reporter right after graduating from St. Patrick High School in Elizabeth. Soon, however, Mitchell found he enjoyed writing comic theatrical skits much more than chasing late-breaking scoops.

He became an actor in 1913, at one point touring with Charles Coburn's Shakespeare Company. Even while playing leading roles on Broadway into the 1920s Mitchell would continue to write. One of the plays he co-authored, *Little Accident*, was eventually made into a film (three times) by Hollywood. Mitchell's first credited screen role was in the 1923 film *Six Cylinder Love*.

Mitchell's breakthrough role was as the embezzler in Frank Capra's 1937 film *Lost Horizon*. Following this performance, he was much in demand in Hollywood. That same year, he was nominated for a Best Supporting Actor Academy Award for his performance *The Hurricane*, directed by John Ford.

Over the next few years, Mitchell appeared in many of the greatest films of the 20th century. In 1939 alone he had key roles in *Stagecoach, Mr. Smith Goes to Washington, Only Angels Have Wings, The Hunchback of Notre*

Dame, and *Gone with the Wind*. While probably better remembered as Scarlett O'Hara's loving but doomed father in *Gone with the Wind*, it was for his performance as the drunken Doc Boone in *Stagecoach*, co-starring John Wayne (in Wayne's breakthrough role), that Mitchell won the Best Supporting Actor Academy Award. In his acceptance speech, he quipped, "I didn't know I was that good".

Throughout the 1940s and 1950s, Mitchell acted in a wide variety of roles in productions such as 1942's *Moontide*, 1944's *The Keys of the Kingdom* (as an atheist doctor) and 1952's *High Noon* (as the town mayor). He is probably best known to audiences today for his role as sad sack Uncle Billy in Capra's 1946 Christmas classic *It's a Wonderful Life* opposite James Stewart. This film, while not well received when released, has become a classic that is shown each year on broadcast television. It ranks regularly as one of the most beloved films of all time.

One of his better roles in the 1950's was as Rags Barnaby in *Destry* (1954) with Audie Murphy. In the film he went from boozing town drunk, to serious Sheriff of Restful, back to drunk, then back to serious Sheriff, then an amazingly heartfelt death scene.

He appeared with Joel McCrea in *Adventure in Manhattan* (1936) and *Buffalo Bill* (1944).

From the 1950s and into the early 1960s, Mitchell worked primarily in television, appearing in a variety of roles in some of the most well-regarded early series of the era, including *Playhouse 90* (1958), *Zane Gray Theatre* (1958-1961), and *Goodyear Theatre* (1959) productions. In 1954, he starred in the TV series *Mayor of the Town*, in 1959 starred in 39 episodes of the TV series *Glencannon* and in the early 1960s originated the stage role *Columbo*, later made famous on television by Peter Falk. *Columbo* was Mitchell's last role.

Mitchell died at age 70, in December 17, 1962, from bone cancer in Beverly Hills, California. He was cremated and his ashes stored in the vault at the Chapel of the Pines Crematory in Los Angeles.

James Mitchum

James Mitchum was born James Robin Spence Mitchum May 8, 1941 in Los Angeles, California and is an American actor. He is the eldest son of actor Robert Mitchum. He is also the brother of actor Christopher Mitchum and the uncle of actor Bentley Mitchum. His first child was born of his marriage to Wende Wagner, an actress who died of cancer in 1997.

He had his first role which was small and unbilled at the age of 8 in the western *Colorado Territory* (1949) with Joel McCrea, Virginia Mayo, and Dorothy Malone. His credited debut was in *Thunder Road* (1958) in which he played his father's much younger "brother," a role written for Elvis Presley, who was eager to do it until his manager demanded too much money. This film became a drive-in cult favorite, revived in the 1970s and 1980s. Curiously, he was again credited as being "introduced" in the *Have Gun Will Travel* episode "Genesis" (1962).

He has appeared in more than thirty films including *The Beat Generation* in 1959, *The Victors* in 1963, as a surfer named Eskimo in *Ride the Wild Surf* in 1964, *In Harm's Way* (1965), *Ambush Bay* (1966), *The Invincible Six* (1970), and *The Last Movie* (1971).

In 1975 he starred in the movie *Moonrunners*, where he played the character Grady Hagg, this movie was the influence for the T.V. show *The Dukes of Hazzard*. He was also in *Zebra Force*, and *Trackdown* co-starring Karen Lamm and Erik Estrada in 1976, *Ransom* (aka *Assault on Paradise*) (1977), *Blackout* (1978), *Monstroid* (1980), *Crazy Jungle Adventure* (1982), *Hollywood Cop* (1987), *Jake Spanner, Private Eye* (1987) and *Fatal Mission* (1990).

John Mitchum

John Newman Mitchum was born in Bridgeport, Connecticut September 6, 1919, and was an American actor from the 1940s in films and, later, television. He was the younger brother of Julie Mitchum and Robert Mitchum. He initially appeared in only unbilled and extra roles before gradually receiving bigger character parts in middle age. Mitchum supported his more famous brother on several occasions and was featured as the cop Frank DiGiorgio in the first three *Dirty Harry* films (1971-1976).

Mitchum was also a writer, poet, singer and played guitar. An autobiography/biography about the life and careers of him and his brother Robert Mitchum was published in the 1998 called *Them Ornery Mitchum Boys*.

He composed the piece "America, Why I Love Her", which John Wayne included in his book and album of the same name. The piece and a short film with Wayne's narration were aired at many television stations at sign-off time before stations began broadcasting 24 hours a day in late 1970s early 1980s. Wayne is often mistakenly credited with composing the piece.

Some of his roles over the years included *Knock on Any Door* (1949), *Flying Leathernecks* (1951), *Stalag 17* (1953), *Nightmare* (1956), *Zane Grey Theater* (1956-1957), *Richard Diamond, Private Detective* (1958), *The Gunfight at Dodge City* (1959) with Joel McCrea, twenty-one episodes as Pickalong in *Riverboat* (1959-1960), *Whispering Smith* (1961) with Audie Murphy, *Twilight Zone* (1961-1964), *Laredo* (1965), *The Munsters* (1965), *El Dorado* (1966), *Warning Shot* (1967), eleven episodes as Trooper Hoffenmueller in *F Troop* (1965-1967), *Batman* (1966-1967), *Paint Your Wagon* (1969), *Chisum* (1970), *Adam-12* (1970), *Bigfoot* (1970), *High Plains Drifter* (1973), *Kolchak: The Night Stalker* (1974), *Breakheart Pass* (1975), *The Misadventures of Sheriff Lobo* (1979), *Jake Spanner, Private Eye* (1989), and *A Family for Joe* (1990).

Mitchum died November 29, 2001, of a stroke, at the age of 82.

Gregory Moffett

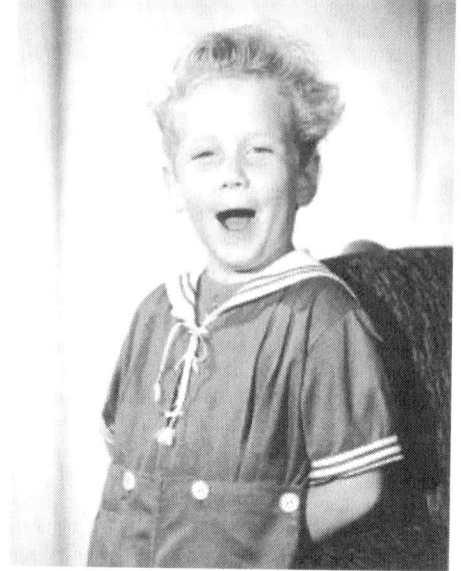

    Gregory Moffett was born James Gregory Moffett on March 14, 1943 in Los Angeles, California. He is an actor, known for *Let's Dance* (1950), *Saddle Tramp* (1950) with Joel McCrea, and *Robot Monster* (1953).

    More of his roles included *The Judge Steps Out* (1949), *Two-Gun Lady* (1955), *Highway Patrol* (1956), and *Adventures of Superman* (1957).

    He is married to Sandy. They have four children.

Henry Mollison

    Henry Mollison was born Evelyn Henry Mollison February 21, 1905 in Dundee, Tayside, Scotland and was a British film actor. He was the brother of the actor Clifford Mollison.

    He was on his way back to Britain from America in 1939 with the intention of joining the armed forces when the ship on which he was traveling was captured by Nazis and he spent five years in a German P.O.W. camp. During this period he organized camp entertainment and produced fifty-six shows for the other prisoners. On his release he returned to Britain where he resumed his acting career. He never fully recovered from his wartime experiences and only made a limited number of post war appearances.

    Some of his roles included Balaclava (1928), The Face at the Window (1932), Manhattan Moon (1935), Youth Takes a Fling (1938) with Joel McCrea, The Man in the White Suit (1951), and Front Page Story (1954).

    He was married to actress Lina Basquette from 1937 until their divorce.

    He eventually died July 19, 1985 a broken man in a home for forgotten actors in Greenwich, London, England.

Anthony C. Montenaro

Anthony C. Montenaro was born on September 16, 1947 in Los Angeles, California. He is a set decorator and actor, known for *Car Wash* (1976), *Smokey and the Bandit* (1977), and *Over the Edge* (1979).

Some of his acting roles included *Wichita Town* (1959) with Joel McCrea, *The Miracle* (1959), *The Adventures of Ozzie & Harriet* (1952-1960), *Guestward Ho!* (1960-1961), *Hennesey* (1962), and *The Lloyd Bridges Show* (1962).

Goodee Montgomery

Goodee Montgomery was born Virginia Montgomery on March 28, 1906 in St. Joseph, Missouri. She was an actress, known for *Charlie Chan Carries On* (1931), *Stolen Harmony* (1935), and *Beware of Ladies* (1936).

More of her roles included *Up the River* (1930), *Lightnin'* (1930) with Joel McCrea, *Transatlantic* (1931), *Stolen Sweets* (1934), and *Mountain Music* (1937).

She was married to Frank McDonald. She died on June 5, 1978 in Hollywood, California at age 72.

Robert Montgomery

Robert Montgomery was born Henry Montgomery, Jr. in Fishkill Landing, New York (now Beacon, New York) May 21, 1904 and was an American film and television actor, director and producer. He was also the father of actress Elizabeth Montgomery of Bewitched.

Montgomery was born to Henry Montgomery, Sr. and his wife, Mary Weed (née Barney). His early childhood was one of privilege as his father was president of the New York Rubber Company. His father committed suicide in 1922 by jumping off the Brooklyn Bridge, and the family's fortune was gone.

Montgomery went to New York City to try his hand at writing and acting. He established a stage career, and became popular enough to turn down an offer to appear opposite Vilma Bánky in the film *This Is Heaven*. Sharing a stage with George Cukor gave him an in to Hollywood, where, in 1929, he debuted in *The Single Standard* and *So This Is College* both with Joel McCrea. He entered the moving picture industry during the revolution of the talkies, which made it more difficult to impress the studio. One writer claimed that Montgomery was able to establish himself because he "proceeded with confidence, agreeable with everyone, eager and willing to take suggestions". During the production of *So This Is College*, Montgomery learned from and questioned crew members from several departments, including sound crew, electricians, set designers, camera crew and film editors. In a later interview, he confessed "it showed [him] that making a motion picture is a great co-operative project." *So This Is College* gained him attention as Hollywood's latest newcomer, and he was put in one production after another, with his popularity growing steadily.

Montgomery initially played exclusively in comedy roles, but portrayed a character in his first drama film in *The Big House* (1930). The studio was initially reluctant to assign him in such a role, until "his earnestness, and his convincing arguments, with demonstrations of how he would play the character" won him the assignment. From *The Big House* on, he was in constant demand. Appearing as Greta Garbo's romantic interest in *Inspiration* (1930) started him toward stardom with a rush. Norma Shearer chose him to star opposite her in *The Divorcee* (1930), *Strangers May Kiss* (1931), and *Private Lives* (1931), which led him to stardom. During this time, Montgomery appeared in the original pre-Code film version of *When Ladies Meet* (1933), which starred Ann Harding and Myrna Loy.

In 1935, Montgomery became President of the Screen Actors Guild, and was elected again in 1946. In 1937, he was nominated for the Academy Award for Best Actor as a psychopath in the chiller *Night Must Fall*, then returned to playing light comedy roles, such as Alfred Hitchcock's *Mr. & Mrs. Smith* (1941) with Carole Lombard, but continued his search for dramatic roles. He was again nominated for an Oscar in 1942 for *Here Comes Mr. Jordan*. During World War II, he joined the United States Navy, rising to the rank of lieutenant commander, and served on the USS *Barton* (DD-722) which was part of the D-Day invasion on June 6, 1944.

In 1945, Montgomery returned to Hollywood, making his uncredited directing debut with *They Were Expendable*, where he directed some of the PT Boat scenes when director John Ford was unable to work for health reasons. Montgomery's first credited film as director was the film noir *Lady in the Lake* (1947), in which he also starred, which received mixed reviews. Adapted from Raymond Chandler's detective novel and sanitized for the censorship of the day, the film was nonetheless noteworthy for the revolutionary way it is filmed entirely from Marlowe's vantage point. Montgomery only appeared on camera a few times, three times in a mirror reflection. He also directed and starred in *Ride the Pink Horse* (1947), also a film noir.

Active in Republican politics and concerned about communist influence in the entertainment industry, Montgomery was a friendly witness before the House Un-American Activities Committee in 1947. The next year, 1948, Montgomery hosted the Academy Awards. He hosted an Emmy Award-winning television series, *Robert Montgomery Presents*, in the 1950s. *The Gallant Hours*, a 1960 film Montgomery directed and co-produced with its star, his friend James Cagney, was the last film or television production he was connected with in any capacity, as actor, director or producer. In 1954, Montgomery took an unpaid position as consultant and coach to President Eisenhower, advising him on how to look his best in his television appearances before the nation. A pioneering media consultant, Montgomery had an office in the White House during this time.

Montgomery has two stars on the Hollywood Walk of Fame, one for movies at 6440 Hollywood Boulevard, and another for television at 1631 Vine Street.

His first marriage, in April 1928, was to actress Elizabeth Daniel Allen (December 26, 1904 – June 28, 1992), sister of Martha-Bryan Allen. The couple had three children: Martha Bryan, who died at 14 months of age in 1931; Elizabeth (April 15, 1933 - May 18, 1995); and Robert, Jr. (January 6, 1936 - February 7, 2000). They divorced on December 5, 1950. His second marriage was to Elizabeth "Buffy" Grant Harkness, whom he wed on December 9, 1950, four days after his divorce from his first wife was finalized.

Montgomery died of cancer on September 27, 1981 at age 77 at Columbia-Presbyterian Hospital in Manhattan. His body was cremated and the ashes were given to the family. His two surviving children, Elizabeth and Robert Montgomery, Jr., both died of cancer as well.

Charles R. Moore

Charles R. Moore was born April 23, 1893, Chicago, Illinois and was an African-American actor who appeared in over 100 films in his acting career, and was sometimes credited as Charles Moore or Charlie Moore.

Moore played small parts such as servants, bootblacks, elevator operators, menial laborers, and, especially, railroad porters and Red Caps. Film buffs may remember him in *Meet John Doe* (1941) where he played the City Hall janitor trying to smoke a cigar while washing the floor on the Christmas Eve that John Doe has threatened to jump off the building.

Moore was part of Preston Sturges' unofficial "stock company" of character actors, appearing in six of Sturges' films. In *Sullivan's Travels* (1941) with Joel McCrea and Veronica Lake, Moore had a memorable moment as the chef who is propelled headfirst through the roof of the land yacht during the chase scene. Moore was also a dancer, but that skill was not often called for in his film appearances.

More of his many roles included *Your Obedient Servant* (1917), *The Homesteader* (1919), *The Ninety and Nine* (1922), *A Daughter of the Congo* (1930), *New Adventures of Get Rich Quick Wallingford* (1931), *Fugitive Lovers* (1934), *The Captain Hates the Sea* (1934), *Internes Can't Take Money* (1937) with Joel McCrea, *God's Step Children* (1938), *Mr. Smith Goes to Washington* (1939), *This Gun for Hire* (1942) with Alan Ladd and Veronica Lake, *I Married a Witch* (1942) a third with Veronica Lake, *The Palm Beach Story* (1942) a third with Joel McCrea, *Son of Dracula* (1943), *Without Reservations* (1946) with John Wayne, and *Welcome Stranger* (1947).

He died July 20, 1947, Los Angeles, California at age 54.

Pauline Moore

Pauline Moore was born Pauline Joless Love in Harrisburg, Pennsylvania June 17, 1914 and was an American actress known for her roles in Western and B movies during the 1930s and 1940s.

After her father died during World War I, her mother remarried in 1925 and Moore took her stepfather's name. She began her career moving to Hollywood in the early 1930s, and also starred on Broadway and worked as a model.

From the late 1930s through the early 1940s, Moore made twenty four films for 20th Century Fox, with whom she was contracted. She later worked for Republic Pictures, starring in four Roy Rogers westerns, as well as the film *King of the Texas Rangers* in 1940, starring football great Sammy Baugh. Moore starred in three Charlie Chan films, starring alongside Cesar Romero, Allan Lane, and Kane Richmond. She also starred alongside Shirley Temple in the 1937 film *Heidi*, and alongside Henry Fonda in the 1939 film *Young Mr. Lincoln*.

More of her roles included *Frankenstein* (1931), *Wagon Wheels* (1934), *Born Reckless* (1937), *Three Blind Mice* (1938), *The Three Musketeers* (1939), *Young Buffalo Bill* (1940), *Arkansas Judge* (1941), *Medic* (1951), *Showdown at Abilene* (1956), and *The Littlest Hobo* (1958).

She was married to the cartoonist Jefferson Machamer from 1934 until his death in 1960. In the early 1940s she retired from acting, and became a mother of three children, but continued to act into the 1950s. From her first uncredited role in 1931 through to her last role in 1958 her career spanned a total of thirty films. She made a few television appearances in the 1950s, including a bit part in *Spoilers of the Forrest* in 1957 alongside Rod Cameron and Vera Ralston, but for the most part her acting career had ended, by her own choice. In 1962, she married Rev. Dodd Watkins, whose death in 1972 left her a widow for the second time. She died of Lou Gehrig's disease in December 7, 2001, at a nursing home in Sequim, Washington at age 87.

Bert Moorhouse

Joel McCrea and Bert Moorhouse in *Gambling Lady*

Bert Moorhouse was born Herbert Green Moorhouse in Chicago, Illinois (sometimes incorrectly billed as Bert Moorehouse) November 20, 1894 and was an American character actor whose career began at the very tail end of the silent era, and lasted through the mid-1950s. He would enter the film industry in 1928 with featured roles in two FBO productions: *Rough Ridin' Red*, and the Hugh Trevor vehicle *Hey Rube!*.

He would appear in either featured or small roles in over 130 films during his twenty-six year career, as well as more than 200 other pictures in which he appeared as an extra.

More of his roles included *Conspiracy* (1930), *The Sport Parade* (1932) with Joel McCrea, *Rockabye* (1932) again with Joel McCrea, *Stage Mother* (1933), *Gambling Lady* (1934) a third with Joel McCrea, *Woman Wanted* (1935) a fourth with Joel McCrea, *Adventure in Manhattan* (1936) a fifth with Joel McCrea, *Wells Fargo* (1937) a sixth with Joel McCrea, *Three Blind Mice* (1938) a seventh with Joel McCrea, *He Married His Wife* (1940) an eight with Joel McCrea, *Dressed to Kill* (1941), *Sullivan's Travels* (1941) a nineth with Joel McCrea, *Yankee Doodle Dandy* (1942), *The Palm Beach Story* (1942) a tenth with Joel McCrea, *Air Raid Wardens* (1943) with Laurel and Hardy, *Jitterbugs* (1943) again with Laurel and Hardy, *Along the Navajo Trail* (1945), *It's a Wonderful Life* (1946), *Samson and Delilah* (1949), *I Was a Communist for the FBI* (1951), *The Long, Long Trailer* (1953), and *Dangerous Mission* (1954).

In 1954 he had small roles in three films, the last of which to be premiered was *Dangerous Mission*, which starred Victor Mature, Piper Laurie, William Bendix, and Vincent Price. All three of these films were released posthumously. Moorhouse was suffering from a severe illness, and on January 26 he would take his own life, via a gunshot wound to the head. He was 59. He was buried with his mother, Fannie, at Forest Lawn Memorial Park in Glendale, California.

Carmen Morales

Carmen Morales was born Maria Del Carmen Morales on October 6, 1911 in Santa Cruz de Tenerife, Canary Islands, Spain. She was an actress, known for *Primrose Path* (1940) with Joel McCrea, *The Long Voyage Home* (1940), and *The Valley of Vanishing Men* (1942).

More of his roles included ***Affectionately Yours*** (1941), ***Two Latins from Manhattan*** (1941), ***Ladies' Day*** (1943), ***They Live by Night*** (1948), and ***The Big Steal*** (1949).

She died on February 3, 2000 in Los Angeles, California at age 88.

Frank Moran

Francis Charles Moran in Cleveland, Ohio March 18, 1887 and was an American boxer and film actor who fought twice for the Heavyweight Championship of the World, and appeared in over 135 movies in a twenty-five year film career.

Born to Martin and Mary Moran, immigrants from County Mayo, Ireland, Moran studied dentistry at the University of Pittsburgh where he also played football. He played professional football for the Pittsburgh Lyceums and Akron Pros as a guard and center.

While Moran was serving in the U.S. Navy in 1908, he knocked out fighter Fred Cooley in the second round. While serving on the U.S.S. Mayflower, he served as a spar partner for President Theodore Roosevelt. He began his career as a prize-fighter that same year with a match against Fred Broad. Soon, Moran, who had a hard right hand punch which he called "Mary Ann", became known as the "White Hope" of the teens. In 1914 he fought Jack Johnson for the Heavyweight Championship of the World, and in 1916 "The Fighting Dentist" went up against Jess Willard for the same title, but lost both bouts. He lost his last fight to Marcel Nilles for the Heavyweight Championship of France on December 22, 1922. He retired from boxing after 66 bouts with a record of 36 wins (28 by a knockout), 13 losses, 16 draws and 1 no contest.

After acting in one show on Broadway in 1926 – a stage adaptation of Theodore Dreiser's novel *An American Tragedy* – Moran made his film debut in 1928 when he did two silent films, *The Chinatown Mystery* and *Ships of the Night*, but his film career didn't start in earnest until 1933, when he appeared as himself in *The Prizefighter and the Lady*, and also in Mae West's *She Done Him Wrong*, in which he played a convict. This was typical of the kinds of roles Moran was to play for the next twenty-five years – gangsters, henchmen, "plug uglies", bartenders, stage hands, sailors, guards, cops, bouncers, moving men, sergeants and other soldiers – roles which belied his personal gentleness and sensitivity.

In the 1940s, Moran was part of Preston Sturges' unofficial "stock company" of character actors, appearing in every American film written and directed by Sturges with one exception. He was seen in *The Great McGinty*, *Christmas in July*, *The Lady Eve*, *Sullivan's Travels* (1941) with Joel McCrea, *The Palm Beach Story* (1942) again with Joel McCrea, *The Miracle of Morgan's Creek*, *Hail the Conquering Hero*, *The Great Moment* (1944) a third with Joel McCrea, *The Sin of Harold Diddlebock* and *Unfaithfully Yours*.

It was Moran who, as a cop in Sturges' *Christmas in July* (1940), halted a tirade by an argumentative Jewish storeowner by barking, "Who do ya think you are, Hitler?" And it was Moran who, as a tough chauffeur in *Sullivan's Travels* (1942), patiently explains to his traveling companions the meaning of the word "paraphrase."

Moran was usually credited for his performances, but almost never received star or featured billing. One exception was Monogram Pictures's *Return of the Ape Man* (1944), starring Bela Lugosi and John Carradine, in which Moran shared credit for the title role with George Zucco, although, in fact, Zucco became ill and Moran replaced him – Zucco does not appear in the film as released. Also, at the beginning of his acting career, Moran was part of the featured cast in Raoul Walsh's *Sailor's Luck* (1933).

Other notable films in which Moran appeared include Charlie Chaplin's *Modern Times* 1936, Fred Astaire and Ginger Rogers's *Follow the Fleet Shall We Dance* and *Carefree* (1938), Frank Capra's *Meet John Doe* (1941), 1943's *Lady of Burlesque* starring Barbara Stanwyck and *Road to Utopia* with Bob Hope and Bing Crosby (1946).

Moran's final film appearance was an uncredited bit part in *The Iron Sheriff*, a Western, in 1957 at the age of 70. He was 80 when he died in Hollywood, California on December 14, 1967 of a heart attack.

Frank Moran was inducted into the Pennsylvania Boxing Hall of Fame in 2012.

Polly Moran

Pauline Theresa "Polly" Moran in Chicago, Illinois June 28, 1883 and was an American actress and comedian.

Moran started out in vaudeville, and widely toured North America, as well as various other locations that included Europe and South Africa. An attractive Irish beauty, she left vaudeville in 1914 after signing for Mack Sennett at Keystone Studios as one of his Sennett Bathing Beauties. There she honed the style of the brash loud-mouth knock-about comedian for which she later became known. She proved effective at slapstick and remained with Sennett for several years until she was signed by MGM.

She partnered with the famous Broadway star Marie Dressler in *The Callahans and the Murphys* (1927), and the two went on to appear in several films together such as *Chasing Rainbows* (1930) and *Caught Short* (1930). After Dressler's death in 1934 Moran's career declined, and she only starred in low-budget comedies or B-movies. In 1940, Moran retired to her home in Laguna Beach, California but maintained an active Hollywood social life and was known for practical jokes. She once ran a failed campaign for a Laguna Beach City Council seat on a "Pro Dogs" platform.

More of her roles included *London After Midnight* (1927), *So This is College* (1929), *Chasing Rainbows* (1930), *The Passionate Plumber* (1932), *Hollywood Party* (1934), *Two Wise Maids* (1937), *Red River Range* (1938), *Meet the Missus* (1940) with Alan Ladd, and *Petticoat Politics* (1941) again with Alan Ladd.

She made a brief comeback appearance in the Tracy-Hepburn classic comedy *Adam's Rib* in 1949. After playing the role, she said, "I worked in the picture two days before I got a look at myself. I never went back."

Moran has a star on the Hollywood Walk of Fame at 6300 Hollywood Boulevard.

After an earlier marriage that ended in divorce in 1917, Moran married attorney Martin T. Malone in 1933. She had one child, a son, who was adopted between her two marriages. She lived at 530 Mountain Road in Laguna Beach, California. Moran died of cardiovascular disease in 1952. Although a number of biographies give Moran's date of death as being January 25, 1952, her grave marker reads, "January 24, 1952".

Antonio Moreno

Antonio "Tony" Moreno was born Antonio Garrido Monteagudo in Madrid, Spain, September 26, 1887 and was a Spanish-born American actor and film director of the silent film era and through the 1950s.

He immigrated to the United States at the age of fourteen and settled in Massachusetts, where he completed his education. He became a stage actor in regional theater productions. In 1912, he moved to Hollywood, California and he was signed to Vitagraph Studios and began his career in bit parts and as a movie extra.

In 1914, Moreno began co-starring in a series of highly successful serials opposite the enormously publicly popular silent film actress Pearl White. These appearances helped to increase Moreno's popularity with the nation's nascent film-goers. By 1915, Antonio Moreno was a highly regarded matinee idol and appearing opposite such successful actors as Tyrone Power, Sr., Gloria Swanson, Blanche Sweet, Pola Negri and Dorothy Gish. Moreno was often typecast in his earliest films as the "Latin Lover", as were other actors of the era with Latin roots, such as Ramón Novarro and Rudolph Valentino.

By the early 1920s, Antonio Moreno joined film mogul Jesse Lasky's Famous Players and became one of the company's most highly paid performers. In 1926 Moreno starred opposite Swedish acting legend Greta Garbo in *The Temptress* and the following year followed up with a starring role in the enormous box-office hit Clara Bow vehicle *It*.

Moreno married American heiress Daisy Canfield Danziger, in 1923, and the couple moved to an estate known as Crestmount, now known as the Canfield-Moreno Estate. The union lasted ten years and ended shortly before Canfield Danziger was killed in an automobile accident on February 23, 1933.

With the advent of talkies in the late 1920s and early 1930s, Moreno's career began to falter, in part because of his heavy Spanish accent. While still acting in English language films, Moreno also began taking parts in Mexican films. During the early 1930s, Moreno directed several well-received Mexican films, among them is the 1932 drama *Santa*, which has been hailed by film critics as one of the best Mexican films of the era. By the mid-1930s, Antonio Moreno began rebuilding his faltering Hollywood career by taking notable roles as a character actor.

By the mid-1940s and throughout the 1950s, Moreno appeared in a number of well received roles, most notably, his 1954 role in the classic horror film *Creature from the Black Lagoon* and his 1955 role as Emilio Figueroa in film director John Ford's influential western epic *The Searchers* opposite John Wayne and Natalie Wood.

More of his roles included *Storm Over the Andes* (1935), *Ambush* (1939), *Valley of the Sun* (1942), *Captain from Castile* (1947), *Saddle Tramp* (1950) with Joel McCrea, *Thunder Bay* (1953), Saskatchewan (1954) with Alan Ladd, and *Catch Me If You Can* (1959).

Moreno retired from film in the late 1950s and died of heart failure February 15, 1967, in Beverly Hills, California; he was laid to rest in the Forest Lawn Memorial Park cemetery in Glendale, California. His film career spanned more than four decades.

In 1994, the Mexican magazine *Somos* published their list of "The 100 best movies of the cinema of Mexico" in its 100th edition and named the 1931 Moreno directed *Santa* its 67th choice.

For his contribution to the motion picture industry, Antonio Moreno was given a star on the legendary Hollywood Walk of Fame at 6651 Hollywood Blvd., Hollywood, California, USA.

Of note is that Moreno was the half-brother of Alfred Moreno Monteagudo, who took over management of the Los Angeles Biltmore Hotel in the 1940s. Antonio Moreno is the granduncle of horror/fantasy author Nicholas Grabowsky.

Ralph Morgan

Ralph Morgan was born Raphael Kuhner Wuppermann in New York City, New York July 6, 1883 and was a Hollywood film, stage, and character actor, and the older brother of Frank Morgan (who played the title role in *The Wizard of Oz*, 1939).

He was the eighth of eleven children of Josephine Wright and George Diogracia Wuppermann. His mother was a Mayflower descendent and his father, George Wuppermann was a Hispanic and Latino German-born citizen, who had moved to U.S. He had made a fortune by distributing Angostura bitters, allowing him to send all of his children to universities. Ralph Morgan graduated from Columbia University with a law degree. However, he abandoned the world of jurisprudence for the vocation of journeyman actor, having already appeared in Columbia's annual Varsity Show. Morgan became so successful in stock and on Broadway that his younger brother, Frank, was encouraged to give acting a try. Frank's career would eventually overshadow that of his elder brother.

His first role on the stage came in *The Bachelor* in 1909 and later played John Marvin in the 1918 hit play, *Lightnin'* .

Ralph Morgan made his film debut in silent films in 1915, appearing in several production made on the East Coast. In the early talkie era he played such leading roles in such productions as *Strange Interlude* in 1932 and *Rasputin and the Empress* also in 1932.

He later settled into secondary character parts. His quiet, dignified demeanor on screen was often employed for murder mysteries in which, more often than not, he would play what is known as a "heavy", being exposed in the last reel as the killer. One of his memorable roles was in the 1942 serial *Gang Busters*, in which he played a brilliant surgeon turned master criminal.

Morgan later worked in both, radio and television, frequently in religious dramas filmed for *Family Theater*.

Among his off-camera activities, he alongside, Grant Mitchell, Berton Churchill, Charles Miller, Alden Gay, and Kenneth Thomson formed the Screen Actors Guild to resolve and stop most of the injustice, which actors faced within the industry. (among which, were prolonged work hours enforced by the studios and the Academy of Motion Pictures Arts and Sciences' membership policy, which was exclusively by invitation.) He was also a founder, charter member and became the first president of SAG in 1933 and was elected to two additional one-year terms in 1938 and 1939, serving until 1940.

More of his credits included *Disorderly Conduct* (1932), *Hell in the Heavens* (1934), *Magnificent Obsession* (1935), *Wells Fargo* (1937) with Joel McCrea, *Forty Little Mothers* (1940) with Veronica Lake, *Adventure in Washington* (1941), *The Monster Maker* (1944), *Song of the Thin Man* (1947), *The Creeper* (1948), *Heart of the Rockies* (1951), *Celanese Theatre* (1951-1952), and *Your Favorite Story* (1953).

Ralph Morgan was married to Georgiana Louise Iverson, who as a stage actress was known as Grace Arnold, although he called her "Daisy" and was the father of Claudia Morgan (1911–1974), an actress best known for creating the role of Vera Claythorne on Broadway in the original production of *Ten Little Indians*, and for her portrayal of Nora Charles on the radio series *The Thin Man*.

He died June 11, 1956 at age 72 in New York City, New York.

Ann Morrison

Ann Morrison was born Anna Mae Parrott on February 15, 1916 in Los Angeles, California. She was an actress, known for *Battle Circus* (1953), *The Brothers Karamazov* (1958), and *General Hospital* (1963).

More of her roles included *Blossoms in the Dust* (1941), *Red Skies of Montana* (1952), *Violent Saturday* (1955), *The Tall Stranger* (1957) with Joel McCrea, *Alcoa Presents: One Step Beyond* (1959), *Gunsmoke* (1961), *Adam-12* (1970), and *Police Woman* (1974-1975).

She was married to Frank Harford. She died on April 18, 1978 in Woodland Hills, Los Angeles at age 62.

Jeff Morrow

Irving "Jeff" Morrow was born January 13, 1907, and was an American actor educated at the Pratt Institute in his native New York City. He was a commercial artist prior to turning to acting.

As early as 1927, Morrow acted onstage as Irving Morrow in Pennsylvania. He later appeared in such plays as *Penal Law*, and *Once in a Lifetime*, as well as repertory in Shakespeare's *A Midsummer Night's Dream*, *Twelfth Night*, *Romeo and Juliet* and *Macbeth*.

After serving in the U.S. Army during World War II, Morrow spent the late 1940s on the stage and in radio, where he won the title role in the *Dick Tracy* radio series. He appeared in many Broadway productions, notably *Three Wishes for Jamie*, *Billy Budd*, the Maurice Evans production of *Macbeth*, and the Katharine Cornell production of *Romeo and Juliet*.

Morrow turned to film acting relatively late in his career, commencing with the Biblical epic *The Robe* in 1953. Often parodied as the 'Cro-Magnon Man' for his prominent brow, Morrow spent much of the 1950s appearing in a mix of A-budget epics in supporting parts, or 'B' Westerns such as *The Siege at Red River* (1954) and science fiction films as a leader and screen hero, usually paired with a busty and beautiful actress.

Morrow carried over much of his acting persona from his radio days to his film acting roles, where his ability to rapidly alter both the tone and volume of his voice for dramatic effect frequently gave sound editors fits. He entered the science fiction/monster movie genre with the 1955 film *This Island Earth*, followed by *The Creature Walks Among Us* (1956), *The Giant Claw* (1957), and *Kronos* (1957).

He also showed up in a boxing movie with Audie Murphy *World in my Corner* (1956), the same year he appeared with Joel McCrea in *The First Texan*.

Morrow returned to television for most of his later roles, making guest appearances on *Twilight Zone* (1960), *Crossroads* (1956-1957), *Bonanza* (1961), *My Friend Flicka* (1955), *The Deputy* (1960), *Perry Mason* (1962-1963), *Daniel Boone* (1966-1968), and *Police Story* (1974-1975).

In 1958-1959, he starred as Bart McClelland, the fictitious supervisor of construction of the Union Pacific Railroad in the syndicated half-hour Western series *Union Pacific,* based loosely on a Joel McCrea and Barbara Stanwyck film of the same name. His *Union Pacific* television co-stars were Judson Pratt and Susan Cummings.

In 1960, Morrow played Tob, the older brother of Boaz (Stuart Whitman), in the biblical drama, *The Story of Ruth*. During the early 1960s, Morrow appeared in such low-budget films as *Harbor Lights* (1963), *Blood Legacy* (1971), and in a bow to his earlier career, a cameo in the 1971 monster film *Octaman* for veteran 1950's monster movie writer/director Harry Essex.

After the 1974 cancellation of the sitcom *The New Temperatures Rising*, Morrow largely retired from acting, though he returned for a 1975 appearance in the series *Police Story*. His last television role was in 1986, with a guest appearance on the second *The Twilight Zone* series.

In his later life, Morrow returned to commercial illustration with occasional acting assignments. He died at the age of eighty-six on December 26, 1993, in Canoga Park in the San Fernando Valley in Los Angeles County, California. He was survived by his wife of nearly fifty years, actress Anna Karen Morrow, and their daughter, Mrs. Lissa Morrow Christian (born 1948). His ashes were scattered off the coast of Palos Verdes, California.

Vic Morrow

Victor Harry "Vic" Morrow was born in the Bronx, New York, February 14, 1929, and was an American actor whose credits include a starring role in the TV series *Combat!* (1962-1967), and prominent roles in a handful of other television and cinema dramas, and numerous guest roles on television.

When he was seventeen, Morrow dropped out of high school and joined the U.S. Navy. He married actress Barbara Turner with whom he had two daughters: actress Jennifer Jason Leigh and Carrie Ann Morrow. Morrow's marriage to Barbara lasted seven years and ended in divorce in 1964. He did not remarry until 1975, over a decade later, when he courted Gale Lester. They were married for five years and were separated just prior to Morrow's death.

Morrow's first movie role was in *Blackboard Jungle* (1955), after which he went into television. Later, he guest starred on John Payne's NBC western series, *The Restless Gun* (1957). Other early roles included *Richard Diamond, Private Detective* (1958), *King Creole* (1958), *Wichita Town* (1959) with Joel McCrea, *Cimarron* (1960), and *Posse from Hell* (1961) with Audie Murphy.

He was cast in the lead role in ABC's *Combat!*, a World War II drama, which aired from 1962–1967. He also worked as a television director. Together with Leonard Nimoy, he produced a 1966 version of *Deathwatch*, an English language film version of Genet's play *Haute Surveillance*, adapted by Morrow and Barbara Turner, directed by Morrow, and starring Nimoy.

After *Combat!* ended, he worked in several films. Morrow appeared in two episodes of Australian-produced anthology series *The Evil Touch* (1973), one of which he also directed. He memorably played the wily local sheriff in director John Hough's road classic *Dirty Mary, Crazy Larry* (1974), as well as the homicidal sheriff, alongside Martin Sheen, in the 1974 TV film *The California Kid*, and had a key role in the 1976 comedy *The Bad News Bears*. He also played Injun Joe in 1973 telefilm *Tom Sawyer*, which was filmed in Upper Canada Village.

Morrow wrote and directed a 1971 Spaghetti Western, produced by Dino DeLaurentis, titled *A Man Called Sledge* starring James Garner. It was Morrow's first and only big screen outing behind the camera. Sledge was filmed in Europe with desert-like settings that were highly evocative of the U.S. southwest.

He also played Capt. Eugene Nathan in the 1980 series *B.A.D. Cats.*

In the early morning hours of July 23, 1982, Morrow and two children, My-Ca Dinh Le (age 7), and Renee Shin-Yi Chen (age 6), died in an accident while filming on location for the *Twilight Zone: The Movie* in Ventura County, California, between Santa Clarita and Piru. Morrow was playing the role of Bill Connor, a racist who is taken back in time and placed in various situations where he would be a persecuted victim: as a Jewish Holocaust victim, a black man about to be lynched by the Ku Klux Klan, and a Vietnamese man about to be killed by U.S. soldiers. Morrow, Le, and Chen were filming a scene for the Vietnam sequence in which their characters attempt to escape from a pursuing U.S. Army helicopter out of a deserted Vietnamese village. The helicopter was hovering at about twenty-five feet above them when pyrotechnic explosions damaged it and caused it to crash on top of them, killing all three instantly. He was decapitated along with one of the child actors.

Morrow is interred in Hillside Memorial Park Cemetery in Culver City, California.

Director John Landis and other defendants, including producer Steven Spielberg and pilot Dorsey Wingo, were ultimately acquitted of involuntary manslaughter and child endangerment. The parents of Le and Chen sued and settled out of court for an undisclosed amount. Morrow's children also sued and settled for an undisclosed amount.

Jack Mower

Jack Mower was born Benjamin Allen Mower on September 5, 1890 in Honolulu, Hawaii. He was an actor and producer, known for *The Shock* (1923), *The Crook Buster* (1925), and *Don't Shoot* (1926).

More of his roles included *The Radio Detective* (1926), *The Cheyenne Kid* (1930), *Palooka* (1934), *Hollywood Hotel* (1937), *The Oklahoma Kid* (1939), *Espionage Agent* (1939) with Joel McCrea, *Yankee Doodle Dandy* (1942), *South of St. Louis* (1949) again with Joel McCrea, *The Lone Ranger* (1950), *House of Wax* (1953), *The Lone Hand* (1953) a third with Joel McCrea, *Maverick* (1958-1959), and *Critic's Choice* (1963).

He died on January 6, 1965 in Hollywood, California at age 74.

Conrad Nagel

Conrad Nagel was born in Keokuk, Iowa March 16, 1897 and was an American screen actor and matinee idol of the silent film era and beyond. He was also a well-known television actor and radio performer.

He was born into an upper-middle-class family, he was the son of a musician father, Frank, and a mother, Frances (née Murphy), who was a locally praised singer. Nagel's mother died early in his life, and he always attributed his artistic inclination to growing up in a family environment that encouraged self-expression. His father, Frank, became dean of the music conservatory at Highland Park College and when Nagel was three, the family moved to Des Moines.

After graduating from Highland Park College at Des Moines, Iowa, Nagel left for California to pursue a career in the relatively new medium of motion pictures where he garnered instant attention from the Hollywood studio executives. With his 6-foot-tall frame, blue eyes, and wavy blond hair; the young, Midwestern Nagel was seen by studio executives as a potentially wholesome matinee idol whose unpretentious all-American charm would surely appeal to the nation's nascent film-goers.

Nagel was immediately cast in film roles that cemented his *unspoiled lover* image. His first film was the 1918 retelling of the Louisa May Alcott classic, *Little Women*, which quickly captured the public's attention and set Nagel on a path to silent film stardom. His breakout role came in the 1920 film, *The Fighting Chance*, opposite Swedish starlet Anna Q. Nilsson.

In 1927, Nagel starred alongside Lon Chaney, Sr., Marceline Day, Henry B. Walthall and Polly Moran in the now lost Tod Browning directed horror film, *London After Midnight*. The film is quite possibly the most famous lost film ever.

Unlike so many silent films stars of the Roaring Twenties, Conrad Nagel had little difficulty transitioning to talkies and spent the next several decades being very well received in high profile films as a character actor. He was also frequently heard on radio and made many notable appearances on television. From 1937 to 1947 he hosted and directed the radio program *Silver Theater*. From 1949 to 1952, he hosted the popular TV game show, *Celebrity Time* and from 1953 to 1954, the DuMont Television Network program *Broadway to Hollywood*. In 1961 he made a guest appearance on *Perry Mason* as art collector and murderer Nathan Claver in "The Case of the Torrid Tapestry."

More of his roles included *The Waning Sex* (1926), *The Mysterious Lady* (1928), *Dynamite* (1929) with Joel McCrea, *The Reckless Hour* (1931), *Death Flies East* (1935), *I Want a Divorce* (1940), *All That Heaven Allows* (1955), *A Stranger in My Arms* (1959), *Gunsmoke* (1962), and *Dr. Kildare* (1965).

On May 11, 1927, Nagel was among thirty-five other film industry insiders to found the Academy of Motion Picture Arts and Sciences (AMPAS); a professional honorary organization dedicated to the advancement of the arts and sciences of motion pictures. Fellow actors involved in the founding included: Mary Pickford, Douglas Fairbanks, Richard Barthelmess, Jack Holt, Milton Sills, and Harold Lloyd. He served as president of the organization from 1932 to 1933. He was also a founding member of the Screen Actors Guild (SAG).

Nagel was the host of the 3rd Academy Awards ceremony held on November 5, 1930, the 5th Academy Awards on November 18, 1932, and a co-host with Bob Hope at the 25th Academy Awards ceremony on March 19, 1953. The 21-year gap between his appearances in 1932 and 1953 is a record for an Oscar ceremonies host.

Nagel married and divorced three times. His first wife, Ruth Helms, gave birth to a daughter, Ruth Margaret, in 1920. His second wife was actress Lynn Merrick. His third wife was Michael Coulson Smith, who gave birth to a son Michael in the late 1950s.

In 1940, Nagel was given an Honorary Academy Award for his work with the Motion Picture Relief Fund. For his contributions to film, radio, and television, Conrad Nagel was given three stars on the Hollywood Walk of Fame at 1719 Vine Street (motion pictures), 1752 Vine Street (radio), and 1752 Vine Street (television).

Nagel died February 24, 1970 in New York City, at age 72, and was cremated at Garden State Crematory in North Bergen, New Jersey. Nagel's remains are interred at the Lutheran Cemetery in Warsaw, Illinois.

Laurence Naismith

Laurence Naismith was born Lawrence Johnson in Thames Ditton, Surrey, England December 14, 1908 and was an English actor.

He appeared in films such as *Carrington VC* (1954), *Richard III* (1955), *Sink the Bismarck!* (1960), *Jason and the Argonauts* (1963), and *Diamonds Are Forever* (1971). He also starred in a children's ghost film *The Amazing Mr Blunden* (1972). He was memorable as Captain Edward Smith of the RMS Titanic in *A Night to Remember* (1958) and in the ABC action drama, *The Fugitive* (1965-1967), starring David Janssen.

In 1965, Naismith played the title role of the Virginia statesman George Mason in the NBC documentary series, *Profiles in Courage*. William Bakewell played George Wythe in the episode, and Arthur Franz was cast as James Madison.

In 1965, Naismith guest-starred as barber Gilly Bright in episode 25, "The Threat" of the ABC military drama, *12 O-Clock High (TV series)*. He played Judge Fulton in the television series *The Persuaders!* (1971), with Tony Curtis and Roger Moore. He portrayed Emperor of Austria Franz Joseph in the BBC production *Fall of Eagles* (1974). Naismith played the *Prince of Verona* in the BBC Television Shakespeare version of *Romeo and Juliet*, and played the non-singing role of Merlin in the 1967 film version of the musical *Camelot*.

More roles included *Kind Hearts and Coronets* (1949), *Whispering Smith Investigates* (1952), *Mogambo* (1953), *Shoot First* (1953) with Joel McCrea, *The Black Knight* (1954) with Alan Ladd, *The Adventures of Robin Hood* (1956), *Boy on a Dolphin* (1957) again with Alan Ladd, *Village of the Damned* (1960), *Jason and the Argonauts* (1963), *Mannix* (1968), *Fall of Eagles* (1974), and *I Remember Nelson* (1982).

In 1939 Naismith married Vera Bocca of Horden, County Durham. He died June 5, 1992 in Southport, Queensland, Australia at age 83 after a short illness. His ashes were scattered into the Pacific Ocean.

Mary Nash

Mary Nash was born Mary Ryan in Troy, New York August 15, 1884 and was an American actress. She is not to be confused with another actress with the same birthname, Mary Ryan (1885-1948).

Mary and her younger sister, writer/actress Florence, were born to James H. Ryan, a lawyer, and his wife, Ellen Frances (née McNamara). The sisters adopted the surname of their stepfather, Philip F. Nash, a vaudeville booking executive, who married their mother after the death of their father. Fortuitously the name change would avoid conflict with the other actress with the same name, who achieved Broadway popularity before Nash. Nash attended the Convent of St. Anne in Montreal and trained for acting at the American Academy of Dramatic Arts.

She was a noted stage actress in New York and London, and vaudeville. After brief appearances as a dancer at the Herald Square Theatre in 1904, she made her off-Broadway debut on Christmas Day 1905 as Leonora Dunbar in James M. Barrie's *Alice-Sit-by-the-Fire*, which starred Ethel Barrymore. She remained with Barrymore for two years, appearing together in *Captain Jinks* and *The Silver Box*. Her last Broadway appearance was a production of *Uncle Tom's Cabin* in 1933, as "Cassie", which starred Otis Skinner and Fay Bainter. She appeared to acclaim on the London stage. She started her Hollywood career in 1936, appearing in eoghteen films.

She moved to Hollywood in 1934, where she was in films until 1946. According to Allmovie: "Nash was often cast as seemingly mild-mannered women who turned vicious when challenged, as witness her work in *College Scandal* (1936) and *Charlie Chan in Panama* (1940). ... Mary Nash's most sympathetic role was as the long-suffering wife of blustering capitalist J. B. Ball in *Easy Living* (1937)."

Nash may be best known for two Shirley Temple films, first as Fraulein Rottenmeier in *Heidi* (1937) and then as Miss Minchin in *The Little Princess* (1939). She played Katharine Hepburn's socialite mother in both stage and movie productions of *The Philadelphia Story* (1940). She played a supporting role in the 1936 Academy Award-winning film *Come and Get It* with Joel McCrea, again with Joel McCrea in *Wells Fargo* (1937), and had a featured role in *In the Meantime, Darling* in 1944.

In 1918, she wed French actor, writer and director Jose Ruben (1888–1969); they divorced after a brief marriage.

She died December 3, 1976 at age 92 in Los Angeles, California.

Howard Negley

Howard Jack Negley was born on April 16, 1898 in Butler, Pennsylvania. He was an actor, known for *Annie Was a Wonder* (1949), *Mr. Whitney Had a Notion* (1949), and *Kansas City Confidential* (1952).

He was a second lieutenant in the US Army during the First World War. When the war ended he was about to be shipped overseas.

More of his roles inlcuded *The Dead March* (1937), *Mama Loves Papa* (1945), *Bud Abbott Lou Costello Meet Frankenstein* (1948), *Saddle Tramp* (1950) with Joel McCrea, *The Day the Earth Stood Still* (1951), *Lost in Alaska* (1952) again with abbott and Costello, *Hopalong Cassidy* (1952-1953), *I Died a Thousand Times* (1955), *Shoot-Out at Medicine Bend* (1957), *Wichita Town* (1959) again with Joel McCrea, *Wanted: Dead or Alive* (1959-1960), and *The Tall Man* (1961).

He was married to Lydia I Powell. He died on November 7, 1983 in Kerrville, Texas at age 83.

George N. Neise

George N. Neise and Joel McCrea in *Fort Massacre*

George N. Neise was born in Chicago, Illinois February 16, 1917 and was an American character actor. He made over 120 film and television appearances between 1942 and 1978.

Neise began his career playing soldiers in war-themed films. After serving in World War II, Neise became an in-demand character actor, playing everything from Greek kings to angry bosses to airline pilots.

He may be best-remembered for the dual role as the patronizing pharmacist Ralph Dimsal and powerful Ancient Greek king, Odius in the Three Stooges feature *The Three Stooges Meet Hercules* (1962). He also appeared as Martian Ogg and an unnamed airline pilot in the trio's next feature *The Three Stooges in Orbit* (1962

His television appearances in Westerns were *The Lone Ranger, Death Valley Days, Cheyenne, Zorro, Have Gun–Will Travel, The Rifleman, Maverick*, and six episodes as the town doctor in *Wichita Town* (1959-1960) with Jpel McCrea.

In addition to his film work, Neise was featured on television drama series' like *Perry Mason* for which he made five appearances. Mostly because of the dishonest character roles he played, he was the murder victim in four of the episodes: Albert Tydings in the 1957 episode, "The Case of the Baited Hook," Wilfred Borden in the 1959 episode, "The Case of the Calendar Girl," Morley Theilman in the 1962 episode, "The Case of the Shapely Shadow," and Stacey Garnett in the 1965 episode, "The Case of the Golden Girls." He also appeared on sitcoms such as *The Dick Van Dyke Show, Green Acres, The Andy Griffith Show, Mister Ed, The Addams Family, Gilligan's Island, Hogan's Heroes, Adam-12*, and *Get Smart*.

Neise died from cancer on April 14, 1996 at age 79. His surviving family included three children from his first wife, Danielle Gentile and two children of his second ex-wife, Lorna Thayer.

Rick Nervick

Rick Nervick is an actor, known for his only two roles in *Gunsmoke* (1961), and *Cry Blood, Apache* (1970) with Joel and Jody McCrea. He was married to Carolyn Stellar.

Cathleen Nesbitt

Cathleen Nesbitt was born Kathleen Mary Nesbitt in Cheshire, England (24 November 24, 1888 and was a British actress of stage, film, and television.

Born to Thomas and Mary Catherine (née Parry) Nebsitt of Welsh and Irish descent, she was educated in Lisieux, France, and at the Queen's University of Belfast and the Sorbonne. Her younger brother, Thomas Nesbitt, Jr., acted in one film in 1925, before his death in South Africa in 1927 from an apparent heart attack.

She made her debut in London in the stage revival of Arthur Wing Pinero's *The Cabinet Minister* (1910). She acted in countless plays after that. In 1911, she joined the Irish Players, went to the United States and debuted on Broadway in *The Well of the Saints*. She also was in the cast of John Millington Synge's *The Playboy of the Western World* with the Irish Players when the whole cast was pelted with fruits and vegetables by the offended Irish American Catholic audience. She became the love of English poet Rupert Brooke in 1912, who wrote love sonnets to her. They were engaged to be married when he died during World War I.

Nesbitt returned to the US and appeared on Broadway in *Quinneys* (1915) and John Galsworthy's *Justice* (1916) as John Barrymore's leading lady in his first dramatic stage role. After five other plays there, she returned to England. For the rest of the decade she performed in London; her roles included the title role in a revival of John Webster's *The Duchess of Malfi*. Her film debut was in the silent *A Star Over Night* (1919). She then performed in *The Faithful Heart* (1922). She did not appear in a film again until 1930, when she played the role of Anne Lymes in *Canaries Sometimes Sing*, which was an early talkie. In 1932, she appeared in *The Frightened Lady*. She appeared in the 1938 film version of *Pygmalion* as "a lady" who attends the Embassy ball. In the opening credits her first name was spelled as "Kathleen", but as "Cathleen" at the end of the film.

Nesbitt's first Hollywood film was *Three Coins in the Fountain* (1954), in which she played the character role of La Principessa. This was followed that same year by *Black Widow*, in which she played Lucia Colletti. She was Cary Grant's Grandmother Janou in 1957's *An Affair to Remember* and, the same year she appeared as Señora Sandoval in *Trooper Hook* with Joel McCrea, the following year, was part of the ensemble cast of *Separate Tables*. She also appeared in *The Parent Trap* (1961), and *Promise Her Anything* (1965).

Other Broadway appearances included Aunt Alicia in the original Anita Loos adaptation of *Gigi* (1951), *Sabrina Fair* (1953), and *Anastasia* (1954). In 1956, she played Mrs. Higgins in *My Fair Lady* starring Rex Harrison. Nesbitt reprised the role in 1981, in her 90s, in a Broadway revival, opposite Harrison, who was in his 70s.

She played Agatha Morley on the TV series *The Farmer's Daughter* from 1963 to 1966, playing the mother of a Congressman (played by William Windom). She guest starred on such shows as *The United States Steel Hour*; *Wagon Train*; *Naked City*, *Dr. Kildare* and *Upstairs, Downstairs* (as Rachel Gurney's mother, Mabel, Countess of Southwold).

In 1969 she played Richard Burton's mother in the film *Staircase* and again in *Villain* two years later. She played an elderly drug addict in *French Connection II* (1975). Her next film was Hitchcock's *Family Plot* (1976), in which she played Julia Rainbird. She then appeared as the grandmother in *Julia* (1977). Her final film was *Never Never Land* (1980) as Edith Forbes.

Nesbit became the love of English poet Rupert Brooke in 1912, who wrote love sonnets to her. They were engaged to be married when he died during World War I.

In 1920 Nesbitt married World War I Military Cross-winner and barrister turned actor Cecil Ramage. They had two children. She and Ramage were separated for many years but remained legally married until her death in 1982.

Nesbitt lived for many years in the United States, but returned to the United Kingdom where she was appointed a Commander of the Order of the British Empire (CBE) in 1978. Her autobiography, *A Little Love and Good Company*, was published in 1973. After a career spanning over 80 years, one of the longest in show business history, Nesbitt died of natural causes at age 93 in London on August 2, 1982.

Ottola Nesmith

Ottola Nesmith was born in Washington, District of Columbia December 12, 1889 and was an American actress. She appeared in over 115 films and television shows between 1913 and 1969.

Some of her roles included *The Still Voice* (1913), *Wife Against Wife* (1921), *The Back Page* (1934), *The Prince and the Pauper* (1937), *Her First Romance* (1940) with Alan Ladd, *The Wolf Man* (1941), *The Great Man's Lady* (1942) with Joel McCrea, *The Return of the Vampire* (1944), *And Now Tomorrow* (1944), *Buck Privates Come Home* (1947) with Abbott and Costello, *Chicago Deadline* (1949) again with Alan Ladd, *The Greatest Show on Earth* (1952), *Witness for the Prosecution* (1957), *The Andy Griffith Show* (1962-1963), *The Wild Wild West* (1965), *Ironside* (1969), and *The Comic* (1969).

She died February 7, 1972 at age 82 in Hollywood, California.

Paul Newlan

Paul Emory Newlan in Plattsburgh, New York June 29, 1903 and was an American film and TV character actor. He was best known for his role as Captain Grey on the NBC police series *M Squad* and for his roles in films including *The Americanization of Emily* and *The Slender Thread*.

Newlan appeared in dozens of films and TV shows between 1935 and 1971. Among his other film roles were with Jopel McCrea, *Millions in the Air*, *Dragnet*, *My Favorite Spy*, *Pirates of Tripoli*, *The Captive City*, *The Great Adventures of Captain Kidd* and *The Buccaneer*, in addition to smaller roles in numerous other films including *You're Never Too Young*, *We're No Angels*, and *To Catch a Thief*.

He appeared with Joel McCrea in *Wells Fargo* (1937), *Sullivan's Travels* (1941), *The Great Moment* (1944), and *Trooper Hook* (1957).

He appeared with Abbott and Costello in *Hold That Ghost* (1941), *Lost in a Harem* (1944), *Lost in Alaska* (1951), *Abbott and Costello Meet Captain Kidd* (1952), and *Abbott and Costello Go to Mars* (1953).

On March 4, 1955, Newlan appeared as the outlaw Jules Beni in an episode of Jim Davis's syndicated western series *Stories of the Century*. Gregg Palmer playedJack Slade, the superintendent of the Central Overland California and Pikes Peak Express Company, based in Julesburg in northeastern Colorado, who sets out to capture Beni.[2]

Newlan portrayed General Prichard on the ABC war series *Twelve O'Clock High* and appearances on series such as *Gunsmoke*, *The Deputy*, *Thriller*, *Wagon Train* and most notable the 1964 *Twilight Zone* episode "The Brain Center at Whipple's". His final credit was in 1971 on Robert Young's *Marcus Welby M.D.*

Newlan died of congestive heart failure on November 23, 1973 in Studio City, California at age 70.

Alex Nicol

Alex Nicol was born Alexander Livingston Nicol Jr., in Ossining, New York January 20, 1916 and was an American actor and director. Nicol appeared in many Westerns including *The Man from Laramie* (1955). He appeared in over forty feature films as well as directing many television shows including *The Wild Wild West* (1967), *Tarzan* (1966), and *Daniel Boone* (1966). He also played many roles on Broadway.

When his movie career started he adjusted the year to 1919. "I was a little older than some of the other people under contract so I thought, 'Well, I'll cure that right now'," he later confessed. His father was the arms keeper at Sing Sing. He studied at the Feagin School of Dramatic Art before joining Maurice Evans' theatrical company, with whom he made his Broadway debut with a walk-on in Henry IV, Part 1 (1939). Later a member of The Actors Studio, Nicol would play Brick in Tennessee Williams's *Cat on a Hot Tin Roof*, under the direction of Studio co-founder Elia Kazan.

However, it was as a character actor that Nicol spent most of his career. He also directed films, and appeared frequently on television.

His acting career was interrupted by a five-year stint in the army. He served with the 101st Cavalry and attained the rank of Technical Sergeant.

Upon discharge, Nicol returned to Broadway in a revival of Clifford Odets' pro-union drama *Waiting for Lefty*(1946). Shortly thereafter, he was admitted to The Actors Studio, where he worked with Elia Kazan; this led to a role in the Studio's 1948 production of *Sundown Beach*, staged by Kazan. Nicol next appeared in *Forward the Heart*, and then as part of the original cast of Rodgers and Hammerstein's musical *South Pacific* (1949), playing one of the marines, but after a few weeks in the show he successfully auditioned to replace Ralph Meeker as Mannion in *Mister Roberts*, and was also made understudy to the play's star Henry Fonda.

While acting in *Mister Roberts*, Nicol was seen by the Universal Studios director George Sherman, who was in New York City to film *The Sleeping City* (1950). He cast Nicol as a young doctor. Nicol was given a contract by Universal, and Sherman also directed his second film, *Tomahawk* (1951), in which he played a cavalry officer with a hatred of Indians.

Small roles as a prisoner of war in *Target Unknown* (1951) and a trainee pilot in *Air Cadet* (1951) preceded Nicol's first major part, co-starring with Frank Sinatra and Shelley Winters in the musical drama *Meet Danny Wilson* (1952). In his next film he was an antagonist again, causing Loretta Young to be wrongly sent to prison in *Because of You* (1952). He played a troublesome sergeant in *Red Ball Express* (1952), directed by Budd Boetticher.

Nicol's first lead role was opposite Maureen O'Hara in *The Redhead from Wyoming* (1953) directed by Lee Sholem.

Going freelance, Nicol was directed by Daniel Mann in *About Mrs Leslie* (1953) starring Shirley Booth and Robert Ryan. Nicol returned to Universal (at a much larger salary than he had been getting as a contract player) to appear in two George Sherman films, *The Lone Hand* (1953) with Joel McCrea and *Dawn at Socorro* (1954). Nicol then made three films in England, most notably Ken Hughes' *The House Across the Lake* (1954).

Anthony Mann directed Nicol in his role as a navigator in *Strategic Air Command* (1955), and it was Mann who then gave the actor his best-remembered role as the weak psychopathic son of a patriarch rancher (Donald Crisp) that menaced Jimmy Stewart in *The Man from Laramie* (1955).

After a supporting role in Jacques Tourneur's *Great Day in the Morning* (1956) Nicol believed his Hollywood career was not progressing. In 1956 he returned to Broadway to replace Ben Gazzara in the lead role of Brick, in *Cat on a Hot Tin Roof*. When the Broadway run ended Nicol starred in the tour.

Nicol starred with Shelley Winters in the play *Saturday Night Kid* (1958). He then returned to Hollywood where he made his first film as a director, *The Screaming Skull* (1958), in which he also acted.

Nicol traveled to Italy when director Martin Ritt gave him a role in *Five Branded Women* (1959). While there he was offered parts in other movies. He and his family remained in Europe for two years.

Returning to the United States in 1961, he played Paul Anka's father in the thriller *Look in Any Window* (1961), then produced and directed a war film in Rome, *Then There Were Three* (1961), in which he co-starred with Frank Latimore. Subsequent acting roles included the *The Twilight Zone* episode "Young Man's Fancy" in 1962; two westerns, *The Savage Guns* (1962) and *Gunfighters of the Casa Grande* (1964); and Roger Corman's *Bloody Mama* (1969), based on the life of Ma Barker.

Nicol later worked as a director in television and did episodes of *Daniel Boone, Wild Wild West*, and many episodes for*Tarzan* starring Ron Ely. The last film in which he acted was *A*P*E* (1976), an independent movie made by a friend of the actor. He retired in the late 1980s and died of natural causes in Montecito, California July 29, 2001 at age 85

Alex Nicol was survived by his wife, Jean and his three children, Lisa Nicol, Alexander Nicol III, and Eric Nicol.

Jane Nigh

Bonnie Lenora "Jane" Nigh in Hollywood, California February 25, 1925 and was an American actress. She was discovered in 1944 by Arthur Wenzler while working in a defense plant. She later signed a contract with Fox Studios. She appeared in more than forty films and television shows, including *State Fair* (1945), *Give My Regards to Broadway* (1948, as June Nigh) and *Sitting Pretty* (1948).

More of her roles included *Something for the Boys* (1944), *House of Dracula* (1945), *The Shocking Miss Pilgrim* (1947), *Captain Carey, U.S.A.* (1950) with Alan Ladd, *Big Town* (1952-1954), *Tales of Wells Fargo* (1957), *Wichita Town* (1960) with Joel McCrea, *Shotgun Slade* (1959-1961), and *Dennis the Menace* (1961).

She married and divorced three times, and had four children, two prematurely, three girls and a boy; the first, a girl, died very soon after birth in 1952. She died on October 5, 1993 of a stroke at the age of 68.

She died October 5, 1993 at age 68 in Kern County, California.

Denny Niles

Denny Niles was born Richard Dennison Niles on August 12, 1933 in Toluca Lake, California. He was an actor, known for *Mister Roberts* (1955), *Men Into Space* (1959), and *Route 66* (1960). He graduated from USC in 1956. He was Golden Gloves boxing champion and, during two-year stint in the army, served as boxing instructor at Ft. Lewis Army Base, Washington.

More of his roles included *The Square Jungle* (1955), *Wichita Town* (1959) with Joel McCrea, *M Squad* (1959), and *The Rebel* (1960).

He was married to Lila Niles. He died on July 11, 2011 in Los Angeles, California at age 77.

Anna Q. Nilsson

Anna Quirentia Nilsson was born in Ystad, Skåne County, Sweden March 30, 1888 and was a Swedish born American actress who achieved success in American silent movies.

Her middle name, "Quirentia " is derived from her date of birth, March 30 Saint Quirinius' Day. When she was 8 years old her father got a job at the local sugar factory in Hasslarp, a small community outside Helsingborg in Sweden where she spent most of her school years. She did very well in school, graduating with highest marks. Due to her good grades she was hired as a sales clerk in Halmstad on the Swedish west coast, unusual for a young woman from a worker's family at the time. But she had set her mind on going to America.

In 1905, she immigrated to the United States through Ellis Island. In the new country, the Swedish teenager started working as a nursemaid and learned English quickly. Soon she started working as a model. In 1907, she was named "Most beautiful woman in America". Penrhyn Stanlaws (1877–1957), one of the most successful and sought after cover artists of his day, picked Anna Q. Nilsson to become one of his models.

Nilsson's modeling led her to getting a role in Kalem's 1911 film *Molly Pitcher*. Another beauty who began appearing in Kalem films at the same time was Alice Joyce. Films of special note for Anna were *Regeneration* (1915) *Seven Keys to Baldpate* (1917), *Soldiers of Fortune* (1919), *The Toll Gate* and *The Luck of the Irish* (both 1920), and *The Lotus Eater* (1921).

She stayed at the Kalem studio for several years, ranked behind their top star Alice Joyce. In the 1920s, she freelanced successfully for Paramount, First National and many other studios and reached a peak of popularity just before the advent of talkies, despite a serious horse-riding accident which kept her from filming for almost two years. In 1923, she portrayed "Cherry Malotte" in the second movie based upon Rex Beach's *The Spoilers*, a role that would be played in later versions by Betty Compson (1930), Marlene Dietrich (1942), and Anne Baxter (1955).

In 1921, she returned to Sweden to film *Värmlänningarna*, her only Swedish movie. In 1926, she was named Hollywood's most popular woman. She welcomed royalty when the Swedish Crown Prince Gustav Adolf (later King Gustaf VI Adolf) and his wife Louise Mountbatten visited Hollywood. In 1928, she struck a record of fan mail, 30,000 letters a month, and that year Joseph P. Kennedy brought her to his newly formed film company RKO Radio Pictures. The following year, as she was horse riding, she fell off the horse, was thrown against a stone wall and broke her hip. After a year of hard training, she was on her feet again.

In 1928, Anna Nilsson made her last film of the silent era, *Blockade*. With the introduction of sound films, Nilsson's career went into a sharp decline, although she continued to play small, often uncredited parts in films into the 1950s. Between 1930 and 1950, she participated in thirty-nine sound films, in smaller roles. She appeared in *The World Changes* (1933), *Wanderer of the Wasteland* (1935), *They Died with Their Boots On* (1941), *The Great Man's Lady* (1942) with Joel McCrea, *The Farmer's Daughter* (1947), *Adam's Rib* (1949), *The Unknown Man* (1951), and *Seven Brides for Seven Brothers* (1954).

Her best known performance in a sound film is arguably her turn as "herself", referred to as one of Swanson's "waxworks" in *Sunset Boulevard* (1950), where she has one small line.

Anna was married to actor Guy Coombs (1916-1916) and to Norwegian-American shoe merchant John Marshall Gunnerson (1923–1925). Nilsson has a star on the Hollywood Walk of Fame at 6150 Hollywood Boulevard for her contribution to motion pictures. She was the first Swedish-born actress to receive such an honor. She died in Sun City, California, on February 11, 1974, of heart failure.

David Niven

David Niven and Joel McCrea in *Three Blind Mice*

James David Graham Niven was born in London, England March 1, 1910 and was an English actor and novelist who was popular in Europe and in the United States. He may be best known for his roles as Squadron Leader Peter Carter in *A Matter of Life and Death*, as Phileas Fogg in *Around the World in 80 Days* and as Sir Charles Lytton, a.k.a. "the Phantom", in *The Pink Panther*. He was awarded the Academy Award for Best Actor for his performance in *Separate Tables* (1958).

Niven attended Heatherdown Preparatory School and Stowe before gaining a place at the Royal Military College, Sandhurst. After Sandhurst he was gazetted a lieutenant in the Highland Light Infantry. Having developed an interest in acting, he left the Highland Light Infantry, travelled to Hollywood and had several minor roles in film. He first appeared as an extra in the British film *There Goes the Bride* (1932). From there, he hired an agent and had several small parts in films from 1933 to 1935, including a non-speaking part in MGM's *Mutiny on the Bounty*. This brought him to wider attention within the film industry and he was spotted by Samuel Goldwyn. Upon the outbreak of the Second World War, Niven returned to Britain and rejoined the army, being re-commissioned as a lieutenant.

Niven resumed his acting career after his demobilisation, and was voted the second most popular British actor in the 1945 Popularity Poll of British film stars. He appeared in *A Matter of Life and Death* (1946), *The Bishop's Wife* (1947), and *Enchantment* (1948), all of which received critical acclaim. Niven later appeared in *The Elusive Pimpernel* (1950), *The Toast of New Orleans* (1950), *Happy Go Lovely* (1951), *Happy Ever After* (1954) and *Carrington V.C.* (1955) before scoring a big success as Phileas Fogg in Michael Todd's production of *Around the World in 80 Days*. Niven appeared in nearly a hundred films, and many shows for TV. He also began writing books, with considerable commercial success. In 1982 he appeared in Blake Edwards' final "Pink Panther" films *Trail of the Pink Panther* and *Curse of the Pink Panther*, reprising his role as Sir Charles Lytton.

James David Graham Niven was born to William Edward Graham Niven (1878–1915) and his wife, Henrietta Julia (née Degacher) Niven. He was named David for his birth on St. David's Day (1 March).

Henrietta was of French and British ancestry. She was born in Wales, the daughter of army officer William Degacher (1841–1879) by his marriage to Julia Caroline Smith, the daughter of Lieutenant General James Webber Smith. Niven's grandfather William Degacher was killed in the Battle of Isandlwana (1879), during the Zulu War. Born William Hitchcock, he and his brother Henry had followed the lead of their father, Walter Henry Hitchcock, in assuming their mother's maiden name of Degacher in 1874.

William Niven, David's father, was of Scottish descent; his paternal grandfather, David Graham Niven, (1811–1884) was from St. Martin's, a village in Perthshire. William served in the Berkshire Yeomanry in the First World War and was killed during the Gallipoli Campaign on August 21, 1915. He was buried in Green Hill Cemetery, Turkey in the Special Memorial Section in Plot F. 10.

Niven's mother remarried, to Sir Thomas Comyn-Platt, in London in 1917. Graham Lord, in *Niv: The Authorised Biography of David Niven*, suggested that Comyn-Platt and Mrs. Niven had been having an affair for some time before her husband's death, and that Sir Thomas may well have been David Niven's biological father, a supposition which has some support from her children. A reviewer of Lord's book stated that Lord's photographic evidence showing a strong physical resemblance between Niven and Comyn-Platt "would appear to confirm these theories, though photographs can often be misleading."

English private schools at the time of Niven's boyhood were noted for their strict and sometimes brutal discipline. Niven suffered many instances of corporal punishment owing to his inclination for pranks, which finally led to his expulsion from Heatherdown Preparatory School at the age of 10.   This ended his chances for Eton College, a significant blow to his family. After failing to pass the naval entrance exam because of his difficulty with math, Niven attended Stowe School, a newly created public school led by headmaster J.F. Roxburgh, who was unlike any of Niven's previous headmasters. Thoughtful and kind, he addressed the boys by their first name, allowed them bicycles and encouraged and nurtured their personal interests. Niven later wrote, "How he did this, I shall never know, but he made every single boy at that school feel that what he said and what he did were of real importance to the headmaster". He attended the Royal Military College at Sandhurst, graduating in 1930 with a commission as a second lieutenant in the regular Army.

He did well at Sandhurst, which gave him the "officer and gentleman" bearing that was to be his trademark. He requested assignment to the Argyll and Sutherland Highlanders or the Black Watch, then jokingly wrote on the form, as his third choice, "anything but the Highland Light Infantry" (because the HLI wore tartan trews rather than kilts). He was assigned to the HLI, and his comment was known in the regiment. Thus Niven did not enjoy his time in the army. He served with the HLI for two years in Malta and then for a few months in Dover. In Malta he became friends with Roy Urquhart, future commander of the British 1st Airborne Division.

Niven grew tired of the peacetime army. Though promoted to lieutenant on January 1, 1933, he saw no opportunity for further advancement. His ultimate decision to resign came after a lengthy lecture on machine guns, which was interfering with his plans for dinner with a particularly attractive young lady. At the end of the lecture, the speaker (a major general) asked if there were any questions. Showing the typical rebelliousness of his early years, Niven asked, "Could you tell me the time, sir? I have to catch a train".

After being placed under close-arrest for this act of insubordination, Niven finished a bottle of whisky with the officer who was guarding him: Rhoddy Rose (later Colonel R.L.C. Rose, DSO, MC). With Rose's assistance, Niven was allowed to escape from a first-floor window. He then headed for America. While crossing the Atlantic, Niven resigned his commission by telegram on September 6, 1933. Niven then moved to New York City, where he began an unsuccessful career in whisky sales, after which he had a stint in horse rodeo promotion in Atlantic City. After detours to Bermuda and Cuba, he arrived in Hollywood in 1934.

When Niven presented himself at Central Casting, he learned that he needed a work permit to reside and work in the U.S. This meant that Niven had to leave the US, so he went to Mexico, where he worked as a "gun-man", cleaning and polishing the rifles of visiting American hunters. He received his Resident Alien Visa from the

American consulate when his birth certificate arrived from England. He returned to the United States and was accepted by Central Casting as "Anglo-Saxon Type No. 2008".

His role in *Mutiny on the Bounty* brought him to the attention of independent film producer Samuel Goldwyn, who signed him to a contract and established his career. Niven appeared in nineteen films in the next four years. He had supporting roles in several major films—*Rose-Marie* (1936), *Dodsworth* (1936), *The Charge of the Light Brigade* (1936), *The Prisoner of Zenda* (1937)—and leading roles in *The Dawn Patrol* (1938), *Three Blind Mice* (1938) with Joel McCrea and *Wuthering Heights* (1939), playing opposite such stars as Errol Flynn, Loretta Young and Laurence Olivier. In 1939 he co-starred with Ginger Rogers in the RKO comedy *Bachelor Mother*, and starred as the eponymous gentleman safe-cracker in *Raffles*.

He also appeared with Joel McCrea in Barbary *Coast* (1935) and *Splendor* (1935).

Niven joined what became known as the Hollywood Raj, a group of British actors in Hollywood which included Rex Harrison, Boris Karloff, Stan Laurel, Basil Rathbone, Ronald Colman, Leslie Howard and C. Aubrey Smith. According to his autobiography, he and Errol Flynn were firm friends and had decided to rent Rosalind Russell's house at 601 North Linden Drive as a bachelor pad. Russell later named the house "Cirrhosis-by-the-Sea".

After Britain declared war on Germany in 1939, Niven returned home and rejoined the Army. He was alone among British stars in Hollywood in doing so; the British Embassy advised most actors to stay. Niven was re-commissioned as a lieutenant in the Rifle Brigade on February 25, 1940, and was assigned to a motor training battalion. He wanted something more exciting however, and transferred into the Commandos. He was assigned to a training base at Inverailort House in the Western Highlands. Niven later claimed credit for bringing future Major General Sir Robert Laycock to the Commandos. Niven commanded "A" Squadron GHQ Liaison Regiment, better known as "Phantom". He worked with the Army Film Unit. He acted in two films made during the war, *The First of the Few* (1942) and *The Way Ahead* (1944). Both were made with a view to winning support for the British war effort, especially in the U.S. Niven's Film Unit work included a small part in the deception operation that used minor actor M.E. Clifton James to impersonate Field Marshal Montgomery. During his work with the Film Unit, Peter Ustinov, though one of the script-writers, had to pose as Niven's batman. (Ustinov also acted in *The Way Ahead*.) Niven explained in his autobiography that there was no military way that he, as a lieutenant-colonel, and Ustinov, who was only a private, could associate, other than as an officer and his subordinate, hence their strange "act". Ustinov later appeared with Niven in *Death on the Nile* (1978).

Niven took part in the Invasion of Normandy, although he was sent to France several days after D-Day. He served in the "Phantom Signals Unit", which located and reported enemy positions, and kept rear commanders informed on changing battle lines. Niven was posted at one time to Chilham in Kent. He remained close-mouthed about the war, despite public interest in celebrities in combat and a reputation for storytelling. He once said:
"I will, however, tell you just one thing about the war, my first story and my last. I was asked by some American friends to search out the grave of their son near Bastogne. I found it where they told me I would, but it was among 27,000 others, and I told myself that here, Niven, were 27,000 reasons why you should keep your mouth shut after the war".

He had particular scorn for those newspaper columnists covering the war who typed out self-glorifying and excessively florid prose about their meagre wartime experiences. Niven stated, "Anyone who says a bullet sings past, hums past, flies, pings, or whines past, has never heard one—they go *crack*!" He gave a few details of his war experience in his autobiography, *The Moon's a Balloon*: his private conversations with Winston Churchill, the bombing of London, and what it was like entering Germany with the occupation forces. Niven first met Churchill at a dinner party in February 1940. Churchill singled him out from the crowd and stated, "Young man, you did a fine thing to give up your film career to fight for your country. Mark you, had you not done so – it would have been despicable."

A few stories have surfaced. About to lead his men into action, Niven eased their nervousness by telling them, "Look, you chaps only have to do this once. But I'll have to do it all over again in Hollywood with Errol Flynn!" Asked by suspicious American sentries during the Battle of the Bulge who had won the World Series in 1943, he answered "Haven't the foggiest idea ... but I did co-star with Ginger Rogers in *Bachelor Mother*!"

Niven ended the war as a lieutenant-colonel. On his return to Hollywood after the war, he received the Legion of Merit, an American military decoration. Presented by Eisenhower himself, it honored Niven's work in setting up the BBC Allied Expeditionary Forces Programme, a radio news and entertainment station for the Allied forces.

Niven resumed his career in 1946, now only in starring roles. His films *A Matter of Life and Death* (1946), *The Bishop's Wife* (1947) with Cary Grant, and *Enchantment* (1948) are all highly regarded. In 1950 he starred in *The Elusive Pimpernel*, which was made in Britain and which was to be distributed by Samuel Goldwyn. Goldwyn pulled out, and the film did not appear in the US for three years. Niven had a long, complex relationship with

Goldwyn, who gave him his first start. But the dispute over *The Elusive Pimpernel* and Niven's demands for more money led to a long estrangement between the two in the 1950s.

During this period Niven was largely barred from the Hollywood studios. Between 1951 and 1956 he made eleven films, two of which were MGM productions and the rest were low-budget British or independent productions. However, Niven won a Golden Globe Award for his work in *The Moon Is Blue* (1953), produced and directed by Otto Preminger. In 1955 Cornel Lucas photographed Niven while filming at the Rank Film Studio in Denham, Buckinghamshire. A limited edition of British postage stamps was produced using one of Lucas's images taken during this portrait sitting.

Niven worked in television. He appeared several times on various short-drama shows, and was one of the "four stars" of the dramatic anthology series *Four Star Playhouse*, appearing in thrity-three episodes. The show was produced by Four Star Television, which was co-owned and founded by Niven, Dick Powell and Charles Boyer. The show ended in 1955, but Four Star TV became a highly successful TV production company.

Niven enjoyed success in 1956, when he starred as Phileas Fogg in producer Michael Todd's *Around the World in 80 Days*. He won the 1958 Academy Award for Best Actor for his role as Major Pollock in *Separate Tables*, his only nomination for an Oscar. Appearing on-screen for only sixteen minutes in the film, this remains the briefest performance ever to win a Best Actor Oscar. He was also a co-host of the 30th, 31st, and 46th Academy Awards ceremonies. After Niven had won the Academy Award, Goldwyn called with an invitation to his home. In Goldwyn's drawing room, Niven noticed a picture of himself in uniform which he had sent to Goldwyn from Britain during the Second World War. In happier times with Goldwyn, he had observed this same picture sitting on Goldwyn's piano. Now years later, the picture was still in exactly the same spot. As he was looking at the picture, Goldwyn's wife Frances said "Sam never took it down."

With an Academy Award to his credit, Niven's career continued to thrive. In 1959 he became the host of his own TV drama series, *The David Niven Show*, which ran for thirteen episodes that summer. He subsequently appeared in another thirty films, including *The Guns of Navarone* (1961) *The Pink Panther* (1963), *Murder by Death* (1976), *Death on the Nile* (1978) and *The Sea Wolves* (1980).

In 1964 he and Boyer appeared in the Four Star series *The Rogues*. Niven played Alexander 'Alec' Fleming, one of a family of retired con-artists who now fleece villains in the interests of justice. This was his only recurring role on television. *The Rogues* ran for only one season, but won a Golden Globe award. In 1965 he starred in *Where the Spies Are*. In 1967 he appeared as one of seven incarnations of 007 in the James Bond spoof *Casino Royale*. Niven had been Bond creator Ian Fleming's first choice to play Bond in *Dr. No*. *Casino Royale* co-producer Charles K. Feldman said later that Fleming had written the book with Niven in mind, and therefore had sent a copy to Niven. Niven was the only James Bond actor mentioned by name in the text of Fleming's novels. In *On Her Majesty's Secret Service*, Bond visits an exclusive ski resort in Switzerland where he is told that David Niven is a frequent visitor and in *You Only Live Twice*, Niven is referred to as the only real gentleman in Hollywood.

While Niven was co-hosting the 46th Annual Oscars ceremony, a naked man appeared behind him, "streaking" across the stage. Niven responded "Isn't it fascinating to think that probably the only laugh that man will ever get in his life is by stripping off and showing his shortcomings?"[

In 1974 he hosted *David Niven's World* for London Weekend Television, which profiled contemporary adventurers such as hang gliders, motorcyclists and mountain climbers: it ran for 21 episodes. In 1975 he narrated *The Remarkable Rocket*, a short animation based on a story by Oscar Wilde. In 1979 he appeared in *Escape to Athena*, which was produced by his son David, Jr. In July 1982, Blake Edwards brought Niven back for cameo appearances in two final "Pink Panther" films (*Trail of the Pink Panther* and *Curse of the Pink Panther*), reprising his role as Sir Charles Lytton. By this time, Niven was having serious health problems. When the raw footage was reviewed, his voice was inaudible, and his lines had to be dubbed by Rich Little. Niven only learned of it from a newspaper report. This was his last film appearance.

Niven wrote four books. The first, *Round the Rugged Rocks*, (published simultaneously in the US under the title "Once Over Lightly") was a novel that appeared in 1951 and was forgotten almost at once. In 1971 he published his autobiography, *The Moon's a Balloon*, which was well received, selling over five million copies. He followed this with *Bring On the Empty Horses* in 1975, a collection of entertaining reminiscences from Hollywood's "Golden Age" in the 1930s and 1940s. It now appears that Niven recounted many incidents from a first-person perspective that actually happened to other people, especially Cary Grant, which he borrowed and embroidered. In 1981 Niven published a second and much more successful novel, *Go Slowly, Come Back Quickly*, which was set during and after the Second World War, and which drew on his experiences during the war and in Hollywood. He was working on a third novel at the time of his death.

After a whirlwind two-week romance in 1940, Niven married Primula Susan Rollo (February 18, 1918, London – May 21, 1946), the aristocratic daughter of British barrister William Hereward Charles Rollo, who was a grandson of the 10th Lord Rollo, and Lady Kathleen Nina Hill, daughter of the 6th Marquess of Downshire. The couple had two sons: David, Jr. and Jamie. Primula, whom he called Primmie, died at age 28, only six weeks after moving to the U.S., of a fractured skull and brain lacerations from an accidental fall in the Beverly Hills, California home of Tyrone Power. While playing "sardines", she walked through a door believing it led to a closet. Instead, it led to a stone staircase to the basement.

Niven recalled this as the darkest period of his life, years afterwards thanking his friends for their patience and forbearance during this time. He claimed to have been so grief-stricken that he thought for a while that he had gone mad. Following a suicide attempt involving a handgun which failed to go off, he eventually rallied and returned to filmmaking.

In 1948 Niven met Hjördis Paulina Tersmeden (née Genberg, 1919–1997), a divorced Swedish fashion model. He recounted their meeting:
"I had never seen anything so beautiful in my life—tall, slim, auburn hair, up-tilted nose, lovely mouth and the most enormous grey eyes I had ever seen. It really happened the way it does when written by the worst lady novelists ... I goggled. I had difficulty swallowing and had champagne in my knees."

They married six weeks later. However, Niven's second marriage was as tumultuous as his first marriage was content. In an unsuccessful effort to bring harmony to the marriage, he and his wife adopted two girls, Kristina and Fiona. Kristina later told biographer Graham Lord that she was convinced that she was Niven's secret child by another fashion model, Mona Gunnarson. All four of Niven's children, as well as many of his friends, told Lord that Hjördis, unable to achieve an acting career, had affairs with other men and became an alcoholic. In October 1951, while pheasant shooting with friends in New England, Hjördis was shot in the face, neck and chest by a member of the hunting party. Local doctors wished to operate immediately to remove the birdshot. However, another doctor advised Niven to allow the swelling of the face to go down. In this way, his wife avoided disfigurement.

While she was convalescing in the Blackstone Hotel in New York, Niven and Hjördis were next-door neighbors with Audrey Hepburn, who made her début on Broadway that season. In 1960, while filming *Please Don't Eat the Daisies* with Doris Day, Niven and Hjördis separated for a few weeks, but later reconciled. Hjördis stopped drinking alcohol for a time after Niven's death in 1983, but returned to it before her own death of a stroke in 1997 at age 78. Niven's friend Billie More noted: "This is not kind, but when Hjördis died I can't think of a single soul who was sorry".

Throughout the 1970s, Niven spent much of his time at his home in Chateau d'Oex in Switzerland, near the ski resort of Gstaad. He had a close group of friends there including actor Roger Moore, writer William F. Buckley, Jr. and former US Ambassador to France Evan G. Galbraith.

In 1980, Niven began experiencing fatigue, muscle weakness and a warble in his voice. His 1981 interviews on the talk shows of Michael Parkinson and Merv Griffin alarmed family and friends; viewers wondered if Niven had either been drinking or suffered a stroke. He blamed his slightly slurred voice on the shooting schedule on the film he had been making, *Better Late Than Never*. He was diagnosed with amyotrophic lateral sclerosis (ALS, or "Lou Gehrig's disease" in the US and Motor Neurone Disease (MND) in the UK) later that year. His final appearance in Hollywood was hosting the 1981 American Film Institute tribute to Fred Astaire.

In February 1983, using a false name to avoid publicity, Niven was hospitalised for ten days, ostensibly for a digestive problem. Afterwards, he returned to his chalet at Chateau d'Oex. His condition continued to decline, but he refused to return to the hospital, and his family supported his decision. He died at his chalet at Chateau d'Oex from ALS on July 29, 1983 at age 73, the same day as his *The Prisoner of Zenda* and *A Matter of Life and Death* co-star Raymond Massey. He was survived by his four children and his second wife. Niven is buried in Chateau D'Oex Cemetery in Chateau d'Oex, Switzerland.

A Thanksgiving service for Niven was held at St Martin-in-the-Fields, London, on October 27, 1983. The congregation of 1,200 included Prince Michael of Kent, Margaret, Duchess of Argyll, Sir John Mills, Sir Richard Attenborough, Trevor Howard, Sir David Frost, Joanna Lumley, Douglas Fairbanks, Jr. and Lord Olivier.

Biographer Graham Lord wrote that "the biggest wreath, worthy of a Mafia Godfather's funeral, was delivered from the porters at London's Heathrow Airport, along with a card that read: 'To the finest gentleman who ever walked through these halls. He made a porter feel like a king'." In 1985 Niven was included in a series of British postage stamps, along with Sir Alfred Hitchcock, Sir Charlie Chaplin, Peter Sellers and Vivien Leigh, to commemorate "British Film Year".

Marian Nixon

Marian Nixon and Joel McCrea in *Chance at Heaven*

Marian Nixon was born Marian Nissinen in Superior, Wisconsin October 20, 1904 and was an American film actress.

Nixon began her career as a teen working as a chorus dancer on the vaudeville circuit. She began appearing in bit part in films in 1922 and landed her first substantial role in the 1923 film *Cupid's Fireman*, opposite Buck Jones. The following year, she was named a WAMPAS Baby Star. Nixon continued to work steadily throughout the mid to late 1920s appearing in *Riders of the Purple Sage* (1925), *Hands Up!* (1926), and *The Chinese Parrot* (1927). In 1929, she made her talkie debut as the lead in *Geraldine*. Later that same year, Nixon appeared opposite Al Jolson in *Say It with Songs* followed by *General Crack* in 1930.

In 1932, she starred as Rebecca in the film adaption of *Rebecca of Sunnybrook Farm* with Ralph Bellamy. Following the release of *Rebecca*, Nixon co-starred in *Winner Take All* with James Cagney. The next year she had a supporting role in John Ford's *Pilgrimage*.

More of her roles included *Silks and Saddles* (1929), *General Crack* (1930), *Winner Take All* (1932), and *Chance at Heaven* (1933) with Joel McCrea.

In 1934, Nixon attempted to change her wholesome image with a role in the comedy *We're Rich Again*. The film wasn't a success and after appearing in eight more films, Nixon retired from acting in 1936. She made her last film, *Captain Calamity* at the age of 32.

On August 11, 1929, Nixon married Chicago department store heir, Edward Hillman, Jr., at the home of his parents. The couple divorced in 1933. The following year, she married her *We're Rich Again* director, William A. Seiter. The marriage lasted until Seiter's death in 1964. They had a son Christopher Seiter (1934-2003). In 1974, she married actor/producer Ben Lyon. After Lyon's death in 1979, Nixon never remarried.

Nixon died of complications following open heart surgery on February 13, 1983 at age 78 and is buried at Forest Lawn Memorial Park, Glendale, California. For her contribution to the motion picture industry, Marian Nixon has a star on the Hollywood Walk of Fame at 1724 Vine Street in Los Angeles, California. Her grandsons are the screenwriters Ted Griffin and Nicholas Griffin.

Jeanette Nolan

Jeanette Nolan was born in Los Angeles, California, December 30, 1911, and was an American radio, film and television actress who was nominated for four Emmy Awards. Nolan was a graduate of Abraham Lincoln High School in Los Angeles.

Nolan began her acting career at the Pasadena Playhouse in Pasadena, California, and, while a student at Los Angeles City College, made her radio debut in 1932 in *Omar Khayyam*, the first transcontinental broadcast from station KHJ, and continued acting until the 1990s. She made her film debut as Lady Macbeth in Orson Welles's 1948 film *Macbeth*, based on Shakespeare's play of the same name. Despite the fact that she and the film received withering reviews at the time, Nolan's film career flourished in largely supporting roles.

She appeared with Joel McCrea in *Saddle Tramp* (1950).

Viewers of film noir may know her best as the corrupt wife of a dead (and equally corrupt) police officer in Fritz Lang's *The Big Heat* (1953).

She appeared in Audie Murphy's *The Guns of Fort Petticoat* (1957) as the Bible toting Cora Melavan who gets her priorities in the correct order by the end of the movie.

Nolan made over three hundred television appearances, including Brian Keith's first series, *Crusader*, in the role of Dr. Marion in "The Healer" (1956). She also appeared on Rod Cameron's syndicated series, *State Trooper*. She also appeared in *The Deep Six* (1958) with Alan Ladd. From 1959 to 1960, she was cast as Annette Deveraux, part-owner of the hotel in the CBS western series *Hotel de Paree*. She appeared in other western films, most notably *The Wild Women of Chastity Gulch* (1982).

She gave an over-the-top performance as a crazed old woman in the "Parasite Mansion" episode of *Thriller*. She appeared in the April 27, 1962, episode "A Book of Faces" on ABC's crime drama *Target: The Corruptors!* She appeared three times on *Wagon Train*, the western series in which her husband John McIntire starred as wagon master Chris Hale from 1961 to 1965. She guest starred three times in 1963 to 1964 on NBC's *Dr. Kildare* and in a 1964 episode of Richard Crenna's short-lived *Slattery's People* political drama on CBS.

Nolan played the role of witches in two of Rod Serling's anthology television series; in *The Twilight Zone* (1963) episode "Jess-Belle" with Anne Francis, and the *Night Gallery* (1971) episode "Since Aunt Ada Came to Stay" with James Farentino and Michele Lee.

On November 4, 1965, she appeared as the treacherous Ma Burns in "The Golden Trail" episode of NBC's *Laredo*, having portrayed a supposedly refined woman trying to hijack a presumed gold shipment, which in actuality is thirty-six bottles of Tennessee whiskey. *Laredo* was a spinoff of the *The Virginian*, whose cast Nolan joined in 1967, along with her husband John McIntire.

She appeared regularly in several radio series: *Young Dr. Malone*, 1939–40; *Cavalcade of America*, 1940–41; Nicolette Moore in *One Man's Family*, 1947–50; and *The Great Gildersleeve*, 1949-52. She appeared episodically in many more.

In 1974, she starred briefly with Dack Rambo in CBS's *Dirty Sally*, a spinoff of the *Gunsmoke* (1955-1975) western series where she had played a recurring guest role for eight episodes. She also played the titular role in the award-winning short film *Peege* (1972) because of her *Gunsmoke* connection. In all, Nolan appeared as a guest star in television's *Gunsmoke* more than any other female.

She guest starred in three of David Janssen's television series *Richard Diamond, Private Detective* (1975-1959), *The Fugitive* (1966), and *Harry O* (1975).

Nolan married actor John McIntire in 1935. They remained married for fifty-six years until his death in 1991. The couple guest starred together in an episode of *Charlie's Angels* in 1979, *The Incredible Hulk* in 1980, *Quincy, M.E.* in 1983, and *Night Court* in 1985, playing Dan Fielding's hick parents. She was the mother of two children, one of whom was the actor Tim McIntire, who was best-known for his turn as the legendary DJ Alan Freed in the 1978 film *American Hot Wax*.

Her final film appearance was in Robert Redford's *The Horse Whisperer* (1998) as Robert Redford's mother.

She died on June 5, 1998, in Los Angeles, California following a stroke at the age of 86. Her interment was in Eureka, Montana's Tobacco Valley Cemetery.

Lloyd Nolan

Lloyd Nolan and Joel McCrea in *Internes Can't Take Money*

Lloyd Benedict Nolan was born in San Francisco, California, August 11, 1902, and was an American film and television actor. Nolan was the son of Margaret and James Nolan, who was a shoe manufacturer. He began his career on stage and was subsequently lured to Hollywood, where he played mainly doctors, detectives, and police officers in many movie roles.

Although Nolan's acting was often praised by critics, he was, for the most part, relegated to B pictures. Despite this, Nolan costarred with a number of well-known actresses, among them Mae West, Dorothy McGuire, and former Metropolitan Opera soprano, Gladys Swarthout.

Under contract to Paramount and 20th Century Fox studios, he assayed starring roles in the late 1930s and early-to-mid 1940s and appeared as the title character in the Michael Shayne detective series of films.

In 1937 he appeared with Joel McCrea in *Internes Can't Take Money* and *Wells Fargo.*

He appeared in Raymond Chandler's novel *The High Window* was adapted from a Philip Marlowe adventure for the seventh film in the Michael Shayne series, *Time to Kill* (1942).

The majority of Nolan's films comprised light entertainment with an emphasis on action. His most famous films include: *Atlantic Adventure* (1935), costarring Nancy Carroll, *Bataan* (1943), and *A Tree Grows in Brooklyn* (1945), with Dorothy McGuire and James Dunn. He also gave a strong performance in the 1957 film *Peyton Place* with Lana Turner.

Nolan subsequently contributed many solid and key character parts in numerous other films. One of these films, *The House on 92nd Street*, was a startling revelation to audiences in 1945. It was a conflation of several true incidents of attempted sabotage by the Nazi regime, incidents which the FBI was able to thwart during World War II, and many scenes were filmed on location in New York City, an unusual occurrence at the time. Nolan portrayed FBI agent Briggs, and actual FBI employees interacted with Nolan throughout the film. He reprised the role in a subsequent 1948 movie, *The Street with No Name.*

He appeared with Alan Ladd in *Wild Harvest* (1947) and *Santiago* (1956), and in *Bad Boy* (1949) as Marshall Brown who takes in Audie Murphy's Danny Lester character at the Variety Club Ranch and subsequently, changes his life.

Later in his career, he returned to the stage and appeared on television to great acclaim in *The Caine Mutiny Court Martial*, for which he received a 1955 Emmy award for portraying Captain Queeg, the role made famous by Humphrey Bogart.

Nolan also starred in a classic 1964 episode of *The Outer Limits,* "Soldier", written by Harlan Ellison. In 1967, he and Strother Martin guest starred in the episode "A Mighty Hunter Before the Lord" of NBC's *The Road West* series starring Barry Sullivan.

Nolan co-starred in all eighty-six episodes in the pioneering NBC series *Julia* (1968-1971), with Diahann Carroll, who became the first African-American to star in her own television series outside of the role of a domestic worker.

He founded the Jay Nolan Autistic Center (now known as Jay Nolan Community Services) in honor of his son Jay who had autism and was chairman of the annual Save Autistic Children Telethon.

He continued working in films and television and his last role in *Hannah and Her Sisters* (1986) was released six months after his death.

Nolan died September 27, 1985, of lung cancer in Los Angeles at the age of 83.

Edgar Norton

Edgar Norton was born in London, England August 11, 1868. He was active on both stage and screen, his theater performances were on both the London and Broadway stages, and his film career spanned both the silent and "talkie" eras in Hollywood.

During his thirty year film career, he would appear in over ninety films. Many consider his most memorable role to be that of Poole, the butler to Dr. Jekyll in the 1931 classic, *Dr. Jekyll and Mr. Hyde.*

More of his roles included *Marriage License?* (1926), *A Certain Young Man* (1928), *Strictly Unconventional* (1930), *Red-Headed Woman* (1932), *The Richest Girl in the World* (1934) with Joel McCrea, *The Bohemian Girl* (1936) with Laurel and Hardy, *The Son of Frankenstein* (1939), *A Chump at Oxford* (1940) again with Laurel and Hardy, *Happy Go Lucky* (1943), *Captain Kidd* (1945), and *The Woman in White* (1948).

He died in the Woodland Hills section of Los Angeles in February 6, 1953 at age 84.

Jack Norton

Jack Norton was born in Brooklyn, New York September 2, 1882 and was an American stage and film character actor who appeared in 184 films between 1934 and 1948, often playing drunks, although in real life he was a teetotaler.

In his early career he had a vaudeville comedy act with his wife Lillian Healy. Norton made his Broadway debut in 1925, in that year's edition of *Earl Carroll's Vanities*, and also appeared in *Florida Girl*, which was produced and staged by Carroll.

Norton's first film work was for a musical short, *School for Romance*, in 1934, in which a young Betty Grable appeared, but his scenes were deleted. His work survived to reach the screen in his next assignment, *The Super Snooper*, a comedy short, and in his third film, his first full-length movie, *Finishing School*, which featured Frances Dee, Billie Burke, Ginger Rogers and Bruce Cabot, Norton played a drunk, setting the pattern for many of his future performances. Although he also played stone sober characters as well, he was best known for his inebriated characterizations, and he improved his work by following genuine drunks around, picking up behavioral tips.

Norton worked continuously and consistently, sometimes appearing in as many as twenty films in one year, although many of his performances went uncredited. One of the few times he was credited as part of the main cast was in 1945 for the film *A Guy, a Gal and a Pal* In the 1940s, Norton was part of Preston Sturges' unofficial "stock company" of character actors, appearing in five films written and directed by Sturges. He is perhaps best known to modern audiences as A. Pismo Clam, the drunken film director whom W.C. Fields is hired to replace in *The Bank Dick* (1940).

More of his roles included *Woman Haters* (1934) with The Three Stooges, *Ruggles of Red Gap* (1935), *The Preview Murder Mystery* (1936), *Pick a Star* (1937) with Laurel and Hardy, *The Roaring Twenties* (1939), *The Spoilers* (1942), *The Palm Beach Story* (1942) with Joel McCrea, *It Ain't Hay* (1943) with Abbott and Costello, *The*

Big Noise (1944) again with Laurel and Hardy, *The Naughty Nineties* (1945) again with Abbott and Costello, *Down to Earth* (1947), and *The Jackie Gleason Show* (1955).

In 1947, Norton retired from films due to illness, his last appearance being in *Alias a Gentlemen*, which was released in 1948, although he did make some live television appearances in the early 1950s.

Jack Norton's final appearance would have been in the 1956 episode of *The Honeymooners* entitled "Unconventional Behavior", but age and infirmity had so overwhelmed him that he was literally written out of the show as it was being filmed, though Jackie Gleason saw to it that Norton was paid fully for the performance he was ready, willing, but unable to give.

Norton died on October 15, 1958 in Saranac Lake, New York at the age of 76. He is buried in Sacred Hearts Cemetery in Southampton, New York on Long Island.

Eva Novak

Eva Barbara Novak was born in St. Louis, Missouri February 14, 1898 and was an American film actress, who was quite popular during the silent film era. She was the younger sister of actress Jane Novak and daughter of Joseph, an immigrant from Bohemia, and Barbara Novak.

She started her film acting career in 1917, with her first film role being in L-KO's *Roped into Scandal*, followed by another seven films that same year. She appeared in seventeen films in 1918, and another eight in 1919. In 1920, she starred opposite Tom Mix in *The Daredevil*, one of six film roles she would have that year, and one of ten films in which she starred opposite Tom Mix.

In 1921, she married stuntman William Reed, whom she met while on location for a film. She was interested in stunt performing herself, having been taught by Mix to perform many of her own stunts. From 1921 to 1928, she appeared in and starred in forty-eight films, including an early version of *Boston Blackie*. She also co-starred with Betty Bronson and Jack Benny in *The Medicine Man* and appeared in the 1922 film *Chasing the Moon*, which was an early forerunner of the 1950s film *D.O.A.* In the late 1920s, she and her husband moved to Australia, where she made numerous films, including *The Romance of Runnibede*. However, with the advent of "talking films", her popularity faded. She would continue to act, but mostly in obscure roles.

More of her roles included *The Beautiful Sinner* (1924), *Phantom of the Desert* (1930), *Dangerous Intrigue* (1936), *Ride a Crooked Mile* (1938), *Corpus Christi Bandits* (1945), *Four Faces West* (1948) with Joel McCrea, *Sunset Blvd.* (1950), *Duel at Apache Wells* (1957), *The Man Who Shot Liberty Valance* (1962), *The Alfred Hitchcock Hour* (1963), and *Laredo* (1966).

She was residing in Woodland Hills, Los Angeles at the time of her death from pneumonia at the age of 90, on April 17, 1988.

Ramon Novarro

Joel McCrea and Ramon Novarro in *The Outriders*

Jose Ramón Gil Samaniego, best known as Ramón Novarro was born in Durango, Mexico, February 6, 1899 was a Mexican film, stage and television actor who began his career as a leading man in silent films in 1917. Novarro was promoted byMGM as a "Latin lover" and became known as sex symbol after the death of Rudolph Valentino.

Novarro was born to Dr. Mariano N. Samaniego, and his wife, Leonor. The family moved to Los Angeles, California, to escape the Mexican Revolution in 1913.

Ramon's father, Dr. Mariano N. Samaniego, was born in Juarez and attended high school in Las Cruces, New Mexico. After receiving his degree in dentistry at the University of Pennsylvania, he moved to Durango, Mexico, and began a flourishing dental practice. In 1891 he married Leonor Pérez-Gavilán, the beautiful daughter of a prosperous landowner. The Pérez-Gaviláns were a mixture of Spanish and Aztec blood, and according to local legend, they were descended from Guerrero, a prince of Montezuma.

The family estate was called the "Garden of Eden". Thirteen children were born there: Emilio; Guadalupe; Rosa; Ramón; Leonor; Mariano; Luz; Antonio; José; a stillborn child; Carmen; Ángel and Eduardo. At the time of the revolution in Mexico, the family moved from Durango to Mexico City and then back to Durango. Three of Ramón's sisters, Guadalupe, Rosa, and Leonor, became nuns. He was a second cousin of the Mexican actresses Dolores del Río and Andrea Palma.

He entered films in 1917 in bit parts. He supplemented his income by working as a singing waiter. His friends, actor and director Rex Ingram and his wife, the actress Alice Terry, began to promote him as a rival to Rudolph Valentino, and Ingram suggested he change his name to "Novarro." From 1923, he began to play more prominent roles. His role in *Scaramouche* (1923) brought him his first major success.

In 1925, Novarro achieved his greatest success in *Ben-Hur*. His revealing costumes caused a sensation. He was elevated into the Hollywood elite. As did many stars, Novarro engaged Sylvia of Hollywood as a therapist (although in her tell-all book, Sylvia erroneously claimed that Novarro slept in a coffin). With Valentino's death in 1926, Novarro became the screen's leading Latin actor, though ranked behind his MGM contemporary, John Gilbert, as a leading man. He was popular as a swashbuckler in action roles and considered one of the great romantic lead actors of his day. Novarro appeared with Norma Shearer in *The Student Prince in Old Heidelberg* (1927) and with Joan Crawford in *Across to Singapore* (1928).

He made his first talking film, starring as a singing French soldier, in *Devil-May-Care* (1929). He starred with Dorothy Janis in *The Pagan* (1929), with Greta Garbo in *Mata Hari* (1931), with Myrna Loy in *The Barbarian* (1933) and opposite Lupe Vélez in *Laughing Boy* (1934).

When his contract with MGM Studios expired in 1935 and the studio did not renew it, Novarro continued to act sporadically, appearing in films for Republic Pictures, a Mexican religious drama, and a French comedy. In the 1940s, he had several small roles in American films, including *We Were Strangers* (1949), directed by John Huston and starring Jennifer Jones and John Garfield. He appeared with Joel McCrea in *The Outriders* (1950). In 1958, he was considered for a role in the television series *The Green Peacock*, with Howard Duff and Ida Lupino, after their CBS Television sitcom *Mr. Adams and Eve* (1957–1958). He appeared in the Louis L'amour movie *Heller in Pink Tights* in 1960. The project, however, never materialized. A Broadway tryout was aborted in the 1960s. Novarro kept busy on television, appearing in NBC's *The High Chaparral* as late as 1968.

At the peak of his success in the late 1920s and early 1930s, Ramón Novarro was earning more than US$100,000 per film. He invested some of his income in real estate, and his Hollywood Hills residence is one of the more renowned designs (1927) by Lloyd Wright, the son of Frank Lloyd Wright. When his career ended, he was still able to maintain a comfortable lifestyle.

Novarro was troubled all his life by his conflicted feelings toward his Roman Catholic religion and his homosexuality. His life-long struggle with alcoholism is often traced to these issues. MGM mogul Louis B. Mayer reportedly tried to coerce Novarro into a "lavender marriage", which he refused.

Along with Dolores del Río, Lupe Vélez and James Cagney, Novarro was accused of promoting Communism in California. It happened after they attended a special screening of the film *¡Que viva México!* by famed Russian filmmaker Sergei M. Eisenstein.

Novarro was murdered on October 30, 1968 at age 69, by brothers Paul and Tom Ferguson, aged 22 and 17, whom he had hired from an agency to come to his Laurel Canyon home for sex. According to the prosecution in the murder case, the two young men believed that a large sum of money was hidden in Novarro's house. The prosecution accused the brothers of torturing Novarro for several hours to force him to reveal where the non-existent money was hidden. They left the house with $20 they took from his bathrobe pocket. Novarro died as a result of asphyxiation—having choked to death on his own blood after being beaten. The two perpetrators were caught and sentenced to long prison terms, but released on probation in the mid-1970s. Both were later re-arrested for unrelated crimes for which they served longer prison terms than for the murder of Novarro.

Ramón Novarro is buried in Calvary Cemetery, in Los Angeles. Ramón Novarro's star on the Hollywood Walk of Fame is at 6350 Hollywood Boulevard.

Jay Novello

Jay Novello was born as Michael Romano in Chicago, Illinois August 22, 1904 and was an American radio, film, and television character actor.

Born of Italian descent, Novello began his career as a radio actor, having played Jack Packard on the Hollywood version of *I Love a Mystery* for a brief period in the middle 1940s. He usually put his suave, cultured voice and dexterity at accents to use in supporting roles, often of an ethnic nature.

He was heard regularly on *Rocky Jordan*, (as Cairo police captain Lt. Sam Sabaaya), the radio version of *The Lone Wolf* (as Jamison the butler), and the long-running serial *One Man's Family* (as Judge Glenn Hunter). He was also heard on *Escape, Crime Classics, Lux Radio Theater, Suspense*, and *Yours Truly, Johnny Dollar*, among others.

In film, Novello alternated between pompous or fussy professionals and assorted ethnic roles, often as Italian or Hispanic characters. One of his earliest and more familiar film appearances is in the 1945 Laurel and Hardy comedy *The Bullfighters*, in which Novello plays a Latin restaurateur. Though prolific in the movies, Novello was limited mostly to bits in minor films, one of his more noteworthy assignments being the officious Spanish consul in Frank Capra's *Pocketful of Miracles*.

More of his roles over his career included *Sergeant Madden* (1939), *They Met in Bombay* (1941) with Alan Ladd, *Captain America* (1944), *Kiss the Blood Off My Hands* (1948), *The George Burns and Gracie Allen Show* (1951), *Biff Baker, U.S.A.* (1952), *Beneath the 12-Mile Reef* (1953), *Son of Sinbad* (1955), *I Love Lucy* (1951-1956), *The Pride and the Passion* (1957), *Richard Diamond, Private Detective* (1958), *Wichita Town* (1960) with Joel McCrea, *Atlantis, the Lost Continent* (1961), *The Outer Limits* (1963), *Harum Scarum* (1965) with Elvis, *Death Valley Days* (1965-1968), *Mannix* (1968-1975), and *The Domino Killings* (1977).

He died September 2, 1982, at age 78, and is interred in Los Angeles, California, at the San Fernando Mission Cemetery.

Elliott Nugent

Elliott Nugent was born September 20, 1896 in Dover, Ohio and was an American actor, playwright, writer, and film director.

Nugent was the son of actor J.C. Nugent, successfully made the transition from silent film to sound. He directed *The Cat and the Canary* (1939), starring Bob Hope and Paulette Goddard. He also directed the Hope films *Never Say Die* (1939) and *My Favorite Brunette* (1947).

Some of his acting roles included *The Single Standard* (1929) with Joel McCrea, *So This Is College* (1929) again with Joel McCrea, *The Last Flight* (1931), *Thunder in the City* (1937), *Welcome Stranger* (1947), and *My Outlaw Brother* (1951).

Nugent was a college classmate (and lifelong friend) of fellow Ohioan James Thurber. Together, they wrote the Broadway play *The Male Animal* (1940) in which Nugent starred with Gene Tierney. He also directed the 1942 Warner Bros. film version of *The Male Animal*, starring Henry Fonda and Olivia de Havilland.

He died August 9, 1980 in New York City, New York at age 83.

Warren Oates

Warren Mercer Oates was born and raised in Depoy, a tiny rural community west of Greenville in Muhlenberg County, Kentucky July 5, 1928 and was an American actor best known for his performances in several films directed by Sam Peckinpah including *The Wild Bunch* (1969) and *Bring Me the Head of Alfredo Garcia*(1974). He starred in numerous films during the early 1970s which have since achieved cult status including *The Hired Hand* (1971), *Two-Lane Blacktop* (1971), and *Race with the Devil* (1975). Oates also portrayed John Dillinger in the biopic *Dillinger* (1973) and Sergeant Hulka in the comedy *Stripes* (1981).

He was the son of Sarah Alice (née Mercer) and Bayless Earle Oates, who owned a general store. He attended Louisville Male High School, Louisville, Kentucky until 1945 but did not graduate. He later earned a high school equivalency degree. After high school he enlisted in the United States Marine Corps for two years serving in the air wing as an aircraft mechanic. He became interested in theater at the University of Louisville and starred in several plays there in 1953 for the Little Theater Company. He got an opportunity in New York City to star in a live production of the television series *Studio One* in 1957.

Oates moved to Los Angeles where he began to establish himself in guest roles in Western television series, including*Wagon Train, Tombstone Territory, Buckskin, Rawhide, Trackdown, Tate, The Rebel, Wanted: Dead or Alive, Have Gun-Will Travel, Lawman, The Big Valley* and *Gunsmoke*. Oates first met Peckinpah when he played a variety of guest roles on *The Rifleman* (1958–1963), a popular television series created by the director. He also played a supporting role in Peckinpah's short-lived series *The Westerner* in 1960. The collaboration continued as he worked on Peckinpah's early films *Ride the High Country* (1962) with Joel McCrea and *Major Dundee* (1965) with Charleton Heston.

In the episode "Subterranean City" (October 14, 1958) of the syndicated *Rescue 8*, Oates played a gang member, Pete, who is the nephew of series character Skip Johnson (Lang Jeffries). In the story line, rescuers Skip Johnson and Wes Cameron (Jim Davis) search for a lost girl in the sewer tunnels and encounter three criminals hiding out underground. Pete soon breaks with his gang companions and joins the firemen Wes and Skip in locating the missing child.

In 1961, Oates guest starred in the episode "Artie Moon" in NBC's *The Lawless Years* crime drama about the 1920s. In 1962, he appeared as "Ves Painter" in the short-lived ABC series *Stoney Burke*, co-starring Jack Lord, a program about rodeo contestants.

Oates also played in a number of guest roles on *The Twilight Zone* (in "The Purple Testament" and "The 7th Is Made Up of Phantoms", in which he costarred with Randy Boone and Ron Foster), *The Outer Limits* ("The Mutant" [1964]), *Combat!* ("The Pillbox" [1964],) and *Lost in Space* ("Welcome Stranger" [1965]). During the 1960s and 1970s, he guest-starred on such shows as *Twelve O'Clock High, Lancer*, and *The Virginian*.

In addition to Peckinpah, Oates worked with several major film directors of his era including Leslie Stevens in the 1960 film *Private Property*, his first starring role;Norman Jewison in *In the Heat of the Night* (1967); Joseph L. Mankiewicz in *There Was a Crooked Man...* (1970); John Milius in *Dillinger* (1973); Terrence Malick in *Badlands* (1973); Philip Kaufman in *The White Dawn* (1974); William Friedkin in *The Brink's Job* (1978); and Steven Spielberg in *1941* (1979).

He appeared in the Sherman Brothers musical version of *Tom Sawyer* as "Muff Potter", the town drunk. He also starred in *The Rise and Fall of Legs Diamond* (1960),*Return of the Seven* (1966), *The Shooting* (filmed in 1965, released in 1968), *The Thief Who Came to Dinner* (1973), *Cockfighter* (1974), *Drum* (1976) and *China 9, Liberty 37* (1978). Oates co-starred three times with friend Peter Fonda in *The Hired Hand* (1971), *Race with the Devil* (1975), and *92 in the Shade* (1975).

June 18 thru June 26, 1967 while making a guest appearance on a segment of *Dundee and the Culhane*, Warren Oates managed to steal the show with his off camera antics and bloopers that had everyone on the set rolling. After a long day of filming, Warren headed over and *set his footprints in cement* along with all the other stars that appeared at Apacheland Movie Ranch. It was during this time that *Heat of the Night* was a blockbuster summer flick. Warren's role as "Officer Sam Wood" is spectacular as he plays a peeping-tom officer and possible killer in the critically acclaimed film.

Oates was cast in Roger Donaldson's 1977 New Zealand film *Sleeping Dogs* together with New Zealand actor Sam Neill. A political thriller with action film elements,*Sleeping Dogs* follows the lead character "Smith" (Neill) as New Zealand plunges into a police state, as a fascist government institutes martial law after industrial disputes flare into violence. Smith gets caught between the special police and a growing resistance movement and reluctantly becomes involved. Oates plays the role of "Willoughby", commander of the American forces stationed in New Zealand and working with the New Zealand fascist government to find and subdue "rebels" (the resistance movement).

His partnership with Peckinpah resulted in two of his most famous film roles. In the 1969 Western classic *The Wild Bunch*, he portrayed Lyle Gorch, a long-time outlaw who chooses to die with his friends during the film's violent conclusion. According to his wife at the time, Teddy, Oates had the choice of starring in *Support Your Local Sheriff*, to be filmed in Los Angeles, or *The Wild Bunch* in Mexico. "He had done *Return of the Seven* in Mexico; he got hepatitis, plus dysentery. But off he went again with Sam (Peckinpah). He loved going on location. He loved the adventure of it. He had great admiration for Sam. Sam Peckinpah and Monte Hellman were the two directors Warren would work with anytime anywhere." In *Bring Me the Head of Alfredo Garcia*, the dark 1974 action/tragedy also filmed in Mexico, Oates played the lead role of Bennie, a hard-drinking down-on-his-luck musician hoping to make a final score. The character was reportedly based on Peckinpah himself. For authenticity, Oates wore the director's sunglasses while filming scenes of the production.

Although the Peckinpah film roles are his best-known, his most critically acclaimed role is GTO in Monte Hellman's 1971 cult classic *Two-Lane Blacktop*. The film, although a failure at the box-office, is studied in film schools as a treasure of the 1970s, in large part due to Oates' heartbreaking portrayal of GTO. Famed film critic Leonard Maltin remarked that Oates' performance in this film was as good as any he'd seen and should have won the Oscar.

He also played Rooster Cogburn in the 1978 television remake of *True Grit*.

A year before his death, Oates co-starred with Bill Murray in the 1981 military comedy *Stripes*. In the role of the drill sergeant, Sergeant Hulka, Oates skillfully played the straight man to Murray's comedic character. The film was a huge financial success, earning $85 million at the box office. In 1982, he co-starred opposite Jack Nicholson in director Tony Richardson's *The Border*.

Warren Oates died in his sleep at his house in Los Angeles, California, of a sudden heart attack brought on by natural causes on April 3, 1982; he was 53 years old. His ashes were scattered at his ranch in Montana.

In 1981, nearly one year before his death, he had co-starred in the CBS TV mini-series *The Blue and the Gray*, which aired in November 1982. His last two films,*Blue Thunder* (which was filmed in early 1980) and *Tough Enough* (which was filmed in late 1981) (both released in 1983), were posthumously dedicated to him. Monte Hellman's film *Iguana* ends with the titles "For Warren" as a dedication.

216

Today, the actor has a dedicated cult following because of his memorable performances in not only Peckinpah's films, but Monte Hellman's independent works, his films with Peter Fonda and a number of B-movies from the 1970s. His occasionally crude facade, likeable persona and uncommon presence are admired by such filmmakers as Quentin Tarantino and Richard Linklater.   During a recent screening of Hellman's *Two-Lane Blacktop*, Linklater introduced the film and announced sixteen reasons why viewers should love the 1971 movie. The sixth was: "Because there was once a god who walked the Earth named Warren Oates."

The documentary film *Warren Oates: Across the Border* was produced by Tom Thurman in 1993 in tribute to the actor's career.

Oates was again recognized in March 2009 with the first-ever biography of his colorful life. Featuring interviews with actor's former wives, children, and friends, *Warren Oates: A Wild Life*, was written by Susan Compo. It has received much acclaim from fans and critics alike.

Oates cast his boot-prints while filming an episode of *Dundee and the Culhane* at Apacheland Movie Ranch on June 23, 1967.

Merle Oberon

Joel McCrea and Merle Oberon in *These Three*

Merle Oberon was born Estelle Merle Thompson in Bombay, British India February 19, 1911 – 23 November 1979 and was an Anglo-Indian actress. She began her film career in British films as Anne Boleyn in *The Private Life of Henry VIII* (1933). After her success in *The Scarlet Pimpernel* (1934), she travelled to the United States to make films for Samuel Goldwyn. She was nominated for an Academy Award for Best Actress for her performance in *The*

Dark Angel (1935). A traffic collision in 1937 caused facial injuries that could have ended her career, but she soon followed this with her most renowned performance in *Wuthering Heights* (1939). Throughout her adult life, in order to conceal her Indian heritage she maintained the fiction that she was born in Tasmania, Australia; the year before she died she finally admitted this story was not true, and records located since her death have confirmed her true origin.

According to some sources, her birth name was Estelle Merle O'Brien Thompson. Merle was given "Queenie" as a nickname, in honor of Queen Mary, who visited India along with King George V in 1911.

Over the years, Oberon obscured her parentage. Some sources claim Merle's parents to have been Arthur Terrence O'Brien Thompson, a British mechanical engineer from Darlington, who worked in Indian Railways, and Charlotte Selby, a Eurasian from Ceylon with partial Māori heritage.

However, at the age of fourteen, Charlotte had in Ceylon given birth to her first child Constance, the result of a relationship with Henry Alfred Selby, an Irish foreman of a tea planter, and some sources have claimed that Constance, twelve at the time of Merle's birth, and not Charlotte, was Merle's biological mother. Whatever the true relationship, Charlotte raised Merle as her own child and as Constance's sister. Charlotte's partner, Arthur Thompson, was listed as the father in Merle's birth certificate, with the forename misspelled as "Arther".

Constance eventually married and had four other children, Edna, Douglas, Harry, and Stanislaus (Stan) with her husband Alexander Soares. Edna and Douglas moved at an early age to the UK and Harry later in life moved to Toronto, Canada and retained Constance's maiden name, Selby. Stanislaus was the only child to keep his father's last name of Soares and he currently resides in Surrey, British Columbia, Canada. All the siblings reportedly believed Merle to be their aunt (the sister of their mother Constance), when in fact she was their half-sister.

When Harry Selby tracked down Merle's birth certificate in Indian government records in Bombay (Mumbai), he was surprised to discover he was in fact Merle's brother and not her nephew. He attempted to visit her in Los Angeles, but she refused to see him. Harry withheld this information from Oberon's biographer Charles Higham, only eventually revealing it to Maree Delofski, the creator of *The Trouble with Merle*, a 2002 documentary produced by the Australian Broadcasting Corporation, which investigated the various conflicting versions of Merle's origin.

In 1914, Arthur Thompson joined the British Army and later died of pneumonia on the Western Front during the Battle of the Somme. Merle, with her "mother" (really her grandmother), led an impoverished existence in shabby Bombay flats for a few years. Then, in 1917, they moved to better circumstances in Calcutta. Oberon received a foundation scholarship to attend La Martiniere Calcutta for Girls, one of the best private schools in Calcutta. There, she was constantly taunted for her unconventional parentage and eventually quit school and received her lessons at home.

Oberon first performed with the Calcutta Amateur Dramatic Society. She was also completely enamored of the films and enjoyed going out to nightclubs. Indian journalist Sunanda K. Datta-Ray claimed that Merle worked as a telephone operator in Calcutta under the name Queenie Thomson, and won a contest at Firpo's Restaurant there, before the outset of her film career.

In 1929, Merle met a former actor named Colonel Ben Finney at Firpo's, and dated him. However, when he saw Oberon's dark-skinned mother one night at her flat, and realised Oberon was mixed-race, he decided to end the relationship. However, Finney promised to introduce her to Rex Ingram of Victorine Studios, if she was prepared to travel to France., which she readily did. After packing all their belongings and moving to France, Oberon and her mother found that their supposed benefactor avoided them, although he had left a good word for Oberon with Ingram at the studios in Nice. Ingram liked Oberon's exotic appearance and quickly hired her to be an extra in a party scene in a film named *The Three Passions*.

Oberon arrived in England for the first time in 1928, aged 17. Initially she worked as a club hostess under the name Queenie O'Brien and played in minor and unbilled roles in various films. "I couldn't dance or sing or write or paint. The only possible opening seemed to be in some line in which I could use my face. This was, in fact, no better than a hundred other faces, but it did possess a fortunately photogenic quality," she modestly told a journalist at *Film Weekly* in 1939. In view of the information discovered since this 1939 article this should be seen as part of a myth perpetrated by Oberon, since apparently she did not reach Europe until 1929.

Her film career received a major boost when the director Alexander Korda took an interest and gave her a small but prominent role, under the name Merle Oberon, as Anne Boleyn in *The Private Life of Henry VIII* (1933) opposite Charles Laughton. The film became a major success and she was then given leading roles, such as Lady Blakeney in *The Scarlet Pimpernel* (1934) with Leslie Howard, who became her lover for a while.

Oberon's career went on to greater heights, partly as a result of her relationship with and later marriage to Alexander Korda, who had persuaded her to take the name under which she became famous. He sold "shares" of her contract to producer Samuel Goldwyn, who gave her good vehicles in Hollywood. Her "mother" stayed behind in England. Oberon earned her sole Academy Award for Best Actress nomination for *The Dark Angel* (1935) produced by Goldwyn. Around this time she had a serious romance with David Niven, and according to his authorized biography, even wanted to marry him, but he wasn't faithful to her.

She then appeared in *These Three* (1936) with Joel McCRea. She was selected to star in Korda's film *I, Claudius* (1937) as Messalina, but a serious car accident resulted in filming being abandoned. Oberon was scarred for life, but skilled lighting technicians were able to hide her injuries from cinema audiences. She went on to appear as Cathy in her most famous film, *Wuthering Heights* (opposite Laurence Olivier; 1939), as George Sand in *A Song to Remember* (1945) and as the Empress Josephine in *Désirée* (1954).

According to *Princess Merle*, the biography written by Charles Higham with Roy Moseley, Oberon suffered even further damage to her complexion in 1940 from a combination of cosmetic poisoning and an allergic reaction to sulfa drugs. Alexander Korda sent her to a skin specialist in New York City, where she underwent several dermabrasion procedures. The results, however, were only partially successful; without makeup, one could see noticeable pitting and indentation of her skin.

Charlotte died in 1937. In 1949 Oberon commissioned paintings of her mother from an old photograph. The paintings hung in all her homes until Oberon's own death.

Merle Oberon had a brief affair in 1941 with Richard Hillary, an RAF fighter pilot who had been badly burned in the Battle of Britain. They met while he was on a good-will tour of the United States. He later became well known as the author of a best-selling book, *The Last Enemy*.

Merle Oberon became Lady Korda upon her husband's knighthood in 1942, when the couple were based at Hills House in Denham, England. She divorced him in 1945, to marry cinematographer Lucien Ballard. Ballard devised a special camera light for her to eliminate her facial scars on film. The light became known as the "Obie".

She married twice more, to Italian-born industrialist, Bruno Pagliai (with whom she adopted two children; they lived in Cuernavaca, Morelos, Mexico) and Dutch actor Robert Wolders – later companion to actresses Audrey Hepburn and Leslie Caron – before her retirement in Malibu, California, where she died, November 23, 1979 at age 68, after suffering a stroke. She was interred at Forest Lawn Memorial Park Cemetery in Glendale, California.

Merle Oberon has a star on the Hollywood Walk of Fame (at 6250 Hollywood Boulevard) for her contributions to Motion Pictures.

Michael Korda, nephew of Alexander Korda, wrote a roman à clef about Oberon after her death entitled *Queenie*. This was also turned into a television miniseries starring Mia Sara.

Pat O'Brien

Joel McCrea and Pat O'Brien in *Gambling Lady*

William Joseph Patrick "Pat" O'Brien was born in Milwaukee, Wisconsin November 11, 1899 and was an American film actor with more than one hundred screen credits. Of Irish descent, he often played Irish and Irish-American characters and was referred to as "Hollywood's Irishman in Residence" in the press. One of the best-known screen actors of the 1930s and 1940s, he played priests, cops, military figures, pilots, and reporters. He is especially well-remembered for his roles in *Knute Rockne, All American* (1940), *Angels with Dirty Faces* (1938), and *Some Like It Hot* (1959). He was frequently paired onscreen with Hollywood legend, James Cagney. O'Brien also appeared on stage and television.

Pat O'Brien was born to an Irish-American Roman Catholic family. All four of his grandparents had come from Ireland. The O'Briens were originally from County Cork. His grandfather, Patrick O'Brien, for whom he was named, was an architect who was killed while trying to break up a saloon fight in New York City. His mother's parents, the McGoverns, emigrated from County Galway in the west of Ireland in the mid- to late-19th century.

As a child, O'Brien served as an altar boy at Gesu Church, while growing up near 13th and Clybourn streets in Milwaukee. He attended Marquette Academy with fellow actor Spencer Tracy, who became a lifelong friend. During World War I, O'Brien and Tracy joined the Navy. They both attended boot camp at the Great Lakes Naval Training Center, but the war ended before their training had finished.

Jack Benny was also at the Great Lakes Naval Training Center at the same time as O'Brien and Tracy. According to his autobiography, Benny performed a number on the violin at a show one evening, when the sailors started booing and heckling him. O'Brien walked on stage and whispered in his ear, "For heaven's sake, Ben, put down the damn fiddle and talk to 'em". Benny stopped playing his violin and made a series of comments that got laughs from the audience. In this way, O'Brien indirectly helped to start Benny's career in comedy.

After the war, O'Brien finished his secondary schooling at Marquette Academy and later attended Marquette University. While still at college, he decided to seek work as an actor. He moved to New York, where he lived for a while with Tracy (who had also become an actor), and began a career on the stage.

After a decade in plays on Broadway and in the New York City area, O'Brien began appearing in movies in 1930. Often playing fast-talking "smart alecs" or romantic leads at first, he soon progressed to playing a string of authority figures, especially cops and priests. His first starring role was as ace reporter Hildy Johnson in the original 1931 version of *The Front Page* with Adolphe Menjou. In 2010, this film was selected by the National Film Preservation Board for preservation in the Library of Congress's National Film Registry as being "culturally, historically, or aesthetically significant."

Warner Brothers hired O'Brien as a contract player in 1933. He remained with the studio until 1940, when he left after a dispute over the terms of his contract renewal. He appeared with James Cagney, also under contract to Warner Brothers, in nine feature films, including *Angels with Dirty Faces* (1938) and Cagney's last film, *Ragtime* (1981). The two originally met in 1926 and remained friends for almost six decades. After O'Brien's death, Cagney referred to him as his "dearest friend." At Warners, O'Brien also played the lead in the boxing film, *The Personality Kid* (1934), as well as in the bio-pic *Oil for the Lamps of China* (1935), which he called "one of my favorite pictures."

He appeared with Joel McCrea and Barbara Stanwyck in *Gambling Lady* (1934).

O'Brien is best known for his role as the famous Notre Dame University football coach Knute Rockne in *Knute Rockne, All American* (1940). In the film, he gave the speech to "win just one for the Gipper," referring to recently deceased football player, George Gipp, portrayed in the film by a young Ronald Reagan. Reagan later used this saying as a slogan for his campaign for president in 1980.

After he left Warner Brothers in 1940, O'Brien briefly worked for Columbia Pictures. Soon he signed a contract with RKO and appeared in several movies for that studio. In 1946 he starred in the successful *film-noir* suspense film, *Crack-Up*.

O'Brien's movie career slowed considerably by the early 1950s, although he still managed to get work in television. In his autobiography, *The Wind At My Back*, he professed to being completely flummoxed about the decline of his career. His close friend, Spencer Tracy, fought with his studio, MGM, to get roles for O'Brien in his films, *The People Against O'Hara* (1951) and *The Last Hurrah* (1958).

In 1959 O'Brien appeared in one of his best-known movies as a police detective opposite George Raft in *Some Like It Hot*, starring Marilyn Monroe, Jack Lemmon, and Tony Curtis. He had a small role as Burt Reynolds' father in the 1978 comedy film *The End*, opposite Myrna Loy, cast as Reynolds' mother.

In later years, O'Brien recalled that he had had three "great" movie roles in his career: Knute Rockne, Hildy Johnson in *The Front Page*, and Father Duffy in *The Fighting 69th*.

In his later years, O'Brien often worked in television. He was cast in 1956 and 1957 in four episodes of the religion anthology series, *Crossroads*. In three of the four programs, he played priests. He also performed in two episodes of *The Virginian* in the mid-1960s.

In the 1960-1961 television season, O'Brien joined Roger Perry in the thirty-four episode ABC sitcom, *Harrigan and Son*, about a father-and-son team of lawyers. He played the lead role of James Harrigan, Sr.

O'Brien made numerous appearances on television as himself, including several on *The Ed Sullivan Show*. In 1957, he guest starred in the first season of the NBC variety program, *The Ford Show, Starring Tennessee Ernie Ford*. Other shows in which he appeared as himself include the interview programs: *The David Frost Show*, *The Tonight Show*, *The Merv Griffin Show*, and *The Joey Bishop Show*. In 1957, Ralph Edwards profiled O'Brien's life and career for an episode of *This Is Your Life*. He was also the mystery guest on the game show *What's My Line?* in 1953 and 1957. His final filmed performance came in a 1982 episode of *Happy Days*.

In the 1960s through the early 1980s, O'Brien often traveled around the United States as a one-man act and in road shows. He also performed frequently in nightclubs. Near the end of his life, he toured in a stage production of *On Golden Pond*, which he considered "absolutely the best play" he had ever read.

In the late 1930s, Pat O'Brien and a small group of his actor friends began to meet to converse and exchange opinions and stories. Hollywood columnist Sidney Skolsky dubbed them the "Irish Mafia," but they preferred to call their social group the "Boys Club." In addition to O'Brien, the original members of the club were James Cagney, Spencer Tracy, and Frank McHugh, all of whom were Irish-Americans. Later Lynne Overman joined their group and then Ralph Bellamy and Frank Morgan. Bert Lahr, Louis Calhern, and James Gleason were occasional guests. The actors gathered to socialize, but they also occasionally used the group to discuss ideas about their latest movies. By the mid-1940s the group began to break up, as members died or moved. Some of the surviving members kept in contact by telephone and occasional meetings.

O'Brien and his wife, Eloise, had four children: Mavourneen, Sean, Terry, and Brigid. Three of his children were adopted. The youngest, Brigid O'Brien (born 1946), was his biological child. Eloise O'Brien occasionally appeared on stage with her husband.

Among those who knew him personally, O'Brien was known for his love of storytelling, jokes, and late-night parties. A friend recalled that he was always "the life, and I mean the lively life, of the party."

Pat O'Brien died on October 15, 1983 from a heart attack at age 83. Ronald Reagan, who was president at the time, released a White House statement noting his sadness over O'Brien's death. The president had called the actor at the hospital days before his death.

Erin O'Brien-Moore

Erin O'Brien-Moore was born May 2, 1902 in Los Angeles, California was an American actress. Moore's acting career began onstage. Noticed in a Broadway stage production, she was signed to a movie contract. Her early movies placed her in second-lead roles, including *Little Men* (1934) and *Ring Around the Moon* (1936). She later performed with actors such as Joel McCrea and Shirley Temple in *Our Little Girl* (1935), Barbara Stanwyck (*The Plough and the Stars*, 1936),Humphrey Bogart (*Black Legion*, 1937), and Paul Muni (*The Life of Emile Zola*, also 1937). Her rising career was interrupted by a fire accident that forced years of surgeries and rehabilitation.

Returning as a character actress, Moore appeared first on television (*Philco Television Playhouse, NBC Presents, General Electric Theater, The Ruggles,* the TV special *Light's Diamond Jubilee*), then again in movies, including *Destination Moon* (1950) *Sea of Lost Ships* (1954), and *Peyton Place* (1957).

Her television career included appearances in *Lux Video Theater, Alfred Hitchcock Presents, Dennis the Menace, Perry Mason, The Time Tunnel, Adam-12,* and for over four seasons on the television version of *Peyton Place* as Nurse Esther Choate, from March 1965 (episode 50) through April 1969 (episode 507).

She retired at the end of the 1960s, and died of cancer on May 3, 1979 in Los Angeles, California at age 77.

Robert Emmett O'Connor

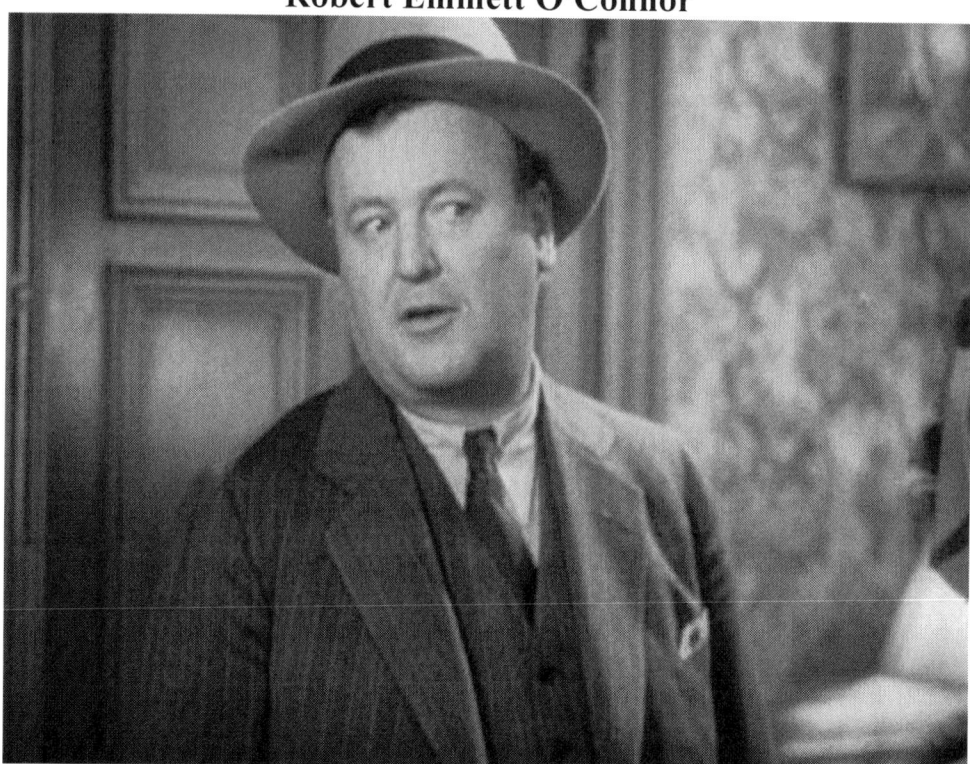

Robert Emmett O'Connor was born in Milwaukee, Wisconsin March 18, 1885 and was an American film actor. He appeared in 204 films between 1919 and 1950. He is probably best known as the warmhearted bootlegger Paddy Ryan in *The Public Enemy* (1931) and as Detective Sergeant Henderson pursuing the Marx Brothers in *A Night at the Opera* (1935). He also appeared as Jonesy, (the older Paramount gate guard) in Billy Wilder's 1950 film *Sunset Boulevard.*

He also made a cameo appearance at the very beginning and very end of the MGM cartoon short *Who Killed Who?*(1943).

More of his roles included *Dressed to Kill* (1928), *Freedom of the Press* (1928) with Joel McCrea, *Up the River* (1930), *Bed of Roses* (1933) again with Joel McCrea, *The Lone Wolf Returns* (1935), *A Star Is Born* (1937), *Wells Fargo* (1937) a third with Joel McCrea, *No Time for Comedy* (1940), *Little Miss Pinkerton* (1943), *Nothing But Trouble* (1944) with Laurel and Hardy, *Bud Abbott and Lou Costello in Hollywood* (1945), *Trail Street* (1947), *Easter Parade* (1948), *Watch the Birdie* (1950), *Annie Oakley* (1954), and *Man Without a Gun* (1958).

He died September 4, 1962 at age 77 in Hollywood, Los Angeles, California.

Spec O'Donnell

Walter "Spec" O'Donnell was born in Fresno, California April 9, 1911 and was an American film actor. He appeared in 191 films between 1923 and 1978. He worked frequently for producer Hal Roach, often appearing in silent comedies as the bratty son of Max Davidson or Charley Chase. His sound era roles were mostly uncredited bits, though he has the unusual distinction of playing the same role (a newsboy) in both an original film and its remake: *Princess O'Hara* (1935) and *It Ain't Hay* (1943) with Abbott and Costello.

More of his roles included *Private Izzy Murphy* (1926), *Call of the Cuckoo* (1927) with Laurel and Hardy, *Show Girl in Hollywood* (1930), *Girl Without a Room* (1933), *The Walking Dead* (1936), *Angels with Dirty Faces* (1938), *A Gentleman After Dark* (1942), *Arsenic and Old Lace* (1944), *The Story of Seabiscuit* (1949), *The Great Caruso* (1951), *Adventures of the Falcon* (1954), *Riverboat* (1960), *The Andy Griffith Show* (1961), *Ride the High Country* (1962) with Joel McCrea, and *Convoy* (1978).

He died October 14, 1986) in Woodland Hills, Los Angeles at age 75.

Damian O'Flynn

Damian O'Flynn was born January 29, 1907, in Boston, Massachusetts, and was an American general purpose actor. He made his first screen appearance in *Marked Woman* (1937). O'Flynn went on to freelance at Warner Brothers, RKO, Paramount, Monogram, and other studios, usually in secondary roles, but occasionally playing leads.

He appeared in *The Great Man's Lady* (1942) with Joel McCrea.

While serving in WWII, he appeared along with several other actors-in-uniform in 20th Century Fox's *Winged Victory* (1944), billed as Corporal Damian O'Flynn. A veteran of many a big-screen Western, like *Saddle Pals* (1947), *Riders of the Whistling Pines* (1949), *Young Daniel Boone* (1950), *The Half-Breed* (1952), *The Far Country*

(1954), *Daniel Boone, Trail Blazer* (1956), *Apache Warrior* (1957), and *Gunfight at Comanche Creek* (1963) with Audie Murphy.

He appeared in thirty-three episodes in the television series *The Life and Legend of Wyatt Earp* (1956-1961) as Doc Goodfellow. Other television programs he appeared in were *Adventures of Wild Bill Hickok* (1956), *The Adventures of Dr. Fu Manchu* (1956), *The New Adventures of Charlie Chan* (1957), *Mr. Adams and Eve* (1957-1958), *Richard Diamond, Private Detective* (1958), *The Jim Backus Show* (1960), *National Velvet* (1962), *Batman* (1966), and his last roles were in *Green Acres* (1967-1969).

He died August 8, 1982, at age 75 in Los Angeles, California.

Maureen O'Hara

Maureen O'Hara and Joel McCrea in *Buffalo Bill*

Maureen O'Hara was born Maureen FitzSimons in Ranelagh, County Dublin, Ireland (now Ranelagh, Dublin, Ireland) August 17, 1920 and is an Irish film actress, and singer. She was first educated at the John Street West Girls' School near Thomas Street in Dublin's Liberties Area. From the age of 6–17 she trained in drama, music, and dance, and at the age of 10 joined the Rathmines Theatre Company and worked in amateur theatre in the evenings, after her lessons. The famously red-headed O'Hara has been noted for playing fiercely passionate heroines with a highly sensible attitude. She often worked with director John Ford and longtime friend John Wayne. Her autobiography, *'Tis Herself*, was published in 2004 and was a New York Times Bestseller.

O'Hara was the second oldest of the six children of Charles Stewart Parnell FitzSimons and Marguerita Lilburn FitzSimons. Her father was in the clothing business and also bought into Shamrock Rovers Football Club, a team O'Hara has supported since childhood. Her mother, a former operatic contralto, was a successful women's clothier. O'Hara was raised as, and still is, a Roman Catholic. Her siblings were Peggy, the oldest, and younger Charles, Florrie, Margot, and Jimmy. Peggy dedicated her life to a religious order, the Sisters of Charity, and the younger children all went on to receive training at the Abbey Theatre and the Ena Mary Burke School of Drama and Elocution in Dublin. O'Hara's dream at this time was to be a stage actress.

O'Hara's father was a very practical man and did not entirely support her theatrical aspirations. He insisted that she learn a skill so that she would have something to fall back on to earn a living with in case her experience in the performing arts was not successful. She enrolled in a business school and became a proficient bookkeeper and typist. Those skills proved helpful many years later when she was able to take and transcribe production notes dictated by John Ford for the screen adaptation of Maurice Walsh's short story *The Quiet Man*.

She did well in her Abbey training and was given an opportunity for a screen test in London. The studio adorned her in a "gold lamé dress with flapping sleeves like wings" and heavy makeup with an ornate hair style. Reportedly, her thoughts concerning the incident were, "If this is the movies, I want nothing to do with them!" The screen test was deemed to be far from satisfactory; however, actor Charles Laughton later saw the test and, despite the overdone makeup and costume, was intrigued, paying particular notice to her large and expressive eyes.

Laughton subsequently asked his business partner Erich Pommer to see the film clip. Pommer agreed with Laughton and O'Hara was offered an initial seven-year contract with their new company, Mayflower Pictures. Her first major film was *Jamaica Inn* (1939) directed by Alfred Hitchcock. Laughton was so pleased with O'Hara's performance that he cast her in the role of Esmeralda opposite him in *The Hunchback of Notre Dame* (1939), which was to be filmed at RKO Studios in Hollywood that same year. After the successful completion of *Hunchback*, World War II began, and Laughton, realising that their studio could no longer film in London, sold O'Hara's contract to RKO. That studio cast her in low-budget films until she was rescued by director John Ford, who cast her as Angharad in *How Green Was My Valley*, which won the 1941 Academy Award for Best Picture.

More early roles included *To the Shores of Tripoli* (1942), *The Fallen Sparrow* (1943), *Buffalo Bill* (1944) with Joel McCrea, *The Spanish Main* (1945), *Sentimental Journey* (1946), and *Sinbad, the Sailor* (1947).

In 1947, she made what is perhaps her best-remembered film, starring as Doris Walker and the mother of a young Natalie Wood in 20th Century Fox's *Miracle on 34th Street*, which, despite being released in May, has become a perennial Christmas classic, with a traditional network television airing every Thanksgiving Day on NBC. The film also helped to further establish O'Hara's career after the film garnered several awards, including an Academy Award Nomination for Best Picture.

In 1946, she became a naturalised citizen of the United States and now holds dual citizenship with the US and her native Ireland.

More of her later roles included *The Redhead from Wyoming* (1953), *Lady Godiva of Coventry* (1955), *Everything But the Truth* (1956), *Our Man in Havana* (1959), *The Parent Trap* (1961), *Mr. Hobbs Takes a Vacation* (1962), *Spencer's Mountain* (1963), *The Rare Breed* (1966), and *The Red Pony* (1973).

In addition to her acting skills, O'Hara had a soprano voice and described singing as her first love. The studio heads never capitalised on her musical talent, as she was already big box office in other genres of film. However, she was able to channel her love of singing through television. In the late 1950s and early 1960s, she was a guest on musical variety shows with Perry Como, Andy Williams, Betty Grable and Tennessee Ernie Ford. In 1960, she starred on Broadway in the musical *Christine* which ran for twelve performances. That year she released two successful recordings, *Love Letters from Maureen O'Hara* and *Maureen O'Hara Sings her Favorite Irish Songs*. *Love Letters from Maureen O'Hara* has been released on CD in Japan and is now out of print.

An icon of Hollywood's Golden Age, at the height of her career, O'Hara was considered one of the world's most beautiful women. She is often remembered for her onscreen chemistry with John Wayne. They made five films together between 1948 and 1972: *Rio Grande, The Quiet Man, The Wings of Eagles, McLintock!* and *Big Jake*. A clip of O'Hara's radiant face as she waves from a gate in John Ford's Academy Award-winning *How Green Was My Valley*, remains one of the most classic images preserved on film and is often featured as a clip in montages and promotions.

In 1939, at the age of 19, O'Hara secretly married Englishman George H. Brown, a film producer, production assistant and occasional scriptwriter whose best known work is the first of Margaret Rutherford's 1960s Miss Marple mysteries, *Murder She Said*. The marriage was annulled in 1941. Later that year, O'Hara married American film director William Houston Price (dialogue director in *The Hunchback of Notre Dame*), but the union ended in 1953, reportedly as a result of his alcohol abuse. They had one child in 1944, a daughter named Bronwyn FitzSimons Price. Bronwyn has one son, Conor Beau FitzSimons, who was born on September 8, 1970. From 1953 until 1967 O'Hara had a relationship with Enrique Parra, a Mexican politician and banker. She wrote in her autobiography; "Enrique saved me from the darkness of an abusive marriage and brought me back into the warm light of life again. Leaving him was one of the most painful things I have ever had to do."

She married her third husband, Charles F. Blair, Jr., on March 12, 1968. Blair was a pioneer of transatlantic aviation, a former Brigadier General of the US Air Force, and a former Chief Pilot at Pan Am. A few years after her marriage to Blair, O'Hara for the most part retired from acting. Blair died in 1978 when an engine of a Grumman Goose he was flying from St. Croix to St. Thomas exploded. She was elected CEO and President of Antilles Airboats, with the added distinction of being the first woman president of a scheduled airline in the US Later she sold the airline with the permission of the shareholders.

O'Hara remained retired from acting until 1991, when she starred in the film *Only the Lonely*, playing Rose Muldoon, the domineering mother of a Chicago cop played by John Candy. In the following years, she continued to work, starring in several made-for-TV movies, including *The Christmas Box* (1995), *Cab for Canada* (1998), and *The Last Dance,* the latter her last film to date, released in 2000.

Now retired, she has homes in Arizona and the Virgin Islands, but lived mainly in Glengarriff, County Cork, after suffering a stroke in 2005. In June 2011, she participated at the Maureen O'Hara Film Festival in Glengarriff.

In May 2012, O'Hara's family contacted social workers regarding claims that O'Hara, who has short-term memory loss, was a victim of elder abuse. In September 2012, O'Hara flew to the US after receiving doctor's permission to fly. She lives with her grandson, Conor Beau FitzSimons, in Idaho.

On May 24-25, 2013, O'Hara made a public appearance at the 2013 John Wayne Birthday "Tribute to Maureen O'Hara" celebration in Winterset, Iowa. The occasion was the ground breaking for the new John Wayne Birthplace Museum; the festivities included an official proclamation from Iowa Governor Terry Branstad declaring May 25, 2013, as "Maureen O'Hara Day" in Iowa. The appearance included a performance by the Shannon Rovers Irish Pipe Band, who travelled from Chicago for the event. About Wayne, O'Hara said; "I was tough. I was tall. I was strong. I didn't take any nonsense from anybody. He was tough, he was tall, he was strong and he didn't take any nonsense from anybody. As a man and a human being, I adored him."

O'Hara received the Heritage Award by the Ireland-American Fund in 1991. For her contributions to the motion picture industry, O'Hara has a star on the Hollywood Walk of Fame at 7004 Hollywood Blvd. In 1993, she was inducted into the Western Performers Hall of Fame at the National Cowboy & Western Heritage Museum in Oklahoma City, Oklahoma. She was also awarded the Golden Boot Award.

In March 1999, O'Hara was selected to be Grand Marshal of New York City's St. Patrick's Day Parade.

In 2004, she was honored with a Lifetime Achievement Award from the Irish Film and Television Academy in her native Dublin. The same year, O'Hara released her autobiography *'Tis Herself,* co-authored with Johnny Nicoletti and published by Simon & Schuster. She has also written the foreword for the cookbook *At Home in Ireland,* and in 2007, she wrote the foreword for the biography of her dear friend, actress Anna Lee.

She was named *Irish America*'s "Irish American of the Year" in 2005, with festivities held at the Plaza Hotel in New York. In 2006, O'Hara attended the Grand Reopening and Expansion of the Flying Boats Museum in Foynes, Limerick, Ireland, as a patron of the museum. A significant portion of the museum is dedicated to her late husband Charles.

O'Hara donated her late husband's seaplane, the *Excambian* (a Sikorsky VS-44A), to the New England Air Museum. The restoration of the plane took eight years and time was donated by former pilots and mechanics in honor of Charles Blair. It is the only surviving example of this type of plane.

In 2011, O'Hara was formally inducted into the Irish America Hall of Fame at an event in New Ross, County Wexford. She was also named president of the Universal Film & Festival Organization (UFFO) which promotes a code of conduct for film festivals and the film industry.

In August 2014 the Academy of Motion Picture Arts and Sciences selected O'Hara to receive an Honorary Academy Award to be presented to her at the Governors Awards held on November 8, 2014 in Los Angeles. With this recognition O'Hara became the second actress, after Myrna Loy in 1991, to have received an Honorary Oscar for acting without ever having been nominated competitively.

Norman Ollestad

Norman Tennyson Ollestad was born on September 7, 1935 in Los Angeles, California. He was an actor, known for *The Good Bad Egg* (1947), *One Spooky Night* (1955), and *Ring of Terror* (1962).

More of his roles included *The Valley of Decision* (1945), *The Son of Rusty* (1947), *Stars in My Crown* (1950) with Joel McCrea, (1950), *Her Twelve Men* (1954), *The Glass Slipper* (1955), *Tea and Sympathy* (1956), and *High School Confidential!* (1958).

He was a passenger on a small chartered plane with his girlfriend Sandra and his son Norman Ollestad, Jr. (age 11) when the plane flew into a snow storm and struck a 8600 foot mountain and all died on February 19, 1979 in San Bernardino County, California. He was 43.

Moroni Olsen

Moroni Olsen was born in Ogden, Utah June 27, 1889 and was an American actor. Olsen was born to Mormon parents Edward Arenholt Olsen and Martha Hoverholst who named him after the Moroni found in the Book of Mormon.

Olsen studied at Weber State Academy, the predecessor of Weber State University. He then went to study at the University of Utah, where one of his teachers was Maud May Babcock. During World War I, he sold war bonds for the United States Navy.

In 1923 Olsen organized the "Moroni Olsen Players" out of Ogden. They performed at both Ogden's Orpheum Theatre and at various other locations spread from Salt Lake City to Seattle.

After having worked on Broadway he made his film debut in a 1935 adaptation of *The Three Musketeers*. He later played a different role in a 1939 comedy version of the story, starring Don Ameche as D'Artagnan and the Ritz Brothers as three dimwitted lackeys who are forced to substitute for the musketeers, who have drunk themselves into a stupor. One of his most famous roles was the voice of the Magic Mirror in Walt Disney's *Snow White and the Seven Dwarfs* (1937).

More of his roles included *Annie Oakley* (1935), *Mummy's Boys* (1936), *Gold Is Where You Find It* (1938), *Susannah of the Mounties* (1939), *Allegheny Uprising* (1939), *Virginia City* (1940), *One Foot in Heaven* (1941), *The Glass Key* (1942) with Alan Ladd and Veronica Lake, *Ali Baba and the Forty Thieves* (1944), *Buffalo Bill* (1944) with Joel McCrea, *Cobra Woman* (1944), *Thirty Seconds Over Tokyo* (1944), *It's a Wonderful Life* (1946), *Call Northside 777* (1948), *Samson and Delilah* (1949), *Lone Star* (1952), *I Love Lucy* (1952), *The Long, Long Trailer* (1953), and *Sign of the Pagan* (1954).

Olsen died on November 22, 1954 from a heart attack at the age of 65. He was buried in Ogden City Cemetery.

Patrick O'Moore

Patrick O'Moore was born on April 8, 1909 in Dublin, Ireland. He was an actor, known for *Sahara* (1943), *The Two Mrs. Carrolls* (1947), and *The Mechanic* (1972).

More of his roles included *Captains of the Clouds* (1942), *The Horn Blows at Midnight* (1945), *Bulldog Drummond at Bay* (1947), *Challenge to Lassie* (1949), *The Son of Dr. Jekyll* (1951), *Million Dollar Mermaid* (1952), *Titanic* (1953), *Adventures of Superman* (1955), *Trooper Hook* (1957) with Joel McCrea, *Cattle Empire* (1958) again with Joel McCrea, *Rawhide* (1959-1960), *Twilight Zone* (1964), *Get Smart* (1966), *Mannix* (1968), *Night Gallery* (1972), *The Sword and the Sorcerer* (1982), *Laverne & Shirley* (1982), *CHiPs* (1983), and The A-Team (1983).

He was married to Maggi O'Moore and Zelma O'Neal. He died on December 10, 1983 in Van Nuys, California at age 74.

Henry O'Neill

Henry O'Neill was born in Orange, New Jersey August 10, 1891 and was a film actor known for playing gray-haired fathers, lawyers, and similarly dignified roles during the 1930s and 1940s.

O'Neill began his acting career on the stage, after dropping out of college to join a traveling theatre company. He served in the military in World War I, and then returned to the stage. In the early 1930s he began appearing in films, including *The Big Shakedown* (1934) with Charles Farrell and Bette Davis, the Joel McCrea film *Wells Fargo* (1937), the Errol Flynn/Olivia de Havilland Western *Santa Fe Trail* (1940), *Air Raid Wardens* (1943 with Laurel and Hardy, the Frank Sinatra/Gene Kelly musical *Anchors Aweigh* (1945), *The Virginian* (1946) again with Joel McCrea, *The Green Years* (1946), and *The Reckless Moment* (1949). His last film was *The Wings of Eagles* (1957), starring John Wayne.

He was on the board of directors of the Screen Actors Guild and has a star on the Hollywood Walk of Fame.

O'Neill died in May 18, 1961 Hollywood, California at the age of 69.

Frank Orth

Frank Orth was born in Philadelphia, Pennsylvania February 21, 1880 and was an American actor. By 1897, he was performing in vaudeville with his wife, Ann Codee, in an act called "Codee and Orth". In 1909, he expanded into song writing, with songs such as "The Phone Bell Rang" and "Meet Me on the Boardwalk, Dearie".

His first contact with motion pictures was in 1928, when he was part of the first foreign-language shorts in sound produced by Warner Bros. He and his wife also appeared together in a series of two-reel comedies in the early 1930s. Orth's first major screen credit was in *Prairie Thunder*, a Dick Foran western, in 1937. From then on, he was often cast as bartenders, pharmacists, and grocery clerks, and always distinctly Irish.

He had a recurring role in the Dr. Kildare series of films and also in the Nancy Drew series as the befuddled Officer Tweedy. Among his better roles were the newspaper man Cary Grant telephones early in *His Girl Friday*, one of the quartet singing "Gary Owen" in *They Died with Their Boots On* (thereby giving Errol Flynnas Gen. Custer the idea of associating the tune with the 7th Cavalry), and as the little man carrying the sign reading "The End Is Near" throughout *Colonel Effingham's Raid.*

More of his roles included *Torchy Blane in Panama* (1938), *Fast and Furious* (1939), *Mexican Spitfire Out West* (1940), *Sergeant York* (1941), *The Ox-Bow Incident* (1943), *Buffalo Bill* (1944) with Joel McCrea, *The Strange Love of Martha Ivers* (1946), *Cheaper by the Dozen* (1950), and *Adventures of Superman* (1952).

However, Orth is probably best remembered for his portrayal of Inspector Faraday in the 1951-1953 television series *Boston Blackie*. A short, plump, round-faced man, often smoking a cigar, Orth as Faraday wore his own dark-rimmed spectacles, though rarely in feature films.

In 1959, Frank Orth retired from show business after throat surgery. His wife died in 1961 after more than sixty years of marriage. Orth lived for ten months without her and then died on St. Patrick's Day (March 17), 1962 at age 82. He is buried in Forest Lawn Cemetery - Hollywood Hills next to his wife.

Vivienne Osborne

Vivienne Osborne was born in Des Moines, Iowa December 10, 1896 and was an American stage and film actress known for her work in Broadway theater and in silent and sound films.

Osborne began her career on stage when she was 5 years old, and by the time she was 18 years old, she had already spent many years touring throughout Washington with a stock theater company. She made her Broadway theater debut when she was in her early twenties, and her screen debut in 1919 in a film that was never released. It was called *The Gray Brother,* but the film did not have distribution and was never released. She continued work on Broadway, and appeared in films when not working theater.

From March through December 1928, she appeared in the Florenz Ziegfeld musical version of *The Three Musketeers.* It was after her performance that Douglas Fairbanks, Sr. offered her a role his last silent film, *The Iron Mask* (1929), made as a sequel to his 1921 film *The Three Musketeers.* Rather than accept the offer, she chose to remain in New York City and continue her career. She signed with Paramount Studios in 1931 and was assigned to character roles, but left them to sign with Warner Studios in order to get better roles. She then left Warners and signed a three year contract with Radio Pictures. She alternated between film and stage roles for the rest of her carer.

Of her work in the *The Three Musketeers* musical, *Theatre Magazine* wrote her voice was "of true operatic quality."

Of her work as Mary Boyd in the 1931 film *Husband's Holiday*, *Spokesman-Review* wrote "Vivienne Osborne does fine work," and noted the several scenes which "tugged at the heartstrings" that were well done by Osborne and her co-star Juliette Compton.

More of her roles included *Over the Hill to the Poorhouse* (1920), *Husband's Holiday* (1931), *The Phantom Broadcast* (1933), *Follow Your Heart* (1936), *Primrose Path* (1940) with Joel McCrea, *Captain Caution* (1940) with Alan Ladd, *I Accuse My Parents* (1944), and *Dragonwyck* (1946).

She died June 10, 1961 at age 64 in Malibu, California.

Oscar O'Shea

Oscar O'Shea October 8, 1881 in Peterborough, Ontario, Canada (8 October 1881 and was a Canadian-born American character actor with over 100 film appearances from 1937 to 1953.

Some of his roles included *Captains Courageous* (1937), *Youth Takes a Fling* (1938) with Joel McCrea, *Of Mice and Men* (1939), *Riders of the Purple Sage* (1941), *Two Weeks to Live* (1943), *The Mummy's Ghost* (1944), *Without Reservations* (1946), *Fury at Furnace Creek* (1948), *The Daughter of Rosie O'Grady* (1950), and *Thy Neighbor's Wife* (1953).

He died 6 April 6, 1960 age 78 in Hollywood, California.

Robert Osterloh

Robert Osterloh was born May 31, 1918, in Pittsburgh, Pennsylvania. After his 1948 film debut in Columbia's *The Dark Past*, American general purpose actor Robert Osterloh was signed to a Warner Brothers contract.

During his Warners tenure, Osterloh was spotted in such fleeting roles as the prisoner whose mail is censored into oblivion in the 1949 James Cagney classic *White Heat* (1949). He then went into his "officer" period, wearing many uniforms and bearing several ranks over the next decade.

Among Robert Osterloh's 1950s film assignments were Major White in *The Day the Earth Stood Still* (1951), Colonel Robert E. Lee in *Seven Angry Men* (1955) and Lieutenant Claybourn in *I Bury the Living* (1958).

Some of his other films include *Fort Massacre* (1958) with Joel McCrea, *Inherit the Wind* (1960), *Young Dillinger* (1965), *The Oscar* (1966), *Rosemary's Baby* (1968), and *Coogan's Bluff* (1968).

He appeared in the television programs *Rebound* (1952), *My Hero* (1953), *Mr. & Mrs. North* (1954), *The Man Behind the Badge* (1955), the *G.E Theatre* episode "Farewell to Kennedy" (1955) with Alan Ladd, *Crusader* (1956), *Gunsmoke* (1958), *Perry Mason* (1957-1959), *Men Into Space* (1960), *Wanted: Dead or Alive* (1960), *Whispering Smith* (1961) with Audie Murphy, *The Outer Limits* (1964), *Ironside* (1971), *Hec Ramsey* (1972).

He died April 16, 2001, at age 82 in Los Osos, San Luis Obispo County, California.

Maureen O'Sullivan

Joel McCrea and Maureen O'Sullivan in *Woman Wanted*

Maureen Paula O'Sullivan was born in Boyle, County Roscommon, Ireland May 17, 1911 and was an Irish actress best known for playing Jane in the *Tarzan* series of films starring Johnny Weissmuller.

O'Sullivan was the daughter of Mary (née Frazer) and Charles Joseph O'Sullivan, an officer in the Connaught Rangers who served in World War I. She was of Irish, English, and Scottish ancestry. She attended a convent school in Dublin, then the Convent of the Sacred Heart at Roehampton (now Woldingham School), England. One of her classmates there was Vivian Mary Hartley, future Academy Award-winning actress Vivien Leigh. After attending finishing school in France, O'Sullivan returned to Dublin to work with the poor.

O'Sullivan's film career began when she met motion picture director Frank Borzage who was doing location filming on *Song o' My Heart* for 20th Century Fox. He suggested she take a screen test. She did and won a part in the movie, which starred Irish tenor John McCormack. She traveled to the United States to complete the movie in Hollywood. O'Sullivan appeared in six movies at Fox, and then made three more at other movie studios.

In 1932, she signed a contract with Metro-Goldwyn-Mayer. After several roles there and at other movie studios, she was chosen by Irving Thalberg to appear as Jane Parker in *Tarzan the Ape Man*, opposite co-star Johnny Weissmuller. She was one of the more popular ingenues at MGM throughout the 1930s and appeared in a number of other productions with various stars. In all, O'Sullivan played Jane in six features between 1932 and 1942.

She also starred with William Powell and Myrna Loy in *The Thin Man* (1934) and played Kitty in *Anna Karenina* (1935) with Greta Garbo and Basil Rathbone. She appeared with Joel McCrea in *Woman Wanted* (1935). She appeared as Molly Beaumont in *A Yank at Oxford* (1938), which was written partly by F. Scott Fitzgerald. At her request, he rewrote her part to give it substance and novelty.

She played another Jane in *Pride and Prejudice* (1940) with Laurence Olivier and Greer Garson, and supported Ann Sothern in *Maisie Was a Lady* (1941). After appearing in *Tarzan's New York Adventure* (1942), O'Sullivan asked MGM to release her from her contract so she could care for her husband who had just left the Navy with typhoid. She retreated from show business, devoting her time to her family. In 1948, she re-appeared on the screen in *The Big Clock,* directed by her husband for Paramount Pictures. She continued to appear occasionally in her husband's movies and on television. However, by 1960 she believed she had permanently retired. In 1958, Farrow's and O'Sullivan's eldest son, Michael, died in a plane crash in California.

Actor Pat O'Brien encouraged her to take a part in summer stock, and the play *A Roomful of Roses* opened in 1961. That led to another play, *Never Too Late*, in which she co-starred with Paul Ford in what was her Broadway debut. Shortly after it opened on Broadway John Farrow died of a heart attack. O'Sullivan stuck with acting after Farrow's death: she was the Today Girl for NBC for a while, then made the movie version of *Never Too Late* (1965) for Warner Bros.. She was also an executive director of a bridal consulting service, Wediquette International. In June and July 1972, O'Sullivan was in Denver, Colorado, to star in the Elitch Theatre production of *Butterflies are Free* with Karen Grassle and Brandon deWilde. The show ended on July 1, 1972. Five days later (on July 6, 1972), while still in Denver, deWilde was killed in a motor vehicle accident.

When her daughter, actress Mia Farrow, became involved with Woody Allen both professionally and romantically, she appeared in *Hannah and Her Sisters*, playing Farrow's mother. She had roles in *Peggy Sue Got Married* (1986) and the science fiction oddity *Stranded* (1987). Mia Farrow named one of her own sons Satchel Ronan O'Sullivan Farrow for her mother.

In 1994, O'Sullivan appeared with Robert Wagner and Stefanie Powers in *Hart to Hart: Home Is Where the Hart Is*, a feature-length made-for-TV movie with the wealthy husband-and-wife team from the popular weekly detective series *Hart to Hart*.

O'Sullivan's first husband was Australian-born writer, award-winning director and Catholic convert John Farrow, from September 12, 1936 until his death on January 28, 1963. She and Farrow were the parents of seven children: Michael Damien (1939–1958), Patrick Joseph (Patrick Villiers Farrow,1942–2009), Maria de Lourdes Villiers (Mia Farrow, born 1945), John Charles (born 1946), Prudence Farrow, Stephanie Farrow, and Theresa Magdalena "Tisa" Farrow.

A widow for twenty years, O'Sullivan was married to her second husband, James Cushing, from August 22, 1983 until her death in 1998.

Maureen O'Sullivan died in Scottsdale, Arizona of complications from heart surgery on June 23, 1998, at age 87. O'Sullivan is buried at Most Holy Redeemer Cemetery, Niskayuna, New York, her widower's hometown. She was survived by her six surviving children, thirty-two grandchildren and thirteen great-grandchildren. Michael, her oldest son, was killed in a plane crash in 1958.

O'Sullivan has a star on the Hollywood Walk of Fame at 6541 Hollywood Boulevard in Hollywood, California, facing the star of Johnny Weissmuller. A black plaque marks her home on Main Street in Boyle, County Roscommon, Ireland. Just around the corner from there, opposite King House, is a tree, ceremonially planted by O'Sullivan to mark her return to her birthplace.

In 1982, O'Sullivan was awarded The George Eastman Award, given by George Eastman House for distinguished contribution to the art of film.

Lynn Overman

Lynne Overman was born in Maryville, Missouri, September 19, 1887 and was an American actor. He began his career in theatre before becoming a film actor in the 1930s and early 1940s. In films he often played a sidekick.

Some of his roles included *Perfect Crime* (1928), *Little Miss Marker* (1934), *Men Without Names* (1935), *Murder Goes to College* (1937), *Union Pacific* (1939) with Joel McCrea, *Caught in the Draft* (1941), *Reap the Wild Wind* (1942), and *The Desert Song* (1943).

He died February 19, 1943 at age 55 in Santa Monica, California.

Reginald Owen

Reginald Owen and Joel McCrea in *Adventure in Manhattan*

John Reginald Owen was born in Wheathampstead, Hertfordshire, England August 5, 1887 and was a British character actor. He was known for his many roles in British and American films and later in television programs.

Owen studied at Sir Herbert Tree's Royal Academy of Dramatic Art and made his professional debut in 1905. In 1911 he starred in the original production of Where the Rainbow Ends as Saint George which opened to very good reviews on December 21, 1911. Reginald Owen had a few years earlier met the author Mrs. Clifford Mills as a young actor and it was he who on hearing her idea of a Rainbow Story persuaded her to turn it into a play and thus "Where the Rainbow Ends" was born.

He went to the United States in 1920 and worked originally on Broadway in New York, but later moved to Hollywood, where he began a lengthy film career. He was always a familiar face in many Metro-Goldwyn-Mayer productions.

Owen is perhaps best known today for his performance as Ebenezer Scrooge in the 1938 film version of Charles Dickens' *A Christmas Carol*, a role he inherited from Lionel Barrymore, who had played the part of Scrooge on the radio every Christmas for years, after Barrymore had broken his hip in an accident.

He was one of only four actors to play both Sherlock Holmes and his companion Dr Watson (Jeremy Brett played Watson on stage in the United States prior to adopting the mantle of Holmes on British television, Carleton Hobbs played both roles in British radio adaptations while Patrick Macnee played both roles in US television films).

Owen first played Watson in the film *Sherlock Holmes* (1932), and then Holmes himself in *A Study in Scarlet* (1933). Having played Ebenezer Scrooge, Sherlock Holmes and Dr. Watson, Owen has the odd distinction of playing three classic characters of Victorian fiction only to live to see those characters be taken over and personified by other actors, namely Alastair Sim as Scrooge, Basil Rathbone as Holmes and Nigel Bruce as Watson.

More roles included *The Countess of Monte Cristo* (1934), *The Call of the Wild* (1935), *Adventure in Manhattan* (1936) with Joel McCrea, *Bad Little Angel* (1939), *They Met in Bombay* (1941) with Alan Ladd, *The Canterville Ghost* (1944), *Green Dolphin Street* (1947), and *Darby's Rangers* (1958).

Later in his career, Owen appeared opposite James Garner in the television series *Maverick* in the episodes "The Belcastle Brand" (1957) and "Gun-Shy" (1958) and in episodes of the series *One Step Beyond* and *Bewitched*. He was also featured in the Walt Disney films *Mary Poppins* (1964) and *Bedknobs and Broomsticks* (1971). He had a small role in the 1962 Irwin Allen production of the Jules Verne novel *Five Weeks in a Balloon*. In August 1964, his Bel-Air mansion was rented out to The Beatles, who were performing at the Hollywood Bowl, when no hotel would book them.

He died November 5, 1972 from a heart attack at age 85 in Boise, Idaho.

Sarah Padden

Sarah Padden was born October 16, 1881 and was a character actress in theater and vaudeville from Chicago, Illinois. She performed on stage in the early 20th century. She is noted for her expressive voice and for her psychological studies of the characters she portrayed. Her finest single-act performance was in *The Clod*, a stage production in which she played an uneducated woman who lived on a farm during the American Civil War.

Padden took part in recitations in the Catholic Church school she attended in Chicago, where her fellow students enjoyed her talent as a mimic. Her parents wanted her to enter a convent, but a liberal-minded priest, Father Dorney, encouraged her ambition to become an actress. He assisted her in obtaining her first stage role, a theatrical featuring Otis Skinner.

For many years, Padden lived in the vicinity of the Broad River, Gaston, South Carolina. On one occasion she ventured onto a dam, reaching its center just as the noon whistle blew near the power station. Frightened, she lost her balance and fell over, but she managed to cling to a steel eyebolt. Fortunately she was rescued by an African

American servant of the power company superintendent. Afterwards Padden's parents hired the man and took him to New York, where he died at age 108.

Padden was a featured player on the Orpheum Circuit, Inc. She had a role in *His Grace de Grammont*, a romantic comedy by Clyde Fitch which came to the Park Theatre in Boston, Massachusetts in September 1905. The production starred Skinner and was based on the life of a chevalier in the court of Charles II. Padden appeared again with Skinner in a four-act play produced by Charles Frohman, *The Honor of the Family*, by Emile Fabre, which was presented in New Rochelle, New York in September 1907.

Another of her theatrical parts was in *Hell-Bent Fer Heaven*, a Pulitzer Prize-winning play by Hatcher Hughes. It was performed at the Wilkes Orange Grove Theater (Majestic Theater), 845 South Broadway (Los Angeles), in November 1925.

Padden was also an active screen actress from 1926 to 1958, appearing in 178 films and television shows.

In 1938, she played "Ma" Thayer in MGM's *Rich Man Poor Girl*, directed by Reinhold Schunzel and starring Robert Young, Ruth Hussey, and Lana Turner. Bill Harrison (Robert Young) a wealthy young businessman moves in with secretary girlfriend Joan Thayer's (Ruth Hussey) eccentric family to convince her they can make their marriage work.

In 1941, she played wealthy spinster Aunt Cassandra ("Cassie") Hildegarde Denham in *Murder by Invitation*, directed by Phil Rosen and starring Wallace Ford and Marian Marsh. In this "closed room" murder comedy, after they unsuccessfully attempt to have her declared legally insane to gain control of her fortune, her nephews and nieces are invited to a week's visit at her mansion where they are murdered one by one.

Other roles included *Our Blushing Brides* (1930), *Red-Headed Woman* (1932) with Jean Harlow, *Marrying Widows* (1934), *Women in Prison* (1938), *Lone Star Raiders* (1940), *This Gun for Hire* (1942) with Alan Ladd and Veronica Lake, *Ghost Guns* (1944), *Marshal of Laredo* (1945), as Mom Palooka in numerous Joe Palooka films starting with *Joe Palooka, Champ* (1946), *Ramrod* (1947) with Joel McCrea and Veronica Lake, *Gunslingers* (1950), *The Lone Ranger* (1950), *The Cisco Kid* (1950), *Big Jim McLain* (1952) with John Wayne and James Arness, *The Abbott and Costello Show* (1953), as Ma Riley in *The Life of Riley* (1953-1955), *Dragnet* (1956), and *No Time for Sergeants* (1958).

She was athletic, taking part in skating, tennis, and swimming. She played eighteen to thirty-six holes of golf daily. In 1919 she was considered one of the best female golfers in the United States. In Los Angeles, California she was fond of playing the municipal links at Griffith Park.

She died December 4, 1967 at age 86 in Los Angeles, California.

Bradley Page

Bradley Page was born on September 8, 1901 in Seattle, Washington. He was an actor, known for *The Affairs of Annabel* (1938), *The Big Store* (1941), and *Sherlock Holmes in Washington* (1943).

More of his roles included *Sporting Blood* (1931), *The Wet Parade* (1932), *Stage Mother* (1933), *The Fighting Ranger* (1934), *Champagne for Breakfast* (1935), *Two in a Crowd* (1936) with Joel McCrea, *The Outcasts of Poker Flat* (1937), *Beyond the Sacramento* (1940), *Sons of the Pioneers* (1942), and *Find the Blackmailer* (1943).

He died on December 8, 1985 in Brookings, Oregon at age 84.

Nester Paiva

Joel McCrea and Nester Paiva in *Ramrod*

Veteran character actor Nestor Paiva was born Nestor Caetano Paiva, June 30, 1905, in Fresno, California, and had one of those nondescript ethnic mugs and a natural gift for dialects that allowed him to play practically any type of foreigner.

He graduated from the University of California at Berkeley and developed an interest in performing while hooking up with college theatrics. Making his debut in a production of Antigone, he played in a Los Angeles production of *The Drunkard* for eleven years, finally leaving the show as his workload grew in number and importance in the mid-1940s.

Film buffs remember him as the main villain, "The Scorpion" in the wartime classic serial *Don Winslow of the Coast Guard* (1943). In hundreds of film and television roles from 1938-67 and in an overall career that spanned forty years, the bald, dark, and bulky Paiva played everything from Spaniards, Greeks, Russians, and Portuguese to Italians, Indians, Arabs, and even African-Americans (the latter on radio). Some were shifty, others excitable, many quite hilarious...and many of them undeserving and small.

Some of his recognizable film and television roles were *Ride a Crooked Mile* (1938), *Union Pacific* (1939) with Joel McCrea, *Beau Geste* (1939), *The Hunchback of Notre Dame* (1939), *Primrose Path* (1940) again with Joel McCrea, *The Sea Hawk* (1940), *The Green Hornet Strikes Again!* (1940), *Hold That Ghost* (1941) with Abbott and Costello, *Reap the Wild Wind* (1942) with John Wayne, *The Dancing Masters* (1943) with Laurel and Hardy, *Badman's Territory* (1946) with Randolph Scott, *Ramrod* (1947) with Joel McCrea and Veronica Lake, *Mighty Joe Young* (1949) with the big monkey, *The Desert Hawk* (1950), *China Smith* (1952), *Viva Zapata!* (1952), *Creature from the Black Lagoon* (1954), *Rocky Jones, Space Ranger* (1954), the Louis L'amour written film *Four Guns to the Border* (1954), *Sheena: Queen of the Jungle* (1955) with Irish McCalla, *Revenge of the Creature* (1955), *Tarantula* (1955), *Hell on Frisco Bay* (1955) with Alan Ladd, *The First Texan* (1956) with Joel McCrea again, *The Mole People* (1956), *The Guns of Fort Petticoat* (1957) with Audie Murphy, *The Deep Six* (1958) again with Alan Ladd, *Alias Jesse James* (1959) with Bob Hope, *Richard Diamond, Private Detective* (1959) with David Janssen, *Wichita Town* (1960) again with Joel McCrea, *Wanted: Dead or Alive* (1960) with Steve McQueen, *Atlantis, the Lost Continent* (1961), *The Four Horsemen of the Apocalypse* (1962), *The Three Stooges in Orbit* (1962) with Moe, Larry, and Curly Joe, *Girls! Girls! Girls!* (1962) with Elvis Presley, *Ballad of a Gunfighter* (1964), *Gunsmoke* (1965), *Get Smart* (1965), *The Addams Family* (1966), *Jesse James Meets Frankenstein's Daughter* (1966), *Let's Kill Uncle, Before Uncle Kills Us* (1966), and *They Saved Hitler's Brain* (1968).

He died September 9, 1966, at age 61 in Hollywood, California.

Eugene Pallette

Joel McCrea and Eugene Pallette in *Girls About Town*

Eugene William Pallette was born in Winfield, Kansas July 8, 1889 and was an American actor. He appeared in over 240 silent era and sound era motion pictures between 1913 and 1946.

After an early career as a slender leading man, Pallette appeared for decades as very obese with a large stomach and deep, gravelly voice, probably best-remembered for comic character roles such as Alexander Bullock, Carole Lombard's father, in *My Man Godfrey* (1936), as Friar Tuck in *The Adventures of Robin Hood* (1938) starring Errol Flynn, and his similar role as Fray Felipe in *The Mark of Zorro* (1940) starring Tyrone Power.

He was the son of William Baird Pallette (1858–?) and Elnora "Ella" Jackson (1860–1906). His sister was Beulah L. Pallette (1880–1968).

Pallette attended Culver Military Academy in Culver, Indiana. He then began his acting career on the stage in stock company roles, appearing for a period of six years.

Pallette began his silent film career as an extra in 1911. His first credited appearance was in the one-reel short western/drama *The Fugitive* (1913) which was directed by Wallace Reid for Flying "A" Studios at Santa Barbara.

Quickly advancing to featured status, Pallette appeared in many westerns. He worked with D. W. Griffith on such films as *The Birth of a Nation* (1915) and *Intolerance* (1916). At this time, he had a slim, athletic figure, a far cry from the portly build that would gain him fame later in his career.

After gaining a substantial amount of weight, Pallette gained status as a recognizable character actor. In 1927, he signed as a regular for Hal Roach Studios and was a reliable comic foil in several early Laurel and Hardy movies. In later years, Pallette's weight may have topped out at 300 pounds.

The advent of the talkies proved to be the second major career boost for Pallette. His inimitable rasping gravel voice (described as "half an octave below anyone else in the cast") made him one of Hollywood's most sought-after character actors in the 1930s and 1940s.

The typical Pallette role was the comically exasperated head of the family (as in *My Man Godfrey* and *The Lady Eve*), the cynical backroom sharpy (as in *Mr. Smith Goes to Washington*), or the gruff detective. However, Pallette's best known role may be as Friar Tuck in *The Adventures of Robin Hood*, and his similar appearance in *The Mark of Zorro*.

BBC commentator Dana Gioia gave this extensive description of Pallette's onscreen appeal:

"Pallette could anchor a scene just by walking downstairs. When he enters Preston Sturges's *The Lady Eve* (1941), trotting down to breakfast singing a merry ballad, he embodies all the small human hopes that screwball comedy exists to shatter.... The mature Pallette character is a creature of provocative contradictions—tough-minded but indulgent, earthy but epicurean, relaxed but excitable. His grit and gravel voice sounds simultaneously tough and comic. Even his corpulence is two-sided. In his best films Pallette made his fatness seem like a sign of moderation and common sense. As Friar Tuck in *The Adventures of Robin Hood* (1938) or Fray Felipe in *The Mark of Zorro* (1940), he shows that a fat priest is no heartless zealot but understands the sins of the flesh. Playing a tubby millionaire like the beer baron in *The Lady Eve* or Alexander Bullock in *My Man Godfrey* (1936), Pallette uses his girth to create a common touch. Stuffed into a tuxedo that seems perpetually near bursting, he seems more down-to-earth than the stylish high society types who surround him. Even Pallette's villains, like the corrupt and cynical politico Chick McCann in *Mr. Smith Goes to Washington*, are immensely likeable. Pushed too far, Pallette confidently uses his weight for physical force. When Bullock finally evicts the free-loading Carlo (Mischa Auer) in *My Man Godfrey*, we are not so much surprised as reassured by Pallette's manly strength. In battle his sword-wielding Friar Tuck is a glory to behold. Pallette may have gained weight, but he never lost his underlying virility."

More of his roles included *The Ten Commandments* (1923), *Whispering Smith* (1926), *The Second 100 Years* (1927), *The Battle of the Century* (1927), *The Virginian* (1929), *Girls About Town* (1931) with Joel McCrea, *Storm at Daybreak* (1933), *The Ghost Goes West* (1935), *One Hundred Men and a Girl* (1937), *The Male Animal* (1942), *It Ain't Hay* (1943) with Abbott and Costello, *In the Meantime, Darling* (1944), and *The Cheaters* (1945).

In increasingly ill health by his late 50s, Pallette made fewer and fewer movies, and for lesser studios. His final movie, *Suspense*, was released in 1946.

In 1946, convinced that there was going to be a "world blow-up" by atom bombs, Pallette received considerable publicity when he set up a "mountain fortress" on a 3,500-acre ranch near Imnaha, Oregon, as a hideaway from universal catastrophe. The "fortress" reportedly was stocked with a sizable herd of prize cattle, enormous supplies of food, and had its own canning plant and lumber mill.

When the "blow-up" he anticipated failed to materialize after two years, he began disposing of the Oregon ranch and returned to Los Angeles and his movie colony friends but, after working steadily from 1913 to 1946, never appeared in another movie.

Eugene Pallette died at age 65 on September 3, 1954 from throat cancer at his apartment, 10835 Wilshire Boulevard, in Los Angeles. His wife, Marjorie, and his sister, Beulah Phelps, were at his side. Private funeral services were conducted on Saturday, September 4, 1954, at the Armstrong Family Mortuary. His cremated remains are interred in an unmarked grave behind the monument of his parents at Green Lawn Cemetery in Grenola, Kansas. He has a star on the Hollywood Walk of Fame for his contribution to motion pictures at 6702 Hollywood Boulevard in Hollywood.

Franklin Pangborn

Franklin Pangborn was born in Newark, New Jersey January 23, 1889 and was an American comedic character actor. Pangborn was famous for small, but memorable roles, with a comic flair. He appeared in many Preston Sturges movies as well as the W.C. Fields films *International House* (1933), *The Bank Dick* (1940), and *Never Give a Sucker an Even Break* (1941).

In the early 1930s, Pangborn worked in short subjects for Mack Sennett, Hal Roach, Universal Pictures, Columbia Pictures, and Pathé Exchange, almost always in support of the leading players. (He played a befuddled photographer opposite "Spanky" McFarland in the *Our Gang* short subject Wild Poses (1933) which and Laurel and Hardy in a Cameo, for example.) He also appeared in scores of feature films in small roles, cameos, and in recurring gags of various types.

One of those character actors who always played essentially the same character no matter the situation, Pangborn portrayed a fussy type of person, polite, elegant, and highly energetic, often officious, fastidious, somewhat nervous, prone to becoming flustered but essentially upbeat, and with an immediately recognizable high-speed patter-type speech pattern. He typically played an officious desk clerk in a hotel, a self-important musician, a fastidious headwaiter, an enthusiastic birdwatcher, and the like, and was usually put in a situation of frustration or was comedically flustered by someone else's topsy-turvy antics.

Pangborn's screen character, which might be described at times as prissy or flighty, was often considered a gay stereotype, although such a topic was too sensitive in his day to be discussed overtly in the dialogue. A rare exception occurred in *International House*, which was filmed before the Hays Office fully censored filmmaking, and was notable for several risqué references (by 1933 standards). In this scene, Fields has just arrived by autogyro at the titular hotel in the Chinese city of Wuhu, but he does not know for sure where he is. Pangborn is the hotel manager:

> Fields: Where am I?
>
> Pangborn: *Wu*-hu!
>
> Fields (giving him a sharp look and removing a flower from his lapel): Don't let the green carnation *fool* you!

(Green carnations are often associated with Oscar Wilde.)

Pangborn was an effective foil for many major comedians, including Fields, Harold Lloyd, Olsen and Johnson, and The Ritz Brothers. He appeared regularly in comedies (including several directed by Preston Sturges) and musicals of the 1940s.

When movie roles became scarce, he worked in television, including *The Red Skelton Show* (1958)(in which he played a murderous bandit!) and a *This Is Your Life* tribute to his old boss, Mack Sennett.

Pangborn was very briefly the announcer on Jack Paar's *The Tonight Show*, but was fired after the first few weeks for a lack of "spontaneous enthusiasm" and replaced by Hugh Downs. The first episode is practically the only one that survives completely intact since the others were wiped by the network to save money (except for select clips), the network's policy through the early 1970s, and the show begins with Pangborn enthusiastically reading the introduction with the coda "...and it's all live!"

More of his numerous roles included *Getting Gertie's Garter* (1927), *Not So Dumb* (1930), *Hollywood Halfbacks* (1931), *Torchy Turns Turtle* (1933), *King Kelly of the U.S.A.* (1934), *Doughnuts and Society* (1936), *It Happened in Hollywood* (1937), *All Over Town* (1937) with Alan Ladd, *Rebecca of Sunnybrook Farm* (1938), *The Villain Still Pursued Her* (1940), *Sullivan's Travels* (1941) with Joel McCrea and Veronica Lake, *The Palm Beach Story* (1942) again with Joel McCrea, *Crazy House* (1943), *The Great Moment* (1944) yet again with Joel McCrea, *Hollywood Victory Caravan* (1945), *The Sin of Harold Diddlebock* (1947), *Romance on the High Seas* (1948), *Down Memory Lane* (1949), *The Alan Young Show* (1951), *Private Secretary* (1953), *The Colgate Comedy Hour* (1955), *Oh, Men! Oh, Women!* (1957), *The Story of Mankind* (1957), and *The Unchained Goddess* (1958).

Pangborn lived in Laguna Beach, California in a house with his mother.

For his contributions to motion pictures, Pangborn has a star on the Hollywood Walk of Fame at 1500 Vine Street.

He died on July 20, 1958 following cancer surgery at age 69. He is buried at Forest Lawn Memorial Park.

Jerry Paris

Jerry Paris was born William Gerald Grossman in San Francisco, California, July 25, 1925, and was an American actor and director best known for playing Jerry Helper, the dentist and next door neighbor of Rob and Laura Petrie, on *The Dick Van Dyke Show* (1961-1966).

After having directed some *Van Dyke* show episodes, Paris devoted himself to directing, both in television and film, most notably on the TV series *Happy Days* (1974-1984), for which he directed 238 episodes.

Paris had roles in films like *Frenchie* (1950) with Joel McCrea, *The Caine Mutiny* (1954), *The Wild One* (1953), *Marty* (1955), *D-Day the Sixth of June* (1956), *Man on the Prowl* (1957), *The Naked and the Dead* (1958), *No Name on the Bullet* (1959) with Audie Murphy, *The Great Impostor* (1961), *Don't Raise the Bridge, Lower the River* (1968), and *Leo and Loree* (1980).

Other television programs he appeared in were *Dragnet* (1952), *The Lone Wolf* (1955), *Those Whiting Girls* (1957), *Steve Canyon* (1959-1960), and also played Martin "Marty" Flaharty, one of Eliot Ness's men in a recurring role in the first season of ABC-TV's *The Untouchables* (1959-1960).

He married the former Ruth Benjamin, and they had three children. She died in 1980. Paris died from complications from brain cancer surgery March 31, 1986, at the age of 60. He was residing in Los Angeles, California, at the time of his death.

In the 1990s sitcom *The Nanny*, Fran Fine's grandmother Yetta Rosenberg played by Ann Morgan Guilbert showed a photo of Paris briefly and claimed it was her late husband. Guilbert played Millie Helper on *The Dick Van Dyke Show*.

Barnett Parker

William Barnett Parker was born September 11, 1886 in Batley, Yorkshire, England. Within the British colony of expatriate actors in Hollywood during the 1930's, Barnett Parker was among the most stereotypical. Harrowgate College-educated, straight-backed, balding and well-intoned, Parker caricatured a multitude of unctuous, stiff-upper-lip butlers, man-servants or waiters, though his performances could, at times, verge on the brink of being camp. When driven to frustration his characters commonly resorted to incoherent twitter or wild gesticulation.

Parker was trained under Marie Tempest and George Alexander in England. He first acted on Broadway at the Lyceum Theatre as Wilfred Tavish in Arthur Wing Pinero's "The "Mind the Paint" Girl" in 1912. He was well served with further roles in hit plays like "Hobson's Choice" (1915), "Artists and Models" (1924) and "The Red Robe" (1928).

He was at first prone to reject film offers, professing to favor acting on stage. Nonetheless, the celluloid medium eventually beckoned, enticing him to sign with the East Coast-based studio Thanhouser in 1915. He worked in films during the daytime (while treading the boards at night) and quickly landed a plum role as a weak socialite, rescuing Gladys Hulette in *Prudence, the Pirate* (1916). He was seldom thereafter afforded the opportunity for heroic acts. During the 1930's, he was primarily in demand for small roles as dandified or 'silly' Britishers, giving value for money in films like *Mr. Deeds Goes to Town* (1936), *Personal Property* (1937), *Live, Love and Learn* (1937) and *Broadway Melody of 1938* (1937).

More of his roles included *The Misleading Lady* (1920), *Adventure in Manhattan* (1936) with Joel McCrea, *Married Before Breakfast* (1937), *Marie Antoinette* (1938), *She Married a Cop* (1939), *He Married His Wife* (1940) again with Joel McCrea, *One Night in the Tropics* (1940) with abbott and Costello, and *New Wine* (1941).

Looking rather older than his years, Barnett Parker died at the Cedars of Lebanon Hospital in Los Angeles after multiple heart attacks at age 54 on August 5, 1941.

Emory Parnell

Emory Parnell was born in St. Paul, Minnesota December 29, 1892 and was an American vaudevillian and actor who appeared in over 250 films in his thirty-six year career. Nicknamed "The Big Swede", Parnell (who was sometimes credited as "Emery" or "Parnel") was married to Effie Laird, and they had two children together, one of whom, James Parnell, also became an actor.

Parnell trained as a musician at Morningside College, a Methodist institution in Sioux City, Iowa, and spent his early years as a concert violinist. He performed on the Chautauqua and Lyceum circuits until 1930, when he relocated to Detroit, Michigan, to narrate and act in commercial and industrial films. Seeking better opportunities in Hollywood, Parnell and his wife moved to Los Angeles, California, where, helped by his red-faced Irish look of frustration, he immediately began to appear in films in a variety of role, such as policemen, doormen, landlords, and small town businessmen.

Although his appearances were often in "B" films, such as the *Ma and Pa Kettle* series, he also made credible showings in "A" films as well. One notable part was as a Paramount studio executive who sang about avoiding libel suits to open 1941's *Louisiana Purchase*. Parnell was also part of writer-director Preston Sturges' unofficial "stock company" of character actors in the 1940s, appearing in five of Sturges' films, including *The Miracle of Morgan's Creek*, where he played the crooked banker, "Mr. Tuerck", the chief antagonist of William Demarest's "Constable Kockenlocker". He also made a memorable appearance as grumpy socialite Ajax Bullion in the Three Stooges short subject *All the World's a Stooge* (1941).

More of his roles included *Arson Gang Busters* (1938), *Union Pacific* (1939) with Joel McCrea, *They Shall Have Music* (1939) again with Joel McCrea, *Foreign Correspondent* (1940) a third with Joel McCrea, *The Maltese Falcon* (1941), *Sullivan's Travels* (1941) a fourth with Joel McCrea, *Arabian Nights* (1943), *The Dancing Masters* (1943) with Laurel and Hardy, *The Great Moment* (1944) a fifth with Joel McCrea, *Badman's Territory* (1946), *The Babe Ruth Story* (1948), *Ma and Pa Kettle* (1949), *The Redhead and the Cowboy* (1951), and *Lost in Alaska* (1952) with Abbott and Costello.

In May 1949, Parnell appeared on Broadway for the first and only time, in the play *Mr. Adam*, which ran for only five performances. In the 1950s, Parnell began to appear on television in both dramatic shows and situation comedies in roles similar to those that he had played in films. He appeared in *The Abbott and Costello Show* (1953), *My Little Margie* (1952-1954), *The Sheriff of Cochise* (1957), *The Life of Riley* (1953-1958), *Lawman* (1958-1960), *Perry Mason* (1964), and *The Andy Griffith Show* (1967).

Parnell's last acting appearance on television was in 1971 as a prospector on CBS's *Gunsmoke*. His last film role was as a bartender in the 1973 film, *Girls on the Road*. His final public appearance came in 1974, when he and his wife were interviewed by TV talk-show host Tom Snyder along with other residents of the Motion Picture Country Home and Hospital.

Parnell died of a heart attack in Woodland Hills, Los Angeles, California June 22, 1979 at age 86.

Milton Parsons

Ernest Milton Parsons was born in Gloucester, Massachusetts May 19, 1904 and was an American actor. He appeared in more than 160 films and television shows between 1939 and 1978.

Some of his roles included *Another Thin Man* (1939), *Hold That Ghost* (1941) with Abbott and Costello, *The Great Man's Lady* (1942) with Joel McCrea, *Who Done It?* (1942) again with Abbott and Costello, *Lost in a Harem* (1944) a third with Bud and Lou, *Dick Tracy vs. Cueball* (1946), *White Heat* (1949), *I Love Lucy* (1952), *The Monster That Challenged the World* (1957), *Elmer Gantry* (1960), *Twilight Zone* (1961-1963), *The Monkees* (1966), *Get Smart* (1969), *The Wild Wild West* (1966-1969), *Night Gallery* (1971), *Kolchak: The Night Stalker* (1975), *Switch* (1976), and *A Love Affair: The Eleanor and Lou Gehrig Story* (1978).

He died May 15, 1980 at age 75 in Los Angeles County, California.

Michael Pate

Joel McCrea and Michael Pate in *The Tall Stranger*

Michael Pate was born Edward John Pate February 26, 1920 in Drummoyne, Sydney, and was an Australian actor, writer, and director.

Initially interested in becoming a medical missionary, but unable to afford the university fees due to the Depression, he worked in Sydney before 1938, when he became a writer and broadcaster for the Australian Broadcasting Commission, collaborating with George Ivan Smith on *Youth Speaks*. For the remainder of the 1930s, he worked primarily in radio drama. He also published theatrical and literary criticism and enjoyed brief success as an author of short stories, publishing works in both Australia and the United States.

During World War II, Pate served in the Australian Army in the South West Pacific Area. He was transferred to the 1st Australian Army Amenities Entertainment Unit, known as "The Islanders", entertaining Australian troops in various combat areas.

After the war, Pate returned to radio, appearing in many plays and serials. Between 1946 and 1950 he began breaking into films. In 1949 he appeared in his first leading role in *Sons of Matthew*. In 1950, he appeared in *Bitter Springs* with Tommy Trinder and Chips Rafferty.

Also in 1950, Pate adapted, produced, and directed two plays — *Dark of the Moon* and *Bonaventure*. Later that year he travelled to the U.S. to appear in a film adaptation of *Bonaventure* for Universal Pictures, which was released in 1951 as *Thunder on the Hill*, starring Claudette Colbert and Ann Blyth.

Pate spent most of the 1950s in the U.S., appearing in over 300 television shows and many films. Most notable among these was a 1953 *Climax!* live production of Ian Fleming's *Casino Royale*, in which Pate played the role of "Clarence Leiter", opposite Barry Nelson's "Jimmy Bond". On the big screen, he played the one-scene role of Flavius in *Julius Caesar*, the 1953 film adaptation of William Shakespeare's play. In the same year he first played a Native American in Australian director John Farrow's western *Hondo* playing opposite John Wayne; he later said that this was his favorite film role. Pate went on to play many Native American roles. In 1956 he appeared in the film *The Court Jester*. Pate also played the lead role of a gunfighting vampire in the 1959 horror film *Curse of the Undead*.

During his time in the U.S., Pate became an acting instructor and lecturer, and wrote many screenplays and plays for the major American networks, including *Rawhide* ("Incident of the Boomerang")(It's actually 'Incident of the Power and the Plow' with Dick Van Patton) and *Most Dangerous Man Alive* ("The Steel Monster"). In 1959, he returned briefly to Australia, where he starred in the TV program *The Shell Hour*.

He returned to the U.S. for another eight years, during which he enjoyed a successful career as a television character actor, appearing repeatedly on such programs as *Gunsmoke* (1957-1964), *Black Saddle* (1959), *Wanted: Dead or Alive* (1959), *Wichita Town* (1960) with Joel McCrea, *The Texan* (1958-1960), *The Rifleman* (1958-1962), *Have Gun - Will Travel* (1957-1962), *Cheyenne* (1957-1962), *Branded* (1966), *Daniel Boone* (1964-1966), *The Virginian* (1963-1970), *Batman* (1966), *Perry Mason* (1963-1964), *Mission: Impossible* (1967), *The Man from U.N.C.L.E.* (1966.), *Get Smart* (1965), *Rawhide* (1959-1964), *Voyage to the Bottom of the Sea* (1964-1968), *Hondo* (1967), and *Wagon Train* (1958-1965).

More of his earlier film work includes *Houdini* (1953), *A Lawless Street* (1955), *7th Cavalry* (1956), *The Oklahoman* (1957) with Joel McCrea, *The Tall Stranger* (1957) again with Joel McCrea, *Westbound* (1959), *Green Mansions* (1959), with Audrey Hepburn, and *McLintock!* (1963).

In the 1963 movie *PT 109*, he played the part of Arthur Reginald Evans, the Australian coast watcher who helped rescue John F. Kennedy and his crew, one of the few times that Pate played an Australian while based in the United States.

In 1968, Pate returned to Australia and became a television producer, winning two Logie Awards while working at the Seven Network. In 1970, he published a textbook on acting, *The Film Actor*. From 1971 to 1975 he starred as Detective Senior Sergeant Vic Maddern in *Matlock Police* for 192 episodes.

After leaving *Matlock Police*, Pate began working more behind the camera, as well as continuing to work in theatre in both Sydney and Melbourne. In 1977 he wrote and produced *The Mango Tree*, starring his son Christopher Pate. In 1979 he adapted the screenplay for *Tim* from the novel by Colleen McCullough, as well as producing and directing the film, which starred Piper Laurie and Mel Gibson. Pate won the Best Screenplay Award from the Australian Writers Guild for his adaptation.

Pate also appeared (as the U.S. President) in *The Return of Captain Invincible* (1982), in which he sings "What the World Needs", a song calling for the return of Captain Invincible to save the world.

During the early 1980s Pate and his son Christopher collaborated in a stage production of *Mass Appeal*. This was a success, and closed with a season at the Sydney Opera House.

Some of his later work included *The Wild Duck* (1984), *Death of a Soldier* (1986), *The Marsupials: The Howling III* (1987), *Mission: Impossible* (1989), *The Existentialist Cowboy's Last Stand* (1995), and *Down Rusty Down* (1997).

Although Pate retired from acting in 2001 he remained busy with voiceover work, and was writing a screenplay at the time of his death.

He died on September 1, 2008 at Gosford Hospital in Sydney, New South Wales, Australia, of complications due to pneumonia at age 88.

Pate was married to Felippa Rock, daughter of American film producer Joe Rock, and had a son, Christopher (also an actor — both had cameos in the film *Howling III*) and a number of grandchildren and great-grandchildren.

Hank Patterson

Hank Patterson was born Elmer Calvin Patterson in Springville, Alabama, October 9, 1888, and was an American actor and musician. He is most known for playing stableman Hank Miller on *Gunsmoke* (1959-1975) and Fred Ziffel on *Petticoat Junction* (1963-1966) and *Green Acres* (1965-1971).

He had intended to be a serious pianist, but became instead a vaudeville piano player, eventually moving to Hollywood where he played in a series of movies, largely Westerns and science fiction from 1939 to 1973.

More of his roles included *Abilene Town* (1946), *Belle Starr's Daughter* (1948), *The Lone Ranger* (1949-1950), *Al Jennings of Oklahoma* (1951), *The Abbott and Costello Show* (1953), *Ride Clear of Diablo* (1954) with Audie Murphy, *Tarantula* (1955), *Gunsight Ridge* (1957) with Joel McCrea, *Attack of the Puppet People* (1958), *Earth vs. the Spider* (1958), *No Name on the Bullet* (1959) again with Audie Murphy, *Gunfighters of Abilene* (1960),

Whispering Smith (1961) a third appearance with Audie Murphy, *Twilight Zone* (1962-1964), *The Wild Wild West* (1965), *Laredo* (1966), *Mod Squad* (1969), and *Love, American Style* (1972).

Hank's great-grandfather, James Pearson, was an original settler of St. Clair County, Alabama as was his mother's great-grandfather, Thomas Newton. Between 1894 and 1897, the family left Alabama to live in Taylor, Texas, where Hank attempted to work as a serious musician only to settle for playing piano in traveling vaudeville shows.

Patterson's great-niece is actress Téa Leoni.

Hank Patterson died August 23, 1975, at age 86 in Woodland Hills, Los Angeles, California.

Kenneth Patterson

Kenneth Gordon Patterson was born on August 3, 1911 in Montana. He was an actor, known for *Invasion of the Body Snatchers* (1956), *...And Justice for All* (1979), and *Being There* (1979).

More of his roles included *The Searching Wind* (1946), *The Boy with Green Hair* (1948), *Cattle Drive* (1951) with Joel McCrea, *Dragnet* (1952), *The Lone Ranger* (1954), *Tombstone Territory* (1958), *Johnny Ringo* (1959-1960), *Perry Mason* (1959-1964), *Little House on the Prairie* (1980), *Lou Grant* (1981), and *Listen to Me* (1989).

He died on February 16, 1990 in Los Angeles County, California at age 78.

Sam Peckinpah

David Edward Samuel Ernest Peckinpah Jr. was born February 21, 1925 in Fresno, California and was an actor, director, writer, and producer. Young Sam was a loner. The child's greatest influence was grandfather Denver Church, a judge, congressman and one of the best shots in the Sierra Nevadas. Sam served in the US Marine Corps during World War II but - to his disappointment - did not see combat. Upon returning to the US he enrolled in Fresno State College, graduating in 1948 with a B.A. in Drama. He married Marie Selland in Las Vegas in 1947 and they moved to Los Angeles, where he enrolled in the graduate Theater Department of the University of Southern California the next year. He eventually took his Masters in 1952.

After drifting through several jobs -- including a stint as a floor-sweeper on The Liberace Show (1952) Sam got a job as Dialogue Director on *Riot in Cell Block 11* (1954) for director Don Siegel. He worked for Siegel on several films, including *Invasion of the Body Snatchers* (1956), in which Sam played Charlie Buckholtz, the town meter reader. His other few acting roles in the 1950s were *Dial Red O* (1955), *An Annapolis Story* (1955), and *Wichita* (1955) with Joel McCrea.

Peckinpah eventually became a scriptwriter for such TV programs as *Gunsmoke* (1955) and *The Rifleman* (1958) (which he created as an episode of Dick Powell's *Zane Grey Theater* (1956) titled "The Sharpshooter' in 1958). In 1961, as his marriage to Selland was coming to an end, he directed his first feature film, a western titled *The Deadly Companions* (1961) starring Brian Keith and Maureen O'Hara.

However, it was with his second feature, *Ride the High Country* (1962),that Peckinpah really began to establish his reputation. Featuring Joel McCrea and Randolph Scott (in his final screen performance), its story about two aging gunfighters anticipated several of the themes Peckinpah would explore in future films, including the controversial *The Wild Bunch*.

Following *Ride the High Country* he was hired by producer Jerry Bresler to direct *Major Dundee* (1965), a cavalry-vs.-Indians western starring Charlton Heston. It turned out to be a film that brought to light Peckinpah's volatile reputation. During hot, on-location work in Mexico, his abrasive manner, exacerbated by booze and marijuana, provoked usually even-keeled Heston to threaten to run him through with a cavalry saber. However, when the studio later considered replacing Peckinpah, it was Heston who came to Sam's defense, going so far as to offer to return his salary to help offset any overages. Ironically, the studio accepted and Heston wound up doing the film for free.

Post-production conflicts led to Sam engaging in a bitter and ultimately losing battle with Bresler and Columbia Pictures over the final cut and, as a result, the disjointed effort fizzled at the box office. It was during this period that Peckinpah met and married his second wife, Mexican actress Begoña Palacios. However, the reputation he earned because of the conflicts on *Major Dundee* contributed to Peckinpah being replaced as director on his next film, the Steve McQueen film *The Cincinnati Kid* (1965), by Norman Jewison.

His second marriage now failing, Peckinpah did not get another feature project for two years. However, he did direct a powerful adaptation of Katherine Anne Porter's *Noon Wine* for ABC Stage 67: *Noon Wine* (1966). This, in turn, helped relaunch his feature career. He was hired by Warner Bros. to direct the film for which he is, justifiably, best remembered. The success of *The Wild Bunch* rejuvenated his career and propelled him through highs and lows in the 1970s. Between 1970-1978 he directed *The Ballad of Cable Hogue* (1970), *Straw Dogs* (1971), *Junior Bonner* (1972), *The Getaway* (1972), *Pat Garrett & Billy the Kid* (1973), *Bring Me the Head of Alfredo Garcia* (1974), *The Killer Elite* (1975), *The Cross of Iron* (1977) and *Convoy* (1978).

Throughout this period controversy followed him. He provoked more rancor over his use of violence in *Straw Dogs*, introduced Ali MacGraw to Steve McQueen in *The Getaway*, fought with MGM's chief James T. Aubrey over his vision for *Pat Garrett & Billy the Kid* that included the casting of Bob Dylan in an unscripted role as a character called "Alias." His last solid effort was the WW II anti-war epic *Cross of Iron,* about a German unit fighting on the Russian front, with Maximilian Schell and James Coburn, bringing the picture in successfully despite severe financial problems.

Peckinpah lived life to its fullest. He drank hard and abused drugs, producers and collaborators. At the end of his life he was considering a number of projects including the Stephen King-scripted *The Shotgunners*. He was returning from Mexico December 28, 1984 when he died from heart failure in a hospital in Inglewood, California, at age 59. At a standing-room-only gathering that held at the Directors Guild the following month, Coburn remembered the director as a man "who pushed me over the abyss and then jumped in after me. He took me on some great adventures". To which Robert Culp added that what is surprising is not that Sam only made fourteen pictures, but that given the way he went about it, he managed to make any at all.

Nat Pendleton

Nathaniel Greene "Nat" Pendleton was born in Davenport, Iowa August 9, 1895 and was an American Olympic wrestler and film actor.

Pendleton was born to Adelaide E. and Nathaniel G. Pendleton. He studied at Columbia University where he began his wrestling career. He was twice Eastern Intercollegiate Wrestling Association (EIWA) champion in 1914 and 1915. Chosen to compete in the US wrestling team at the 1920 Summer Olympics in Antwerp, Belgium, Pendleton lost only one match during the competition, and was awarded a silver medal. Returning to the US he became a professional wrestler, and with the celebrity status he had achieved, drifted into films in the late 1920s.

His early roles were largely uncredited. Then he was chosen to appear in *Horse Feathers* (1932) with the Marx Brothers as one of the two college football players who kidnap Harpo and Chico, and his career began to develop. His role as circus strongman Eugen Sandow in *The Great Ziegfeld* (1936) brought him the strongest reviews of his career. Pendleton was most often cast in supporting roles as thugs, gangsters, or policemen and was usually typecast playing characters that depended on their brawn but were "none too bright".

Some of his other films include *The Thin Man* (1934) and *At the Circus* (1939), again with the Marx Brothers. He appeared in recurring roles in two MGM film series of the late 1930s and 1940s - as Joe Wayman, the ambulance driver in the *Dr. Kildare* series, and its spin-off, the *Dr. Gillespie* series.

More of his roles included *The Sea Wolf* (1930), *The Beast of the City* (1932), *Fugitive Lovers* (1934), *Two in a Crowd* (1936) with Joel McCrea, *Young Dr. Kildare* (1938), *Buck Privates* (1941) with Abbott and Costello, Swing Fever (1943), and *Death Valley* (1946).

He made his final film appearances in *Scared to Death* with Bela Lugosi, and *Buck Privates Come Home* (both 1947).

Pendleton died in San Diego, California in October 12, 1967 from a heart attack at age 72.

Steve Pendleton

Gaylord "Steve" Pendleton was born September 16, 1908, and was an American film actor. He appeared in over 150 films during his career.

The younger brother of comic actor Nat Pendleton, he entered films in 1923. He was usually cast as collegiate types (undergrads, military school cadets), with a few weaklings and villains thrown in. Fans of Bob Hope and Bing Crosby will remember Pendleton as tuxedoed "other man" Gordon Wycott in *Road to Singapore* (1940). Active in films and television until 1976, Gaylord Pendleton was generally confined to minor roles, with a handful of leads and second leads in serials and comedy two-reelers.

Some of his works include *Twentieth Century* (1934), *Internes Can't Take Money* (1937) with Joel McCrea, *Ride a Crooked Mile* (1938), *The Grapes of Wrath* (1940), *Sergeant York* (1941), *The Return of Rin Tin Tin* (1947), *Beyond Glory* (1949) with Alan Ladd and Audie Murphy, *Rio Grande* (1950), *Indian Uprising* (1952), *The Great Jesse James Raid* (1953), *Target Earth* (1954), *Battle Hymn* (1957), *Guns of the Timberland* (1960) again with Alan Ladd, *Blood Bath* (1966), *Pit Stop* (1969), and *Cannon* (1976).

He died October 3, 1984 in Pasadena, California, at age 76.

Barbara Pepper

Barbara Pepper was born Marion Pepper May 31, 1915 in New York City, New York and was an American actress. Barbara Pepper's signature roles were as worldly "dames" during the Hollywood's 1930s and 1940s Golden Era, fitting snugly alongside other flashy broads of that period such as Iris Adrian, Joan Blondell and Veda Ann Borg. Barbara patented her own unique, hard-boiled style, however, and should have gone further than she did. Most people who remember this fine character actress today as Doris Ziffel, the shrill, slovenly barnyard neighbor of Eddie Albert and Eva Gabor on TV's highly popular bucolic Green Acres (1965) series, will find it almost impossible to visualize the hefty, porcine-like actress from that sitcom as a blue-eyed, platinum-blonde knockout and former Ziegfeld/Goldwyn Girl way back when.

By age 16, her mind was already set for a show biz career. Within a short time, and against her parents' wishes, she nabbed a show girl spot in Florenz Ziegfeld, Jr.'s Follies and changed her first name to Barbara. Here is where she met fellow chorine Lucille Ball and the two became lifetime, dedicated friends. After appearing as a member of the "George White's Scandals" on Broadway, Barbara soon integrated radio and film work as well, paying her dues primarily in bit parts as saloon girls, clerks, chippies, and the like.

Her film debut was as a slave girl extra (along with Lucy) in Eddie Cantor's *Roman Scandals* (1933). A couple of movies gave her the chance for brassy stardom, including *Our Daily Bread* (1934) as a floozie named Sally, and a love interest role opposite comedian Bert Wheeler (of Wheeler and Woolsey) in *Mummy's Boys* (1936), but the roles were basically one-dimensional and she remained in the secondary ranks for the rest of her career.

Her father, Dave Pepper, a non-professional, put together a brief, minor character career when he visited his daughter on the film set of *Wanted! Jane Turner* (1936) and was cast by director Edward Killy in the unbilled role of a detective. Father and daughter both also appeared in another movie the following year: *The Outcasts of Poker Flat* (1937).

More of her early work included *Hollywood Stadium Mystery* (1938), *Of Mice and Men* (1939), *Foreign Correspondent* (1940) with Joel McCrea, and *My Favorite Spy* (1942).

Trained by acting guru Maria Ouspenskaya at one stage, she married actor Craig Reynolds (ne Harold Hugh Enfield) in 1943 and the marriage proved a loving one despite later financial hardships when both could only find sporadic work. On stage in 1944, they appeared together in a modern version of "Lady Chatterly's Lover" at the Geary Theater in San Francisco. They went on to have two sons, Dennis Michael and John Hugh Enfield.

In 1949, however, her husband died tragically in a motorcycle accident. Barbara was absolutely devastated. Overwhelmed with her loss and the prospect of raising two sons alone, severe depression and a debilitating alcohol problem set in. Forced to find work as a laundress and waitress in between sparse acting parts, her weight quickly ballooned while her features grew coarse and bloated. During this period she could only muster up tiny roles on film and TV as various comic snoops and harridans.

Friends like Lucy stepped in to help. Over the years, Barbara would be glimpsed several times on I Love Lucy (1951), including the classic episode "Friends of the Friendless" and as a frightened hospital nurse who is taken aback by Ricky Ricardo's severe voodoo make-up when Lucy gives birth to Little Ricky. Barbara also brightened up other TV comedies with small parts on Jack Benny's program as well as George Burns and Gracie Allen's popular show. She could also be found occasionally on the *Perry Mason* (1957) series playing minor but colorful characters.

In the 1960s, Barbara was glimpsed as a minor, plus-sized foil for Jerry Lewis in several of his slapstick film vehicles (*Rock-a-Bye Baby* (1958), *Who's Minding the Store?* (1963), *The Patsy* (1964) and *Hook, Line and Sinker* (1969), the last mentioned released posthumously). One bright respite from all her financial miseries during this time came with a steady paycheck and her semi-regular series role as "mother" to a TV-watching pig on the popular *Green Acres* (1965) series. Barbara worked very well alongside crusty veteran character actor Hank Patterson as her close-to-deaf, dirt-farmer husband Fred Ziffel, although "son" Arnold the Pig received more fan mail than the two adults put together!

While Barbara was quite fun in her cranky bucolic role, the fun wouldn't last very long. Her health began to deteriorate rapidly during the run of this sitcom and she was eventually forced to relinquish the part during the 1968-1969 season, with actress Fran Ryan taking over the part. Plagued by a heart condition, Barbara died of a coronary in July 18, 1969, at the age of 54.

Dorothy Peterson

Dorothy Peterson was born Bergetta Peterson in Hector, Minnesota December 25, 1897 and was an American film and television actress.

Peterson was of Swedish immigrant ancestry. She made her screen debut in 1930s *Mothers Cry*, a domestic drama that required the 29-year-old actress to age nearly three decades in the course of the film. *Mothers Cry* instantly typecast Peterson in careworn maternal roles, which she continued to essay for the rest of her career.

Most of her subsequent film assignments were supporting roles like Mrs. Hawkins in *Treasure Island* (1934). In 1942, she briefly replaced Olive Blakeney as Mrs. Aldrich in the comedy series entry *Henry Aldrich for President*.

More of his roles included *Traveling Husbands* (1931), *Business and Pleasure* (1932) with Joel McCrea, *The Mayor of Hell* (1933), *The Country Doctor* (1936), *Five Little Peppers and How They Grew* (1939), *Cheers for Miss Bishop* (1941), *The Woman in the Window* (1944), and *Sister Kenny* (1946).

Her last screen appearance was as the mother of Shirley Temple in *That Hagen Girl* (1947). Peterson remained active on the New York TV and theatrical scene until the early 1960s. She appeared in eighty-three films, and made several television appearances between 1930 and 1964.

She died October 3, 1979 in New York City at age 81.

Howard Petrie

Joel McCrea and Howard Petrie in *Border River*

Howard Alexander Petrie was born in Beverly, Massachusetts November 22, 1906 and was an American radio, television, and film actor.

When Howard was three years old his family moved to Concord, Massachusetts. The Petries later lived in Arlington, Massachusetts and then Somerville, Massachusetts, where Howard Petrie received his secondary school education. A talented musician, he conducted his high school glee club and played with various instrumental groups. He was a member of the debating team, a captain in the School Regiment and Chairman of the Senior Night Committee.

Petrie appeared in school dramatic productions including a starring role as "Marquis de la Seigliere" in the senior class play and the Jules Sandeau three-act comedy, *Mademoiselle de la Seigliere.*

After he graduated from Somerville High School in 1924, Petrie worked briefly as a bank clerk and a securities salesman. While on a sales call to a radio station, his sonorous bass voice landed him a job. He joined WBZ Radio in Boston in 1929 as a junior announcer. After ten months at the WBZ studios, Petrie left for New York City in June, 1930 where he joined the staff of NBC. Petrie soon became the head announcer for many of the network's shows. His first major network assignment was on *Everything Goes,* starring Garry Moore. He was the announcer for scores of shows including *Abbie's Irish Rose, Big Sister, Camel Caravan, Blondie, The Ray Bolger Show, The Judy Canova Show, The Jimmy Durante Show,* and *The Garry Moore Show.*

While at NBC he met his future wife, Alice Wood who was employed at NBC between 1931 and 1936. The Petries had one son.

In 1936, Petrie won the prestigious Batten, Barten and Durstine Award for Good Announcing. In 1942 he was the recipient of the H.P. Davis Memorial Announcers' Award for "personality, adaptability, diction, voice and versatility." Petrie moved to California in 1943 to become the announcer for *The Judy Canova Show.* As a "personality announcer," he became a character in the show.

In 1947, a movie producer who was looking for a tall man for a character role, saw Petrie on the radio stage and offered him the part. At 6 feet four and 240 pounds, Petrie played numerous "big man" roles. He worked as a character actor in over thirty feature films and forty television shows. He often appeared in Westerns in both mediums.

Some of his roles included *The Fabulous Joe* (1947), *Cattle Drive* (1951) with Joel McCrea, *Carbine Williams* (1952), *Border River* (1954) again with Joel McCrea, *Rage at Dawn* (1955), *Gunsmoke* (1956), *The Tin Star* (1957), *Wanted: Dead or Alive* (1959-1960), *Rawhide* (1960-1961), and *Death Valley Days* (1960-1962).

Howard Petrie had been living in semi-retirement at his home, Autumn Hill, in Walpole, New Hampshire, when he died in Keene, New Hampshire, on March 24, 1968.

Buster Phelps

Buster Phelps was born Silas Vernon Phelps, Jr. on November 5, 1926 in Los Angeles, California. He was an actor, known for *Little Orphan Annie* (1932), *Broken Dreams* (1933), and *Anna Karenina* (1935).

More of his roles included *Stepping Sisters* (1932), *One Man's Journey* (1933) with Joel McCrea, *The World Gone Mad* (1933), *The Affair of Susan* (1935), *Libeled Lady* (1936), *Little Tough Guy* (1938), *Slightly Tempted* (1940), *The Wagons Roll at Night* (1941), *And the Angels Sing* (1944), *Tomorrow Is Forever* (1946), and *Mother Is a Freshman* (1949).

He died on January 10, 1983 in Los Angeles at age 56.

Lee Phelps

Lee Phelps was born Napoleon Bonaparte Kukuck May 15, 1893 in Philadephia, Pennsylvania and was an American film actor. He appeared in over 600 films between 1917 and 1953, mainly in uncredited roles. He also appeared in three films that won the Academy Award for Best Picture (*Grand Hotel*, *You Can't Take it With You* and *Gone with the Wind*).

Some of his roles included *The Little Shepherd of Kingdom Come* (1920), *Putting Pants on Philip* (1927), *Puttin' on the Ritz* (1930), *The Public Enemy* (1931), *The Beast of the City* (1932), *King Kong* (1933), *Dancing Lady* (1933), *Roast-Beef and Movies* (1934), *Gambling Lady* (1934) with Joel McCrea, *Public Hero #1* (1935), *Woman Wanted* (1935) again with Joel McCrea, *The Bohemian Girl* (1936), *Our Relations* (1936), *Internes Can't Take Money* (1937) a third with Joel McCrea, *Wells Fargo* (1937) a fourth with Joel McCrea, *Convicts at Large* (1938), *They Shall Have Music* (1939) a fifth with Joel McCrea, *Knute Rockne All American* (1940), *Pacific Blackout* (1941), *The Great Man's Lady* (1942) a sixth with Joel McCrea, *Air Raid Wardens* (1943), *Arsenic and Old Lace* (1944), *Scarlet Street* (1945), *Ding Dong Williams* (1946), *Red River* (1948), *The Cisco Kid* (1950), *Carbine Williams* (1952), *The Lone Ranger* (1950-1952), and *The Beast from 20,000 Fathoms* (1953).

He died March 19, 1953 at age 59 in Culver City, Los Angeles, California.

Carmen Phillips

Carmen Phillips was born January 10, 1937 in Chicago, Illinois. She was an actress, known for *Ask Any Girl* (1959), *Please Don't Eat the Daisies* (1960), and *Easy Rider* (1969).

Some of her other roles included *Alfred Hitchcock Presents* (1958), *Alcoa Presents: One Step Beyond* (1959), *Perry Mason* (1960), *Ocean's Eleven* (1960), *Laramie* (1961), *Ride the High Country* (1962) with Joel McCrea, *The Lieutenant* (1963-1964), *Destry* (1964), *The Alfred Hitchcock Hour* (1962-1965), *Laredo* (1966), and *Games* (1967).

She was married to David Morin. She died on September 22, 2002 in Hollywood, California at age 65.

Phillip Phillips

Philip Phillips is an actor, known for *Hot Shots* (1956), Louis L'amour's *The Tall Stranger* (1957) with Joel McCrea, and *Wanted: Dead or Alive* (1958) with Steve McQueen.

Some of his other roles included *The Jack Benny Program* (1957), *M Squad* (1959), *The Loretta Young Show* (1958-1960), *McKeever & the Colonel* (1962-1963), and *Make Room for Daddy* (1956-1963).

William Phipps

William Edward "Bill" Phipps was born in Vincennes, Indiana February 4, 1922 and is a retired American actor and producer, perhaps best known for his roles in dozens of classic sci-fi and westerns, both in films and on television.

Phipps grew up in St. Francisville in Lawrence County in southeastern Illinois. His parents divorced when he was six years old. By the time he was in high school, he was using his stepfather's last name of Couch. He developed a love of acting at a young age and performed in several plays in grade school and high school. One of the plays in which he performed, during his junior year of high school in 1937, was *Before Morning*, a 1933 play made into a film that same year.

After graduating from high school in 1939, he attended Eastern Illinois University in Charleston, Illinois, where he majored in accounting, was elected freshman class president and served as head cheerleader. After two years of college, he moved to Hollywood, to pursue a career in acting and resumed his original last name of Phipps.

During that same year, the United States entered into World War II, and Phipps enlisted in the United States Navy, serving as a radio operator on several ships all across the Pacific. He served three years, and then settled in Los Angeles to begin his career. He enrolled in the Actors' Lab in Hollywood, alongside fellow actor Russell Johnson.

Phipps' big break came when he and Johnson were double-cast in a play at the Actors Lab. They drew straws to see which actor would perform in the matinée, and which would take the evening show. Phipps drew the evening show, which was attended that same evening by actor Charles Laughton. Laughton was impressed by Phipps' performance, and came backstage afterwards to ask Phipps to perform in Laughton's own play. Phipps' career took off, and he was soon in his first feature film, *Crossfire* (1947). In 1949, Phipps auditioned for the speaking voice of Prince Charming in the upcoming Disney film Cinderella. The studio was pleased with his performance and Phipps was offered the part by Walt Disney himself.

More roles followed such as *The Arizona Ranger* (1948), *The Outriders* (1950) with Joel McCrea, the post-apocalyptic *Five* (1951) (his only leading role), *Invaders from Mars* (1953), *The War of the Worlds* (1953), *Jesse James vs. the Daltons* (1954), *The First Texan* (1956) again with Joel McCrea, *M Squad* (1957-1960), *Twilight Zone* (1960), *The Life and Legend of Wyatt Earp* (1956-1961), *The Evil of Frankenstein* (1964), *Harlow* (1965), *The Munsters* (1965), *The Green Hornet* (1966), *The Guns of Will Sonnett* (1968-1969), *Police Woman* (1976), *Baretta* (1976), *Charlie's Angels* (1977), *Eight Is Enough* (1981), *Boone* (1983-1984), narrating the television version of *Dune* (1984), *T.J. Hooker* (1986), *Highway to Heaven* (1984-1988), *Empty Nest* (1990), and *Homeward Bound: The Incredible Journey* (1993).

After nearly thirty years in the business, performing in film and television in a wide variety of roles, Phipps took a break from Hollywood and moved to Hawaii. While there, he hosted a movie presentation program called "Hollywood Oldies", on Maui's Cable 7. After a little more than five years in Hawaii, he returned to Hollywood to portray President Theodore Roosevelt in the 1976 television movie *Eleanor and Franklin*.

Phipps' last movie role to date was in the 2000 independent film *Sordid Lives*, in which he also served as one of the film's producers. In 2005, several of Phipps' films were the subject of an EIU (Eastern Illinois University) film festival in his honor. He received an honorary doctorate from the university the following year.

Paul Picerni

Paul Picerni with Joel McCrea in *Saddle Tramp* and with author in 2002

Paul Vincent Picerni was born in New York, December 1, 1922, and was an American actor. As a child Paul Picerni had aspirations to become an attorney until he acted in an eighth-grade play and later learned that the school principal liked his performance and called him "a born actor".

He was an Eagle Scout who joined the United States Army Air Forces during World War II, where he served as a B-24 Liberator bombardier in the China-Burma-India Theater. He flew twenty-five combat missions with the 493rd Bomb Squadron of the 7th Bomb Group and received the Distinguished Flying Cross. He was part of a mission that attacked and destroyed the real bridge made famous in the film *The Bridge on the River Kwai* (1957). After the Japanese surrendered, Picerni became a Special Services officer in India. Following his discharge, he enrolled at Loyola Marymount University, at Los Angeles.

As a young actor returning from the war, he appeared in military pictures: his first film was in *Beyond Glory* (1948) with Alan Ladd and Audie Murphy, and *Twelve O'Clock High* (1949) as a bombardier and as Private Edward P. Rojeck in *Breakthrough* (1950).

He made an appearance in *Saddle Tramp* (1950) with Joel McCrea and Wanda Hendrix, Audie Murphy's wife at the time. This led to a Warner Brothers contract for Picerni and a succession of roles at that studio including a starring turn as the hero in the 1953 horror classic *House of Wax*.

After his departure from Warners, he appeared with Audie Murphy again in Universal Studio's *To Hell and Back* (1955).

He then appeared in the pilot episode for the 1957-1958 NBC detective series, *Meet McGraw*, starring Frank Lovejoy. Picerni appeared in two episodes, "Gun Hand" and "Badge to Kill" of the 1957-1959 syndicated western series *26 Men*, true stories of the Arizona Rangers, starring Tristram Coffin. In 1957, he played a deserter in an episode of the syndicated *Boots and Saddles*. In 1959, he appeared in an episode of NBC's *Northwest Passage* adventure series about Major Robert Rogers's exploits during the French and Indian War. That same year, he appeared as a police detective in the episode "The Quemoy Story" of Bruce Gordon's short-lived NBC docudrama about the Cold War, *Behind Closed Doors*.

More roles followed in *Omar Khayyam* (1957), *The Deep Six* (1958) again with Alan Ladd, *The Young Philadelphians* (1959), *Shotgun Slade* (1960), and *Whispering Smith* (1961) with Audie Murphy for a third time.

When Italian organizations began to complain about the use of Italian gangsters on TV's, *The Untouchables*, starring Robert Stack as G-man Eliot Ness, Picerni joined the cast of the show as Ness's number-one aide, Lee Hobson, from 1960-1963.

In 1964, he portrayed Pierre Lafitte in, *The Great Adventure*. Some more roles include *The Fugitive* (1964), *The Big Valley* (1966), *Batman* (1967), *The Scalphunters* (1968), *Airport* (1970), *Kelly's Heroes* (1970), *Here's Lucy* (1970-1971), *O'Hara, U.S. Treasury* (1971-1972), *The Sixth Sense* (1972), *Adam-12* (1970-1974), *Gunsmoke* (1967-1974), *Kolchak: The Night Stalker* (1975), *Mannix* (1970-1975), *Starsky and Hutch* (1976-1977), *The Red Hand Gang* (1977), *Kojak* (1974-1978), *Capricorn One* (1977), *Beyond the Poseidon Adventure* (1979), *The Incredible Hulk* (1979), *Alcatraz: The Whole Shocking Story* (1980), *Vega$* (1980), *The Fall Guy* (1981), *Strike Force* (1982), *T.J. Hooker* (1982-1983), *Sledge Hammer!* (1986), *Dirty Dozen: The Deadly Mission* (1987), *Diagnosis Murder* (1998-2000), and *Three Days to Vegas* (2007).

For some thirty years, Picerni was the half-time master of ceremonies for the Los Angeles Rams home games.

Picerni married former ballet dancer Marie Mason, in 1947; they had eight children and ten grandchildren. Many of their children and family are employed as Hollywood stunt people, including son Paul V. Picerni, Jr., grandson Rick Picerni, and sister Paula Picerni.

His autobiography *Steps to Stardom: My Story* was published in 2007.

He has attended Audie Murphy Days in Greenville, Texas, a record six times between 2001 and 2010.

Picerni died from a heart attack on January 12, 2011, in Palmdale, California at age 88.

John Pickard

John M. Pickard was born in Lascassas in Rutherford County, near Murfreesboro in central Tennessee June 25, 1913 and was an American actor who appeared primarily in television westerns.

He graduated from the Nashville Conservatory in Nashville, Tennessee. His first acting roles were small parts in films, mostly uncredited, beginning in 1936 as a dueling soldier in the picture *Mary of Scotland*, based on the 16th-century queen, Mary of Scotland.

From 1942 to 1946, Pickard served in the United States Navy, having been the model for naval recruitment posters during World War II.

Pickard returned to acting after the war and appeared in supporting roles in scores of westerns and action dramas before landing the starring role in the syndicated television series, *Boots and Saddles*, set on an Arizona fort in the late 19th century. His second film role, also uncredited, came in John Wayne's *Wake of the Red Witch* (1948).

More film roles followed in *White Heat* (1949), *Frenchie* (1950) with Joel McCrea, *Hoodlum Empire* (1952), *The Lawless Breed* (1953), *Black Horse Canyon* (1954) again with Joel McCrea, *Shotgun* (1955), *Tension at Table Rock* (1956), *The Oklahoman* (1957) a third with Joel McCrea, *The Power of the Resurrection* (1958), *Cimarron* (1960), *A Gathering of Eagles* (1963), *The Greatest Story Ever Told* (1965), *Charro!* (1969), *True Grit* (1969), *Chisum* (1970), *The Hindenburg* (1975), and *Mayday at 40,000 Feet!* (1976).

Pickard's first television guest-starring roles were in crime dramas in 1951 and 1952, respectively -- *Racket Squad*, with Reed Hadley, and *Boston Blackie*. In 1954, he guest starred on the legal drama, *The Public Defender*, again with Reed Hadley. He was also cast on the syndicated western anthology series, *Stories of the Century*, with Jim Davis, and later on Davis' other series, *Rescue 8*, based on stories of the Los Angeles County Fire Department. Pickard appeared on *Hopalong Cassidy* and in 1956 on the CBS children's western *My Friend Flicka*. That same year he was cast in another anthology series, *Navy Log*, and in an episode of Jack Webb's NBC series, *Dragnet*. He appeared in a 1956 episode of the TV Series *The Lone Ranger* entitled "Trouble at Tylerville".

From 1957 to 1958, he filled the lead role of Captain Shank Adams on *Boots and Saddles*, with episodes set in the Arizona Territory on a United States Army fort. Afterwards, Pickard guest starred in many more westerns including the role of the gunfighter Johnny Ringo on *The Life and Legend of Wyatt Earp*, starring Hugh O'Brian as Wyatt Earp.

Other appearances were on *Tales of the Texas Rangers*, *Dick Powell's Zane Grey Theater*, *Yancy Derringer*, *Wagon Train*, *Johnny Ringo*, *Tales of Wells Fargo*, *The Texan*, *The Rebel*, *Laramie*, *The Rifleman*, *Empire*, *Rawhide*, *The Wild Wild West*, and *The Virginian*. From 1960 to 1975, he appeared in twelve episodes of the long-running CBS western, *Gunsmoke*, with James Arness, who in 1955 had beaten out Pickard for the series lead as Marshal Matt Dillon.

In 1959, Pickard was cast, uncredited, as a Mississippi River pirate in the episode "The Unwilling" of the NBC western series, *Riverboat*, starring Darren McGavin and Burt Reynolds. In the story line, businessman Dan Simpson, played by Eddie Albert, attempts to open a general store in the American West despite a raid from river pirates who stole from him $20,000 in merchandise. Debra Paget is cast in this episode as Lela Russell, and Russell Johnson, as Darius.

Other television roles included *Wichita Town* (1959-1960) also with Joel McCrea, *Twilight Zone* (1963), and *Hondo* (1967).

Pickard's final on-screen appearanceswas in a 1987 episode of the CBS detective series, *Simon and Simon*.

On August 4, 1993, Pickard, at the age of 80, was killed by a bull on the family farm in Rutherford County, Tennessee. He was survived by his wife, Ann M. Pickard, and one adult child, three grandchildren, and numerous great-grandchildren.

Slim Pickens

Louis Burton Lindley, Jr. was born in Kingsburg, California June 29, 1919, known by the stage name Slim Pickens, was an American rodeo performer and film and television actor who epitomized the profane, tough, sardonic cowboy, but who is best remembered for his comic roles, notably in *Dr. Strangelove* and *Blazing Saddles*.

Pickens was the son of Sally Mosher (née Turk) and Louis Bert Lindley, Sr. He was an excellent rider from age 4. He graduated from Hanford High School, Hanford, California and was a member of the FFA. After graduating school he joined the rodeo. He was told that working in the rodeo would be "slim pickings" (very little money), giving him his name, but he did well and eventually became a well-known rodeo clown.

After twenty years on the rodeo circuit, his distinctive Oklahoma-Texas drawl (even though he was a lifelong Californian), his wide eyes and moon face and strong physical presence gained him a role in the western film, *Rocky Mountain* (1950) starring Errol Flynn. He appeared in many more westerns, playing both villains and comic sidekicks to the likes of Rex Allen.

Pickens appeared in dozens of films, including *Old Oklahoma Plains* (1952), *Down Laredo Way* (1953), *Gunsight Ridge* (1957) with Joel McCrea, *Tonka* (1959), *One-Eyed Jacks* (1961) with Marlon Brando, *Dr. Strangelove* (1964), *Major Dundee* (1965) with Charlton Heston, the remake of *Stagecoach* (1966; Pickens played the driver, portrayed in the 1939 film by Andy Devine), *Never a Dull Moment* (1968), *The Cowboys* (1972) with John Wayne, *Ginger in the Morning* (1974) with Fred Ward, *Blazing Saddles* (1974), *Poor Pretty Eddie* (1975), *Rancho Deluxe* (1975), *The Getaway* with Steve McQueen, *Tom Horn* (1980), also with McQueen, *An Eye for an Eye* (1966) and *Pat Garrett and Billy the Kid* (1973) in a small but memorable role.

He also had a small role in Steven Spielberg's *1941* (1979) in scenes with Toshiro Mifune and Christopher Lee; during one scene, he names the objects that he has with himself, and sounds like he does in *Dr. Strangelove* during the "Survival Kit Contents Check" scene. In 1978, Pickens lent his voice to theme park Silver Dollar City as a character named Rube Dugan, for a ride called "Rube Dugan's Diving Bell", The diving bell was a simulation ride that took passengers on a journey to the bottom of Lake Silver and back. The ride was in operation from 1978 to 1984.

He also played werewolf sheriff Sam Newfield in *The Howling* (1981).

In 1960, he appeared in the NBC western series, *Overland Trail* in the episode "Sour Annie" with fellow guest stars Mercedes McCambridge and Andrew Prine. Pickens appeared five times on NBC's *Outlaws* (1960–62) western series as the character "Slim." The program, starring Barton MacLane, was the story of a U.S. marshal in Oklahoma Territory — deputies played by Don Collier, Jock Gaynor and Bruce Yarnell — and the outlaws that they pursued. In 1967, Pickens had a recurring role as the scout California Joe Milner on the ABC military western *Custer*, starring Wayne Maunder in the title role.

In 1975, Pickens was in another western, playing the evil, limping bank robber in Walt Disney's *The Apple Dumpling Gang*; that same year, the exploitation classic *Poor Pretty Eddie* was released, with Pickens portraying twisted Sheriff Orville. He provided the voice of B.O.B. in the 1979 Disney science fiction thriller *The Black Hole*. That same year he played Jack Bigelow in Louis L'amour's *The Sacketts* miniseries. His last film was his least notable, *Pink Motel* (1982) with Phyllis Diller.

Pickens played B-52 pilot Major T.J. "King" Kong. in *Dr. Strangelove*. Stanley Kubrick cast Pickens after Peter Sellers, who played three other roles in the film, sprained his ankle and was unable to perform in the role due to having to work in the cramped cockpit set. Pickens was chosen because his accent and comic sense were perfect for the role of Kong, a cartoonishly patriotic and gung-ho B-52 commander. He was not given the script to the entire film, but only those portions in which he played a part.

Pickens credited *Dr. Strangelove* as a turning point in his career. Previously he was "Hey you" on sets and afterward he was addressed as "Mr. Pickens." Pickens once said, "After *Dr. Strangelove* the roles, the dressing rooms, and the checks all started gettin' bigger." Pickens said he was amazed at the difference a single movie could make. However, working with Kubrick proved too difficult, especially the more than 100 takes of the H-bomb riding scene. In the late 1970s, Pickens was offered the part of Dick Halloran in Kubrick's adaptation of Stephen King's *The Shining*, but Pickens stipulated that he would appear in the film only if Kubrick was required to shoot Pickens' scenes in fewer than 100 takes. Instead, Pickens' agent showed the script to Don Schwartz, the agent of Scatman Crothers, and Crothers accepted the role.

Pickens lent his voice to the 1975 studio recording of Bobby Bridger's collection of Western ballads *A Ballad of the West*, in which he narrated part 1, "Seekers of the Fleece", the story of Jim Bridger and the mountain man fur trade era. Slim's interest in this project blossomed in 1970 when his daughter, Daryle Ann, was cast in Max Evans' independent film *The Wheel*. Evans had also hired Jim Bridger's great-grandnephew, Bobby Bridger, to sing the film's theme song. Aware of her father's interest in mountain men, Daryle Ann set up a meeting for Evans and Pickens, and Pickens immediately volunteered to narrate the heroic couplets. In July, Bobby, Slim and the Lost Gonzo Band recorded Seekers of the Fleece outside Denver in a tipi studio, where Slim's old mountain-man pal Timberjack Joe had decorated with grizzly bear robes and beaver pelts to set the mood.

Pickens appeared in numerous television guest shots, including four episodes of the syndicated western series *Annie Oakley* (1956), with Gail Davis and Brad Johnson, and three episodes of NBC's *The Wide Country* (1962), a rodeo series starring Earl Holliman and Andrew Prine. In 1961, he had a recurring role as Johnson in the 17-episode NBC series, *The Americans*, the story of how the American Civil War divided families. He was a credited semi-regular in the role of "Slim" in the second season of the NBC western series, *Outlaws*. Thereafter, he was cast in a first-season episode of NBC's espionage series, *The Man from U.N.C.L.E.*.

Pickens appeared in episodes of *The Lone Ranger*, *Frontier Doctor*, *The Tall Man*, Maverick , *Riverboat*, *The Fugitive*, *The Travels of Jaimie McPheeters*, *The Legend of Jesse James*, *Alias Smith and Jones*, *Daniel Boone*, *The Virginian*, *That Girl*, and *Kung Fu*.

Pickens was cast in recurring roles in *The Legend of Custer*, *Bonanza*, *Hee Haw*, *B. J. and the Bear* with Greg Evigan, and *Filthy Rich*.

One of Pickens' most memorable television roles was in an episode of CBS's *Hawaii Five-O*, in which he portrayed the patriarch of a family of serial killers.

Pickens also emceed NBC's short-lived country music variety series *The Nashville Palace* in 1981.

In 1982, Pickens was inducted into the Western Performers Hall of Fame at the National Cowboy & Western Heritage Museum in Oklahoma City, Oklahoma.

Pickens was inducted into the Pro Rodeo Cowboy Hall of Fame in Colorado Springs, CO for his work as a Rodeo Clown.

In his last years Pickens lived with his wife, Margaret, in Columbia, California. He was a civilian pilot with a multi-engine rating and enjoyed flying in a green U.S. Air Force flight suit while wearing a cowboy hat, similar to the wardrobe worn in Dr. Strangelove. He died on December 8, 1983, after surgery for a brain tumor at age 64. Pickens' brother, Samuel T. Lindley, acted under the name Easy Pickens. His most notable appearance was as "Easy" in Sam Peckinpah's *The Ballad of Cable Hogue*.

Walter Pidgeon

Walter Davis Pidgeon was born in Saint John, New Brunswick, Canada September 23, 1897 and was a Canadian American actor who starred in many films, including *Mrs. Miniver*, *The Bad and the Beautiful*, *Forbidden Planet*, *Advise & Consent*, *Voyage to the Bottom of the Sea*, *Funny Girl* and *Harry in Your Pocket*.

Pidgeon was the son of Hannah (née Sanborn), a housewife, and Caleb Burpee Pidgeon, a haberdasher. Pidgeon attended local schools and the University of New Brunswick, where he studied law and drama. His university education was interrupted by World War I, and he enlisted in the 65th Battery, Royal Canadian Field Artillery. Pidgeon never saw action, however, as he was severely injured in an accident. He was crushed between two gun carriages and spent seventeen months in a military hospital. Following the war, he moved to Boston, Massachusetts, where he worked as a bank runner, at the same time studying voice at the New England Conservatory of Music. He was a classically trained baritone.

Discontented with banking, Pidgeon moved to New York City, where he walked into the office of E.E. Clive, announced that he could act and sing and could prove it. After acting on stage for several years, he made his Broadway debut in 1925.

Pidgeon made a number of silent films in the 1920s. He became a huge star with the arrival of talkies, thanks to his singing voice. He starred in extravagant early Technicolor musicals, including *The Bride of the Regiment* (1930), *Sweet Kitty Bellairs* (1930), *Viennese Nights* (1930) and *Kiss Me Again* (1931). He appeared in *Rockabye* (1932) with Joel McCrea. He became associated with musicals, and when the public grew weary of them his career began to falter. In 1935 he took a break from Hollywood and did a stint on Broadway, appearing in the plays *Something Gay*, *Night of January 16th*, and *There's Wisdom in Women*. When he returned to movies, he was relegated to playing secondary roles in films like *Saratoga* and *The Girl of the Golden West*. One of his better known roles was in *The Dark Command*, where he portrayed the villain (loosely based on American Civil War guerrilla William C. Quantrill) opposite John Wayne, Claire Trevor, and a young Roy Rogers.

It was not until he starred in the Academy Award-winning Best Picture *How Green Was My Valley* (1941) that his popularity returned. He then starred opposite Greer Garson in *Blossoms in the Dust* (1941), *Mrs. Miniver* (1942) (for which he was nominated for the Academy Award for Best Actor) and its sequel, *The Miniver Story* in 1950. He was also nominated in 1944 for *Madame Curie*, again opposite Garson. His partnership with her continued throughout the 1940s and into the 1950s with *Mrs. Parkington* (1944), *Julia Misbehaves* (1948), *That Forsyte Woman* (1949), and finally *Scandal at Scourie* (1953). He also starred as Chip Collyer in the comedy *Week-End at the Waldorf* (1945) and later as Colonel Michael S. 'Hooky' Nicobar, who is given the difficult task of repatriating Russians in post-World War II Vienna in the drama film *The Red Danube* (1949).

Although he continued to make films, including *The Bad and the Beautiful* and *Forbidden Planet*, Pidgeon returned to work on Broadway in the mid-1950s after a twenty-year absence, and was featured in *Take Me Along* with Jackie Gleason. He received a Tony Award nomination for the musical play.

In 1962, he portrayed General Augustus Perry in the episode "The Reunion" on CBS's *Rawhide*.

He continued making films, playing Admiral Harriman Nelson in 1961's *Voyage to the Bottom of the Sea*, James Haggin in Walt Disney's *Big Red* (1962), and the Senate Majority Leader in Otto Preminger's *Advise & Consent*. His role as Florenz Ziegfeld in *Funny Girl* (1968) was well received. Later, he played Casey, James Coburn's sidekick, in *Harry in Your Pocket* (1973).

Pidgeon guest-starred in the episode "King of the Valley" (November 26, 1959) of CBS's *Dick Powell's Zane Grey Theater*.

His other television credits included *Breaking Point*, *The F.B.I.*, *Marcus Welby, M.D.*, and *Gibbsville*. In 1963 he guest starred as corporate attorney Sherman Hatfield in the fourth of four special episodes of *Perry Mason* while Raymond Burr was recovering from surgery.

Pidgeon was active in the Screen Actors Guild, and served as president from 1952 to 1957. He tried to stop the production of *Salt of the Earth*, which was made by a team blacklisted during the Red Scare. He retired from acting in 1978.

Walter Pidgeon has a star on the Hollywood Walk of Fame at 6414 Hollywood Blvd.

Pidgeon married twice. In 1919, he wed the former Edna Muriel Pickles, who died in 1921 during the birth of their daughter, also named Edna. In 1931, Pidgeon married his secretary, Ruth Walker, to whom he remained married until his death September 25, 1984 at age 87 in Santa Monica, California, following a series of strokes.

Phillip Pine

Phillip Pine was born July 16, 1920 in Hanford, California and was an American film and television actor, writer, director, and producer.

In a career that spanned seven decades, Pine in 1955 portrayed the outlaw John Wesley Hardin in the ninth episode "John Wesley Hardin" of the ABC/Desilu western television series, *The Life and Legend of Wyatt Earp*, starring Hugh O"Brian in the title role.[1] In a later episode of the same series in 1957, Pine again played Hardin, along with Mike Ragan as Clay Allison, Denver Pyle as Ben Thompson, and Mason Alan Dinehart as Bat Masterson, all of whom come to Earp's aid in a shootout with the owner and foreman of the Big T Ranch, Rance Purcell (Richard Devon) and Gus Andrews (Grant Withers).

Pine appeared in a *Wagon Train* episode titled "The Ben Corutney Story" in 1958. He subsequently played the character Colonel Phillip Green in the classic *Star Trek* episode "The Savage Curtain". Pine was in the second episode of *The Outer Limits* entitled "The Hundred Days of the Dragon". He also appeared in two episodes of *The Twilight Zone*, "The Four of Us Are Dying", and "The Incredible World of Horace Ford". Pine appeared as mobster Jack Zuta in the third episode of *The Untouchables* titled "The Jake Lingle Killing"and in *The Fugitive*. He made a 1964 appearance as Phillip Stewart in the *Perry Mason* episode, "The Case of the Wednesday Woman." In 1967, Pine appeared in an episode of *The Invaders* entitled "Genesis". Pine also appeared in an episode of "Rawhide" entitled "Incident at Dangerfield Dip". He also played a gangster known only as "Mark" in Irving Lerner's film noir classic, *Murder by Contract*.

More of his roles included *Wichita Town* (1959) with Joel McCrea, *Get Smart* (1965), *Adam-12* (1969), *The Sixth Sense* (1972), *Harry O* (1974), *Get Christie Love!* (1975), *Baretta* (1976), *Hill Street Blues* (1984), and *Creep* (2005).

He died December 22, 2006 at age 86 in Las Vegas, Nevada.

Snub Pollard

Harry "Snub" Pollard was born as Harold Fraser in Melbourne, Australia November 9, 1889 and was a silent film comedian, popular in the 1920s.

Often mistaken as the brother of Australian actress Daphne Pollard, though the two were not related. Harry Pollard took the name Pollard as his stage name. In addition, the two both acted with "Pollard's Lilliputian Opera Co." in Australia, which gave stage performances featuring children and performers of small stature. This was a very well known troupe in its time, and many of its performers adopted the surname "Pollard".

Pollard played supporting roles in the early films of Harold Lloyd. The long-faced Pollard sported a Kaiser Wilhelm mustache turned upside-down; this became his trademark. Lloyd's producer, Hal Roach, gave Pollard his own starring series of one- and two-reel shorts. The most famous is 1923's *It's a Gift*, in which he plays an inventor of many Rube Goldberg-like contraptions, including a car that runs by magnet power.

Pollard left Roach in 1924 and joined the low-budget Weiss Brothers studio in 1926. There he co-starred with Marvin Loback as a poor man's version of Laurel and Hardy, copying that team's plots and gags.

In the 1930s, Pollard played small parts in talking comedies, and was featured as comic relief in "B" westerns. Pollard's silent-comedy credentials guaranteed him work in slapstick revivals. He appeared with other film veterans in *Hollywood Cavalcade* (1939), *The Perils of Pauline* (1947), and *Man of a Thousand Faces* (1957). He also appeared regularly as a supporting player in Columbia Pictures' two-reel comedies of the mid-1940s.

Forsaking his familiar mustache, he landed much steadier work as a bit player. He played incidental roles in scores of Hollywood features and shorts, almost always as a mousy, nondescript fellow, usually with no dialogue. In Wheeler & Woolsey's *Cockeyed Cavaliers* (1934), he's a drunken doctor. At the end of *Miracle on 34th Street* (1947), when a squad of bailiffs hauling sacks of mail enters the courtroom, Pollard brings up the rear. He appeared as a bartender in *Stars in My Crown* (1950) with Joel McCrea. In Frank Capra's *Pocketful of Miracles* (1961), Pollard plays a Broadway beggar. His last film, *Twist Around the Clock* (1962), shows him wordlessly reacting to a curvaceous woman dancing energetically.

Snub Pollard died of cancer on January 19, 1962, at age 72, after nearly 50 years in the movie business. His interment was at Forest Lawn Memorial Park (Hollywood Hills).

For his contributions to motion pictures, Pollard has a star on the Hollywood Walk of Fame at 6415½ Hollywood Boulevard.

Victor Potel

Victor Potel was born in Lafayette, Indiana October 12, 1889 and was an American film character actor who began in the silent era and appeared in over 430 films in his 38 year career.

His acting career goes back almost to the beginning of the commercial film industry in the United States. He made his first silent film in 1910, a comedy short filmed in Chicago by Essanay Film Manufacturing Company called *A Dog on Business*. Potel continued to make films for Essanay, appearing in dozens of films every year, including most of the Broncho Billy series, and played a character called "Slippery Sam" in 80 movies. He also appeared in Universal Pictures' "Snakeville" series.

Potel's first talking picture was *Melody of Love*, starring Walter Pidgeon, made for Universal in 1928, and in the sound era he continued to work continuously and constantly, playing small parts and sometimes uncredited bit parts, all primarily comic roles due to his height (6 ft 1) and gawkiness.

In addition to acting, on several occasions Potel also wrote and directed. In the 1920s he directed two silent shorts, *The Rubber-Neck* in 1924 and *Action Craver* in 1927, and contributed the story for *Saxophobia* in 1927. In the following decade, in the sound era, he was the dialogue director for *The Big Chance* (1933), and wrote the story for *Inside Information* in 1934. In 1935 he provided continuity and dialogue for *Million Dollar Haul* and the screenplay for *Hot Off the Press*. In the 1940s, Potel was part of Preston Sturges' unofficial "stock company" of character actors, appearing in nine films written and directed by Sturges.

More of his roles included *Broncho Billy and the Schoolmistress* (1912), *Two Bold, Bad Men* (1915), *At the Sign of the Jack O'Lantern* (1922), *The Little Shepherd of Kingdom Come* (1928), *Ruggles of Red Gap* (1935), *Barbary Coast* (1935) with Joel McCrea, *Married Before Breakfast* (1937), *Sullivan's Travels* (1941) with Joel McCrea and Veronica Lake, *The Palm Beach Story* (1942) a third with Joel McCrea, *The Great Moment* (1944) a fourth film with Joel McCrea, *Heldorado* (1946), The *Egg and I* (1947), and *Relentless* (1948).

Potel continued to work right up until his death on March 8, 1947 at age 57 in Hollywood, California.

Russ Powell

Russ Powell was born in Indianapolis, Indiana September 16, 1875 and was an American film actor. He appeared in 186 films between 1915 and 1943.

Some of his roles included *The Soul of Youth* (1920), *The Hunchback of Notre Dame* (1923), *Her Wild Oat* (1927), *The Big Trail* (1930), *Business and Pleasure* (1932) with Joel McCrea, *King Kong* (1933), *One Man's Journey* (1933) again with Joel McCrea, *Barbary Coast* (1935) a third with Joel McCrea, *These Three* (1936) a fourth with Joel McCrea, *Come and Get It* (1936) a fifth with Joel McCrea, *Banjo on My Knee* (1936) a sixth with Joel McCrea, *Union Pacific* (1939) a seventh with Joel McCrea, *The Son of Davy Crockett* (1941), *To Be or Not to Be* (1942), and *Action in the North Atlantic* (1943).

He died in Los Angeles, California November 28, 1950 at age 75.

Purnell Pratt

Purnell Pratt was born in Bethel, Illinois October 20, 1885 and was an American film actor. He appeared in 114 films between 1914 and 1941.

Some of his roles included *The Flame Fighter* (1925), *Thru Different Eyes* (1929), *The Silver Horde* (1930) with Joel McCrea, *Grand Hotel* (1932), *Billion Dollar Scandal* (1933), *The Man Who Reclaimed His Head* (1934), *Hollywood Boulevard* (1936), *Colorado Sunset* (1939), and *Doctors Don't Tell* (1941).

He July 25, 1941 died in Hollywood, California at age 55.

Guy Prescott

Guy Prescott was born on January 19, 1914 in Lincoln County, Oklahoma. He was an actor and writer, known for *Shotgun* (1955), *The Unearthly* (1957) and *Pharaoh's Curse* (1957).

More of his roles included *The Desert Rats* (1953), *Rocky Jones, Space Ranger* (1954), *Rage at Dawn* (1955), *The Tall Stranger* (1957) with Joel McCrea, *Queen of Outer Space* (1958), *The Hypnotic Eye* (1960), *Atlantis, the Lost Continent* (1961), and *Gunsmoke* (1962).

He died on March 7, 1998 in Los Angeles, California

Robert Preston

Robert Preston and Joel McCrea in *Union Pacific*

Robert Preston was born Robert Preston Meservey in Newton, Massachusetts June 8, 1918 and was an American stage and film actor best remembered for originating the role of Harold Hill in the 1957 musical *The Music Man* and the subsequent film adaptation. He is also known for his Oscar-nominated role as homosexual Carroll "Toddy" Todd in *Victor Victoria* (1982).

Preston was the son of Ruth L. (née Rea; 1895-1973) and Frank Wesley Meservey (1899–1996), a garment worker and billing clerk for American Express, respectively. After attending Abraham Lincoln High School in Los Angeles, he studied acting at the Pasadena Community Playhouse.

Following the attack on Pearl Harbor and the United States entry into World War II, he joined the United States Army Air Corps and served as an intelligence officer in the U.S. 9th Air Force with the 386th Bomb Group (Medium). At the end of the war in Europe, the 386th and Captain Robert Meservy, an S-2 Officer (intelligence), were stationed in St. Trond, Belgium. Meservey's job had been receiving intelligence reports from 9th Air Force headquarters and briefing the bomber crews on what to expect in accomplishing their missions.

When he began appearing in films, the studio ordered Meservey to stop using his actual family name. As Robert Preston, the name by which he would be known for his entire professional career, he appeared in many Hollywood films, predominantly Westerns but not exclusively, he was "Digby Geste" in the sound remake of *Beau Geste* (1939) with Gary Cooper and Ray Milland, and featured in *North West Mounted Police* (1940) also with "Coop".

More of his early roles included *Union Pacific* (1939) with Joel McCrea, *Reap the Wild Wind* (1942), *This Gun for Hire* (1942) with Alan Ladd and Veronica Lake, *Wild Harvest* (1947) again with Alan Ladd, *Whispering Smith* (1948) a third with Alan Ladd, *Tulsa* (1949), *Best of the Badmen* (1951), *The Last Frontier* (1955), *Craft Theatre* (1957), and *How the West was Won* (1962).

Preston appeared on the cover of *Time* magazine on July 21, 1958.

However, Preston is probably best remembered for his performance as "Professor" Harold Hill in Meredith Willson's musical *The Music Man* (1962). He had already won a Tony Award for his performance in the original Broadway production in 1957. When Willson adapted his story for the screen, he insisted on Preston's participation over the objections of Jack L. Warner, who had wanted Frank Sinatra for the role.

In 1961, Preston was asked to make a recording as part of a program by the President's Council on Physical Fitness to get schoolchildren to do more daily exercise. The song, "Chicken Fat", which was written and composed by Meredith Willson and performed by Preston with full orchestral accompaniment, was distributed to schools across the nation and played for students in calisthenics every morning. The song later became a surprise novelty hit and part of many baby-boomers' childhood memories.

He took a nine yer break from films and telelvision and reentered the acting profession in Junior Bonner (1972) with Steve McQueen. Another poplular role was as Big Ed Bookman in Semi-Tough (1977) with Burt Reynolds.

In 1979 and 1980, Preston portrayed determined family patriarch Hadley Chisholm in the CBS western miniseries, *The Chisholms*. Rosemary Harris played his wife, Minerva. The Preston character died in the ninth of the thirteen episodes of the program. Other co-stars were Ben Murphy, Lance Kerwin, Brett Cullen, and James Van Patten. In the storyline, the Chisholms lost their land in Virginia by fraud and left for California to begin a new life.

Although he was not known for his singing voice, Preston appeared in several other stage and film musicals, notably *Mame* (1974) and *Victor Victoria* (1982), for which he received an Academy Award nomination. He appeared in an unusual film called *S.O.B.* (1981) with Julie Andrews and William Holden. This was the film in which Julie Andrews appeared topless and caused quite a stir.

His last role in a theatrical film was in *The Last Starfighter* (1984), in which he portrayed an interstellar con man/military recruiter called "Centauri". He said that he based his approach to the character of Centauri on that which he had taken to Professor Harold Hill. He also starred in the HBO 1985 movie *Finnegan, Begin Again* along with Mary Tyler Moore. His final role was in the television film *Outrage!* (1986).

An intensely private person, no official biographies exist for the actor, although several interviews given late in his career shed light on the guarded actor.

Preston died of lung cancer in Montecito, California on March 21, 1987, at the age of 68.

Sherwood Price

Sherwood Price was born November 15, 1933. He is an American character actor who has appeared in dozens of films and television programs from 1952 to 1995.

Some of those appearances include *Scorching Fury* (1952), *I Led 3 Lives* (1956), numerous episodes of *The Gray Ghost* (1957-1958) as General Jeb Stuart, *Westinghouse Desilu Playhouse* (1959-1960), *Wichita Town* (1960) with Joel McCrea, *The Roaring 20's* (1961), *Whispering Smith* (1961) with Audie Murphy, *Cheyenne* (1961-1962), *The Untouchables* (1963), *Gunsmoke* (1965), *The Big Valley* (1965-1968), *The Protectors* (1972-1973), *Police Woman* (1976), *SST: Death Flight* (1977), *The Misadventures of Sheriff Lobo* (1979), and *Last of the Dogmen* (1995).

Lucien Prival

Lucien Prival was born on July 14, 1901 in New York City, New York. He was an actor, known for *Hell's Angels* (1930) with Jean Harlow, *The Bride of Frankenstein* (1935), and *Mr. Wong, Detective* (1938).

More of his roles included *The Great Deception* (1926), *The Last of the Lone Wolf* (1930), *Sherlock Holmes* (1932), *The Bride of Frankenstein* (1935), *Espionage Agent* (1939) with Joel McCrea, *Hitler - Beast of Berlin* (1939) with Alan Ladd, *The Secret Code* (1942), *The Falcon's Alibi* (1946), *Bodyguard* (1948), *China Smith* (1952), *High Noon* (1952), *Biff Baker, U.S.A.* (1953), and *Ramar of the Jungle* (1953).

He died on June 3, 1994 in Daly City, California at age 92.

Jed Prouty

Jed Prouty was born in Boston, Massachusetts April 6, 1879 and was an American film actor.

Prouty was a vaudeville performer before becoming a film actor. Mostly appearing in comedies, he occasionally performed a serious character role, for instance a small part as an oily publicist in *A Star is Born* (1937). After a significant career in silent films, a large part of Prouty's later career was the Jones Family series. They were seventeen low-budget 20th Century Fox family comedies between 1936 and 1940, along with Spring Byington as Mrs. Jones, for such directors as Malcolm St. Clair and Frank R. Strayer. Prouty appeared in all but the final entry.

More of his roles included *Unknown Treasures* (1926), *His Captive Woman* (1929), *Business and Pleasure* (1932) with Joel McCrea, *Hollywood Party* (1934), *The Texas Rangers* (1936), *The Duke of West Point* (1938), *Go West, Young Lady* (1941), *Citizen Saint* (1947), *Guilty Bystander* (1950), and *Short Short Dramas* (1952).

He died May 10, 1956 at age 77 in New York City, New York.

Frank Puglia

Frank Puglia was born in Sicily, Italy March 9, 1892 and was an Italian film actor. Puglia had small, but memorable roles in films including *Casablanca* (a Moroccan rug merchant), *Now Voyager* and *The Jungle Book*, all in 1942.

The actor started his career as a teen on stage in Italian operas. He immigrated to the U.S. in 1907 and worked in a laundry before joining an Italian language theatre group in New York. While appearing on stage, he was discovered by D. W. Griffith, which began an acting career spanning over 150 films. He usually played ethnic types in films, and claimed to have learned English from reading newspapers.

More of his roles included *The Man Who Laughs* (1928), *Bordertown* (1935), *Wife vs. Secretary* with Jean Harlow, *Spawn of the North* (1938), *Mr. Smith Goes to Washington* (1939), *The Mark of Zorro* (1940), *The Boogie Man Will Get You* (1942), *Phantom of the Opera* (1943), *Tall in the Saddle* (1944), *Without Reservations* (1946), *My Favorite Brunette* (1947), *Colorado Territory* (1949) with Joel McCrea, *Captain Carey, U.S.A.* (1950) again with Alan Ladd, *Son of Belle Starr* (1953), *The First Texan* (1956) again with Joel McCrea, Louis L'amour's *The Burning Hills* (1956), *20 Million Miles to Earth* (1957), *The Texan* (1960), *Girls! Girls! Girls!* (1962) with Elvis, *The Outer Limits* (1964), *I Dream of Jeannie* (1967), *The Fugitive* (1967), *Mannix* (1969), *The Rookies* (1973), and *Mr. Ricco* (1975).

He was originally cast as the undertaker, Bonasera, in Francis Ford Coppola's The Godfather (1972), even participating in Marlon Brando's infamous screen test, but he fell ill before filming could begin. He was replaced by Sicilian actor Salvatore Corsitto, thus losing out on delivering one of the most famous opening lines ("I believe in America... America has made me my fortune") in film history.

He died October 25, 1975 at age 83.

Napoleon Pukui

Napoleon Pukui was born in December 1875 in Honolulu, Hawaii Territory as Napoleon Kalolii Pukui. He is an actor, known for his only role in *Bird of Paradise* (1932) with Joel McCrea. A date of death was not found.

Bernard Punsly

Bernard Punsly was born in New York City July 11, 1923 and was an American actor who later left show business to become a physician. His last name was often spelled incorrectly in film credits as Punsley.

Punsly auditioned for a part in the play *Dead End* in 1935 because he thought it might be fun. The success of the play led to a series of film appearances for the cast, including Punsly. The first film of the "Dead End Kids" (or Bowery Boys) series was *Dead End*, also produced in 1937 with Joel McCrea and Humphrey Bogart. Punsly played the parts of "Milt" and later "Ape."

More of his roles included *Little Tough Guy* (1938), *The Angels Wash Their Faces* (1939), *Junior G-Men* (1940), *Sea Raiders* (1941), and *Mug Town* (1942).

He continued with similar film parts until he joined the army. Even as an actor, he was known to read medical books in his spare time. After receiving medical training in the army, Punsley entered the Medical College of the University of Georgia, subsequently obtaining his medical degree. He returned to the west to set up a medical practice in Torrance, California, never returning to show business.

He became chief of staff in the South Bay Hospital in Redondo Beach, California. He was married to Lynne and had two children, Bryan and Richard.

On January 20, 2004, at age 80, he died of cancer in Torrance, California.

Denver Pyle

Denver Dell Pyle was born May 11, 1920, and was an American film and television actor. He is best remembered for playing Uncle Jesse in *The Dukes of Hazzard* (1979-1985).

Pyle was born in Bethune in Kit Carson County, Colorado, to farmer Ben H. Pyle (1895–1988) and his wife Maude (1899–1985). After graduating from high school, Pyle briefly attended Colorado State University but dropped out to enter show business.

He was a drummer and band member until the United States entered the Second World War, when he enlisted in the Merchant Marines.

After the war, Pyle embarked on his film career. He starred in several movies and on television during the 1950s and 1960s. He had roles in *The Flying Saucer* (1950), *The Cisco Kid* (1951-1952), *The Maverick* (1952), *Goldtown Ghost Riders* (1953), *The Lone Wolf* (1954), *Hopalong Cassidy* (1952-1954), *Adventures of Superman* (1954), *The Adventures of Kit Carson* (1952-1954), *The Gene Autry Show* (1951-1954), *Drum Beat* (1954) with Alan Ladd, *Top Gun* (1955), *The Lone Ranger* (1951-1956), *Destination 60,000* (1957), *The Left Handed Gun* (1958), *The Horse Soldiers* (1959), *Wichita Town* (1960) with Joel McCrea, *The Man Who Shot Liberty Valance* (1962), *The Dick Van Dyke Show* (1963)

He also appeared on an episode of the *Twilight Zone* in 1964 called "Black Leather Jackets" where he played the father. He appeared in the 1963-1964 season in ABC's drama about college life, *Channing*. He also is known for portraying both the suspect and the murder victim on the final *Perry Mason* (1958-1966) episode; he was the only actor to play a victim, a suspect and the actual murderer (in a previous episode) on the series out of six appearances. He was Grandpa Tarleton in all twenty-six episodes of *Tammy* in the 1965-66 season.

He was a regular co-star of Audie Murphy's in the films *Gunsmoke* (1953), *Column South* (1953), *Ride Clear of Diablo* (1954), *To Hell and Back* (1955), *Cast a Long Shadow* (1959), and *Gunpoint* (1966).

In addition, he played the antagonist Frank Hamer in *Bonnie and Clyde* (1967), Buck Webb (Doris Day's father) during the first two seasons of CBS's *The Doris Day Show* (1968–1970), and Briscoe Darling on *The Andy Griffith Show* (1960–1968). He appeared in fourteen episodes of Gunsmoke (1956-1973).

He did some writing and directing for the short-lived half-hour *Gunsmoke* spin-off western *Dirty Sally* starring Jeanette Nolan, which ran on CBS in the first half of 1974. He also played the role of Arkansas in Michael Dante's film *Winterhawk* (1975).

Pyle played the role of Mad Jack in the NBC series *The Life and Times of Grizzly Adams* (1977–1978).

In his later years, Pyle played mostly cameo television roles and retired from full-time acting. He played the title role in *Podunk Possum* (1997). His last cinematic movie role was alongside Mel Gibson, Jodie Foster, and James Garner in the 1994 film *Maverick*, playing a cheating card player who jumps off a riverboat to keep his dignity. His last acting role was a reprisal of Jesse Duke in the 1997 made-for-TV movie *The Dukes of Hazzard: Reunion!*

Denver married his first wife, Marilee Carpenter (1924–2010), in 1955. The aspiring actor took a Twentieth Century Fox production assistant as his bride. They had sons David and Tony in 1956 and 1957, respectively.

According to her obituary, "Marilee advised and assisted Denver throughout his fifty-year career in motion pictures and television—uninterrupted by their divorce in 1970—until his death in 1997".

Denver married Tippie Johnston in 1983. They were married until Pyle's death.

Pyle died of lung cancer on Christmas Day in, 1997. He is buried in Forreston, Texas.

Robert Quarry

Robert Walter Quarry was born in Santa Rosa, California November 3, 1925 and was an American actor, known for several prominent horror film roles.

Quarry was the son of Mable (née Shoemaker) and Paul Quarry, a doctor. His grandmother was an actress. He left school at the age of 14 to pursue a career in radio.

In November 1943, Quarry joined the Army, where he formed a theatrical troupe. After the war he acted again, first for RKO and then for MGM. It was at this time that he befriended Katharine Hepburn.

His films include Shadow of a Doubt (1943), Soldier of Fortune (1955), A Kiss Before Dying (1956), Crime of Passion (1957), *Count Yorga, Vampire* (1970), its sequel *The Return of Count Yorga* (1971), and *Dr. Phibes Rises Again* (1972), in which he played alchemist Dr. Biederbeck pitted against Vincent Price's Phibes in a race to find the mythical elixir of eternal life. Although it is well known that Price did not care for his co-star— once, when Quarry was singing in his dressing room during the making of *Dr Phibes Rises Again*, he said to Price, "You didn't know I could sing did you?" and Price replied: "Well I knew you couldn't act"— the two were later also paired in *Madhouse* (1974).

American International Pictures had plans for Quarry to succeed Price, signing him to a long term contract, but the decline in the company's fortunes, and old style horror films falling out of fashion, meant that it never happened. Quarry did make further horror film appearances, as the hippy guru vampire Khorda in 1973's *The Deathmaster* and as a gangster in the 1974 zombie movie *Sugar Hill*. A third Count Yorga film was often rumored to be in the works, but never materialised.

Quarry made several guest appearances on TV shows, including *Mike Hammer* (1958), *Richard Diamond, Private Detective* (1957-1959) with David Janssen, *Wichita Town* (1960) with Joel McCrea, *The Fugitive* (1963) again with David Janssen, *Perry Mason* (1965), *Ironside* (1973), *Cannon* (1974), *The Rockford Files* (1977-1979), and *Buck Rogers in the 25th Century* (1979).

In 1980 he was in a in an accident, in which he was struck by a drunk driver. It resulted in serious facial injuries. He was also mugged in Hollywood shortly thereafter.

In 1987, Quarry returned to film with *Cyclone* directed by Fred Olen Ray. Quarry would be cast in over twenty of Ray's films in the remainder of his career. Some of his later roles included *Moon in Scorpio* (1987), *Sexbomb* (1989), *Teenage Exorcist* (1991), *Inner Sanctum II* (1994), *Hybrid* (1998), and *Fugitive Mind* (1999).

Quarry died February 20, 2009 at the Motion Picture & Television Country House and Hospital in Woodland Hills, California at the age of 83.

Nina Quartero

Nina Quartero was born in New York City March 17, 1908 and was a motion picture actress whose career spanned the years 1928 - 1943. Often she played supporting roles and sometimes a diversive love interest for the lead male actor.

In *One Stolen Night* (1929) Quartero was cast with Betty Bronson and William Collier. The story concerns a British World War I soldier who comes to the assistance of an enslaved dancer. In *Frozen River* (1929) she was paired with Raymond McKee as the motion picture's romantic leads. Wonder dog Rin Tin Tin, is the most unlikely of heroes in the screen drama.

In 1931 Quartero appeared in *Arizona*, an early John Wayne movie. Playing "Conchita," she is a source of strife in Wayne's relationship to the characters depicted by Laura La Plante and June Clyde. She performed again with Wayne in *The Man from Monterey* (1933).

She appeared in *The Devil's Brother* and *Sons of the Desert*, both in 1933 and with Laurel and Hardy. She appeared with Jean Harlow in *Wife vs. Secretary* (1936) the same year she appered with Joel McCrea in *Two in a Crowd*.

Her final screen performances show Quartero playing smaller parts, such as the role of a Cuban dancer in *Torchy Blane In Panama* (1938), a native dancer in *Green Hell* (1940) and a bar-girl in *A Lady Takes a Chance* (1943).

Quartero once tried a publicity stunt by claiming that she was betrothed to Notre Dame All-American Quarterback Frank Carideo. Carideo demanded a retraction of Quartero's engagement announcement, although admitted he knew her from a time when each resided in Mount Vernon, New York. He had also visited her home, in Beverly Hills, California, prior to the 1930 University of Southern California game, to exchange greetings.

Nina Quartero died in Woodland Hills, California in November 23, 1985 at age 77.

Anthony Quinn

Joel McCrea and Anthony Quinn in *Buffalo Bill*

Antonio Rodolfo Quinn Oaxaca in Chihuahua, Mexico, April 21, 1915, more commonly known as Anthony Quinn, was a Mexican American actor, as well as a painter and writer. He starred in numerous critically acclaimed and commercially successful films, including *La Strada, The Guns of Navarone, Lawrence of Arabia, Zorba the Greek, Guns for San Sebastian, The Message* and *Lion of the Desert*. He won the Academy Award for Best Supporting Actor twice: for *Viva Zapata!* in 1952 and *Lust for Life* in 1956.

Quinn was born during the Mexican Revolution. His mother, Manuela "Nellie" Oaxaca, was of Aztec ancestry. His father, Francisco (Frank) Quinn, was also born in Mexico, to an Irish immigrant father from County Cork and a Mexican mother. Frank Quinn rode with Mexican revolutionary Pancho Villa, then later moved to the East Los Angeles neighborhood of City Terrace and became an assistant cameraman at a movie studio. In Quinn's autobiography *The Original Sin: A Self-portrait by Anthony Quinn* he denied being the son of an "Irish adventurer" and attributed that tale to Hollywood publicists.

When he was six years old, Quinn attended a Catholic church (even thinking he wanted to become a priest). At age eleven, however, he joined the Pentecostals in the International Church of the Foursquare Gospel (the Pentecostal followers of Aimee Semple McPherson). For a time he played in the church's band and was an apprentice preacher with the renowned evangelist. "I have known most of the great actresses of my time, and not one of them could touch her," Quinn once said of the spellbinding McPherson, whom he credited with inspiring Zorba's gesture of the dramatically outstretched hand.

Quinn grew up first in El Paso, Texas, and later the Boyle Heights and the Echo Park areas of Los Angeles, California. He attended Hammel Street Elementary School, Belvedere Junior High School, Polytechnic High School and finally Belmont High School in Los Angeles, with future baseball player and *General Hospital* star John

Beradino, but left before graduating. Tucson High School in Arizona, many years later, awarded him an honorary high school diploma.

As a young man, Quinn boxed professionally to earn money, then studied art and architecture under Frank Lloyd Wright, at Wright's Arizona residence and his Wisconsin studio, Taliesin. The two very different men became friends. When Quinn mentioned that he was drawn to acting, Wright encouraged him. Quinn said he had been offered $800 per week by a film studio and didn't know what to do. Wright replied, "Take it, you'll never make that much with me." In a 1999 interview *Private Screenings with Robert Osborne*. Quinn said that the contract was for only $300 per week.

After a short time performing on the stage, Quinn launched his film career performing character roles in the 1936 films *Parole* (his debut) and *The Milky Way*. He played "ethnic" villains in Paramount films such as *The Last Train from Madrid* (1937) with Alan Ladd, *Dangerous to Know* (1938) and *Road to Morocco*, and played a more sympathetic Crazy Horse in *They Died with Their Boots On* with Errol Flynn. By 1947, he had appeared in over fifty films and had played Indians, Mafia dons, Hawaiian chiefs, Filipino freedom-fighters, Chinese guerrillas, and Arab sheiks, but was still not a major star. He returned to the theater, playing Stanley Kowalski in *A Streetcar Named Desire* on Broadway. In 1947, he became a naturalized citizen of the United States.

He came back to Hollywood in the early 1950s, specializing in tough roles. He was cast in a series of B-adventures such as *Mask of the Avenger* (1951). His big break came from playing opposite Marlon Brando in Elia Kazan's *Viva Zapata!* (1952). Quinn wanted to play the lead role of Zapata but Brando, coming off his recent success in the film *Streetcar Named Desire*, was Kazan's first choice. However, his supporting role as Zapata's brother won Quinn an Oscar while Brando lost the Oscar for Best Actor to Gary Cooper in *High Noon*. He was the first Mexican-American to win any Academy Award. He appeared in several Italian films starting in 1953, turning in one of his best performances as a dim-witted, thuggish and volatile strongman in Federico Fellini's *La strada* (1954) opposite Giulietta Masina. Quinn won his second Oscar for Best Supporting Actor by portraying the painter Paul Gauguin in Vincente Minnelli's van Gogh biographical film, *Lust for Life* (1956). The following year, he received an Oscar nomination for his part in George Cukor's *Wild Is the Wind*. In *The River's Edge* (1957), he played the husband of the former girlfriend (played by Debra Paget) of a killer (Ray Milland), who turns up with a stolen fortune and forces Quinn and Paget at gunpoint to guide him safely to Mexico. Quinn starred in *The Savage Innocents* 1959 (film) as Inuk, an Eskimo who finds himself caught between two clashing cultures. The film later inspired the song Quinn the Eskimo (Mighty Quinn) by Bob Dylan.

As the decade ended, Quinn allowed his age to show and began his transformation into a major character actor. His physique filled out, his hair grayed, and his once smooth, swarthy face weathered and became more rugged. He played a Greek resistance fighter in *The Guns of Navarone* (1961), an aging boxer in *Requiem for a Heavyweight*, and the Bedouin shaikh Auda abu Tayi in *Lawrence of Arabia* (both 1962). That year he also played the title role in *Barabbas*, based on a novel by Pär Lagerkvist. The success of *Zorba the Greek* in 1964 was the high-water mark of his career and resulted in another Oscar nomination for Best Actor. Other films included *The 25th Hour* (1967), with Virna Lisi; *The Magus* (1968), with Michael Caine and Candice Bergen, based on the novel by John Fowles; La Bataille de San Sebastian (*Guns for San Sebastian*) with Charles Bronson; and *The Shoes of the Fisherman*, where he played a Catholic Archbishop in a Soviet Siberian prison who becomes Pope. In 1969, he starred in *The Secret of Santa Vittoria* with Anna Magnani, and each were nominated for a Golden Globe Award.

In 1971, after the success of a TV movie named *The City*, where Quinn played Mayor Thomas Jefferson Alcala, he starred in the single-season ABC television series entitled *The Man and the City*. Though the program was filmed in Albuquerque, New Mexico, the name of the city is not disclosed on the program. His subsequent television appearances were sporadic, among them *Jesus of Nazareth*.

In 1976, he starred in the movie *Mohammad, Messenger of God* (also known as *The Message*), about the origin of Islam, as Hamza, a highly revered warrior instrumental in the early stages of Islam. In 1981, he starred in the *Lion of the Desert*, together with Irene Papas, Oliver Reed, Rod Steiger, and John Gielgud. Quinn played the real-life Bedouin leader Omar Mukhtar who fought Benito Mussolini's Italian troops in the deserts of Libya. The film, produced and directed by Moustapha Akkad, is now critically acclaimed, but performed poorly at the box office because of negative publicity in the West at the time of its release, stemming from its having been partially funded by Libya. In 1983, he reprised his most famous role, playing Zorba the Greek for 362 performances in a successful revival of the Kander and Ebb musical *Zorba*. Quinn performed in this musical both on Broadway in New York City and at the Kennedy Center in Washington, D.C.

Quinn's film career slowed during the 1990s, but he nonetheless continued to work steadily, appearing in *Revenge* (1990), *Jungle Fever* (1991), *Last Action Hero* (1993), *A Walk in the Clouds* (1995) and *Seven Servants* (1996). In 1994, he played Zeus in the five TV movies that led to the syndicated series *Hercules: The Legendary*

Journeys. (However, he did not continue in the actual series, and the role was eventually filled by several other actors).

Quinn made an appearance at the John Gotti trial, according to John H. Davis, author of *Mafia Dynasty: The Rise and Fall of the Gambino Crime Family*. He told reporters he wanted to play Paul Castellano, the boss of the Gambino family after Carlo Gambino. Gotti had Castellano murdered, becoming the boss of the Gambino family thereafter. Gotti was on trial concerning a variety of felony charges when Quinn visited the courtroom. Although he tried to shake hands with Gotti, federal marshals prevented him from doing so, Davis says. The actor interpreted the testimony of Sammy ("The Bull") Gravano, Gotti's underboss, against Gotti as "a friend who betrays a friend." He hadn't come to "judge" Gotti, Quinn insisted, but because he wanted to portray Castellano, who inspired the actor because he had had a "thirty-year-old" mistress, which Quinn believed was "a beautiful thing." He would later portray Gambino family underboss Aniello Dellacroce in the 1996 HBO film *Gotti*. Armand Assante portrayed John Gotti and Richard C. Sarafian portrayed Paul Castellano. Quinn was nominated for a Golden Globe for his performance as Dellacroce.

Art critic Donald Kuspit, explains, "examining Quinn's many expressions of creativity together—his art and acting—we can see that he was a creative genius..."

Early in life Quinn had an interest in painting and drawing. Throughout his teenage years he won various art competitions in California and focused his studies at Polytechnic High School in Los Angeles on drafting. Later, Quinn studied briefly under Frank Lloyd Wright through the Taliesin Fellowship—an opportunity created by winning first prize in an architectural design contest. Through Wright's recommendation, Quinn took acting lessons as a form of post-operative speech therapy, which led to an acting career that spanned over six decades.

Apart from art classes taken in Chicago during the 1950s, Quinn never attended art school; nonetheless, taking advantage of books, museums, and amassing a sizable collection, he managed to give himself an effective education in the language of modern art. Although Quinn remained mostly self-taught, intuitively seeking out and exploring new ideas, there is observable history in his work because he had assiduously studied the modernist masterpieces on view in the galleries of New York, Mexico City, Paris, and London. When filming on location around the world, Quinn was exposed to regional contemporary art styles exhibited at local galleries and studied art history in each area.

In an endless search for inspiration, he was influenced by his Mexican ancestry, decades of residence in Europe, and lengthy stays in Africa and the Middle East while filming in the 1970s and 1980s.

By the early 1980s, his work had caught the eyes of various gallery owners and was exhibited internationally, in New York, Los Angeles, Paris, and Mexico City. His work is now represented in both public and private collections throughout the world.

He wrote two memoirs, *The Original Sin* (1972) and *One Man Tango* (1997), a number of scripts, and a series of unpublished stories currently in the collection of his archive.

Quinn's personal life was as volatile and passionate as the characters he played in films. His first wife was the adopted daughter of Cecil B. DeMille, the actress Katherine DeMille, whom he married in 1937. The couple had five children: Christopher (1939-1941), Christina (born December 1, 1941), Catalina (born November 21, 1942), Duncan (born August 4, 1945), and Valentina (born December 26, 1952). Their first child, Christopher, aged two, drowned in the lily pond of next-door neighbor W.C. Fields.

In 1965, Quinn and DeMille were divorced, because of his affair with Italian costume designer Jolanda Addolori, whom he married in 1966. They had three children: Francesco Quinn (March 22, 1963 – August 5, 2011), Danny (born April 16, 1964), and Lorenzo Quinn (born May 7, 1966).

The union ended in 1997, after Quinn had children with his secretary, Katherine Benvin. He then married Benvin, with whom he had two children, Antonia Quinn (born July 23, 1993) and Ryan Nicholas Quinn (born July 5, 1996). Quinn and Benvin remained together until his death.

Quinn also had two children with Friedel Dunbar: Sean Quinn (born February 7, 1973), a New Jersey real estate agent, and Alexander Anthony Quinn (born December 30, 1976), an event producer in Los Angeles, California.

He had a personal relationship with New York Mafia Crime Boss Frank Costello and other Genovese gangsters.

Quinn spent his last years in Bristol, Rhode Island. He died at age 86 in Boston, Massachusetts from pneumonia and respiratory failure while suffering from throat cancer shortly after completing his role in his last film, *Avenging Angelo* (2002).

His funeral was held in the First Baptist Church in America in the College Hill section of Providence, Rhode Island;. Late in life, he had joined the Foursquare evangelical Christian community. He is buried in a family plot in Bristol, Rhode Island.

Steve Raines

Steve Raines was born in Grants Pass, Oregon June 17, 1916 and was an American actor. Raines appeared in many television series and several films, including *Naked Gun* (1956), *Street of Darkness* (1958), and *Macho Callahan* (1970) with David Janssen.

Steve was the adopted son of Mr. and Mrs Henry Savage of San Antonio, Texas. The Savages had a riding stable across the road from an orphan's home where Steve was. Steve started coming over to the stable and eventually was adopted by the Savages. He and Mr. Savage performed in some "B" movies with Henry Garcia a local actor. After a while, he decided he would go to California to be in the movies.

Raines is known for playing the role of Jim Quince in the CBS western series, *Rawhide* (1959–1965), starring Clint Eastwood and Eric Fleming.

More of his roles included *Under Colorado Skies* (1947), *Sheriff of Wichita* (1949), *Broken Lance* (1954), *Brave Eagle* (1955-1956), *Cattle Empire* (1958) with Joel McCrea, *Maverick* (1961), *Laredo* (1966), *The Wild Wild West* (1969), and *The Virginian* (1966-1971).

His last appearance of thirteen since 1959 was in a 1974 episode of CBS's *Gunsmoke*, starring James Arness. January 4, 1996.

He died January 4, 1996 at age 79 in Grants Pass, Oregon.

Marjorie Rambeau

Marjorie Rambeau was born in San Francisco, California July 15, 1889 and was an American film and stage actress.

Rambeau was born to Marcel and Lilian Garlinda (née Kindelberger) Rambeau. Her parents separated when she was a child. She and her mother went to Nome, Alaska where young Marjorie dressed as a boy, sang and played the banjo in saloons and music halls. Her mother insisted she dress as a boy to thwart amorous attention from drunken grown men in such a wild and woolly outpost as Nome. She began performing on the stage at the age of 12. She attained theatrical experience in a rambling early life as a strolling player. Finally she made her Broadway debut on March 10, 1913 in a tryout of Willard Mack's play, *Kick In*.

In her youth she was a Broadway leading lady. In 1921, Dorothy Parker memorialized her in verse: "If all the tears you shed so lavishly / Were gathered, as they left each brimming eye. / And were collected in a crystal sea, / The envious ocean would curl up and dry— / So awful in its mightiness, that lake, / So fathomless, that clear and salty deep. / For, oh, it seems your gentle heart must break, / To see you weep. ..."

Her silent films with the Mutual company included *Mary Moreland* and *The Greater Woman* (1917). The films were not major successes but did expose Rambeau to film audiences. By the time talkies came along she was in her early forties and she began to take on character roles in films such as *Min and Bill*, *The Secret Six*, *Laughing Sinners*, *Grand Canary*, *Joe Palooka*, and *Primrose Path* (1940) with Joel McCrea, for which she was nominated for the Academy Award for Best Supporting Actress.

In 1940, Rambeau had the title role in *Tugboat Annie Sails Again* as well as second billing under Wallace Beery (the co-star of the original *Tugboat Annie*) in *20 Mule Team*; she also played an Italian mother in *East of the River*. Other films included *Tobacco Road*, *A Man Called Peter*, and *Broadway*. In 1953, she was again nominated for an Oscar, this time for *Torch Song*. In 1957, she appeared in a supporting role in her last film *Man of a Thousand Faces* about the life of Lon Chaney, although she never worked with the real Chaney in silent films.

For her contribution to the motion picture industry, Rambeau has a star on the Hollywood Walk of Fame at 6336 Hollywood Blvd.

According to author and *New York Mirror* theatre critic Bernard Sobel the Reuben sandwich was invented for Marjorie Rambeau upon a visit to Reuben's Restaurant and Delicatessen in New York City.

Rambeau was married three times but bore no children: The first was in 1913 to Canadian writer, actor, and director Willard Mack. They divorced in 1917. She then married another actor, Hugh Dillman McGaughey, in 1919. They divorced in 1923. Dillman later married Anna Thompson Dodge, widow of automobile magnate Horace Elgin Dodge, Sr., and one of the wealthiest women in the world. Rambeau's last marriage was to Francis Asbury Gudger in 1931, with whom she remained until his death in 1967. Gudger was from Asheville, North Carolina. In the winters they often stayed there, and in the summer they lived in Sebring, Florida. His previous wife was killed in an automobile accident in Tampa two years before, but Rambeau and Gudger had been sweethearts years before when the former was the "toast of Broadway".

She died July 6, 1970 at her home in Palm Springs, California at age 80 and was buried at the Desert Memorial Park in Cathedral City, California.

Mikail Rasumny

Mikail Rasumny was born Mikhail Razumnyy May 13, 1890 in Odessa, Kherson Governorate, Russian Empire [now Ukraine]. The son of a cantor, Rasumny made his stage debut at 14 and toured Europe and South America with the Moscow Art Theatre. Rasumny settled in the U.S. in 1935 and took jobs as a bill collector and dishwasher between acting jobs.

His surname "Rasumny" has a nice sound in Russian: it means "reasonable," "rational," "sensible," even "intelligent." Strictly transliterated into English, letter by letter, it would be spelled "Razumnyy." He'd acted a few years in Germany before immigrating to the US, and in Germany he acquired the spelling "Rasumny." He never bothered to change that spelling after arriving in Hollywood.

His first film American appearance was in *Comrade X* (1940). He spent the remainder of his career playing several ethnic roles. Some more of his roles included *The Shanghai Gesture* (1941), *For Whom the Bell Tolls* (1943), *The Unseen* (1945) with Joel McCrea, *Our Hearts Were Growing Up* (1946), *Song of My Heart* (1948), *Anything Can Happen* (1952), *The Goldbergs* (1954), *Producers' Showcase* (1955), and *Hot Blood* (1956).

He died February 17, 1956 at age 65 in Woodland Hills, California.

John Raven

John Raven is an actor, known for *Rancho Notorious* (1952), *The San Francisco Story* (1952) with Joel McCrea, and *Gang Busters* (1952).

Some of his other roles included *Three Guys Named Mike* (1951), *The Great Caruso* (1951), *Pat and Mike* (1952), *Hot Blood* (1956), *Doctor Who* (1966), *Sergeant Cork* (1966), and *Let's Go Out* (1968).

Cyril Raymond

Cyril Raymond and Joel McCrea in *Shoot First*

Cyril William North Raymond was born February 13, 1899 in Rowley Regis, Staffordshire and was a British character actor. Of dozens of film and television appearances, probably his best-remembered role was as Fred Jesson, the husband of Celia Johnson's Laura Jesson in *Brief Encounter* (1945).

During the Second World War he served as a RAF fighter controller during the Battle of Britain and was awarded the MBE in the 1945 King's Birthday Honours. He reached the rank of Wing Commander.

When he was 12, he was a schoolboy living at the Grand Hotel, Broad Street, Bristol. His mother Rose Raymond, 44-years-old, was managing the hotel. His father Herbert Linton Raymond had died in 1906 at the hotel, Herbert and Rose are buried at Arnos Vale Cemetery, Bristol.

He was married twice. First to Iris Hoey and then to Gillian Lind, both of whom were actresses.

On December 4, 1923 with Iris Hoey he had a son John North Blagrave Raymond, who was born in Bristol. He divorced her in 1936.

In 1937 he married Gillian Pratt (Lind) in, Hailsham, who was related to Boris Karloff. Her nephew is production designer, Anthony D. G. Pratt.

More of his roles included *These Charming People* (1931), *The Shadow* (1933), *Thunder in the City* (1937), *The Spy in Black* (1939), *Spitfire* (1942), *Men of Two Worlds* (1946), *The Jack of Diamonds* (1949), *Shoot First* aka *Rough Shoot* (1953) with Joel McCrea, *Charley Moon* (1956), *The Safecracker* (1958), *Beware of Children* (1961), and *Night Train to Paris* (1964).

Cyril died on March 20, 1973 at Ripe, Sussex, UK at age 74.

Phillip Reed

Phillip Reed was born Milton Le Roy Treinis March 25, 1908 in New York City, New York March 25, 1908 and was an American actor. He was perhaps best known for his role as Steve Wilson in a series of four films (1947–1948) based on the Big Town radio series.

Television appearances include a lead role in the 1955 anthology drama series *Police Call*. More of his roles included *College Coach* (1933), *Gambling Lady* (1934) with Joel McCrea, *The Woman in Red* (1935), *The Last of the Mohicans* (1936), *Weekend for Three* (1941), *Rendezvous with Annie* (1946), *Unknown Island* (1948), *Davy Crockett, Indian Scout* (1950), *The Girl in the Red Velvet Swing* (1955), *The Tattered Dress* (1957), *Riverboat* (1959), *Alfred Hitchcock Presents* (1956-1962), *The Alfred Hitchcock Hour* (1962), and *Burke's Law* (1963).

He also appeared as King Toranshah in the 1965 Elvis Presley musical film *Harum Scarum*, which was his last role. Reed died in December 7, 1996 at age 88 and was buried at Forest Lawn Memorial Park Cemetery in Glendale, California.

Ralph Reed

Ralph Reed was born Ralph Redd Freeto August 12, 1931 in Wichita, Kansas and was an actor from 1938 to 1958. He attended UCLA in 1953. He was a Korean War Veteran, discharged in 1955.

Some of his roles included *Since You Went Away* (1944), *Red Skies of Montana* (1952), *High Noon* (1952), *How to Marry a Millionaire* (1953), *Somebody Up There Likes Me* (1956), *The Tall Stranger* (1957) with Joel McCrea, *North by Northwest* (1959), *Cimarron* (1960), *Perry Mason* (1962), *Destry* (1964), and *Rawhide* (1959-1965).

He moved to Orange County, California in 1962 and had been in Real Estate for the past 35 years. He died January 21, 1997 at age 65 in El Toro, California.

George Reeves

George Reeves was born George Keefer Brewer in Woolstock, Iowa January 5, 1914 and was an American actor best known for his role as Superman in the 1950s television program *Adventures of Superman*.

His death at age 45 from a gunshot remains a polarizing issue; the official finding was suicide, but some believe he was murdered or the victim of an accidental shooting.

He was the son of Don Brewer and Helen Lescher (his death certificate erroneously lists his birthplace as Kentucky). Reeves was born five months into their marriage (the reason Reeves's mother subsequently claimed a false April birth date for her son, something he was unaware of until adulthood). They separated soon after his birth and Helen moved back to her home in Galesburg, Illinois.

Later, Reeves' mother moved to California to stay with her sister. There, Helen met and married Frank Bessolo. George's father married Helen Schultz in 1925 and had children with her. Don Brewer never saw his son again.

In 1927, Frank Bessolo adopted George as his own son, and the boy took on his new stepfather's last name to become George Bessolo. Frank and Helen Bessolo's marriage lasted fifteen years and ended in divorce while Reeves was away visiting relatives. His mother told Reeves that Frank had committed suicide. Reeves' cousin, Catherine Chase, told biographer Jim Beaver that Reeves did not know for several years that Bessolo was still alive, or that he was his stepfather and not his biological father.

George began acting and singing in high school and continued performing on stage as a student at Pasadena Junior College. He also boxed as a heavyweight in amateur matches until his mother Helen ordered him to stop, fearing his good looks might be damaged.

While studying acting at the Pasadena Playhouse, Reeves met his future wife, Ellanora Needles. They married on September 22, 1940, in San Gabriel, California, at the Church of Our Savior. They had no children and divorced ten years later.

At the Pasadena Playhouse, Reeves met fellow actor Frank Wilcox, who was best man at Reeves' wedding. The two were subsequently cast together in eleven films.

Reeves' film career began in 1939 when he was cast as Stuart Tarleton (incorrectly listed in the film's credits as Brent Tarleton), one of Scarlett O'Hara's suitors in *Gone with the Wind*. It was a minor role but he and Fred Crane, both in brightly dyed red hair as "the Tarleton Twins," were in the film's opening scenes. Like Wilcox, Reeves was contracted to Warner Brothers soon after being cast. Warner changed his professional name to "George Reeves." His *Gone with the Wind* screen credit reflects the change. Between the start of *Gone with the Wind* production and its release twelve months later, several films on his Warner contract were made and released, making *Gone with the Wind* his first film role, but his fifth film released. One of those was *Espionage Agent* (1939) with Joel McCrea.

He starred in a number of two-reel short subjects and appeared in several B-pictures, including two with Ronald Reagan and three with James Cagney *Torrid Zone* (1940), *The Fighting 69th* (1940), and *The Strawberry Blonde* (1941)). Warner loaned him to producer Alexander Korda to co-star with Merle Oberon in *Lydia* (1941), a box-office failure.

Released from his Warner contract, he signed a contract at Twentieth Century-Fox but was released after only a handful of films, one of which was the Charlie Chan movie *Dead Men Tell* (1941). He freelanced, appearing in five Hopalong Cassidy westerns before director Mark Sandrich cast Reeves as Lieutenant John Summers opposite Claudette Colbert and Veroncia Lake in *So Proudly We Hail!* (1942), a war drama for Paramount Pictures. He won critical acclaim for the role and garnered considerable publicity.

Reeves was drafted into the U.S. Army in early 1943. He was assigned to the U.S. Army Air Forces and performed in the USAAF's Broadway show *Winged Victory*. The long Broadway run was followed by a national tour and a movie version in 1944. Reeves was then transferred to the Army Air Forces' First Motion Picture Unit, where he made training films. He looked forward to working with *So Proudly We Hail!* director Mark Sandrich. Sandrich felt that Reeves had the potential to become a major star, but Sandrich died in 1945. Reeves would later comment on the impact Sandrich's death had on his film career.

Discharged at the war's end, Reeves returned to Hollywood. However, many studios were slowing down their production schedules, and some production units had shut down completely. He appeared in a pair of outdoor thrillers with Ralph Byrd, another Veronica Lake film *The Sainted Sisters* (1948), and in a Sam Katzman-produced serial, *The Adventures of Sir Galahad* (1949). Reeves fit the rugged requirements of the roles and, with his retentive memory for dialogue, he did well under rushed production conditions. He was able to play against type and starred as a villainous gold hunter in a Johnny Weissmuller *Jungle Jim* (1948) film.

Separated from his wife (their divorce became final in 1950), Reeves moved to New York City in 1949. He performed on live television anthology programs as well as on radio and then returned to Hollywood in 1951 for a role in a Fritz Lang film, *Rancho Notorious*. Meanwhile, DC Comics was planning a television adaptation of its most famous character.

In 1953, Reeves played a minor character, Sergeant Maylon Stark, in the motion picture *From Here To Eternity*. The film won the Academy Award for Best Picture and gave Reeves a second motion picture appearance in a film that ultimately won the Oscar (the other being *Gone with The Wind*).

In June 1951, Reeves was offered the role of Superman in a new television series titled *Adventures of Superman*. He was initially reluctant to take the role because, like many actors of his time, he considered television unimportant and believed few would see his work. He received low pay and only for the weeks of production. The half-hour films were shot on tight schedules; at least two shows were made every six days. According to commentaries on the *Adventures of Superman* DVD sets, multiple scripts would be filmed simultaneously to take advantage of the standing sets, so that, e.g., all the "Perry White's office" scenes for three or four episodes would be shot the same day and the various "apartment" scenes would be done consecutively.

Reeves' career as Superman had begun with *Superman and the Mole Men* (1951), a film intended both as a B-picture and as the pilot for the TV series. Immediately after completing it, Reeves and the crew began production of the first season's episodes, all shot over thirteen weeks in the summer of 1951. The series went on the air the following year, and Reeves was amazed at becoming a national celebrity. In 1952, the struggling ABC Network purchased the show for national broadcast, which gave him greater visibility.

The Superman cast members had restrictive contracts which prevented them from taking other work that might interfere with the series. Except for the second season, the Superman schedule was brief (thirteen shows shot two per week, a total of seven weeks out of a year), but all had a "thirty day clause," which meant that the producers could demand their exclusive services for a new season on four weeks' notice. This prevented long-term work on major films with long schedules, stage plays which might lead to a lengthy run, or any other series work.

However, Reeves had earnings from personal appearances beyond his meager salary, and his affection for his young fans was genuine. Reeves took his role model status seriously, avoiding cigarettes where children could see him and eventually quitting smoking. He kept his private life discreet. Nevertheless, he had a romantic relationship with a married ex-showgirl eight years his senior, Toni Mannix, wife of Metro-Goldwyn-Mayer general manager Eddie Mannix.

In the documentary *Look, Up in the Sky: The Amazing Story of Superman*, Jack Larson described how when he first met Reeves he told him that he enjoyed his performance in *So Proudly We Hail!* According to Larson, Reeves said that if Mark Sandrich had not died, he would not be there in "this monkey suit." Larson said it was the only time he heard Reeves say anything negative about being Superman.

In between the first and second seasons of *Superman*, Reeves got sporadic acting assignments in one-shot TV anthology programs and in two feature films, *Forever Female* (1953) and Fritz Lang's *The Blue Gardenia* (1953). But by the time the series was airing nationwide, Reeves found himself so associated with Superman and Clark Kent that it was difficult for him to find other roles. An untrue but often-repeated story suggests that he was upset when his scenes as Sergeant Maylon Stark in the classic film *From Here to Eternity* were cut after a preview audience kept yelling "There's Superman!" whenever he appeared on screen. *Eternity* director Fred Zinnemann, the screenwriter Daniel Taradash, and others have maintained that every scene written for Reeves' character was shot and included as part of the released film. Zinnemann has also asserted that there were no post-release cuts, nor was there even a preview screening. Everything in the first production draft of the script is still present in the final product seen since 1953. If audiences yelled "There's Superman!" during the film's theatrical release, there is no evidence it affected its success at the box office.

With Toni Mannix, Reeves worked tirelessly to raise money to fight myasthenia gravis. He served as national chairman for the Myasthenia Gravis Foundation in 1955. During the second season, Reeves appeared in a short film for the Treasury Department, *Stamp Day for Superman*, in which he caught the villains and told children why they should invest in government savings stamps.

In the 104 episodes of the show, Reeves got along well with his costars. Larson, who played Jimmy Olsen, recalled that Reeves enjoyed playing practical jokes on the crew and cast. Reeves insisted his original Lois Lane, Phyllis Coates, be given equal billing in the credits. He also stood by Robert Shayne (who played Police Inspector William "Bill" Henderson) when Shayne was subpoenaed by FBI agents on the set of *Superman*. (Shayne's political activism in the Screen Actors Guild in the 1940s was used by his embittered ex-wife as an excuse to label him a Communist, although Shayne had never been a Communist Party member.) When Coates was replaced by Noel Neill (who had played Lois Lane in the Kirk Alyn serials), Reeves defended her nervousness on her first day when he felt that the director was being too harsh with her. On the other hand, he liked to stand outside camera range, mugging at the other cast members to see if he could break them up. According to Larson, Reeves took on-set photos with his Minox and handed out prints. By all accounts, there was strong camaraderie among the show's actors.

After two seasons, Reeves was dissatisfied with the one-dimensional role and low salary. Now 40 years old, he wished to quit and move on with his career. The producers looked elsewhere for a new star, allegedly contacting Kirk Alyn, the actor who had first portrayed Superman in the original movie serials and who had initially refused to play the role on television. Alyn turned them down again.

Reeves established his own production company and conceived a TV adventure series, *Port of Entry*, which would be shot on location in Hawaii and Mexico, writing the pilot script himself. However, *Superman* producers offered him a salary increase and he returned to the series. He was reportedly making $5,000 per week, but only while the show was in production (about eight weeks each year). As for *Port of Entry*, Reeves was never able to gain financing for the project, and the show was never made.

In 1957, the producers considered a theatrical film, *Superman and the Secret Planet*. A script was commissioned from David Chantler, who had written many of the TV scripts. In 1959, however, negotiations began for a renewal of the series, with twenty-six episodes scheduled to go into production. (John Hamilton, who had played Perry White, died in 1958, so the former film-serial Perry White Pierre Watkin was to replace him.)

By mid 1959, contracts were signed, costumes refitted, and new teleplay writers assigned. Noel Neill was quoted as saying that the cast of Superman was ready to do a new series of the still-popular show. Producers reportedly promised Reeves that the new programs would be as serious and action-packed as the first season, guaranteed him creative input, and slated him to direct several of the new shows as he had done with the final three episodes of the 1957 season. In the documentary *Look, Up in the Sky: The Amazing Story of Superman*, Neill remembered that Reeves was excited to go back to work. Jack Larson, however, told biographer Beaver: "Anyone who thought another season of Superman would make George Reeves happy didn't know George."

Attempting to showcase his versatility, Reeves sang on the Tony Bennett show in August 1956. He appeared on *I Love Lucy* (Episode #165, Lucy Meets Superman") in 1956 as Superman. Character actor Ben Welden had acted with Reeves in the Warner Bros. days and frequently guest-starred on *Superman*. He said, "After the *I Love Lucy* show, Superman was no longer a challenge to him.... I know he enjoyed the role, but he used to say, 'Here I am, wasting my life.'"His good friend Bill Walsh, a producer at Disney Studios, gave Reeves a prominent role in *Westward Ho, the Wagons!* (1956), in which Reeves wore a beard and mustache. It was to be his final feature film appearance.

Reeves, Noel Neill, Natividad Vacío, Gene LeBell, and a trio of musicians toured with a public appearance show from 1957 onward. The stage show was a gigantic hit for the excited children who got to see their hero in person, though not a huge moneymaker for Reeves. The first half of the show was a *Superman* sketch in which Reeves and Neill performed with LeBell as a villain called "Mr. Kryptonite" who captured Lois Lane. Kent then rushed offstage to return as Superman, who came to the rescue and fought with the bad guy. The second half of the show was Reeves out of costume and as himself, singing and accompanying himself on the guitar. Vacio and Neill accompanied him in duets.

Reeves and Toni Mannix split in 1958 and Reeves announced his engagement to society playgirl Leonore Lemmon. He complained to friends, columnists, and his mother of his financial problems. He received royalties from syndication of the Superman show, but these were insubstantial, particularly in view of his lifestyle. Under these circumstances, the planned revival of *Superman* was apparently a small lifeline. Reeves had also hoped to direct a low-budget science-fiction film written by a friend from his Pasadena Playhouse days, and he had discussed the project with his first Lois Lane, Phyllis Coates, the previous year. However, Reeves and his partner failed to find financing and the film was never made. There was another Superman stage show scheduled for Julyand a planned stage tour of Australia. Reeves had options for making a living, but those options apparently all involved playing Superman again - a role he was not eager to reprise at age 45.

Jack Larson and Noel Neill both remembered Reeves as a noble Southern gentleman (even though he was from Iowa) with a sign on his dressing room door that said *"Honest George, the people's friend."* After Reeves had been made a "Kentucky Colonel" during a publicity trip in the South, the sign on his dressing room door was replaced with a new one that read *Honest George", also known as Col. Reeves,* created by the show's prop department. A photo of a smiling Reeves and the sign appear in Gary Grossman's book about the show.

According to the Los Angeles Police Department report, between approximately 1:30 and 2:00 a.m. on June 16, 1959, George Reeves died of a gunshot wound to his head in the upstairs bedroom at his home in Benedict Canyon. The police arrived within the hour. Present in the house at the time of the incident were Leonore Lemmon (who had been Reeves's fiancee at the time), William Bliss, writer Richard Condon, and Carol Van Ronkel, who lived a few blocks away with her husband, screenwriter Rip Van Ronkel.

According to these witnesses, Lemmon and Reeves had been dining and drinking earlier in the evening in the company of writer Condon, who was ghostwriting an autobiography of prizefighter Archie Moore. Reeves and Lemmon had had an argument at the restaurant in front of Condon, and the three of them returned home. However, Lemmon stated in news interviews with Reeves' biographer Jim Beaver that she and Reeves had not accompanied friends to the restaurant but rather to wrestling matches. Contemporaneous news items indicate that Reeves' friend Gene LeBell was wrestling that night—yet LeBell's own recollections are that he did not see Reeves after a workout session earlier in the day. In any event, Reeves went to bed, but sometime near midnight an impromptu party began when Bliss and Carol Van Ronkel arrived. Reeves angrily came downstairs and complained about the noise. After blowing off steam, he stayed with the guests for a while, had a drink, and then retired upstairs again in a bad mood.

The guests later heard a single, gunshot from upstairs. Bliss ran upstairs into Reeves' bedroom and found him lying across the bed dead, his naked body facing upward and his feet on the floor. It is believed that this corroborated Reeves' sitting position on the edge of the bed when he allegedly shot himself, after which the bullet struck his head, his body fell back on the bed and the 9 mm Luger pistol fell between his feet.

Statements from the witnesses that were made to the police and the press essentially agree. Neither Leonore Lemmon nor even other guests who were at the scene made any apology for their delay in calling the police after hearing the fatal gunshot that killed Reeves; the shock of the death, the lateness of the hour, and their state of intoxication were given as reasons for the delay. Police said that all of the witnesses present were extremely inebriated and that coherent stories were very difficult to obtain from them.

In contemporary news articles, Lemmon attributed Reeves' alleged suicide to depression caused by his "failed career" and inability to find more work. The report made by the Los Angeles Police states, "[Reeves was]... depressed because he couldn't get the sort of parts he wanted." Newspapers and wire-service reports possibly misquoted LAPD Sergeant V.A. Peterson as saying: "Miss Lemmon blurted, 'He's probably going to go shoot himself.' A noise was heard upstairs. She continued, 'He's opening a drawer to get the gun.' A shot was heard. 'See there—I told you so!'"However, this statement may have been embellished by journalists. Lemmon and her friends were downstairs at the time the shot was fired, with music playing downstairs. It would have been nearly impossible to hear a drawer opening in the upstairs bedroom through the music. Lemmon later claimed that she had never said anything so specific but rather had made an offhand remark along the lines of "Oh, he'll probably go shoot himself now."

While the official story given by Lemmon to the police placed her in the living room with party guests at the time of the shooting, statements from Fred Crane, who was Reeves' friend and colleague from *Gone with The Wind*, put Leonore Lemmon either inside or in direct proximity to Reeves' bedroom—minimally as a witness to the shooting. According to Crane, Bill Bliss had told Millicent Trent that after the shot rang out and while Bliss was having a drink, Leonore Lemmon came downstairs and said, "Tell them I was down here, tell them I was down here!" In an interview with Carl Glass, Crane expanded on this: "It needed to be said and that is the way I heard it from Millie as it was told to her by Bill Bliss. Janet Bliss and Millie were very close friends. I met Millie at Bill and Janet's house up in Benedict Canyon on Easton Drive. We lived on the same street."

Witness statements and the examination of the crime scene by the Los Angeles Police led to the official inquiry conclusion that Reeves's death was a suicide. Reeves' will, dated 1956, bequeathed his entire estate to Toni Mannix, much to Lemmon's surprise and devastation. Her statement to the press read, "Toni got a house for charity, and I got a broken heart," referring to the Myasthenia Gravis Foundation.

Reeves is interred at Mountain View Cemetery and Mausoleum in Altadena, California. In 1985, he was posthumously named one of the honorees by DC Comics in the company's 50th anniversary publication *Fifty Who Made DC Great*.

Carl Benton Reid

Carl Benton Reid was born in Lansing, Michigan August 14, 1893 and was an American actor. He achieved fame on the Broadway stage in 1939 as Oscar Hubbard, one of Regina Giddens's (Tallulah Bankhead) greedy, devious brothers in the play *The Little Foxes*, and made his film debut reprising his role opposite Bette Davis in the 1941 film version. He also appeared in several Shakespeare plays on Broadway, and in the original production of Eugene O'Neill's *The Iceman Cometh*, as Harry Slade.

His stern, cold demeanor quickly stereotyped him in villainous, and/or unpleasant characters, although he could play a sympathetic role, as he did occasionally in such films as the 1957 TV-movie version of *The Pied Piper of Hamelin*. Here he played the Mayor of Hamelout, who unsuccessfully requests help from the Mayor of Hamelin (Claude Rains), when Hamelout is the victim of a flood. The flood leads to the famous plague of rats which invade Hamelin, and set the main plot in motion.

More of his roles included *In a Lonely Place* (1950), *Carbine Williams* (1952), *Escape from Fort Bravo* (1953), *Wichita* (1955) with Joel McCrea, *The First Texan* (1956) again with Joel McCrea, *Battle Hymn* (1957), *Tarzan's Fight for Life* (1958), *Pork Chop Hill* (1959), *Wichita Town* (1960) also with Joel McCrea, *The Underwater City* (1962), *Perry Mason* (1958-1963), and *Burke's Law* (!965-1966).

His last two roles came in 1966; as the judge in the film version of *Madame X* and as Claude Townsend in the TV series *The F.B.I.*. March 16, 1973.

He died March 16, 1973 atage 79 in Hollywood, California.

Vincent Renno

Vincent Renno was born Dominic Negrelli on October 4, 1914 in Lawrence, Massachusetts. He was an actor, known for *Abbott and Costello Meet the Killer, Boris Karloff* (1949), *Frenchie* (1950) with Joel McCrea, and *The Great Caruso* (1951).

Some of his other roles included *Criss Cross* (1949), *Black Hand* (1950), *Sirocco* (1951), and *My Six Convicts* (1952).

He died on November 5, 1955 in Los Angeles, California at age 41.

Adeline DeWalt Reynolds

Adeline DeWalt Reynolds was born September 19, 1862 in Benton County, Iowa. She survived the death of her husband in 1905, the San Francisco earthquake in 1906, and raising four children with no money. In 1926, when she was 64 she became one of the most mature freshman ever to enter the University of California. She graduated 6 years later with her B.A. degree.

In 1940, at age 78, she went to Hollywood, where she began her acting career. She was best known for her role in *Shirley Temple's Storybook* production of "Sleeping Beauty", although she is probably seen most often in *Going My Way* (1944) as Father Fitzgibbon's elderly mother.

More of her roles included *Shadow of the Thin Man* (1941), *Tales of Manhattan* (1942), *Son of Dracula* (1943), *A Tree Grows in Brooklyn* (1945), *The Girl from Manhattan* (1948), *Stars in My Crown* (1950) with Joel McCrea, *Here Comes the Groom* (1951), *Pony Soldier* (1952), *Witness to Murder* (1954), *The Ten Commandments* (1956), *Have Gun - Will Travel* (1958), *Peter Gunn* (1959), *Zane Grey Theater* (1959), and *Playhouse 90* (1960).

She died August 13, 1961 at age 98 in Hollywood, Los Angeles, California.

Gene Reynolds

Gene Reynolds was born Eugene Reynolds Blumenthal in Cleveland, Ohio April 4, 1923 and is a former American actor turned award-winning television writer, director, and producer. He was one of the producers of the popular TV series *M*A*S*H*.

He was born to Frank Eugene Blumenthal and Maude Evelyn Blumenthal, and was raised in Detroit, Michigan, where his father Frank was a businessman and entrepreneur.

He made his screen debut in the 1934 *Our Gang* short *Washee Ironee*, and for the next three decades made numerous appearances in films such as *In Old Chicago* (1937), *Captains Courageous* (1937), *Love Finds Andy Hardy* (1938), *Boys Town* (1938), *They Shall Have Music* (1939) with Joel McCrea, *Eagle Squadron* (1942), *The Country Girl* (1954), and *The McConnell Story* (1955) with Alan Ladd, and on television series like *The Lone Ranger* (1950), *I Love Lucy* (1957), *Armstrong Circle Theatre* (1951), *Whirlybirds* (1957), and *Hennesey* (1959), and *Captain Nice* (1967).

In 1957, Reynolds joined forces with Frank Gruber and James Brooks to create *Tales of Wells Fargo* for NBC. During the program's five-year run he wrote and directed numerous episodes. Additional directing credits include multiple episodes of *Leave It to Beaver*, *The Andy Griffith Show*, *The Farmer's Daughter*, *My Three Sons*, *F Troop*, *Hogan's Heroes*, *Room 222*, and *Many Happy Returns*.

As a writer, director, and producer, Reynolds was involved with two highly successful CBS series in the 1970s and early 1980s. Between 1972 and 1983, he produced 121 episodes of *M*A*S*H*, which he co-created with Larry Gelbart, and for which he also wrote eleven episodes and directed twenty-four. During that same period, he produced twenty episodes of *Lou Grant*, for which he wrote (or co-wrote) four episodes and directed eleven.

Reynolds has been nominated for twenty-four Emmy Awards and won six times, including Outstanding Comedy Series for *M*A*S*H* and Outstanding Drama Series twice for *Lou Grant*, which also earned him a Humanitas Prize. He won the Directors Guild of America Award for Outstanding Direction of a Comedy Series twice for his work on *M*A*S*H* and the Directors Guild of America Award for Outstanding Direction of a Drama Series once for his work on *Lou Grant*.

Reynolds was elected President of the Directors Guild of America in 1993, a post he held for four years until 1997.

Reynolds was married to actress-turned author Bonnie Jones, who appeared in five episodes of *M*A*S*H* as Lt. Barbara Bannerman, from 1967 until 1976, when the couple divorced. He and his current wife, actress Ann Sweeny, who also appeared on *M*A*S*H* as Nurse Carrie Donovan in two episodes, married in 1979 and have one son, Andrew "Buzzy" Reynolds, a semi-professional figure skater.

Erik Rhodes

Erik Rhodes was born Ernest Sharpe at El Reno, Indian Territory, now Oklahoma February 10, 1906 and was an American film and Broadway singer and actor. He is best remembered today for appearing in two classic Hollywood musical films with popular dancing team of Fred Astaire and Ginger Rogers, *The Gay Divorcee* (1934) and *Top Hat* (1935).

Rhodes started performing on the Broadway stage in *A Most Immoral Lady* (1928) using his birth name Ernest Sharpe. This was followed by two musicals *The Little Show* (1929) and *Hey Nonny Nonny!* (1932).

He first used the name Erik Rhodes when he appeared on Broadway in *Gay Divorce* (1932) and again in London in 1933. In this show, he gave a memorable comic portrayal of a spirited, feather-brained, thick-accented Italian character that impressed RKO executives enough to bring him to Hollywood to reprise the role in the film version, *The Gay Divorcee* (1934).

More of his early roles included *Old Man Rhythm* (1935), *One Rainy Afternoon* (1936), *Woman Chases Man* (1937) with Joel McCrea, and *Dramatic School* (1938).

His last film in the pre-war years was *On Your Toes* (1939). By the end of the war, he was very socially active in New York City often seen with Baron Nicolas de Gunzburg, his onetime companion, and the Nordstrom Sisters at popular watering holes such as the Stork Club and 21 Club.

Between 1947 and 1964, he was back on Broadway in *The Great Campaign*, *Dance Me a Song*, *Collector's Item*, *Shinbone Alley*, *Jamaica*, *How to Make a Man*, and *A Funny Thing Happened on the Way to the Forum*. In the Cole Porter musical *Can-Can*, he appeared as a lecherous art critic, and introduced the song "Come Along With Me".

Among his television appearances, he played the role of murder victim Herman Albright in the 1961 *Perry Mason* episode, "The Case of the Violent Vest."

He married his wife Emala in 1972 and they lived in New York City until the early 1980s. He died of pneumonia February 17, 1990 in Oklahoma City at age 84 and is interred with his wife in the El Reno Cemetery in El Reno, Oklahoma.

Addison Richards

Joel McCrea and Addison Richards in *Gunsight Ridge*

Addison Richards was born Addison Whitaker Richards, Jr. October 20, 1887, in Zanesville, Ohio, and was an American film actor. He appeared in almost 400 films between 1933 and 1964 and could be counted upon to play upstanding, law-abiding citizens and/or officers of good moral fiber; only occasionally menacing.

Some of those credits included *The Girl from Missouri* (1934) with Jean Harlow, *The Eagle's Brood* (1935), *The Walking Dead* (1936), *Boys Town* (1938), *Nick Carter, Master Detective* (1939), *Gangs of Chicago* (1940) with Alan Ladd, *My Little Chickadee* (1940), *The Strawberry Blonde* (1941), *I Wanted Wings* (1941) with Veronica Lake, *Private Buckaroo* (1942), *A-Haunting We Will Go* (1942) with Laurel and Hardy, *The Deerslayer* (1943), *The Fighting Seabees* (1944), *The Fighting Sullivans* (1944), *Duffy's Tavern* (1945), *Mighty Joe Young* (1949), *Robert Montgomery Presents* (1952-1954), *Fury at Gunsight Pass* (1956), *The Fastest Gun Alive* (1956), *Walk the Proud Land* (1956) with Audie Murphy, *The Deerslayer* (1957), *Richard Diamond, Private Detective* (1957), *Gunsight Ridge* (1957) with Joel McCrea, *The People's Choice* (1957-1958), *Trackdown* (1958-1959), *Fibber McGee and Molly* (1959), *Wanted: Dead or Alive* (1958-1960), *The Deputy* (1960-1961), *The Fugitive* (1964), and *No Time for Sergeants* (1964).

He died March 22, 1964 at age 76, from a heart attack. His interment was located at Oak Park Cemetery in Claremont, California.

Tom Ricketts

Thomas "Tom" Ricketts was born in London, England January 15, 1853 and was an English-American silent film actor, director and screenwriter who was involved in almost 350 motion pictures.

Ricketts directed the first motion picture ever in Hollywood in 1909, entitled *Justified*. Starting in the honkytonks of London, he became one of the most able Shakespearean actors of his day. Ricketts directed over 100 silent films between 1909 and 1919, but in 1919 he decided to concentrate on his career as an actor. A hard worker, Ricketts acted in almost 200 films, right until his death.

Some of his roles included *The Killer* (1921), *Black Oxen* (1923), *The Cat's Pajamas* (1926), *Venus of Venice* (1927), *Freedom of the Press* (1928) with Joel McCrea, *The Life of the Party* (1930), *The Common Law* (1931) again with Joel McCrea, *The Sign of the Cross* (1932), *The Eleventh Commandment* (1933), *The Girl from Missouri* (1934), *The Three Musketeers* (1935), *After the Thin Man* (1936), *Dead End* (1937) a third with Joel McCrea, and *The Young in Heart* (1938).

He appeared in one of the most popular films of the late 1930s, *Son of Frankenstein*, shortly before his death.

He died of pneumonia on January 20, 1939 at age 86.

John Ridgely

John Ridgely was born John Huntington Rea in Chicago, Illinois September 6, 1909 and was an American film character actor with over 100 film credits. He appeared in the 1946 Humphrey Bogart film *The Big Sleep* as blackmailing gangster Eddie Mars and had a memorable role as a suffering heart patient in the film noir *Nora Prentiss* (1947).

More of his roles included *Hollywood Hotel* (1937), *Cowboy from Brooklyn* (1938), *Each Dawn I Die* (1939), *The Fighting 69th* (1940), *They Died with Their Boots On* (1941), *Arsenic and Old Lace* (1944), *Two Guys from Milwaukee* (1946), *Command Decision* (1948), *Saddle Tramp* (1950) with Joel McCrea, *Al Jennings of Oklahoma* (1951), *The Greatest Show on Earth* (1952), *Off Limits* (1953), *Woman with a Past* (1954), and *Adventures of Wild Bill Hickok* (1952-1955).

Freelancing after 1948, John Ridgely continued to essay general-purpose parts until he left films in 1953; thereafter he worked in summer-theater productions and television until his death from a heart attack at the age of 58 on January 18, 1968.

Stanley Ridges

Stanley Ridges was born in Southampton, Hampshire, England July 17, 1890 and was a British-born actor who made his mark in films by playing a wide assortment of character parts. Stanley Ridges would become a protégé of Beatrice Lillie, a star of musical stage comedies, and spent a great many years learning and honing his craft on the stage. He was seldom cast in roles where he could really make an impression.

Eventually making his way to America, Ridges started out as a song-and-dance man on Broadway, but later turned to dramatic roles onstage, appearing in such plays as Maxwell Anderson's *Mary of Scotland* (as Lord Morton) and *Valley Forge* (as Lieutenant Colonel Lucifer Tench), becoming a romantic leading man.

Ridges' silent film debut was in 1923's *Success*. With his excellent diction and rich speaking voice, he easily made the transition into sound films, with his career taking off at age 43, in *Crime Without Passion* (1934), opposite Claude Rains. Ridges found himself cast in character roles, as his graying hair put his romantic leading man days at an end. His most famous roles probably were two different professors, one of them the kindly Professor Kingsley in the thriller *Black Friday* (1940). The Jekyll and Hyde transformations gave Ridges a chance to display his acting ability.

Ridges was often cast in supporting roles in many classic films, and played the lead only once, in the B-picture *False Faces* (1943).

Ridges's other notable film roles were in *Internes Can't Take Money* (1937) with Joel McCrea, again with Joel McCrea in *Union Pacific* (1939) and *Espionage Agent* (1939), as the Scotland Yard inspector who is shadowing Charles Laughton in the film *The Suspect* (1944), as Major Buxton (Gary Cooper's commanding officer) in the film *Sergeant York* (1942), as Professor Siletsky in *To Be or Not to Be* (1942), and as Cary Travers Grayson, the official White House physician in the film *Wilson* (1944).

By 1950, he had just begun an appearing in television anthologies such as *Studio One* and *Philco Television Playhouse*. His last feature film, the Ginger Rogers comedy *The Groom Wore Spurs*, in which he played a mobster, was released a month before his death. Stanley Ridges died April 22, 1951, in Westbrook, Connecticut, at age 60.

Fritzi Ridgeway

Fritzi Ridgeway was born in Butte, Montana April 8, 1898 and was an American actress of the silent era. She appeared in sixty-three films between 1916 and 1934. She married film composer Constantin Bakaleinikoff. In 1928 she built the Hotel del Tahquitz in Palm Springs, California.

Some of her roles included *The Old Homestead* (1922), *Getting Gertie's Garter* (1927), *The Enemy* (1927) with Joel McCrea, *Hell's Heroes* (1929), *Ladies of the Big House* (1931), *Frisco Jenny* (1932), and *We Live Again* (1934).

She died March 29, 1961 in Lancaster, California from a heart attack at age 62.

Suzanne Ridgeway

Suzanne Ridgway was born Ione D. Ahrens January 27, 1918, in Los Angeles, California, and was an American actress. An attractive, raven-haired model actress mostly appeared in comedies and musicals. She appeared in over 150 films and television programs from 1937 to 1959.

Some of those credits include *The Buccaneer* (1938), *Gone with the Wind* (1939), *Citizen Kane* (1941), *Hit the Ice* (1943), *Heaven Only Knows* (1947), *Mexican Hayride* (1948), *The West Point Story* (1950), *Abbott and Costello Meet Captain Kidd* (1952), *Ma and Pa Kettle on Vacation* (1953), *East of Sumatra* (1953), *Border River* (1954) with Joel McCrea, *The She-Creature* (1956), *Tension at Table Rock* (1956), *Around the World in Eighty Days* (1956), *A Merry Mix-up* (1957), *From Hell It Came* (1957), "The Flight" episode of *Suspicion* (1957) with Audie Murphy, and *The Purple Gang* (1959).

She died May 6, 1996 at age 78 in Burbank, California.

Cyril Ring

Cyril Ring and Joel McCrea in *Business and Pleasure*

292

Cyril Ring was born in Boston, Massachusetts December 5, 1892 and was an American film actor. He began his career in silent films in 1921. By the time of his final performance in 1951, he had appeared in over 350 films, almost all in small and/or uncredited parts.

He is best remembered as a con artist captured and hand-cuffed to fellow con artist Kay Francis at the very end of the Marx Brothers film *The Cocoanuts* (1929).

More of his roles included *Tongues of Flame* (1924), *The Social Lion* (1930), *Business and Pleasure* (1932) with Joel McCrea, *Meet the Baron* (1933), *Everybody's Old Man* (1936), *Topper* (1937), *Wells Fargo* (1937) again with Joel McCrea, *Zenobia* (1939) with Oliver Hardy, *Union Pacific* (1939) a third with Joel McCrea, *Espionage Agent* (1939) a fourth with Joel McCrea, *One Night in the Tropics* (1940) with abbott and Costello, *Great Guns* (1941) with Laurel and Hardy, *Keep 'Em Flying* (1941) again with Bud & Lou, *Sullivan's Travels* (1941) a fifth with Joel McCrea, *Batman* (1943), *The Dancing Masters* (1943) again with Stan & Ollie, *In Society* (1944) yet again with Abbott and Costello, *The Bullfighters* (1945) also with Laurel and Hardy, *The Naughty Nineties* (1945) also with Abbott and Costello, *Return of the Bad Men* (1948), *Tulsa* (1949), and *Iron Man* (1951).

He was the brother of actress Blanche Ring and the first husband of actress/dancer Charlotte Greenwood (from 1915–1922; divorced). He died on July 17, 1967 in Hollywood, California, at age 74.

Elisabeth Risdon

Elisabeth Risdon was born Elizabeth Evans in London, England, April 26, 1887, and was an English film actress. She appeared in over 140 films between 1913 and 1952. An attractive beauty in her youth she usually played in society parts. In later years in films she switched to playing character parts.

Some of her credits include *The Idol of Paris* (1914), *Florence Nightingale* (1915), *A Star Over Night* (1919), *Crime and Punishment* (1935), *Dead End* (1937) with Joel McCrea, *The Girl from Mexico* (1939), *Sorority House* (1939) with Veronica Lake, *Abe Lincoln in Illinois* (1940), *The Howards of Virginia* (1940) with Alan Ladd, *High Sierra* (1941), *Reap the Wild Wind* (1942), *Mexican Spitfire's Blessed Event* (1943), *The Canterville Ghost* (1944), *The Unseen* (1945), *The Egg and I* (1947), *Sierra* (1950) with Audie Murphy, *It's a Big Country* (1951), *Schlitz Playhouse* (1953), *The Ford Television Theatre* (1955-1956), and *Ethel Barrymore Theater* (1956).

She died December 20, 1958, in Santa Monica, California from a cerebral hemorrhage. She was married to prolific silent film director George Loane Tucker who left her a widow in 1921.

Bert Roach

Bert Roach was born in Washington, D.C. August 21, 1891 and was an American film actor. He appeared in 327 films between 1914 and 1951.

Some of those roles included *Officer Cupid* (1921), *Money Talks* (1926), *The Battle of the Century* (1927), *The Time, the Place and the Girl* (1929), *Bird of Paradise* (1932) with Joel McCrea, *Half a Sinner* (1934) again with Joel McCrea, *God's Country and the Woman* (1937), *Another Thin Man* (1939), *Time Out for Rhythm* (1941), *Shine on Harvest Moon* (1944), *Little Giant* (1946) with Abbott and Costello, *Good Sam* (1948), *The Tall Target* (1951).

He died February 16, 1971 in Los Angeles, California at age 79.

Jason Robards, Sr.

Jason Nelson Robards, Sr. was born Jason Nelson Robards on a farm in Hillsdale, Michigan December 31, 1892 and was an American stage and screen actor, and the father of Oscar-winning actor Jason Robards, Jr. Robards appeared in many films, initially as a leading man, then in character roles and occasional bits.

Robards was the son of Elizabeth (née Loomis), a schoolteacher, and Frank P. Robards, Sr., a farmer and post office inspector who managed Theodore Roosevelt's 1912 Presidential campaign in Michigan. He was raised in Chicago, Illinois. He trained at the American Academy of Dramatic Arts. He was consistently billed as "Jason Robards," as his more famous son, also named Jason Robards, did not come into prominence until the end of the elder Robards' career. He is only referred to as Jason Robards, Sr. in retrospect. He died in 1963, having lived to see his namesake son and grandson (Jason Robards III) carry on the family acting tradition.

Robards' film career lasted from 1921 through 1961. His Broadway credits include the musical *Turn To The Right* (1917). Robards' best known stage role was John Marvin in the long-running hit *Lightnin'*. Robards' connection to the part caused his son to equate him to the character of James Tyrone in *Long Day's Journey Into Night,* which Jason, Jr. played on Broadway in 1956 and on screen in 1962. In the play, Tyrone is an actor whose career is limited by his identification with a single part, The Count of Monte Cristo. Jason, Jr. would later say "One of the most damaging things for me, I realize now, was playing a drunk in the play *Long Day's Journey Into Night.* In the play, the drunk's father is a failed artist and his mother was a drug addict. It was only after years of analysis I realized I was acting out events in my own life on stage."

More of his roles included *The Cohens and Kellys* (1926), *The Isle of Lost Ships* (1929), *Caught Plastered* (1931), *The Super Snooper* (1934), *Zorro Rides Again* (1937), *Half a Sinner* (1940) with Joel McCrea, *Sherlock Holmes in Washington* (1943), *Zombies on Broadway* (1945), *Badman's Territory* (1946), *Dick Tracy Meets Gruesome* (1947), *Return of the Bad Men* (1948), *Horsemen of the Sierras* (1949), *Broken Arrow* (1958), *Laramie* (1960), *Wild in the Country* (1961), *Tales of Wells Fargo* (1962), and *The Adventures of Ozzie & Harriet* (1963).

The Robardses, father and son, acted on stage together only once, in Budd Schulberg's *The Disenchanted*, a play inspired by the story of F. Scott Fitzgerald. Jason, Jr., won his only Tony Award for his performance.

Robards, Sr. died April 4, 1963 at age 70, in Sherman Oaks, California, of a heart attack.

Chuck Roberson

Charles Hugh "Chuck" Roberson was born near Shannon, Texas May 10, 1919 and was an American cowboy, actor, and stuntman. He was nicknamed "Bad Chuck" by director John Ford, for whom he worked many times, to distinguish him from "Good Chuck," stuntman Chuck Hayward. Roberson was reportedly the rowdier of the two, thus the nicknames.

Roberson was the son of farmer Ollie W. Roberson and Jannie Hamm Roberson. Raised on cattle ranches in Shannon, Texas, and Roswell, New Mexico, he left school at 13 to become a cowhand and oilfield roughneck. He married and took his wife and daughter to California, where he joined the Culver City Police Department and guarded the gate at MGM studios. Following army service in World War II, he returned to the police force.

During duty at Warner Bros. studios during a labor strike, he met stuntman Fred Kennedy, who alerted him to a stunt job at Republic Pictures. Roberson got the job, due both to his expert horsemanship and his resemblance to John Carroll, whom Roberson doubled in his first picture, *Wyoming* (1947). His close physical resemblance to John

Wayne led to nearly thirty years as Wayne's stunt double. He often played small roles and stunted in other roles in the same film, which frequently resulted in his "shooting" himself once the picture was cut together. He graduated to larger supporting roles in westerns for Wayne and John Ford, and to a parallel career as a second-unit director.

More of his roles included *Albuquerque* (1948), *The Fighting Kentuckian* (1949), *Atom Man vs. Superman* (1950), *Cattle Drive* (1951) with Joel McCrea, *Cattle Town* (1952), *Hondo* (1953), *The Second Greatest Sex* (1955), *The Big Country* (1958), *Rio Bravo* (1959), *Have Gun - Will Travel* (1960-1961), *Cat Ballou* (1965), *Lost in Space* (1966), *Mod Squad* (1969), *McQ* (1974), and *99 and 44/100% Dead* (1974).

In 1979 he published an autobiography entitled *The Fall Guy: 30 Years as the Duke's Double.* Roberson died June 8, 1988 of cancer in Bakersfield, California at age 69 and is buried next to his brother, actor Lou Roberson in Los Angeles.

Florence Roberts

Florence Roberts was born in Frederick, Maryland March 16, 1861 and was an actress of the stage and in motion pictures.

She began acting on the stage in New York, New York at the age of 19. Her career began at the Brooklyn, New York Opera House in *Hoop of Gold*. She secured her first stage role with the Denman Thompson Company and played leads with the N.B. Curtis Company. This experience led to appearances on Broadway. She once starred in *Zala*, a production of David Belasco. She headed a stock company in Philadelphia, Pennsylvania for a period of fifteen years. The actress made three world tours in stock. There was a South African repertoire and a tour of Australia with the Henry Duffy players. She also played in stock companies in Boston and other cities.

Roberts' success in motion pictures began with a Mack Sennett comedy. The film producer saw her on the stage in *Your Uncle Dudley* and cast her in *Grandma's Girl* (1930) Her earliest roles were in *A Wife's Suspicion* and *A Wise Dummy*, both in 1917.

Among her film performances, the *Jones Family* series is the most renowned. She played the role of 'Grandma' in seventeen of the films, including *Young as You Feel* (1940) with Veronica Lake.

Some of her other films included *Kept Husbands* (1931) with Joel McCrea, *Babes in Toyland* (1934) with Laurel and Hardy, *Les Misérables* (1935), *The Prisoner of Zenda* (1937), *Personal Secretary* (1938), *Abe Lincoln in Illinois* (1940), and *Double Alibi* (1940).

She died June 6, 1940 at age 79 in Hollywood, California.

Roy Roberts

Roy Roberts was born Roy Barnes Jones March 19, 1906, in Tampa, Florida, and was an American actor. He proudly claimed over 900 performances in a forty-year career. He might not have been known necessarily by name but the face was so distinct and obviously familiar. The prototype of the steely executive, the no-nonsense mayor, the assured banker, the stentorian leader, Roberts looked out of place without his patented dark suit and power tie. His silvery hair, perfectly trimmed mustache, non-plussed reactions and take-charge demeanor reminded one of the "Mr. Monopoly" character from the classic game board.

He was the youngest of six children. The year 1900 is given as his birth date in several reference books, which seems compatible with his noticeably aged appearance in the last decade or so of his life, but his final resting stone bears the year 1906.

His early career was on the Broadway stage, gracing such plays as *Old Man Murphy* (1931), *Twentieth Century* (1932), *The Body Beautiful* (1935), and *My Sister Eileen* (1942). In 1943 he made a successful switch to films, debuting as a Marine officer in *Guadalcanal Diary* (1943).

Usually billed around tenth in the credits, he played a reliable succession of stalwart roles such as captains, generals, politicians, sheriffs, judges, etc. He was also a semi-standard presence in film noir, appearing in such classics as *Force of Evil* (1948), *He Walked by Night* (1948), and *The Enforcer* (1951) as both good cop and occasional heavy.

More of his film roles include *My Darling Clementine* (1946), *Chicago Deadline* (1949) with Alan Ladd, *Calamity Jane and Sam Bass* (1949), *Sierra* (1950) with Audie Murphy, *The Cimarron Kid* (1952) again with Audie Murphy, *House of Wax* (1953), *Tumbleweed* (1953) a third appearance with Audie Murphy, *Dawn at Socorro* (1954), *Stranger on Horseback* (1955) with Joel McCrea, *The First Texan* (1956) again with Joel McCrea, *Kid Galahad* (1962), *It's a Mad Mad Mad Mad World* (1963), *I'll Take Sweden* (1965), *The Million Dollar Duck* (1971), *Chinatown* (1974), and *The Strongest Man in the World* (1975).

When Roberts made the move to TV he began to include more work in comedies. The 1950s and 1960s would prove him to be a most capable foil to a number of prime sitcom stars including Gale Storm and Lucille Ball. His patented gruff and exasperated executives often displayed their prestige by the mere use of initials, such as "W.W." and "E.J." While he never landed the one role on film or TV that could have led to top character stardom, he nevertheless remained a solid and enjoyable presence, a character player who added stature no matter how far down the credits list.

Some of those television credits include *Mr. & Mrs. North* (1952-1953), *My Little Margie* (1952-1955), *Crossroads* (1956-1957), *The Gale Storm Show* (1956-1960), *Have Gun - Will Travel* (1962), *Twilight Zone* (1963), *The Munsters* (1964), *McHale's Navy* (1963-1965), *The Addams Family* (1965), *Laredo* (1966), *The Beverly*

Hillbillies (1963-1967), *The Lucy Show* (1966-1968), *Bewitched* (1967-1970), *Petticoat Junction* (1963-1970), *Gunsmoke* (1961-1975), and *Here's Lucy* (1969-1974).

A stocky man for most his life, Roberts gained considerable girth in the late 1960s, which made his characters even more imposing. He died of a heart attack on May 28, 1975, in Los Angeles and was buried in Fort Worth, Texas. He was survived by his wife, actress Lillian Moore.

Willard Robertson

Willard Robertson was born in Runnels, Texas January 1, 1886 and was an American actor. He appeared in 147 films between 1924 and 1948. He was a lawyer who abandoned his profession to take up the actor's calling.

Robertson acted in Hollywood films until the year he died, typically portraying men of authority such as doctors, elected officials, military officers and - yes - lawyers.

Some of his film roles included *Daughters of the Night* (1924), *The Lawyer's Secret* (1931), *The Rider of Death Valley* (1932), *Guilty as Hell* (1932), *Supernatural* (1933), *Gambling Lady* (1934) with Joel McCrea, *Three Godfathers* (1936), *Island in the Sky* (1938), *Union Pacific* (1939) again with Joel McCrea, *My Little Chickadee* (1940), *I Wanted Wings* (1941) with Veronica Lake, *Sullivan's Travels* (1941) again with Veronica Lake and Joel McCrea, *The Ox-Bow Incident* (1943), *The Virginian* (1946) a fourth with Joel McCrea, *My Favorite Brunette* (1947) with Alan Ladd, and *Fury at Furnace Creek* (1948).

He died in Hollywood, California April 5, 1948 at age 52.

Dewey Robinson

Dewey Robinson was born in New Haven, Connecticut, August 17, 1898, and was an American film character actor who appeared in over 250 films between 1931 and 1952.

Dewey Robinson made his Broadway debut in 1922 in a melodrama called *The Last Warning*, which ran for seven months and 238 performances. Several years later, in 1925, he appeared in a comedy, *Solid Ivory*, which was not a success, and was also his final Broadway production.

In 1931 Robinson, a big, barrel-chested man at 6' 1" who easily conveyed physical menace, made his first film when he played a waiter in George Cukor's *Tarnished Lady*, starring Tallulah Bankhead. That performance did not receive screen credit, and this was often the case over Robinson's career, although he was in the billed main cast in *Murder on the Campus* (1934), *Navy Secrets* (1939), and *There Goes Kelly* (1945). Because of his size and physical presence, Robinson worked often during periods when gangster movies were the rage.

Notable early roles for Robinson include a polo-playing hood in *Little Giant* (1933) starring Edward G. Robinson, a supervisor of slaves in Eddie Cantor's *Roman Scandals* that same year, and the Ben Turpin short *Keystone Hotel* in 1935. In the 1940s, Robinson was part of Preston Sturges' unofficial 'stock company' of character actors, appearing in eight films written and directed by Sturges.

He appeared in *The Great Moment* (1944) with Joel McCrea and *Texas, Brooklyn & Heaven* (1948) with Audie Murphy.

In 1950, near the end of his career, Robinson played a Brooklyn Dodgers fan in *The Jackie Robinson Story* who progressed from bigotry to exuberant support of Jackie Robinson.

Robinson died in Las Vegas, Nevada on December 11, 1950, from a heart attack, but because he worked so prolifically, films in which he appeared continued to be seen until 1952, when *At Sword's Point*, a Musketeer adventure, was released.

Edward G. Robinson

Joel McCrea and Edward G. Robinson in *Barbary Coast*

Edward Goldenberg Robinson was born Emmanuel Goldenberg in Bucharest, Romania December 12, 1893 and was American actor. A popular star during Hollywood's Golden Age, he is best remembered for his roles as gangsters, such as Rico in his star-making film *Little Caesar* and as Rocco in *Key Largo*.

Other memorable roles include insurance investigator Barton Keyes in the film noir *Double Indemnity* (1944), Dathan (adversary of Moses) in *The Ten Commandments* (1956), and his final performance as Sol Roth in the science-fiction story *Soylent Green* (1973).

Robinson was selected for an Honorary Academy Award for his work in the film industry, which was posthumously awarded two months after the actor's death in 1973.

Robinson was born to a Yiddish-speaking Romanian Jewish family in Bucharest, the son of Sarah (née Guttman) and Morris Goldenberg, a builder.

After one of his brothers was attacked by an anti-Semitic mob, the family decided to immigrate to the United States. Robinson arrived in New York City on February 14, 1903. He grew up on the Lower East Side, had his Bar Mitzvah at First Romanian-American congregation, and attended Townsend Harris High School and then the City College of New York. An interest in acting led to him winning an American Academy of Dramatic Arts scholarship, after which he changed his name to *Edward G. Robinson* (the G. signifying his original surname).

He began his acting career in the Yiddish Theater District in 1913 and made his Broadway debut in 1915. He made his film debut in a minor uncredited role in 1916; in 1923 he made his named debut as 'E. G. Robinson' in *The Bright Shawl*. He played a snarling gangster in the 1927 Broadway police/crime drama *The Racket* that led to his being cast in similar film roles. One of many actors who saw his career flourish in the new sound film era rather than falter, he made only three films prior to 1930 but left his stage career that year and made fourteen films between 1930–1932.

Robinson went on to make a total of 101 films in his fifty year career. An acclaimed performance as the gangster Caesar Enrico "Rico" Bandello in *Little Caesar* (1931) led to him being further typecast as a "tough guy" for much of his early career, in works such as *Five Star Final* (1931), *Smart Money* (1931; his only movie with James Cagney), *Tiger Shark* (1932), *Barbary Coast* (1935) with Joel McCrea, *Kid Galahad* (1937) with Bette Davis and Humphrey Bogart, and *A Slight Case of Murder* (1938).

He volunteered for military service but due to age, he could not qualify during World War II. However, Robinson did become an outspoken public critic of fascism and Nazism, and donated more than US$ 250,000 to 850 political and charitable groups between 1939 and 1949. He was host to the *Committee of 56* who gathered at his home on December 9, 1938, signing a "Declaration of Democratic Independence" which called for a boycott of all German-made products. He played FBI agent Turrou in *Confessions of a Nazi Spy*, the first American film which showed Nazism as a threat to the United States in 1939, and in 1940 played Paul Ehrlich in *Dr. Ehrlich's Magic Bullet* and Paul Julius Reuter in *A Dispatch from Reuter's*, both biographies of prominent Jewish public figures.

Meanwhile, throughout the 1940s Robinson also demonstrated his knack for both film noir and comedic roles, including Raoul Walsh's *Manpower* (1941) with Marlene Dietrich and George Raft, *Larceny, Inc.* (1942) with Jane Wyman and Broderick Crawford, Billy Wilder's *Double Indemnity* (1944) with Fred MacMurray and Barbara Stanwyck, Fritz Lang's *The Woman in the Window* (1944) with Joan Bennett and *Scarlet Street* (1945) with Joan Bennett and Dan Duryea, and Orson Welles' *The Stranger* (1946) with Welles and Loretta Young. He appeared for director John Huston as gangster Johnny Rocco in *Key Largo* (1948), the last of five films he made with Humphrey Bogart and the only one in which Bogart did not play a supporting role.

On three occasions in 1950 and 1952, he was called to testify in front of the House Un-American Activities Committee (HUAC) and was threatened with blacklisting. Robinson took steps to clear his name, such as having a representative go through his check stubs to ensure that none had been issued to subversive organizations. He did not give names of Communist sympathizers, but he repudiated the organizations he had belonged to in the 1930s and 1940s. His own name was cleared, but in the aftermath his career noticeably suffered, as he was offered smaller roles and those less frequently. Robinson continued his "ritual of rehabilitation by humiliation" in October 1952, when he wrote an article titled "How the Reds made a Sucker Out of Me", that was published in the *American Legion Magazine*. In spite of this, he was once again called to testify before the House Un-American Activities Committee in January 1954.

His career rehabilitation received a boost in 1954, when noted anti-communist director Cecil B. DeMille cast him as the traitorous Dathan in *The Ten Commandments*. The film was released in 1956, as was the psychological thriller *Nightmare*. He also appeared in *Hell on Frisco Bay* with Alan Ladd that was released in 1955. After a subsequent short absence from the screen, Robinson's film career—augmented by an increasing number of television roles— restarted for good in 1958-1959, when he was second-billed after Frank Sinatra in the 1959 release *A Hole in the Head*.

Some of his television and later film roles included *Zane Grey Theater* (1959), *The Detectives* (1961), *My Geisha* (1962), *Robin and the 7 Hoods* (1964), *Cheyenne Autumn* (1964), *The Cincinnati Kid* (1965) with Steve McQueen, *Batman* (1967), *Never a Dull Moment* (1968), *Mackenna's Gold* (1969), *The Old Man Who Cried Wolf* (1970), *Night Gallery* (1971), and *Neither by Day Nor by Night* (1972).

The last-ever scene Robinson filmed was a euthanasia sequence in the science fiction cult film *Soylent Green* (1973); it is sometimes claimed that he told friend and co-star Charlton Heston that he, Robinson, had in fact only weeks to live at best. As it turned out, Robinson died only twelve days later.

Robinson married his first wife, stage actress Gladys Lloyd, in 1927; born Gladys Lloyd Cassell, she was the former wife of Ralph L. Vestervelt and the daughter of Clement C. Cassell, an architect, sculptor and artist. The couple had one son, Edward G. Robinson, Jr. (a.k.a. Manny Robinson, 1933–1974), as well as a daughter from Gladys Robinson's first marriage. In 1956 he was divorced from his wife. In 1958 he married 38-year-old Jane Bodenheimer, a dress designer known as Jane Arden.

In noticeable contrast to many of his onscreen characters, Robinson was a sensitive, softly-spoken and cultured man, who spoke seven languages. Remaining a liberal Democrat despite his difficulties with HUAC, he attended the 1960 Democratic Convention in Los Angeles, California. He was a passionate art collector, eventually building up a significant collection and partnering with Vincent Price to run a gallery. In 1956, however, he sold his collection to Greek shipping tycoon Stavros Niarchos to raise cash for his divorce settlement with Gladys Robinson; his finances had suffered due to underemployment in the early 1950s. Another of his chief pastimes was collecting records of the world's leading concerts.

Robinson died of bladder cancer January 26, 1973, and is buried in a crypt in the family mausoleum at Beth-El Cemetery in the Ridgewood area of the borough of Queens in New York City.

Robinson has been the inspiration for a number of animated television characters, usually caricatures of his most distinctive 'snarling gangster' guise. An early version of the gangster character Rocky, featured in the Bugs Bunny cartoon *Racketeer Rabbit*, shared his likeness. This version of the character also appears briefly in *Justice League*, in the episode "Comfort and Joy", as an alien with Robinson's face and non-human body, who hovers past the screen as a background character. Similar caricatures also appeared in *The CooCooNut Grove*, *Thugs with Dirty Mugs* and *Hush My Mouse*. Another character based on Robinson's tough-guy image was The Frog from the cartoon series *Courageous Cat and Minute Mouse*. The voice of B.B. Eyes in *The Dick Tracy Show* was based on Robinson, with Mel Blanc and Jerry Hausner sharing voicing duties.

In more modern terms, voice actor Hank Azaria has said that the voice of *Simpsons* character police chief Clancy Wiggum is an impression of Robinson. This has been explicitly joked about in episodes of the show. In "The Day the Violence Died" (1996), a character states that Chief Wiggum is clearly based on Robinson. In 2008's "Treehouse of Horror XIX", Wiggum and Robinson's ghost each accuse the other of being rip-offs. Another caricature of Robinson appears in two episodes of *Star Wars: The Clone Wars* season two, in the person of Lt. Tan Divo.

Robinson was never nominated for an Academy Award, but in 1973 he was awarded an honorary Oscar in recognition that he had "achieved greatness as a player, a patron of the arts, and a dedicated citizen ... in sum, a Renaissance man". He had been notified of the honor, but died two months before the award ceremony, thus the award was collected by his widow, Jane Robinson. He was included at #24 in the American Film Institute's list of the 25 greatest male stars in American cinema.

May Robson

May Robson was born Mary Jeanette Robison in Melbourne, Victoria, Australia April 19, 1858 and was an actress and playwright whose career spanned fifty-eight years, starting in 1883 when she was 25 years of age. A major stage actress of the late 19th and early 20th century, Robson is best known today for the dozens of 1930s motion pictures she appeared in when she was well into her seventies, usually playing cross old ladies with hearts of gold.

Robson was the earliest-born person to enjoy a major Hollywood career and receive an Academy Award nomination.

She was the fourth child born to Captain Henry Robison and his wife, Julia,. Capt. Robison served in the British Royal Navy and retired in Australia for his health. He died when Mary was seven years old. Julia Robison packed up her family and returned to London. She was educated in England, Brussels, and Paris.

At age 17, in 1875, Mary married her first husband, Charles Leveson Gore, in London. The couple first ran a cattle ranch in Fort Worth, Texas, and later moved to New York City, where most sources agree that Charles Gore died in or around 1883. Biographer Jan Jones posits that Robson and Gore divorced because Robson did not wish to return to England. Without her husband, Mary did embroidery work and gave painting lessons to support her three children.

By the time she began her acting career in 1883, two of Robson's three children had died; the surviving child was Edward Hyde Leveson Gore (December 2, 1876 - September 23, 1954). Six years after beginning her stage career, Robson married Augustus Homer Brown, a police surgeon, on May 29, 1889. They remained together until his death on April 1, 1920.

On September 17, 1883, she became an actress on the Brooklyn Grand Opera House stage. Her name was incorrectly spelled "Robson" in the billing, which she used from that point forward "for good luck". Over the next several decades, she flourished on the stage as a comedienne and character actress. Her success was partly due to her affiliation with powerful manager and producer Charles Frohman and the Theatrical Syndicate. Robson established her own touring theatrical company by 1911.

She appeared as herself at her Long Island home in a cameo with one of her adult daughters in the 1915 silent *How Molly Made Good*, a film that's available on DVD. She starred in the 1916 silent film *A Night Out*, an adaptation of the play she co-wrote, *The Three Lights*.

In 1927 Robson attended Edinburgh University, then went to Hollywood where she would have a successful film career as a senior aged woman. Among her starring roles was in *The She-Wolf* (1931) as a miserly millionaire businesswoman based on the real-life miser Hetty Green. She also starred in the final segment of the anthology film *If I Had a Million* (1932) as a rest home resident who gets a new lease on life when she is given a $1,000,000 check by a dying business tycoon. She played in *One Man's Journey* (1933) with Joel McCrea, the Queen of Hearts in *Alice in Wonderland* (1933), Countess Vronsky in *Anna Karenina* (1936), Aunt Elizabeth in *Bringing Up Baby* (1938), Aunt Polly in *The Adventures of Tom Sawyer* (1938), and a sharp-tongued Granny in *A Star Is Born* (1937). Robson was top-billed as late as 1940, starring in *Granny Get Your Gun* at age 82. Her last film was 1942's *Joan of Paris* with Alan Ladd.

In 1933, Robson was nominated for an Academy Award at age 75 in the Best Actress category for *Lady for a Day*. She lost to Katharine Hepburn; the two actresses would both appear in the Hepburn-Grant classic film, *Bringing Up Baby* (1938).

Robson was the first Australian-born person to be nominated for an acting Oscar, and for many years she held the record as the oldest performer nominated for an Oscar.

She died October 20, 1942 at age 84 in Beverly Hills, Los Angeles, California.

Gil Rogers

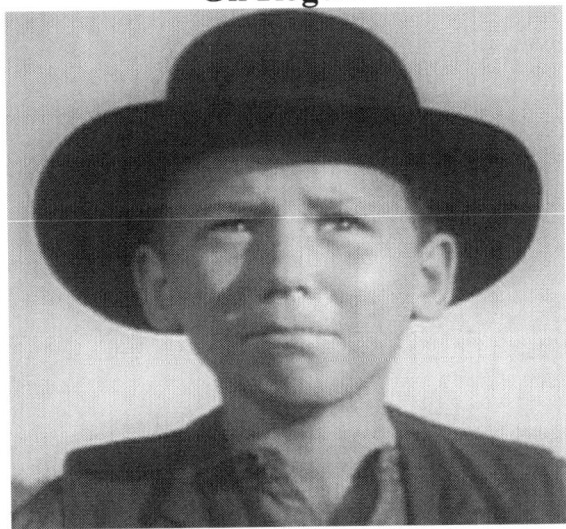

Gil Rogers was born Gilbert John Reigers on October 13, 1949 in Kern County, California. He is an actor, known for *Leave It to Beaver* (1957), *My Three Sons* (1963-1969), and *Yours, Mine and Ours* (1968).

More of his roles included *Wichita Town* (1960) with Joel McCrea, *Perry Mason* (1960), *Riverboat* (1960), *Make Room for Daddy* (1960), *Lassie* (1961), *The Virginian* (1963), and *Lost in Space* (1968).

Later he was a guitarist for Johnny Mathis.

Ginger Rogers

Ginger Rogers and Joel McCrea in *Primrose Path*

Ginger Rogers was born Virginia Katherine McMath in Independence, Missouri July 16, 1911 and was an American actress, dancer and singer who appeared in films, and on stage, radio, and television throughout much of the 20th century.

During her long career, she made seventy-three films, collaborating with Fred Astaire as a romantic lead actress and dancing partner in a series of ten Hollywood musical films that revolutionized the genre. She achieved great success on her own in a variety of film roles and won the Academy Award for Best Actress for her performance in *Kitty Foyle* (1940). She ranks #14 on the AFI's 100 Years...100 Stars list of actress screen legends.

Rogers was the only child of William Eddins McMath, an electrical engineer, and his wife, Lela Emogene (née Owens; 1891–1977). Ginger's parents separated soon after her birth, and she and her mother went to live with her grandparents, Walter and Saphrona (née Ball) Owens, in nearby Kansas City. Rogers' parents fought over her custody. After her mother denied him visitation, her father reportedly absconded with his daughter twice.

After her parents divorced, Rogers stayed with her grandparents while her mother wrote scripts for two years in Hollywood. Rogers was to remain close to her grandfather (much later, when she was a star in 1939, she bought him a home at 5115 Greenbush Avenue in Sherman Oaks, California so that he could be close to her while she was filming at the studios).

One of Rogers' young cousins, Helen, had a hard time pronouncing "Virginia", shortening it to "Ginga"; the nickname stuck.

When "Ginga" was nine years old, her mother remarried, to John Logan Rogers. Ginger took the surname Rogers, although she was never legally adopted. They lived in Fort Worth, Texas. Her mother became a theater critic for a local newspaper, the *Fort Worth Record*. She attended, but did not graduate from, Fort Worth's Central High School (later renamed R.L. Paschal High School).

As a teenager, Rogers thought of becoming a school teacher, but with her mother's interest in Hollywood and the theater, her early exposure to the theater increased. Waiting for her mother in the wings of the Majestic Theatre, she began to sing and dance along with the performers on stage.

Rogers' entertainment career was born one night when the traveling vaudeville act of Eddie Foy came to Fort Worth and needed a quick stand-in. She then entered and won a Charleston dance contest which allowed her to tour for six months, at one point in 1926 performing at an 18-month-old theater called *The Craterian* in Medford, Oregon. This theater honored her many years later by changing its name to the *Craterian Ginger Rogers Theater*.

At 17, Rogers married Jack Culpepper, a singer/dancer/comedian/recording artist of the day who worked under the name Jack Pepper (according to Ginger's autobiography, she knew Culpepper when she was a child, as her cousin's boyfriend). They formed a short-lived vaudeville double act known as "Ginger and Pepper". The marriage was over within months, and she went back to touring with her mother. When the tour got to New York City, she stayed, getting radio singing jobs and then her Broadway theater debut in a musical called *Top Speed*, which opened on Christmas Day, 1929.

Within two weeks of opening in *Top Speed*, Rogers was chosen to star on Broadway in *Girl Crazy* by George Gershwin and Ira Gershwin, the musical play widely considered to have made stars of both her and Ethel Merman. Fred Astaire was hired to help the dancers with their choreography. Her appearance in *Girl Crazy* made her an overnight star at the age of 19.

Rogers' first movie roles were in a trio of short films made in 1929—*Night in the Dormitory, A Day of a Man of Affairs*, and *Campus Sweethearts*. In 1930, she was signed by Paramount Pictures to a seven-year contract.

Rogers soon got herself out of the Paramount contract—under which she had made five feature films at Astoria Studios in Astoria, Queens—and moved with her mother to Hollywood. When she got to California, she signed a three-picture deal with Pathé Exchange. She made feature films for Warner Bros., Monogram, and Fox in 1932 and was named one of fifteen "WAMPAS Baby Stars". She then made a significant breakthrough as "Anytime Annie" in the Warner Brothers film *42nd Street* (1933). She went on to make a series of films with Fox, Warner Bros. (*Gold Diggers of 1933*), Universal, Paramount, and RKO Radio Pictures.

Rogers was most famous for her partnership with Fred Astaire. Together, from 1933 to 1939, they made nine musical films at RKO: *Flying Down to Rio* (1933), *The Gay Divorcee* (1934), *Roberta* (1935), *Top Hat* (1935), *Follow the Fleet* (1936), *Swing Time* (1936), *Shall We Dance* (1937), *Carefree* (1938), and *The Story of Vernon and Irene Castle* (1939) (*The Barkleys of Broadway* (1949) was produced later at MGM). They revolutionized the Hollywood musical, introducing dance routines of unprecedented elegance and virtuosity, set to songs specially composed for them by the greatest popular song composers of the day.

Arlene Croce, Hannah Hyam and John Mueller all consider Rogers to have been Astaire's finest dance partner, principally because of her ability to combine dancing skills, natural beauty, and exceptional abilities as a dramatic actress and comedienne, thus truly complementing Astaire, a peerless dancer who sometimes struggled as an actor and was not considered classically handsome. The resulting song and dance partnership enjoyed a unique credibility in the eyes of audiences. Of the thirty-three partnered dances she performed with Astaire, Croce and Mueller have highlighted the infectious spontaneity of her performances in the comic numbers "I'll Be Hard to Handle" from *Roberta* (1935), "I'm Putting All My Eggs in One Basket" from *Follow the Fleet* (1936) and "Pick Yourself Up" from *Swing Time* (1936). They also point to the use Astaire made of her remarkably flexible back in classic romantic dances such as "Smoke Gets in Your Eyes" from *Roberta* (1935), "Cheek to Cheek" from *Top Hat* (1935) and "Let's Face the Music and Dance" from *Follow the Fleet* (1936). For special praise, they have singled out her performance in "Waltz in Swing Time" from *Swing Time* (1936), which is generally considered to be the most virtuosic partnered routine ever committed to film by Astaire. She normally had no solo dance routines at RKO (apart from the "I've Got a New Lease on Life" and "Out of Sight, Out of Mind" numbers from "In Person" (1935)). Astaire always included at least one virtuoso solo routine in each film, while Rogers performed the solo tap dance "Let Yourself Go" in the Astaire and Rogers musical *Follow the Fleet* (1936).

Although the dance routines were choreographed by Astaire and his collaborator Hermes Pan, both have acknowledged Rogers's input and have also testified to her consummate professionalism, even during periods of intense strain, as she tried to juggle her many other contractual film commitments with the punishing rehearsal schedules of Astaire, who made at most two films in any one year. In 1986, shortly before his death, Astaire remarked, "All the girls I ever danced with thought they couldn't do it, but of course they could. So they always cried. All except Ginger. No no, Ginger never cried". John Mueller summed up Rogers's abilities as follows: "Rogers was outstanding among Astaire's partners, not because she was superior to others as a dancer, but, because, as a skilled, intuitive actress, she was cagey enough to realize that acting did not stop when dancing began ... the reason so many women have fantasized about dancing with Fred Astaire is that Ginger Rogers conveyed the impression that dancing with him is the most thrilling experience imaginable". According to Astaire, when they were first teamed together in *Flying Down to Rio*, "Ginger had never danced with a partner before. She faked it an awful lot. She couldn't tap and she couldn't do this and that ... but Ginger had style and talent and improved as she went along. She got so that after a while everyone else who danced with me looked wrong." Author Dick Richards, in his book "Ginger: Salute to a Star", quoted Astaire saying to Raymond Rohauer, curator at the New York Gallery of Modern Art "Ginger was brilliantly effective. She made everything work for her. Actually she made things very fine for both of us and she deserves most of the credit for our success."

Rogers also introduced some celebrated numbers from the Great American Songbook, songs such as Harry Warren and Al Dubin's "The Gold Diggers' Song (We're in the Money)" from *Gold Diggers of 1933* (1933), "Music Makes Me" from *Flying Down to Rio* (1933), "The Continental" from *The Gay Divorcee* (1934), Irving Berlin's "Let Yourself Go" from *Follow the Fleet* (1936), the Gershwins' "Embraceable You" from *Girl Crazy* and "They All Laughed (at Christopher Columbus)" from *Shall We Dance* (1937). Furthermore, in song duets with Astaire, she co-introduced Berlin's "I'm Putting All My Eggs in One Basket" from *Follow the Fleet* (1936), Jerome Kern and Dorothy Fields's "Pick Yourself Up" and "A Fine Romance" from *Swing Time* (1936) and the Gershwins' "Let's Call the Whole Thing Off" from *Shall We Dance* (1937).

After 15 months apart and with RKO facing bankruptcy, the studio hired Fred and Ginger for another movie called *Carefree*, but it lost money. Next came *The Story of Vernon and Irene Castle*, but the serious plot and tragic ending resulted in the worst box office receipts of any of their films. This was driven not by diminished popularity, but by the hard 1930s economic reality. The production costs of musicals, always significantly more costly than regular features, continued to increase at a much faster rate than admissions.

Both before and immediately after her dancing and acting partnership with Fred Astaire ended, Rogers starred in a number of successful dramas and comedies. *Stage Door* (1937) demonstrated her dramatic capacity, as the loquacious yet vulnerable girl next door, a tough minded, theatrical hopeful, opposite Katharine Hepburn. Successful comedies included *Vivacious Lady* (1938) with James Stewart, *Fifth Avenue Girl* (1939), where she played an out-of-work girl sucked into the lives of a wealthy family, and *Bachelor Mother* (1939), with David Niven, in which she played a shop girl who is falsely thought to have abandoned her baby.

In 1941, Rogers won the Academy Award for Best Actress for her role in 1940's *Kitty Foyle*. She enjoyed considerable success during the early 1940s, and was RKO's hottest property during this period. In *Roxie Hart* (1942), based on the same play which served as the template for the later musical *Chicago*, Rogers played a wisecracking wife on trial for a murder her husband committed.

In the neo-realist *Primrose Path* (1940), directed by Gregory La Cava, she played a prostitute's daughter trying to avoid the fate of her mother. The film also starred Joel McCrea with whom she starred in 1933 with in *Chance at Heaven*. Further highlights of this period included *Tom, Dick, and Harry*, a 1941 comedy in which she dreams of marrying three different men; *I'll Be Seeing You* (1944), with Joseph Cotten; and Billy Wilder's first Hollywood feature film: *The Major and the Minor* (1942), in which she played a woman who masquerades as a 12-year-old to get a cheap train ticket and finds herself obliged to continue the ruse for an extended period. This film featured a performance by Rogers's own real mother, Lela, playing her film mother.

Becoming a free agent, Rogers made hugely successful films with other studios in the mid-'40s, including *Tender Comrade* (1943), *Lady in the Dark* (1944), and *Week-End at the Waldorf* (1945), and became the highest-paid performer in Hollywood. However, by the end of the decade, her film career had peaked. Arthur Freed reunited her with Fred Astaire in *The Barkleys of Broadway* in 1949.

Rogers's film career entered a period of gradual decline in the 1950s, as parts for older actresses became more difficult to obtain, but she still scored with some solid movies. She starred in *Storm Warning* (1950) with Ronald Reagan and Doris Day, the noir, anti Ku Klux Klan film by Warner Brothers, and in *Monkey Business* (1952) with Cary Grant and Marilyn Monroe, directed by Howard Hawks. In the same year, she also starred in *We're Not Married!*, also featuring Marilyn Monroe, and in *Dreamboat*. She played the female lead in *Tight Spot* (1955), a mystery thriller, with Edward G. Robinson. After a series of unremarkable films she scored with a great popular success, playing Dolly Levi in the long-running *Hello, Dolly!* on Broadway in 1965.

In later life, Rogers remained on good terms with Astaire: she presented him with a special Academy Award in 1950, and they were co-presenters of individual Academy Awards in 1967, during which they elicited a standing ovation when they came on stage in an impromptu dance. In 1969, she had the lead role in another long-running popular production of *Mame*, from the book by Jerome Lawrence and Robert Edwin Lee, with music and lyrics by Jerry Herman, at the Theatre Royal Drury Lane in the West End of London, arriving for the role on the liner *Queen Elizabeth 2* from New York. Her docking there occasioned the maximum of pomp and ceremony at Southampton. She became the highest paid performer in the history of the West End up to that time. The production ran for fourteen months and featured a Royal Command Performance for Queen Elizabeth II.

From the 1950s onwards, Rogers made occasional appearances on television, even substituting for a vacationing Hal March on *The $64,000 Question*. In the later years of her career, she made guest appearances in three different series by Aaron Spelling: *The Love Boat* (1979), *Glitter* (1984), and *Hotel* (1987), which was her final screen appearance as an actress. In 1985, Rogers fulfilled a long-standing wish to direct when she directed the musical *Babes in Arms* off-Broadway in Tarrytown, New York, at 74 years old. That production starred Broadway talents Randy Skinner and Karen Ziemba.

The Kennedy Center honored Ginger Rogers in December 1992. This event, which was shown on television, was somewhat marred when Astaire's widow, Robyn Smith, who permitted clips of Astaire dancing with Rogers to be shown for free at the function itself, was unable to come to terms with CBS Television for broadcast rights to the clips (all previous rights holders having donated broadcast rights gratis).

Rogers was an only child, and maintained a close relationship with her mother throughout her life. Lela Rogers (1891–1977) was a newspaper reporter, scriptwriter, and movie producer. She was also one of the first women to enlist in the Marine Corps, was a founder of the successful "Hollywood Playhouse" for aspiring actors and actresses on the RKO set, and a founder of the Motion Picture Alliance for the Preservation of American Ideals.

Mother and daughter had an extremely close professional relationship as well. Lela Rogers was credited with many pivotal contributions to her daughter's early successes in New York and in Hollywood, and gave her much assistance in contract negotiations with RKO.

In her classic 1930s musicals with Astaire, Ginger Rogers, co-billed with him, was paid less than Fred, the creative force behind the dances, who also received 10% of the profits. But she was also paid less than many of the supporting "farceurs" billed beneath her, in spite of her much more central role in the films' great financial success. This was personally grating to her, and had effects upon her relationships at RKO, especially with director Mark Sandrich, whose purported disrespect of Rogers prompted a sharp letter of reprimand from producer Pandro Berman, which she deemed important enough to publish in her autobiography. Rogers fought hard for her contract and salary rights and for better films and scripts.

Rogers' first marriage was at age 17 to her dancing partner Jack Pepper (real name Edward Jackson Culpepper) on March 29, 1929. They divorced in 1931, having separated soon after the wedding. In 1934, she married actor Lew Ayres (1908–1996). They divorced seven years later.

In 1943, Rogers married her third husband, Jack Briggs, a Marine. Upon his return from World War II, Briggs showed no interest in continuing his incipient Hollywood career. They divorced in 1949. In 1953, she married Jacques Bergerac, a French actor 16 years her junior, whom she met on a trip to Paris. A lawyer in France, he came to Hollywood with her and became an actor. They divorced in 1957. Her fifth and final husband was director and producer William Marshall. They married in 1961, and divorced in 1971, after his bouts with alcohol, and the financial collapse of their joint film production company in Jamaica.

Rogers was lifelong friends with actresses Lucille Ball and Bette Davis. She appeared with Ball in an episode of *Here's Lucy* on November 22, 1971, in which Rogers danced the Charleston for the first time in many years. Rogers starred in one of the earliest films co-directed and co-scripted by a woman, Wanda Tuchock's *Finishing School* (1934). Rogers maintained a close friendship with her cousin, writer/socialite Phyllis Fraser, but was not Rita Hayworth's natural cousin, as has been reported. Hayworth's maternal uncle, Vinton Hayworth, was married to Rogers's maternal aunt, Jean Owens.

In 1977, Rogers's mother died. Rogers remained at the 4-Rs (Rogers's Rogue River Ranch) until 1990, when she sold the property and moved to nearby Medford, Oregon. Her last public appearance was on March 18, 1995, when she received the Women's International Center (WIC) Living Legacy Award. For many years, Rogers regularly supported, and held in-person presentations, at the Craterian Theater, in Medford, where she had performed in 1926 as a vaudevillian. The theater was comprehensively restored in 1997, and posthumously renamed in her honor, as the Craterian Ginger Rogers Theater.

Rogers spent winters in Rancho Mirage and summers in Medford, Oregon. She continued making public appearances (chiefly at award shows) until suffering a stroke that left her partially paralyzed and dependent on a wheelchair. Despite her stroke, Rogers never saw a doctor or went to a hospital. Rogers died at her Rancho Mirage home on April 25, 1995, at the age of 83. An autopsy concluded that the cause of death was a heart attack. She was cremated and her ashes interred in the Oakwood Memorial Park Cemetery in Chatsworth, California, with her mother's remains.

Kasey Rogers

Joel McCrea and Kasey Rogers in *The Gunfight at Dodge City*

Kasey Rogers was born Josie Imogene Rogers in Morehouse, Missouri December 15, 1925 and was an American actress, best known for playing the second Louise Tate on the popular U.S. television sitcom *Bewitched*.

She moved with her family to California at the age of two. As a child, her prowess at the game of baseball led her friends to nickname her Casey (after the famous poem "Casey at the Bat"). While under contract to Paramount she used the stage name Laura Elliot.

Rogers began work under the names Laura Elliott and Laura Elliot for Paramount Pictures. She appeared in movies such as *Special Agent* (1949), *Samson and Delilah* (1949), *Paid in Full* (1950), *Two Lost Worlds* (1951), and, in perhaps her best-known film role, Alfred Hitchcock's *Strangers on a Train* (1951), playing Miriam, the scheming, adulterous wife of Guy Haines (Farley Granger).

In 1955 she began working with a press agent in Hollywood, Walter Winslow Lewis III (aka "Bud"). It was Bud who suggested she use the nickname with her maiden name and changed the "C" to a "K." They would later marry and have three children together.

More of her roles included *The Lone Ranger* (1955), *The Adventures of Jim Bowie* (1956), *Richard Diamond, Private Detective* (1958), *The Gunfight at Dodge City* (1959) with Joel McCrea, *Wanted: Dead or Alive* (1959-1960), *Thriller* (1962), *Deadline for Murder* (1964), *The Lucy Show* (1967-1968), and *Adam-12* (1971).

In 1964, she landed a starring spot on *Peyton Place* as Julie Anderson, the mother of Betty Anderson (Barbara Parkins). She left the role after 103 episodes in 1966 to replace Irene Vernon in the role of "Louise Tate" on *Bewitched*.

In 1972, she made her final appearance of thirty-three episodes as Louise Tate in the episode "Serena's Youth Pill." Rogers then retired from acting, appearing in only a few guest television spots, and making appearances on the *Bewitched* edition of *E! True Hollywood Story*. Twice-married and the mother of four (and a grandmother), Rogers had in recent years turned her talents to writing and development, including a proposed new TV series, *Son of a Witch*.

In the 1970s, she became involved with motorcycles after her son began riding and then racing at the age of 9. Rogers became involved in the world of motocross racing. She worked closely with the AMA and established PURR ("PowderPuffs Unlimited Riders and Racers"), an association that brought women into the male-dominated sport, in 1974. PURR would later evolve into what is now the Women's Pro-Class division.

Rogers wrote five books with Mark Wood. The first was *The Bewitched Cookbook: Magic in the Kitchen* (1996), a cookbook based on the TV-series *Bewitched* with the foreword written by Rogers' co-star and friend Sandra Gould. The other books were *Halloween Crafts: Eerily Elegant Décor* (2001), *Character Wreaths: Holiday Projects for Year 'Round Decor* (2002), *Decorating for Christmas* (2003), and *Create a Bewitched Falloween: 55 Projects for Decorating and Entertaining* (2003). The two filmed an unaired pilot for a proposed how-to craft series, *Hands on Holidays*. The pilot was released on DVD in 2006. In 2013, *Bewitched and Beyond: The Fan Who Came to Dinner* by Mark Wood (with Eddie Lucas) was published by BearManor Media, a recounting of the friendship of Wood and Rogers.

The title of Charles Tranberg's biography of Agnes Moorehead, *I Love the Illusion*, comes from Rogers' recounting of Moorehead using this phrase when asked about acting. Adam Gerace, a friend of Rogers and Mark Wood, dedicated his 2009 PhD dissertation to her.

After battling throat cancer for many years, Rogers went into cardiac arrest. She then suffered a stroke, and died in Los Angeles, California on July 6, 2006, aged 80.

Will Rogers

Will Rogers and Joel McCrea in *Lightnin'*

William Penn Adair "Will" Rogers was born in Oologah, Indian Territory, [now Oklahoma] November 4, 1879 and was an American cowboy, vaudeville performer, humorist, social commentator and motion picture actor. He was one of the world's best-known celebrities in the 1920s and 1930s.

Known as "Oklahoma's Favorite Son," Rogers was born to a prominent Cherokee Nation family. He traveled around the world three times, made seventy-one movies (nearly fifty silent films and twenty-one "talkies"), wrote more than 4,000 nationally syndicated newspaper columns, and became a world-famous figure. By the mid-1930s, the American people adored Rogers. He was the leading political wit of the Progressive Era, and was the top-paid Hollywood movie star at the time. Rogers died in 1935 with aviator Wiley Post, when their small airplane crashed in Alaska.

Rogers' vaudeville rope act led to success in the Ziegfeld Follies, which in turn led to the first of his many movie contracts. His 1920s syndicated newspaper column and his radio appearances increased his visibility and popularity. Rogers crusaded for aviation expansion, and provided Americans with first-hand accounts of his world travels. His earthy anecdotes and folksy style allowed him to poke fun at gangsters, prohibition, politicians, government programs, and a host of other controversial topics in a way that was appreciated by a national audience, with no one offended. His aphorisms, couched in humorous terms, were widely quoted: "I am not a member of an organized political party. I am a Democrat." Another widely quoted Will Rogers comment was "I don't make jokes. I just watch the government and report the facts."

Rogers even provided an epigram on his most famous epigram:

> When I die, my epitaph, or whatever you call those signs on gravestones, is going to read: "I joked about every prominent man of my time, but I never met a man I dident [sic] like." I am so proud of that, I can hardly wait to die so it can be carved.

The house he was born in had been built in 1875 and was known as the "White House on the Verdigris River." His parents, Clement Vann Rogers (1839–1911) and Mary America Schrimsher (1838–1890), were both of part Cherokee ancestry, making Rogers himself 9/32 (just over 1/4) Cherokee. Rogers quipped that his ancestors did not come over on the *Mayflower*, but they "met the boat." His mother was quarter-Cherokee and a hereditary member of the Paint Clan. She died when Will was 11, and his father remarried less than two years after her death.

Rogers was the youngest of eight children. He was named for the Cherokee leader Col. William Penn Adair. Only three of his siblings, sisters Sallie Clementine, Maude Ethel, and May (Mary), survived into adulthood.

His father, Clement, was a leader within Cherokee society. A Cherokee judge, he was a Confederate veteran and served as a delegate to the Oklahoma Constitutional Convention. Rogers County, Oklahoma is named in honor of Clement Rogers. He served several terms on the Cherokee Senate. Clement Rogers achieved financial success as a rancher and used his influence to help soften the negative effects of white acculturation on the tribe. Clement had high expectations for his son and desired him to be more responsible and business-minded. Will was more easygoing and oriented toward the loving affection offered by his mother, Mary, rather than the harshness of his father. The personality clash increased after his mother's death, and young Will went from one venture to another with little success. Only after Will won acclaim in vaudeville did the rift begin to heal, but Clement's death in 1911 precluded a full reconciliation.

Rogers was a good student and an avid reader of *The New York Times,* but he dropped out after the 10th grade. He later claimed he was a poor student, saying that he "studied the Fourth Reader for ten years." He was much more interested in cowboys and horses, and learned to rope and use a lariat.

Rogers worked the Dog Iron Ranch for a few years. Near the end of 1901, he and a friend left home with aspirations to work as gauchos in Argentina. They arrived in Argentina in May 1902, and spent five months trying to make it as ranch owners in the pampas. Rogers and his partner lost all their money, and in his words, "I was ashamed to send home for more," so the two friends separated and Rogers sailed for South Africa. It is often claimed he took a job breaking in horses for the British Army, but the Boer War had ended three months earlier. Rogers actually got work at James Piccione's ranch near Mooi River Station in the Pietermaritzburg district of Natal.

He began his show business career as a trick roper in "Texas Jack's Wild West Circus":

> "He (Texas Jack) had a little Wild West aggregation that visited the camps and did a tremendous business. I did some roping and riding, and Jack, who was one of the smartest showmen I ever knew, took a great interest in me. It was he who gave me the idea for my original stage act with my pony. I learned a lot about the show business from him. He could do a bum act with a rope that an ordinary man couldn't get away with, and make the audience think it was great, so I used to study him by the hour, and from him I learned the great secret of the show business— knowing when to get off. It's the fellow who knows when to quit that the audience wants more of."

Grateful for the guidance but anxious to move on, Rogers quit the circus and went to Australia. Texas Jack gave him a reference letter for the Wirth Brothers Circus there, and Rogers continued to perform as a rider and trick roper, and worked on his pony act. He returned to the United States in 1904, appeared at the St. Louis World's Fair, and then began to try his roping skills on the vaudeville circuits.

On a trip to New York City, Rogers was at Madison Square Garden when a wild steer broke out of the arena and began to climb into the viewing stands. Rogers roped the steer to the delight of the crowd. The feat got front page attention from the newspapers, giving him valuable publicity and an audience eager to see more. Willie Hammerstein, father of later librettist Oscar Hammerstein II, came to see his vaudeville act, and signed Rogers to appear on the Victoria Roof—which was literally on a rooftop—with his pony. For the next decade, Rogers estimated he worked for fifty weeks a year at the Roof and at the city's myriad vaudeville theaters.

Rogers described these early years at the Fifteenth Anniversary of the Columbia Theater in New York City. "I got a job on Hammerstein's Roof at $140 a week for myself, my horse, and the man who looked after it. I remained on the roof for eight weeks, always getting another two week extension when Willie Hammerstein would say to me after the Monday matinee, 'you're good for two weeks more'... Marty Shea, the booking agent for the Columbia, came to me and asked if I wanted to play burlesque. They could use an extra attraction... I told him I would think about it, but 'Burlesque' sounded to me then as something funny." Shea and Sam A. Scribner, the general manager of the Columbia Amusement Company, approached Rogers a few days later. Shea told Scribner Rogers was getting $150 and would take $175. "'What's he carrying?', Scribner asked Shea. 'Himself, a horse, and a man', answered Shea." Scribner replied, "'Give him eight weeks at $250'".

In 1908, Rogers married Betty Blake (1879–1944), and the couple had four children: Will Rogers, Jr., Mary Amelia, James Blake, and Fred Stone. Will, Jr. became a World War II hero, played his father in two films, and became a member of Congress. Mary became a Broadway actress, and Jim was a newspaperman and rancher; Fred died of diphtheria at age two. The family lived in New York, but they managed to make it home to Oklahoma during the summers. In 1911, Rogers bought a 20-acre ranch near Claremore, Oklahoma, which he intended to use as his retirement home, for $500 per acre.

In the fall of 1915, Rogers began to appear in Florenz Ziegfeld's *Midnight Frolic*. The variety revue began at midnight in the top-floor night club of Ziegfeld's New Amsterdam Theatre, and drew many influential—and regular—customers. By this time, Rogers had refined his act to a science. His monologues on the news of the day followed a similar routine every night. He appeared on stage in his cowboy outfit, nonchalantly twirling his lasso, and said, "Well, what shall I talk about? I ain't got anything funny to say. All I know is what I read in the papers." He then made jokes about what he had read in that day's newspapers. The line "All I know is what I read in the papers" is often incorrectly described as Rogers' most famous punch line, when it was, in fact, his opening line.

His run at the New Amsterdam ran on into 1916, and Rogers' obvious popularity led to an engagement on the more famous *Ziegfeld Follies*. At this stage, Rogers' act was strictly physical, a display of daring riding and clever tricks with his lariat. He discovered that audiences identified the cowboy as the archetypical American—doubtless aided by Theodore Roosevelt's image as a cowboy. Rogers' cowboy showed an unfettered man free of institutional restraints, with no bureaucrats to order his life. When he came back to the United States and worked in Wild West shows, he noticed that audiences were just as fascinated by his frontier, Oklahoma twang. By 1916, a featured star in Ziegfeld's Follies on Broadway, he moved into satire by transforming the "Ropin' Fool" to the "Talkin' Fool". At one performance, with President Woodrow Wilson in the audience, he improvised a "roast" of presidential policies that had Wilson, and the entire audience, in stitches and proved his remarkable skill at off-the-cuff, witty commentary on current events. The rest of his career he built around that skill.

An editorial in *The New York Times* said that "Will Rogers in the Follies is carrying on the tradition of Aristophanes, and not unworthily." Rogers branched into silent films too, for Samuel Goldwyn's company Goldwyn Pictures. He made his first silent movie, *Laughing Bill Hyde*, filmed in Fort Lee, New Jersey, in 1918. Many early films were made near the major New York performing market, so Rogers could make the film, yet still rehearse and perform in the *Follies*. He eventually appeared in most of the *Follies*, from 1916 to 1925.

Hollywood discovered Rogers in 1918, as Samuel Goldwyn gave him the title role in *Laughing Bill Hyde*. A three-year contract with Goldwyn, at triple the Broadway salary, moved Rogers west. He bought a ranch in Santa Monica and set up his own production company. While Rogers enjoyed film acting, his appearances in silent movies suffered from the obvious restrictions of silence—not the strongest medium for him, having gained his fame as a commentator on stage. It helped somewhat that he wrote a good many of the title cards appearing in his films. In 1923, he began a one-year stint for Hal Roach and made twelve pictures. Among the films he made for Roach in 1924 were three directed by Rob Wagner: *Two Wagons Both Covered, Going to Congress,* and *Our Congressman*. He made two other feature silents and a travelogue series in 1927, and did not return to the screen until his time in the 'talkies' began in 1929.

He made 48 silent movies, but with the arrival of sound in 1929 he became a top star in that medium. His first sound film, *They Had to See Paris* (1929), finally gave him the chance to exercise his verbal magic. He played a homespun farmer (*State Fair)* in 1933, an old-fashioned doctor (*Dr. Bull*) in 1933, a small town banker (*David Harum*) in 1934, and a rustic politician (*Judge Priest*) in 1934. He was also in *County Chairman* (1935), *Steamboat 'Round the Bend* (1935), and *In Old Kentucky* (1935). His favorite director was John Ford.

Rogers appeared in 21 feature films alongside such noted performers as Lew Ayres, Billie Burke, Richard Cromwell, Jane Darwell, Andy Devine, Janet Gaynor, Rochelle Hudson, Boris Karloff, Myrna Loy, Joel McCrea, Hattie McDaniel, Ray Milland, Maureen O'Sullivan, ZaSu Pitts, Dick Powell, Bill "Bojangles" Robinson, Mickey Rooney, and Peggy Wood. He was directed three times by John Ford. He appeared in three films with his friend Stepin Fetchit (aka Lincoln T. Perry): *David Harum* (1934), *Judge Priest* (1934) and *The County Chairman* (1935).

He appeared in two films with his friend Joel McCrea: *Lightnin'* (1930) and *Business and Pleasure* (1932).

With his voice becoming increasingly familiar to audiences, he was able to basically play himself, without normal makeup, in each film, managing to ad-lib and even work in his familiar commentaries on politics at times. The clean moral tone of his films led to various public schools taking their classes, during the school day, to attend special showings of some of them. His most unusual role may have been in the first talking version of Mark Twain's novel *A Connecticut Yankee in King Arthur's Court*. His popularity soared to new heights with films including *Young As You Feel*, *Judge Priest*, and *Life Begins at 40* with Richard Cromwell and Rochelle Hudson.

Rogers demonstrated multiple skills, and was an indefatigable worker. He toured the lecture circuit. *The New York Times* syndicated his weekly newspaper column from 1922 to 1935. Going daily in 1926 his short "Will Rogers Says" reached forty million newspaper readers. He wrote frequently for the mass-circulation upscale magazine, *The Saturday Evening Post*, where Rogers advised Americans to embrace the frontier values of neighborliness and democracy on the domestic front while remaining clear of foreign entanglements. He took a strong, highly popular stand in favor of aviation, including a military air force of the sort his flying buddy General Billy Mitchell advocated.

He began a weekly column, titled "Slipping the Lariat Over," at the end of 1922. He had already published a book of wisecracks and had begun a steady stream of humor books. Through the continuing series of columns for the McNaught Syndicate between 1922 and 1935, as well as in his personal appearances and radio broadcasts, he won the loving admiration of the American people, poking jibes in witty ways at the issues of the day and prominent people—often politicians. He wrote from a non-partisan point of view and became a friend of presidents and a confidant of the great. Loved for his cool mind and warm heart, he was often considered the successor to such greats as Artemus Ward and Mark Twain. Rogers was not the first entertainer to use political humor before his audience. Others, such as Broadway comedian Raymond Hitchcock and Britain's Sir Harry Lauder, preceded him by several years. The legendary Bob Hope is the best known political humorist to follow Rogers' example.

From about 1925 to 1928, Rogers traveled the length and breadth of the United States in a "lecture tour". (He began his lectures by pointing out that "A humorist entertains, and a lecturer annoys.") During this time he became the first civilian to fly from coast to coast with pilots flying the mail in early air mail flights. The National Press Club dubbed him "Ambassador at Large of the United States." He visited Mexico City, along with Charles Lindbergh, as a guest of U.S. Ambassador Dwight Morrow. Rogers gave numerous after-dinner speeches, became a popular convention speaker, and gave dozens of benefits for victims of floods, droughts, or earthquakes.

He made a trip to the Orient in 1931 and to Central and South America the following year. In 1934, he made a globe-girdling tour and returned to play the lead in Eugene O'Neill's stage play *Ah, Wilderness!* He had tentatively agreed to go on loan from Fox to MGM to star in the 1935 movie version of the play; however, his concern over a fan's reaction to the 'facts-of-life' talk between his character and its son caused him to decline the role—and that freed up his schedule allowing him to fly with Wiley Post that summer.

Radio was the exciting new medium, and Rogers became a star there as well, recycling his newspaper pieces. From 1930 to 1935, he made radio broadcasts for the Gulf Oil Company. This weekly Sunday evening show, *The Gulf Headliners*, ranked among the top radio programs in the country. Since he easily rambled from one subject to another, reacting to his studio audience, he often lost track of the half-hour time limit in his earliest broadcasts, and was cut off in mid-sentence. To correct this, he brought in a wind-up alarm clock, and its on-air buzzing alerted him to begin wrapping up his comments. By 1935, his show was being announced as "Will Rogers and his famous Alarm Clock."

In January 1934, Rogers used a racial slur in a radio skit, referring to a song as a "nigger spiritual," which resulted in a protest by the National Association for the Advancement of Colored People (NAACP). Rogers had used the word in print in his syndicated newspaper columns on a few occasions, but this was evidently the first time he had used it on the radio.

Rogers was a staunch Democrat, but he also supported Republican Calvin Coolidge. Democrat Franklin D. Roosevelt was his favorite. Although he supported Roosevelt's New Deal, he could just as easily joke about it:

Lord, the money we do spend on Government and it's not one bit better than the government we got for one-third the money twenty years ago.

He served as a goodwill ambassador to Mexico, and a brief stint as mayor of Beverly Hills. The California city was incorporated, and thus run by an appointed city manager. The "mayor's office" was merely a ceremonial one that enabled Will to make more jokes about do-nothing politicians such as himself. During the depths of the Great Depression, angered by Washington's inability to feed the people, he embarked on a cross country fundraising tour for the Red Cross.

Rogers thought all campaigning was bunk. To prove the point he mounted a mock campaign in 1928 for the presidency. His only vehicle was the pages of *Life,* a weekly humor magazine. Rogers ran as the "bunkless candidate" of the Anti-Bunk Party. His only campaign promise was that, if elected, he would resign. Every week, from Memorial Day through Election Day, Rogers caricatured the farcical humors of grave campaign politics. On election day he declared victory and resigned.

Rogers became an advocate for the aviation industry after noticing advancements in Europe and befriending Charles Lindbergh, the most famous aviator of the era. During his 1926 European trip, he witnessed the European advances in commercial air service and compared them to the almost nonexistent facilities in the United States. Rogers' newspaper columns frequently emphasized the safety record, speed, and convenience of this means of transportation, and he helped shape public opinion on the subject.

In 1935 the famed aviator Wiley Post, an Oklahoman, became interested in surveying a mail-and-passenger air route from the West Coast to Russia. He attached a Lockheed Explorer wing to a Lockheed Orion fuselage, fitting floats for landing in the lakes of Alaska and Siberia. Rogers visited Post often at the airport in Burbank, California while he was modifying the aircraft, and asked Post to fly him through Alaska in search of new material for his newspaper column. When the floats Post had ordered did not arrive at Seattle in time, he used a set that was designed for a larger type, making the already nose-heavy hybrid aircraft still more nose-heavy. However, according to the research of Bryan Sterling, the floats were the correct type for the aircraft.

After making a test flight in July, Post and Rogers left Lake Washington near Seattle in the Lockheed Orion-Explorer in early August and then made several stops in Alaska. While Post piloted the aircraft, Rogers wrote his columns on his typewriter. Before they left Fairbanks they signed and mailed a burgee belonging to the South Coast Corinthian Yacht Club. The signed burgee is on display at South Coast Corinthian Yacht Club in Marina del Rey, California. On August 15, they left Fairbanks, Alaska for Point Barrow. They were a few miles from Point Barrow when they became uncertain of their position in bad weather and landed in a lagoon to ask directions. On takeoff, the engine failed at low altitude, and the aircraft plunged into the lagoon, shearing off the right wing, and ended up inverted in the shallow water of the lagoon. Both men died instantly. He was 55.

Carlos Romero

Joel McCrea and Carlos Romero in *Wichita Town*

Carlos Romero was born in Hollywood, California, February 15, 1927, and was an American actor, noted for his many appearances on television.

Some of his film and television credits included *The World Was His Jury* (1958), *The Gale Storm Show* (1958), *The Gun Runners* (1958) with Audie Murphy, *Richard Diamond, Private Detective* (1959), *Wanted: Dead or Alive* (1959), several episodes as Rico in *Wichita Town* (1959-1960) with Joel McCrea, *Zorro* (1958-1961), *77 Sunset Strip* (1961-1962), *Island of the Blue Dolphins* (1964), *Perry Mason* (1963-1966), *The Fugitive* (1966-1967), *The F.B.I.* (1967-1969), *D.A.: Murder One* (1969), *O'Hara, U.S. Treasury* (1972), *Adam-12* (1972-1974), *Soylent Green* (1973), *Kolchak: The Night Stalker* (1975), *The New Adventures of Wonder Woman* (1977), *Hart to Hart* (1979-1983), *T.J. Hooker* (1983), *Falcon Crest* (1982-1983), *The A-Team* (1985), *Dynasty* (1986), *Magnum, P.I.* (1987), and *L.A. Law* (1989).

Romero died in Ferndale, California, on June 21, 2007.

Cesar Romero

Cesar Romero and Joel McCrea

Cesar Julio Romero, Jr. was born in New York City, New York February 15, 1907 and an American actor, singer, dancer, voice artist, and comedian who was active in film, radio, and television for almost sixty years. His wide range of screen roles included Latin lovers, historical figures in costume dramas, characters in light domestic comedies, and as the Joker in the *Batman* television series, which was included in *TV Guide's* 2013 list of The 60 Nastiest Villains of All Time.[1]

Romero was the son of Cesar Julio Romero, Sr. and Maria Mantilla (daughter of Cuban national hero José Martí). His father was an Italian-born importer-exporter of sugar refining machinery, and his mother was a Cuban concert singer. He had a privileged childhood, being educated at the Collegiate School and the Riverdale Country Day School. However, that lifestyle changed dramatically when his parents lost their sugar import business and suffered losses in the Stock Market Crash of 1929. Romero's Hollywood earnings allowed him to support his large family, all of whom followed him to the American West Coast years later. Romero lived on and off with various family members (especially his sister) for the rest of his life.

In October 1942, he voluntarily enlisted in the U.S. Coast Guard and served in the Pacific Theater of Operations. He reported aboard the Coast Guard-manned assault transport USS *Cavalier* in November 1943. According to a press release from the period, Romero saw action during the invasions of Tinian and Saipan. The same article mentioned that he preferred to be a regular part of the crew and was eventually promoted to the rating of Chief Boatswain's Mate.

Romero played "Latin lovers" in films from the 1930s until the 1950s, usually in supporting roles. He starred as the Cisco Kid in six westerns made between 1939 and 1941. Romero danced and performed comedy in the 20th Century Fox films he starred in opposite Carmen Miranda and Betty Grable, such as *Week-End in Havana* and *Springtime in the Rockies*, in the 1940s. He also played a minor role as Sinjin, a piano player in Glenn Miller's band, in the 1942 20th Century Fox musical, *Orchestra Wives*.

In *The Thin Man* (1934), Romero played a villainous supporting role opposite the film's main star William Powell. Many of Romero's films from this early period saw him cast in small character parts, such as Italian gangsters and East Indian princes. Romero had a lead role as the Pathan rebel leader, Khoda Khan, in John Ford's 1937 British Raj-era actioner *Wee Willie Winkie* alongside Shirley Temple. He also appeared in a comic turn as a subversive opponent to Frank Sinatra and his crew in *Ocean's 11*.

Romero was also a romantic if aggressive leading man in films such as Allan Dwan's *15 Maiden Lane* (1936) opposite Claire Trevor, in which he spins Trevor around in a dance sequence, and played the key role of the Doc Holliday character (with name changed to "Doc Halliday") in Dwan's Wyatt Earp saga *Frontier Marshal* three years later.

He appeared in *He Married His Wife* (1940) with Joel McCrea.

20th Century Fox, along with mogul Darryl Zanuck, personally selected Romero to co-star with Tyrone Power in the Technicolor historical epic *Captain from Castile* (1947), directed by Henry King. While Power played a fictionalized character, Romero played Hernán Cortés, a historical conquistador in Spain's conquest of the Americas.

Among many television credits, Romero appeared several times on *The Martha Raye Show* in the mid 1950s. He portrayed Don Diego de la Vega's uncle in a number of Season 2 *Zorro* episodes.

In 1958, he guest-starred as Ramon Valdez, a South American businessman, who excels at doing the Cha-Cha with Barbara Eden in her syndicated romantic comedy, *How to Marry a Millionaire* in the episode entitled "The Big Order". He performed the mambo with Gisele MacKenzie on her NBC variety show, *The Gisele MacKenzie Show*. He guest-starred in 1957 on CBS's *The Lucy-Desi Comedy Hour* on the first episode of the seventh season ("Lucy Takes a Cruise to Havana"). He also played a card shark on the episode, "The Honorable Don Charlie Story," of NBC's *Wagon Train*.

In 1959, Romero was cast as Joaquin in the episode "Caballero" from *The Texan*. In 1960, he was cast as Ricky Valenti in "Crime of Passion" from *Pete and Gladys*. In 1965, Romero played the head of THRUSH in France in "The Never Never Affair" from *The Man from U.N.C.L.E.*.

From 1966 to 1968, Romero portrayed the Joker in *Batman*. He refused to shave his mustache for the role and so, the Joker's white face makeup was simply smeared over it when playing the supervillain throughout the series' run and in the 1966 film. However, Romero's facial hair can still be seen in some shots. He also appeared in an episode of *Daniel Boone* as Esteban de Vaca in 1966.

In the 1970s, Romero portrayed the absent father of the Freddie Prinze character Chico Rodriguez in *Chico and the Man*, and later Peter Stavros in the television series *Falcon Crest* (1985–1987). Among Romero's guest star work in the 1970s was a recurring role on the western comedy *Alias Smith and Jones*, starring Pete Duel and Ben Murphy. Romero played Señor Armendariz, a Mexican rancher feuding with Patrick McCreedy (Burl Ives), the owner of a ranch on the opposite side of the border. He appeared in three episodes. He also appeared as Count Dracula on Rod Serling's *Night Gallery*, and guest-starred in an episode of *Bewitched*.

Apart from these television roles, Romero appeared as A.J. Arno, a small-time criminal who continually opposes Dexter Riley (played by Kurt Russell) and his schoolmates of Medfield College in a series of films by Walt Disney Productions in the 1970s.

Romero never married but made frequent appearances at Hollywood events, escorting actresses such as Joan Crawford, Linda Darnell, Barbara Stanwyck, Lucille Ball, Ann Sheridan, Jane Wyman, and Ginger Rogers; he was almost always described in interviews and articles as a "confirmed bachelor".

Romero was a registered Republican and in October 1960 he appeared in the Nixon-Lodge Bumper Sticker Motorcade Campaign.

On January 1, 1994, Romero died of bronchitis and pneumonia in Santa Monica, California at age 86. His body was cremated and the ashes were interred at Inglewood Park Cemetery in Inglewood, California.

Mickey Rooney

Mickey Rooney was born Joseph Yule, Jr. in the Brooklyn borough of New York City September 23, 1920 and is an American film actor and entertainer whose film, television, and stage appearances span nearly his entire lifetime.

He has received multiple awards, including a Juvenile Academy Award, an Honorary Academy Award, two Golden Globes, and an Emmy Award. Working as a performer since he was a child, he was a superstar as a teenager for the films in which he played Andy Hardy, and he has had one of the longest careers of any actor, to date spanning 91 years actively making films in ten decades, from the 1920s to the 2010s. For a younger generation of fans, he gained international fame for his leading role as Henry Dailey in The Family Channel's The Adventures of the Black Stallion (1979).

Along with Jean Darling, Carla Laemmle, and Baby Peggy, he is one of the last surviving stars who worked in the silent film era. He is also the last surviving cast member of several films in which he appeared during the 1930s and 1940s.

His father, Joe Yule (born Ninnian Joseph Ewell), was from Glasgow, Scotland, and his mother, Nellie W. (née Carter), was from Kansas City, Missouri. Both of his parents were in vaudeville, appearing in a Brooklyn production of A Gaiety Girl when Joseph, Jr. was born. He began performing at the age of seventeen months as part of his parents' routine, wearing a specially tailored tuxedo.

When he was fourteen months old, unknown to everyone, he crawled onstage wearing overalls and a little harmonica around his neck. He sneezed and his father, Joe, Sr., grabbed him up, introducing him to the audience as Sonny Yule. He felt the spotlight on him and has described it as his mother's womb. From that moment on, the stage was his home.

His father was a womanizer and a heavy drinker, leaving the family when Joe, Jr. was only three. While Joe, Sr. was traveling, Joe, Jr. and his mother moved from Brooklyn to Kansas City to live with his aunt. While his mother was reading the entertainment newspaper, Nellie was interested in getting Hal Roach to approach her son to participate in the Our Gang series in Hollywood. Roach offered $5 a day to Joe, Jr., while the other young stars were paid five times more.

As he was getting bit parts in films, he was working with other established film stars such as Joel McCrea, Colleen Moore, Clark Gable, Douglas Fairbanks, Jr., and Jean Harlow. While selling newspapers around the corner, he also entered into Hollywood Professional School, where he went to school with dozens of unfamiliar students such as: Joseph A. Wapner, Nanette Fabray, Judy Garland, Lana Turner, among many others, and later Hollywood High School, where he graduated in 1938.

The Yules separated in 1924 during a slump in vaudeville, and in 1925, Nell Yule moved with her son to Hollywood, where she managed a tourist home. Fontaine Fox had placed a newspaper ad for a dark-haired child to play the role of "Mickey McGuire" in a series of short films. Lacking the money to have her son's hair dyed, Mrs. Yule took her son to the audition after applying burnt cork to his scalp. Joe got the role and became "Mickey" for seventy-eight of the comedies, running from 1927 to 1936, starting with Mickey's Circus, released September 4, 1927. These had been adapted from the Toonerville Trolley comic strip, which contained a character named Mickey McGuire. Joe Yule briefly became Mickey McGuire legally in order to trump an attempted copyright lawsuit (if it were his legal name, the film producer Larry Darmour did not owe the comic strip writers royalties). His mother also changed her surname to McGuire in an attempt to bolster the argument, but the film producers lost. The litigation settlement awarded damages to the owners of the cartoon character, compelling the twelve-year-old actor to refrain from calling himself Mickey McGuire on- and offscreen.

Rooney later claimed that, during his Mickey McGuire days, he met cartoonist Walt Disney at the Warner Brothers studio, and that Disney was inspired to name Mickey Mouse after him, although Disney always said that he had changed the name from "Mortimer Mouse" to "Mickey Mouse" on the suggestion of his wife.

During an interruption in the series in 1932, Mrs. Yule made plans to take her son on a ten-week vaudeville tour as McGuire, and Fox sued successfully to stop him from using the name. Mrs. Yule suggested the stage name of Mickey Looney for her comedian son, which he altered slightly to Rooney, a less frivolous version. Rooney made other films in his adolescence, including several more of the McGuire films, and signed with Metro-Goldwyn-Mayer in 1934. He played in *Half a Sinner* (1934) with Joel McCrea. MGM cast Rooney as the teenage son of a judge in 1937's *A Family Affair,* setting Rooney on the way to another successful film series.

In 1937, Rooney was selected to portray Andy Hardy in *A Family Affair,* which MGM had planned as a B-movie. Rooney provided comic relief as the son of Judge James K. Hardy, portrayed by Lionel Barrymore (although Lewis Stone would play the role of Judge Hardy in subsequent films). The film was an unexpected success, and led to thirteen more Andy Hardy films between 1937 and 1946, and a final film in 1958. Rooney also received top billing as "Shockey Carter" in Hoosier Schoolboy (1937).

Also in 1937, Rooney made his first film alongside Judy Garland with Thoroughbreds Don't Cry. Garland and Rooney became close friends and a successful song-and-dance team. Besides three of the Andy Hardy films, where she portrayed Betsy Booth, a younger girl with a crush on Andy, they appeared together in a string of successful musicals, including the Oscar-nominated *Babes in Arms* (1939). During an interview in the 1992 documentary film MGM: When the Lion Roars, Rooney describes their friendship:

"Judy and I were so close we could've come from the same womb. We weren't like brothers or sisters but there was no love affair there; there was more than a love affair. It's very, very difficult to explain the depths of our love for each other. It was so special. It was a forever love. Judy, as we speak, has not passed away. She's always with me in every heartbeat of my body."

Rooney's breakthrough-role as a dramatic actor came in 1938's Boys Town opposite Spencer Tracy as Whitey Marsh, which opened shortly before his 18th birthday. Rooney was awarded a special Juvenile Academy Award in 1939 and was named the biggest box-office draw in 1939, 1940, and 1941. A well-known entertainer by the early 1940s, his picture appeared on the cover of the March 18, 1940 issue of Time magazine, timed to coincide with the release of Young Tom Edison; the cover story began:

"Hollywood's No. 1 box office bait in 1939 was not Clark Gable, Errol Flynn, or Tyrone Power, but a rope-haired, kazoo-voiced kid with a comic-strip face, who until this week had never appeared in a picture without mugging or overacting it. His name (assumed) was Mickey Rooney, and to a large part of the more articulate U. S. cinemaudience, his name was becoming a frequently used synonym for brat."

Rooney, with Garland, was one of many celebrities caricatured in Tex Avery's 1941 Warner Bros. cartoon Hollywood Steps Out. As of 2013[update], Rooney is the only surviving entertainer depicted in the cartoon. In 1991, Rooney was honored by the Young Artist Foundation with its Former Child Star "Lifetime Achievement" Award recognizing his achievements within the film industry as a child actor. After presenting the award to Rooney, the foundation subsequently renamed the accolade "The Mickey Rooney Award" in his honor.

In 1944, Rooney entered military service. He served more than twenty-one months, until shortly after the end of World War II. During and after the war he helped entertain the troops in America and Europe, and spent part of the time as a radio personality on the American Forces Network and was awarded the Bronze Star Medal for entertaining troops in combat zones. In addition to the Bronze Star Medal, Rooney also received the Army Good Conduct Medal, American Campaign Medal, European-African-Middle Eastern Campaign Medal, and World War II Victory Medal for his military service.

After his return to civilian life, his career slumped. He appeared in a number of films, including Words and Music in 1948, which paired him for the last time with Garland on film (he appeared with her on one episode as a guest on her CBS variety series in 1963). He briefly starred in a CBS radio series, Shorty Bell, in the summer of 1948, and reprised his role as "Andy Hardy", with most of the original cast, in a syndicated radio version of The Hardy Family in 1949 and 1950 (repeated on Mutual during 1952).

His first television series, The Mickey Rooney Show: Hey, Mulligan (created by Blake Edwards with Rooney as his own producer), appeared on NBC television for thirty-two episodes between August 28, 1954 and June 4, 1955. In 1951, he directed a feature film for Columbia Pictures, My True Story starring Helen Walker. Rooney also starred as a ragingly egomaniacal television comedian in the live ninety minute television drama The Comedian, in the Playhouse 90 series on the evening of Valentine's Day in 1957, and as himself in a revue called The Musical Revue of 1959 based on the 1929 film The Hollywood Revue of 1929, which was edited into a film in 1960, by British International Pictures.

In 1958, Rooney joined Dean Martin and Frank Sinatra in hosting an episode of NBC's short-lived Club Oasis comedy and variety show. In 1960, Rooney directed and starred in The Private Lives of Adam and Eve, an ambitious comedy known for its multiple flashbacks and many cameos. In the 1960s, Rooney returned to theatrical entertainment. He still accepted film roles in undistinguished films, but occasionally would appear in better works, such as the Rod Serling written Requiem for a Heavyweight (1962), It's a Mad, Mad, Mad, Mad World (1963), and The Black Stallion (1979).

One of Rooney's more controversial roles came in the highly-acclaimed 1961 film Breakfast at Tiffany's where he played a stereotyped buck-toothed myopic Japanese neighbor (Mr. Yunioshi) of the main character, Holly Golightly, played by Audrey Hepburn. Despite Rooney's protests that he was congratulated for the role by Asians, that role would later be held up as one of the most notorious examples of Hollywood's history of stereotypical depictions of that racial group.

On December 31, 1961, he appeared on television's What's My Line and mentioned that he had already started enrolling students in the MRSE (Mickey Rooney School of Entertainment). His school venture never came to fruition. This was a period of professional distress for Rooney; as a childhood friend, director Richard Quine put it: "Let's face it. It wasn't all that easy to find roles for a 5-foot-3 man who'd passed the age of Andy Hardy." In 1962, his debts had forced him into filing for bankruptcy.

In 1966, while Rooney was working on the film Ambush Bay in the Philippines, his wife Barbara Ann Thomason (aka's: Tara Thomas, Carolyn Mitchell), a former pinup model and aspiring actress who had won seventeen straight beauty contests in Southern California, was found dead in their bed. Beside her was her lover, Milos Milos, an actor friend of Rooney's. Detectives ruled it murder-suicide, which was committed with Rooney's own gun.

Rooney was awarded an Academy Juvenile Award in 1938, and in 1983 the Academy of Motion Picture Arts and Sciences voted him their Academy Honorary Award for his lifetime of achievement. He was mentioned in the 1972 song "Celluloid Heroes" by The Kinks: "If you stomped on Mickey Rooney/ He'd still turn 'round and smile..."

In addition to his movie roles, Rooney made numerous guest-starring roles as a character actor for nearly six decades, beginning with an episode of Celanese Theatre. The part led to other roles on such television series as Schlitz Playhouse (1957), Playhouse 90 (1957), Producers' Showcase (1957), Alcoa Theatre (1958), Wagon Train (1959-1960), General Electric Theater (1960), Hennesey (1961), The Dick Powell Theatre (1961-1963), Arrest and Trial (1964), Burke's Law (1964), Combat! (1964), The Fugitive (1966), Bob Hope Presents the Chrysler Theatre (1964-1965), The Jean Arthur Show (1966), The Name of the Game (1970), Dan August (1971), Night Gallery (1972), The Love Boat (1982), Kung Fu: The Legend Continues (1996), among many others.

Rooney made a successful transition to television and stage work. In 1961, he guest-starred in the thirteen week James Franciscus adventure–drama CBS television series The Investigators. In 1962, he was cast as himself in the episode "The Top Banana" of the CBS sitcom, Pete and Gladys, starring Harry Morgan and Cara Williams.

In 1963, he entered The Twilight Zone, giving a one-man performance in the episode "The Last Night of a Jockey". Also in 1963, in 'The Hunt' episode 9, season 1 for Suspense Theater, he played the sadistic sheriff hunting the young surfer played by James Caan. In 1964, he launched another half-hour sitcom, Mickey, on ABC. The story line had "Mickey" operating a resort hotel in southern California. Son Tim Rooney appeared as Rooney's teenaged son on this program, and Emmaline Henry starred as Rooney's wife. It lasted seventeen episodes, ending primarily due to the suicide of co-star Sammee Tong in October 1964.

He won a Golden Globe and an Emmy Award for his role in 1981's Bill. Playing opposite Dennis Quaid, Rooney's character was a mentally-challenged man attempting to live on his own after leaving an institution. He reprised his role in 1983's Bill: On His Own, earning an Emmy nomination for the role.

Rooney provided the voices for four Christmas TV animated/stop action specials: Santa Claus Is Comin' to Town (1970), The Year Without a Santa Claus (1974), Rudolph and Frosty's Christmas in July (1979), and A Miser Brothers' Christmas (2008)—always playing Santa Claus.

He continued to work on stage and television through the 1980s and 1990s, appearing in the acclaimed stage play Sugar Babies with Ann Miller beginning in 1979. Following this, he toured as Pseudelous in Stephen Sondheim's A Funny Thing Happened on the Way to the Forum. In the 1990s, he returned to Broadway for the final months of Will Rogers Follies, playing the ghost of Will's father. On television, he starred in the short-lived sitcom, One of the Boys, along with two unfamiliar young stars, Dana Carvey and Nathan Lane, in 1982. He toured Canada in a dinner theatre production of The Mind with the Naughty Man in the mid-1990s. He played The Wizard in a stage production of The Wizard of Oz with Eartha Kitt at Madison Square Garden. Kitt was later replaced by Jo Anne Worley. In 1995 he starred with Charlton Heston, Peter Graves, and Deborah Winters in the Warren Chaney docudrama America: A Call to Greatness. He also appeared in the documentaries That's Entertainment! and That's Entertainment! III, in both films introducing segments paying tribute to Judy Garland.

Rooney voiced Mr. Cherrywood in The Care Bears Movie (1985), and starred as the Movie Mason in a Disney Channel Original Movie family film 2000's Phantom of the Megaplex. He voiced himself in the Simpsons episode "Radioactive Man" of 1995. In 1996–97, Rooney played Talbut on the TV series, Kleo The Misfit Unicorn. He costarred in Night at the Museum in 2006 with Dick Van Dyke and Ben Stiller; Rooney filmed a cameo with Van Dyke for the 2009 sequel, Night at the Museum: Battle of the Smithsonian, which was cut from the film but included as an extra on the DVD release.

After starring in one unsuccessful TV series and turning down an offer for a huge TV series, Rooney finally hit the jackpot, at 70, when he was offered a starring role on The Family Channel's The Adventures of the Black Stallion (1990-1993), where he reprised his role as Henry Dailey in the film of the same name, eleven years earlier. The show was based on a novel by Walter Farley. For this role, he had to travel to Vancouver. Like the show itself, the Black Stallion TV series, Rooney became one of the most beloved stars. The show became an immediate hit with teenagers, young adults, and people all over the world, being seen in seventy countries.

Rooney appeared in television commercials for Garden State Life Insurance Company in 1999, alongside his wife Jan Rooney. In commercials shown in 2007, he can be seen in the background washing imaginary dishes.

In 2003, Rooney and his wife began their association with Rainbow Puppet Productions, providing their voices to the 100th Anniversary production of Toyland!, an adaptation of Victor Herbert's Babes in Toyland. He created the voice for the Master Toymaker while Jan provided the voice for Mother Goose. Since that time, they have created voices for additional Rainbow Puppet Productions including Pirate Party, which also features vocal performances by Carol Channing. Both productions continue to tour theaters across the country.

He continues to work in film and tours with his wife in a multi-media live stage production called Let's Put On a Show! His first performance of this show after the September 11, 2001 terrorist attack was in Bend, Oregon, in which Mickey and Jan requested that the show begin with the singing of the "Star Spangled Banner" by Jan offstage with only the American flag visible on stage.

On May 26, 2007, he was grand marshal at the Garden Grove Strawberry Festival. Rooney made his British pantomime debut, playing Baron Hardup in Cinderella, at the Sunderland Empire Theatre over the 2007 Christmas period, a role he reprised in 2009 at the Milton Keynes theatre.

In 2008, Rooney starred as Chief, a wise old ranch owner, in the independent family feature film Lost Stallions: The Journey Home, marking a return to starring in equestrian-themed productions for the first time since the 1990s TV show Adventures of the Black Stallion. Even though they acted together before, Lost Stallions: The Journey Home is the sole film to date in which Rooney and Jan portrayed a married couple onscreen.

In December 2009, he appeared as a guest at a dinner-party hosted by David Gest on Come Dine With Me.

Rooney made a brief cameo appearance in The Muppets (2011), making his career span ten decades.

In 2011, Rooney appeared in an episode of Celebrity Ghost Stories, recounting how, during a down period in his career, his deceased father appeared to him one night, telling him not to give up on his career. He claims that the experience bolstered his resolve and soon afterwards his career experienced resurgence.

Even more roles continued with Bamboo Shark (2011), Driving Me Crazy (2012), The Voices from Beyond (2012), and The Woods (2012).

Rooney has been married eight times. In the 1950s and 1960s, he was often the subject of comedians' jokes for his alleged inability to stay married. He is currently married to Jan Chamberlin. In 2013, this eighth marriage reached a milestone for reaching the same span of time from Rooney's first marriage to his last divorce. He has a total of nine children, as well as nineteen grandchildren and several great-grandchildren.

In 1942, he married future Hollywood starlet Ava Gardner, but the two were divorced well before she became a star in her own right. While stationed in the military in Alabama in 1944, Rooney met and married local beauty-queen Betty Jane Phillips. This marriage ended in divorce after he returned from Europe at the end of World War II. His subsequent marriages to Martha Vickers (1949) and Elaine Mahnken (1952) were also short-lived and ended in divorce. In 1958, Rooney married Barbara Ann Thomason (stage name Carolyn Mitchell), but tragedy struck when she was murdered in 1966. Falling into deep depression, he married Barbara's friend, Marge Lane, who helped him take care of his young children. The marriage lasted only 100 days. He was married to Carolyn Hockett from 1969 to 1974, but financial instability ended the relationship. Finally, in 1978, Rooney married Jan Chamberlin, his 8th wife. They both are outspoken advocates for veterans and animal rights, and Rooney is an outspoken advocate for veterans and senior rights.

On September 23, 2010, Rooney celebrated his 90th birthday at Feinstein's at Loews Regency in the Upper East Side of New York City. Among the people who were attending the party were: Donald Trump, Regis Philbin, Nathan Lane, and Tony Bennett. In December 2010 he was honored as Turner Classic Movies Star of the Month.

On February 16, 2011, Rooney was granted a temporary restraining order against Christopher Aber, one of Jan Rooney's two sons from a previous marriage. On March 2, 2011 Rooney appeared before a special U.S. Senate committee that was considering legislation to curb elder abuse. Rooney stated that he was financially abused by unnamed family members. On March 27, 2011, all of Rooney's finances were permanently handed over to lawyers over the claim of missing money.

In April 2011, the temporary restraining order that Rooney was previously granted was replaced by a confidential settlement between Rooney and his stepson. Christopher Aber and Jan Rooney have denied all the allegations.

In May 2013, Mickey sold his house of many years, separated from his wife Jan Rooney and split the proceeds.

He died April 6, 2014 at age 93 in North Hollywood, Los Angeles, California.

Harry Rosenthal

Harry Rosenthal was born May 15, 1900 in New York City, New York and was an orchestra leader, composer, pianist and actor.

By the 1920s he was in London where he had a thriving musical career as a composer, bandleader and pianist, including composing five operettas which met with great success. He came to the United States by 1929, when he wrote songs for Herbert Stothart's musical *Polly* on Broadway, and in 1930 acted in Ring Lardner and George S. Kaufman's play *June Moon*, which was revived in 1933. After he met Edward, the Prince of Wales at a reception, he accompanied the heir to the British throne on a world tour.

Rosenthal's film career began in 1931 and ended in 1948, during which time he worked on nineteen films, playing pianists, orchestra leaders and also non-musical roles, as well as composing music (for *The Sin of Harold Diddlebock*) and conducting (on *For Me and My Gal*).

In the early 1940s, Rosenthal was part of writer-director Preston Sturges' unofficial "stock company" of character actors, appearing in all of Sturges' films from *The Great McGinty* (1940) through *The Sin of Harold Diddlebock* (1947) with the exception of *Hail the Conquering Hero*.

He appeared with Joel McCrea in *Sullivan's Travels* (1941), *The Palm Beach Story* (1942), and *The Great Moment* (1944).

Both in New York and in Hollywood, Rosenthal was often mentioned in gossip columns, surprisingly so, given the small size of the parts he played. His death May 10, 1953 at age 52 in Beverly Hills, California, from a heart attack, was similarly noted.

Bodil Rosing

Bodil Rosing was born Bodil Hammerich December 27, 1877 in Copenhagen, Denmark December 27, 1877 and was an American film actress in the silent and sound eras. She made one or two stage appearances on Broadway and in the meantime raised four children.

Some of her roles included *Pretty Ladies* (1925), *The Law of the Range* (1928), *All Quiet on the Western Front* (1930), *Grand Hotel* (1932), *Crimson Romance* (1934), *Libeled Lady* (1936), *You Can't Take It with You* (1938), *Hitler - Beast of Berlin* (1939) with Alan Ladd, *Reaching for the Sun* (1941) with Joel McCrea, and *Marry the Bo$$'$ Daughter* (1941).

She died December 31, 1941 age 64 in Hollywood, California.

Myrna Ross

Myrna Ross was born in 1939 in Akron, Ohio. She was an actress, known for *Beach Blanket Bingo* (1965), *How to Stuff a Wild Bikini* (1965), and *The Swinger* (1966).

More of her roles included *Highway Patrol* (1958), *Ocean's Eleven* (1960), *Ride the High Country* (1962) with Joel McCrea, *A House Is Not a Home* (1964), *Get Smart* (1967), *Live a Little, Love a Little* (1968), and *2000 Years Later* (1969).

She had two daughters: Tiffany Blake Nelson born in June of 1970 and Sabrina Blythe Nelson who was born in February 1973.

Myrna Ross along with her mother, husband Stuart C. Nelson, two small daughters and some friends were on their way to the Little King Ranch for a skiing vacation when the plane they had chartered crashed, killing all on board December 26, 1975 in Rollinville, Colorado. She was 36.

Peggy Ross

Joel McCrea and Peggy Ross in *Business and Pleasure*

Peggy Ross was born Margaret Campbell on August 11, 1912 in Vancouver, British Columbia, Canada. She was an actress, known for her only two roles in *Business and Pleasure* (1932) with Joel McCrea and *Splendid Fellows* (1934). She died on July 8, 1985 in San Francisco, California.

Gene Roth

Gene Roth was born Eugene Oliver Edgar Stutenroth in Redfield, South Dakota, January 8, 1903, and was an American film actor. He appeared in over 250 films between 1922 and 1967.

He began his acting career doing uncredited bit roles in silent pictures in the early 1920s. Moreover, Roth worked as a movie theater manager and built and installed pipe organs before his acting career took off in the 1940s following his arrival in Hollywood, California in 1943. Often cast as threatening heavies and scruffy working class types, and rough-around-the-edges law officers.

Roth is remembered for his portrayals of heavies and bad guys in Three Stooges short films such as *Slaphappy Sleuths* (1950), *Hot Stuff* (1956), *Quiz Whizz* (1958), *Outer Space Jitters* (1957), and *Pies and Guys* (1958). His most memorable role was as Russian spy Bortsch in *Dunked in the Deep* (1949), as well as its remake, *Commotion on the Ocean* (1956). His most famous line was his threat to Shemp Howard: "Give me dat fill-um!" ('fill-um' being 'film' with a Russian accent). He also appeared in their movie *The Three Stooges Meet Hercules* (1962).

Some non-Three Stooges roles include *Secret Agent X-9* (1945), *Jesse James Rides Again* (1947), *Four Faces West* (1948) with Joel McCrea, *Dick Tracy* (1950), *The Amos 'n Andy Show* (1951), *Carbine Williams* (1952), *Jack McCall Desperado* (1953), *Seven Brides for Seven Brothers* (1954), *The Lone Ranger* (1949-1954), *The Cisco Kid* (1956), *Utah Blaine* (1957), *She Demons* (1958), *Earth vs. the Spider* (1958), *Attack of the Giant Leeches* (1959), *G.I. Blues* (1960), *Atlantis, the Lost Continent* (1961), *Twilight Zone* (1961), *Whispering Smith* (1961) with Audie Murphy, *How the West Was Won* (1962), *The Courtship of Eddie's Father* (1963), *The Greatest Story Ever Told* (1965), and *Rosie!* (1967).

After retiring from acting in the early 1970s, Roth worked part time as a liquor counterman at a drug store and was an active participant in the nostalgia convention circuit. He was married four times and was the father of three children. Gene's life came to a tragic untimely end at age 73 when he was struck and killed by a hit-and-run driver while crossing the street in Los Angeles, California on July 19, 1976.

Jean Rouverol

Jean Rouverol was born in St. Louis, Missouri July 8, 1916 and is an American author, actress and screenwriter who was blacklisted by the Hollywood movie studios in the 1950s.

She is the daughter of playwright Aurania Rouverol (1886–1955), who created Andy Hardy and wrote many of the films in the MGM series. After being spotted in a high school production, Rouverol first acted in a Hollywood motion picture at the age of seventeen, appearing as W. C. Fields' daughter in the comedy *It's a Gift* (1934). She continued to perform mainly in supporting roles, making another eleven films until 1940 when she married screenwriter Hugo Butler.

She also appeared in *Private Worlds* in 1935 with Joel McCrea.

With four children coming in quick order, Rouverol did not return to film acting but throughout the 1940s performed on radio, including playing Betty Carter on *One Man's Family*. While her husband was away serving in the U.S. military during World War II, Rouverol wrote her first novella which she sold to *McCall's* magazine in 1945. By 1950, she had her first screenplay made into a film, but her career was interrupted as a result of the investigations by the House Committee on Un-American Activities (HUAC) into Communist influence in Hollywood.

In 1943, Rouverol and her husband had joined the American Communist Party. In 1951, when agents for HUAC attempted to subpoena them, Rouverol and her husband chose self-exile to Mexico with their four small children rather than face a possible prison sentence as endured by some of their friends who were dubbed the 'Hollywood Ten'. Labeled as subversives and dangerous revolutionaries by the U.S., government, they did not return to the United States on a permanent basis for thirteen years, during which time they had two more children.

While in exile, Rouverol continued to write screenplays. She also wrote short stories and articles for various American magazines to help earn money. Three screenplays she co-wrote with her husband were accepted for filming by the Hollywood studios because agent Ingo Preminger (brother of director Otto Preminger) arranged for friends from the Writers Guild of America to put their names on the scripts.

In 1960 the family moved to Italy so Rouverol and her husband could work on a film script. After a few years, in 1964 they briefly lived in Mexico again, and then returned to the United States for good. Living in California again, she and her husband continued their screenplay collaboration. She also wrote a book on Harriet Beecher Stowe. However, her husband was diagnosed with arteriosclerotic brain disease and died in 1968.

In the 1970s, Rouverol returned to writing. She scripted an episode of *Little House on the Prairie*, and after publishing three books in three years, she was hired as co-head writer for the CBS soap opera *Guiding Light*. For this show she received a Daytime Emmy nomination and a Writers Guild of America Award. Rouverol, by then sixty years old, left the show in 1976. In 1984 Jean authored *Writing for the Soaps*. She taught writing at the University of Southern California and at UCLA Extension. She also wrote scripts for *Search for Tomorrow* and *As the World Turns*.

Rouverol served four terms on the board of directors of the Writers Guild of America and in 1987 she received the Guild's Morgan Cox Award as a member "whose vital ideas, continuing efforts and personal sacrifice" best exemplified the ideal of service to the guild.

In 2000, the very active eighty-four-year-old Rouverol published *Refugees from Hollywood: A Journal of the Blacklist Years*, that told the story of her family's life in exile.

Jean Rouverol lived with actor Cliff Carpenter, another former blacklisted artist, for several years.

Herbert Rudley

Herbert Rudley was born in Philadelphia, Pennsylvania, March 22, 1910, and was a prolific character actor who appeared on stage, in films, and on television.

He attended Temple University. He left Temple after winning a scholarship to Eva Le Gallienne's Civic Repertory Theatre.

He began appearing on stage in 1926. His Broadway debut was in *Did I Say No* in 1931. He also appeared in stage productions of *The Threepenny Opera, Abe Lincoln in Illinois*, and *Macbeth*.

In 1940, he appeared in the film version of *Abe Lincoln in Illinois*. For the next four decades he appeared in dozens of supporting film roles, including *A Walk in the Sun* (1945), *Joan of Arc* (1948), *The Silver Chalice* (1954), *Raw Edge* (1956), *The Bravados* (1958), *The Jayhawkers!* (1959), *Hell Bent for Leather* (1960) with Audie Murphy, *Follow That Dream* (1962), *Falling in Love Again* (1980), and *Forever and Beyond* (1981).

On television, he appeared in both drama, often as a military person, and comedy, such as *Robert Montgomery Presents* (1950-1953), *Science Fiction Theatre* (1955), *My Friend Flicka* (1955-1956), *The George Burns and Gracie Allen Show* (1956-1957), *Gunsmoke* (1956-1957), thirty-seven episodes as Sam Brennan in *The Californians* (1957-1958), *The Bob Cummings Show* (1957-1959), *Wichita Town* (1959) with Joel McCrea, *Hawaiian Eye* (1960), twenty-eight episodes as Will Gentry in *Michael Shayne* (1960-1961), *The Beverly Hillbillies* (1963), *My Favorite Martian* (1963-1964), *The Munsters* (1965), twenty-six episodes as General Crone in *Mona McCluskey* (1965-1966), *I Dream of Jeannie* (1970), *Owen Marshall: Counselor at Law* (1972), *Project U.F.O.* (1978), and *House Calls* (1982).

Rudley, however, is best remembered for his role as Eve Arden's husband, attorney Herb Hubbard, in fifty-six episodes of *The Mothers-in-Law* (1967-1969).

In 1981, he made four appearances on the series *Dallas* as Howard Barker, an attorney who represented J. R. Ewing in his divorce and child custody fight with his former wife, Sue Ellen.

He died of a heart attack September 9, 2006, at age 96 in Los Angeles County, California.

Marcus Rudnick

Marcus Rudnick is an actor, known for his only role in *Cry Blood, Apache* (1970) with Joel and Jody McCrea.

Oscar Rudolph

Oscar Rudolph was born in Cleveland, Ohio April 2, 1911 and was an American film and television director, producer and actor. He is the father of film director, screewriter and producer Alan Rudolph.

Rudolph started his Hollywood entertainment career as a bit actor at the age of 14 after he moved from Cleveland, Ohio, where he was born, to Southern California with his family in 1924 and began his Hollywood career as a child actor. His first film was *Little Annie Rooney* which starred now legendary silent film actress Mary Pickford.

More of his roles included *So This Is College (*1929) with Joel McCrea, *The Secret Six* (1931), *Gridiron Flash* (1934), *Wells Fargo* (1937) again with Joel McCrea, and *Emergency Squad* (1940).

He would appear in a total a thirty-six films, in mostly uncredited or bit roles, from 1925 until 1947, when he appeared in his last role in the film *Easy Come, Easy Go*, which co-starred actress Diana Lynn and actors Sonny Tufts and Barry Fitzgerald.

Oscar began his directorial career as an assistant director on numerous film projects throughout the 1940s before transitioning over to the burgeoning genre of television in the 1950s. He directed more than 500 television shows including such popular series as *The Donna Reed Show*, *The Lone Ranger*, *McHale's Navy*, *The Phyllis Diller Show*, *My Favorite Martian*. *Batman* and *The Brady Bunch*.

His directorial film credits included *Rocket Man* (1954), *Twist Around the Clock* (1961) and *Don't Knock the Twist* (1962).

Rudolph died at age 79 February 1, 1991 at Encino Hospital Medical Center in Encino, California of complications following a stroke. He was survived by his wife of 53 years, Sylvia, his son Alan, and a daughter.

Charles Ruggles

Charles Sherman "Charlie" Ruggles was born in Los Angeles, California February 8, 1886 and was a comic American actor. In a career spanning six decades, Ruggles appeared in close to 100 feature films. He was also the brother of director, producer, and silent actor Wesley Ruggles (1889–1972).

Despite training to be a doctor, Ruggles soon found himself on the stage, appearing in a stock production of *Nathan Hale* in 1905. At Los Angeles's Majestic Theatre, he played the romantic lead Private Jo Files in L. Frank Baum and Louis F. Gottschalk's musical, *The Tik-Tok Man of Oz* in 1913. He moved to Broadway to appear in *Help Wanted* in 1914. His first screen role came in the silent *Peer Gynt* the following year. Throughout the 1910s and 1920s Ruggles continued to appear in silent movies, though his passion remained the stage, appearing in long-running productions such as *The Passing Show of 1918*, *The Demi-Virgin*, and *Battling Butler*. His most famous stage hit was one of his last before a twenty year hiatus, *Queen High*, produced in 1930.

From 1929, Ruggles appeared in talking pictures. His first was *Gentleman of the Press* in which he played a comic, alcoholic newspaper reporter. Throughout the 1930s he was teamed with comic actress Mary Boland in a string of domestic farces, notably *Six of a Kind* (1934), *Ruggles of Red Gap* (1935), and *People Will Talk* (1935); Boland was the domineering wife and Ruggles the mild-mannered husband. Ruggles is best remembered today as the big-game hunter in *Bringing Up Baby* (1938). In other films he often played the "comic relief" character in otherwise straight films.

The next decade of work included *The Farmer's Daughter* (1940), *The Invisible Woman* (1940), *Friendly Enemies* (1942), *The Doughgirls* (1944) with Joe DeRita, *Incendiary Blonde* (1945), *Ramrod* (1947) with Joel McCrea and Veronioca Lake, and *Look for the Silver Lining* (1949).

In 1949, Ruggles halted his film career to return to the stage and to move into television. He was the headline character in the TV series *The Ruggles*, a family comedy in which he played a character also called Charlie Ruggles, and *The World of Mr. Sweeney*. He guest starred on NBC's *The Martha Raye Show*. In 1961, Ruggles was cast in "Hassie's European Tour", in which he portrays a wealthy neighbor who offers to finance a European trip for series character Hassie McCoy (Lydia Reed) on ABC's *The Real McCoys*, starring Walter Brennan.

Ruggles returned to the big screen in 1961, playing Charles McKendrick in *The Parent Trap* and Mackenzie Savage in *The Pleasure of His Company*. In the latter film, he reprised the role for which he had won a Tony Award in 1959. He appeared in *Son of Flubber* (1963) with Fred Mac Murray.

He also appeared in *Destry* (1964), *Burke's Law* (1963-1964), *Wagon Train* (1965), *The Munsters* (1965), *Laredo* (1966), *Please Don't Eat the Daisies* (1966), and *The Danny Thomas Hour* (1968).

Both of his marriages, to Adele Rowland (1914–1921) and Marion LaBarba (1942–1970), ended in divorce.

Ruggles died of cancer at his Hollywood home December 23, 1970 at the age of 84. He was interred in Glendale's Forest Lawn Memorial Park Cemetery.

He has a star on the Hollywood Walk of Fame on Hollywood Boulevard.

Bing Russell

Bing Russell was born Neil Oliver Russell in Brattleboro, Vermont May 5, 1926 and was an American actor and baseball club owner. He was the father of Golden Globe-nominated actor Kurt Russell and grandfather of ex-major league baseball player Matt Franco.

Russell was the son of Ruth Stewart (née Vogel) and Warren Oliver Russell. He always wanted to become an actor and studied drama at Brattleboro High School. As a boy, he was dubbed an unofficial mascot of the New York Yankees, becoming good friends with the likes of Lefty Gomez and Joe DiMaggio. Also, Lou Gehrig, who was already weakened by illness, gave him the last bat he used to hit a home run before his retirement.

Russell made his debut in the film *Big Leaguer* (1953) and had some uncredited roles in his early career in roles such as *Cult of the Cobra* (1955), *Tarantula* (1955), *The Deadly Mantis* (1957), *Gunfight at the O.K. Corral* (1957), *Cattle Empire* (1958) with Joel McCrea, *Rio Bravo* (1959), *Wanted: Dead or Alive* (1959-1960), *The*

Untouchables (1960-1962), *Twilight Zone* (1961-1963), *The Munsters* (1965), *The Fugitive* (1963-1965), *Adam-12* (1969-1973), and *O'Hara, U.S. Treasury* (1971).

Best known as Deputy Clem Foster on *Bonanza* (1959) and Robert in *The Magnificent Seven* (1960), he guest starred in episodes of many television series.

In 1963, he was cast as John Quigley, a Chicago mobster, in the episode "Five Tickets to Hell" of Jack Webb's CBS anthology series, *GE True*. In the story line, Quigley travels to Chihuahua, Mexico, where he robs the mint of $500,000 and kills seven men in the commission of the crime. Police Lieutenant Juan Garcia (Carlos Romero) tracks down Quigley and his three accomplices. Barbara Luna also appears in the episode.

Russell played Vernon Presley to his son Kurt's Elvis Presley in the 1979 television movie, *Elvis*. One of his last roles was as a van driver in his son's movie *Tango & Cash* (1989).

Russell owned the Portland Mavericks, the only independent team in the Class A Northwest League. Russell kept a thirty-man roster because he believed that some of the players deserved to have one last season. His motto was *fun*. He created a park that kept all corporate sponsorship outside the gates, hired the first female general manager, Lanny Moss in professional baseball, and named the first Asian American GM/Manager. His team set a record for the highest attendance in minor league history, but lost the 1977 pennant to the Bellingham Mariners. Subsequently, Major League Baseball regained interest in Portland and resurrected the Portland Beavers minor league franchise. The Portland area was recovered but paid Russell the highest payout in history for a minor league territory after Russell took the matter to arbitration. Ex-major leaguers and never-weres who could not stop playing the game flocked to his June try-outs, which were always open to anyone who showed up. The team and archival footage of Russell were featured in the 2014 documentary *The Battered Bastards of Baseball*.

Russell died from complications of cancer on April 8, 2003 in Thousand Oaks, California at age 76.

Gail Russell

Joel McCrea and Gail Russell in *The Unseen*

327

Gail Russell was born Elizabeth L. Russell in Chicago, Illinois September 21, 1924 and was an American film and television actress.

She was born to George and Gladys (Barnet) Russell, and then moved to the Los Angeles, California, area when she was a teenager. Russell's extraordinary beauty brought her to the attention of Paramount Pictures in 1942. Although she was almost clinically shy and had no acting experience, Paramount had great expectations for her and employed an acting coach to work with her.

At the age of 19 she appeared in her first film, *Henry Aldrich Gets Glamour* (1943). Russell appeared in several more films in the early and mid-1940s, the most notable being *The Uninvited* (1944) with Ray Milland and *Our Hearts Were Young and Gay* (1944), in which she co-starred with Diana Lynn. Russell later appeared in the more popular films *Salty O'Rourke* (1945) and *Calcutta* (1947) with Alan Ladd and the two with John Wayne, *Angel and the Badman* (1947) and *Wake of the Red Witch* (1948). She also appeared in *The Unseen* (1945) with Joel McCrea.

She continued working after 1947, and married actor Guy Madison in 1949, but by 1950 it was well known that she had become a victim of alcoholism, and Paramount did not renew her contract. She had started drinking on the set of *The Uninvited* to ease her paralyzing stage fright and lack of self-confidence. Alcohol made a shambles of her career, appearance, and personal life. She was divorced by Madison in 1954 and, after a five-year absence, returned to work in a co-starring role with Randolph Scott in the western *Seven Men from Now* (1956), produced by her friend Wayne, and had a substantial role in *The Tattered Dress* (1957).

On July 5, 1957, she was photographed by a *Los Angeles Times* photographer after she drove her convertible into the front of Jan's coffee shop at 8424 Beverly Blvd. After failing a sobriety test, Russell was arrested and charged with driving under the influence.

She appeared in two more films after that but was not able to control her addiction, and on August 26, 1961, Russell was found dead in her apartment in Brentwood, Los Angeles, California, at the age of 36. She died from liver damage attributed to long-term alcohol abuse. She was also found to have been suffering from malnutrition at the time of her death. She was buried in Valhalla Memorial Park Cemetery in North Hollywood, California.

John Russell

Joel McCrea and John Russell in *Fort Massacre*

John Lawrence Russell was born in Los Angeles, California, January 3, 1921 and was an American actor, and World War II veteran, most noted for playing Marshal Dan Troop in the successful ABC western television series *Lawman* from 1958 to 1962.

He fit the Hollywood image of tall, dark, and handsome. He attended the University of California as a student athlete. Following the outbreak of World War II, he joined the United States Marines, though he was initially rejected because of his height 6 ft 3 in. He was commissioned as second lieutenant on November 11, 1942, and was assigned to the 6th Marine Regiment. His division was sent to Guadalcanal, where he served as an assistant intelligence officer. He contracted malaria and returned home with a medical discharge.

Russell's first film appearance was in Frank Capra's *Mr. Smith Goes to Washington* (1939) as Otis Hopper. Russell was contracted to 20th Century Fox in several supporting roles, and later was signed with Republic Pictures. He primarily played secondary roles, often in western films, including William A Wellman's 1948 *Yellow Sky*, but in 1952 starred opposite Judy Canova in *Oklahoma Annie*.

More roles included *Slattery's Hurricane* (1949) with Veronica Lake, *Saddle Tramp* (1950) with Joel McCrea, *Frenchie* (1950) again with Joel McCrea, *Man in the Saddle* (1951), *Hoodlum Empire* (1952), and *Jubilee Trail* (1954)/

In 1955 Russell was given the lead role in a television drama called *Soldiers of Fortune*. The half-hour adventure show placed him and his sidekick, played by Chick Chandler, in a dangerous jungle setting. While the show proved popular with young boys, it did not draw enough adult viewers to its prime slot and was canceled in 1957.

In 1957 Russell made a memorable appearance as a tough lawman in *Untamed Youth*. In 1959, Russell guest starred in an episode of NBC's adventure series *Northwest Passage*, a fictionalized account of the exploits of Major Robert Rogers in the French and Indian War.

In 1958, Russell appeared in *Fort Massacre* again with Joel McCrea.

He was next cast in his best-known role as Marshal Dan Troop, the lead character in *Lawman*, an ABC/Warner Brothers hit western series that ran for four years. Co-starring with Peter Brown, who played Deputy Johnny McKay, and Peggie Castle as Birdcage saloon owner Lily Merrill, Russell portrayed a U.S. frontier peace officer mentoring his younger compatriot. At the same time that *Lawman* premiered, Russell played an outlaw, along with Edd Byrnes and Rodolfo Hoyos, Jr., in the 1958 season premiere episode "Ring of Sand" of *Sugarfoot*, another ABC/WB western with Will Hutchins in the title role.

Russell appeared in other motion pictures for Warner Brothers, notably as the villain in *Yellowstone Kelly* (1959) with other Warner Brothers Television contract stars as well as the Howard Hawks 1959 western, *Rio Bravo*, which starred John Wayne, Dean Martin, Ricky Nelson, and Walter Brennan.

More roles continued in *Apache Uprising* (1965), *Hostile Guns* (1967), *Buckskin* (1968), and *If He Hollers, Let Him Go!* (1968).

In 1969, Russell appeared in five episodes of *It Takes a Thief* starring Robert Wagner as SIA agent William Dover.

Throughout the 1960s to the 1980s, he returned to secondary roles, appearing in more than twenty films, including three directed by his friend Clint Eastwood. One of these was as Marshal Stockburn, the chief villain in Eastwood's 1985 film *Pale Rider*.

Russell appeared in the second season of the Filmation children's science fiction series *Jason of Star Command* (1979). He played the role of Commander Stone, a blue-skinned alien from Alpha Centauri. He replaced James Doohan, who played the Commander in the previous season but left to start working on *Star Trek: The Motion Picture* (1979).

His later roles included *Six Tickets to Hell* (1981), *Simon & Simon* (1982), *Honkytonk Man* (1982), as Marshal Dan Troop in *The Fall Guy* (1984) in the episode "King of the Cowboys" with other old western television stars, such as Peter Breck and Roy Rogers, and *Under the Gun* (1988).

John Russell died from emphysema January 19, 1991 at age 70 and was interred in the Los Angeles National Cemetery, a former U.S. Veterans Administration cemetery in Los Angeles, California.

Mary Ruth

Joel McCrea and Mary Ruth in *They Shall Have Music*

Mary Ruth was born as Mary Ruth Kizziar. She is an actress, known for *Song of the Buckaroo* (1938), *They Shall Have Music* (1939) with Joel McCrea, and *Boy Meets Joy* (1939).

More of her roles included *Nobody's Children* (1940), *Pot o' Gold* (1941), *The Hard-Boiled Canary* (1941), *Gentleman from Dixie* (1941), and *Riot Squad* (1941).

Basil Ruysdael

    Basil Ruysdael was born in Jersey City, New Jersey July 24, 1888 and was an American film actor and opera singer.

    He started as a bass-baritone with the Metropolitan Opera Company from 1910 to 1918. In the World War One era, he was a leading bass at The Met, appearing with opera stars such as Enrico Caruso and Geraldine Farrar. Starting in 1918, he appeared on the New York stage. He moved to California in 1923 to teach voice. His most famous pupil was opera star Lawrence Tibbett.

    Ruysdael is probably best known to modern audiences as Detective Hennessey in the first Marx Brothers film *The Cocoanuts*. He also appeared in *Pinky, The File on Thelma Jordon, Colorado Territory* (1949) with Joel McCrea, *Broken Arrow, People Will Talk, Carrie, The Violent Men, Blackboard Jungle,* and *The Horse Soldiers*. In 1955, Ruysdael played General Andrew Jackson in the ABC miniseries *Davy Crockett,* broadcast on the *Disneyland* television series. In his final television role he appeared on *Perry Mason* as Henry W. Dameron in the 1959 episode, "The Case of Paul Drake's Dilemma." His last on-screen role was in *The Story of Ruth* in 1960. His last film role was *One Hundred and One Dalmatians,* in which he provided a voice characterization; the film itself was released one year after his death.

    Ruysdael narrated the NBC Blue Network series *Stones of History* which was broadcast in 1934 and 1935. He was the announcer on a syndicated programme for Rexall in 1939 before becoming the commercial spokesman for DuPont on *Cavalcade of America* on the NBC Blue Network in 1940.

    By 1941, he was a pitch-man for Lucky Strike cigarettes, which sponsored several shows including *Your Hit Parade, Information Please* and *The Jack Benny Show*. He appeared, transcribed, on the latter show from October 1, 1944 to November 28, 1948 and gave his name near the end of the final commercial. Ruysdael was also the announcer on a 1944 summer replacement show, *Mother and Dad,* starring Parker Fennelly on CBS, and *The Radio Reader's Digest* in 1946 on CBS.

    Ruysdael died on October 10, 1960 at the age of 72 of complications following surgery in a hospital in Hollywood, California. He was survived by his widow, Kathleen. He was buried in Omaha, Nebraska's Forest Lawn Memorial Park.

Walter Sande

Joel McCrea and Walter Sande in *Wichita*

Walter Sande was born in Denver, Colorado, July 9, 1906, and was an American actor, notable for film roles.

He was one of those stern, heavyset character actors in Hollywood no person could recognize by name. He showed an early interest in music as a youth and by his college years managed to start his own band. This led to a job as musical director for 20th Century-Fox's theater chain, which, in turn, led him to acting in films beginning in 1937.

Usually providing atmospheric bits with no billing, he made an initial impression in serial cliffhangers as a third-string heavy with the popular *The Green Hornet Strikes Again!* (1940) and *Sky Raiders* (1941).

His first top featured role, however, would come with *The Iron Claw* (1941) as Jack "Flash" Strong, a photographer who, uncharacteristically for Walter, served as a comic sidekick to our serial hero. Best of all would be his role in another serial as Red Pennington, the amusing sidekick to *Don Winslow of the Navy* (1942). He repeated his role again in *Don Winslow of the Coast Guard* (1943), the successful sequel.

The Pennington role would spark a long and steady career in movies and television, usually a step or two behind Hollywood's elite, in *Citizen Kane* (1941) with Alan Ladd, *Sergeant York* (1941), *Great Guns* (1941) with Laurel &

Hardy and Alan Ladd, *A-Haunting We Will Go* (1941) again with Laurel & Hardy, *Son of Dracula* (1943), *To Have and Have Not* (1944), *The Blue Dahlia* (1946) with Alan Ladd and Veronica Lake, *Bad Boy* (1949) with Audie Murphy, *The Kid from Texas* (1950) again with Audie Murphy, *Red Mountain* (1951) yet again with Alan LAdd, *The Duel at Silver Creek* (1952) a third appearance with Audie Murphy, *The War of the Worlds* (1953), *Wichita* (1955) with Joel McCrea, *The Adventures of Tugboat Annie* (1957), *Richard Diamond, Private Detective* (1959), *Wanted: Dead or Alive* (1959-1960), *Laramie* (1959-1962), *The Quick Gun* (1964) a fourth appearance with Audie Murphy, *The Navy vs. the Night Monsters* (1966), *Death of a Gunfighter* (1969), *Adam-12* (1971), and *Michael O'Hara the Fourth* (1972).

He died of a heart attack on November 22, 1971, at the age of sixty-five in Chicago, Illinois.

George Sanders

George Sanders and Joel McCrea in *Foreign Correspondent*

George Henry Sanders was born July 3, 1906, and was a Russian-born English film and television actor, singer-songwriter, music composer, and author. His prominent English accent and baritone voice often led him to be cast as sophisticated but villainous characters. He is perhaps best known as Addison DeWitt in *All About Eve* (1950), Jack Favell in *Rebecca* (1940), and the malevolent tiger Shere Khan in *The Jungle Book* (1967). His career spanned more than forty years.

Sanders was born in Saint Petersburg, Imperial Russia, at number 6 Petrovski Ostrov. His English parents were Henry Sanders (1873–1961) and Margaret Sanders (1875–1967). Actor Tom Conway (1904–1967) was his elder brother. His younger sister, Margaret Sanders, was born in 1912. George was eleven when, in 1917, at the outbreak of the Russian Revolution, the family went back to England. Like his brother, he attended Brighton College, a boys' independent school in Brighton, Sussex, then went on to Manchester Technical College. After graduation he worked at an advertising agency, where the company secretary, aspiring actress Greer Garson, suggested he take up a career in acting.

Sanders made his British film debut in 1929. Seven years later, after a series of British films, his first role in an American production was *Lloyd's of London* (1936) as Lord Everett Stacy. His smooth, upper-crust English accent and sleek British manner, along with a suave, snobbish and somewhat threatening air, put him in demand for American films throughout the following decade.

He played supporting roles in high-end productions such as Alfred Hitchcock's *Foreign Correspondent* (1940) with Joel McCrea, and *Rebecca* (1940), in which he and Judith Anderson played cruel foils to Joan Fontaine's character. He had leading roles in somewhat lower-budget pictures such as *Rage in Heaven* (1941). He also played the lead in both The Falcon and The Saint film series. In 1942, Sanders handed the Falcon role to his brother Tom, in *The Falcon's Brother*. The only other film in which the two brothers appeared together was *Death of a Scoundrel* (1956), in which they also played brothers.

Sanders played Lord Henry Wotton in the 1945 film version of *The Picture of Dorian Gray*. In 1947, he co-starred with Gene Tierney and Rex Harrison in *The Ghost and Mrs. Muir*. That same year, he gave one of his most critically noted performances, starring with Angela Lansbury in director Albert Lewin's little-known film *The Private Affairs of Bel Ami*, taken from an 1885 novel by Guy de Maupassant. He and Lansbury also featured in Cecil B. deMille's biblical epic *Samson and Delilah* in 1949.

In 1950, Sanders drew his greatest popular and commercial success as the acerbic, cold-blooded theatre critic Addison DeWitt, in *All About Eve*, for which he won an Academy Award for Best Supporting Actor. He then starred as Sir Brian de Bois-Guilbert in the 1952 film *Ivanhoe*, dying in a duel with Robert Taylor after professing his love for Jewish maiden Rebecca, played by Elizabeth Taylor.

Sanders went into television with the successful series *The George Sanders Mystery Theater*. He played an upper-crust English villain, G. Emory Partridge, in the 1965 *The Man From U.N.C.L.E.* episode "The Gazebo in the Maze Affair", and reprised the role later in that same year in "The Yukon Affair". He also portrayed Mr. Freeze in two episodes of the live-action *Batman* TV series which were shown in February 1966. He also appeared in the under-rated film *Trunk to Cairo* (1966) with Audie Murphy.

In 1967, Sanders voiced the malevolent Shere Khan in the Walt Disney production of *The Jungle Book*. During the production of *The Jungle Book*'s soundtrack, Sanders was unavailable to provide the singing voice for Shere Khan during the final recording of the song, "That's What Friends Are For" despite being an accomplished singer. Mellomen member Bill Lee was called in to substitute for Sanders and can be heard on the soundtrack. In the film, however, all the singing was done live and Sanders provided Khan's singing voice.

Sanders' smooth voice, urbane manner and upper-class British accent inspired Peter Sellers' character "Hercules Grytpype-Thynne" in the famous 1950s BBC radio comedy series *The Goon Show*. In 1964, Sellers and Sanders appeared together in the Pink Panther sequel *A Shot in the Dark*. In 1969, he had a supporting role in John Huston's *The Kremlin Letter*, in which his first scene showed him dressed in drag and playing piano in a snooty San Francisco gay bar. One of Sanders' final screen roles was in a 1972 feature film version of the BBC television series *Doomwatch*.

Two ghostwritten crime novels were published under his name to cash in on his fame. The first was *Crime on My Hands* (1944), written in the first person and mentioning his "Saint" and "Falcon" movies. This was followed by *Stranger at Home* in 1946. Both were actually written by female authors: the former by Craig Rice, and the latter by Leigh Brackett.

In 1958, Sanders recorded an album called *The George Sanders Touch: Songs for the Lovely Lady*. The album was released by ABC-Paramount Records, and carried lush string arrangements of romantic ballads, crooned by Sanders in a fit baritone/bass (spanning from low to middle C), including "Such is My Love", a song of Sanders' own composition. After going to great lengths, he got himself signed to sing in *South Pacific* but was overwhelmed with anxiety over the role and quickly dropped out.

He also signed on for the role of Sheridan Whiteside in the stage musical *Sherry!* (1967), based on the Kaufman Hart play *The Man Who Came to Dinner*, but found the ongoing stage production highly demanding. He quit when his wife Benita Hume discovered she had terminal bone cancer.

On October 27, 1940, Sanders married Susan Larson; they divorced in 1949. From later that year until 1954, Sanders was married to Hungarian actress Zsa Zsa Gabor (with whom he starred in the 1956 film *Death of a Scoundrel* after their divorce). On February 10, 1959, Sanders married actress Benita Hume, widow of actor Ronald Colman. She died in 1967.

His autobiography *Memoirs of a Professional Cad* was published in 1960, and gathered critical praise for its wit. Sanders suggested the title *A Dreadful Man* for his biography, which was later written by Sanders' friend Brian Aherne, and published in 1979.

Sanders's last marriage was on December 4, 1970, to Magda Gabor, the elder sister of his second wife. This marriage lasted only six weeks, after which he began drinking heavily.

In his later years, Sanders suffered from bewilderment and bouts of anger, worsened by waning health. He can be seen teetering in his last films, owing to a loss of balance. According to Aherne's biography, he also had a minor stroke. Sanders could not bear the notion of losing his health or needing help from someone else, and he became deeply depressed. At about this time, Sanders found he could no longer play his grand piano, which he dragged outside and smashed with an axe. His last girlfriend, who was Mexican and much younger than he, persuaded Sanders to sell his beloved house in Majorca, Spain, which he later bitterly regretted. From then on, he drifted.

On April 23, 1972, Sanders checked into a hotel in Castelldefels, a coastal town near Barcelona. He was found dead two days later April 25, 1972, having taken five bottles of Nembutal. Sanders was 65 years old. He left behind a suicide note, which read:

Dear World, I am leaving because I am bored. I feel I have lived long enough. I am leaving you with your worries in this sweet cesspool. Good luck.

Sanders's body was cremated, and the ashes were scattered in the English Channel. David Niven wrote in his autobiography, *The Moon's a Balloon* (1972), that in 1937 his friend Sanders had predicted he would commit suicide when he was 65.

Sanders garnered two stars on the Hollywood Walk of Fame, for motion pictures at 1636 Vine Street and for television at 7007 Hollywood Boulevard. He is mentioned in The Kinks' song "Celluloid Heroes" and his ghost makes an appearance in Clive Barker's 2001 novel *Coldheart Canyon*, as well as in the 2007 animated feature *Dante's Inferno*.

Dick Sargent

Dick Sargent was born in Carmel-by-the-Sea, California April 19, 1930, notable as the second actor to portray Darrin Stephens on the television series *Bewitched*. The actor took the name Dick Sargent from a *Saturday Evening Post* illustrator/artist of the same name.

Sargent had appeared in films since his debut in *Prisoner of War* (1954). More of his early roles included *The Beast with a Million Eyes* (1955), *Love Me Tender* (1956), *Black Saddle* (1959), *Wichita Town* (1960) with Joel McCrea, *Gunsmoke* (1962), *Wagon Train* (1963-1964), and *Daniel Boone* (1966-1967).

When Dick York was forced to leave the *Bewitched* series owing to health problems in 1969, Sargent stepped into the role. He had previously appeared on the short-lived sitcom *Broadside* and the even shorter-lived *Tammy Grimes Show*. He appeared in *The Great Locomotive Chase* starring Fess Parker, *Operation Petticoat* starring Cary Grant, and *The Ghost and Mr. Chicken* starring Don Knotts. Sargent played Darrin until *Bewitched* ended in 1972. Later in the 1970s, he appeared in the 1979 film *Hardcore* as Jake Van Dorn's straight laced brother in law, Wes DeJong.

Sargent continued to work in film roles such as playing Harry in *Live a Little, Love a Little* in 1968 starring opposite *Elvis Presley* and *Michele Carey* and made numerous guest appearances on various television shows, including one episode of *Three's Company*, *The Waltons*, *Charlie's Angels*, *Knots Landing*, *Family Ties*, *Fantasy Island*, and two episodes of *The Dukes of Hazzard*. He also portrayed himself in a 1993 *Columbo* episode. In the mid-1980s, he landed the steady role of Richard Preston, the widowed father, in the syndicated sitcom *Down to Earth*. He also appeared in the witch-themed movie *Teen Witch* in 1989. He also appeared in *Diff'rent Strokes*.

Throughout the 1980s, he joined actress Sally Struthers as an advocate for Christian Children's Fund, which brought relief to developing nations' children.

On National Coming Out Day in 1991, Sargent publicly declared his homosexuality and supported gay rights issues. The high rate of suicide among young homosexuals was the main reason, jokingly referring to himself as a "retroactive role model". Sargent recognized his ill health from prostate cancer may have led people to assume he suffered from AIDS. He lived with his domestic partner, Albert Williams, until his death.

In June 1992, Sargent was a Grand Marshal of the Los Angeles Gay Pride parade along with Elizabeth Montgomery. She died of colorectal cancer in 1995.

Sargent was diagnosed with prostate cancer in 1989. Doctors were initially optimistic that it could be treated; however, the disease continued to spread and by early 1994, he had become seriously ill. Sargent died from the disease on July 8, 1994 at age 64. His remains were cremated.

Former *Bewitched* co-star Elizabeth Montgomery commented, "He was a great friend, and I will miss his love, his sense of humor and his remarkable courage." Montgomery herself died of cancer less than a year later.

Ann Savage

Ann Savage was born Bernice Maxine Lyon in Columbia, South Carolina February 19, 1921 and was an American film and television actress. She is best-remembered as the cigarette-puffing femme fatale in the critically acclaimed film noir *Detour* (1945), and starred in more than twenty B movies between 1943 and 1946.

Effectively leaving the film business in the mid-1950s, Savage made occasional appearances on television and worked for industrial and inspirational film producers during the 1950s–1970s. She made a number of live appearances at film festivals, especially for screenings of *Detour*.

In 2007, she was cast by director Guy Maddin as his mother in *My Winnipeg*, "a part that had been tipped to bring her an Academy Award and which introduced her to a legion of new fans".

During her early years, her family was on the move constantly as her United States Army officer father moved from base to base. After he died when Bernice was four years old, her mother moved the two of them to Los Angeles. Growing up around the corner from the Jewelry District, the Broadway movie palaces of downtown Los Angeles... served as her babysitter while her mother worked selling jewelry.

She attended 64th Street Grammar School, and Mount Vernon Junior High, and first stepped on a soundstage at the age of 17 at MGM Studios, screentested by Edgar Selwyn, Ann spent time among the more famous Hollywood kids of the day like Lana Turner, Judy Garland, Freddie Bartholomew and Deanna Durbin. Her MGM-test did not work out, prompting her to "get her teeth capped and acquire theatre training at the Max Reinhardt workshop on Sunset Boulevard. Reinhardt oversaw her namechange, and Bernice became Ann Savage. The Reinhardt school's manager, Bert D'Armand, would also become Savage's agent, and the two would later marry. Savage was offered a screentest by Fox, but she decided not to turn up as she knew the studio already had a bevy of pretty blondes".

Savage instead made a screen test with Columbia Pictures—after playing Lorna in a Reinhardt acting showcase of Odets' *Golden Boy*— and was offered a contract. Recalling Columbia mogul Harry Cohn as a friendly Uncle type, Savage recalled Cohn was intimidated by acid-tongued Rosalind Russell. The two actresses featured together in *What a Woman!*, one of a dozen films featuring Savage to be released in 1943.

Although Columbia typically groomed its girls to look like Rita Hayworth, Savage's look echoed Ann Sheridan, although her perpetually blonde locks were reddened for *Footlight Glamour* (1943) *"so that the star, Penny Singleton, would be the only blonde on screen"*. She joined Joan Davis and Jinx Falkenberg in *Two Senoritas from Chicago* (1943), and starred (as a brunette) in the first of several outings with Tom Neal in *Klondike Kate* (1943).

She also appeared in *The More the Merrier* in 1943 with Joel McCrea.

Although Savage and Neal did not see eye-to-eye—she thought him "childlike"—the duo would star together in *Two Man Submarine* and *The Unwritten Code* (both 1944), before their most famous film, the 1945 surreal film noir *Detour*. Reminiscing in the 1980s about her career as a stalwart B movie actress, Savage would dismiss "most of her roles as 'mindless'," saying:

> "The actresses were just scenery. The stories all revolved around the male actors; they really had the choice roles. All the actresses had to do was to look lovely, since the dialogue was ridiculous."

Detour, she felt, was different. The two leads underwent role reversal, with Savage's Vera blackmailing Neal's Al, in a part described by her manager Kent Adamson as "vicious and predatory... [and] very sexually aggressive".

Although the B-feature was shot quickly in twenty-eight days, its status has been cemented over the years. Director Wim Wenders called her work "at least fifteen years ahead of its time", while *The Guardian* termed Ann "a Garbo for our times". More recently, critics including Derek Malcolm and Barry Norman have particularly praised the film, with Norman calling Savage "sultry and sexy... a feline film noir star at its finest". After *Detour*, although Savage starred in a half-dozen more films during the later 1940s—including *Scared Stiff* (1945), *The Spider* (1945), *The Dark Horse* (1946) and *Satan's Cradle* (1949) (a rare Western)—her most prolific years were behind her.

When the film entered the public domain, it was frequently shown on syndicated television stations, and released in numerous VHS home video incarnations. Gaining "cult status" and garnering critical acclaim as "arguably film noir's greatest low-budget feature", this exposure earned Savage a new, younger, following. From the 1980s, Savage also attended a number of film festivals, helping to bolster her personal status, and leading her to emerge once more as "a glamorous figure about Hollywood at film festivals and galas".

In 1983, she attended a screening of *Detour* held as a tribute to director Edgar Ulmer and met up with Ulmer's widow, Shirley.

Savage drifted towards television, and "found she liked the pace", featuring in showcase programs *Fireside Theater*, *Schlitz Playhouse of the Stars* and *The Ford Television Theatre* between 1950 and 1955. She also guest-starred in episodes of *Front Page Detective*, *Gang Busters*, *City Detective* and *Death Valley Days* (AKA *The Pioneers*), but ultimately found herself being offered fewer and fewer roles. She continued to act on the big screen, including in Allan Dwan's *Women They Almost Lynched* (1953) with Audrey Totter, Joan Leslie and John Lund.

She eventually started appearing in commercials and industry films before essentially withdrawing from acting almost entirely in the mid-1950s.

Savage was a popular World War II pin-up model, an *Esquire* centerfold shot by Hurrell and a tireless barnstorming seller of War Bonds on two tours. She was briefly married to Clark Tennesen between 1939 and 1941, before marrying her agent (and the Max Reinhardt school manager) Burt (or Bert) D'Armand c. 1942–1945. The two lived in New York throughout the latter part of the 1950s and the 1960s until his sudden death in 1969.

After her husband's death, Savage returned to Los Angeles to be near her mother, and took odd jobs to finance flying lessons, becoming a licensed pilot in 1979. Her manager quoted her as saying that she "loved flying because it put her 'closer to God and Bert'." She also became part-owner of a small tool company, and later took a secretarial course and became a docket clerk receptionist and then a secretary at a law firm [Loeb & Loeb] in Los Angeles.

Having grown up and worked through the latter part of Hollywood's 'Golden Age', Savage was very keen on the preservation and celebration of all things Hollywood, becoming a volunteer and advisory board member of *Hollywood Heritage*.

Savage's exposure and the praise heaped on *Detour* led to her appearing in the 1986 film *Fire with Fire* and in a guest role on the television show *Saved by the Bell* (1991).

In 2007, she enjoyed a comeback, and rave reviews when Canadian filmmaker Guy Maddin cast her as his mother in his personal portrait of his hometown, *My Winnipeg* (2008). Maddin, according to Savage's manager, is a fan of *Detour*, while Savage's role in his film—"a part that had been tipped to bring her an Academy Award"—also "introduced her to a legion of new fans, including Steven Spielberg, John Travolta and Martin Scorsese". Maddin has stated that he cast Savage because she would have scared the pants off Bette Davis. *My Winnipeg* was critically acclaimed and won prizes from both the Toronto Film Critics Association and the San Francisco Film Critics Circle, as well as the Best Canadian Feature Film at the Toronto International Film Festival and a Genie Award nomination.

Her renewed following also prompted her to create her own MySpace web page and a Facebook account.

Remaining blonde throughout her eighties, and continuing to attend film festivals and galas, Savage had a series of strokes and became a resident of the Motion Picture & Television Country House and Hospital in California. She died in her sleep on December 25, 2008, at age 87. She is buried next to D'Armand at the Hollywood Forever Cemetery (in Los Angeles, California). Her personal and career memorabilia will become part of the Harry Ransom Center at The University of Texas at Austin, alongside the archives of Robert De Niro, David Mamet, David O. Selznick and Gloria Swanson (among others).

In 2005, Savage was elevated to the status of "icon and legend" by the Academy of Motion Picture Arts and Sciences. In 2007, *TIME* magazine named Savage's role as Vera in *Detour* one of the "Top 10 Movie Villains", and *Detour* itself as one of the hundred best movies. In 2010, McFarland and Co. published *Savage Detours: The Life and Work of Ann Savage*, by Kent Adamson and Lisa Morton.

Joe Sawyer

Joe Sawyer was born Joseph Sauers in Guelph, Ontario, Canada August 29, 1906 and was a Canadian film actor. He appeared in more than 200 films between 1930 and 1962, and was sometimes billed under his birth name.

Joe Sawyer's familiar mug appeared everywhere during the 1930s and 1940s, particularly as a stock player for Warner Bros. in its more standard college musicals, comedies, and crime yarns.

Trained at the Pasadena Playhouse, he had a perfect "tough guy" look: sturdy build, jutting chin and beady eyes, made more distinctive by his shock of light hair and a slightly high-pitched voice.

Sawyer made his film debut in 1931 under his real name, which, contrary to popular opinion, was German and not Irish, though he made a career out of playing Irishmen, and appeared mostly in strong-arm bit parts in his early career until hitting his stride playing a variety of coaches, cops, and sidekicks with imposing names like "Spud," "Slug" and "Whitey."

He appeared in films, in just about every genre, over a four-decade-long career, among them *College Humor* (1933), *Saturday's Millions* (1933) with Alan Ladd, *College Rhythm* (1934), *The Westerner* (1934), *The Informer* (1935) in which his portrayal of an IRA gunman got him noticed by the public and critics alike, *Pride of the Marines* (1936), *Black Legion* (1937), *The Petrified Forest* (1936) (another "tough-guy" role that got him good reviews), *Union Pacific* (1939) with Joel McCrea, *The Grapes of Wrath* (1940), *They Died with Their Boots On* (1941), *Sergeant York* (1941), *Tarzan's Desert Mystery* (1943), *Hit the Ice* (1943) with Abbott and Costello, *The Naughty Nineties* (1945) again with Bud and Lou, *Gilda* (1946), *It Came from Outer Space* (1953) the author's favorite roles of his, *North to Alaska* (1960) and *How the West Was Won* (1962).

He also guest-starred on many TV series such as *The Abbott and Costello Show* (1953), was a regular on *The Adventures of Rin Tin Tin* (1954) as Sgt. Aloysius "Biff" O'Hara, *Maverick* (1959), and *Bat Masterson* (1961).

His first wife was actress Jeane Wood, the daughter of *Gone with the Wind* (1939) uncredited director Sam Wood. His second wife, June, died in 1960.

He died April 21, 1982 in Ashland, Oregon from liver cancer at age 75.

William Schallert

William Joseph Schallert was born in Los Angeles, California July 6, 1922) is an American character actor who has appeared in many films and in such television series as *Perry Mason, The Smurfs, Jefferson Drum, Philip Marlowe, The Rat Patrol, Gunsmoke, Star Trek, The Patty Duke Show, 87th Precinct, The Many Loves of Dobie Gillis, The Waltons, The Partridge Family, Bonanza, Wanted: Dead or Alive, Leave It to Beaver, The Dick Van Dyke Show, Love, American Style, Get Smart, Lawman, Combat!, The Wild Wild West, Wichita Town* with Joel McCrea, and in later years, *Star Trek: Deep Space Nine, Medium* and *True Blood*.

As with many character actors with long careers, Schallert's face is more recognizable than his name.

William "Bill" Schallert, the son of Edwin Francis Schallert, a longtime drama critic for the *Los Angeles Times*, and Elza Emily Schallert (née Baumgarten) a magazine writer and radio host. He began acting while a student at the University of Southern California, Los Angeles, and in 1946, helped found the Circle Theatre with Sydney Chaplin and several fellow students. And, in 1948, Schallert was directed Sydney's father, the famous Charlie Chaplin in a staging of Somerset Maugham's "Rain."

Schallert has appeared in supporting roles on numerous television programs since the early 1950s, including *Gunsmoke* (season 3, episode 16 "Twelfth Night") in 1957 and (season 4, episode 16 "Gypsum Hills Feud") in 1958 and *The Partridge Family*, as a very humble folk-singing guitar player with "Stage Fright", in 1971. He appeared three times as Major Karl Richmond on NBC's *Steve Canyon*, starring Dean Fredericks in the title role.

Schallert has also appeared in several movies. One of his early cinematic roles is a brief uncredited performance as a police detective in *The Reckless Moment* (1949) with Joan Bennett and James Mason. He can be seen too in *The Man from Planet X* (1951) with Robert Clarke, *The Tarnished Angels* (1958) with Robert Stack, *Blue Denim* (1959) with Brandon deWilde, *Pillow Talk* (1959) with Doris Day and Rock Hudson, *Speedway* (1968) with Elvis Presley, *The Jerk* (1979) with Steve Martin, *Teachers* (1984) with Nick Nolte, and *Innerspace* (1987), in which he played Martin Short's doctor. He also played (uncredited) an ambulance attendant in the early minutes of the 1950s sci-fi classic, *Them!* (1954). He is a founding member of the Circle Players at The Circle Theatre, started in 1946, now known as El Centro Theatre.

Schallert starred in *Philbert*, an innovative 1964 TV pilot for ABC, which combined live action camera work and animation. Created by Warner Brothers animator Friz Freleng and directed by Richard Donner, ABC backed out of the series shortly before full production was to begin, though the completed pilot was released in theaters by Warner Brothers as a short subject.

He is probably best known as Martin Lane on *The Patty Duke Show*. He also appeared as a wise teacher, Mr. Leander Pomfritt on *The Many Loves of Dobie Gillis*, and as The Admiral on *Get Smart*. Coincidentally, on the two former shows he worked opposite actress Jean Byron. Schallert made three guest appearances on CBS's *Perry Mason* between 1957-1962, including the role of Donald Graves in the series' fifth episode, "The Case of the Sulky Girl," and Dr. Bradbury in the 1961 episode, "The Case of the Misguided Missile."

He is also remembered for playing the role of Nilz Baris in the *Star Trek* episode "The Trouble With Tribbles". He also appeared in the archive footage of that episode which was used in the *Star Trek: Deep Space Nine* episode "Trials and Tribble-ations". Schallert appeared in DS9 himself, in the second season episode "Sanctuary", in which he played Varani, a Bajoran musician.

Schallert played the role of Carson Drew in the television series *The Hardy Boys/Nancy Drew Mysteries* (1977–1979), featuring Pamela Sue Martin as Nancy Drew.

In addition to his onscreen performances, Schallert has done voiceover work for numerous television and radio commercials over the years. Among these were a recurring role as "Milton the Toaster" in animated commercials for Kellogg's Pop-Tarts.

Schallert has the rare distinction of appearing in both the original movie version of *In The Heat of The Night* (1967) and the later NBC TV version in 1992. In 2004, *TV Guide* recognized Schallert's portrayal of Martin Lane on *The Patty Duke Show* as No. 39 on its list of "50 Greatest TV Dads."

Schallert served as president of the Screen Actors Guild (SAG) from 1979 to 1981, and has remained active in SAG projects since then, including serving as a Trustee of the SAG Pension and Health Plans since 1983, and of the Motion Picture and Television Fund since 1977. (His former co-star and television daughter, Patty Duke, also served as SAG president from 1985 to 1988.) During Schallert's tenure as SAG President, he founded the Committee for Performers with Disabilities, and in 1993, he was awarded the Ralph Morgan Award for service to the Guild.

Schallert has also continued to work steadily as an actor in later life, appearing in a 2008 episode of *How I Met Your Mother*, the HBO television movie *Recount* (2008) as U.S. Supreme Court Associate Justice John Paul Stevens, the HBO series *True Blood* and his distinctive voice continues to bring him work for commercial and animation voiceovers. 2009 appearances included a guest role on *Desperate Housewives* on March 15, 2009, in which he played the role of a small newspaper editor, and he also appeared in an episode of *According to Jim*. More recently, he appeared in the January 21, 2010 pilot episode of *The Deep End* on ABC as a retiring CEO with Alzheimer's Disease. He also made an appearance on *Medium* on the February 5, 2010 episode and a cameo on the June 26, 2011 season premiere of *True Blood* as the Mayor of Bon Temps. He played Max Devore, a secondary antagonist, in the A&E adaptation of Stephen Kings *Bag of Bones*.

His most recent roles was in an episode of 2 Broke Girls in 2014.

In 2010, Schallert made a series of Public Service Announcement videos with Patty Duke and other castmates from *The Patty Duke Show* for the Social Security Administration, which can be found at www.ssa.gov.

Since 1949, Schallert has been married to actress Leah Waggner, who has appeared with him in various shows, including episodes of *The Patty Duke Show* and *The Dick Van Dyke Show.* They have four children.

Schallert has had both legs amputated and wears prosthetic legs.

Billy Kent Schaefer

Billy Kent Schaefer was born on September 26, 1920 in Los Angeles, California. He is an actor, known for *The Home Maker* (1925), *The Little Pest* (1927), and *The Wind* (1928).

More of his roles included *Arizona Sweepstakes* (1926), *The Truthful Sex* (1926), *The Enemy* (1927) with Joel McCrea, *Warming Up* (1928), and *As Good as Married* (1937).

Douglas Scott

Douglas Scott was born on May 31, 1925 in Seattle, Washington. He was an actor, known for *Lloyd's of London* (1936), *Wuthering Heights* (1939), and *Intermezzo: A Love Story* (1939).

More of his roles included *Dynamite* (1929) with Joel McCrea, *Cimarron* (1931), *The Eagle and the Hawk* (1933), *Wee Willie Winkie* (1937), *We Are Not Alone* (1939), *Naval Academy* (1941), *Get Hep to Love* (1942), and *Sweet Rosie O'Grady* (1943).

He died on June 23, 1988 in Concord, California at age 63.

Randolph Scott

Randolph Scott and Joel McCrea in *Ride the High Country*

Randolph Scott was born George Randolph Scott in Orange County, Virginia January 23, 1898 and was an American film actor whose career spanned from 1928 to 1962. As a leading man for all but the first three years of his cinematic career, Scott appeared in a variety of genres, including social dramas, crime dramas, comedies, musicals (albeit in non-singing and non-dancing roles), adventure tales, war films, and a few horror and fantasy films. However, his most enduring image is that of the tall-in-the-saddle Western hero. Out of his exactly 100 film appearances over sixty were in Westerns; thus, "of all the major stars whose name was associated with the Western, Scott most closely identified with it."

Scott's more than thrty years as a motion picture actor resulted in his working with many acclaimed screen directors, including Henry King, Rouben Mamoulian, Michael Curtiz, John Cromwell, King Vidor, Allan Dwan, Fritz Lang, and Sam Peckinpah. He also worked on multiple occasions with prominent directors: Henry Hathaway (eight times), Ray Enright (seven), Edwin R. Marin (seven), André de Toth (six), and most notably, his seven film collaborations with Budd Boetticher. Scott also worked with a diverse array of cinematic leading ladies, from Shirley Temple and Irene Dunne to Mae West and Marlene Dietrich.

Tall (6ft 2½in), lanky and handsome, Scott displayed an easygoing charm and courtly Southern drawl in his early films that helped offset his limitations as an actor, where he was frequently found to be stiff or "lumbering". As he matured, however, Scott's acting improved while his features became burnished and leathery, turning him into the ideal "strong, silent" type of stoic hero. *The BFI Companion to the Western* noted:

"In his earlier Westerns ... the Scott persona is debonair, easy-going, graceful, though with the necessary hint of steel. As he matures into his fifties his roles change. Increasingly Scott becomes the man who has seen it all, who has suffered pain, loss, and hardship, and who has now achieved (but at what cost?) a stoic calm proof against vicissitude."

During the early 1950s, Scott was a consistent box-office draw. In the annual *Motion Picture Herald* Top Ten Polls, he ranked 10th in 1950, 8th in 1951, and again 10th in 1952. Scott also appeared in the Quigley's *Top Ten Money Makers Poll* from 1950 to 1953.

He was reared in Charlotte, North Carolina, the second of six children born to parents of Scottish-American descent. His father was George Grant Scott, born in Franklin, Virginia, an administrative engineer in a textile firm. His mother was Lucille Crane Scott, born in Luray, Virginia, a member of a wealthy North Carolina family. The Scott children in order of birth were: Margaret, Randolph, Katherine, Virginia, Joseph, and Barbara, most born in North Carolina.

Because of his family's financial status, young Randolph was able to attend private schools such as Woodberry Forest School. From an early age, Scott developed and displayed an athletic trait, excelling in American football, baseball, horse racing, and swimming.

In April 1917, the United States entered World War I and shortly afterwards, Scott, then 19 years old, joined the United States Army. He served in France as an artillery observer with the 2nd Trench Mortar Battalion, 19th Field Artillery. His wartime experience would give him training that would be put to use in his later film career, including the use of firearms and horsemanship.

After the Armistice brought World War I to an end, Scott stayed in France and enrolled in an artillery officers' school. Although he eventually received a commission, Scott decided to return to America and thus journeyed home around 1919.

With his military career over, Scott continued his education at Georgia Tech where he set his sights on becoming an all-American football player. However a back injury prevented him from achieving this goal. Scott then transferred to the University of North Carolina, where he majored in textile engineering and manufacturing. As with his military career, however, he eventually dropped out of college and went to work as an accountant in the textile firm where his father was employed.

Around 1927, Scott developed an interest in acting and decided to make his way to Los Angeles and seek a career in the motion picture industry. Fortunately, Scott's father had become acquainted with Howard Hughes and provided a letter of introduction for his son to present to the eccentric millionaire filmmaker. Hughes responded by getting Scott a small part in a George O'Brien film called *Sharp Shooters* (1928). Despite its title and the presence of O'Brien, *Sharp Shooters* is not a western, as some film historians claimed. Rather, it's a romantic comedy. A print of the film survives in the UCLA Film and Television Archive.

In the next few years, Scott continued working as an extra and bit player in several films, including *Weary River* (1929) with Richard Barthelmess and *The Virginian* (1929) with Gary Cooper. Reputedly, Scott also served as Cooper's dialect coach in this latter film.

On the advice of director Cecil B. DeMille, Scott also gained much-needed acting experience by performing in stage plays with the Pasadena Playhouse.

In 1931 Scott played his first leading role (with Sally Blane) in *Women Men Marry*, a film, now apparently lost, that was made by a Poverty Row studio called Headline Pictures. He followed that movie with a supporting part in a Warner Bros. production starring George Arliss, *A Successful Calamity*. In 1932 Scott appeared in a play at the Vine Street Theatre in Hollywood entitled *Under a Virginia Moon*. His performance in this play resulted in several offers for screen tests by the major movie studios. Scott eventually signed a seven-year contract with Paramount Pictures at a salary of US$400 per week (adjusted for inflation, US$400 in 1932 is the equivalent of approximately US$4800 in 2006).

Scott's first role under his new Paramount contract was a small supporting part in a comedy called *Sky Bride* (1932) starring Richard Arlen and Jack Oakie. Following that, however, Paramount cast him as the lead in *Heritage of the Desert* (1932), his first significant starring role and also the one that established him as a Western hero. As with *Women Men Marry*, Sally Blane was his leading lady. The film was the first of ten "B" Western films that Scott made for Paramount in a series loosely based on the novels of Zane Grey. Around the same time, Fox also remade some Zane Grey titles that they owned, with George O'Brien as their star. Henry Hathaway made his directorial debut with *Heritage of the Desert*; he would go on to direct a total of seven out of the ten Zane Grey adaptations that Scott would appear in. Henry Hathaway also directed one film in the Zane Grey series without Scott: *Under the Tonto Rim* (1933) starring Stuart Erwin.

Many of these Grey adaptations were remakes of earlier silent films. In an effort to save on production costs, Paramount utilized stock footage from the silent version and even hired some of the same actors, such as Raymond Hatton and Noah Beery, to repeat their roles. For the 1933 films *The Thundering Herd* and *Man of the Forest*, Scott's hair was darkened and he sported a trim moustache so that he could easily be matched to footage of Jack

Holt, the star of the silent versions. Around this time, Warner Bros. did the same thing. John Wayne starred in a series of Westerns for them that utilized footage from an earlier series from the silent era that starred Ken Maynard.

In his book, *The Hollywood Western: Ninety Years of Cowboys and Indians, Train Robbers, Sheriffs and Gunslingers*, film historian William K. Everson refers to the Zane Grey series as being "uniformly good". He also writes:

"To the Last Man was almost a model of its kind, an exceptionally strong story of feuding families in the post-Civil War era, with a cast worthy of an "A" feature, excellent direction by Henry Hathaway, and an unusual climactic fight between the villain (Jack LaRue) and the *heroine* (Esther Ralston, in an exceptionally appealing performance). *Sunset Pass*... was not only one of the best but also one of the most surprising in presenting Randolph Scott and Harry Carey as *heavies."*

The Zane Grey series were a boon for Scott, as they provided him with "an excellent training ground for both action and acting".

In between his work in the Zane Grey Western series, Paramount cast Scott in several non-Western roles, such as "the other man" in *Hot Saturday* (1932), with Nancy Carroll and Cary Grant; *Hello, Everybody!* (1933), an odd one-shot attempt to make a film star out of the popular but heavy-set radio singer Kate Smith; and *Go West, Young Man* (1936).

Paramount also cast Scott in two fairly good horror films: *Murders in the Zoo* (1933) with Lionel Atwill, and *Supernatural* (1933) with Carole Lombard. Paramount also loaned him to work at other studios, including Columbia, where he appeared with Bebe Daniels in a minor romantic comedy called *Cocktail Hour* (1933).

By 1935 Scott was firmly established as a popular movie star and, thus, following the release of *Rocky Mountain Mystery* (1935), Paramount moved him up from his "B" Western status to a star of "A" features, many on loan out.

Scott made four films for RKO Radio Pictures during 1935–1936. Two of these were in the popular series of musicals starring Fred Astaire and Ginger Rogers: *Roberta* (1935), also starring Irene Dunne, and *Follow the Fleet* (1936). In both of these films Scott played Astaire's lunkheaded but likable pal. The other two were among the best in Scott's career: *Village Tale* (1935), "a touching, still-obscure melodrama about small-town gossip and hypocrisy" directed by John Cromwell, and *She* (1935), a superb adventure-fantasy adapted from H. Rider Haggard's 1886 novel.

In 1936, Scott, on loan to independent producer Edward Small, starred in another adventure classic, *The Last of the Mohicans*, adapted from the 1826 novel by James Fenimore Cooper. A big hit in its day, the film "gave Scott his first unqualified 'A' picture success as a lead."

Scott's films at Paramount include the aforementioned *Go West, Young Man* (1936), which reunited him with director Henry Hathaway and is Mae West's adaptation of Lawrence Riley's Broadway hit comedy *Personal Appearance*; *So Red the Rose* (1936), directed by King Vidor and starring Margaret Sullavan; and *High, Wide, and Handsome*. This last film, a musical directed by Rouben Mamoulian, featured Scott in his "most ambitious performance," The film is set in 1859 in Pennsylvania, and follows the exploits of oil prospector Scott as he struggles against various varmints and vested interests out to wreck his business, and tries to keep his marriage to Irene Dunne intact, despite the tempting presence of saloon singer Dorothy Lamour.

In 1938 Scott finished his contract with Paramount and began freelancing. Some of the roles that he took over the next few years were supporting ones, while his other roles during the same time frame had him occasionally lapse into villainy. One missed opportunity also came about around this time. Due to his Southern background, Scott was considered for the role of Ashley Wilkes in *Gone with the Wind*, but it was Leslie Howard who eventually got the part.

For 20th Century Fox Scott supported child star Shirley Temple in *Rebecca of Sunnybrook Farm* (1938) and *Susanna of the Mounties* (1939). For the same studio he played a supporting role in his first Technicolor film, *Jesse James* (1939), a lavish highly romanticized account of the famous outlaw (Tyrone Power) and his brother Frank (Henry Fonda). Shortly after making this film, Scott portrayed Wyatt Earp in *Frontier Marshal* (1939) and, for Universal, starred with Kay Francis in *When the Daltons Rode* (1940).

Scott followed this by co-starring with Errol Flynn in *Virginia City* (1940) and played the "other man" role in the Irene Dunne–Cary Grant romantic comedy *My Favorite Wife* (1940).

In 1941 Scott returned to Zane Grey country by co-starring with Robert Young in the Technicolor production *Western Union*, directed by Fritz Lang. Scott played a "good bad man" in this film and gave one of his finest performances. Bosley Crowther of the *New York Times* wrote:

"Randolph Scott, who is getting to look and act more and more like William S. Hart, herein shapes one of the truest and most appreciable characters of his career as the party's scout."

In 1941, Scott also co-starred with a young Gene Tierney in another western, *Belle Starr*. Scott's only role as a truly evil villain was in Universal's *The Spoilers*, a rip-roaring adaptation of Rex Beach's 1905 tale of the Alaskan gold rush co-starring Marlene Dietrich and John Wayne. The movie's climax featured Scott and Wayne (and their stunt doubles) in one of the most spectacular fistfights ever filmed. The Dietrich-Scott-Wayne combination worked so well that Universal recast the trio the following year in *Pittsburgh*, a war-time action-melodrama which had Wayne and Scott slugging it out once more.

In 1943 Scott starred in *The Desperados*, Columbia Pictures' first feature in Technicolor. The film was produced by Harry Joe Brown, with whom Scott would form a business partnership several years later.

Shortly after the United States entered World War II, Scott attempted to obtain an officer's commission in the Marines, but because of a back injury years earlier, he was rejected. However, he did his part for the war effort by touring in a comedy act with Joe DeRita (who later became a member of the Three Stooges) for the Victory Committee showcases, and he also raised food for the government on a ranch that he owned.

In 1942 and 1943, Scott appeared in several war films, notably *To the Shores of Tripoli*, *Bombardier*, the Canadian warship drama *Corvette K-225*, *Gung Ho!* and *China Sky*.

In 1946, after playing roles that had him wandering in and out of the saddle for many years, including a role alongside Charles Laughton in the cheaply made production *Captain Kidd* (1945), Scott appeared in *Abilene Town*, a UA release which cast him in what would become one of his classic images, the fearless lawman cleaning up a lawless town. The film "cemented Scott's position as a cowboy hero" and from this point on all but two of his starring films would be Westerns. The Scott Westerns of the late 1940s would each be budgeted around US$1,000,000, equal to $12,093,857 today.

Scott renewed his acquaintance with producer Harry Joe Brown and together they began producing many of Scott's Westerns, including several that were shot in the two-color Cinecolor process. Their collaboration produced the superior *Coroner Creek* (1948) with Scott as a vengeance-driven cowpoke who "predates the Budd Boetticher/Burt Kennedy heroes by nearly a decade," *Gunfighters* (1947) based on the Zane Grey novel *Two Sombreros*, and *The Walking Hills* (1949), a modern-day tale of gold hunters.

He also made Westerns for Nat Holt. Some of these movies, *Badman's Territory*, *Trail Street*, and *Rage at Dawn* were released by RKO, while others, like *Fighting Man of the Plains*, *Canadian Pacific*, and *The Cariboo Trail* were released by Twentieth Century Fox. In the late 1940s and early 1950s Scott's films were made mainly for Columbia or Warner Bros. His salary for the latter studio was US$100,000 per picture (equal to $991,189 today).

Scott's pictures from this period include the 1950 *Colt .45*, the 1951 films *Fort Worth*, *Man in the Saddle* and *Carson City*, and the 1952 films *Hangman's Knot* (which Scott produced), *The Man Behind the Gun*, *The Stranger Wore a Gun* (filmed in 3-D), and *Thunder Over the Plains*. Also in 1953, Scott appeared in *Riding Shotgun*, an unusual Western that presents (probably unintentionally) some McCarthyistic overtones. In 1954, Scott played a laconic good guy in *The Bounty Hunter*. Most of these were directed by André de Toth.

Scott also made *Rage at Dawn* in 1955 for Nat Holt, which was released by RKO starring Scott and Forrest Tucker, and featuring Denver Pyle, Edgar Buchanan, and J. Carrol Naish. It purports to tell the true story of the Reno Brothers, an outlaw gang which terrorized the American Midwest, particularly Southern Indiana, soon after the American Civil War.

Also of interest is *Shootout at Medicine Bend* shot in 1955, but released in 1957, which was Scott's last movie in black and white. The movie co-stars James Garner and Angie Dickinson.

By 1956, Scott turned 58, an age where the careers of most leading men would be winding down. Scott, however, was about to enter his finest and most acclaimed period.

In 1955, screenwriter Burt Kennedy wrote a script entitled *Seven Men from Now* which was scheduled to be filmed by John Wayne's Batjac Productions with Wayne as the film's star and Budd Boetticher as its director. However, Wayne was already committed to John Ford's *The Searchers*. Wayne therefore suggested Scott as his replacement. The resulting film, released in 1956, did not make a great impact at the time but is now regarded by many as one of Scott's best, as well as the one that launched Scott and Boetticher into a successful collaboration that totaled seven films. While each film is independent and there are no shared characters or settings, this set of films is often called the Ranown Cycle, for the production company run by Scott and Harry Joe Brown, which was involved in their production. Kennedy scripted four of them. In these films Boetticher achieved works of great beauty, formally precise in structure and visually elegant, notably for their use of the distinctive landscape of the California Sierras. As the hero of these "floating poker games" (as Andrew Sarris calls them), Scott tempers their innately pessimistic view with quiet, stoical humour, as he pits his wits against such charming villains as Richard Boone in *The Tall T* and Claude Akins in *Comanche Station*.

The Scott and Boetticher films were *Seven Men from Now* (1956), *The Tall T* (1957), *Decision at Sundown* (1957), *Buchanan Rides Alone* (1958), *Westbound* (1959), *Ride Lonesome* (1959), and *Comanche Station* (1960).

In 1962 Scott made his final film appearance in *Ride the High Country*, a film now regarded as a classic. It was directed by Sam Peckinpah and co-starred Joel McCrea, an actor who had a screen image similar to Scott's and who also from the mid-1940s on devoted his career almost exclusively to Westerns.

Scott and McCrea's farewell Western is characterized by a nostalgic sense of the passing of the Old West; a preoccupation with the emotionality of male bonding and of the experiential 'gap' between the young and the old; and the fearful evocation, in the form of the Hammonds (the villains in the film), of these preoccupations transmuted into brutal and perverse forms.

McCrea, like Scott, retired from filmmaking after this picture, although he returned to the screen twice in later years.

Following *Ride the High Country*, Scott retired from film at the age of 64. Having made shrewd investments throughout his life, he eventually accumulated a fortune worth a reputed $100 million.

During his retirement years he remained friends with Fred Astaire and also became friends with the Reverend Billy Graham. Scott was described by his son Christopher as being a deeply religious man. He was an Episcopalian and a member of St. Peter's Episcopal Church in Charlotte, North Carolina.

Scott married twice. In 1936, he became the second husband of heiress Marion duPont, daughter of William Du Pont, Sr. and great-granddaughter of Éleuthère Irénée Du Pont de Nemours, the founder of the E.I. du Pont de Nemours and Company. Marion had previously married George Somerville, with Scott serving as best man at the wedding; the marriage ended in divorce three years later. In 1944, Scott married Patricia Stillman, with whom he adopted two children. The marriage lasted until Scott's death.

Scott died of heart and lung ailments March 2, 1987 at the age of 89 in Beverly Hills, California. He was interred at Elmwood Cemetery in Charlotte, North Carolina.

Zachary Scott

Joel McCrea and Zachary Scott in *South of St. Louis*

Zachary Scott was born Zachary Thomson Scott, Jr. in Austin, Texas February 21, 1914 and was an American actor, most notable for his roles as villains and 'mystery men'.

He was a distant cousin of George Washington, and his grandfather had been a very successful cattle rancher.

Scott intended to be a doctor like his father, Zachary Scott, Sr. (1880–1964), but after attending the University of Texas for a while, he decided to switch to acting. He signed on as a cabin boy on a freighter which took him to

England, where he acted in repertory theatre for a while, before he returned to Austin, and began acting in local theater.

Alfred Lunt discovered Scott in Texas and convinced him to move to New York City, where he appeared on Broadway. Scott made his debut on Broadway in a revival of *Ah, Wilderness!* in 1941 with a small role as a bartender. Three years later, Jack Warner saw him in a performance of *Those Endearing Young Charms* and signed him to appear in *The Mask of Dimitrios* (1944).

He appeared the next year in *Mildred Pierce* to much acclaim. In the film, Scott was Joan Crawford's somewhat sleazy love interest, whose mysterious murder formed the basis of the plot. (The character was equally sleazy but was not killed in the novel on which the movie was based.) In 1946 exhibitors voted him the third most promising "star of tomorrow".

During this period, Scott and his first wife Elaine socialized regularly with Angela Lansbury and her first husband, Richard Cromwell. Elaine Scott had met Zachary Scott back in Austin and she made a name for herself behind the scenes on Broadway as stage manager for the original production of *Oklahoma!*. The Scotts had one child together, Waverly Scott.

Zachary Scott enjoyed playing scoundrels and the public enjoyed those portrayals, too. Scott went on to star in such movies as *The Southerner* (1945), *The Unfaithful* (1947), *Cass Timberlane* (1947), *South of St. Louis* (1949) with Joel McCrea, *Flamingo Road* (1949), *Flaxy Martin* (1949), *Guilty Bystander* (1950), and *Shadow on the Wall* (1950), opposite Nancy Davis Reagan and Ann Sothern. He also appeared in *Stronghold* (1951) with Veronica Lake.

In 1950, Scott was involved in a rafting accident. Also during that year, he divorced his first wife, Elaine, who subsequently married writer John Steinbeck. Possibly as a result of these developments or due to a box-office slump, Scott succumbed to a depression which in turn limited his acting. Since Warner Bros. did not continue to promote his films, he turned back to the stage, and also appeared on television. During this period Scott remarried and he and his second wife, actress Ruth Ford, had a child together as well (he adopted her daughter from a previous marriage).

Some of his later roles and television credits included *Dead on Course* (1952), *Appointment in Honduras* (1953), *The United States Steel Hour* (1954), *Treasure of Ruby Hills* (1955), *Shotgun* (1955), *Violent Stranger* (1957), *Natchez Trace* (1960), *Rawhide* (1961), *The Expendables* (1962), *The Doctors and the Nurses* (1963), and *The Rogues* (1965).

He moved back to Austin, where he died from a brain tumor October 3, 1965 at the age of 51.

In 1968 the Austin Civic Theatre was renamed the Zachary Scott Theatre Center to honor their native son. His family has endowed two chairs at the University of Texas's theatre department in his name. A street at the old airport Mueller Redevelopment in Austin is named in his honor.

Scott has a star on the Hollywood Walk of Fame.

Gay Seabrook

Gay Seabrook was born Gladys Johnson in Seattle, Washington April 1, 1901 and was a film, Broadway, and radio actress.

Seabrook was teamed with comedian Emerson Treacy to form the double-act Treacy and Seabrook. The team was very successful on radio and in theater during the early 1930s, with routines similar to those of real husband-and-wife team Burns and Allen.

Seabrook also appeared as the ditzy mother of Spanky McFarland in the *Our Gang* short films *Bedtime Worries* (1933) and *Wild Poses* (1933) which also featured a cameo by Laurel and Hardy.

More of her roles included *Misbehaving Ladies* (1931), *Strictly Personal* (1933), *Half a Sinner* (1934), *Helldorado* (1935), *The Higgins Family* (1938), *Love, Honor and Oh-Baby!* (1940), and *Escort Girl* (1941).

In addition to her work with Treacy, Seabrook sometimes supplied the voice of Sniffles, an early character on the Warner Bros. roster created by Chuck Jones, though several other voice actresses, most notably Marjorie Tarlton and Leone Ledoux, are also credited with doing the voice of Sniffles from time to time.

Seabrook died on April 18, 1970 at age 69 in Bedford Hills, New York.

Dorothy Sebastian

Dorothy Sebastian was born in Birmingham, Alabama April 26, 1903 and was an American film and stage actress.

In her youth, she aspired to be a dancer and a film actress. Her family frowned on both ambitions, however, so she fled to New York at the age of 15. Upon her arrival in New York City, Sebastian's southern drawl was thick enough to "cut with a knife".She followed around theatrical agents before returning at night to a $12-a-month room, after being consistently rejected.

Sebastian's first contact in Hollywood was Robert Kane, who gave her a film test at United Studios. She performed in *George White's Scandals* and later co-starred with Joan Crawford and Anita Page for a popular series of MGM romantic dramas including *Our Dancing Daughters* (1928) and *Our Blushing Brides* (1930). Sebastian also appeared in 1929's *Spite Marriage*, wherein she was cast opposite her then-lover Buster Keaton.

More of her roles included *Bluebeard's Seven Wives* (1925), *The Demi-Bride* (1927), *The Single Standard* (1929) with Joel McCrea, *Montana Moon* (1930), *They Never Come Back* (1932), and *The Life of Vergie Winters* (1934).

By the mid-1930s, Sebastian was semi-retired from acting after marrying Hopalong Cassidy star William Boyd. After their 1936 divorce, she returned to acting appearing in mostly bit parts.

More of those later roles included *Rough Riders' Round-up* (1939), *Reap the Wild Wind* (1942), and *George White's Scandals* (1945).

Her last onscreen appearance was in the 1948 film *The Miracle of the Bells*.

Sebastian is credited with co-writing the Moon Mullican blues ballad "The Leaves Mustn't Fall". Mullican recorded this in 1950 and 1958 and it has since become a bluegrass standard.

In 1947, Sebastian married Miami Beach businessman Harold Shapiro to whom she remained married until her death.

On November 7, 1938, Sebastian was found guilty of drunk driving in a Beverly Hills, California Justice Court. The night she was arrested, she had been dining at the home of Buster Keaton with her nephew. She was given a thirty-day suspended jail sentence and paid a fine of $75.[5]

In 1940, Sebastian was denied an award of $10,000 from a San Diego court. She appeared at a Red Cross benefit in San Francisco in 1937, and failed to pay her hotel bill. She contended the promoter should have met the expense. An employee of the Plaza Hotel took out the suit, charging "defrauding an innkeeper". The State Supreme Court of California reversed the decision, which awarded her the money on grounds of malicious prosecution.

On April 8, 1957, Sebastian died of cancer at the Motion Picture & Television Country House and Hospital in Woodland Hills, California at age 53. She is buried at Holy Cross Cemetery in Culver City, California.

For her contribution to the motion picture industry, Dorothy Sebastian has a star on the Hollywood Walk of Fame at 6655 Hollywood Blvd.

Charles Seel

Joel McCrea and Charles Seel in *Wichita Town*

Charles Frederick Seel was born April 29, 1897 in New York City, New York. He was a balding, narrow-eyed American character player, a former vaudevillian and radio actor from 1929. He acted in early silent films on the East Coast. Regularly on screen after 1937, he was seen in innumerable small roles as clerks, bartenders, and shopkeepers. He was most familiar for his recurring role as the telegrapher Barney on TV's *Gunsmoke* (1961-1974) and as newsman Mr. Krinkie in *Dennis the Menace* (1960-1963).

More of his roles included *Comet Over Broadway* (1938), *Here Comes Mr. Jordan* (1941), *Hopalong Cassidy* (1952), *I Was a Teenage Frankenstein* (1957), *Wanted: Dead or Alive* (1959), *Wichita Town* (1959-1960) with Joel McCrea, *Alcoa Presents: One Step Beyond* (1959-1961), *The Man Who Shot Liberty Valance* (1962), *Twilight Zone* (1962-1963), *Destry* (1964), *The Munsters* (1965), *Star Trek* (1968), *The Virginian* (1962-1969), *Night Gallery* (1971), *Hec Ramsey* (1972), *Ssssss* (1973), *Adam-12* (1970-1974), and *Marcus Welby, M.D.* (1972-1976).

He died April 19, 1980 at age 82 in Los Angeles County, California.

Rocky Shahan

Rocky Shahan was born Robert Ray Shahan on March 4, 1919 in Texas. He is known for his work on *Ride a Violent Mile* (1957), *Blood Arrow* (1958), and *Rawhide* (1959).

More of his roles included *Son of Zorro* (1947), *The James Brothers of Missouri* (1949), *The Longhorn* (1951), *Man from the Black Hills* (1952), *Hopalong Cassidy* (1953), *Stories of the Century* (1954-1955), *Have Gun - Will Travel* (1957-1958), *Cattle Empire* (1958) with Joel McCrea, *Gunsmoke* (1957-1964), and *The Guns of Will Sonnett* (1969).

He died on December 8, 1981 in Denton, Texas at age 62.

Reginald Sheffield

Reginald Sheffield was born as Matthew Reginald Sheffield Cassan in the St. George's, Hanover Square district of London, England February 18, 1901 and was an English actor.

He was born to Matthew Sheffield Cassan and Alice Mary Field. He had a brother, Edward Sheffield Cassan and a sister, Flora Kathleen Sheffield Cassan, who became an actress known as Flora Sheffield.

His father was born in Ireland and his mother in England. They were married in London in 1892. Matthew died when Reginald was nine. In 1913 Reginald Sheffield (billed as Eric Desmond) appeared in *David Copperfield*. In 1914, Alice Sheffield and her children immigrated to the United States where they lived in Queens, New York. Reginald acted on the stage and in films. While his sister, Flora, was an actress, brother Edward worked as an accountant in a bank and later became a theatrical agent.

Sheffield's Broadway performances credited as Reggie Sheffield include *Evidence* (1914), in which his mother, Alice Sheffield, also appeared, *The Merry Wives of Windsor* (1916), *If* (1917), *The Betrothal* (1918) and *Helena's*

Boys (1924). His performances credited as Reginald Sheffield include *Youth* (1920), *The Way Things Happen* (1924), *Hay Fever* (1925), playing Sandy Tyrell, *Slaves All* (1926), *Soldiers and Women* (1929), playing Lieutenant Mason and *Dear Old England* (1930).

Reginald Sheffield was married in 1927 to Louise Van Loon (b. January 21, 1905 - d. April 14, 1987), a New York-born, Vassar College graduate with a liberal arts education. The couple had three children: Mary Alice Sheffield Cassan (born 1928), Jon Matthew Sheffield Cassan (born 11 April 1931 - 15 October 2010) (aka actor Johnny Sheffield), and William Hart Sheffield Cassan (born 1936) (actor Billy Sheffield).

As film production became more and more located in Southern California, Sheffield and his wife travelled back and forth between New York and Los Angeles. After several years they moved permanently to the West Coast.

Being a trained stage actor, Sheffield easily made the transition from silent films to talkies. He was a working actor who became memorable in numerous character and supporting roles and appeared with some of the greatest film stars of the day, including Constance Bennett, William Powell, George Arliss, Loretta Young, Gary Cooper, Errol Flynn, Rosalind Russell, Cary Grant and Joan Fontaine.

Some of his roles included *Classmates* (1924), *The College Widow* (1927), *Old English* (1930), *The House of Rothschild* (1934), *Splendor* (1935) with Joel McCrea, *The Adventures of Robin Hood* (1938), *Suspicion* (1941), *Appointment in Berlin* (1943), *The Great Moment* (1944) again with Joel McCrea, *Captain Kidd* (1945), *The Three Musketeers* (1948), *Rogues of Sherwood Forest* (1950), and *Forbidden* (1953).

In 1954, he began starring as Professor Mayberry in the television series *Rocky Jones, Space Ranger*. And after his son, Johnny Sheffield, appeared in his last jungle film in 1955, Reginald created, produced and directed a pilot for a television series, *Bantu, the Zebra Boy*, but a sponsor was not found and the show was never produced as a weekly series.

Sheffield acted in both versions of Cecil B. DeMille's *The Buccaneer* in (1938) and (1958), the latter being his last screen appearance.

Reginald Sheffield died December 8, 1957 in Pacific Palisades, California at age 56.

Jan Shepard

Jan Shepard was born Josephine Angela Sorbello on March 19, 1928 in Quakertown, Pennsylvania. She is an actress, known for *King Creole* (1958), *Attack of the Giant Leeches* (1959), and *That Certain Summer* (1972).

More of her roles included *Sabre Jet* (1953), *The Adventures of Kit Carson* (1954), *The Lone Ranger* (1955), *Science Fiction Theatre* (1955-1957), *Wichita Town* (1959) with Joel McCrea, *Wanted: Dead or Alive* (1960), *Laramie* (1961-1962), *Perry Mason* (1962-1965), *Paradise, Hawaiian Style* (1966), *Gunsmoke* (1961-1967), *The Virginian* (1965-1969), *Longstreet* (1972), and *The Rookies* (1973).

She has been married to Ray Boyle since 1954.

Fred Sherman

Fred Sherman was born Clarence E. Kolegraff May 14, 1905 in South Dakota and began his career in tent shows and vaudeville eventually working in films and television.

Some of his roles included *Too Many Women* (1942), *Behind Green Lights* (1946), *Chain Lightning* (1950), *Adventures of Superman* (1952), *Hopalong Cassidy* (1953), *Seven Men from Now* (1956), *The Oklahoman* (1957) with Joel McCrea, *Richard Diamond, Private Detective* (1957), *Space Master X-7* (1958), *Wichita Town* (1959) again with Joel McCrea, *Laramie* (1961), and *Wagon Train* (1959-1962).

After completing an episode of the *Andy Griffith Show* in 1962 he suffered a stroke which confined him to hospitals and the Motion Picture Country Home where he died May 20, 1969 at age 64 in Woodland Hills, Los Angeles, California.

Gale Sherwood

Gale Sherwood was born Jacqueline Nash in Hamilton, Ontario March 4, 1929 and was a Canadian singer and actress best known as the singing partner of Nelson Eddy from 1953 until his death in 1967. Sherwood graduated from High School in 1945.

Her film and television roles included juvenile roles as Betty in *They Shall Have Music* (1939) with Joel McCrea and in *Let's Make Music* (1941). As an adult, she appeared as Meelah in *Blonde Savage* (1947), Ellen Forrester in *Rocky* (1948), Sophia in *Song of My Heart* (1948), Yvonne in *Naughty Marietta* (TV 1955), Morgan Le Fay in *A Connecticut Yankee* (1955), and Margot in *The Desert Song* (TV 1955).

She sang with Eddy on television and in his nightclub act from 1953 until his death in 1967. Her stage roles included an appearance in *Show Boat* in 1967 with the Los Angeles Civic Light Opera.

Marion Shilling

Marion Shilling was born Marion Schilling in Denver, Colorado December 3, 1910 and was an American film actress of the 1930s. She started her acting career as a stage actress, starring in stage plays such as *Miss Lulu Betts* and *Mrs. Wiggs of the Cabbage Patch*. In 1929 she received her first screen role in *Wise Girls*. After a couple of roles in other films, she starred opposite William Powell in the 1930 crime drama *Shadow of the Law*. That movie springboarded her into roles as a B-movie heroine.

In 1931 she was one of thirteen girls selected as "WAMPAS Baby Stars", a list that included future Hollywood star Marian Marsh. From 1930 to 1936 she starred in forty two films, mostly westerns or mysteries. She often starred opposite Tom Keene and Guinn "Big Boy" Williams. In the 1934 film serial *The Red Rider*, she starred opposite early western film legend Buck Jones, with a supporting cast that included William Desmond and football legend Jim Thorpe.

More of her roles included *Shadow of the Law* (1930), *The Common Law* (1931), *A Parisian Romance* (1932), *Thunder Over Texas* (1934), *Rio Rattler* (1935), and *Cavalcade of the West* (1936).

Despite her success in films, Shilling retired in 1936, to marry and have a family. She was married to Edward Cook from 1937 until his death in 1998. They had two children, Edward and Frances.

She never returned to acting, and died from natural causes on November 6, 2004, in Torrance, California at age 93.

Ann Shoemaker

Ann Shoemaker was born January 10, 1891, in Brooklyn, New York and was an American actress who appeared in seventy films and TV movies between 1928 and 1976.

Some of her roles included *Walls Tell Tales* (1928), *Chance at Heaven* (1933) with Joel McCrea, *Cheating Cheaters* (1934), *Stella Dallas* (1937), *An Angel from Texas* (1940), *Ellery Queen, Master Detective* (1940) with Alan Ladd, *Thirty Seconds Over Tokyo* (1944), *Magic Town* (1947), *House by the River* (1950), *The Web* (1951-1954), *The Kaiser Aluminum Hour* (1956), *Sunrise at Campobello* (1960), *The Doctors and the Nurses* (1962), *Rawhide* (1965), *The Fortune Cookie* (1966), *Mission: Impossible* (1969), and *Gemini Man* (1976).

She was married to the actor Henry Stephenson. She died September 18, 1978, in Los Angeles, California at age 87.

Short Gertrude

Short Gertrude was born Carmen Gertrude Short April 6, 1902 in Cincinnati, Ohio. Gertrude was in vaudeville for five years then moved to the legit stage and onto Hollywood in 1922. From 1924 to 1925, Short played in a series of "Telephone Girl" comedies, directed by her husband. She continued playing telephone operators in several of her sound films. In fact, her last screen appearance was as an operator in the 1945 film *Weekend at the Waldorf.*

More of her roles included *The Man Life Passed By* (1923), *The Square Sex* (1924), *The Masked Woman* (1927), *Once a Gentleman* (1930), *The Thin Man* (1934), *Woman Wanted* (1935) with Joel McCrea, *You Can't Get Away with Murder* (1939), and *Sheriff of Cimarron* (1945).

During WWII Short left the screen to work at Lockheed and stayed there until she retired in 1967. She was married to director/writer Scott Pembroke, daughter of actor Lew Short and sister of actress Florence Short.

She died July 31, 1968 at age 66 in Hollywood, California.

Lee Shumway

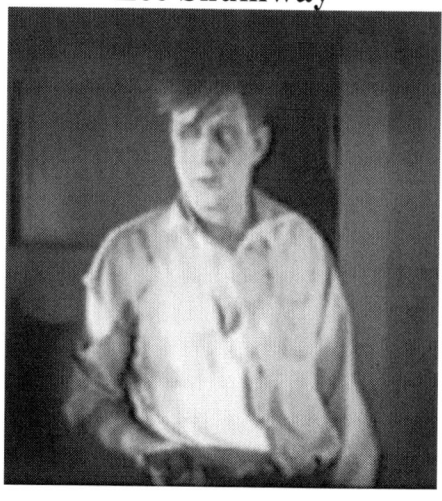

Lee Shumway was born Leonard Charles Shumway March 4, 1884 in Salt Lake City, Utah. A stage actor, Shumway turned to movies in 1909 mainly starring in westerns and serials.

Some of his roles included *The Texas Bearcat* (1925), *His Foreign Wife* (1927), *The Son of the Golden West* (1928), *So This Is College* (1929) with Joel McCrea, *Mystery of the Wax Museum* (1933), *The Lone Wolf Returns* (1935), *Come and Get It* (1936) again with Joel McCrea, *Wells Fargo* (1937) a third with Joel McCrea, *Homicide Bureau* (1939), *King of the Texas Rangers* (1941), *Sherlock Holmes in Washington* (1943), *The Lost Weekend* (1945), *Buck Privates Come Home* (1947), *Trigger, Jr.* (1950), *The Lone Ranger* (1950-1953), and *Calamity Jane* (1953).

Shumway retired from the screen in 1947. He died January 4, 1959 at age 74 in Los Angeles, California.

Sylvia Sidney

Sylvia Sidney and Joel McCrea in *Dead End*

Sylvia Sidney born Sophia Kosow in The Bronx, New York August 8, 1910 and was an American actress of stage, screen and film, who rose to prominence in the 1930s appearing in numerous crime dramas.

Sidney was the daughter of Rebecca (née Saperstein), a Romanian Jew, and Victor Kosow, a Russian Jewish immigrant who worked as a clothing salesman. Her parents divorced by 1915, and she was adopted by her stepfather, Sigmund Sidney, a dentist. Her mother became a dressmaker and renamed herself Beatrice Sidney. Now using the surname Sidney, she became an actress at the age of fifteen as a way of overcoming shyness. As a student of the Theater Guild's School for Acting, Sidney appeared in several of their productions during the 1920s and earned praise from theater critics. In 1926, she was seen by a Hollywood talent scout and made her first film appearance later that year.

During the Depression, Sidney appeared in a string of films, often playing the girlfriend or the sister of a gangster. Among her films from this period were: *An American Tragedy, City Streets* and *Street Scene* (all 1931), Alfred Hitchcock's *Sabotage* and Fritz Lang's *Fury* (both 1936), *You Only Live Once, Dead End* with Joel McCrea (both 1937) and *The Trail of the Lonesome Pine*, an early three-strip Technicolor film. It was during this period that she developed a reputation for being difficult to work with.

Her career diminished somewhat during the 1940s. In 1949 exhibitors voted her "box office poison". In 1952, she played the role of Fantine in *Les Misérables*, and her performance was widely praised and allowed her opportunities to develop as a character actress.

She appeared three times on CBS's *Playhouse 90* anthology series. On May 16, 1957, she appeared as Lulu Morgan, mother of singer Helen Morgan in "The Helen Morgan Story". Four months later, Sidney joined her former co-star Bergen again on the premiere of the short-lived NBC variety show, *The Polly Bergen Show*.

In 1973, Sidney received an Academy Award nomination for her supporting role in *Summer Wishes, Winter Dreams*. As an elderly woman Sidney continued to play supporting screen roles, and was identifiable by her husky voice, the result of a lifetime cigarette smoking habit. She was the formidable Miss Coral in the film version of *I*

Never Promised You a Rose Garden and later was cast as Aidan Quinn's grandmother in the television production of *An Early Frost* for which she won a Golden Globe Award. She played Aunt Marion in *Damien: Omen II* and had key roles in *Beetlejuice* (directed by longtime Sidney fan Tim Burton), as Juno, for which she won a Saturn Award, and *Used People* (which co-starred Jessica Tandy, Marcello Mastroianni, Marcia Gay Harden, Kathy Bates and Shirley MacLaine).

Her final role was in another film by Burton, *Mars Attacks!*, in which she played an elderly woman whose beloved Slim Whitman records help stop an alien invasion from Mars; when played over a loudspeaker, they cause the Martians' heads to explode.

On television, she appeared in episodes of *My Three Sons, Dear John*, the pilot episode of *WKRP in Cincinnati* as the imperious owner of the radio station; on *Thirtysomething*, and at the beginning of each episode as the crotchety travel clerk on the short-lived late-1990s revival of *Fantasy Island*.

Her Broadway career spanned five decades, from her debut performance as a graduate of the Theatre Guild School in June 1926 at age 15, in the three-act fantasy *Prunella* to the Tennessee Williams play *Vieux Carré* in 1977. Other stage credits included *The Fourposter, Enter Laughing*, and *Barefoot in the Park*. In 1982, Sidney was awarded The George Eastman Award by George Eastman House for distinguished contribution to the art of film.

Sidney was married three times. She first married publisher Bennett Cerf on October 1, 1935, but the couple were divorced six months later, on April 9, 1936. She later married actor and acting teacher Luther Adler in 1938, by whom she had her only child, a son, Jacob ("Jody"; 1939–1987), who died of Lou Gehrig's disease. Adler and Sidney divorced in 1947. During her marriage to Luther Adler she was a sister-in-law to acclaimed stage actress and drama teacher Stella Adler. On March 5, 1947, she married radio producer and announcer Carlton Alsop; they were divorced on March 22, 1951.

Sidney died July 1, 1999 from esophageal cancer at the age of 88 in New York City, after a career spanning more than seventy years. She was cremated.

She had published two popular instruction books: *Sylvia Sidney's Needlepoint Book* (1968) and *The Sylvia Sidney Question and Answer Book on Needlepoint* (1975).

Sidney has a star on the Hollywood Walk of Fame for her contribution to Motion Pictures at 6245 Hollywood Boulevard.

Bernard Siegel

Bernard Siegel was born in the city of Lemberg (today known as Lviv, Ukraine), in the province of Galicia in the Austria-Hungarian Empire on April 19, 1868. He was an American character actor, whose career spanned both the silent film era, as well as carrying over into the beginning of sound pictures. His career spanned over twenty-five years, during which time he appeared in 127 films.

His film career began with a small featured role in the 1913 silent film, *The Third Degree* (which would be remade in 1919, and again in 1926, the latter film being the first film directed by Michael Curtiz).

More of his roles included *The Orgy* (1915), *The Song of the Soul* (1918), *Sidewalks of New York* (1923), *The Vanishing American* (1925), *Open Range* (1927), *Freedom of the Press* (1928) with Joel McCrea, *Sea Fury* (1929), *Beau Ideal* (1931), *East of Java* (1935), *Wells Fargo* (1937) again with Joel McCrea, and *Broadway Serenade* (1939).

Siegel died in July 9, 1940 of a heart attack in Los Angeles at the age of 72.

Mario Siletti

Mario Giovanni Siletti was born on July 22, 1903 in Turin, Piedmont, Italy. He was an actor, known for *The House on Telegraph Hill* (1951), *The Great Caruso* (1951), and *Kansas City Confidential* (1952).

More of his roles included *My Little One* (1933), *We Were Seven Widows* (1939), *Four Steps in the Clouds* (1942), *The Razor's Edge* (1946), *East Side, West Side* (1949), *Go for Broke!* (1951), *Wings of the Hawk* (1953), *Bring Your Smile Along* (1955), *I Love Lucy* (1953-1956), *Richard Diamond, Private Detective* (1958-1959), *Wichita Town* (1960) with Joel McCrea, *The Honeymoon Machine* (1961), *4 for Texas* (1963), and *Hazel* (1962-1964).

He died on April 19, 1964 in Los Angeles, California at age 60.

David Silva

David Silva was born David Silva Guglielmeti. on October 9, 1917 in Mexico City, Distrito Federal, Mexico. He was an actor and producer. Most of his films were Spanish speaking.

Some of his English speaking roles included *Beneath the Sky of Mexico* (1937), *I Shall Live Again* (1940), *Peach Blossom* (1945), *Toast to Love* (1951), *The First Texan* (1956) with Joel McCrea, *Looking for Death* (1961), *Narcotics Division* (1963), *The Batwoman* (1968), *The Champions of Justice* (1971), and *The Mansion of Madness* (1973).

He died on September 21, 1976 in Mexico City, Mexico at age 58.

Ivan F. Simpson

Ivan Freebody Simpson was born in Glasgow, Scotland February 8, 1875 and was a Scottish film and theatre actor.

Ivan Simpson went as a young man to New York City, where he worked for four decades on Broadway from 1906 until his death. In 1915 he started his film silent career and starred in notable silent films like *The Green Goddess* from 1923, where he played Mister Watkins. He also acted in this role seven years later again. In 1929 he portrayed Hugh Myers in *Disraeli*, together with his close friend George Arliss. Arliss and Simpson played together in seven films.

Especially in the 1930s, Simpson was a successful character actor in supporting and bit parts and appeared in many classics. He often played servants, like in *David Copperfield* and *Mark of the Vampire*. He also portrayed priests, judges or doctors. Ivan Simpson played together with Errol Flynn in credited parts in *The Adventures of Robin Hood*, *The Prince and the Pauper* and *Captain Blood*.

More of his roles included *Sherlock Holmes* (1932), *Splendor* (1935) with Joel McCrea, *The Adventures of Sherlock Holmes* (1939), *The Uninvited* (1944), and *Robert Montgomery Presents* (1950-1951).

Ivan F. Simpson starred in over 100 Hollywood films; his last was *My Girl Tisa* from 1948. He died October 12, 1951 at the age of 76. His was buried in Kensico Cemetery. His daughter was actress Pamela Simpson (1905-2002).

Russell Simpson

Russell McCaskill Simpson was born in San Francisco, California June 17, 1880 and was an American character actor.

Simpson is best known for his work in the films of John Ford and, in particular, for his portrayal of Pa Joad in *The Grapes of Wrath* in 1940.

Simpson reportedly prospected for gold in Alaska in his youth, but by 1909 had gone into the theatre. He appeared in at least two plays on Broadway between 1909 and 1912, and made his motion picture debut in Cecil B. DeMille's 1914 original film version of *The Virginian* in a bit part. By 1923, when the film was remade, Simpson had progressed to playing the lead villain.

Gaunt, lanky, and rustic-sounding, Simpson was a familiar character actor for almost forty-five years, particularly as a member of the John Ford Stock Company.

More of his roles included *Rustling for Cupid* (1926), *The Lone Star Ranger* (1930), *The Riding Tornado* (1932), *Frontier Marshal* (1934), *Mountain Justice* (1937), *Mr. Smith Goes to Washington* (1939), *Coroner Creek* (1948), *The Outriders* (1950) with Joel McCrea, *Saddle Tramp* (1950) again with Joel McCrea, *Oklahoma!* (1955), and *The Tin Star* (1957).

He worked up to 1959, the year of his death. His final film was *The Horse Soldiers*, his tenth film for Ford. He died December 12, 1959 at age 82 in Woodland Hills, California.

He was survived by his wife Gertrude. They had two children, Russell, Jr. and Roberta.

Robert F. Simon

Robert F. Simon was born in Mansfield in Richland County in north central Ohio December 2, 1908 and was an American character actor, often portraying military or authority figure roles. Though his face was recognized by audiences, he was mostly unknown by name. A life member of The Actors Studio, Simon appeared in films and on television between 1950 and 1985, having mastered the genre of westerns, drama, and comedy.

Simon was an all-state high school basketball champion in the 1920s. He played basketball in one-on-one games well into his forties. Before he entered acting, he was a traveling salesman. He initially thought that acting would help him to overcome his natural shyness, but he enjoyed appearing on stage and later film so much that he decided to make a career as an actor. His first professional job was in Marc Blitzstein's *No For an Answer* in which he displayed his song-and-dance abilities. He was also involved with The Cleveland Play House and then with The Actors Studio, through which he became an understudy to Lee J. Cobb for the lead in Arthur Miller's *Death of a Salesman*.

Simon had two daughters, Barbara Ann Simon Callet (born 1941) and Susan Simon Thompson, and two sons, Robert Louis Simon (born 1950) and James A. Simon (born 1951).

Simon appeared on Broadway in Clifford Odets's play, *Clash by Night*. In 1949, he succeeded Lee J. Cobb as Willy Loman in *Death of a Salesman*.

His first film appearances were as Inspector Foley in *Where the Sidewalk Ends* (1950) and as a psychiatrist in *Bright Victory* (1951). His first television role was at the age of 43 in 1952 as Captain Scott in the episode "Woman with a Sword" on *Hallmark Hall of Fame* anthology series. Simon appeared as Ackerman in the 1954 film *Rogue Cop*. Between 1951 and 1954, he appeared on *The Philco Television Playhouse* and *Justice*.

In 1955, he appeared on television in episodes of *Medic* and *Alfred Hitchcock Presents* as well as such feature films as *Chief Crazy Horse*, *Seven Angry Men*, and *The Court-Martial of Billy Mitchell*. Actress Elizabeth Montgomery, who would later play Simon's daughter-in-law, Samantha, on *Bewitched*, made her film debut in *The Court-Martial of Billy Mitchell*.

In 1956, Simon achieved his first significant film role as Dave Goodman, the father of musician Benny Goodman, in *The Benny Goodman Story*. Between 1953 and 1956, Simon appeared in four episodes of *Kraft Television Theatre* and twice in the anthology series *Studio One*.

In 1956 and 1957, he appeared in episodes of *State Trooper*, *The Millionaire* and *M Squad*. In 1957, he appeared as George Nordmann in the feature film *Edge of the City*, starring John Cassavetes and Sidney Poitier. In 1958, Simon guest-starred as Captain Woods in "The Coward of Fort Bennett" on *General Electric Theater*. In 1957 and 1958, he appeared in four episodes of the anthology series, *Playhouse 90*. In 1959, he appeared on *Peter Gunn* and *Adventures in Paradise*.

There were few television westerns in which Simon did not guest star. From 1956 to 1970, he appeared in *Broken Arrow*, *Disneyland*, *Dick Powell's Zane Grey Theater*, *Laramie*, *Black Saddle*, *Law of the Plainsman*, *Johnny Ringo*, *Cheyenne*, and *The Dakotas*, *Wichita Town* (1960) with Joel McCrea, *The Man From Blackhawk*, *The Texan*, *Tombstone Territory*, *Tate*, *Shotgun Slade*, *Stagecoach West*, *Bat Masterson*, *Lawman*, *Klondike*, and *Frontier Circus*, *Have Gun - Will Travel*, *Wagon Train*, *The Legend of Jesse James*, *The Road West*, *Gunsmoke*, *Laredo*, *The Virginian*, *Bonanza*, and *The Guns of Will Sonnett*.

In 1962, he played the part of Mackie in the episode "House of the Hunter" on CBS's *Rawhide*.

Simon appeared as Handy Strong in the acclaimed feature film *The Man Who Shot Liberty Valance*.

Simon appeared in such programs as *Crusader*, *Route 66*, *Dante*, *The DuPont Show with June Allyson*, *Johnny Midnight*, *Straightaway*, *The Roaring 20s*, *Sea Hunt*, and *State Trooper*. In the 1961–1962 season, he appeared on episodes of *The Dick Powell Show*, *The Lloyd Bridges Show*, *Cain's Hundred*, *The Defenders*, and *Sam Benedict*.

Simon guest-starred three times on *Perry Mason.*, including the role of murderer Edward Bannister in the 1958 episode, "The Case of the Desperate Daughter." Simon appeared as Harvey, friend of the main character Paul Driscoll in the 1963 *The Twilight Zone* episode "No Time Like the Past". In 1965, Simon appeared in episodes of *Slattery's People*, *Voyage to the Bottom of the Sea*, and *Dr. Kildare*.

In 1966, Simon starred as Mr. Rellik in the Highway Safety Films' production *The Third Killer*. Simon's role was that of a "Death" salesman charged with three accounts, including traffic fatalities.

In addition to *Bewitched* and *Nancy*, Simon appeared in other sitcoms, such as *McHale's Navy*, *Mrs. G. Goes to College*, *Get Smart*, and *The Andy Griffith Show*.

In 1967, Simon appeared as "Cervantes" in *The Reluctant Astronaut*. He appeared in a 1970 episode of *Love, American Style*, in a 1971 episode of *Nichols*, starring James Garner, and a 1973 episode of *The Partridge Family*. In 1973, he made three guest appearances as General Maynard M. Mitchell on *M*A*S*H*.

From 1969 to 1985, Simon appeared in *Marcus Welby, M.D.*, *The Mod Squad*, *The Interns*, *Barnaby Jones*, *Hawaii Five-O*, *Cannon*, *Ellery Queen*, *Columbo*, *McCloud*, *Quincy M.E.*, *Eight Is Enough*, and *The Feather and Father Gang*. His last television appearance was in a 1985 episode of *Airwolf*.

Simon died of a heart attack in Tarzana, California on November 29, 1992, three days before what would have been his 84th birthday. He is interred at Oakwood Memorial Park Cemetery in Chatsworth, California.

Betty Sinclair

Betty Sinclair was born on February 7, 1907 in Liverpool, England. She was an actress and production manager, known for *City Streets* (1931), *Mr. Muggs Rides Again* (1945), and *Something in the City* (1950).

More of her roles included *Lightnin'* (1930) with Joel McCrea, *Smart Alecks* (1942), *Docks of New York* (1945), *Mister Peepers* (1952), *Robert Montgomery Presents* (1951-1956), *The United States Steel Hour* (1953-1963), *The Jackie Gleason Show* (1966), and *Great Performances* (1971).

She died on September 20, 1983 in Tenafly, New Jersey at age 76.

Alison Skipworth

Alison Skipworth was born Alison Mary Elliott Margaret Groom in London, England July 25, 1863 and was an English stage and screen actress.

Skipworth made her first stage appearance at Daly's Theatre in London in 1894, in *A Gaiety Girl*. Her first American performance came the following year at the Broadway Theatre in New York City. She sang in light opera in *An Artist's Model*. In this production she served as understudy to Marie Tempest. After performing in two London plays, Skipworth returned to the United States, and made it her home. She joined the company of Daniel Frohman at the Lyceum. There she made her debut as *Mrs. Ware* in *The Princess and the Butterfly* in 1897.

In 1905 and 1906 Skipworth toured with Viola Allen in three productions of Shakespeare, *Cymbeline*, *Twelfth Night* and *As You Like It*. In the following years she played with James K. Hackett and John Drew, Jr., among other theatre celebrities. Productions in which she was featured are *The Swan*, *The Enchanted April*, *The Grand Duchess and the Waiter*, *Mrs. Dane's Defence* and *Marseilles*.

She appeared in her first film in 1912, *A Mardi Gras Mix-Up*. The same year she performed in *The Pilgrimage*, *Into the Jungle*, and *A Political Kidnapping*. She excelled in the new sound medium in films which arrived at the close of the 1920s. In 1930 she made her first talkie, *Strictly Unconventional*.

Skipworth appeared opposite W.C. Fields in four films: *If I Had a Million* (1932), *Tillie and Gus* (1933), *Alice in Wonderland* (1933), and *Six of a Kind* (1934). Her later screen credits include *Two in a Crowd* (1936) with Joel McCrea, *The Casino Murder Case*, *The Girl from 10th Avenue*, *King of the Newsboys*, *Wide Open Faces* and *Ladies In Distress*.

Nicknamed *Skippy*, Skipworth resided in an ordinary Hollywood flat, drove a Ford, and drank tea daily in her own garden each afternoon when she was not working.

Alison Skipworth died of natural causes in July 5, 1952 at her home in New York City, three weeks short of her 89th birthday.

Alexis Smith

Alexis Smith and Joel McCrea in *South of St. Louis*

Alexis Smith was born Gladys Smith in Penticton, British Columbia June 8, 1921 and was a Canadian-born stage, film, and television actress. She appeared in several major Hollywood movies in the 1940s and had a notable career on Broadway in the 1970s, winning a Tony Award in 1972.

She first began acting as a teen, in summer stock in Canada before moving with her family to the United States. She was raised in Los Angeles.

After being discovered by a talent scout while attending college, Smith was signed to a contract by Warner Bros. Her earliest film roles were uncredited bit parts, and it took several years for her career to gain momentum. Her first credited role was in the feature film *Dive Bomber* (1941), playing the female lead opposite Errol Flynn. Her appearance in *The Constant Nymph* (1943) was well received and led to bigger parts.

During the 1940s, Smith appeared alongside some of the most popular male stars of the day, including Errol Flynn in *Gentleman Jim* (1942), and *San Antonio* (1945) (in which she sang a special version of the popular ballad "Some Sunday Morning"), Fredric March in *The Adventures of Mark Twain* (1944), Humphrey Bogart in *Conflict* (1945) and *The Two Mrs. Carrolls* (1947), Cary Grant in a sanitized, fictionalized version of the life of Cole and Linda Porter in *Night and Day* (1946), *South of St. Louis* (1949) with Joel McCrea, and Bing Crosby in *Here Comes the Groom* (1951), her favorite role.

She also appeared on the Dean Martin and Jerry Lewis Radio (NBC) broadcast on January 25, 1952.

While Smith was under contract at Warner Bros., she met fellow actor Craig Stevens; they wed in 1944. In later years, Smith toured in several stage hits including the 1955 National company of *Plain and Fancy*, co-starring with her husband in Jean Kerr's *Mary, Mary* and *Cactus Flower*.

Smith appeared on the cover of the May 3, 1971, issue of *Time* as the result of the critical acclaim for her singing and dancing role in Hal Prince's Broadway production of Stephen Sondheim's *Follies*, which marked her long-awaited Broadway debut. In 1972, she won the Tony Award for Best Actress in a Musical for her performance.

Her stage career continued through the 1970s, with appearances in the 1973 all-star revival of *The Women* (1973), the short-lived re-working of William Inge's drama *Picnic*, re-titled *Summer Brave* (1975), and the ill-fated musical *Platinum* (1978), which earned Smith another Tony nomination for her performance but closed after a brief run. She then toured for more than a year as the madam in *The Best Little Whorehouse in Texas*, including a seven-month run in Los Angeles.

Smith returned to the big screen with star billing at the age of 54 in Jacqueline Susann's *Once Is Not Enough* (1975) opposite Kirk Douglas, followed by *The Little Girl Who Lives Down the Lane* with Martin Sheen and Jodie Foster the following year and *Casey's Shadow* with Walter Matthau in 1978.

Smith appeared in six episodes of *The Love Boat* from 1982 to 1985, and had a recurring role on the television series *Dallas* as Clayton Farlow's sister Lady Jessica Montford in 1984, and again in 1990. She also starred in the short-lived 1988 series *Hothouse,* and was nominated for an Emmy Award for her guest appearance on *Cheers* in 1990.

Smith died of brain cancer in Los Angeles June 9, 1993 on the day after her 72nd birthday. She had no children and her sole survivor was her husband of 49 years, actor Craig Stevens. Smith's final film, *The Age of Innocence* (1993), was released shortly after her death. Her body was cremated and her ashes were scattered over the Pacific.

Art Smith

Arthur Gordon "Art" Smith in Chicago, Illinois March 23, 1899 and was an American film stage and television actor, best known for playing supporting roles in the 1940s.

He was a member of the Group Theatre and performed in many of their productions, including *Rocket to the Moon*, *Awake and Sing!*, *Golden Boy* and *Waiting for Lefty*, all by Clifford Odets; *House of Connelly* by Paul Green; and Sidney Kingsley's *Men in White*.

Smith appeared in many black-and-white noirish films in supporting roles alongside more handsome and popular movie leads, such as John Garfield in *Body and Soul* (1947) and Humphrey Bogart in *In a Lonely Place* (1950). In 1957, he originated the role of Doc in the stage version of *West Side Story*.

More of his roles included *None But the Lonely Heart* (1944), *A Tree Grows in Brooklyn* (1945), *Ride the Pink Horse* (1947), *Mr. Peabody and the Mermaid* (1948), *South of St. Louis* (1949) with Joel McCrea, *South Sea Sinner* (1950), *Rose of Cimarron* (1952), *The Hustler* (1961), and *The Moving Finger* (1963).

The grey-haired actor usually played studious types in films. He worked on television in CBS Playhouse (1967) before finally retiring in 1967.

Smith was one of the victims of the Hollywood blacklist, which mostly ended his film career in 1952. He died February 24, 1973, at age 73, in Long Island, New York, from a heart attack.

C. Aubrey Smith

Sir Charles Aubrey Smith was born in London, England July 21, 1863, known to film-goers as C. Aubrey Smith, was an England Test cricketer who became a stage and film actor, acquiring a niche as the officer-and-gentleman type, as in the first sound version of *The Prisoner of Zenda* (1937). In Hollywood, he organized English actors into a cricket team, playing formal matches that much intrigued local spectators.

Smith was born to parents C. J. Smith, a medical doctor and Sarah Ann (*neé* Clode). His sister, Beryl Faber (died 1912), was married to Cosmo Hamilton.

He was educated at Charterhouse School and St John's College, Cambridge. He settled in South Africa to prospect for gold in 1888-1889. While there he developed pneumonia and was wrongly pronounced dead by doctors. He married Isabella Wood in 1896.

As a cricketer, Smith was primarily a right arm fast bowler, though he was also a useful right-hand lower-order batsman and a good slip fielder. He was regarded by his contemporaries as one of the best bowlers to play the game.

His oddly curved bowling run-up, which started from deep mid-off, earned him the nickname "Round the Corner Smith". When he bowled round the wicket his approach was concealed from the batsman by the umpire until he emerged, leading W.G. Grace to comment "it is rather startling when he suddenly appears at the bowling crease." He played for Cambridge University (1882–1885) and for Sussex at various times from 1882 to 1892. While in South Africa he captained the Johannesburg English XI. He captained England to victory in his only Test match, against South Africa at Port Elizabeth in 1888-1889, taking five wickets for nineteen runs in the first innings. The English team who played was by no means representative of the best players of the time and nobody at the time realized that the match would enter the cricket records as an official Test match. In 1932, he founded the Hollywood Cricket Club and created a pitch with imported English grass. He attracted fellow expatriates such as David Niven, Laurence Olivier, Nigel Bruce (who served as captain), Leslie Howard and Boris Karloff to the club as well as local American players.

Smith's stereotypical Englishness spawned several amusing anecdotes: while fielding at slip for the Hollywood Club, he dropped a difficult catch and ordered his English butler to fetch his spectacles; they were brought on to the field on a silver platter. The next ball looped gently to slip, to present the kind of catch that "a child would take at midnight with no moon." Smith dropped it and, snatching off his lenses, commented, "Damned fool brought my reading glasses." Decades after his cricket career had ended, when he had long been a famous face in films, Smith was spotted in the pavilion on a visit to Lord's. "That man over there seems familiar", remarked one member to another. "Yes", said the second, seemingly oblivious to his Hollywood fame, "Chap called Smith. Used to play for Sussex."

He began acting on the London stage in 1895. His first major role was in *The Prisoner of Zenda* the following year, playing the dual lead roles of king and look-alike. Forty-one years later, he appeared in the most acclaimed film version of the novel, this time as the wise old advisor. When Raymond Massey asked him to help him understand the role of Black Michael, he answered "My dear Ray, in my time I have played every part in *The Prisoner of Zenda* except Princess Flavia. And I *always* had trouble with Black Michael!" He made his Broadway debut in a revival of George Bernard Shaw's *Pygmalion* in the starring role of Henry Higgins.

Smith appeared in early films for the nascent British film industry, starring in *The Bump* in 1920 (written by A.A. Milne for the company Minerva Films, which was founded in 1920 by the actor Leslie Howard and his friend and story editor Adrian Brunel). Smith later went to Hollywood where he had a successful career as a character actor playing either officer or gentleman roles. He was also regarded as being the unofficial leader of the British film industry colony in Hollywood, which Sheridan Morley characterized as the Hollywood Raj, a select group of British actors who were seen to be colonizing the capital of the film business in the 1930s. Other film stars considered to be "members" of this select group were David Niven (whom Smith treated like a son), Ronald Colman, Rex Harrison, Robert Coote, Basil Rathbone, Nigel Bruce (whose daughter's wedding he had attended as best man), Leslie Howard (whom Smith had known since working with him on early films in London) and Patric Knowles.

Smith became infamous for expecting his fellow countrymen to report for regular duty at his Hollywood Cricket Club. Anyone who refused was known to "incur his displeasure". Fiercely patriotic, Smith became openly critical of the British actors of enlistment age who did not return to fight after the outbreak of World War II in 1939.

He loved playing on his status as Hollywood's "Englishman in Residence". His bushy eyebrows, beady eyes, handlebar moustache and height of 6'4" made him one of the most recognizable faces in Hollywood. He starred alongside such screen legends as leading ladies Greta Garbo, Elizabeth Taylor and Vivien Leigh and the actors Clark Gable, Laurence Olivier, Ronald Colman, Maurice Chevalier and Gary Cooper. His films include such classics as *The Prisoner of Zenda* (1937), *The Four Feathers* (1939), *Dr. Jekyll and Mr. Hyde* (1941) and *And Then There Were None* (1945) in which he played General Mandrake.

More of his roles included *Such Is the Law* (1930), *Just a Gigolo* (1931), *Tarzan the Ape Man* (1932), *Gambling Lady* (1934) with Joel McCrea, *Lloyd's of London* (1936), *Another Thin Man* (1939), *The Adventures of Mark Twain* (1944), *Terror by Night* (1946), and *Little Women* (1949).

Commander McBragg in the TV cartoon *Tennessee Tuxedo and His Tales* is a parody of him. The cartoon character also appears in *The Simpsons* episode "The Seemingly Never-Ending Story".

Smith died from pneumonia in Beverly Hills December 20, 1948, at age 85. His body was cremated and nine months later, in accordance with his wishes, his ashes were returned to England and interred in his mother's grave at St Leonard's churchyard in Hove, Sussex.

Smith has a star on the Hollywood Walk of Fame and was an officer in the Legion of Frontiersmen. In 1933, he was on the first board of the Screen Actors Guild.

He was appointed a Commander of the Order of the British Empire (CBE) in 1938 and was knighted by King George VI in 1944 for services to Anglo-American amity.

John Smith

John Smith was born Robert Errol Van Orden in Los Angeles, California March 6, 1931 and was an American actor remembered in particular for his leading roles in two NBC western television series, *Cimarron City* and *Laramie.*

A descendant of Peter Stuyvesant, the Dutch governor of New Netherland in the 17th century, Smith was born, to Errol and Margaret Van Orden, graduated from Susan Miller Dorsey High School in Los Angeles and enrolled at the University of California at Los Angeles. He sang with a dance band and played football and basketball and engaged in gymnastics during his school years.

In the early 1940s, Smith joined the Robert Mitchell Boys Choir and appeared in several films, including Bing Crosby's *Going My Way* and *The Bells of St. Mary's,* as an uncredited choir member.

By 1950, he was working as a messenger for Metro-Goldwyn-Mayer and in 1952, the studio cast him as James Stewart's brother in *Carbine Williams,* although the part was uncredited. He was renamed by his agent Henry Willson in contrast to the more exciting names of Willson's other clients as he was "the only John Smith in the business".

In 1954, Smith appeared as the newlywed Milo Buck, opposite Karen Sharpe as Nell Buck, in the Academy Award-winning airplane disaster film, *The High and the Mighty,* starring and produced by John Wayne.

In 1955, Smith played the part of James Earp, older brother of Wyatt Earp in the film *Wichita,* starring Joel McCrea and Vera Miles. That same year, he played the part of Willie McGill or the "Colfax Kid" in the episode "Paper Gunman" of NBC's anthology series *Frontier,* hosted and narrated by Walter Coy.

Smith guest starred in 1955 in the role of John Sontag in the syndicated television series *Stories of the Century,* the first western series to win an Emmy Award. The episode is entitled "Sontag and Evans," referring to Sontag's older partner in crime, Chris Evans, played by Morris Ankrum. Sontag and Evans turn to crime to fight the encroachment of the Southern Pacific Railroad.

In 1956, Smith had a small role as Caleb Cope in the film *Friendly Persuasion,* starring Gary Cooper. He was Jeff Northrup in another 1956 film, *Hot Rod Girl.* He appeared as Thursday October Christian in another film, *The Women of Pitcairn Island.* That same year, he was the lead guest in "The Story of Lucky Swanson" on CBS's fantasy drama, *The Millionaire,* and as a character called "Utah" on *Father Knows Best,* the Robert Young situation comedy. He was further cast in 1956 as Steve Maguire in the episode "The Singing Preacher", with Dick Foran in the lead role, on the religion anthology series, *Crossroads.* He appeared as David in the 1956 episode "Cholera" of CBS's *Gunsmoke.*

In 1957, Smith starred with Fay Spain as a young prizefighter, Tommy Kelly, in the film, *The Crooked Circle.* He was cast as Private Reynolds that year in the picture *Tomahawk Trail,* starring Chuck Connors.

Smith appeared twice on the ABC/Warner Brothers western series, *Colt .45,* starring Wayde Preston. He was cast as The Comanche Kid in "Gallows at Granite Gap" (November 8, 1957), with Virginia Gregg as Martha Naylor and

Stuart Randall, later a recurring character with Smith on *Laramie*, as Sheriff Pat Monohan. The child actor Ken Osmond was cast as Tommy. Smith subsequently appeared on *Colt .45* as Shelby Taylor in "Point of Honor" (March 21, 1958). In this episode Cameron Mitchell portrayed Dr. Alan McMurdo.

In 1958, Smith appeared in the episode "The Irwin Brown Story" of the United States Navy television drama *Men of Annapolis*.

In the 1958–1959 television season, Smith landed a starring role as the blacksmith/deputy sheriff Lane Temple on *Cimarron City*. The episodes rotated among Smith and two other stars, George Montgomery as Mayor Matt Rockford and Audrey Totter as Beth Purcell, the owner of the Cimarron City boarding house.

In 1958, he played the part of Smitty in "Letter of the Weak" in the detective series, Mickey Spillane's *Mike Hammer*, starring Darren McGavin. In 1959, he appeared as Irving Randall in the episode of "A Night with the Boys" of CBS's *Alfred Hitchcock Presents*. That same year, Smith played a pilot, Joe Walker, in the film *Island of Lost Women*.

And in 1959, he was cast as the young rancher Slim Sherman, the lead role on *Laramie* (1959–1963) with Robert Fuller, Hoagy Carmichael, Robert L. Crawford, Jr., Stuart Randall, and later Spring Byington and Dennis Holmes. From their stint on *Laramie*, Smith and Robert Fuller developed a lifelong friendship, until Smith's own death in early 1995. On the first episode of the second season "Queen of Diamonds," he introduced Julie London to Fuller, who also developed a lifelong friendship with Smith's co-star, until London's own death, late in 2000.

In 1964, John Wayne asked director Henry Hathaway to cast Smith in the role of Steve McCabe in Wayne's film *Circus World*. According to a Smith biography, Hathaway developed an intense dislike for Smith for unknown reasons and tried to keep him from working again in Hollywood.

In 1966, Smith guest-starred as Noble Vestry in the short-lived 1966 ABC comedy/western series *The Rounders*, starring Chill Wills. That same year, he played the part of Joe Gore in the film entitlede *Waco*.

In 1967, Smith was cast as Ed Dow in three episodes of ABC's short-lived *Hondo* western series, starring Ralph Taeger. He appeared in three episodes: "Hondo and the Ghost of Ed Dow", "Hondo and the War Cry", and "Hondo and the Eagle Claw.".

In 1968 and 1970, he appeared in two episode of NBC's *The Virginian*, starring James Drury and Doug McClure. In 1972, he appeared in two episodes of Robert Fuller's & Julie London's *Emergency!* in the role of "Captain Hammer." He also appeared in 1968 in an episode of Robert Culp's *I Spy* crime drama. In 1971, he appeared as Dr. Carl Isenburg in the horror film, *Legacy of Blood.*

In 1972, he guest starred on NBC's police drama *Adam-12*. That same year, he had his last film role as Mr. Ames in Walt Disney's *Justin Morgan Had a Horse*. His last television appearances came in 1974 and 1975, when he portrayed different physicians in two episodes of ABC's medical-drama *Marcus Welby, M.D.*, starring Robert Young. And in 1975, he appeared on Angie Dickinson's NBC drama, *Police Woman*.

Smith died on January 25, 1995 at the age of 63 of cirrhosis of the liver and heart problems. He was survived by one daughter. Smith was cremated, and his ashes were scattered at sea.

Abraham Sofaer

Abraham Sofaer was born October 1, 1896 in Rangoon, Burma. [now Yangôn, Myanmar] October 1, 1896 and was an American stage actor who became a familiar supporting player on film and television in his later years. Sofaer's strong features and resonant voice complemented the many exotic character parts he played.

He began his acting career on the London stage in 1921, but soon was alternating between London and Broadway. By the 1930s, he was appearing in both British and American films. Among his more prominent performances were the dual role of the Judge and Surgeon in Powell and Pressburger's *A Matter of Life and Death* (1946) and St. Paul in *Quo Vadis* (1951).

More of his roles included *Little Miss Nobody* (1933), *The House of the Spaniard* (1936), *A Voice in the Night* (1941), *Stairway to Heaven* (1946), *Christopher Columbus* (1949), *Judgment Deferred* (1952), *The First Texan* (1956) with Joel McCrea, *Song Without End* (1960), *4 for Texas* (1963), *The Greatest Story Ever Told* (1965) as Joseph of Arimathaea, *Journey to the Center of Time* (1967), and *Chisum* (1970) Chief White Buffalo.

He also appeared on television from its earliest days in the late 1930s and on radio. Although his film appearances diminished after the 1950s, he continued to have guest roles on dozens of major U.S. television series throughout the 1960s. He appeared again with Joel McCrea in an episode of *Wichita Town* (1960). He made three appearances on *Perry Mason*, including the role of defendant Elihu Laban in the 1963 episode, "The Case of the Two-Faced Turn-a-Bout." He also featured in *Star Trek* ("Charlie X" and "Spectre of the Gun" - voice only), *The Twilight Zone* ("The Mighty Casey"), *Daniel Boone* ("Not in Our Stars"), *Lost in Space* ("The Flaming Planet"), *The Asphalt Jungle* ("The McMasters Story"), and *The Outer Limits* ("Demon with a Glass Hand"), and *Kolchak: The Night Stalker* which was his last role in 1974 before retiring.

He may be best-remembered for his recurring role as Hadji, the master of all genies, on *I Dream of Jeannie* and as The Swami who advises Peter Tork in the "Sauna" scene in The Monkees' 1968 film Head.

Sofaer married Psyche Angela Christian, with whom he had two sons and four daughters. He died in Woodland Hills, Los Angeles, California, as the result of congestive heart failure in January 21, 1988 at age 91.

The noted jurist of the same name is the son of one of the actor's cousins.

Arthur Space

Charles Arthur Space was born in Brunswick, New Jersey October 12, 1908 and was an American film, television, and stage actor. He was best known as Doc Weaver, the veterinarian, in thirty-nine episodes of long-running CBS television series, *Lassie*.

Space began his career in summer stock theater and eventually began appearing on Broadway. He made his film debut in the 1941 crime drama *Riot Squad* opposite Richard Cromwell. The following year, Space appeared alongside Abbott and Costello in *Rio Rita*. He also had roles in *Tortilla Flat* (1942), *The Dancing Masters* (1943) with Laurel and Hardy, *The Big Noise* (1944) again with Laurel and Hardy, *Bud Abbott and Lou Costello in*

Hollywood (1945), *Our Vines Have Tender Grapes* (1945), *The Fuller Brush Man* (1948), and *The Fuller Brush Girl* (1950). In the early 1950s, Space appeared in various film serials including *Government Agents vs. Phantom Legion, Canadian Mounties vs. Atomic Invaders*, and *Panther Girl of the Kongo*.

In 1954, Space played the bandit Black Bart, or Charles Bolles, in an episode of the syndicated western television series *Stories of the Century*.

Throughout the mid-1950s, Space continued appearing in films such as *The Spirit of St. Louis* with James Stewart while guest starring on various television series. He appeared four times as Col. Tomkin in the ABC western series, *Colt .45*, starring Wayde Preston. During this time, Space had a recurring role on *Lassie*. More of his television roles included *The Amos 'n Andy Show* (1952), *Annie Oakley* (1954), *Crusader* (1956), *Broken Arrow* (1957-1958), and *Wichita Town* (1959) with Joel McCrea.

In 1960, Space landed the role of the practical farmer Herbert Brown in the 58-episode NBC television series *National Velvet*, with Lori Martin as his equestrian daughter, Velvet Brown, and Ann Doran as his wife, Martha. After the series ended in 1962, Space continued acting in both television and films. Among his roles were four *Perry Mason* appearances between 1958 and 1964. In his first appearance he played murderer Willard Scott in "The Case of the Rolling Bones," and his final role was as murderer Edgerton Cartwell in "The Case of the Silver Bullets."

More of his later television roles included *The Big Valley* (1965-1968), *The Wild Wild West* (1965-1968), *Ironside* (1968-1972), *The Six Million Dollar Man* (1975), *Baretta* (1978), *Charlie's Angels* (1980), and *Lou Grant* (1978-1981).

His last role was in a 1981 episode of the television series, *Walking Tall*.

He died of cancer at his home Hollywood on January 13, 1983 at the age of 74.

Ned Sparks

Ned Sparks was born Edward Arthur Sparkman in Guelph, Ontario November 19, 1883 and was a Canadian-born character actor. Sparks was well known for his deadpan expression and deep, gravelly voice.

Sparks left home at age 16 and attempted to work as a gold prospector on the Klondike Gold Rush. After running out of money, he won a spot as a singer on a traveling musical company's tour. At age 19, he returned to Canada and briefly attended a Toronto seminary. After leaving the seminary, he worked for the railroad and worked in theater in Toronto. In 1907, he left Toronto to try his hand in the Broadway theatre in New York City.

While working on Broadway, Sparks developed his trademark deadpan expression while portraying the role of a desk clerk in the play *Little Miss Brown*. His success on the stage soon caught the attention of MGM's Louis B. Mayer who signed Sparks to a six picture deal. Sparks began appearing in numerous silent films before finally making his "talkie" debut in the 1928 film *The Big Noise*.

In the 1930s, Sparks became known for portraying dour-faced, sarcastic, cigar-chomping characters. He became so associated with the type that, in 1936, *The New York Times* reported that Sparks had his face insured for

USD$100,000 with Lloyd's of London. The market agreed to pay the sum to any photographer who could capture Sparks smiling (Sparks later admitted that the story was a publicity stunt and he was only insured for $10,000).

Sparks was also caricatured in cartoons including the Jack-in-the-Box character in the Disney short *Broken Toys* (1935), and the jester in *Mother Goose Goes Hollywood* (1938), a hermit crab in both Tex Avery's *Fresh Fish* (1939) Bob Clampett's Goofy Groceries (1941), a chicken in Bob Clampett's *Slap Happy Pappy* (1940) and brief appearances in Friz Freleng's Warner Brothers cartoon *Malibu Beach Party* (1940), and Tex Avery's *Hollywood Steps Out* (1940).

Sparks appeared in ten stage productions and over 80 films. Some of those roles included *The Canary Murder Case* (1929), *Kept Husbands* (1931) with Joel McCrea, *Servants' Entrance* (1934), *Hawaii Calls* (1938), *Stage Door Canteen* (1943), and *Magic Town* (1947).

He retired from films in 1947.

On April 3, 1957, Sparks died of an intestinal blockage in Victorville, California at age 73.

Barbara Stanwyck

Joel McCrea and Barbara Stanwyck in *The Great Man's Lady*

Barbara Stanwyck was born Ruby Catherine Stevens in Brooklyn, New York July 16, 1907 and was an American actress. She was a film and television star, known during her sixty-year career as a consummate and versatile professional with a strong, realistic screen presence, and a favorite of directors including Cecil B. DeMille, Fritz Lang and Frank Capra. After a short but notable career as a stage actress in the late 1920s, she made eighty-five films in thirty-eight years in Hollywood, before turning to television.

Orphaned at the age of four and partially raised in foster homes, by 1944 Stanwyck had become the highest-paid woman in the United States. She was nominated for the Academy Award for Best Actress four times, for *Stella Dallas* (1937), *Ball of Fire* (1941), *Double Indemnity* (1944) and *Sorry, Wrong Number* (1948). For her television work, she won three Emmy Awards, for *The Barbara Stanwyck Show* (1961), *The Big Valley* (1966) and *The Thorn Birds* (1983). *The Thorn Birds* also won her a Golden Globe. She received an Honorary Oscar at the 1982 Academy Award ceremony and the Golden Globe Cecil B. DeMille Award in 1986. She was also the recipient of honorary lifetime awards from the American Film Institute (1987), the Film Society of Lincoln Center (1986), the Los

Angeles Film Critics Association (1981) and the Screen Actors Guild (1967). Stanwyck received a star on the Hollywood Walk of Fame in 1941 and was ranked as the 11th greatest female star of all time in 1999, by the American Film Institute.

She was the fifth and youngest child of Catherine Ann (née McPhee) and Byron E. Stevens. The couple was working class, her father a native of Massachusetts and her mother an immigrant from Nova Scotia. Ruby was of English and Scottish ancestry, by her father and mother, respectively. When she was four, her mother died of complications from a miscarriage after a drunken stranger accidentally knocked her off a moving streetcar. Two weeks after the funeral, Byron Stevens joined a work crew digging the Panama Canal and was never seen again. Ruby and her brother, Byron, were raised by their older sister Mildred, who was only five years older than Ruby. When Mildred got a job as a John Cort showgirl, Ruby and Byron were placed in a series of foster homes (as many as four different homes in a year), from which Ruby often ran away.

During the summers of 1916 and 1917, Ruby toured with Mildred, and practiced her sister's routines backstage. Watching the movies of Pearl White, whom Ruby idolized, also influenced her drive to be a performer. At age 14, she dropped out of school to take a job wrapping packages at a department store in Brooklyn. Ruby never attended high school, although early biographical thumbnail sketches had her attending Brooklyn's famous Erasmus Hall High School. Soon after, she took a job filing cards at the Brooklyn telephone office for a salary of $14 a week, a salary that allowed her to become financially independent. She disliked both jobs; her real interest was to enter show business even as her sister Mildred discouraged the idea. She then took a job cutting dress patterns for *Vogue* magazine, but because customers complained about her work, she was fired. Her next job was as a typist for the Jerome H. Remick Music Company, a job she reportedly enjoyed. However, her continuing ambition was to work in show business and her sister finally gave up trying to dissuade her.

In 1923, a few months before her 16th birthday, Ruby auditioned for a place in the chorus at the Strand Roof, a night club over the Strand Theatre in Times Square. A few months later, she obtained a job as a dancer in the 1922 and 1923 seasons of the Ziegfeld Follies, dancing at the New Amsterdam Theater. "I just wanted to survive and eat and have a nice coat," Stanwyck said. For the next several years, she worked as a chorus girl, performing from midnight to seven a.m. at nightclubs owned by Texas Guinan. She also occasionally served as a dance instructor at a speakeasy for gays and lesbians owned by Guinan. One of her good friends during those years was pianist Oscar Levant, who described her as being "wary of sophisticates and phonies."

In 1926, Billy LaHiff, who owned a popular pub frequented by showpeople, introduced Ruby to impresario Willard Mack. Mack was casting his play *The Noose* and LaHiff suggested that the part of the chorus girl be played by a real chorus girl. Mack agreed and after a successful audition, gave the part to Ruby. She co-starred with actors Rex Cherryman and Wilfred Lucas. As initially staged, the play was not a success. In an effort to improve it, Mack decided to expand Ruby's part to include more pathos. *The Noose* re-opened on October 20, 1926, and became one of the most successful plays of the season, running on Broadway for nine months and 197 performances. At the suggestion of either Mack or David Belasco, Ruby changed her name to Barbara Stanwyck by combining the first name of her character, Barbara Frietchie, with Stanwyck, after the name of another actress in the play, Jane Stanwyck.

Stanwyck became a Broadway star soon after when she was cast in her first leading role in *Burlesque* (1927). She received rave reviews and it was a huge hit. Film actor Pat O'Brien would later say on a talk show in the 1960s: "The greatest Broadway show I ever saw was a play in the 1920s called 'Burlesque'." In Arthur Hopkins' autobiography, *To a Lonely Boy,* he describes how he came about casting Stanwyck, saying: "After some search for the girl, I interviewed a nightclub dancer who had just scored in a small emotional part in a play that did not run (*The Noose*). She seemed to have the quality I wanted, a sort of rough poignancy. She at once displayed more sensitive, easily expressed emotion than I had encountered since Pauline Lord. She and (Hal) Skelly were the perfect team, and they made the play a great success. I had great plans for her, but the Hollywood offers kept coming. There was no competing with them. She became a picture star. She is Barbara Stanwyck." He also describes Stanwyck as "The greatest natural actress of our time," noting with sadness, "One of the theater's great potential actresses was embalmed in celluloid."

Around this time, Stanwyck was summoned by film producer Bob Kane to make a screen test for his upcoming 1927 silent film *Broadway Nights.* She lost the lead role because she could not cry in the screen test but was given a minor part as a fan dancer. This was Stanwyck's first film appearance.

While playing in *Burlesque,* Stanwyck had been introduced to her future husband, actor Frank Fay, by Oscar Levant. Stanwyck and Fay were married on August 26, 1928, and soon moved to Hollywood.

Stanwyck's first sound film was *The Locked Door* (1929), followed by *Mexicali Rose,* released in the same year. Neither film was successful; nonetheless, Frank Capra chose Stanwyck for his *Ladies of Leisure* (1930). Numerous prominent roles followed, among them the children's nurse who saves two little girls from being gradually starved to death by Clark Gable's vicious character in *Night Nurse* (1931); *So Big!*, as a valiant midwest farm woman (1932); *Shopworn* 1932; the ambitious woman from "the wrong side of the tracks" in *Baby Face* (1933); the title character in *Gambling Lady* (1934) with Joel McCrea, again with Joel McCrea in *Banjo on My Knee* (1936), the self-sacrificing title character in *Stella Dallas* (1937); *Internes Can't Take Money* (1937) also with Joel McCrea, Molly Monahan in *Union Pacific* (1939) a fourth with with Joel McCrea; the con artist who falls for her intended victim (played by Henry Fonda) in *The Lady Eve* (1941); the extremely successful, independent doctor Helen Hunt in *You Belong to Me* (1941) also with Fonda; a nightclub performer who gives a professor (played by Gary Cooper) a better understanding of "modern English" in the comedy *Ball of Fire* (1941); *The Great Man's Lady* (1942) a fifth with Joel McCrea, the woman who talks an infatuated insurance salesman (Fred MacMurray) into killing her husband in *Double Indemnity* (1944); the columnist caught up in white lies and a holiday romance in *Christmas in Connecticut* (1945); and the doomed wife in *Sorry, Wrong Number* (1948). She also played a doomed concert pianist in *The Other Love* (1947); the piano music was played by Ania Dorfmann, who drilled Stanwyck for three hours a day until she was able to move her arms and hands to match the music. Stanwyck was reportedly one of the many actresses considered for the role of Scarlett O'Hara in *Gone with the Wind* (1939), although she did not receive a screen test. In 1944, Stanwyck was the highest-paid woman in the United States.

Many of her roles involved strong characters. In *Double Indemnity,* Stanwyck brought out the cruel nature of the "grim, unflinching murderess," marking her as the "most notorious femme" in the film noir genre. Yet, Stanwyck was known for her accessibility and kindness to the backstage crew on any film set. She knew the names of their wives and children. Frank Capra said of Stanwyck: "She was destined to be beloved by all directors, actors, crews and extras. In a Hollywood popularity contest she would win first prize hands down."

William Holden and Stanwyck were friends of long standing. When Stanwyck and Holden were presenting the Best Sound Oscar, Holden paused to pay a special tribute to her for saving his career when Holden was cast in the lead for *Golden Boy* (1939). After a series of unsteady daily performances, he was about to be fired, but Stanwyck staunchly defended him, successfully standing up to the film producers. Shortly after Holden's death, Stanwyck recalled the moment when receiving her honorary Oscar: "A few years ago I stood on this stage with William Holden as a presenter. I loved him very much, and I miss him. He always wished that I would get an Oscar. And so tonight, my golden boy, you got your wish".

She appeared in a few westerns such as *Cattle Queen of Montana* (1954), *The Maverick Queen* (1956), *Trooper Hook* (1957) a fifth film with Joel McCrea, and *Forty Guns* (1957).

When Stanwyck's film career declined in 1957, she moved to television. Her 1961–1962 series *The Barbara Stanwyck Show* was not a ratings success but earned her an Emmy Award. The 1965–1969 Western series *The Big Valley* on ABC made her one of the most popular actresses on television, winning her another Emmy. She was billed as "Miss Barbara Stanwyck". She also appeared in the television series, *The Untouchables* with Robert Stack. She appeared in 1963 episode of *Wagon Train*, the "Molly Kincaid Story", and alongside Elvis Presley in the movie *Roustabout* in 1964.

Years later, Stanwyck earned her third Emmy for *The Thorn Birds*. In 1985, she made three guest appearances in the primetime soap opera *Dynasty* prior to the launch of its short-lived spin-off series *The Colbys* in which she starred alongside Charlton Heston, Stephanie Beacham, and Katharine Ross. Unhappy with the experience, Stanwyck remained with the series for only one season (it lasted for two), and her role as Constance Colby Patterson, who was killed off in the series, would prove to be her last. Earl Hamner, Jr. (producer of *The Waltons*) had initially wanted Stanwyck for the lead role of Angela Channing on the 1980s soap opera *Falcon Crest*, but she turned it down and the role went to her best friend, Jane Wyman.

While playing in *The Noose*, Stanwyck fell in love with her married co-star, Rex Cherryman, who became her fiancé in 1928. Cherryman had become ill early in 1928 and his doctor advised him to take a sea voyage to Paris where he and Stanwyck had arranged to meet. While still at sea, he died of septic poisoning, at the age of 31.

On August 26, 1928, Stanwyck married her *Burlesque* co-star, Frank Fay. She and Fay later claimed that they disliked each other at first, but became close after the sudden death of Cherryman. A botched abortion at age fifteen had resulted in complications which left Stanwyck unable to have children. After moving to Hollywood, the couple adopted a son, Dion Anthony "Tony" Fay, on December 5, 1932. The marriage was a troubled one. Fay's successful career on Broadway did not translate to the big screen, whereas Stanwyck achieved Hollywood stardom. Fay engaged in physical confrontations with his young wife, especially when he was inebriated. The couple divorced on December 30, 1935. Stanwyck won custody of their troubled adoptive son whom she had raised with a strict authoritarian hand and demanding expectations. Stanwyck and her son were estranged after his childhood, meeting only a few times after he became an adult. The child whom she had adopted in infancy, "resembled her in just one respect: both were, effectively orphans."

In 1936, while making the film *His Brother's Wife* (1936), Stanwyck became involved with her co-star, Robert Taylor. Rather than a torrid romance, their relationship was more one of mentor and pupil. Stanwyck served as support and adviser to the younger Taylor, a transplant from a small Nebraska town, guiding his career and acclimating him to the sophisticated Hollywood culture. The couple began living together, sparking newspaper reports about the two. Stanwyck was hesitant to remarry after the failure of her first marriage. However, their 1939 marriage was arranged with the help of Taylor's studio Metro-Goldwyn-Mayer, a common practice in Hollywood's golden age. Louis B. Mayer had insisted on the two stars marrying and went as far as presiding over arrangements at the wedding. She and Taylor enjoyed time together outdoors during the early years of their marriage, and owned acres of prime West Los Angeles property. Their large ranch and home in the Mandeville Canyon section of Brentwood, Los Angeles, is still referred to by the locals as the old "Robert Taylor ranch."

In 1950, Stanwyck and Taylor mutually decided to divorce, and after his insistence, she proceeded with the official filing of the papers. There have been many rumors regarding the cause of their divorce, but after World War II, Taylor had attempted to create a life away from Hollywood, a goal that Stanwyck did not share. After the divorce, they acted together in Stanwyck's last feature film, *The Night Walker* (1964). Stanwyck never remarried and cited Taylor as the love of her life, according to her friend and *Big Valley* co-star, Linda Evans. She took his death in 1969 very hard and took a long break from film and television work.

Stanwyck was one of the most well-liked actors in Hollywood and was friends with many of her fellow actors (as well as crew members of her films and TV shows), including Joel McCrea and his wife Frances Dee, George Brent, Robert Preston, Henry Fonda (who had a lifelong crush on her), James Stewart, Linda Evans, Joan Crawford, Jack Benny and his wife Mary Livingstone, William Holden, Gary Cooper, Fred McMurray, and many others.

Stanwyck had a romantic affair with actor Robert Wagner, whom she met on the set of *Titanic* (1953). Wagner, who was 22, and Stanwyck, who was 45 at the beginning of the relationship, had a four-year romance, which is described in Wagner's memoir, *Pieces of My Heart* (2008). Stanwyck ended the relationship. In the 1950s, Stanwyck also, reportedly, had a one-night-stand with the much younger Farley Granger, which he wrote about in his autobiography *Include Me Out: My Life from Goldwyn to Broadway* (2007).

Stanwyck's retirement years were active, with charity work outside the limelight. She was robbed and assaulted inside her Beverly Hills home in 1981. The following year, while filming *The Thorn Birds*, the inhalation of special-effects smoke on the set may have caused her to contract bronchitis. The illness was compounded by her cigarette habit; she had been a smoker from age nine until four years before her death.

Stanwyck died on January 20, 1990 of congestive heart failure and chronic obstructive pulmonary disease at age 82 at Saint John's Health Center. She had indicated that she wished for no funeral service. In accordance with her wishes, her remains were cremated and the ashes scattered from a helicopter over Lone Pine, California, where she had made some of her western films.

Ron Starr

Joel McCrea and Ron Starr in *Ride the High Country*

Ron Starr was born Ronald Starr on March 10, 1942 in Los Angeles, California. He is an actor, known for *G.I. Blues* (1960) with Elvis, *Ride the High Country* (1962) with Joel McCrea, and *This Is Not a Test* (1962).

More of his roles included *M Squad* (1959), *The Texan* (1960), *The Deputy* (1960), *The Tall Man* (1961), *Perry Mason* (1963), *Bonanza* (1964), *I Spy* (1965), and *Angels Hard as They Come* (1971).

He is the father, with Meg Foster, of Christopher Starr.

Sally Starr

Sally Starr was born Sarah Kathryn Sturm in Pittsburgh, Pennsylvania January 23, 1909 and was a movie actress.

She was a Broadway actress before making her debut in motion pictures. She performed on stage from the age of fourteen. Starr debuted in *Frolics* featuring Ted Lewis as a teenager. She later appeared in George White's Scandals of 1924.

When Starr came to Hollywood she signed a contract with MGM. She played leading roles in *So This Is College* (1929) with Joel McCrea, *The Woman Racket* (1930), *Not So Dumb* (1930), *Personality* (1930), *Pardon My Gun* (1930) and *For The Love o' Lil* (1930). Starr was signed among the cast of *Swing High* (1930), a production of Pathe Pictures.

Starr continued her theatrical performances after her motion picture career began. She played with Eleanor Powell and George Hassell in *The Optimists*, staged at the Century Roof Theater in January 1928. The same year she was cast with Elliott Nugent, Robert Montgomery, and Phyllis Crane in *College Life*. Her final films are *Meet The Bride* (1937), *Getting An Eyeful* (1938), *Love and Onions* (1938), and *Money on Your Life* (1938).

She died May 5, 1996 age 87 in South Park Township, Allegheny County, Pennsylvania.

Jack Starrett

Jack Starrett was born Claude Ennis Starrett, Jr. in Refugio, Texas November 2, 1936 and was an American actor and film director. Starrett is perhaps best known for his role as *Gabby Johnson*, a parody of George "Gabby" Hayes, in the 1974 classic parody film *Blazing Saddles* and is also known for his role as the brutal deputy Art Galt in the 1982 action film *First Blood*. He also played the cruel foreman Swick in *The River*. Starrett was often typecast as a tough-talking police officer and played essentially the same character in a trio of biker films: *The Born Losers* (the film that introduced Billy Jack), *Hells Angels on Wheels* (both from 1967), and *Angels from Hell* (1968). He acted in another biker film, *Hell's Bloody Devils* (1970), and directed two more: *Run, Angel, Run* in 1969 and *Nam's Angels* (1970). He also appeared in *Cry Blood, Apache* (1970) with Joel and Jody McCrea.

He was raised in Refugio, Texas and worked in the oil fields before coming to Hollywood.

Starrett starred in the 1961 film *Like Father Like Son* as Coach Jennings, and later reprised the role in *The Young Sinner* in 1965 and *Like Father Like Son* in 1987.

Valerie Starrett, Jack's wife stated that Jack had always wished to direct rather than act. He made an uncredited first attempt at direction when the original director of *The Girls from Thunder Strip*.

Through his career, Starrett directed feature films and episodes of television programs. In addition, he made guest appearances on TV shows including *Hill Street Blues*, *Hunter*, *The A-Team*, and *Knight Rider* (in which he made three guest appearances as different characters.)

Starrett died March 27, 1989 from renal failure in Sherman Oaks, California at the age of 52. At the time of his death he was married to Valerie Starrett. His daughter is Jennifer Starrett, who is also an actress.

Myrtle Stedman

Myrtle Stedman was born in Chicago, Illinois March 3, 1883 was a leading lady and later character actress in motion pictures beginning in silent films in 1910. She was educated at a private finishing school. Miss Stedman performed in light opera and musical comedies. Her voice was cultivated in France. Her tutor was Marchesi, who was known as one of the finest instructors of voice culture in his country. Myrtle did not enter the field of light opera because of her preference for light opera. She starred for a number of seasons in *Isle of Spice* and *The Chocolate Soldier*. She performed for a year at the Whitney Theater in Chicago and was a prima donna of the Chicago Grand Opera Company.

Her first appearances in movies were in Selig studio western and action short films. Among her feature films are *Flaming Youth*, *The Valley of the Moon*, *The Dangerous Age*, and *The Famous Mrs. Fair*. In 1936, she was signed by Warner Brothers to play bit and extra roles. More of her roles included *The Man in the Shadow* (1926), *The Jazz Age* (1929) with Joel McCrea, *Forbidden Company* (1932), *Song of the Saddle* (1936), *Expensive Husbands* (1937), and *Love, Honor and Behave* (1938).

Her last release was *Accidents Will Happen*, in 1938.

Myrtle Stedman died of a heart attack in Hollywood, California in January 8, 1938 at the age of 54. Interment at Inglewood Park Cemetery, Inglewood California. Her husband Marshall Stedman was a drama school conductor. They were divorced by 1920. Their son Lincoln Stedman was a prolific silent film character actor.

Bob Steele

Joel McCrea and Bob Steele in *Cattle Drive*

Bob Steele was born Robert Adrian Bradbury January 23, 1907, and was an American actor. He was born in Portland, Oregon, into a vaudeville family. After years of touring, the family settled down in Hollywood in the late 1910s, where his father, Robert N. Bradbury, soon found work in the movies, first as an actor, later as a director, and by 1920, he hired Bob and his twin brother Bill (1907–1971) as juvenile leads for a series of adventure movies titled *The Adventures of Bob and Bill*.

Bob's career began to take off for good in 1927, when he was hired by production company Film Booking Offices of America (FBO) to star in a series of Westerns. Bob, who was re-christened Bob Steele at FBO, soon made a name for himself, and in the late 1920s, 1930s, and 1940s starred in B-Westerns for almost every minor film studio, including Monogram, Supreme, Tiffany, Syndicate, Republic (including several films of the *Three Mesquiteers* series) and Producers Releasing Corporation (PRC) (including the initial films of their "Billy the Kid" series), plus he had the occasional role in an A-movie, as in the adaptation of John Steinbeck's novel, *Of Mice and Men* from 1939.

In the 1940s, Bob's career as a cowboy hero was on the decline, but he kept himself working by accepting supporting roles in many big movies like Howard Hawks' *The Big Sleep* (1946), or the John Wayne vehicles *Island in the Sky* (1953), *Rio Bravo* (1959), *The Comancheros* (1961), *The Longest Day* (1962), *McLintock!* (1963), and *Rio Lobo* (1970).

Besides these he also made occasional appearances in science fiction films like *Atomic Submarine* (1959) and *Giant from the Unknown* (1958) and did lots of television work, culminating in a regular supporting role in the army comedy *F Troop* (1965–1967), which allowed him to show his comic talent. Steele played the character of Trooper Duffy, who claimed to have been "shoulder to shoulder with Davy Crockett at the Alamo". In fact Steele played in *Davy Crockett at the Fall of the Alamo* in 1926.

Other notable roles over the years included *Westward Ho* (1942), *Fort Worth* (1951), *Cattle Drive* (1951) with Joel McCrea, *The Spoilers* (1955), *The Life and Legend of Wyatt Earp* (1955), *Decision at Sundown* (1957), *Pork Chop Hill* (1959), *National Velvet* (1960), *4 for Texas* (1963), *Taggart* (1964), *The Bounty Killer* (1965), *Something Big* (1971), *Charley Varrick* (1973), and *Nightmare Honeymoon* (1974).

He worked with Audie Murphy in *Column South* (1953), *Drums Across the River* (1954), *Ride a Crooked Trail* (1958), *No Name on the Bullet* (1959), *Hell Bent for Leather* (1960), *Whispering Smith* (1961), *Six Black Horses* (1962), *Showdown* (1963), and *Bullet for a Badman* (1964),

Bob Steele died on December 21, 1989, from emphysema after a long sickness.

Carolyn Stellar

Carolyn Stellar was born Carolyn Golda Underwood on November 6, 1934 in San Francisco, California. She is an actress and costume designer, known for *Cry Blood, Apache* (1970), *Brock's Last Case* (1973), and *Devil Times Five* (1974).

More of her roles included *The Love God?* (1969), *My Three Sons* (1970-1972), *Aloha Means Goodbye* (1974), *Police Story* (1975), *Police Woman* (1975), *Walking Tall Part II* (1975), *God's Gun* (1976), *Sgt. Pepper's Lonely Hearts Club Band* (1978), and *Knots Landing* (1983).

She was previously married to Rick Nervick and John Stellern. Together with Rick Nervick, their children are actor/singer Leif Garrett and actress Dawn Lynn.

Karel Štěpánek

Karel Štěpánek was born October 29, 1899 in Brünn, Austria-Hungary [now Brno, Czech Republic] Though born in Czechoslovakia, actor Karel Stepanek was generally regarded as a German actor due to his extensive film work in Germany (as Karl Stepanek) in the years before World War II.

Stepanek fled to England in 1940, where, like many European refugee actors, he specialized in portraying Teutonic villains. He tried to stay away from out-and-out Nazi roles, but his predilection for wearing black uniforms and barking out guttural commands left little doubt as to the political preferences of Stepanek's screen characters. One of his most typical characterizations could be found in the 1946 POW drama, *The Captive Heart*; Stepanek also registered well as a friendlier foreigner in *The Fallen Idol* (1949).

More of his roles included *The Unknown* (1936), *Another Experience* (1940), *They Met in the Dark* (1943), *Give Us This Day* (1949), *Shoot First* (1953) with Joel McCrea, *Private's Progress* (1956), *The Adventures of Robin Hood* (1956-1957), *The 2nd Best Secret Agent in the Whole Wide World* (1965), *The Frozen Dead* (1966), *Before Winter Comes* (1969), and *Been Down So Long It Looks Like Up to Me* (1971).

Commuting between London and Hollywood, Karel Stepanek continued to fight World War II, usually on the wrong side, into such 1960s films as *Sink the Bismarck!* (1960), *I Aim at the Stars* (1960) and *Operation Crossbow* (1965).

Henry Stephenson

Henry Stephenson was born Harry Stephenson Garraway in Grenada, British West Indies. April 16, 1871, sometimes credited as Harry Stephenson, was a British stage and film actor.

He Stephenson was educated in Britain and started acting in his twenties. He made his Broadway debut in 1901, playing the messenger in *A Message from Mars*.

He appeared in a few silent films, but made his mark in talkies, starting in 1932. That year, he played tycoon 'C.B.' Gaerste in *Red-Headed Woman* with Jean Harlow, Doctor Alliott in *A Bill of Divorcement*, as well as John Tring in *Cynara* (1932), a role Stephenson had successfully portrayed, a year earlier, on stage. He received excellent reviews for his work in *Cynara*. The following year, the English-born actor appeared as the intimidating yet warm-hearted Mr. Laurence in *Little Women*.

He eventually appeared in ninety films from 1917 to 1951, mostly portraying British Gentlemen. Some of his roles included *The Richest Girl in the World* (1934) with Joel McCrea, *Captain Blood* (1935), *The Charge of the Light Brigade* (1936), *The Adventures of Sherlock Holmes* (1939), *Rings on Her Fingers* (1942), *The Hour Before the Dawn* (1944) with Veronica Lake, *Tarzan and the Amazons* (1945), *Time Out of Mind* (1947), *Oliver Twist* (1948), and *Challenge to Lassie* (1949).

He appeared in two television programs before retiring. Those shows were *Pulitzer Prize Playhouse* (1951) and *Studio One in Hollywood* (1951).

He married actress Ann Shoemaker. They had one daughter. Henry Stephenson died in San Francisco, California on April 24, 1956, after a long illness at 85. He was survived by Ann and his daughter.

James Stephenson

James Albert Stephenson in Selby, Yorkshire, England April 14, 1889 and was a British actor. The son of chemist and druggist John G. Stephenson and Emma Stephenson, James Stephenson grew up in the West Riding of Yorkshire and Burnley, Lancashire, with his brothers, Alan and Norman. He became a bank clerk and later had a career as a merchant. In the 1930s, he immigrated to the United States and took U.S. nationality in 1938.

British stage actor James Stephenson made his film debut in 1937 at the age of 48 initially with parts in four films. Warner Brothers signed him the following year, and he began playing urbane villains and disgraced gentlemen.

Some of his roles included *The Perfect Crime* (1937), *Cowboy from Brooklyn* (1938), *Espionage Agent* (1939) with Joel McCrea, and *The Sea Hawk* (1940).

Stephenson's big break came when director William Wyler cast him, in spite of studio resistance, in *The Letter* (1940) opposite Bette Davis. He was nominated for an Academy Award for Best Supporting Actor for that role. Later that year he played the title role in *Calling Philo Vance*, and in 1941 he was first-billed in *Shining Victory*, in which he played the character of Dr. Paul Venner.

Just as Stephenson's acting career was starting to rise he died July 29, 1941 due to a heart attack at the age of 52 in Pacific Palisades, California . His wife was Lorna Anderson Stephenson.

John Stephenson

August John Stephenson was born August 9, 1923, in Kenosha, Wisconsin, and is a veteran voice actor, dating back to network radio in the 1950's.

In the 1950s and 1960s, Stephenson was a frequent announcer/narrator on early television series, serving as the closing credits announcer on *I Love Lucy* (1951-1957) and the voice on the 1967 version *Dragnet* (1967-1969) who solemnly intoned, "And now, the results of the trial." He also supplied countless cartoon voices for Hanna-Barbera, including Mr. Slate in *The Flintstones* (1960-1966) and additional voices for the cartoon series *Abbott & Costello* (1967), *Darkwing Duck* (1991), *Duck Dodgers* (2003), and *Scooby-Doo! Abracadabra-Doo* (2010).

Some of his live-action roles include *The Lone Ranger* (1954), *I Died a Thousand Times* (1955), *The People's Choice* (1955-1958), *Wichita Town* (1959) with Joel McCrea, *Whispering Smith* (1961) with Audie Murphy, *The Beverly Hillbillies* (1963-1964), *F Troop* (1965), *Get Smart* (1965), *Green Acres* (1966), *Iron Horse* (1967), *Hellfighters* (1968), *Hogan's Heroes* (1965-1970), *Mission: Impossible* (1972), *McMillan & Wife* (1973), *Herbie Rides Again* (1974), *The Streets of San Francisco* (1975), and *Lou Grant* (1977).

John Stephenson died December 29, 2012 at age 89.

K.T Stevens

K. T. Stevens was born Gloria Wood July 20, 1919, in Los Angeles, California, and was an American film actress. The daughter of director Sam Wood, Stevens made her first film appearance when she was just two years old in her father's second 1921 silent film, *Peck's Bad Boy*.

As an adult, she changed her name to distance herself from her father's fame. In 1946, Stevens married actor Hugh Marlowe. They divorced in 1968. She and Marlowe were the parents of two sons. Stevens and Marlowe acted in the Broadway production of *Laura* in which, credited as "A Girl" so as not to alert the audience, she played the part filmed by Gene Tierney. Marlowe played the detective that Dana Andrews played in the film.

Stevens appeared in a number of films in the 1940s and 1950s, including *The Great Man's Lady* (1942) with Joel McCrea and Barbara Stanwyck, *Address Unknown* (1944), *Port of New York* (1949) with Yul Brynner, *Harriet Craig* (1950) with Joan Crawford, *Tumbleweed* (1953) with Audie Murphy, *Jungle Hell* (1956), and *Missile to the Moon* (1958).

In addition, she acted on episodic television in such series as *The Brothers Brannagan* (1961), and appeared on the daytime soap opera *The Young and the Restless* (1976-1980) as the veiled facially burned Vanessa Prentiss.

Additional roles included *The Rifleman* (1960-1963), *Iron Horse* (1966), *Adam-12* (1975), *Buck Rogers in the 25th Century* (1979), *They're Playing with Fire* (1984, and *Knots Landing* (1989).

Her last film role before her death June 13, 1994, from lung cancer was in the 1994 Whoopi Goldberg film *Corrina, Corrina*.

Mark Stevens

Mark Stevens was born Richard William Stevens in Cleveland, Ohio December 13, 1916 and was an American actor.

He first studied to become a painter before becoming active in theater work. He then launched a radio career as an announcer in Akron, Ohio.

Moving to Hollywood, he became a Warner Brothers contract actor at $100 a week in 1943. The studio darkened and straightened his curly ginger-colored hair and covered his freckles. At first he was billed as Stephen Richards, but it was changed to Mark Stevens at the suggestion of Darryl Zanuck when he moved to 20th Century Fox.

Stevens emerged as a film noir leading man in such films as *Within These Walls* (1945) and *The Dark Corner* (1946), the latter pairing him with Lucille Ball. In 1946 exhibitors voted him the fifth-most promising "star of tomorrow".

He played an FBI man going undercover to arrest a gangster played by Richard Widmark in *The Street With No Name* (1948), and appeared as Olivia de Havilland's loyal husband in *The Snake Pit* (1948). Stevens also performed in musicals including *I Wonder Who's Kissing Her Now?* (1947) and *Oh, You Beautiful Doll* (1949).

In 1951, he starred in the DuMont series *News Gal* which was later syndicated on ABC in 1957. From 1954-1956 he played a newspaper managing editor in the CBS Television series *Big Town*, having replaced Patrick McVey, who starred in the role from 1950-1954. Reruns of *Big Town* began airing on DuMont under the title *City Assignment* while new episodes of the series were still appearing on CBS.

In the 1950s Stevens was also a television actor, producer and writer. He also directed and starred in four features, notably a 1956 crime film, *Time Table*. He later worked in semi-retirement in the 1960s in Europe.

Some of his later roles included Gunsight Ridge (1957) with Joel McCrea, Gunsmoke in Tucson (1958), Escape from Hell Island (1963), Spain Again (1969), S.W.A.T. (1976), *Murder, She Wrote* (1986), and *Magnum, P.I.* (1987).

On September 15, 1994, Stevens died of cancer in Majores, Spain, at the age of 77.

For his contribution to the television industry, Mark Stevens has a star on Hollywood's Walk of Fame, located at 6637 Hollywood Blvd.

Naomi Stevens

Naomi Stevens was born in Trenton, New Jersey November 29, 1926 and is an American prolific character actress of film and television from the 1950s through the 1980s. She has appeared in almost 100 roles over the years, usually depicting someone's ethnic mother, or neighbor. Her most frequent characterizations were Italian, Jewish, Latin, or East European, and often with a comic touch.

Co-starring with Jack Lemmon and Shirley MacLaine in *The Apartment* (1960) she gives advice on living as the wife of Dr. Dreyfus, Baxter's neighbor, who is commandeered by C.C. Baxter to revive a mistress, Fran Kubelik, of his married boss. The young woman has taken an overdose of sleeping pills to combat her feelings of rejection and futility. Ms. Stevens is the supportive "Jewish mother," intent on scolding Baxter (who she thinks is the offender) while she shores up the flagging spirits of the victim.

More of her roles included *Cheyenne* (1957), *Wichita Town* (1960) with Joel McCrea, *Twilight Zone* (1960), *Have Gun - Will Travel* (1957-1962), *Perry Mason* (1961-1964), *My Favorite Martian* (1965), *The Fugitive* (1966), *The Shakiest Gun in the West* (1968), *Adam-12* (1969), *Love, American Style* (1969-1973), *Kolchak: The Night Stalker* (1974), *The Montefuscos* (1975), *Vega$* (1978-1979), *Trapper John, M.D.* (1984), and *To Heal a Nation* (1988).

Onslow Stevens

Onslow Stevens was born Onslow Ford Stevenson in Los Angeles, California March 29, 1902 and was an American stage, television, and film actor.

He was the son of character actor Houseley Stevenson. Stevens became involved in performing in 1928, appearing in *Under the Roof* at the Pasadena Community Playhouse, where his entire family worked as performers, directors, and teachers. His first major success came from his performance in the Broadway play *Stage Door*. He then went on to star in over eighty films, at first as the lead actor, but mostly in character roles later in his career.

Some of his roles included *Heroes of the West* (1932), *Once in a Lifetime* (1932) with Alan Ladd, *This Side of Heaven* (1934), *The Three Musketeers* (1935), *The Man Who Wouldn't Talk* (1940), *House of Dracula* (1945), *O.S.S.* (1946) again with Alan Ladd, *Night Has a Thousand Eyes* (1948), *Lorna Doone* (1951), *The San Francisco Story* (1952) with Joel McCrea, *Fangs of the Wild* (1954), *Tribute to a Bad Man* (1956), *The Ten Commandments* (1956), *Wanted: Dead or Alive* (1958), *Gunsmoke* (1959), *All the Fine Young Cannibals* (1960), and *The Couch* (1962).

He spent the last years of his life in a nursing home in Van Nuys, Los Angeles, California. He died of pneumonia January 5, 1977 after suffering a broken hip at the age of 74. His interment was located in Valhalla Memorial Park Cemetery with an unmarked grave.

For his contribution to the motion picture industry, Onslow Stevens has a star on the Hollywood Walk of Fame at 6349 Hollywood Boulevard.

Hayden Stevenson

Hayden Stevenson was born in Georgetown, Kentucky July 2, 1877 and was an American film actor. He appeared in 108 films between 1915 and 1942.

Some of those roles included *I'll Show You the Town* (1925), *Man, Woman and Sin* (1927), *Freedom of the Press* (1928) with Joel McCrea, *The Lightning Warrior* (1931), *Love Me Forever* (1935), The Light That Failed (1939), and *Reap the Wild Wind* (1942).

He died January 31, 1952 in Los Angeles, California at age 74.

Houseley Stevenson

Houseley Stevenson was born July 30, 1879 in London, England, and was a British-born American character actor.

He labored in a San Francisco glass factory until his thirties, and then embarked on an acting career. He became a respected teacher, director, and performer at famed Pasadena Community Playhouse in California. He appeared in numerous films in the Thirties and Forties, his craggy face enlivening many movies.

Some of those films included *Bengal Tiger* (1936), *The Adventurous Blonde* (1937), *The Body Disappears* (1941), *Happy Land* (1943), *Without Reservations* (1946), *Ramrod* (1947) with Joel McCrea, *The Ghost and Mrs. Muir* (1947), *Four Faces West* (1948), *Knock on Any Door* (1949), *Colorado Territory* (1949), *Sierra* (1950) with Audie Murphy, *The Gunfighter* (1950), *Hollywood Story* (1951), *The Wild North* (1952), and *Oklahoma Annie* (1952).

Several of his children had effective careers in front of or behind the camera, including actor Onslow Stevens and actor-editor Houseley Stevenson, Jr.

He died August 6, 1953, at age 74 in Duarte, Los Angeles County, California.

Eleanor Stewart

Eleanor Stewart was born in Chicago, Illinois February 2, 1913 and was an American film actress of the 1930s and 1940s, appearing mostly in western films.

Stewart attended Northwestern University, and after winning a talent contest, moved to Hollywood in the mid-1930s. Initially on contract with MGM, she eventually worked freelance for various studios, starring often as the heroine opposite Bob Steele, Tex Ritter, Jack Randall, Bob Custer, Ken Maynard and Tom Keene, among others. She is probably best known for her role in the serial *The Fighting Devil Dogs*, which was released throughout 1938. During the 1940s she did three Hopalong Cassidy films.

More of her roles included *The Gun Ranger* (1936), *The Rangers Step In* (1937), *The Mexicali Kid* (1938), *Flaming Lead* (1939), *Waterloo Bridge* (1940), *Pirates on Horseback* (1941), *The Great Man's Lady* (1942) with Joel McCrea, and *Frenchman's Creek* (1944).

During World War II, she was a Gray Lady volunteer at the Veterans Administration Hospital in Los Angeles. She was also a voice actor and a writer. She was the author of *A Fair Vision*, a book about the Pilgrims. Her career spanned a total of thirty six films. Retiring from film in the 1940s, her last role of the era was in the 1944 Hopalong Cassidy film *Mystery Man*. She had no acting roles until 1979, when she played a small role in the film *The Orphan*.

Twice married, she had one child, a daughter, Karen Peterson, from her first marriage to MGM publicity man Les Peterson. Her second marriage was to Maurice Greiner, from 1991 until her death. She died July 4, 2007 from complications of Alzheimer's disease, at the age of 94.

Janet Stewart

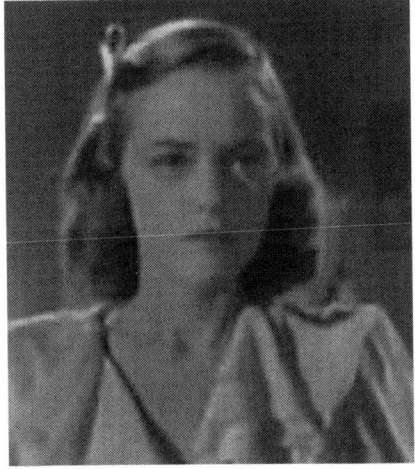

Janet Stewart is an actress, known for *Strangers on a Train* (1951), *Small Town Girl* (1953), and *The Andy Griffith Show* (1960).

More of her roles included *Goodbye, My Fancy* (1951), *Dragnet* (1952), *Girls in the Night* (1953), *Them!* (1954), *A Man Called Peter* (1955), *Perry Mason* (1957), *Richard Diamond, Private Detective* (1959), and *Wichita Town* (1960) with Joel McCrea.

Peggy Stewart

Peggy Stewart was born Margaret O'Rourke in West Palm Beach, Florida June 5, 1923 and is an American actress known for her roles in Western B movies and television series.

She distinguished herself as a swimming champion in high school; her sister, Patricia O'Rourke, was an Olympic swimmer. In the 1930s, her family moved to California, where she met character actor Henry O'Neill. He recommended her to Paramount Pictures executives who were looking for a new actress for the part of Joel McCrea's teenage daughter in *Wells Fargo* (1937). Her work in the film led to numerous other film roles.

In April 1944, Stewart signed a contract with Republic Pictures and began starring in Western B movies opposite such actors as Allan Lane, Sunset Carson, and Wild Bill Elliott. During that time she played in several episodes of *Adventures of Red Ryder*. She usually played the part of the tough heroine, rather than a passive girl needing to be saved. From 1944 to 1951 she starred in thirty-five films, most of which were Westerns and film serials. She also starred with Gene Autry several times during that period as well as appearing on several episodes of *The Cisco Kid*, including "Oil Land", which first aired on October 10, 1950.

In 1949, she played alongside Jim Bannon in *Ride, Ryder, Ride*. She again played the part of heroine to Bannon in 1949, starring in *The Fighting Redhead*. In 1952 she starred with Bill Elliott in *Kansas Territory*. In 1957, she had a minor role on CBS's *Have Gun-Will Travel* episode "The Outlaw". In 1958, she was cast as Etta Jackson, the romantic interest of the painter Hurley Abbott, played by Brad Johnson, in the episode "The Underdog" of the ABC/Desilu western series, *The Life and Legend of Wyatt Earp*, with Hugh O'Brian in the title role.

Her career slowed in the 1960s, and by the 1970s she was residing in Studio City, California. Stewart won the Golden Boot Awards in 1984. Semi-retired, Stewart still continued to act on occasion. She played a bit role on one episode of *Seinfeld* in 1990 titled "The Implant"; in that episode she played the part of the aunt of George Costanza's temporary girlfriend.

In 2009 through 2010, Stewart played Pam Beesly's "old-fashioned" grandmother Mee-Maw on The Office episode "Niagara", and once more in the episode when they baptize Jim's and Pam's daughter Cece. In 2012, she played Grandma Delores in Adam Sandler's comedy film, *That's My Boy*. Her last roles to date was as Mrs. Decker in an episode of *Getting On* in 2014.

In recent decades, Stewart has appeared regularly as a guest speaker at Western film festivals. Since 1993, Stewart has appeared as a special guest at the annual Lone Pine Film Festival.

Stewart was married twice. In 1940 she married actor Don "Red" Barry; the marriage ended in divorce in 1944. She was married to actor Buck Young from 1953 until his death on February 9, 2000.

Jan Stine

Jan Randall Stine was born on April 29, 1938 in Fort Wayne, Indiana. Jan was the son of Jan J. N. Stine and Bernardine Anne Bowers. His father was employed as a spray painter, later becoming a plant foreman, and his mother was employed as a glove inspector.

Jan became interested in acting during his high school years at Fort Wayne Central High School, appearing in a number of high school plays and becoming the leader of the local affiliate of The National Thespian Society. He relocated to California and trained at the Pasadena Playhouse as an actor.

He was in over thirty movies and television programs and was known for *The Donna Reed Show* (1958), *Wise Use of Credit* (1960), *Claudelle Inglish* (1961) and *Munroe* (1963).

More of his roles included *Mackenzie's Raiders* (1958), *Black Saddle* (1959), *Wichita Town* (1959) with Joel McCrea, *Wanted: Dead or Alive* (1960), *The Rifleman* (1960-1961), *Perry Mason* (1962), *Hawaiian Eye* (1963), and *The Lieutenant* (1963-1964).

His final acting appearances were as Timmy and Runt in two episodes of the television series *Hank* (1966). Following his acting career he completed a Master of Arts degree, became a school teacher followed by a change in career to become a nursing home and rehabilitation center administrator. He died on November 13, 2010 from complications caused by throat cancer in La Verne, California at age 72.

Dean Stockwell

Dean Stockwell and Joel McCrea in *Cattle Drive*

Dean Stockwell was born Robert Dean Stockwell in North Hollywood, Los Angeles, California March 5, 1936 and is an American actor of film and television, with a career spanning over sixty-five years. As a child actor under contract to Metro-Goldwyn-Mayer he first came to the public's attention in films such as *Anchors Aweigh* and *The Green Years*; as a young adult he played a lead role in the 1957 Broadway and 1959 screen adaptations of Meyer Levin's *Compulsion*, a novel based on the true-life story of Leopold and Loeb.

More recently he became widely known for television roles, playing Rear Admiral Albert "Al" Calavicci in the 1989–1993 television series *Quantum Leap*, and Brother Cavil in the Sci Fi Channel 21st century revival of *Battlestar Galactica*.

In 1945, he appeared in a main character role (Donald Martin) in the musical movie *Anchors Aweigh* alongside Frank Sinatra and Gene Kelly. Some of his other notable child roles included that of Robert Shannon in *The Green Years* (1946), Gregory Peck's son in *Gentleman's Agreement* (1947), as the son of William Powell and Myrna Loy as Nick and Nora Charles, Nick Jr., in *Song of the Thin Man* (1947), as an orphaned runaway longing to go to sea in *Deep Waters* (1948) and as Lionel Barrymore's grandson and Richard Widmark's protege in *Down to the Sea in Ships* (1949). He also starred in the lead role of *The Boy with Green Hair* in 1948, and in *The Secret Garden* in 1949. In 1950, he appeared in a lead role alongside Errol Flynn in *Kim*, the film of Rudyard Kipling's novel.

He appeared in two westerns with Joel McCrea in *Stars in My Crown* (1950) and *Cattle Drive* (1951).

Unlike many child actors, he continued to act past his teenage years. In 1957, he starred as Judd Steiner in the Broadway adaptation of *Compulsion*, based on the Leopold and Loeb story; he played the same role in the 1959 film adaptation *Compulsion*. In 1958, he joined Gloria Talbott and Dan Blocker as guest stars in the episode "Mercyday" of the NBC western series *The Restless Gun*, starring John Payne.

In 1960, he played coal miner's son Paul Morel in the British film *Sons and Lovers*, an American actor cast as an Englishman, working alongside Trevor Howard and Wendy Hiller. In 1961, Stockwell appeared in the premiere episode of ABC's *Bus Stop* series, which starred Marilyn Maxwell. In 1962, he appeared in an adaptation of Eugene O'Neill's play *Long Day's Journey Into Night* along with Katharine Hepburn, Ralph Richardson and Jason Robards. In 1964, Stockwell guest-starred in an episode of NBC's medical drama *The Eleventh Hour*.

In the early 1960s, Stockwell dropped out of show business, becoming active in the hippie subculture.

Stockwell appeared in a 1969 episode of Bonanza as a down-and-out former Union soldier. He then appeared in two episodes of the mystery series *Columbo*. In 1973, he was the leading actor in a horror B-film called *The Werewolf of Washington*. Stockwell played Jack Whittier, a reporter who had an affair with the daughter of the U.S. President and is sent to Hungary. There he is bitten by a werewolf, and then gets transferred back to Washington, D.C., where he gets a job as the press secretary to the President. During the mid-1970s Stockwell worked as a real-estate broker.

In 1984, he appeared in Wim Wenders' critically acclaimed film *Paris, Texas*, and in that same year, in David Lynch's film version of *Dune* as Wellington Yueh. The following year he turned in a brief but significant role as attorney Bob Grimes in William Friedkin's *To Live and Die in L.A.* In 1986, Stockwell made an appearance in another Lynch production, the neo-noir thriller *Blue Velvet*. In 1988, he was nominated for an Academy Award for Best Supporting Actor for his performance as Mafia boss Tony "the Tiger" Russo in the comedy *Married to the Mob*. He received a star on the Hollywood Walk of Fame on February 29, 1992 (Leap Day) following the success of *Quantum Leap*.

Some of his later roles included Stephen King's *The Langoliers* (1995), *Air Force One* (1997), *Star Trek: Enterprise* (2002), *Stargate SG-1* (2002), *JAG* (2002-2004), *NCIS: New Orleans* (2014), and *Entertainment* (2015).

Along with Jack Lemmon and Marcello Mastroianni, Stockwell won the award for best actor at the Cannes Film Festival twice, for *Compulsion* and *Long Day's Journey Into Night*.

Stockwell joined the cast of *Battlestar Galactica* starting with its second season finale, portraying what became the lead antagonist, Cylon John Cavil.

Robert Dean Stockwell was the younger son of Nina Olivette, an actress and dancer, and Harry Stockwell, an actor and singer. His elder brother was actor Guy Stockwell. He married Millie Perkins on April 15, 1960; they divorced on July 30, 1962. He married Joy Marchenko on December 15, 1981. They had two children: a son, Austin, born November 5, 1983 and a daughter, Sophia, born August 5, 1985. Stockwell and Marchenko divorced in 2004.

Stockwell has been widely reported to be the godfather of actress Amber Tamblyn; however, in a 2009 interview with Parade Magazine, Tamblyn explained that Stockwell was one of three famous friends of her father, actor Russ Tamblyn, who were always around the house when she was growing up, and who were big influences on her life. The other two, in addition to Stockwell, were actor Dennis Hopper, and musician Neil Young. The word "godfather" was "just a loose term I've always used for all of them," Tamblyn explained in the interview, suggesting that Stockwell's "godfather" moniker is informal, at best.

He is an accomplished artist who creates both digitally enhanced photographs and original collages in the style of his friend and fellow artist, Wallace Berman. During his time at the University of California, Berkeley, Stockwell immersed himself in music and wrote several small compositions. As part of his friendship with musician Neil Young, Stockwell designed the album cover art for *American Stars 'N Bars*. Together, they directed *Human Highway*, which Stockwell also co-wrote. The title track from Young's 1970 album *After the Gold Rush* is based on the title of a screenplay written by Stockwell.

Stockwell is an avid golfer and would play golf during breaks in filming episodes of *Quantum Leap*. He's a martial artist, holding instructor rank in Modern Arnis.

He is an "avowed environmentalist," a personality aspect which has permeated his onscreen characters at times.

Lewis Stone

Lewis Shepard Stone in Worcester, Massachusetts November 15, 1879 and was an American actor best known for his role as Judge James Hardy in Metro-Goldwyn-Mayer's Andy Hardy film series and as an MGM contract player.

Born to Bertrand Stone and Philena Heald Ball, Lewis Stone's hair turned gray very prematurely (reportedly by age 20). Lewis served in the United States Army in the Spanish-American War, and then returned to a career as a writer. He soon began acting. In 1912 Stone found great success in the popular play *Bird of Paradise* which starred Laurette Taylor. The play was later filmed in 1932 and 1951. Stone's career was interrupted by World War I where he served again in the United States Army in the cavalry. By then he had a white-haired, distinguished appearance and began appearing in roles which matched his demeanor. He showed up in First National's 1920 Nomads of the North (a wonderfully preserved silent film) to good effect playing a Royal Canadian Mounted Policeman. He portrayed the title role in the 1922 silent film version of *The Prisoner of Zenda*, as well as the role of "Rudolf Rassendyll".

Stone was nominated for the Academy Award for Best Actor in 1929 for *The Patriot*. After that, he appeared in seven films with Greta Garbo, spanning both the silent and early sound periods. He played the role of Dr. Otternschlag in the Garbo film *Grand Hotel*, in which, completely unaware of all the high drama that has just occurred, he utters the famous closing line: "Grand Hotel. People come. People go. Nothing ever happens". He played a larger role in the 1933 Garbo film *Queen Christina*. His appearance in the highly successful prison film *The Big House* furthered his career, and he starred with some of the biggest names in Hollywood in the 1930s, such stars as Norma Shearer, John Gilbert, Ramón Novarro, Clark Gable, and Jean Harlow.

He played adventurers in the dinosaur epic *The Lost World* (1925) with Wallace Beery and *The Mask of Fu Manchu* (1932) with Boris Karloff, and a police captain in *Bureau of Missing Persons* (1933). In 1937 Stone essayed the role which would become his most famous, that of Judge James Hardy in the Mickey Rooney "Andy Hardy" series. Stone appeared as the judge in fifteen movies, beginning with *You're Only Young Once* (1937).

More of his roles included *Freedom of the Press* (1928) with Joel McCrea, *The Secret Six* (1931), *Woman Wanted* (1935) again with Joel McCrea, *The Bugle Sounds* (1942), *Stars in My Crown* (1950) a third with Joel McCrea, and *All the Brothers Were Valiant* (1953).

Stone died in Hancock Park in Beverly Hills, Los Angeles, California on September 12, 1953, at age 73. Stone reportedly suffered a heart attack while chasing away some neighborhood kids who were throwing rocks at his garage. Another published report states that on that date Stone and his third wife were watching television when they heard a racket in the back yard. When he investigated, Stone found lawn furniture once again floating in the pool and glimpsed three or perhaps four teenage boys running towards the street. Stone gave chase despite his wife's warning not to exert himself. Upon reaching the sidewalk, Stone suddenly collapsed. A gardener, Juan Vergara, witnessed the chase and summoned aid.

A photo published in newspapers of the day showed Stone's body on the sidewalk immediately after the incident. Decades later, the photo was included in Kenneth Anger's Hollywood scandals book, *Hollywood Babylon*.

Lewis Stone was later honored with a star on the Hollywood Walk of Fame at 6524 Hollywood Blvd.

Milburn Stone

Milburn Stone was born Hugh Milburn Stone in Burrton, Kansas July 5, 1904 and was an American film and television actor, a nephew of actors Fred Stone and Madge Blake, best known as "Doc" (Dr. Galen Adams) on the CBS western series *Gunsmoke* (1955-1975). He also played a Dr. Blake in the 1943 film Gung Ho!

His parents were Herbert and Laura (née Belfield) Stone. Acting must have been in his blood as the nephew of Broadway comedian Fred Stone for Milburn left home as a teenager to find work with touring repertory troupes. Emulating his famous uncle Fred, he appeared in vaudeville as part of a song-and-dance team called 'Stone and Strain'.

Following a minor appearance on Broadway in *The Jayhawkers*, Milburn moved to Los Angeles in 1935 to try his luck in films. He toiled for years in mostly unbilled parts for 'poverty row' Monogram Pictures, apprenticing in a number of background roles as both benign fellows (clerks, reporters, sailors, detectives) and bad guys (convicts, robbers, henchmen). Out of the blue he would nab a heroic film lead in films as *Federal Bullets* (1937) or serial thrillers as *The Great Alaskan Mystery* (1944) and *The Master Key* (1945), then invariably go right back to unbilled status in his very next role.

In 1940, he appeared with Marjorie Reynolds, Tristram Coffin, and I. Stanford Jolley in the comedy espionage film *Chasing Trouble*. Also in 1940 Stone co-starred with Roy Rogers in the film *Colorado*, in which he played Rogers's brother-gone-wrong.

390

He played the liberal minded warden in Monogram Pictures' *Prison Mutiny* in 1943. He was signed by Universal Pictures in 1943 and became a familiar face in its features and serials. One of his film roles was a radio columnist in the Gloria Jean-Kirby Grant musical *I'll Remember April*. He made such an impression in this film that Universal gave him a starring role (and a similar characterization) in the 1945 serial *The Master Key*.

More of his roles included *The Three Mesquiteers* (1936), *Banjo on My Knee* (1936) with Joel McCrea, *Paroled from the Big House* (1938), *The Great Plane Robbery* (1940), *The Great Train Robbery* (1941), *Reap the Wild Wind* (1942), *Captive Wild Woman* (1943), *Sherlock Holmes Faces Death* (1943), *The Royal Mounted Rides Again* (1945), *Buck Privates Come Home* (1947) with Abbott and Costello, *Calamity Jane and Sam Bass* (1949), *Branded* (1950) with Alan Ladd, *Flying Leathernecks* (1951), *Dragnet* (1952), *The Private War of Major Benson* (1955), *Drango* (1957), and *Climax!* (1958).

One of CBS Radio's hit series, the western *Gunsmoke*, was adapted for television in 1955 and recast with experienced screen actors. Howard McNear, radio's "Doc Adams," was replaced by Milburn Stone, who gave the role a harder edge consistent with his screen portrayals. He stayed with *Gunsmoke* through its entire run and was often shown sparring in a friendly manner with costars Dennis Weaver and Ken Curtis, who played, respectively, Chester Goode and deputy Festus Haggen.

In March 1971, Stone had heart bypass surgery at UAB Hospital, Birmingham, Alabama. Afterward, he had to be revived two times after his heart stopped.

He last appeared in *When the West Was Fun: A Western Reunion* (1979) as himself with a whole lot of western television stars.

He died on June 12, 1980 and was survived by his second wife, the former Jane Garrison (who died in 2002), and their daughter, Shirley Stone Gleason.

A painting of the Doc Adams character was commissioned from Gary Hawk, a painter from Stone's home state of Kansas. When then-President Ronald Reagan, a friend of Milburn Stone, heard about the painting, Gary Hawk was invited to the Oval Office to present the artwork to the President. Stone lived to see Reagan emerge as the likely Republican nominee for President in 1980 but not to witness Reagan's election.

For his contribution to the television industry, Milburn Stone has a star on the Hollywood Walk of Fame at 6801 Hollywood Blvd. He died of a heart attack June 12, 1980) in La Jolla, California. In 1981, he was inducted posthumously into the Western Performers Hall of Fame at the National Cowboy & Western Heritage Museum in Oklahoma City, Oklahoma. After his death he left a legacy for the Performing Arts, in Cecil County, Maryland, by way of the Milburn Stone Theatre in North East, Maryland.

John St. Polis

John St. Polis was born in New Orleans, Louisiana November 24, 1873 and was an American actor.

Before starting his film career, Polis had made a name for himself on the Broadway stage, most notably in the role of Frederik in the original production of *The Return of Peter Grimm* (1911–1912) and the play's revival in 1921, both performed at the Belasco Theatre.

He appeared in 126 films between 1914 and 1943. In all of his early roles, the actor is billed as John Sainpolis. His best-known performances are as Etienne Laurier in *The Four Horsemen of the Apocalypse* (1921), and as Comte Phillipe de Chagny in *The Phantom of the Opera* (1925).

St. Polis successfully made the transition from silent cinema to "talkies" with one of his most praised performances as Dr. John M. Besant, the father of Norma Besant (played by Mary Pickford) in *Coquette* (1929).

More of his roles included *The Grain of Dust* (1928), *The Three Sisters* (1930), *Gambling Sex* (1932), *A Night at the Opera* (1935), *International Crime* (1938), *They Shall Have Music* (1939) with Joel McCrea, *Reap the Wild Wind* (1942), and *Assignment in Brittany* (1943).

He died on October 8, 1946 in Los Angeles, California from undisclosed causes at age 72.

Erich von Stroheim

Erich von Stroheim was born Erich Oswald Stroheim in Vienna, Austria September 22, 1885 and was an Austrian director, actor and producer, most notable as being a film star of the silent era, subsequently noted as an auteur for his directorial work.

Stroheim was the son of Benno Stroheim, a middle-class hat-maker, and Johanna Bondy, both of whom were practicing Jews.

Stroheim immigrated to America at the end of 1909. On arrival at Ellis Island he claimed to be Count Erich Oswald Hans Carl Maria von Stroheim und Nordenwall, the son of Austrian nobility like the characters he played in his films, but both Billy Wilder and Stroheim's agent Paul Kohner claimed that he spoke with a decidedly lower-class Austrian accent. However Jean Renoir writes in his memoirs: "Stroheim spoke hardly any German. He had to study his lines like a schoolboy learning a foreign language." Later, while living in Europe, Stroheim claimed in published remarks to have "forgotten" his native tongue. In Renoir's movie *la Grande Illusion*, Stroheim speaks German with a strong American accent.

By 1914 he was working in Hollywood. He began working in movies in bit-parts and as a consultant on German culture and fashion. His first film, in 1915, was *The Country Boy* in which he was uncredited. His first credited role came in *Old Heidelberg*.

He began working with D. W. Griffith, taking uncredited roles in *Intolerance*. Additionally, Von Stroheim acted as one of the many assistant directors on *Intolerance*, a film remembered in part for its huge cast of extras. Later, with America's entry into World War I, he played sneering German villains in such films as *Sylvia of the Secret Service* and *The Hun Within*. In *The Heart of Humanity*, he tears the buttons from a nurse's uniform with his teeth, and when disturbed by a crying baby, throws it out of a window.

Following the end of the war, Stroheim turned to writing and then directed his own script for *Blind Husbands* in 1919. He also starred in the film. As a director, Stroheim was known to be dictatorial and demanding, often antagonizing his actors. He is considered one of the greatest directors of the silent era, creating films that represent cynical and romantic views of human nature. (In the 1932 film *The Lost Squadron*, with Joel McCrea, Stroheim played a parody of himself as a fanatic German film director making a World War I movie who orders extras playing dead soldiers to "Stay dead!")

His next directorial efforts were the lost film *The Devil's Pass Key* (1919) and *Foolish Wives* (1922), in which he also starred. Studio publicity for *Foolish Wives* claimed that it was the first film to cost one million dollars.

In 1923, Stroheim began work on *Merry-Go-Round*. He cast the American actor Norman Kerry in a part written for himself 'Count Franz Maximilian Von Hohenegg' and newcomer Mary Philbin in the lead actress role. However studio executive Irving Thalberg fired Von Stroheim during filming and replaced him with director Rupert Julian.

Probably Stroheim's best remembered work as a director is *Greed*, a detailed filming of the novel *McTeague* by Frank Norris. He originally started it as a project with Samuel Goldwyn's Goldwyn Pictures. Stroheim had long wanted to do a film version of the book. He originally intended it to be a highly detailed reproduction of the original, shot mostly at the locations described in the book in San Francisco and Death Valley. The original print ran for an astonishing ten hours. Knowing this version was far too long, Stroheim cut out almost half the footage, reducing it to a six-hour version to be shown over two nights. It was still deemed too long, so Stroheim and director Rex Ingram edited it into a four-hour version that could be shown in two parts.

However, in the midst of filming, Goldwyn was bought by Marcus Loew and merged into Metro-Goldwyn-Mayer. After rejecting Stroheim's attempts to cut it to less than three hours, MGM removed *Greed* from his control and gave it to head scriptwriter June Mathis, with orders to cut it down to a manageable length. Mathis gave the print to a routine cutter, who reduced it to 2.5 hours. In what is considered one of the greatest losses in cinema history, a janitor destroyed the cut footage.

The shortened release version was a box-office failure, and was angrily disowned by Stroheim. In particular, he blamed Mathis for destroying his pet project, since she was credited as a writer due to contractual obligations. However, Mathis had worked with Stroheim before and had long admired him, so it is not likely she would have indiscriminately butchered his film. The film was partially reconstructed in 1999 by Producer Rick Schmidlin, using the existing footage mixed with surviving still photographs, but *Greed* has passed into cinema lore as a lost masterpiece.

Stroheim followed with a commercial project, *The Merry Widow* (his most commercially successful film) and the more personal *The Wedding March* and the now-lost *The Honeymoon*.

Stroheim's unwillingness or inability to modify his artistic principles for the commercial cinema, his extreme attention to detail, his insistence on near-total artistic freedom and the resulting costs of his films led to fights with the studios. As time went on he received fewer directing opportunities.

In 1929, Stroheim was dismissed as the director of the film *Queen Kelly* after disagreements with star Gloria Swanson and producer and financier Joseph P. Kennedy over the mounting costs of the film and Stroheim's introduction of indecent subject matter into the film's scenario.

After *Queen Kelly* and *Walking Down Broadway*, a project from which Stroheim was also dismissed, Stroheim returned to working principally as an actor, in both American and French films. He appeared as a guest star in the 1953 anthology drama television series *Orient Express* in the episode entitled *The Man of Many Skins*.

Working in France on the eve of World War II, Stroheim was prepared to direct the film *La dame blanche* from his own story and screenplay. Jean Renoir wrote the dialogue, Jacques Becker was to be assistant director and Stroheim himself, Louis Jouvet and Jean-Louis Barrault were to be the featured actors. Max Cossvan was to produce the film for Demo-Film. The production was prevented by the outbreak of the war on September 1, 1939, and Stroheim returned to the United States.

He is perhaps best known as an actor for his role as von Rauffenstein in Jean Renoir's *La Grande Illusion* (1937) and as Max von Mayerling in Billy Wilder's *Sunset Boulevard* (1950).

For the latter film, which co-starred Gloria Swanson, Stroheim was nominated for the Academy Award for Best Supporting Actor. Excerpts from *Queen Kelly* were used in the film. The Mayerling character states that he used to be one of the three great directors of the silent era, along with D.W. Griffith and Cecil B. DeMille; many film critics agree that Stroheim was indeed one of the great early directors. Stroheim's character in *Sunset Boulevard* thus had an autobiographical basis that reflected the humiliations suffered through his career.

Stroheim was married three times. He was married to Margaret Knox from 1913 to 1915; His second marriage was to Mae Jones from 1916 to 1919. He was never divorced from his third wife Valerie Germonprez, though he lived with actress Denise Vernac, from 1939 until his death. Vernac also starred with him in several films. Two of Stroheim's sons eventually joined the film business: Erich, Jr. (1916–1968) as an assistant director and Josef (1922–2002) as a sound editor.

Stroheim spent the last part of his life in France, where his silent film work was much admired by artists in the French film industry. In France he acted in films, wrote several novels that were published in French, and worked on various unrealized film projects. He was awarded the French Légion d'honneur shortly before his death May 12, 1957 in Maurepas, France at the age of 71.

Chuck Stubbs

Chuck Stubbs was born March 26, 1926 in Detroit, Michigan. A former child actor, Chuck Stubbs served during World War II. Some of his early acting roles included *Babes in Toyland* (1934) with Laurel and Hardy, *Heidi* (1937), *Boys Town* (1938), *Angels with Dirty Faces* (1938), *Stagecoach* (1939), *They Shall Have Music* (1939) with Joel McCrea, *One Million B.C.* (1940), and *Dumbo* (1941).

After the war, he became a Los Angeles businessman and civic leader. He died August 23, 2003 at age 77 in Leucadia, California.

Barry Sullivan

Joel McCrea and Barry Sullivan in *The Outriders*

Barry Sullivan was born Patrick Barry Sullivan in New York City August 29, 1912, and was an American movie actor who appeared in over 100 movies from the 1930s to the 1980s.

Sullivan fell into acting when in college playing semi-pro football. During the later Depression years, Sullivan was told that because of his 6 ft 3 in stature and rugged good looks he could "make money" simply standing on a Broadway stage. This began a successful career on Broadway, movies, and television.

One of Sullivan's most memorable roles was in *The Great Gatsby* (1949) with Alan Ladd, and another was playing a movie director in *The Bad and the Beautiful* (1952) opposite Kirk Douglas. Sullivan toured the US with Bette Davis in theatrical readings of the poetry of Carl Sandburg and starred opposite her in the 1951 film *Payment on Demand*. In 1950, Sullivan appeared in *The Outriders* with Joel McCrea, and the the film *A Life of Her Own* and replaced Vincent Price in the role of Leslie Charteris' Simon Templar on the NBC Radio show *The Saint*.

Unfortunately, Sullivan only lasted two episodes before the show was cancelled, and then resurrected five weeks later with Vincent Price once again playing the starring role.

In the 1953-1954 television season, Sullivan appeared with other celebrities as a musical judge in ABC's *Jukebox Jury*. Sullivan's first starring television role was a syndicated adaptation of the radio series *The Man Called X* for Ziv Television in 1956-1957, as secret agent Ken Thurston, the role Herbert Marshall originally portrayed before the microphone. In the 1957-1958 season, Sullivan starred in the adventure/drama television series *Harbormaster*. He played a commercial ship's captain, David Scott, and Paul Burke played his partner, Jeff Kittridge, in five episodes of the series, which aired first on CBS and then ABC under the revised title *Adventure at Scott Island*.

In 1960, Sullivan played frontier sheriff Pat Garrett opposite Clu Gulager as outlaw Billy the Kid in the NBC western television series *The Tall Man* (although the series ran for seventy-five half-hour episodes, the one in which Garrett kills Billy was never filmed). That same year he played outlaw Jim Flood in *Seven Ways from Sundown* (1960) with Audie Murphy. In additional to *The Tall Man*, Sullivan also starred in the television series *The Road West*, which aired on NBC on Monday, alternating with Perry Como), during the 1966-1967 season. Sullivan played the role of family patriarch Ben Pride.

Sullivan appeared in Sam Peckinpah's *Pat Garrett & Billy the Kid* (1973) as John Chisum, but his scene was excised from the release print (though later restored to the film). He had a featured role in the 1976 miniseries *Rich Man, Poor Man Book II*.

Sullivan guest starred in many series, including *Pursuit* (1958), *Route 66* (1963), *Ben Casey* (1963-1964), *Perry Mason* (1965), *Mission: Impossible* (1967), *The High Chaparral* (1970), *Rod Serling's Night Gallery* (1969-1972), *The Sixth Sense* (1972), *Harry O* (1974), *The Bionic Woman* (1976), *Charlie's Angels* (1979), *The Love Boat* (1979), and *Vega$* (1979).

Sullivan was consistently in demand for the entirety of his career. His acting career spanned romantic leading man roles to villains and finally to character roles. In his later years, Sullivan had roles in the films, *Oh, God!* (1977) with George Burns and *Earthquake* (1974), where he shared scenes with Ava Gardner.

Sullivan has two stars on the Hollywood Walk of Fame: one at 1500 Vine St. for his work in television, and another at 6160 Hollywood Blvd. for motion pictures.

His daughter Jenny Sullivan wrote the play *J for J* (*Journals for John*) after she found a packet of unsent letters (in 1995) written by Barry decades earlier to her older brother, Johnny, who was mentally disabled. The play premiered on October 20, 2001. John Ritter, who in real life had a handicapped brother, played Johnny, Jenny played herself, and actor Jeff Kober portrayed Sullivan.

Sullivan was a Democratic Party activist and a tireless advocate for the mentally disabled. He had three children. Sullivan was married and divorced three times. Marie Brown, a Broadway actress, was mother to both Jenny and John Sullivan. Gita Hall, model and actress, was the mother of Patricia. His third marriage to Desiree Sumara produced no children.

Sullivan died of respiratory failure at age 81 on June 6, 1994, in Sherman Oaks, California.

His daughter, Jenny Sullivan, a former actress, is now a theater director. Younger daughter Patricia "Patsy" was twelve years old when signed to a cosmetic company contract as their "face" and was a cover girl featured on many national magazines as well as in commercials. As a teen she married songwriter Jimmy Webb, with whom she had five sons and a daughter. Three of Patsy's sons formed the rock group "The Webb Brothers" and have enjoyed success. Jenny Sullivan married musician Jim Messina; they have no children.

Frank Sully

Frank Sully was born in St. Louis, Missouri June 17, 1908 and was an American film actor. He appeared in over 240 films between 1934 and 1968.

Sully was often cast as a heavy or villain throughout his career. Modern viewers will recognize Sully in his appearances in several late Three Stooges films such as *Fling in the Ring*, *Pardon My Backfire*, and *Guns a Poppin*. In comedy, perhaps his most memorable role was as the bewildered waiter who thinks he is seeing triple in the Stooges' *A Merry Mix Up*.

Dramatically, Sully is remembered as one of the Joad family members 'Noah Joad', whose family treks across country for a new life, in the 1940 classic John Ford film *The Grapes of Wrath*.

More of his roles included his first movie *Murder at the Vanities* (1934) with Alan Ladd, *Criminals of the Air* (1937), *Youth Takes a Fling* (1938) with Joel McCrea, *The Fighting 69th* (1940), *To the Shores of Tripoli* (1942), *Yankee Doodle Dandy* (1942), *The More the Merrier* (1943) again with Joel McCrea, *Boston Blackie and the Law* (1946), *Wild Harvest* (1947) again with Alan Ladd, *Blondie's Hero* (1950), *I Love Lucy* (1952), *Battle of Rogue River* (1954), *Fury at Gunsight Pass* (1956), *The Life and Legend of Wyatt Earp* (1957), *The Gunfight at Dodge City* (1959) a third with Joel McCrea, *Riverboat* (1960), *Leave It to Beaver* (1958-1963), *The Wild Wild West* (1967), *The Virginian* (1963-1967), and *Funny Girl* (1968).

Frank Sully died on December 17, 1975 at age 67. He is buried in Forest Lawn Memorial Park in Long Beach, California.

Grady Sutton

Grady Harwell Sutton in Chattanooga, Tennessee April 5, 1906 and was an American film and television actor from the 1920s to the 1970s.

Sutton was raised in Florida where he attended St. Petersburg High School. He began his career during the silent film era and made the transition to sound films with the college themed serials *The Boy Friends*. He moved on to countless character roles, where he frequently played dimwitted country boys. His most well-known roles were as Frank Dowling, Katharine Hepburn's dancing partner, in *Alice Adams* (1935) and as a foil to W.C. Fields in two films, *You Can't Cheat an Honest Man* (1939), *Pigskin Parade* (1936) with Alan Ladd, and *The Bank Dick* (1940).

Film historian William J. Mann characterizes Sutton as a typical "Hollywood Sissy," that is as a gay actor who ordinarily portrayed an effeminate character for comedic effect.

More of his roles included *So This Is College* (1929) with Joel McCrea, *This Reckless Age* (1932), *The Story of Temple Drake* (1933), *Man on the Flying Trapeze* (1935), *Love Takes Flight* (1937), *He Stayed for Breakfast* (1940), *Whispering Ghosts* (1942), *The Great Moment* (1944) again with Joel McCrea, *Salty O'Rourke* (1945) again with Alan Ladd, *Plainsman and the Lady* (1946), *Grand Canyon* (1949), *A Star Is Born* (1954), *The Life and Legend of Wyatt Earp* (1956), *Lawman* (1960-1962), *4 for Texas* (1963), *Tickle Me* (1965) with Elvis, *The Bounty Killer* (1965), *Paradise, Hawaiian Style* (1966) again with Elvis, *Batman* (1967), *Myra Breckinridge* (1970), *Support Your Local Gunfighter* (1971), *Hawaii Five-O* (1972), *The Odd Couple* (1974), and *Rock 'n' Roll High School* (1979).

He finally retired from acting in 1979. The strength of his association with Fields was such that it was mentioned in the commentary for *My Fair Lady*. Sutton has a non-speaking role in some of the formal-dress scenes, and subtly performs some comic shtick. The commentator refers to him as "an old W. C. Fields actor".

Sutton died September 17, 1995 at the Motion Picture & Television Country House and Hospital in Woodland Hills, California at the age of 89.

Blanche Sweet

Sarah Blanche Sweet was born in Chicago, Illinois June 18, 1896 and was an American silent film actress who began her career in the earliest days of the Hollywood motion picture film industry.

Born into a family of stock theater and vaudeville performers, Blanche Sweet entered the entertainment industry at an early age. At age 4 she toured in a play called *The Battle of the Strong* whose star was stage luminary Maurice Barrymore. A decade later Sweet would act with Barrymore's son Lionel in a D. W. Griffith directed film. In 1909, she started work at Biograph Studios under contract to director D. W. Griffith. By 1910 she had become a rival to Mary Pickford, who had also started for Griffith the year before.

Sweet is renowned for her energetic, independent roles, at variance with the 'ideal' Griffith type of vulnerable, often fragile, femininity. After many starring roles, her first real landmark film was the 1911 Griffith thriller *The Lonedale Operator*. In 1913 she starred in Griffith's first feature-length movie, *Judith of Bethulia*. In 1914 Sweet was initially cast by Griffith in the part of Elsie Stoneman in his epic *The Birth of a Nation* but the role was eventually given to rival actress Lillian Gish, who was Sweet's senior by three years. That same year Sweet parted ways with Griffith and joined Paramount (then Famous Players-Lasky) for the much higher pay that studio was able to afford.

Throughout the 1910s, Sweet continued her career appearing in a number of highly prominent roles in films and remained a publicly popular leading lady. She often starred in vehicles by Cecil B. DeMille and Marshall Neilan, and she was recognised by leading film critics of the time to be one of the foremost actresses of the entire silent era. It was during her time working with Neilan that the two began a publicized affair, which brought on his divorce from former actress Gertrude Bambrick. Sweet and Neilan married in 1922. The union ended in 1929 with Sweet charging that Neilan was a persistent adulterer.

During the early 1920s Sweet's career continued to prosper, and she starred in the first film version of *Anna Christie* in 1923. The film is also notable as being the first Eugene O'Neill play to be made into a motion picture. In successive years, she starred in *Tess of the d'Urbervilles* and *The Sporting Venus*, both directed by Neilan. Sweet soon began a new career phase as one of the newly formed MGM studio's biggest stars.

As the Roaring Twenties wound down, Sweet's career faltered with the advent of talkies. Sweet made just three talking pictures, including her critically lauded performance in 1930's *Show Girl in Hollywood*, and *The Silver Horde* (1930) with Joel McCrea, before retiring from the screen that same year and marrying stage actor Raymond Hackett in 1935. The marriage lasted until Hackett's death in 1958.

Sweet spent the remainder of her performing career in radio and in secondary Broadway stage roles. Eventually, her career in both of these fields petered out, and she began working in a Los Angeles department store. In the late 1960s, her acting legacy was resurrected when film scholars invited her to Europe to receive recognition for her work.

On September 24, 1984, a tribute to Blanche Sweet was held at the Museum of Modern Art in New York City. Miss Sweet introduced her 1925 film, *The Sporting Venus.*

Sweet died in New York City of a stroke, on September 6, 1986, just weeks after her 90th birthday. Her ashes were later scattered at the Brooklyn Botanical Gardens.

Gloria Talbott

Joel McCrea and Gloria Talbot in *The Oklahoman*

Gloria Talbot was born Gloria Talbott in Glendale, California, February 7, 1931, and was an American film and television actress.

Talbot began her career as a child actor in such films as *Maytime* (1937), *Sweet and Lowdown* (1943), and *A Tree Grows In Brooklyn* (1945).

After leaving school, Talbot formed a dramatic group and played shows at various clubs. She stopped acting following her marriage, and resumed after her divorce, having worked extensively in film and television. She worked on a regular basis in the 1950s, having appeared in *Crashout* (1955), the Humphrey Bogart comedy *We're No Angels* (1955), and *All That Heaven Allows* (1955). In that same year, Talbot appeared in *TV Reader's Digest* episode *America's First Great Lady* as Pocahontas. Other films she was in include *Strange Intruder* (1956), *The Oklahoman* (1957) with Joel McCrea, *The Cyclops* (1957), *Cattle Empire* (1958) again with Joel McCrea, *Alias Jesse James* (1959), *Oklahoma Territory* (1960), *Arizona Raiders* (1965) with Audie Murphy, and *An Eye for an Eye* (1966).

She became known as a 'scream queen' after appearing in a number of horror films including *The Daughter of Dr. Jekyll* (1957), *The Cyclops* (1957), and *I Married a Monster from Outer Space* (1958).

Her multiple television credits include *The Abbott and Costello Show* (1953), *Hopalong Cassidy* (1953), *The Roy Rogers Show* (1954), *Richard Diamond, Private Detective* (1958), *Zorro* (1959), *Wanted: Dead or Alive* (1958-1960), *Whispering Smith* (1961) again with Audie Murphy, and *Perry Mason* (1961-1966).

She came out of retirement and appeared in *The Naked Monster* (2005) which was filmed in 1985 and released five years after her death.

Married four times, Talbot died September 19, 2000, from kidney failure and was survived by her fourth husband, Dr. Patrick Mullally and by two children. Her sister, Lori Talbott, also became an actress.

Daughter Mea Mullally, born to Gloria and Dr. Steven J. Capabianco, her second husband, won three gold medals in local ice-skating competitions and is an aspiring actress.

Lyle Talbot

Lyle Talbot was born Lisle Henderson in Pittsburgh, Pennsylvania, February 8, 1902, and was an American actor on stage and screen, best known for his long career in movies from 1931 to 1960 and for his frequent appearances on television in the 1950s and '60s, including his decade-long role as Joe Randolph on television's *The Adventures of Ozzie and Harriet* (1955-1966).

He began his movie career under contract to Warner Brothers in the early days of "talking pictures" and went on to appear in more than 150 films, first as a young matinee idol and later as a character actor and star of many B movies. He was a founding member of the Screen Actors Guild (SAG) and later served on the board.

Talbot was raised in Brainard, Nebraska. He began his career as a magician's assistant and became a leading actor in traveling tent shows in the Midwest and briefly established his own theater company in Memphis. He went to Hollywood in 1931 when the film industry began producing movies with sound and needed "actors who could talk".

Most notable among his film work was his appearance in the classic pre-noir *Three on a Match* (1932) with Humphrey Bogart and Bette Davis, co-starring with Spencer Tracy in the prison movie *20,000 Years in Sing Sing* (1932), romancing opera singer Grace Moore in *One Night of Love* (1934), and pursuing Mae West in *Go West, Young Man* (1936). He appeared opposite many famous actresses including Carole Lombard, Barbara Stanwyck, Mary Astor, Ginger Rogers, and Shirley Temple.

He appeared in *He Married His Wife* (1940) with Joel McCrea.

Talbot's activism in union affairs affected his career path. Warner Brothers dropped him from its roster, and Talbot seldom received starring roles again. He became a capable character actor, playing affable neighbors or crafty villains with equal finesse.

In countless low-budget B-movie work, Talbot's roles spanned the gamut. He played cowboys, pirates, detectives, cops, surgeons, psychiatrists, soldiers, judges, newspaper editors, storekeepers, and boxers. In later life he proudly claimed to have never rejected any role offered to him, which explains his participation in three infamous Edward D. Wood, Jr. films: *Glen or Glenda* (1953), *Jail Bait* (1954), and *Plan 9 from Outer Space* (1959).

Talbot also worked with The Three Stooges in *Gold Raiders* (1951), portrayed Lex Luthor in *Atom Man vs. Superman* (1950), played villains in four comedies with The Bowery Boys, and took the role of Commissioner Gordon in the 1949 serial *Batman and Robin*. He appeared with Audie Murphy in *Tumbleweed* (1953).

As his film career tapered off, Talbot became a familiar character actor on American television in the 1950s and 1960s as a regular on *Ozzie and Harriet*.

Talbot had a recurring role as Robert Cummings' United States Air Force buddy Paul Fonda on *The Bob Cummings Show*. Talbot also guest starred frequently on such classic TV series as *The Abbott and Costello Show* (1953), *Hopalong Cassidy* (1953), *Stories of the Century* (1954), *Commando Cody: Sky Marshal of the Universe* (1955), *The George Burns and Gracie Allen Show* (1954-1958), *Richard Diamond, Private Detective* (1960), *Petticoat Junction* (1964), *Green Acres* (1965-1971), *O'Hara, U.S. Treasury* (1972), *Adam-12* (1973), *Charlie's Angels* (1979), *The Dukes of Hazzard* (1984), *The New Leave It to Beaver* (1986), and *Newhart* (1987).

Having started his career in the theater and later co-starred on Broadway in 1940-41 in *Separate Rooms*, Talbot returned to the stage in the 1960s and 1970s, starring in national road company versions of Thornton Wilder's *The Matchmaker*, Gore Vidal's political drama *The Best Man*, Neil Simon's *The Odd Couple* and *Barefoot in the Park*, Arthur Sumner Long's "Never Too Late," and appearing as Capt. Braddock in a 1967 revival of *South Pacific*, at New York's Lincoln Center.

He continued to appear occasionally on TV shows well into his 80s, and narrated two PBS biographies, *The Case of Dashiell Hammett* and *World Without Walls* about pioneering pilot Beryl Markham, both produced and written by his son, Stephen Talbot.

Talbot was the first live action actor to play two prominent DC Comics characters on-screen: the aforementioned Commissioner Gordon in *Batman and Robin* (1949), and supervillain Lex Luthor in *Atom Man vs. Superman* (1951),who at the time was simply known as Luthor. Talbot began a longstanding tradition of actors in these roles that were most recently filled by Gary Oldman and Kevin Spacey, respectively.

After several brief marriages, Talbot in 1948 married a young singer and actress, Margaret Epple, who often used the stage name, Paula. They had four children together and remained married for over forty years until her death in 1989.

Three of his four children became journalists: Stephen Talbot was for many years a documentary producer for the PBS series *Frontline* and *Frontline World* and is now the executive producer of *Sound Tracks: Music Without Borders*. David is an author of *Brothers* about John and Robert Kennedy and the founder and editor of www.Salon.com, and Margaret is a staff writer for *The New Yorker*. His other daughter, Cynthia Talbot, is a family physician and residency director in Portland, Oregon.

Talbot died on March 2, 1996, at his home in San Francisco, California, at age 94 from pneumonia. His remains were cremated and given to his family.

Hal Taliaferro

Wally Wales was born Floyd Taliaferro Alderson in Sheridan, Wyoming November 13, 1895 and was an American film actor who also appeared in many films under the name Hal Taliaferro. He appeared in over 220 films between 1921 and 1964.

He was raised on his family's ranch, near Birney in Rosebud County, Montana.

Young Floyd's first "outside" job was on a cattle drive for John B. Kendrick. He also drove a tourist stage for the Buffalo Bill Stage line before drifting west in 1915 ending up in Los Angeles where he went to work as a wrangler on Universal's Ranch.

In 1917 he joined the army and served in the American Expeditionary Forces in France.

From 1921 through 1928 he appeared in twenty-two silent films, starring in many (mainly Westerns) under the name Wally Wales, and in 1929 made the successful transition to sound. Subsequently his star faded and he began appearing in much smaller roles, usually as Hal Taliaferro.

Some of his roles included *Western Hearts* (1921), *The Hurricane Horseman* (1925), *The Cyclone Cowboy* (1927), *The Soda Water Cowboy* (1927), *The Utah Kid* (1930), *The Fighting Texans* (1933), *Secrets of Hollywood* (1933), *Smoking Guns* (1934), *The Cactus Kid* (1935), *The Gun Ranger* (1936), *Wells Fargo* (1937) with Joel McCrea, *The Great Adventures of Wild Bill Hickok* (1938), *Daughter of the Tong* (1939), *Dark Command* (1940), *Young Bill Hickok* (1940), *American Portrait* (1940) with Alan Ladd, *Jesse James at Bay* (1941), *Tombstone: The Town Too Tough to Die* (1942), *Hoppy Serves a Writ* (1943), *The Fighting Seabees* (1944), *Federal Operator 99* (1945), *Ramrod* (1947) with Joel McCrea and Veronica Lake, *Red River* (1948), *Colt .45* (1950), *The Sea Hornet* (1951), and *Junction City* (1952).

He retired from films in the early 1950s and returned to the family ranch, now known as the Bones Brothers Ranch (listed on the National Historical Register in 2004). He built a cabin there and lived out his remaining active years painting landscapes.

He died in a Sheridan, Wyoming nursing home from complications of a stroke and pneumonia in 1980, at age 84.

Akim Tamiroff

Akim Mikhailovich Tamiroff was born in Tiflis, Russian Empire (now Tbilisi, Georgia), Russian October 29, 1899 and was an ethnic Armenian actor. He won the first Golden Globe Award for Best Supporting Actor.

He trained at the Moscow Art Theatre drama school. He arrived in the U.S. in 1923 on a tour with a troupe of actors and decided to stay. Tamiroff managed to develop a career in Hollywood despite his thick Russian accent.

Tamiroff's film debut came in 1932 in an uncredited role in *Okay, America!* He performed in several more uncredited roles until 1935, when he co-starred in *The Lives of a Bengal Lancer*. The following year, he was cast in the title role in *The General Died at Dawn*, for which he was nominated for the Academy Award for Best Supporting Actor. He appeared in the 1937 musical *High, Wide, and Handsome* and the 1938 proto-noir *Dangerous to Know* opposite Anna May Wong, frequently singled out as his best role.

In the following decade, he appeared in such films as *The Buccaneer* (1938), *Union Pacific* (1939) with Joel McCrea, *The Great McGinty* (1940), *The Corsican Brothers* (1941), *Tortilla Flat* (1942), *Five Graves to Cairo* (1943), *His Butler's Sister* (1943), *For Whom the Bell Tolls* (1943), for which he received another Oscar nomination, and *The Miracle of Morgan's Creek* (1944). In later years, Tamiroff appeared in *Desert Legion* (1953) with Alan Ladd, *Ocean's 11* (1960), *Topkapi* (1964), *Alphaville* (1965) and had a long collaboration with Orson Welles including *Touch of Evil* (1958), *Mr Arkadin* (1955), *The Trial* (1962) and Welles' unfinished version of *Don Quixote*, in which he played Sancho Panza.

While Tamiroff may not be a household name now, his malapropistic performance as the boss in *The Great McGinty* inspired the cartoon character Boris Badenov, the male half of the villainous husband-and-wife team Boris and Natasha on *The Rocky and Bullwinkle Show*. He was also spoofed in a 1969 episode of the TV show *H.R. Pufnstuf* entitled "The Stand-in" in which a frog named "Akim Toadanoff" directs a movie on Living Island.

Tamiroff died on September 17, 1972 from cancer at age 72 in Palm Springs, California.

Julius Tannen

Julius Tannen was born in New York City, New York May 16, 1880 and was a comedian – or monologist, as those of his era were known – who had a long and successful career in vaudeville. He was known to stage audiences (and respected by other monologists) for his witty improvisations and creative word games. He had a successful career as a character actor in films, appearing in over fifty films in his twenty-five year film career. He is best known to film audiences from the musical *Singin' in the Rain* (1952), in which he appears as the man demonstrating a talking picture early in the film.

Tannen never intended to become a performer. As a young man, he was a salesman whose pitch was so good that he began to get offers to entertain at parties. He made his professional vaudeville debut at the age of 21, and soon developed into a monologist, the predecessor to today's stand up comic. He would frequently end his routines before the payoff of the story, allowing the audience to complete it for themselves, and exited with the phrase "My father thanks you, my mother thanks you, my sister thanks you, and I thank you," which was co-opted by the young George M. Cohan.

He made his Broadway debut in 1905, in a musical comedy called *Lifting the Lid* and went on to appear in three other productions in the next year. As a vaudevillian, he played the Palace Theatre in New York City – the apex of vaudeville performing – more often than almost anyone else, indicating that he was at the peak of his profession. He appeared again on Broadway in 1916, and returned again in 1920, in a comic play with music, *Her Family Tree*, for which he received credit for writing his own scenes. Tannen was also seen in two editions of *Earl Carroll's Vanities*, in 1925 and 1926, and in *George White's Scandals.*

The advent of talking pictures created a need in Hollywood for performers with stage experience, and Tannen appeared in his first film in 1935, when he did an uncredited bit in *Stranded*. This set him upon his twenty-five year career as a character man, although his work frequently went without credit. Some more of his early work included *Pigskin Parade* (1936) with Alan Ladd, *Mama Runs Wild* (1937), *A Man to Remember* (1938), and *Danger Flight* (1939).

In the 1940s, Tannen was part of Preston Sturges' unofficial "stock company" of character actors, appearing in eight films written and directed by Sturges, with the size of his roles increasing over time.

Some of his later roles included *Sullivan's Travels* (1941) with Joel McCrea, *The Ghost of Frankenstein* (1942), *The Palm Beach Story* (1942) again with Joel McCrea, *The Great Moment* (1944) a third with Joel McCrea, *House of Frankenstein* (1944), *The Dolly Sisters* (1945), *The Sin of Harold Diddlebock* (1947), *Always Leave Them Laughing* (1949), *Clash by Night* (1952), *Loving You* (1957) with Elvis, and *The Last Hurrah* (1958).

Undoubtedly, Tannen's most memorable and prominent performance came at the age of 72, when he portrayed a man demonstrating the technology of talking pictures in a film-within-the-film in *Singin' in the Rain* in 1952.

Tannen continued to appear in films until 1959, when he was seen in an uncredited role in director John Sturges' *Last Train from Gun Hill*. He continued to work until he suffered a stroke in 1964. He died the following year January 3, 1965, at the age of 84, at the Motion Picture Country Home in Woodland Hills, California. His sons, William Tannen and Charles Tannen, were both successful film and television actors; William had a recurring role on *The Life and Legend of Wyatt Earp*; Charles later became a television executive.

Lucille Ball said that seeing Tannen perform in her hometown of Jamestown, New York when she was a child inspired her to go into show business.

William Tannen

William Tannen was born November 17, 1911 in New York City, New York, and was an American character actor who appeared in nearly 300 films and television programs from 1934 to 1969.

Some of his roles included *The Band Plays On* (1934), *Tough Guy* (1936), *Another Thin Man* (1939), *Flight Command* (1940), *Dr. Jekyll and Mr. Hyde* (1941), *Air Raid Wardens* (1943) with Laurel and Hardy, *The Canterville Ghost* (1944), *Bud Abbott and Lou Costello in Hollywood* (1945), *All the King's Men* (1949), *The Adventures of Kit Carson* (1951-1955), *Jesse James vs. the Daltons* (1955), *The First Texan* (1956) with Joel McCrea, *Blackjack Ketchum, Desperado* (1956), *Jailhouse Rock* (1957) with Elvis Presley, *Richard Diamond, Private Detective* (1958), *Wanted: Dead or Alive* (1960), *Whispering Smith* (1961) and *The Quick Gun* (1964) with Audie Murphy, *Get Smart* (1966), *Batman* (1966), *Support Your Local Sheriff!* (1969), and *Lancer* (1969).

He died December 2, 1976, at age 65 in Woodland Hills, Los Angeles, California.

Lilyan Tashman

Lilyan Tashman (was born in Brooklyn, New York October 23, 1896 and was a Brooklyn-born Jewish American vaudeville, Broadway, and film actress. Tashman was best known for her supporting roles as tongue-in-cheek villainesses and the vindictive "other woman".She made sixty-six films over the course of her Hollywood career and although never obtained superstar status, her cinematic performances are "sharp, clever and have aged little over the decades."

Lilyan Tashman was the tenth and youngest child of Brooklyn, New York clothing manufacturer Maurice Tashman and his wife Rose. Tall, blonde, and slender with fox-like features and a throaty voice, Tashman freelanced as a fashion and artist's model in New York City. By 1914 she was an experienced vaudevillian, appearing in Ziegfeld Follies between 1916 and 1918. In 1921 Tashman made her film debut in *Experience*, and over the next decade and a half she appeared in numerous silent films. With her husky contralto singing voice she easily navigated the transition to the talkies.

More of her roles included *Whispering Smith* (1926), *A Texas Steer* (1927), *Bulldog Drummond* (1929), *The Cat Creeps* (1930), *Girls About Town* (1931) with Joel McCrea, *Wine, Women and Song* (1933), and *Riptide* (1934).

Tashman married vaudevillian Al Lee in 1914 but they divorced in 1921. She married actor Edmund Lowe in 1925. Her lesbian affairs in Hollywood were an open secret, and her wardrobe and lavish parties the talk of the town.

She died of cancer in New York City on March 21, 1934, at the age of 37. Her last film, *Frankie and Johnny*, was released posthumously in 1936.

Dub Taylor

Dub Tayor and his son Buck Taylor with David Williams in 2004

Walter Clarence Taylor, Jr. was born in Richmond, Virginia. February 26, 1907 — known as Dub Taylor — was an American character actor who worked extensively in westerns, but also in comedy from the 1940s into the 1990s. He was the father of actor Buck Taylor, who played the character Newly O'Brien on CBS's *Gunsmoke*.

The name Walter was shortened to "W" by his friends and then "Dub." His family moved to Augusta, Georgia, when he was five years old and lived in that city until he was thirteen. During that time he befriended Ty Cobb's son and namesake, Ty Cobb, Jr. He had four siblings: Minnie Margret Taylor, Maud Clare Taylor, George Taylor and Edna Fay Taylor. Taylor was particularly close to a grandson, Walter Tac Tharp.

A vaudeville performer, Taylor made his film debut in 1938, having portrayed the cheerful ex-football captain Ed Carmichael in Frank Capra's *You Can't Take It with You*. The following year, Taylor appeared in *The Taming of the West*, in which he originated the character of "Cannonball," a role he continued to play for the next ten years, in over fifty films. "Cannonball" was a comic sidekick to "Wild Bill" Saunders (played by Bill Elliott), a pairing that continued through thirteen features, during which Elliott's character became Wild Bill Hickok.

During this period, a productive relationship with Tex Ritter as Elliott's co-hero began with *King of Dodge City* (1941). That partnership lasted through ten films, but Taylor left after the first one, carrying his "Cannonball" character over to a new series with Russell "Lucky" Hayden. ("Wild Bill" brought in Frank Mitchell to play a very different character, also named "Cannonball," in the remainder of his shows with Ritter.)

Taylor moved again to a series of films starring Charles Starrett, who eventually became "The Durango Kid", once again, playing his sidekick, Cannonball. These films had been produced at Columbia Pictures, Capra's studio, and had a certain quality of production that seemed to be lacking at the Monogram lot, where Taylor brought his "Cannonball" character in 1947. There he joined up with Jimmy Wakely for a concluding run of sixteen films (in two years). These final episodes may have been unpleasant experiences for Taylor, as he never wanted to talk about them thereafter. After 1949, Taylor turned away from Cannonball, and went on to a busy and varied career.

His acting roles, even during his Cannonball period, were not confined to these films. He had bit parts in a number of classic films, including *Mr. Smith Goes to Washington* (1939) with Jimmy Stewart, *A Star Is Born* (1954), and *Them!* (1954), along with dozens of television roles.

He also appeared in *The McConnell Story* (1955) with Alan Ladd. Taylor was cast regularly alongside Alan Hale, Jr., in the syndicated *Casey Jones* (1957-1958) television series, in the role of Jones' fireman, Wally. Taylor can also be seen in a brief role in *No Time for Sergeants* (1958) as the Callville representative of the draft board who summons Andy Griffith from his rural home to the United States Air Force. *A Hole in the Head* (1959) directed by Frank Capra, Taylor plays the Garden of Eden Hotel clerk for hotel owner Frank Sinatra.

Observant fans who saw the 1954 feature film *Dragnet* watched him in an uncredited role at the start of the movie; his character, gangster Miller Starkie, is killed in the opening scene. He had a small role in the 1959 Walt Disney film *Tonka* as a rustler of stray horses for sale.

He also appeared in Joel McCrea's series *Wichita Town* (1960) and an episode of *Twilight Zone* (1962).

He joined Sam Peckinpah's stock company in 1965's *Major Dundee* as a professional horse thief, and appeared subsequently in that director's *The Wild Bunch* (as a prohibitionist minister who gets his flock shot up by the title outlaws in the film's infamous opening scene), *Junior Bonner* (1972), *The Getaway* (1972), and *Pat Garrett and Billy The Kid* (1973) as an aging, eccentric outlaw friend of Billy's. He also appeared in Michael Cimino's crime film *Thunderbolt and Lightfoot*.

Despite his extensive career as a character actor in a wide array of varying roles, Taylor's niche was in westerns, of which he appeared in literally dozens of films. He was in *The Undefeated* with John Wayne and Rock Hudson, in which he played an ill-tempered chuckwagon cook with a cat. Arguably, his most memorable role was playing the father of Michael J. Pollard's C.W. Moss in *Bonnie and Clyde* (1967). Taylor also co-starred in the 1971 movie, *Support Your Local Gunfighter,* as the drunken Doc Shultz, who removes star James Garner's chest tattoo, which reads "I Love Goldie."

He is also remembered for his trademark bowler hat, which he wore in most of his appearances. He was also known for his wild gray hair, an unshaven bristly face, squinty eyes, and his raspy voice and cackle. He put that voice to use, alongside fellow western veterans like Jeanette Nolan and Pat Buttram, in the Disney animated feature *The Rescuers* (1977), as Digger the mole. In the early 1980s, Taylor appeared as the cartoonish sidekick of a John Wayne-like cowboy called "The Gumfighter", exclaiming "Hubba Bubba wins again!" in a series of Western-themed Hubba Bubba bubble gum commercials. He also wore it when he played Mr. Tucker, a political party chairman, in *Used Cars* (1980).

Taylor played a recurring character, Houston Lamb, over the course of four episodes of *Little House On The Prairie* in seasons six and seven (1979 to 1981). His character worked and lived at the school for the blind in Sleepy Eye.

His later years on television was consumed by his weekly appearances on the long-running Country music/comedy show *Hee-Haw*. Taylor's participation lasted six seasons, 1985–1991, where he was mostly seen as a regular in the Lulu's Truck Stop skit featuring Lulu Roman and Gailard Sartain. Taylor's routine was to complain about the food being served. And, in a classic portrayal of his comic abilities, Taylor appeared in several episodes of CBS's *Designing Women* (1989-1990) as a somewhat off-the-beam rustic who becomes enamored of the women from Sugarbaker's during a camping expedition.

Dub Taylor made at least two cameos in the early nineties. In *Back to the Future Part III* (1990, he appeared alongside veteran Western actors Pat Buttram and Harry Carey, Jr.. he also appeared in *The Gambler Returns: The Luck of the Draw* (1991). His last appearance was in the film *Maverick* (1994), as a hotel room clerk.

In 1994, he appeared in a commercial for Pace Foods, where he portrays one of four participants in a fair's "Dip-Off" contest, where he and two other competitors use their "secret ingredient" of Pace Picante Sauce in their dips. When the fourth participant holds up a jar of "Mexican Sauce" as a "secret ingredient", Taylor shouts, "That stuff's made in New York City!", causing his competitors to shout "NEW YORK CITY?!" and all three give the "Mexican Sauce" user the rough treatment.

Dub loved shotgunning and was seen often with his much loved 28 gauge Parker shotguns. He was a common fixture at many of the popular Southern California trap and skeet ranges about Los Angeles.

Taylor died of heart failure on October 3, 1994 in Los Angeles at age 87. He was cremated, with his ashes scattered near Westlake Village, California. In addition to son, Buck Taylor, he had a daughter, Faydean Taylor Tharp (born c. 1931) of the Greater Los Angeles Area.

Before he joined the *Gunsmoke* cast, Buck Taylor appeared in ten episodes of the largely forgotten ABC western, *The Monroes* in 1966-1967. Dub Taylor appeared in two of those episodes and also guest starred numerous times on *Gunsmoke*. Buck and Dub Taylor appeared together in the 1991 Turner Network Television Louis L'amour film *Conagher* starring Buck Taylor's friend Sam Elliott and Elliott's wife, Katharine Ross, and *Gunsmoke* veteran Ken Curtis, who made his last screen appearance.

In early 2006, filmmaker Mark Stokes directed a feature-length documentary on the life of Dub Taylor, *That Guy: The Legacy of Dub Taylor*, which has received support from the Taylor Family and many of Dub's previous co-workers, including Bill Cosby, Peter Fonda, Dixie Carter, John Mellencamp, Don Collier, and Cheryl Rogers-Barnett. The project is from executive producers Stokes and James Kicklighter from JamesWorks Entertainment and Professor Pauper Productions.

I met and talked with Dub's son Buck Taylor at the Red River Western Film Festival in July of 2004, and again at the Memephis Film Festival in June of 2014. He is a really nice guy and a great artist.

Phil Tead

Phillips Tead was born in Somerville, Massachusetts September 29, 1893, sometimes billed as Phil Tead, was an American character actor in film and television.

His film career began in silent pictures in 1914 and ran some 40 years. Among his many roles he might be best remembered as the semi-recurring character "Professor Pepperwinkle", an eccentric inventor in several of the color episodes of the 1950s TV series *Adventures of Superman*. His appearances included the final episode, "All That Glitters". His first appearance had been as a shopkeeper named Mr. Willy, a similarly eccentric character.

One visible early role is an appearance in *Horse Feathers*, the 1932 Marx Brothers comedy, in which he plays a radio play-by-play announcer at the film's climactic college football game.

In the early 1950s he turned his attention primarily to television, appearing in various western series as well as *Superman*.

More of his roles included *Reaching for the Moon* (1930), *The Dark Horse* (1932), *The Most Dangerous Game* (1932) with Joel McCrea, *Meet the Baron* (1933), *The Woman in Red* (1935), *Woman Wanted* (1935) again with Joel McCrea, *I Stole a Million* (1939), *You Can't Escape Forever* (1942), *The Dolly Sisters* (1945), *Jim Thorpe -- All-American* (1951), *The Lawless Breed* (1953), *Hopalong Cassidy* (1954), *The Lone Ranger* (1950-1955), *I Love Lucy* (1957), *The George Burns and Gracie Allen Show* (1952-1958),

Tead's final television work came in several episodes of the western series, *The Lawman*, during 1958-1959.

He died June 9, 1974 at age 80 in Los Angeles, California.

Ray Teal

Ray Teal was born in Grand Rapids, Michigan, January 12, 1902, and was an American actor who appeared in more than 250 movies and some ninety television programs in his thirty-seven-year career. His longest-running role was as Sheriff Roy Coffee on NBC's western television series *Bonanza* (1960–1972). He also played a sheriff in the film *Ace in the Hole* (1951).

Teal, a saxophone player, worked his way through University of California, Los Angeles, located in Los Angeles, California, as a bandleader before becoming an actor.

He had a recurring role as a police officer in the 1953-1955 ABC sitcom with a variety show theme, *Where's Raymond?*, renamed *The Ray Bolger Show*. Ray Bolger played Raymond Wallace, a song-and-dance man who was repeatedly barely on time for his performances.

He was a bit-part player in western films for several years before landing a substantial role in *Northwest Passage* (1940). Other roles followed such as *Captain Midnight* (1942), *See Here, Private Hargrove* (1944), *Back to Bataan* (1945), *Captain Kidd* (1945), *The Best Years of Our Lives* (1946), *Whispering Smith* (1948) with Alan Ladd, *Bad Boy* (1949) with Audie Murphy, *The Great Gatsby* (1949) again with Alan Ladd, *The Kid from Texas* (1950) again with Audie Murphy, *Winchester '73* (1950), *Hangman's Knot* (1952), *Apache Ambush* (1955), Louis L'amour's *The Burning Hills* (1956) and *Utah Blaine* (1957), *The Guns of Fort Petticoat* (1957) again with Audie Murphy, another Louis L'amour western *The Tall Stranger* (1957) with Joel McCrea, *Wanted: Dead or Alive* (958), *Inherit the Wind* (1960), *Posse from Hell* (1961) a fourth time with Audie Murphy, *Dennis the Menace* (1962), *Twilight Zone* (1963), *The Fugitive* (1963), *Bullet for a Badman* (1964) a fifth appearance with Audie Murphy, *Taggart* (1964) a fourth Louis L'amour western, *Chisum* (1970), and his final film *The Hanged Man* (1974).

He died April 2, 1976, of natural causes at age seventy-four in Santa Monica, California.

Shirley Temple

Joel McCrea and Shirley Temple in *Our Little Girl*

Shirley Jane Temple was born in Santa Monica, California April 23, 1928 and was an American film and television actress, singer, dancer and public servant, most famous as a child star in the 1930s. As an adult, she entered politics and became a diplomat, serving as United States Ambassador to Ghana and later to Czechoslovakia, and as Chief of Protocol of the United States.

Temple began her film career in 1932 at the age of three. In 1934, she found international fame in *Bright Eyes*, a feature film designed specifically for her talents. She received a special Juvenile Academy Award in February 1935 for her outstanding contribution as a juvenile performer to motion pictures during 1934, and film hits such as *Curly Top* and *Heidi* followed year after year during the mid-to-late 1930s. Licensed merchandise that capitalized on her wholesome image included dolls, dishes and clothing. Her box office popularity waned as she reached adolescence. She appeared in a few films of varying quality in her mid-to-late teens, and retired completely from films in 1950 at the age of 22. She was the top box-office draw in Hollywood for four years in a row (1935–1938) in a *Motion Picture Herald* poll.

She returned to show business in 1958 with a two-season television anthology series of fairy tale adaptations. She made guest appearances on television shows in the early 1960s and filmed a sitcom pilot that was never released. She sat on the boards of corporations and organizations including The Walt Disney Company, Del Monte Foods and theNational Wildlife Federation. She began her diplomatic career in 1969, with an appointment to represent the United States at a session of the United Nations General Assembly. In 1988, she published her autobiography, *Child Star*.

Temple was the recipient of numerous awards and honors including the Kennedy Center Honors and a Screen Actors Guild Life Achievement Award. She ranks 18th on the American Film Institute's list of the greatest female American screen legends of all time.

She was the daughter of Gertrude Amelia Temple (née Krieger), a homemaker, and George Francis Temple, a bank employee. The family was of English, German and Dutch ancestry. She had two brothers, George Francis, Jr. and John Stanley. Temple's mother encouraged her infant daughter's singing, dancing, and acting talents, and in September 1931 enrolled her in Meglin's Dance School in Los Angeles. About this time, Temple's mother began styling her daughter's hair in ringlets similar to those of silent film star Mary Pickford.

While at Meglin's, she was spotted by Charles Lamont, a casting director for Educational Pictures. Although Shirley hid behind the piano while in the studio, Lamont took a shine to her, inviting her to audition, and in 1932 signed her to a contract. Educational Pictures were about to launch their *Baby Burlesks*, series of short films satirizing recent film and political events, using pre-school children in every role. Because the children were dressed as adults and given mature dialogue the series was eventually seen as dated and exploitive.

Baby Burlesks was a series of one-reelers; another series of two-reelers called *Frolics of Youth* followed, with Temple playing Mary Lou Rogers, a youngster in a contemporary suburban family. To underwrite production costs at Educational, Temple and her child co-stars modeled for breakfast cereals and other products. She was lent to Tower Productions for a small role in her first feature film (*The Red-Haired Alibi*) in 1932 and, in 1933, to Universal, Paramount, and Warner Bros., for various bit parts. After Educational Pictures declared bankruptcy in 1933, her father purchased her contract for $25.

It was while walking out of the viewing of her last *Frolics of Youth* picture that Fox Film songwriter Jay Gorney saw Temple dancing in the movie theater lobby. Recognizing her from the screen, he arranged for her to have a tryout for the movie *Stand Up and Cheer!*. Arriving for the audition on December 7, 1933, she won the part and was signed to a $150/week contract guaranteed for two weeks by the Fox Film Corporation. The role turned out to be a breakthrough performance for her. Her charm was evident to Fox heads, as she was ushered into corporate offices almost immediately after the completion of the *Baby Take a Bow* song and dance number she did with James Dunn. On December 21, 1933, her contract was extended to a year at the same $150/week with a seven year option and her mother Gertrude was hired on at $25/week as her hairdresser and personal coach. Released in May 1934, *Stand Up and Cheer!* became Temple's breakthrough film. Within months, she became the symbol of wholesome family entertainment. In June, her success continued with a loan-out to Paramount for *Little Miss Marker*.

Following the success of her first three 1934 movies, it soon became apparent to the Temples that the amount of money she was being paid was not commensurate to the amount of money her films generated for the studios. Her image also started to appear on numerous commercial products without approval and without compensation. In an effort to get control over the corporate piracy of her image and to negotiate with Fox, Temple's parents hired the lawyer Loyd Wright to represent them. On July 18, 1934, Temple's contract was raised to $1,000 a week and her mother's salary was raised to $250 a week, with an additional $15,000 bonus for each movie completed. Cease and desist letters were sent out to several companies and the process was started for awarding corporate licenses.

On December 28, 1934, *Bright Eyes* was released. It was the first feature film crafted specifically for Temple's talents and the first in which her name appeared above the title. Her signature song, "On the Good Ship Lollipop", was introduced in the film and sold 500,000 sheet music copies. The film demonstrated Temple's ability to portray a multi-dimensional character and established a formula for her future roles as a lovable, parentless waif whose charm and sweetness mellow gruff older men. In February 1935, Temple became the first child star to be honored with a miniature Juvenile Oscar for her 1934 film accomplishments, and she added her foot- and handprints to the forecourt at Grauman's Chinese Theatre a month later.

Fox Films merged with Twentieth Century Pictures to become 20th Century Fox in 1935. Producer and studio head Darryl F. Zanuck focused his attention and resources upon cultivating Temple's superstar status. With four successful films to her credit, she was the studio's greatest asset. Nineteen writers known as the Shirley Temple Story Development team created eleven original stories and some adaptations of the classics for her.

Biographer Anne Edwards writes about the tone and tenor of Temple films under Zanuck, "This was mid-Depression, and schemes proliferated for the care of the needy and the regeneration of the fallen. But they all required endless paperwork and demeaning, hours-long queues, at the end of which an exhausted, nettled social worker dealt with each person as a faceless number. Shirley offered a natural solution: to open one's heart." Edwards points out that the characters created for Temple would change the lives of the cold, the hardened, and even the criminal with positive results. Edwards quotes a nameless filmographer: "She assaults, penetrates, and opens [the flinty characters] making it possible for them to *give* of themselves. All of this returns upon her at times forcing her into situations where she must decide who needs her most. It is her agony, her Calvary, and it brings her to her most despairing moments ... Shirley's capacity for love ... was indiscriminate, extending to pinched misers or to common hobos, it was a social, even a political, force on a par with democracy or the Constitution." Temple films were seen as generating hope and optimism, and President Franklin D. Roosevelt said, "It is a splendid thing that for just fifteen cents an American can go to a movie and look at the smiling face of a baby and forget his troubles."

Most films Temple starred in were cheaply made at $200,000 or $300,000 per picture and were comedy-dramas with songs and dances added, sentimental and melodramatic situations aplenty, and little in the way of production values. Her film titles are a clue to the way she was marketed—*Curly Top* and *Dimples*, and her "little" pictures such as *The Little Colonel* and *The Littlest Rebel*. Temple often played a fixer-upper, a precocious Cupid, or the good fairy in these films, reuniting her estranged parents or smoothing out the wrinkles in the romances of young couples. She was very often motherless, sometimes fatherless, and sometimes an orphan confined to a dreary asylum. Elements of the traditional fairy tale were woven into her films: wholesome goodness triumphing over meanness and evil, for example, or wealth over poverty, marriage over divorce, or a booming economy over a depressed one. As Temple matured into a pre-adolescent, the formula was altered slightly to encourage her naturalness, naïveté, and tomboyishness to come forth and shine while her infant innocence, which had served her well at six but was inappropriate for her tweens (or later childhood years), was toned down.

In the contract they signed in July 1934, Temple's parents agreed to four films a year from their daughter (rather than the three they wished). A succession of films followed: *The Little Colonel*, *Our Little Girl* with Joel McCrea, *Curly Top* (with the signature song "Animal Crackers in My Soup"), and *The Littlest Rebel* in 1935. *Curly Top* and *The Littlest Rebel* were named to *Variety's* list of top box office draws for 1935. In 1936, *Captain January*, *Poor Little Rich Girl*, *Dimples*, and *Stowaway* were released. *Curly Top* was Temple's last film before the merger of 20th Century and Fox.

Based on Temple's many screen successes, Zanuck increased budgets and production values for her films. By the end of 1935, Temple's salary was raised to $2,500 a week. In 1937, John Ford was hired to direct the sepia-toned *Wee Willie Winkie* (Temple's own favorite) and an A-list cast was signed that included Victor McLaglen, C. Aubrey Smith and Cesar Romero. Elaborate sets were built at the famed Iverson Movie Ranch in Chatsworth, Calif., for the production, with a rock feature at the heavily filmed location ranch eventually being named in honor of Temple and becoming known as Shirley Temple Rock.

The film was a critical and commercial hit. but British writer and critic Graham Greene muddied the waters in October 1937 when he wrote in a British magazine that Temple was a "complete totsy" and accused her of being too nubile for a nine-year-old:

"Her admirers—middle-aged men and clergymen—respond to her dubious coquetry, to the sight of her well-shaped and desirable little body, packed with enormous vitality, only because the safety curtain of story and dialogue drops between their intelligence and their desire".

Temple and Twentieth Century-Fox sued for libel and won. The settlement remained in trust for Temple in an English bank until she turned twenty-one, when it was donated to charity and used to build a youth center in England.

The only other Temple film released in 1937 was *Heidi*. Midway through the shooting of the movie, the dream sequence was added into the script. There were reports that Temple was behind the dream sequence and that she was enthusiastically pushing for it but in her autobiography she vehemently denied this. Her contract gave neither her nor her parents any creative control over the movies she was in. She saw this as the collapse of any serious attempt by the studio to build upon the dramatic role from the previous movie *Wee Willie Winkie*.

The Independent Theatre Owners Association paid for an advertisement in the *Hollywood Reporter* in May 1938 that included Temple on a list of actors who deserved their salaries while others, such as Katharine Hepburn and Joan Crawford, were described as "whose box-office draw is nil". That year *Rebecca of Sunnybrook*

Farm, *Little Miss Broadway* and *Just Around the Corner* were released. The latter two were panned by the critics, and *Corner* was the first Temple film to show a slump in ticket sales. The following year, Zanuck secured the rights to the children's novel, *A Little Princess*, believing the book would be an ideal vehicle for Temple. He budgeted the film at $1.5 million (twice the amount of *Corner*) and chose it to be her first Technicolor feature. *The Little Princess* was a 1939 critical and commercial success with Temple's acting at its peak. Convinced Temple would successfully move from child star to teenage actress, Zanuck declined a substantial offer from MGM to star Temple as Dorothy in *The Wizard of Oz* and cast her instead in *Susannah of the Mounties*, her last money-maker for Twentieth Century-Fox. The film was successful, but because she made only two films in 1939 instead of the usual three or four, Temple dropped from number one box-office favorite in 1938 to number five in 1939.

In 1939, Temple was the subject of the Salvador Dalí painting *Shirley Temple, The Youngest, Most Sacred Monster of the Cinema in Her Time* and she was animated and was with Donald Duck in *The Autograph Hound*.

In 1940, Temple starred in two consecutive flops at Twentieth Century-Fox, *The Blue Bird* and *Young People*. Temple's parents bought up the remainder of her contract and sent her at the age of 12 to Westlake School for Girls, an exclusive country day school in Los Angeles. At the studio, Temple's bungalow was renovated, all traces of her tenure expunged, and the building reassigned as an office complex.

Within a year of her departure from Twentieth Century-Fox, MGM signed Temple for her comeback, and made plans to team her with Judy Garland and Mickey Rooney for the Andy Hardy series. The idea was quickly abandoned, with MGM teaming Temple with Garland and Rooney for the musical *Babes on Broadway*. Fearing that either Garland or Rooney could easily upstage Temple, MGM replaced her with Virginia Weidler. As a result, Temple's only film for Metro became *Kathleen* in 1941, a story about an unhappy teenager. The film was not a success and her MGM contract was canceled after mutual consent. *Miss Annie Rooney* followed for United Artists in 1942, but it too was unsuccessful. The actress retired for almost two years from films, throwing herself into school life and activities.

In 1944, David O. Selznick signed Temple to a personal four-year contract. She appeared in two wartime hits for him: *Since You Went Away* and *I'll Be Seeing You*. Selznick however became involved with Jennifer Jones and lost interest in developing Temple's career. She was loaned to other studios with *Kiss and Tell*, *The Bachelor and the Bobby-Soxer*, and *Fort Apache* being her few good films at the time.

According to biographer Robert Windeler, her 1947–1949 films neither made nor lost money, but "had a cheapie B look about them and indifferent performances from her".Selznick suggested she move abroad, gain maturity as an actress, and even change her name. She had been typecast, he warned her, and her career was in perilous straits. After auditioning for and losing the role of Peter Pan on the Broadway stage in August 1950, Temple took stock, admitted her recent movies had been poor fare, and announced her official retirement from films on December 16, 1950.

Many Temple-inspired products were manufactured and released during the 1930s. Ideal Toy and Novelty Company in New York City negotiated a license for dolls with the company's first doll wearing the polka-dot dress from *Stand Up and Cheer!*. Shirley Temple dolls realized $45 million in sales before 1941. A mug, a pitcher, and a cereal bowl in cobalt blue with a decal of Temple were given away as a premium with Wheaties.

Successfully-selling Temple items included a line of girls' dresses and accessories, soap, dishes, cutout books, sheet music, mirrors, paper tablets, and numerous other items. Before 1935 ended, Temple's income from licensed merchandise royalties would exceed $100,000, doubling her income from her movies. In 1936, her income would top $200,000 from royalties. She endorsed Postal Telegraph, Sperry Drifted Snow Flour, the Grunow Teledial radio, Quaker Puffed Wheat, General Electric and Packard automobiles.

At the height of her popularity, Temple was often the subject of a number of myths and rumors, some of which were propagated by 20th Century Fox/Fox Films. In addition to forging her birth certificate to make her a year younger, Fox also publicized her as a natural talent with no formal acting or dance training. As a way of explaining how she knew stylized buck and weave dancing, she was enrolled in the Elisa Ryan School of Dancing for two weeks.

One persistent rumor that was especially prevalent in Europe was the idea that Temple was not a child at all but rather a 30-year old midget due in part to her stockier body type. So prevalent were these rumors that the Vatican dispatched Father Silvio Massante in part to investigate whether or not she was indeed a child. The fact that she never seemed to miss any teeth led some people to conclude she had all her adult teeth. Temple was actually constantly losing teeth throughout her tenure with 20th Century Fox, most notably during the sidewalk ceremony in front of Grauman's Theatre, where she took off her shoes and placed her bare feet in the cement to take attention away from her face. To combat this, she wore dental plates and caps to hide the gaps in her teeth. Another rumour pertaining to her teeth was the idea that they were filed to make them appear like baby teeth, which was false.

Her biggest trademark, her hair, also was the subject of rumors. One rumor that circulated was that she actually wore a wig. On more than one occasion, fans would yank at her hair to test this theory. As she would later state, she wished all she had to do was wear a wig. The actual nightly process she went through in the setting of her curls was actually tedious and often grueling, with once a week vinegar rinses burning her eyes. Rumors also spread about her hair color, namely that she was not a natural blonde, but this was untrue. During the making of *Rebecca of Sunnybrook Farm*, news spread that she was going to do extended scenes without her trademark curls. During production, she also caught a cold which caused her to miss a couple days. As a result, a spurious myth began in Britain that all of her hair had been cut off.

In 1943, 15-year-old Temple met John Agar (1921–2002), an Army Air Corps sergeant, physical training instructor, and a member of a Chicago meat-packing family. On September 19, 1945, when Temple was 17 years old, they were married before 500 guests in an Episcopal ceremony at Wilshire Methodist Church in Los Angeles. On January 30, 1948, Temple gave birth to their daughter, Linda Susan. Agar became a professional actor and the couple made two films together: *Fort Apache* (1948, RKO) and *Adventure in Baltimore* (1949, RKO). The marriage became troubled, and Temple divorced Agar on December 5, 1949. She received custody of their daughter and the restoration of her maiden name. The divorce was finalized on December 5, 1950.

In January 1950, Temple met Charles Alden Black, a WWII United States Navy intelligence officer and Silver Star recipient who was Assistant to the President of the Hawaiian Pineapple Company. Conservative and patrician, he was the son of James B. Black, the president and later chairman of Pacific Gas and Electric, and reputedly one of the richest young men in California. Temple and Black were married in his parents' Del Monte, California, home on December 16, 1950, before a small assembly of family and friends.

The family relocated to Washington, D.C., when Black was recalled to the Navy at the outbreak of the Korean War. Temple gave birth to their son, Charles Alden Black, Jr., in Washington, D.C., on April 28, 1952. Following the war's end and Black's discharge from the Navy, the family returned to California in May 1953. Black managed television station KABC-TV in Los Angeles, and Temple became a homemaker. Their daughter Lori was born on April 9, 1954. Lori went on to be a bassist in the grunge band the Melvins. In September 1954, Charles, Sr. became director of business operations for the Stanford Research Institute and the family moved to Atherton, California. The couple remained married for 54 years until his death on August 4, 2005, at home in Woodside of complications from a bone marrow disease.

Between January and December 1958, Temple hosted and narrated a successful NBC television anthology series of fairy tale adaptations called *Shirley Temple's Storybook*. Temple acted in three of the sixteen hour-long episodes, and her son made his acting debut in the Christmas episode, "Mother Goose".The series was popular but faced some problems. The show lacked the special effects necessary for fairy tale dramatizations, sets were amateurish, and episodes were telecast in no regular time-slot, making it difficult to generate a following. The show was reworked and released in color in September 1960 in a regular time-slot as *The Shirley Temple Show*. It faced stiff competition from *Maverick*, *Lassie*, *Dennis the Menace*, the 1960 telecast of *The Wizard of Oz*, and the Walt Disney anthology television series however, and was canceled at season's end in September 1961.

Temple continued to work on television, making guest appearances on *The Red Skelton Show*, *Sing Along with Mitch*, and other shows. In January 1965, she portrayed a social worker in a sitcom pilot called *Go Fight City Hall* that was never released. In 1999, she hosted the *AFI's 100 Years... 100 Stars* awards show on CBS, and, in 2001, served as a consultant on an ABC-TV production of her autobiography, *Child Star: The Shirley Temple Story*.

Motivated by the popularity of *Storybook* and television broadcasts of Temple's films, the Ideal Toy Company released a new version of the Shirley Temple doll and Random House published three fairy tale anthologies under Temple's name. Three hundred thousand dolls were sold within six months and 225,000 books between October and December 1958. Other merchandise included handbags and hats, coloring books, a toy theater, and a recreation of the *Baby, Take a Bow* polka-dot dress.

Following her venture into television, Temple became active in the Republican Party in California. In 1967, she ran unsuccessfully in a special election in California's 11th congressional district to fill the seat left vacant by the death of eight-term Republican J. Arthur Younger from leukemia. She ran as a conservative and lost to law school professor Pete McCloskey, a liberal Republican who was a staunch opponent of the Vietnam War.

Temple was extensively involved with the Commonwealth Club of California, a public-affairs forum headquartered in San Francisco. She spoke at several of the meetings through the years and served as its president in 1984.

Temple got her start in foreign service after her failed run for Congress in 1967, when Henry Kissinger overheard her talking about Namibia at a party and was surprised that she knew anything about it. She was appointed Representative to the 24th United Nations General Assembly by President Richard M. Nixon (September – December 1969), and was appointed United States Ambassador to Ghana (December 6, 1974 – July 13, 1976) by

President Gerald R. Ford. She was appointed first female Chief of Protocol of the United States (July 1, 1976 – January 21, 1977), and was in charge of arrangements for President Jimmy Carter's inauguration and inaugural ball. She served as the United States Ambassador to Czechoslovakia (August 23, 1989 – July 12, 1992), having been appointed by President George H. W. Bush. She was the first and only female US ambassador to Czechoslovakia. Temple was a personal witness to two crucial moments in the history of Czechoslovakia's fight against Communism. Temple was in Prague in August 1968, as a representative of the International Federation of Multiple Sclerosis Societies and was actually going to meet up with Czechoslovakian party leader Alexander Dubček on the very day that Soviet-backed forces invaded the country. Dubček fell out of favor with the Soviets after a series of reforms known as the Prague Spring. Temple, who was stranded at a hotel as the tanks rolled in, sought refuge on the roof of the hotel. It was from here she saw an unarmed woman on the street gunned down by Soviet forces, a sight which stayed with her for the rest of her life. Later, after she became ambassador to Czechoslovakia, she was present during the Velvet Revolution, which brought about the end of Communism in Czechoslovakia. Temple played a critical role in hastening the end of the Communist regime by openly sympathizing with anti-Communist dissidents and later establishing formal diplomatic relations with the newly elected government led by Václav Havel. She took the unusual step of personally accompanying Havel on his first official visit to Washington, riding along on the same plane.

In 1972, Temple was diagnosed with breast cancer. The tumor was removed and a modified radical mastectomy performed. Following the operation, she announced it to the world via radio, television, and a February 1973 article for the magazine *McCall's*. In doing so, she became one of the first prominent women to speak openly about breast cancer.

Temple served on numerous boards of directors of large enterprises and organizations including The Walt Disney Company, Del Monte, Bank of America, the Bank of California, BANCAL Tri-State, Fireman's Fund Insurance, the United States Commission for UNESCO, the United Nations Association and the National Wildlife Federation.

Shirley Temple died on February 10, 2014, at the age of 85. She was at her home in Woodside, California, surrounded by family and caregivers. Her family stated only that she died of natural causes. The specific cause, according to her death certificate released on March 3, 2014, was chronic obstructive pulmonary disease. A lifelong smoker, she avoided revealing her habit in public to avoid setting a bad example for her fans. She is survived by her three children, as well as a granddaughter and two great-grandchildren.

Robert Tessier

Robert W. Tessier was born in Lowell, Massachusetts June 2, 1934 and was an American actor and stuntman who was best known for playing heavy, menacing characters on film and television.

Born of Algonquian descent, Tessier served as a paratrooper in the Korean War earning both a Silver Star and Purple Heart.

Tessier was an accomplished motorcycle rider doing stunts in the circus. These skills helped him secure his first film role in *The Born Losers* (1967) directed by Tom Laughlin.

With his shaven head, size and threatening-looking appearance, Tessier went on to play a series of villainous roles on both TV and in film. He later formed a stunt troupe called Stunts Unlimited with director Hal Needham.

Although Tessier starred in many films and TV roles over his career, probably two of his best remembered film roles were as the menacing, karate-wielding convict "Shokner" in the 1974 comedy-drama *The Longest Yard* with Burt Reynolds (whom he counted as one of his friends) and as Kevin in *The Deep* (1977). He also played a bare knuckle fighter in the Charles Bronson film *Hard Times* (1975).

More of his roles included *Cry Blood, Apache* (1970) with Joel and Jody McCrea, *The Velvet Vampire* (1971), *Kung Fu* (1974), *Little House on the Prairie* (1975), *Doc Savage: The Man of Bronze* (1975), *Last of the Mohicans* (1977), *Hooper* (1978), *Centennial* (1978-1979), *Starsky and Hutch* (1979), *The Villain* (1979), *Buck Rogers in the 25th Century* (1979), *Hart to Hart* (1979), *The Dukes of Hazzard* (1980), *The Incredible Hulk* (1980), *Vega$* (1980), *The Cannonball Run* (1981), *Fantasy Island* (1981), *CHiPs* (1982), *Magnum, P.I.* (1984), *The A-Team* (1983-1985), *Spenser: For Hire* (1985), *The Fall Guy* (1981-1986), *B.L. Stryker* (1989), *Fertilize the Blaspheming Bombshell* (1990), and *Fists of Steel* (1991).

In his spare time, Tessier was an accomplished cabinet maker often making pieces for his co-stars.

Tessier died of cancer in October 11, 1990 at age 56 in Lowell, Massachusetts.

Walter Tetley

Walter Tetley was born Walter Campbell Tetzlaff in New York City, New York June 2, 1915 and was an American voice actor, was a child impersonator in radio's classic era, with regular roles on *The Great Gildersleeve* and *The Phil Harris-Alice Faye Show*, as well as continuing as a voice-over artist in animated cartoons, commercials, and spoken-word record albums. He is perhaps best known as the voice of "Sherman" in the Jay Ward-Bill Scott *Mr. Peabody* TV cartoons.

Tetley was born to a Scottish-born mother, Jessie Smith Campbell, and father Frederick Tetzlaff who was born in New York of German parents.

He was a precocious performer even when he was a child, beginning at age seven performing Harry Lauder imitations. He established himself in radio, usually playing smart-aleck kids. Tetley moved to Hollywood in 1938 and acted in a number of films (he is the wisecracking messenger or pageboy in several Universal Pictures comedies), but radio was his truest metier.

Some of his film roles included *You Can't Cheat an Honest Man* (1939), *They Shall Have Music* (1939) with Joel McCrea, *Let's Make Music* (1941), *Horror Island* (1941), *The Pride of the Yankees* (1942), and *Who Done It?* (1942) with Abbott and Costello,

Walter Tetley's perennially adolescent voice was the result of a medical condition. While this has been cited as a hormonal problem, one of Tetley's employers, Bill Scott, offered a more specific explanation. According to Scott, Tetley's mother was reluctant to give up the revenue generated from her son's busy radio career and, in Scott's words, "She had him fixed (castrated). Walter Tetley, the world's tallest midget." Whatever the medical reason, the condition arrested Tetley's development, preventing his voice from breaking into maturity as well as preventing his further physical growth. Tetley would sound forever as though he was stranded on the bridge between boyhood and pre-teen adolescence. Combined with his excellent delivery and spot-on comic timing, he parlayed his condition into a radio career that lasted nearly a quarter of a century, with some of radio's biggest stars including Tetley in their shows, including but not limited to Fred Allen, Jack Benny, W.C. Fields and others.

Fans of vintage radio remember Walter Tetley best for two roles. He was cast to play spunky nephew Leroy on *The Great Gildersleeve*, beginning in 1941. (Leroy's "Ah, you kiddin'?" and "Aw, for corn's sake!" became almost as much of a pair of show catch-phrases as the title character's booming trill, "Leeee-rooooy!") Tetley stayed with that role for just about the entire life of that show, voicing Leroy in and out of jams from making nitroglycerin with his home chemistry set to helping Uncle Gildersleeve (Harold Peary) break out of the public library into which they got locked accidentally, after hours. The bad news: his unique appearance and true age obstructed him from playing the shorter, younger Leroy in the four *Gildersleeve* feature films (though he did appear in a speaking role as a bellhop in the third of those films, 1943's *Gildersleeve on Broadway*).

But Tetley might have been an even bigger hit beginning in 1948, when he took on a concurrent continuing role on an equally popular comedy, playing obnoxious grocery boy Julius Abruzzio on *The Phil Harris-Alice Faye Show* until the show's finish in 1954. (Surviving episodes that include pre-air audience warmups by Phil Harris usually included Harris alluding to Tetley as "the kid who steals the show every week"—even though Tetley was almost 40 years old when the Harris-Faye show ended production.) Julius combined an obsession with getting the better of his clumsy elders Phil and Remley to an unconcealed crush on Alice and was as much a fixture on the show as Harris's in-character malapropping vanity and Faye's tart but loving earthiness. He also played minor roles, such as a boy in a drugstore in the radio drama *Dr. Christian* (1937–1939). An example is in the "Dog Story" episode.

"I wondered what a radio show would be like if the audience could see the actors on stage," Tetley was quoted as saying once about his radio work. "But then they couldn't be allowed to read scripts. It would be like a movie. That wouldn't be any good. Radio would then be the same as movies." To the same interviewer, Tetley admitted that adulthood in the body of a child troubled him enough, finding it difficult for many years to make adult friends or even to assert himself to his own family. But he finally made peace with the dichotomy, accepted himself, and distinguished between his meal ticket and his self successfully.

Walter's foray into voices for theatrical cartoons began in the 1930s, as the voice of Felix the Cat in Van Beuren's *Rainbow Parade* cartoons in shorts such as "Neptune Nonsense". In "Bold King Cole", Tetley starts the cartoon short singing "Nature and Me", showcasing his song styling abilities.

In the late 1940s, he was the voice of Andy Panda in the Walter Lantz cartoons distributed by Universal Pictures.

In 1946, Tetley supplied the voice of the electric utility mascot Reddy Kilowatt in the short film *Reddy Made Magic*, produced by Lantz with Reddy Kilowatt creator Ashton B. Collins, Sr.; Tetley also performed the film's theme song. In 1959 he reprised the role in a John Sutherland-produced remake called *The Mighty Atom*.

In the late 1950s and early 1960s, Walter would become familiar to a new generation as the voice of Sherman, the nerdy, freckled, bespectacled boy sidekick of time-traveling dog genius Mr. Peabody, in the "Peabody's Improbable History" segments of Jay Ward's *The Rocky Show* (also known as *The Bullwinkle Show*), which made its debut in 1959.

Tetley worked for Capitol Records in the 1950s, providing an array of juvenile voices for the label's spoken-word and comedy albums, including *Stan Freberg Presents the United States of America Volume One: The Early Years* (1961). His *Gildersleeve* co-star, Harold Peary, had made three albums for Capitol a decade earlier, telling children's stories Gildersleeve-style.

In 1973 Tetley made an appearance on the Rod Serling radio series *The Zero Hour*. He can be heard in the "Princess Stakes Murder" episodes beginning the week of November 19.

In 1971, after several more years' voiceover work, Tetley was seriously injured in a motorcycle accident and used a wheelchair for the rest of his life. Numerous sources have suggested Tetley may have lost his southern California home in the same period and lived out his days in a trailer. He died September 4, 1975 at age 60, having never fully recovered from his injuries. His interment was in Chatsworth's Oakwood Memorial Park.

Frank M. Thomas

Frank Marion Thomas was born in St. Joseph, Missouri July 13, 1889 and was an American actor on the stage, screen, and television.

Thomas' parents were Jesse and Virginia Thomas. He first appeared on Broadway in 1914. Thomas also played many supporting roles in films from the 1930s through the 1970s. His best-known roles were *Special Investigator* (1936), *We Who Are About To Die* (1937), *A Man to Remember* (1938), *Law of the Underworld* (1938), *The Mysterious Miss X* (1939) with Alan Ladd, *Mr. Smith Goes to Washington* (1939), *A Shot In the Dark* (1941), *Reap the Wild Wind* (1942), *The Great Man's Lady* (1942) with Joel McCrea, *Desert Trail* (1942), and *No Place for a Lady* (1943), *Martin Kane* (1950-1952), *The Phil Silvers Show* (1957-1959), and *Paradise Bay* (1965).

Thomas and his wife, actress Mona Bruns, were the parents of actor Frankie Thomas. Frank died November 25, 1989 in Tujunga, California at the age of 100.

Dee J.Thompson

Dee J. Thompson was born as Dee Jeanette Thompson. She is an actress, known for *The Killer Is Loose* (1956), *Love in a Goldfish Bowl* (1961), and *The Glass Bottom Boat* (1966).

Some of her other roles included *It Grows on Trees* (1952), *Dragnet* (1953-1954), *Trooper Hook* (1957) with Joel McCrea, *Rawhide* (1959), *Alfred Hitchcock Presents* (1962), *My Favorite Martian* (1963), *Gunsmoke* (1956-1965), *The Alfred Hitchcock Hour* (1962-1965), and *The Big Valley* (1967).

Jim Thorpe

James Francis "Jim" Thorpe -*Wa-Tho-Huk*, translated as "Bright Path"; was born in Prague, Indian Territory, USA. [now Oklahoma] May 28, 1888 and was an American athlete of Native American and European ancestry. Considered one of the most versatile athletes of modern sports, he won Olympic gold medals for the 1912 pentathlon and decathlon, played American football (collegiate and professional), and also played professional baseball and basketball. He lost his Olympic titles after it was found he was paid for playing two seasons of semi-professional baseball before competing in the Olympics, thus violating the amateurism rules that were then in place. In 1983, thirty years after his death, the International Olympic Committee (IOC) restored his Olympic medals.

Thorpe grew up in the Sac and Fox Nation in Oklahoma. He played as part of several all American Indian teams throughout his career, and "barnstormed" as a professional basketball player with a team composed entirely of American Indians.

From 1920 to 1921, Thorpe was nominally the first president of the American Professional Football Association (APFA), which would become the National Football League (NFL) in 1922.

He played professional sports until age 41, the end of his sports career coinciding with the start of the Great Depression. Thorpe struggled to earn a living after that, working several odd jobs. Thorpe suffered from alcoholism, and lived his last years in failing health and poverty.

In a poll of sports fans conducted by ABC Sports, Thorpe was voted the Greatest Athlete of the Twentieth Century out of fifteen other athletes including Muhammad Ali, Babe Ruth, Jesse Owens, Wayne Gretzky, Jack Nicklaus, and Michael Jordan.

Information about Thorpe's birth, name and ethnic background varies widely. He was baptized "Jacobus Franciscus Thorpe" in the Catholic Church. Thorpe was born in Indian Territory, but no birth certificate has been found. He was generally considered to have been born on May 28, 1888, near the town of Prague, Oklahoma.

Thorpe himself said in an article in *The Shawnee News-Star* in 1949 that he was born May 28, 1888, on his mother's allotment "near and south of Bellemont – Pottawatomie County – along the banks of the North Fork River . . . hope this will clear up the inquiries as to my birthplace." Bellemont was a small community, now disappeared, on the line between Pottawatomie and Lincoln Counties. While the town of Prague, Lincoln County, now claims to be the birthplace of Thorpe, there is no evidence that Thorpe himself called Prague his hometown. All his personal references were either Shawnee (the county seat of Pottawatomie County and about ten miles southwest of his birthplace) or "Pott County". The Sak And Fox agency is in Stroud, Lincoln County, which could cause some of the confusion.

Thorpe's parents were both of mixed-race ancestry. His father, Hiram Thorpe, had an Irish father and a Sac and Fox Indian mother. His mother, Charlotte Vieux, had a French father and a Potawatomi mother, a descendant of Chief Louis Vieux. He was raised as a Sac and Fox, and his native name, *Wa-Tho-Huk*, translated as "path lit by great flash of lightning" or, more simply, "Bright Path". As was the custom for Sac and Fox, he was named for something occurring around the time of his birth, in this case the light brightening the path to the cabin where he was born. Thorpe's parents were both Roman Catholic, a faith which Thorpe observed throughout his adult life.

Thorpe attended the Sac and Fox Indian Agency school in Stroud, Oklahoma, with his twin brother, Charlie. Charlie helped him through school until he succumbed to a bout of pneumonia when they were nine years old. He ran away from school several times. His father then sent him to the Haskell Institute, an Indian boarding school in Lawrence, Kansas, so that he would not run away again. When his mother died of childbirth complications two years later, he became depressed. After several arguments with his father, he left home to work on a horse ranch.

In 1904 the sixteen-year-old Thorpe returned to his father and decided to attend Carlisle Indian Industrial School in Carlisle, Pennsylvania. There his athletic ability was recognized and he was coached by Glenn Scobey "Pop" Warner, one of the most influential coaches of early American football history. Later that year he became orphaned after Hiram Thorpe died from gangrene poisoning after being wounded in a hunting accident, and Jim again dropped out of school. He resumed farm work for a few years and then returned to Carlisle Indian Industrial School.

Thorpe began his athletic career at Carlisle in 1907 when he walked past the track and beat all the school's high jumpers with an impromptu 5-ft 9-in jump still in street clothes. His earliest recorded track and field results come from 1907. He also competed in football, baseball, lacrosse and even ballroom dancing, winning the 1912 intercollegiate ballroom dancing championship.

Pop Warner was hesitant to allow Thorpe, his best track and field athlete, to compete in a physical game such as football. Thorpe, however, convinced Warner to let him try some rushing plays in practice against the school team's defense; Warner assumed he would be tackled easily and give up the idea. Thorpe "ran around past and through them not once, but twice". He then walked over to Warner and said "Nobody is going to tackle Jim," while flipping him the ball.

Thorpe gained nationwide attention for the first time in 1911. As a running back, defensive back, placekicker and punter, Thorpe scored all his team's points—four field goals and a touchdown—in an 18–15 upset of Harvard, a top ranked team in those early days of the National Collegiate Athletic Association. His team finished the season 11–1. In 1912 Carlisle won the national collegiate championship largely as a result of his efforts – he scored 25 touchdowns and 198 points during the season.

Carlisle's 1912 record included a 27–6 victory over Army. In that game, Thorpe's 92-yard touchdown was nullified by a teammate's penalty, but on the next play Thorpe rushed for a 97-yard touchdown. Future President Dwight Eisenhower, who played against him that season, recalled of Thorpe in a 1961 speech:
"Here and there, there are some people who are supremely endowed. My memory goes back to Jim Thorpe. He never practiced in his life, and he could do anything better than any other football player I ever saw."

He was awarded All-American honors in both 1911 and 1912.

Football was - and would remain - Thorpe's favorite sport. He competed only sporadically in track and field, even though this turned out to be the sport in which he gained his greatest fame.

In the spring of 1912, he started training for the Olympics. He had confined his efforts to jumps, hurdles and shot-puts, but now added pole vaulting, javelin, discus, hammer and 56 lb weight. In the Olympic trials held at Celtic Park in New York, his all-round ability stood out in all these events and so he riveted a claim to a place on the team that went to Sweden.

For the 1912 Summer Olympics in Stockholm, Sweden, two new multi-event disciplines were included, the pentathlon and the decathlon. A pentathlon, based on the ancient Greek event, had been introduced at the 1906 Summer Olympics. The 1912 version consisted of the long jump, javelin throw, 200-meter dash, discus throw and 1500-meter run.

The decathlon was a relatively new event in modern athletics, although it had been part of American track meets since the 1880s and a version had been featured on the program of the 1904 St. Louis Olympics. The events of the new decathlon differed slightly from the American version. Both seemed appropriate for Thorpe, who was so versatile that he served as Carlisle's one-man team in several track meets. He could run the 100-yard dash in 10 seconds flat, the 220 in 21.8 seconds, the 440 in 51.8 seconds, the 880 in 1:57, the mile in 4:35, the 120-yard high hurdles in 15 seconds, and the 220-yard low hurdles in 24 seconds. He could long jump 23 ft 6 in and high-jump 6 ft 5 in. He could pole vault 11 feet, put the shot 47 ft 9 in, throw the javelin 163 feet, and throw the discus136 feet.

Thorpe entered the U.S. Olympic trials for both the pentathlon and the decathlon. He won the awards easily, winning three events, and was named to the pentathlon team, which also included future International Olympic Committee president Avery Brundage. There were only a few candidates for the decathlon team, however, and the trials were cancelled.

His schedule in the Olympics was busy. Along with the decathlon and pentathlon, he competed in the long jump and high jump. The first competition was the pentathlon. He won four of the five events and placed third in the javelin, an event he had not competed in before 1912. Although the pentathlon was primarily decided on place points, points were also earned for the marks achieved in the individual events. He won the gold medal. That same day, he qualified for the high jump final in which he placed fourth, and also took seventh place in the long jump. Even more remarkably, because someone had stolen his shoes just before he was due to compete, he found some discarded ones in a rubbish bin and won his medals wearing them. He is shown in the 1912 photo wearing two different shoes and extra socks because one shoe was too big.

Thorpe's final event was the decathlon, his first — and as it turned out, his only — Olympic decathlon. Strong competition from local favorite Hugo Wieslander was expected. Thorpe, however, easily defeated Wieslander by more than 700 points. He placed in the top four in all ten events, and his Olympic record of 8,413 points would stand for nearly two decades. Overall, Thorpe won eight of the fifteen individual events comprising the pentathlon and decathlon.

As was the custom of the day, the medals were presented to the athletes during the closing ceremonies of the games. Along with the two gold medals, Thorpe also received two challenge prizes, which were donated by King Gustav V of Sweden for the decathlon and Czar Nicholas II of Russia for the pentathlon. Several sources recount that, when awarding Thorpe his prize, King Gustav said, "You, sir, are the greatest athlete in the world", to which Thorpe replied, "Thanks, King".Contemporary sources from 1912 are lacking, suggesting that the story was apocryphal, however. The anecdote appeared in newspapers as early as 1948, 36 years after his appearance in the Olympics, and in books as early as 1952.

Thorpe's successes had not gone unnoticed at home, and he was honored with a ticker-tape parade on Broadway. He remembered later, "I heard people yelling my name, and I couldn't realize how one fellow could have so many friends."

Apart from his track and field appearances, he also played in one of two exhibition baseball games at the 1912 Olympics, which featured two teams composed of U.S. track and field athletes. It was not Thorpe's first try at baseball, as the public would soon learn.

After his victories at the Olympic Games in Sweden, on September 2, 1912, he returned to Celtic Park, the home of the Irish American Athletic Club, in Queens, New York (where he had qualified four months earlier for the Olympic Games), to compete in the Amateur Athletic Union's All-Around Championship. Competing against Bruno Brodd of the Irish American Athletic Club and J. Bredemus of Princeton University, he won seven of the ten events contested and came in second in the remaining three. With a total point score of 7,476 points, Thorpe broke the previous record of 7,385 points set in 1909, (also set at Celtic Park), by Martin Sheridan, the champion athlete of the Irish American Athletic Club. Sheridan, a five-time Olympic gold medalist, was present to watch his record broken, approached Thorpe after the event and shook his hand saying, "Jim, my boy, you're a great man. I never expect to look upon a finer athlete." He told a reporter from *The New York World*, "Thorpe is the greatest athlete that ever lived. He has me beaten fifty ways. Even when I was in my prime, I could not do what he did today."

In 1912, strict rules regarding amateurism were in effect for athletes participating in the Olympics. Athletes who received money prizes for competitions, were sports teachers or had competed previously against professionals were not considered amateurs and were barred from competition.

In late January 1913, the *Worcester Telegram* published a story announcing that Thorpe had played professional baseball, and other U.S. newspapers followed up the story. Thorpe had indeed played professional baseball in the Eastern Carolina League for Rocky Mount, North Carolina, in 1909 and 1910, receiving meager pay; reportedly as little as US$2 ($51 today) per game and as much as US$35 ($886 today) per week. College players, in fact, regularly spent summers playing professionally but most used aliases, unlike Thorpe.

Although the public didn't seem to care much about Thorpe's past, the Amateur Athletic Union (AAU), and especially its secretary James Edward Sullivan, took the case very seriously. Thorpe wrote a letter to Sullivan, in which he admitted playing professional baseball:[

..."I hope I will be partly excused by the fact that I was simply an Indian schoolboy and did not know all about such things. In fact, I did not know that I was doing wrong, because I was doing what I knew several other college men had done, except that they did not use their own names...."

His letter didn't help. The AAU decided to withdraw Thorpe's amateur status retroactively and asked the International Olympic Commission (IOC) to do the same. Later that year, the IOC unanimously decided to strip Thorpe of his Olympic titles, medals and awards and declare him a professional.

Although Thorpe had played for money, the AAU and IOC did not follow the rules for disqualification. The rulebook for the 1912 Olympics stated that protests had to be made "within" 30 days from the closing ceremonies of the games. The first newspaper reports did not appear until January 1913, about six months after the Stockholm Games had concluded. There is also some evidence that Thorpe's amateur status had been questioned long before the Olympics, but the AAU had ignored the issue until being confronted with it in 1913.

The only positive element of this affair for Thorpe was that, as soon as the news was reported that he had been declared a professional, he received offers from professional sports clubs.

Because the minor league team that last held Jim Thorpe's contract had disbanded in 1910, he found himself in the rare position of being a sought after free agent at the major league level during the era of the reserve clause, and thus had a choice of baseball teams for which to play. In January 1913, he turned down a starting position with the American League cellar-dwelling St. Louis Browns, choosing instead to join the 1912 National League champion New York Giants, who, with Thorpe playing in 19 of their 151 games, would repeat as the 1913 National League champions. Immediately following the Giants' October loss in the 1913 World Series, Thorpe and the Giants joined the Chicago White Sox for a world tour. Barnstorming across the United States and then around the world, Thorpe was the celebrity of the tour. Thorpe's presence increased the publicity, attendance and gate receipts for the tour. He met with Pope Pius X and Abbas II Hilmi Bey (the last Khedive of Egypt), and played before 20,000 people in London including King George V. While in Rome, he was filmed wrestling with another baseball player on the floor of the Colosseum, although no known copy of that film has survived.

Thorpe signed with the New York Giants baseball club in 1913 and played sporadically with them as an outfielder for three seasons. After playing in the minor leagues with the Milwaukee Brewers in 1916, he returned to the Giants in 1917 but was sold to the Cincinnati Reds early in the season. In the "double no-hitter" between Fred Toney of the Reds and Hippo Vaughn of the Chicago Cubs, Thorpe drove in the winning run in the 10th inning. Late in the season, he was sold back to the Giants. Again, he played sporadically for them in 1918 before being traded to the Boston Braves on May 21, 1919, for Pat Ragan. In his career, he amassed 91 runs scored, 82 runs batted in and a .252 batting average over 289 games. He continued to play minor league baseball until 1922.

But Thorpe had not abandoned football either. He first played professional football in 1913 as a member of the Indiana-based Pine Village Pros, a team that had a several-season winning streak against local teams during the 1910s. He then signed with the Canton Bulldogs in 1915. They paid him $250 ($5,828 today) a game, a tremendous wage at the time. Before signing him Canton was averaging 1,200 fans a game, but 8,000 showed up for his debut against the Massillon Tigers. The team won titles in 1916, 1917, and 1919. He reportedly ended the 1919 championship game by kicking a wind-assisted 95-yard punt from his team's own 5-yard line, effectively putting the game out of reach. In 1920, the Bulldogs were one of 14 teams to form the American Professional Football Association (APFA), which would become the National Football League (NFL) two years later. Thorpe was nominally the APFA's first president, but spent most of the year playing for Canton and a year later was replaced as president by Joseph Carr. He continued to play for Canton, coaching the team as well. Between 1921 and 1923, he helped organize and played for the Oorang Indians (LaRue, Ohio), an all-Native American team. Although the team's record was 3–6 in 1922, and 1–10 in 1923, he played well and was selected for the *Green Bay Press-Gazette's* first All-NFL team in 1923, which would later be formally recognized by the NFL as the league's official All-NFL team in 1931).

Thorpe never played for an NFL championship team. He retired from professional football at age 41, having played 52 NFL games for six teams from 1920 to 1928.

Until 2005, most of Thorpe's biographers were unaware of his basketball career until a ticket discovered in an old book that year documented his career in basketball. By 1926, he was the main feature of the "World Famous Indians" of LaRue which sponsored traveling football, baseball, and basketball teams. "Jim Thorpe and His World-Famous Indians" barnstormed for at least two years (1927–1928) in parts of New York and Pennsylvania as well as Marion, Ohio. Although pictures of Thorpe in his WFI basketball uniform were printed on postcards and published in newspapers, this period of his life was not well documented.

Thorpe married three times and had eight children (one of whom died in childhood). In 1913 Thorpe married Iva Miller, whom he had met at Carlisle. They had four children: Jim Jr. (who died at age 2), Gale, Charlotte and Grace. Miller filed for divorce from Thorpe in 1925, claiming desertion.

In 1926 Thorpe married Freeda V. Kirkpatrick (September 19, 1905 – March 2, 2007). She was working for the manager of the baseball team for which he was playing at the time. They had four sons: Carl, a lieutenant colonel in the U.S. Army, William, Richard and John ("Jack").Kirkpatrick divorced Thorpe in 1941 after 15 years of marriage.

Lastly, Thorpe married Patricia Askew on June 2, 1945; she was with him when he died.

After his athletic career, Thorpe struggled to provide for his family. He found it difficult to work a non-sports-related job and never held a job for an extended period of time. During the Great Depression in particular, he had various jobs, among others as an extra for several movies, usually playing an American Indian chief in Westerns.

Some of his film roles included *Touchdown* (1931), *Wild Horse Mesa* (1932), *King Kong* (1933), *Barbary Coast* (1935) with Joel McCrea, *Treachery Rides the Range* (1936), *Pick a Star* (1937) with Laurel and Hardy, *Start Cheering* (1938) with The Three Stooges, *The Man from Texas* (1939), *They Died with Their Boots On* (1941), *Outlaws of Santa Fe* (1944), *The Vampire's Ghost* (1945), *White Heat* (1949) with James Cagney, and *Wagon Master* (1950).

He also worked as a construction worker, a doorman (bouncer), a security guard and a ditchdigger, and briefly joined the United States Merchant Marine in 1945. Thorpe was a chronic alcoholic during his later life.

He ran out of money sometime in the early 1950s. When hospitalized for lip cancer in 1950, he was admitted as a charity case. At a press conference announcing the procedure, his wife, Patricia, wept and pleaded for help, saying, "[W]e're broke.... Jim has nothing but his name and his memories. He has spent money on his own people and has given it away. He has often been exploited."

In early 1953, Thorpe went into heart failure for the third time while dining with Patricia in their home in Lomita, California. He was briefly revived by artificial respiration and spoke to those around him, but lost consciousness shortly afterward and died on March 28 at the age of 64.

Chief Thundercloud

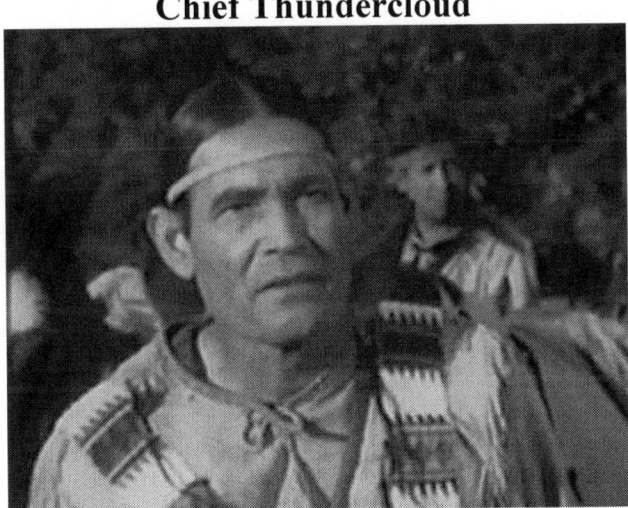

Chief Thundercloud wasborn Victor Daniels, April 12, 1899 and was an American character actor in Westerns.

Information about Thundercloud is vague. Most biographies state that he was a full blooded Cherokee (or Muskogee), although others state that he had some German, Scottish and/or Irish ancestors; and that he was educated at the University of Arizona, although no record exists of his enrollment. The pressbook for *The Lone Ranger Rides Again* announced his parents as "Dark Cloud and Morning Star, aristocrats of the Muskogee tribe" but his death certificate lists his father as "Joseph Mahawa."

Daniels worked many jobs before becoming a stuntman. From there he graduated to character actor status. His title "Chief" was a Hollywood invention. He had the title role in *Geronimo* (1939) and played Tonto in both Republic Lone Ranger serials, *The Lone Ranger* (1938) and *The Lone Ranger Rides Again* (1939).

More of his roles included *The Rustlers of Red Dog* (1935), *Custer's Last Stand* (1936), *The Riders of the Whistling Skull* (1937), *The Law West of Tombstone* (1938), *Union Pacific* (1939) with Joel McCrea, *Young Buffalo Bill* (1940), *Western Union* (1941), *Shut My Big Mouth* (1942), *Daredevils of the West* (1943), *Buffalo Bill* (1944) again with Joel McCrea, *Badman's Territory* (1946), *The Traveling Saleswoman* (1950), *Buffalo Bill in Tomahawk Territory* (1952), *My Little Margie* (1954), and *The Searchers* (1956).

In later years, he worked with other western actors, performing in live shows at the Corriganville Movie Ranch, now the Corriganville Regional Park near Simi Valley, California. One of his last appearances was on March 1, 1955, as the Apache Geronimo in the premiere episode of the syndicated television series *Buffalo Bill, Jr.*, starring Dick Jones in the fictional title role of a young Texas frontier marshal.

He died December 1, 1955 at age 56 in Ventura, California.

Zeffie Tilbury

Zeffie Agnes Lydia Tilbury was born in Paddington, Middlesex, England November 20, 1863 and was an English actress.

Zeffie Tilbury was the daughter of the variety performer Lydia Thompson and John Christian Tilbury, a riding-master, who died in a steeplechasing accident in 1864, when he was rolled on by his horse.

Tilbury was married twice. First to Arthur Frederick Lewis in June, 1887, and later to L. E. Woodthorpe, who died on April 8, 1915.

She was known first on the London stage and on the Broadway in New York. She is today best-known for playing wise or evil older characters in films, such as the distinguished lady gambler at dinner with Greta Garbo and Joel McCrea in *The Single Standard* (1929), as the pitful Grandma Joad in *The Grapes of Wrath* (1940) and Grandma Lester in *Tobacco Road* (1941).

She appeared in over 70 films. Her earliest surviving silent film is the Valentino/Nazimova 1921 production of *Camille*. Tilbury is probably best remembered as the old lady who is befriended by Spanky and his friends on her birthday and, as a result, is transformed from a lonely, disagreeable recluse to a happy and loving carefree soul in the 1936 Hal Roach *Our Gang* comedy *Second Childhood*. In the same year she also portrayed the Gypsy Queen in the Laurel and Hardy film *The Bohemian Girl* (1936).

More of her roles included *Werewolf of London* (1935), *After the Thin Man* (1936), *It Happened in Hollywood* (1937), *The Story of Alexander Graham Bell* (1939), *Sheriff of Tombstone* (1941), and *Flying with Music* (1942).

She died in Los Angeles, California July 241950 at the age of 86.

Regis Toomey

John Regis Toomey was born in Pittsburgh, Pennsylvania, August 13, 1898, and was an American film and television actor. He was one of four children of Francis X. and Mary Ellen Toomey and attended Peabody High School. He initially pondered a law career, but acting won out and he established himself as a musical stage performer.

Educated in dramatics at the University of Pittsburgh, where he became a brother of Sigma Chi, Toomey began as a stock actor and eventually made it to Broadway. Toomey was a singer on stage until throat problems (acute laryngitis) while touring in Europe stopped that aspect of his career. In 1929, he appeared in his first films such as *Alibi*, *The Wheel of Life,* and *Rich People*, initially starting out as a leading man, but finding more success as a character actor, sans his toupee.

In 1941, Toomey appeared in *You're in the Army Now*, in which he and Jane Wyman had the longest screen kiss in cinema history: 3 minutes and 5 seconds.

Toomey appeared in over 180 films, including classics such as *Union Pacific* (1939) with Joel McCrea, *Reaching for the Sun* (1941) again with Joel McCrea, *The Big Sleep* (1946) with Humphrey Bogart.

Other roles included *The Bishop's Wife* (1947), *The Boy with Green Hair* (1948), *Mighty Joe Young* (1949), *Frenchie* (1950) a third with Joel McCrea, *The Battle at Apache Pass* (1952), *Son of Belle Starr* (1953), *The High and the Mighty* (1954), and *Drums Across the River* (1954) with Audie Murphy.

In the 1954-1955 television season, Toomey appeared as Joe Mulligan, a police officer in Los Angeles and the father of the Mickey Rooney character Mickey Mulligan, in NBC's short-lived sitcom, *The Mickey Rooney Show: Hey, Mulligan.*

He portrayed Lt. Dennis "Mac" McGough to David Janssen's character of *Richard Diamond, Private Detective* (1957-1958).

He appeared in *The Mysterious Miss X* (1939) and *Guns of the Timberland* (1960) with Alan Ladd.

In the 1961–1962 television season, he appeared in a supporting role with George Nader in the syndicated crime drama *Shannon* about insurance investigators. From 1963–1966, Toomey was one of the stars of the ABC crime drama, *Burke's Law*, starring Gene Barry. He played Sergeant Les Hart, one of the detectives assisting the murder investigations of the millionaire police captain Amos Burke.

He played Dr. Barton Stuart in *Petticoat Junction* (1968-1969). More roles continued in *Change of Habit* (1969) with Elvis Presley, *The F.B.I.* (1972), *Adam-12* (1973), *The Phantom of Hollywood* (1974), *Won Ton Ton: The Dog Who Saved Hollywood* (1976), *Fantasy Island* (1978), *C.H.O.M.P.S.* (1979), *It's a Living* (1982), and *Evil Town* (1987).

His 1925 marriage to Kathryn Scott produced two children. They met in 1924 when he appeared in the musical Rose Marie which Kathryn had assistant choreographed.

Toomey died of natural causes on October 12, 1991, at the Motion Picture Country House in Woodland Hills, California, at age 93.

Fred 'Snowflake' Toones

Fred 'Snowflake' Toones was born January 5, 1906 in North Carolina. Toones is one of the most colorful character faces in B-Westerns and cliffhangers. He appeared in over 200 films between 1928 and 1951; and during 1936 and 1947, Toones often worked under contract for Republic Pictures, appearing in about forty of its films.

Toones often played a bootblack or shoeshine man in at least six of his movies, and Toones actually ran the shoeshine stand at Republic Studios.

Toones first appeared as a porter in 1932 in *The Hurricane Express*, and was usually typecast as a porter - appearing in over fifty films in such a role. He also played a variety of other service-oriented or domestic worker roles such as stable grooms, janitors, elevator operators, valets, cooks, bellhops, doormen, butlers, and bartenders.

His standard characterization was that of a middle-aged "colored" man with a high-pitched voice and childlike mannerisms. "Snowflake" was the stage name Toones was best known by, and he used this name as his credit as early as his third film, 1931's *Shanghaied Love*. Likewise, in *Shanghaied Love* and over 35 other films, "Snowflake" was also Toones' character name.

Toones acted in films such as *Mississippi* (1935), *Hawk of the Wilderness* (1938), and *Daredevils of the Red Circle* (1939) with Bruce Bennett and in many "B" westerns such as *The Lawless Nineties* (1936) with John Wayne.

He also appeared in dozens of two-reeler's such as Columbia's *Woman Haters* (1934) which was the Three Stooges first official Columbia short, and had a bit role in Laurel and Hardy's classic feature *Way Out West* (1937).

Toones is also a familiar face in four Preston Sturges comedies: *Twentieth Century* (1934), *Remember the Night* (1940), *Christmas in July* (1940), *The Great Man's Lady* (1942) with Joel McCrea, and *The Palm Beach Story* (1942) also with Joel McCrea.

More of his roles included *The Galloping Ghost* (1931), *I Am a Fugitive from a Chain Gang* (1932), *The Mayor of Hell* (1933), *Meet the Baron* (1933) also with The Three Stooges, *Half a Sinner* (1934) with Joel McCrea, *Stolen Harmony* (1935), *Come and Get It* (1936) a fourth with Joel McCrea, *Heroes of the Alamo* (1937), *Dodge City* (1939), *The People vs. Dr. Kildare* (1941), *Mystery of the 13th Guest* (1943), *The Lost Weekend* (1945), *The Crimson Key* (1947), and *Racket Squad* (1951).

He died February 13, 1962 at age 56 in Los Angeles, California.

Henry Travers

Henry Travers was born Travers John Heagerty March 5, 1874, and was an English actor. His most memorable role was that of the angel, Clarence, in the 1946 film *It's A Wonderful Life*.

Travers was the son of Daniel Heagerty, an Irish doctor from Cork. He grew up in Berwick-upon-Tweed, which is his birthplace according to many biographies, but had actually been born in Prudhoe, some sixty miles further south near the River Tyne. The family were only in Prudhoe for a couple of years, moving there from Woodburn, on the A68 road near Corsenside, Northumberland in about 1866 and then moving on to Tweedmouth at Berwick-upon-Tweed in about 1876.

Initially he trained as an architect at Berwick before taking to the stage under the name Henry Travers.

A stage actor in England, he immigrated to the United States and appeared in Hollywood film productions beginning in 1933 with Reunion in Vienna. More roles followed in *The Invisible Man* (1933), *Death Takes a Holiday* (1934), *Dodge City* (1939), *Stanley and Livingstone* (1939), *Primrose Path* (1940) with Joel McCrea, *Random Harvest* (1942), *The Naughty Nineties* (1945) with Abbott and Costello, *The Yearling* (1946), *Beyond Glory* (1948) with Alan Ladd and Audie Murphy, and *The Girl from Jones Beach* (1949).

Travers' most famous role was as the angel Clarence who comes to save James Stewart's character from suicide in Frank Capra's classic *It's a Wonderful Life* (1946).

He was also an Oscar-nominated actor for his role in the film *Mrs. Miniver* (1942).

After a long and successful career, he retired from the screen in 1949, and died October 18, 1965, at age 91 in Hollywood, Los Angeles, California.

Arthur Treacher

Arthur Veary Treacher was born in Brighton, East Sussex, England July 23, 1894 and was an English actor. Arthur was the son of a Sussex solicitor; he was educated at a boarding school in Uppingham in Rutland.

Treacher was a veteran of World War I serving as an officer in the Royal Garrison Artillery; his father had served with the Sussex Volunteer Artillery before his son's birth. After the war, he established a stage career and in 1926, he went to America as part of a musical-comedy revue called Great Temptations. He was featured in the 1930 Billy Rose production *Sweet and Low*.

He began his film career in the 1930s, which included roles in four Shirley Temple films: *Curly Top*, uncredited *Stowaway* (1936), *Heidi* (1937), and *The Little Princess* (1939). Scenes intentionally put the 6' 4" Treacher standing or dancing side-by-side with the tiny child actress. They sing and dance together in *The Little Princess* an old song "Knocked 'em in the Old Kent Road". This can currently be seen on YouTube. Treacher filled the role of the ideal butler, and he portrayed P.G. Wodehouse's perfect valet character Jeeves in the films *Thank You, Jeeves!* (1936) and *Step Lively, Jeeves* (1937). He also played a valet or butler in several other films, including *Personal Maid's Secret*, *Mister Cinderella* and *Bordertown*.

More early roles included *Gambling Lady* (1934) with Joel McCrea, *The Captain Hates the Sea* (1934) with The Three Stooges, *You Can't Have Everything* (1937), *Brother Rat and a Baby* (1940) with Alan Ladd, *In Society* (1944) with Abbott and Costello, *The Countess of Monte Cristo* (1948), and *Love That Brute* (1950).

In 1961 and 1962, he and William Gaxton starred in Guy Lombardo's production of the musical *Paradise Island*, which played at the Jones Beach Marine Theater.

In 1962, he replaced Robert Coote as King Pellinore (with over-the-title star billing) in the original Broadway production of Lerner and Loewe's musical *Camelot*, and he remained with the show through the Chicago engagement and post-Broadway tour that closed in August 1964.

In 1964, Treacher played the role of stuffy English butler Arthur Pinkney in two episodes of *The Beverly Hillbillies*. Pinkney mistakenly believed the hillbillies were the domestic servants of the family he was hired by, while the hillbillies believed Pinkney was a boarder at their Beverly Hills mansion.

Treacher played the role of Constable Jones in Disney's *Mary Poppins* (1964) and made many guest appearances on television, in addition to being Merv Griffin's announcer and sidekick on *The Merv Griffin Show* from 1965–70 ("...and now, here's the dear boy himself, Merrr-vin!") When Griffin switched from syndication to CBS in 1969, the network brass insisted that Treacher was too old for the show, but Griffin fought to keep Treacher and eventually won out. However, when Griffin moved his show to Los Angeles the following year, Treacher stayed behind, telling Griffin "at my age, I don't want to move, especially to someplace that shakes!"

During this period of latter-day popularity, Treacher also capitalized on his name recognition through the use of his name and image for such franchized business concerns as the Call Arthur Treacher Service System (a household help agency) and Arthur Treacher's Fish and Chips. The restaurant chain became popular in the 1970s and grew to nearly 900 outlets, although it is unclear whether or not Treacher had any financial involvement with the company. The fish and chips chain continues to exist, although there are believed to be only around 45 franchises left throughout the United States.

He died December 14, 1975 at age 81 in Manhasset, New York. He was survived by his wife, Virginia Taylor who married him in 1940. Treacher's ashes were scattered into the Atlantic Ocean.

Chief Many Treaties

Chief Many Treaties was born William Malcolm Hazlett on April 11, 1874 in Montana. He was an Was a Blackfoot Indian actor, known for *Go West, Young Lady* (1941), *The Law Rides Again* (1943), and *Buffalo Bill Rides Again* (1947).

More of his roles included *Battling with Buffalo Bill* (1931), *Gordon of Ghost City* (1933), *Drums of Destiny* (1937), *Kit Carson* (1940), *Springtime in the Rockies* (1942), *Buffalo Bill* (1944) with Joe McCrea, *Last of the Redmen* (1947), and *Black Bart* (1948).

He died on February 29, 1948 in Los Angeles, California at age 73.

Mary Treen

Mary Treen was born Mary Louise Summers March 27, 1907, in St. Louis, Missouri. About as reliable as one could ever find, character actress Mary Treen was a familiar face to most and could always be counted on to bring a bit of levity to any film scene.

A minor actress for much of her career, she managed to secure a plain, unassuming niche for herself in 1940s, 1950s and 1960s Hollywood. Her father died while she was still an infant. Raised in California by her mother, who once performed under the stage name Helene Sullivan, and her stepfather, a physician, she attended the Westlake School for Girls as well as a convent where she tried out successfully in school plays.

Mary began dancing in vaudeville shows and revues before seeking her fame in the movies. Tall (5'9") and stringy-framed, she formed a musical comedy duo with Marjorie Barnett, who was 5'3", billing themselves as "Treen and Barnett: Two Unsophisticated Vassar Co-eds". Much of their comedy was centered on their difference in height. Not a beauty by Hollywood standards, Mary relied on humor to get attention.

In 1934, Warner Brothers signed her up after seeing her in a local play. After three years, she freelanced. Her scores of pudgy-cheeked nurses, waitresses, career girls, wallflowers, and confidantes enhanced many a comedy or, at the very least, offered a brief respite in a heavier drama. In the long run, however she deserved better. A few of Mary's highlights would include the films *Kentucky Moonshine* (1938), *I Love a Soldier* (1944) (the role was written especially for her), *Don Juan Quilligan* (1945), and the Christmas classic *It's a Wonderful Life* (1946) as James Stewart's cousin Tilly.

Other roles included The Great Man's Lady (1942) with Joel McCrea, *So Proudly We Hail!* (1943) with Veronica Lake, *Texas, Brooklyn & Heaven* (1948) with Audie Murphy, *The Gene Autry Show* (1952), *Willy* (1954-1955), *The Last Stagecoach West* (1957), *The Sad Sack* (1957), *I Married a Monster from Outer Space* (1958), *Wagon Train* (1960), *The Andy Griffith Show* (1960-1961), and *The Errand Boy* (1961).

Mary actually stole a few scenes as the arch maid Hilda on *The Joey Bishop Show* (1962-1965) for three seasons.

She continued acting in such films and television programs as *Perry Mason* (1965), *Green Acres* (1966), *Please Don't Eat the Daisies* (1967), *The Bill Cosby Show* (1971), *Here's Lucy* (1974), *The Strongest Man in the World* (1975), *The Love Boat* (1977), *The Dukes of Hazzard* (1981), *The Fall Guy* (1981), and *Wait Till Your Mother Gets Home!* (1983).

She appeared in three Elvis Presley movies like *Girls! Girls! Girls!* (1962), *Fun in Acapulco* (1963), and *Paradise, Hawaiian Style* (1966).

Perhaps because she could play old maid types so easily in later years, she was often thought to have never married. She actually did marry, quite late in life, to a whole-sale liquor dealer. They had no children. He died in 1965 and she eventually moved in with her ex-vaudeville partner, Marjorie Barnett-Klein, who was also widowed.

In later years the two performed their old routines to the delight of other senior citizens. Mary was living in Balboa Beach, California when she died of cancer July 20, 1989 at the age of 82.

Claire Trevor

Claire Trevor was born as Claire Wemlinger in Bensonhurst, Brooklyn, New York March 8, 1910 and was an American film actress. She was nicknamed the "Queen of Film Noir" because of her many appearances in "bad girl" roles in film noir and other black-and-white thrillers. She appeared in over sixty films. She won the Academy Award for Best Supporting Actress for her role as the hopelessly alcoholic gangster moll in *Key Largo* and was nominated for her roles in *The High and the Mighty* and *Dead End*.

Trevor iwas the only child of Noel Wemlinger, a Fifth Avenue merchant tailor, and his wife, Benjamina ("Betty"), and grew up in Larchmont, New York. For many years her year of birth was misreported as 1909, rare instance of an actress actually being younger than her given age, which is why her age at death was initially given as 91, not 90. Her family was of German, Irish and Frenchdescent.

According to her biography on the website of Claire Trevor School of the Arts, "Trevor's acting career spanned more than seven decades and included successes in stage, radio, television, and film. . . . [S]he often played the hard-boiled blonde, and every conceivable type of 'bad girl' role."

After completing high school, Trevor began her career with six months of art classes at Columbia University and six months at the American Academy of Dramatic Arts, performing in stock in the late 1920s . By 1932 she was starring on Broadway; that same year she began appearing in Brooklyn-filmed Vitaphone shorts. Her first credited film role was in the 1933 film *Life in the Raw*, with her feature film debut coming that same year in *Jimmy and Sally* (1933) as "Sally Johnson".

From 1933–1938, Trevor starred in twenty-nine films, often having either the lead role or the role of heroine. In 1937, she was the second lead actress (after top-billed Sylvia Sydney) in *Dead End*, playing opposite Joel McCrea and Humphrey Bogart, which led to her nomination for Best Supporting Actress. From 1937–1940, she appeared with Edward G. Robinson in the popular radio series *Big Town*, while continuing to make movies. By 1939, she was well established as a solid "leading lady". Some of her most memorable performances during this period were opposite John Wayne, including the classic 1939 western *Stagecoach*, which was Wayne's breakthrough role. She starred opposite Wayne again in *Allegheny Uprising* that same year, and yet again in 1940 in *Dark Command*. Over a decade later, she would again costar with Wayne, gaining her final Oscar nomination for *The High and the Mighty* (1954).

Two of Trevor's most memorable roles were opposite Dick Powell in *Murder, My Sweet* (1944) and with Lawrence Tierney in *Born to Kill* (1947), in the latter playing a divorcee who gets more than she bargained for by falling in love with a bad boy who impulsively commits a murder. *Key Largo*, the following year, gave Trevor the role of Gaye Dawn, the washed-up nightclub singer and gangster's moll, for which she won the Academy Award for Best Supporting Actress.

In 1957 she won an Emmy for her role in the Producers' Showcase episode entitled *Dodsworth*. Trevor moved into supporting roles in the 1950s, with her appearances becoming increasingly rare after the mid-1960s. A few of her television roles included *Wagon Train* (1959), *The Untouchables* (1959), *Alfred Hitchcock Presents* (1956-1961), *Dr. Kildare* (1962), *The Love Boat* (1983), and *Murder, She Wrote* (1987).

She returned for one final theatrical film, as Charlotte in *Kiss Me Goodbye* (1982). Her last film was the 1987 television movie *Norman Rockwell's Breaking Home Ties*. Trevor made a guest appearance at the 70th Academy Awards in 1998.

Trevor married Clark Andrews, director of her radio show, in 1938, but they divorced four years later. Her second marriage, in 1943, to Navy lieutenant Cylos William Dunsmoore produced a son, Charles. The marriage ended in divorce in 1947. The next year, Trevor married Milton Bren, a film producer with two sons from a previous marriage, and moved to Newport Beach, California.

In 1978, her son Charles Dunsmoore Bren died in the crash of PSA Flight 182 in San Diego, followed by the death of her husband Milton Bren from a brain tumor in 1979. Devastated by these losses, she returned to Manhattan for some years, living in a Fifth Avenue apartment and taking a few acting roles amid a busy social life. Eventually she returned to California, where she remained for the rest of her life, becoming a generous supporter of the arts.

Claire Trevor died of respiratory failure in Newport Beach, April 8, 2000 at age 90. She was survived by her two stepsons and extended family. For her contribution to the motion picture industry, Claire Trevor has a star on the Hollywood Walk of Fame at 6933 Hollywood Blvd.

The Claire Trevor School of the Arts at the University of California, Irvine was named in Trevor's honor. Her Oscar and Emmy statuettes are on display in the Arts Plaza there, next to the Claire Trevor Theatre.

Ivan Triesault

Ivan Triesault was born July 14, 1898 in Reval, Russian Empire [now Tallinn, Estonia] January 3, 1980 in Los Angeles, California and was an American actor. His parents are from the island of Hiiumaa.

His first stage appearance was at the German Theatre in Tallinn aged 14, before moving to the United States at age 18. There he began to train in acting and dance, working on Broadway before moving into film.

His notable roles include appearances in *Cry of the Werewolf* (1944), *The Story of Dr. Wassell* (1944), *A Song to Remember* (1945),*Notorious* (1946), *5 Fingers* (1952), *Ma and Pa Kettle on Vacation* (1953), *Border River* (1954) with Joel McCrea, *Jet Pilot* (1957), *Journey to the Center of the Earth* (1959), *Alcoa Presents: One Step Beyond* (1959), *It Happened in Athens*(1962), *Viva Las Vegas* (1964), *Von Ryan's Express* (1965), *Batman* (1966), *Mission: Impossible* (1967), and *The Wild Wild West* (1967-1969).

He died in Los Angeles, California January 3, 1980 due to cardiac failure at age 87.

Forrest Tucker

Forrest Tucker and Joel McCrea in *Fort Massacre*

Forrest Meredith Tucker was born in Plainfield, Indiana February 12, 1919 and was an American actor in both movies and television from the 1940s to the 1980s. Tucker, who stood 6'4"tall and weighed 200 lb, appeared in nearly 100 action films in the 1940s and 1950s.

Tucker was a son of Forrest A. Tucker and his wife Doris Heringlake. He began his performing career at age 14 at the 1933 Chicago World's Fair, pushing the big wicker tourist chairs by day and singing "Throw Money" at night. After his family moved to Washington, D.C., Tucker attracted the attention of Jimmy Lake, the owner of the Old Gaiety Burlesque Theater, by winning its Saturday night amateur contest on consecutive weeks. After his second win, Tucker was hired full-time as master of ceremonies at the theatre. However, his initial employment there was short-lived; it was soon discovered that Tucker was underage. Tucker graduated from Washington-Lee High School, Arlington, Virginia, near Washington, D.C. in 1938.

Lying about his age, Tucker then joined the United States Army cavalry. He was stationed at Fort Myer in Arlington, Virginia, but was discharged when his age became known. He returned to work at the Old Gaiety after his 18th birthday.

When Lake's theatre closed for the summer in 1939, Tucker travelled to California and began auditioning for movie roles. He was cast as Wade Harper in *The Westerner* (1940), which starred Gary Cooper. He stood out in a fight scene with Cooper and was signed to Columbia Pictures.

In 1941, he played his first lead in PRC's *Emergency Landing*, and the following year he costarred in the classic *Keeper of the Flame*.

Tucker enlisted in the Army again during World War II, earning a commission as a second lieutenant. He resumed his acting career at the war's end, appearing in the classic 1946 film *The Yearling* and stealing a few scenes from Errol Flynn in *Never Say Goodbye* the same year.

In 1948, Tucker left Columbia and signed with Republic Pictures. At Republic, he made his breakthrough in *Sands of Iwo Jima* (1949), as PFC Thomas, a Marine with a score to settle with John Wayne's Sergeant Stryker. Graduating to top billing, Tucker starred in numerous action films during the 1950s, including *Rock Island Trail*(1950), *California Passage* (1950), *Rage at Dawn* (1955, where he played Frank Reno), *The Abominable Snowman* (1957), *The Quiet Gun* (1957), and *The Crawling Eye* (1958).

In 1958 he also co-starred with Joel McCrea in *Fort Massacre.*

430

The year 1958 brought another turning point in his career, when he won the role of Beauregard Burnside, Mame's first husband in *Auntie Mame,* the highest grossing U.S. film of the year. Tucker showed a flair for light comedy under the direction of Morton DaCosta that had largely been unexplored in his roles in westerns and science fiction films.

A two-year stint on television in the series *Crunch and Des* from 1955-1956 with Sandy Kenyon, featuring Forrest as a charter-boat captain in the Bahamas was well received. Tucker was cast as "Professor" Harold Hill by director Da Costa in the national production of *The Music Man* and played the role 2,008 times over the next five years, including a fifty-six week run at the Shubert Theatre in Chicago. Following his *Music Man* run, Tucker starred in the Broadway production of *Fair Game for Lovers* (1964) and then turned to television for his most famous role, starring as frontier capitalist Sgt. Morgan O'Rourke in *F Troop* (1965–1967). Though *F Troop* lasted only two seasons on ABC, the series has been in constant syndication since, reaching three generations of viewers. (Two of his *Gunsmoke* episodes feature Tucker in his cavalry uniform again, as the comic "Sergeant Holly," (1970) who in one scene "marries" and spends a hectic night with Miss Kitty.)

He appeared in many television series, including CBS's *Appointment with Adventure* in the 1956 series finale entitled "Two Falls for Satan, ABC's *Channing* a drama about college life which aired during the 1963-1964 season.

Following *F Troop*, Tucker returned to films in character parts (*Barquero* and *Chisum*, both 1970) and occasional leads (1975's *The Wild McCullochs*). On television, Tucker was a frequent guest star, including an episode of *Night Gallery* (1971), a total of six appearances on *Gunsmoke* and the recurring role of Jarvis Castleberry, Flo's estranged father on the 1976-1985 TV series, *Alice* and its spinoff, *Flo*. Tucker was a regular on three series after *F Troop*: *Dusty's Trail* (1973) with Bob Denver; *The Ghost Busters* (1975–1976) which reunited him with *F Troop* co-star Larry Storch; guest star on *The Bionic Woman* (1976), several episodes of *The Love Boat* (1980-1983), as J.T. Conners and *Filthy Rich* (1982) playing the second Big Guy Beck. (1982–1983), and *Murder, She Wrote* (1984). He continued to be active on stage as well, starring in the national productions of *Plaza Suite*, *Show Boat*, and *That Championship Season*.

Tucker suffered from severe alcoholism in his final years, but returned to the big screen after an absence of several years, in the Cannon Films action film *Thunder Run* (1986), playing the hero, trucker Charlie Morrison. His final film appearance was *Outtakes*, a low-budget imitation of *The Groove Tube*.

His feature film comeback unfortunately was short-lived. He died from lung cancer and emphysema on October 25, 1986 at age 67, a few months after the theatrical release of*Thunder Run* and *Outtakes*. He was interred in Forest Lawn - Hollywood Hills Cemetery in Los Angeles.

Tucker married four times: (1) to Sandra Jolley (1919–1986), divorced in 1950, daughter of the character actor I. Stanford Jolley (who also died of emphysema) and the sister of the Academy Award-winning art director Stan Jolley, (2) to Marilyn Johnson on March 28, 1950, and after her death in 1960 (3) to Marilyn Fisk on October 23, 1961. He had a daughter (Pamela "Brooke" Tucker) by his first marriage, and a daughter (Cindy Tucker) and son (Forrest Sean Tucker) by his third. (4) In 1986, he married Sheila Forbes.

Sonny Tufts

Joel McCrea and Sonny Tufts in *The Virginian*

Sonny Tufts was born Bowen Charlton Tufts III in Boston, Massachusetts July 16, 1911 and was an American film actor.

Tufts was born into a prominent banking family, whose patriarch had supposedly sailed to America from England in 1638. He broke with the family banking tradition by studying opera at Yale, where he was an editor of campus humor magazine *The Yale Record*, as well as a member of the Delta Kappa Epsilon fraternity (Phi chapter) and Skull and Bones.

After graduating from college in 1935, he auditioned with the Metropolitan Opera in New York but eventually worked on the Broadway stage. In 1942, Tufts went to Hollywood. He attained some fame during World War II, principally because, due to an old college football injury, he was one of the few handsome male actors not serving overseas in the war. In 1944 he was voted the number one "Star of Tomorrow" by exhibitors.

Some of his credits over his twenty-five year acting career from 1943 to 1968 include *So Proudly We Hail!* (1943) with Veronica Lake, *Here Come the Waves* (1944), *Bring on the Girls* (1945) again with Veronica alke, *Miss Susie Slagle's* (1946) a third with Veronica Lake, *The Virginian* (1946) with Joel McCrea, *Blaze of Noon* (1947), *Easy Living* (1949), *Glory at Sea* (1952), *Cat-Women of the Moon* (1953), *The Seven Year Itch* (1955) with Mariyn Monroe, *The Parson and the Outlaw* (1957), *The Virginian* (1963), *Town Tamer* (1965), *The Loner* (1965), *Cottonpickin' Chickenpickers* (1967), and *Land's End* (1968).

He was married to Spanish dancer Barbara Dare from 1938 to 1953.

He is a relative of Charles Tufts, for whom Tufts University is named.

Tufts died of pneumonia at age 58 in Santa Monica, California, on June 4, 1970.

Tom Tully

Tom Tully was born in Durango in southwestern Colorado August 21, 1908 and was an American actor.

Thomas Kane Tully served in the United States Navy, was a private pilot, and worked as a junior reporter for the *Denver Post* in Denver, Colorado, before he entered acting with the expectation of better pay. Tully started out on stage before eventually acting in Hollywood films starting in 1943. He changed his surname for professional reasons, from Tulley to Tully.

He received an Academy Award nomination for the role of the first commander of the *Caine* in 1954's *The Caine Mutiny*, with Humphrey Bogart. From 1954 through 1960, he played the role of Police Inspector Matt Grebb on the CBS television series, *The Lineup*, with co-star Warner Anderson, a gripping police drama. In repeats, *The Lineup* was known as *San Francisco Beat*.

He made two appearances as Rob Petrie's (Dick Van Dyke) father on CBS's *The Dick Van Dyke Show* in 1964 and 1966.

Tully's Hollywood film career spanned from the early 1940s until 1973, and he continued to accept many guest-starring roles on television.

More of his early roles included *The Sign of the Cross* (1932), *Destination Tokyo* (1943), *The Unseen* (1945) with Joel McCrea, *The Virginian* (1946) again with Joel McCrea, *Branded* (1950) with Alan Ladd, *Trouble Along the Way* (1953), *Love Me or Leave Me* (1955), *The Wackiest Ship in the Army* (1962), and *The Carpetbaggers* (1964) again with Alan Ladd.

In 1962, he appeared on the NBC modern western series, *Empire* in the role of Tom Cole in the episode "Long Past, Long Remembered." The series starred Richard Egan as New Mexico rancher Jim Redigo. In 1963, he was cast as Danny Mundt in "A Taste for Pineapple" of the ABC crime drama, *The Untouchables*. That same year he portrayed Jethro Tate in "Who Killed Billy Jo?" on another ABC crime drama, *Burke's Law*, with Gene Barry.

In 1964, Tully delivered two memorable appearances on CBS's *Perry Mason*. The first was as defendant Carey York in "The Case of the Arrogant Arsonist;" the second was as murder victim Harvey Scott in "The Case of the Nautical Knot." During the 1966 season of ABC's *Shane* western series, he made seventeen appearances as Tom Starett.

In November 1969, Tully traveled to the former South Vietnam for the United Service Organization. His "handshake tour" took him to hospitals, radio interviews, and flight behind enemy lines, courtesy of the 173rd Airborne Brigade, to visit strategic military outposts such as the "Hawks Nest" in the Phum Valley. While in Vietnam entertaining troops, Tully contracted a filarial worm similar to the creature that causes elephantiasis. After returning to the United States, his condition worsened. Because a blood clot in a major vein shut off circulation, his left leg was amputated close to the hip. The amputation was performed in Laguna Beach, California, close to his home in San Juan Capistrano.

Not to be held down, Tully continued his acting in television dramas such as *Mission: Impossible* (1972) and *The Rookies* (1972-1973). His last feature film role was as a crooked gun dealer in Don Siegel's thriller *Charley Varrick* (1973), with Walter Matthau. His gritty portrayal in a seedy storefront seemed particularly poignant as he wheeled around his cramped shop in his wheelchair.

Complications from his surgery caused pleuritis, deafness, and serious debilitation. Tully died of cancer at the age of 73 on April 27, 1982, in Newport Beach. His death was brought about in part from the tragedy that he suffered in Vietnam.

At the time of his death, Tully had completed a manuscript about his grandmother and grandfather, David F. Day, a Medal of Honor winner in the American Civil War. Day was the owner of the newspaper in Ouray, Colorado, formerly known as *The Solid Muldoon*, now the *Durango Herald*.

Felipe Turich

Felipe Turich was born on December 5, 1898 in Hidalgo, Mexico. He was an actor, known for *Beauty and the Bandit* (1946), *Jesse James Meets Frankenstein's Daughter* (1966), and *Hook, Line and Sinker* (1969).

More of his roles included *The Kid Ranger* (1936), *Outlaws of the Rio Grande* (1941), *Beauty and the Bandit* (1946), *Mexican Hayride* (1948) with Abbott and Costello, *My Favorite Spy* (1951), *Border River* (1954) with Joel McCrea, *Tales of Wells Fargo* (1957), *Holiday for Lovers* (1959), *Temple Houston* (1963), *Firecreek* (1968), *Fuzz* (1972), *Adam-12* (1973), *Wanted: The Sundance Woman* (1976), *How the West Was Won* (1978), and *Matt Houston* (1983).

He was married to Rosa Sinohui. He died on March 9, 1992 in Los Angeles County, California at age 93.

Brandon Tynan

Brandon Tynan was born on April 11, 1875 in Dublin, Ireland. He was an actor, known for *Success* (1923), *Loyal Lives* (1923), and *Unrestrained Youth* (1925).

More of his roles included *Wells Fargo* (1937) with Joel McCrea, Youth Takes a *Fling* (1938) again with Joel McCrea, *Virginia City* (1940), and *Marry the Bo$$'S Daughter* (1941).

He was married to Lily Cahill and Caroline Whyte. He died on March 19, 1967 in New York City, New York at age 91.

Minerva Urecal

434

Minerva Urecal was born Minerva Holzer September 22, 1894, in Eureka, California, and was an American actress. Of Scottish descent, cruel-eyed, hatchet-faced veteran actress Minerva Urecal was a radio-trained player who spent some time on the clock with stage work before setting her sights on film and TV. Her subsequent stage moniker would become a partial anagram of her hometown name.

Strictly a West Coast-based performer, she finally turned to films in 1933 at the age of 39, and appeared for the next three decades making a number of top stars miserable even in the smallest of parts. Obviously inspired by the cranky dowager instincts of Marie Dressler, Urecal was equipped with extremely coarse and intimidating features that showed no fear to anyone. Her beady eyes, hawk-like nose, firm-set jaw, angry demeanor, and immovable stance could tear right through a person. She could easily shrink a film husband by at least three inches with a simple withering glance.

Evidently a little of her went a long way, for Urecal appeared primarily in uncredited parts over the years. Still noticeable, however, she could be glimpsed as a secretary, laundress, spinster, neighbor, or townsperson somewhere along the line. She was a typically unsatisfied store customer and proved a most brutal and narrow-minded gossip when called upon. Her unhappy kind was ideally suited for big-city tenement settings, the western frontier or on the open seas, and she also played a number of ethnic types (Italian, Swedish, etc.). Primarily diffused in "B" quality pictures and two-reel short comedies, she was often confused with another scene-stealing character harridan, Marjorie Main, who resembled her in looks, tone, and style. Some of Urecal's more visible roles were in *Oh, Doctor* (1937), *Love in a Bungalow* (1937), *The Ape Man* (1943), *Louisiana Hayride* (1944), *Moonlight and Cactus* (1944), *Salty O'Rourke* (1945) with Alan Ladd, *The Virginian* (1946) with Joel McCrea, *Rainbow Over Texas* (1946), and *The Lovable Cheat* (1949).

Tucked away in the shadows in many of her 200+ film parts, she began tackling TV assignments in the 1950s and appeared to have an affinity for westerns, guesting on *The Lone Ranger* (1949), *The Range Rider* (1951), *My Friend Flicka* (1955), and both *Gene Autry* and *Roy Rogers'* popular weekly series, among others.

She finally stepped up to the plate with her own series as the titular whiskey-voiced heroine in *The Adventures of Tugboat Annie* (1957). She played Annie Brennan, the weather-beaten widow of a sea captain who takes over the tugboat "Nemesis" herself and the repercussions therein. The comedy series lasted only one season. She later replaced the similarly formidable Hope Emerson as Mother for the 1959-60 season of the detective series *Peter Gunn* (1958).

Urecal continued in character film roles until the mid-1960s, and proved a standout as James Stewart's touchy Scandinavian cook in *Mr. Hobbs Takes a Vacation* (1962). One of her acid-tongued shrews finally got her comeuppance in her next-to-last film. As the intolerant, highly indignant townswoman Mrs. Lindquist, whose cruel orbs could turn any ordinary man to stone, it is she who suffers that exact same fate when she visits Tony Randall's traveling circus in *7 Faces of Dr. Lao* (1964).

Some of Urecal's final TV roles were on *Wagon Train* (1957), *Perry Mason* (1957), *Whispering Smith* (1961) with Audie Murphy, and *Petticoat Junction* (1963).

Never married, the California die-hard succumbed to a heart attack at age 71 in February 26, 1966.

Charles Unger

Charles Unger is a blond child actor, known for *The Night Is Young* (1935), *Come and Get It* (1936) with Joel McCrea, and *Go West Young Man* (1936).

More of his roles included *Unwelcome Stranger* (1935), *The Plough and the Stars* (1936), *Drums of Destiny* (1937), and *Kidnapped* (1938).

Rudy Vallee

Joel McCrea and Rudy Vallee in *The Palm Beach Story*

Rudy Vallée was born Hubert Prior Vallée in Island Pond, Vermont July 28, 1901 and was an American singer, actor, bandleader, and entertainer. He was one of the first modern pop stars of the teen idol type.

Rudy Vallée was the son of Charles Alphonse and Catherine Lynch Vallée. Both of his parents were born and raised in Vermont; however his grandparents were immigrants. The Vallées were francophone Canadians from neighboring Quebec, while the Lynches were from Ireland. Vallée grew up in Westbrook, Maine.

In 1917, he decided to enlist for World War I, but was discharged when the Navy authorities found out that he was only 15. He enlisted in Portland, Maine on March 29, 1917, under the false birthdate of July 28, 1899. He was discharged at the Naval Training Station, Newport, Rhode Island, on May 17, 1917 with 41 days of active service.

After playing drums in his high school band, Vallée played clarinet and saxophone in various bands around New England as a teenager. From 1924 through 1925, he played with the Savoy Havana Band at the Savoy Hotel in London, where his fellow band-members discouraged his attempts to become a vocalist. He then returned to the United States to obtain a degree in philosophy from Yale, where he played in the Yale Collegians with future *New Yorker* cartoonist Peter Arno.

After graduation, he formed his own band, "Rudy Vallée and the Connecticut Yankees", having named himself after influential saxophonist Rudy Wiedoeft. With this band, which featured two violins, two saxophones, a piano, a banjo and drums, he started singing (supposedly reluctantly at first). He had a rather thin, wavering tenor voice and seemed more at home singing sweet ballads than jazz numbers. However, his singing, together with his suave manner and boyish good looks, attracted great attention, especially from young women. Vallée was given a recording contract and in 1928, he started performing on the radio.

Vallée became the most prominent and, arguably, the first of a new style of popular singer, the crooner. Previously, popular singers needed strong projecting voices to fill theaters in the days before the electric microphone. Crooners had soft voices that were well suited to the intimacy of the new medium of the radio. Vallée's trombone-like vocal phrasing on "Deep Night" would inspire later crooners such as Bing Crosby, Frank Sinatra, and Perry Como to model their voices on jazz instruments.

Vallée also became what was perhaps the first complete example of the 20th century mass media pop star. Flappers mobbed him wherever he went. His live appearances were usually sold out, and even if his singing could hardly be heard in those venues not yet equipped with the new electronic microphones, his screaming female fans went home happy if they had caught sight of his lips through the opening of the emblematic megaphone he often sang through. A brief caricature of him in the Fleischer Brothers' color Betty Boop theatrical short cartoon from 1934 *Poor Cinderella* depicts him singing through a megaphone.

His recording career began in 1928 recording for Columbia Records' cheap labels (Harmony, Velvet Tone, and Diva). He signed to Victor in February 1929 and remained with them through to late 1931, leaving after a heated dispute with company executives over title selections. He then recorded for the short-lived, but extremely popular "Hit of the Week" label (which sold records laminated onto cardboard). In August 1932, he signed with Columbia and stayed with them through 1933; he returned to Victor in June 1933. His records were issued on Victor's new budget label, Bluebird, until November 1933 when he was moved up to the full-priced Victor label. He stayed with Victor until signing with ARC in 1936, who released his records on their Perfect, Melotone, Conqueror and Romeo labels until 1937 when he returned to Victor.

Along with his group, The Connecticut Yankees, Vallée's best known popular recordings included: "The Stein Song" (aka University of Maine fighting song) in 1929 and "Vieni, Vieni" in the latter 1930s. Vallée sang fluently in three Mediterranean languages, and always varied the keys, thus paving the way for later pop crooners such as Dean Martin, Andy Williams, and Vic Damone. Another memorable rendition of his is "Life Is Just a Bowl of Cherries", in which he imitates Willie Howard's voice in the final chorus. One of his record hits was "The Drunkard Song," popularly known as "There Is a Tavern in the Town." Vallée couldn't stop laughing for the last couple of verses – supposedly he struggled to keep a straight face at the corny lyrics, and the band members egged him on. He managed a second take reasonably well. The "laughing" version was so infectious, however, that Victor released both takes (take 1 was issued on Victor 24721 with a regular Victor label, and take 2 was issued on Victor 24739 on a special white label that read in bright red: "Dear Rudy, What do you say we let the public have this one? The slip-up makes the record sound funnier" – E. Wallerstein" and "O.K. – R. Vallée".)

Vallée's last hit song was the 1943 reissue of the melancholy ballad "As Time Goes By", popularized in the feature film *Casablanca* in 1943 (due to the mid-1940s recording ban, Victor reissued the version he had recorded twelve years earlier). During World War II, Vallée enlisted in the United States Coast Guard to help direct the 11th district Coast Guard band as a Chief Petty Officer. Eventually he was promoted to Lieutenant and led the forty piece band to great success. In 1944 he was placed on the inactive list and he returned to radio.

Vallée's song compositions included "Oh! Ma-Ma! (The Butcher Boy)" in 1938, recorded by Glenn Miller and his Orchestra, "Deep Night", which was recorded by Duke Ellington and his Orchestra, "If You Haven't Got a Girl", "Violets", "Where To", "Will You Remember Me?", "We'll Never Get Drunk Any More", "Sweet Summer Breeze", "Actions Speak Louder Than Words", "Ask Not", "Forgive Me", "Charlie Cadet", "Somewhere In Your Heart", "You Took Me Out Of This World", "Old Man Harlem" with Hoagy Carmichael, which was recorded by the Dorsey Brothers band, "I'm Just a Vagabond Lover", and "Betty Co-Ed".

In middle age, Vallée's voice matured into a robust baritone. In 1967 he recorded a new record album. Called "Hi-Ho Everybody" it was produced by Snuff Garrett and Ed Silvers for Dot Records on its Viva label; arranged by Al Capps. The engineers were Dave Hassinger and Henry Leroy. Included on the album were songs: "Winchester Cathedral", "Michelle", "My Blue Heaven", "Sweet Heart of Sigma Chi", "Who Likes Good Pop Music?", "Bluebird", "Who", "Lady Godiva", "Mame", "The Whiffenpoof Song", "Strangers in The Night", and "One of Those Songs".

In 1995, a Golden Palm Star on the Palm Springs, California, Walk of Stars was dedicated to him. In 1929, Vallée began hosting *The Fleischmann's Yeast Hour*, a very popular radio show at the time. Vallée continued hosting popular radio variety shows through the 1930s and 1940s. *The Royal Gelatin Hour* featured various film performers of the era, such as Fay Wray and Richard Cromwell in dramatic skits.

When Vallée took his contractual vacations from his national radio show in 1937, he insisted his sponsor hire Louis Armstrong as his substitute (this was the first instance of an African-American fronting a national radio program). Vallée also wrote the introduction for Armstrong's 1936 book *Swing That Music*.

In 1929, Vallée made his first feature film, *The Vagabond Lover* for RKO Radio. His first films were made to cash in on his singing popularity. His initial performances were rather wooden, but his acting greatly improved in the late 1930s and 1940s, and by the time he began working with Preston Sturges in the 1940s he had become a successful comedic supporting player. He appeared opposite Joel McCrea and Claudette Colbert in the 1942 Preston Sturges screwball comedy *The Palm Beach Story* in 1940. Other films in which he appeared include *I Remember Mama*, *Unfaithfully Yours* and *The Bachelor and the Bobby-Soxer*.

In 1955, Vallée was featured in *Gentlemen Marry Brunettes,* co-starring Jane Russell, Alan Young, and Jeanne Crain. The production was filmed on location in Paris. The film was based on the Anita Loos novel that was a sequel to her acclaimed *Gentlemen Prefer Blondes*. *Gentlemen Marry Brunettes* was popular throughout Europe at the time and was released in France as *A Paris Pour les Quatre ("Paris for the Four"),* and in Belgium as *Tevieren Te Parijs.*

Vallée performed on Broadway as J.B. Biggley in the 1961 musical *How to Succeed in Business Without Really Trying* and reprised the role in the 1967 film version. He appeared in the campy 1960s *Batman* television show as the villain Lord Marmaduke Ffogg and in 1971 made a television appearance as a vindictive surgeon in the *Night Gallery* episode "Marmalade Wine." He toured with a one-man theater show into the 1980s, occasionally opening for The Village People.

Vallée was married briefly to actress Jane Greer, but that ended in divorce in 1944. His previous marriage to Leonie Cauchois was annulled and the one to Fay Webb ended in divorce. After divorcing Jane Greer, he married Eleanor Norris in 1946, who wrote a memoir, *My Vagabond Lover*. Their marriage lasted until his death in 1986.

Always loyal to Yale University, he never forgot his Maine roots, and maintained an estate at Kezar Lake in Maine.

Vallée died of cancer at his home on July 3, 1986. He is interred in St. Hyacinth's Cemetery in Westbrook, Maine at age 84.

Monte Vandergrift

Monte Vandergrift was born on January 12, 1893 in Pittsburgh, Pennsylvania. He was an actor, known for *Shotgun Pass* (1931), *The Mandarin Mystery* (1936), and *The Phantom Creeps* (1939.

More of his roles included *Behind Office Doors* (1931), *King Kong* (1933), *Gambling Lady* (1934) with Joel McCrea, *Private Worlds* (1935) again with Joel McCrea, *The Texas Rangers* (1936), *Woman Chases Man* (1937) a third with Joel McCrea, *The Beloved Brat* (1938), and *Missing Evidence* (1939).

He died on July 29, 1939 in North Hollywood, California at age 46.

Dale Van Sickel

Dale Harris Van Sickel was born in Eatonton, Georgia, November 29, 1907, and was an American college football, basketball, and baseball player during the 1920s, who later became a Hollywood motion picture actor and stunt performer for over forty years. Van Sickel played college football for the University of Florida, and was recognized as the first first-team All-American in the history of the Florida Gators football program.

He grew up in Gainesville, Florida. Van Sickel attended Gainesville High School, where he played high school football for the Gainesville Purple Hurricanes. In 2007, eighty-one years after he graduated from high school, the Florida High School Athletic Association (FHSAA) recognized Van Sickel as one of the "100 Greatest Players of the First 100 Years" of Florida high school football. He is generally regarded as the best high school football player produced in the state of Florida before the 1930s.

Van Sickel attended the University of Florida in Gainesvile He played right end for the Florida Gators football team for three seasons from 1927 to 1929, on the opposite side of the line from left end Dutch Stanley. During his three years as a member of the Gators varsity, the team won twenty-three of twenty-nine games. Led by future Hall of Fame coach Charlie Bachman in 1928, Van Sickel and the Gators posted an 8–1 record during his junior season, outscoring their competition 366–44 the most points scored in the nation. The Gators' sole 1928 loss was to Tennessee in Knoxville—by a single point, 12–13. The Associated Press, Newspaper Enterprise Association and Grantland Rice of *Collier's Weekly* named Van Sickel to their respective 1928 first-team All-America squads, making him the first player from the University of Florida to be named a first-team All-American. As was typical of the 1920s era, Van Sickel played both offense and defense; his College Hall of Fame biography describes him as "a swift and sure-handed receiver on offense and a gifted defensive player". Van Sickel was injured during his senior football season in 1929, and while he was productive, he was unable to post the same sort of numbers in 1929 that he did during his 1928 All-American season.

Van Sickel was also the team captain and a varsity letterman for the Florida Gators basketball and Gators baseball teams. He was later inducted into the University of Florida Athletic Hall of Fame as a "Gator Great," and he was also the first Gator to be inducted into the College Football Hall of Fame in 1975.

Van Sickel graduated from the University of Florida with a bachelor's degree in 1930, and he remained at the university to be an assistant coach for the Gators football and basketball teams during the 1930 and 1931 seasons. Afterward, he moved to Hollywood to begin a career as a movie stuntman, and had his first on-screen stunt role in the Marx Brothers' film *Duck Soup* (1933)

Over the next thirty-eight years, Van Sickel appeared as an extra and occasional leading man in over 280 films and television episodes, and performed on-screen stunts in another 140. He was a founding member, and the first president, of the Stuntmen's Association of Motion Pictures.

Some of the films and television programs he appeared in included *The Richest Girl in the World* (1934), *Mr. Deeds Goes to Town* (1936), *Kid Galahad* (1937), *Gone with the Wind* (1939), *Hellzapoppin'* (1941), *Reap the Wild Wind* (1942), *Captain America* (1944), *The Purple Monster Strikes* (1945), *Son of Zorro* (1947), *Jesse James Rides Again* (1947), *Mighty Joe Young* (1949), *The Fighting Kentuckian* (1949), *The Greatest Show on Earth* (1952), *Abbott and Costello Go to Mars* (1953), *The War of the Worlds* (1953), *Rocky Jones, Space Ranger* (1954), *Seven Brides for Seven Brothers* (1954), *Commando Cody: Sky Marshal of the Universe* (1955), *Earth vs. the Flying Saucers* (1956), *Gunsight Ridge* (1957) with Joel McCrea, *The Wings of Eagles* (1957), *Wanted: Dead or Alive* (1959), *Spartacus* (1960), *Birdman of Alcatraz* (1962), *The Greatest Show on Earth* (1963), *Murderers' Row* (1966), *The Green Hornet* (1967), *The Love Bug* (1968), and *Duel* (1971).

He also appeared in *Cast a Long Shadow* (1959), *Seven Ways from Sundown* (1960), *Six Black Horses* (1962), and *Showdown* (1963) with Audie Murphy.

Van Sickel died January 25, 1977, in Newport Beach, California, as a result of injuries received while filming a car crash stunt in 1975; he was 69 years old. Van Sickel was survived by his wife Iris and their daughter.

Victor Varconi

Victor Varconi was born Mihály Várkonyi in Kisvárda, Austria-Hungary March 31, 1891 and was a highly successful silent film star in Hungary. He was the first Hungarian actor to make a film in the United States.

He worked under contract to Cecil B. DeMille, and played Pontius Pilate in DeMille's 1927 production of *The King of Kings*.

Varconi's popularity waned with the advent of sound films- because of his accent he was cast in smaller parts, often playing Hispanic characters. He worked on the New York City stage and wrote for radio.

More of his roles included *Dance Fever* (1925), *The Divine Lady* (1929) with Joel McCrea, *When London Sleeps* (1934), *The Story of Vernon and Irene Castle* (1939), *Reap the Wild Wind* (1942), *Dakota* (1945), *Samson and Delilah* (1949), *The Man Who Turned to Stone* (1957), and *The Atomic Submarine* (1959).

He died from a heart attack in Santa Barbara, California on June 6, 1976, at the age of 85 and was interred at the Calvary Cemetery, East Los Angeles, California, USA.

Queenie Vassar

Queenie Vassar was born October 28, 1870 in Glasgow, Scotland. Coming to the U.S. in 1884, Vassar performed as a musical/comic star during the 1890s. She played in *The Lady of the Slipper; Or, A Modern Cinderella* which opened at the Globe Theatre in New York in 1912 and ran for 232 performances.

She appeared in only three films: *Primrose Path* (1940) with Joel McCrea, *Lady in a Jam* (1942), and *None But the Lonely Heart* (1944).

She died September 11, 1960 at age 89 in Hollywood, California.

Hilda Vaughn

Hilda Vaughn was born December 27, 1898 in Baltimore, Maryland. Thin and tart-tongued, theater actress Hilda Vaughn, had a decade of intense activity at the beginning of the sound period, mainly at MGM. Although she always played a pleb (a maid, a charwoman, a governess, a saleswoman, a slavey, ...) and never a patrician, the characters she embodied did not lack ... character! Which is best exemplified by her best part, Tina, Jean Harlow's blackmailing domestic in George Cukor's *Dinner at Eight* (1933).

Some of her other roles included *Three Live Ghosts* (1929), *The Phantom of Crestwood* (1932), *The Trail of the Lonesome Pine* (1936), *Banjo on My Knee* (1936) with Joel McCrea, and *Charlie Chan at the Wax Museum* (1940).

After 1940, Hilda Vaughn returned to the theatre. She died December 28, 1957 at age 59 in Baltimore, Maryland.

Robert Vaughn

Robert Francis Vaughn was born in New York City November 22, 1932 and is an American actor noted for his stage, film, and television work. His best-known TV roles include the suave spy Napoleon Solo in the 1960s series *The Man from U.N.C.L.E.* and the wealthy detective Harry Rule in the 1970s series *The Protectors*. In film, he portrayed one of the title characters in *The Magnificent Seven* and Major Paul Krueger in *The Bridge at Remagen*, and provided the voice of Proteus IV, the computer villain of *Demon Seed*.

As grifter and card sharp Albert Stroller, Vaughn appeared in all but one of the forty-eight episodes of the British television drama series *Hustle* (2004–2012). From January to February 2012, he appeared in the long-running British soap opera *Coronation Street* as Milton Fanshaw, a love interest for Sylvia Goodwin, played by veteran English actress Stephanie Cole.

Vaughn was born to performer parents: Marcella Frances (née Gaudel), a stage actress, and Gerald Walter Vaughn, a radio actor. His ancestry includes Irish, French, and German. After his parents divorced, Vaughn lived in Minneapolis with his grandparents while his mother traveled. He attended North High School and later enrolled in the University of Minnesota as a journalism major. He quit after a year and moved to Los Angeles with his mother. He enrolled in Los Angeles City College, then transferred to Los Angeles State College of Applied Arts and Sciences, where he earned a Master's degree in theater. Continuing his higher education even through his successful acting career, Vaughn earned a Ph.D. in communications from the University of Southern California, in 1970. In 1972, he published his dissertation as the book *Only Victims: A Study of Show Business Blacklisting*.

Vaughn made his television debut on the November 21, 1955 "Black Friday" episode of the American TV series *Medic*, the first of more than two hundred episodic roles by the middle of 2000.

Vaughn appeared as Stan Gray with Virginia Christine as his older sister, Hester, in the surprise-ending episode "The Twisted Road" of the western syndicated series, *Frontier Doctor*, starring Rex Allen in the title role as Dr. Bill Baxter.

His first film appearance was as an uncredited extra in *The Ten Commandments* (1956), playing a golden calf idolater also visible in a scene in a chariot behind that of Yul Brynner. Vaughn's first credited movie role came the following year in the Western *Hell's Crossroads* (1957), in which he played the real-life Bob Ford, the killer of outlaw Jesse James. After being seen by Burt Lancaster in Calder Willingham's play *End as a Man*, Vaughn was signed to a contract with Lancaster's film company and was to have played the Steve Dallas role in *Sweet Smell of Success* but was drafted into the United States Army before he could begin the film.

Vaughn's first notable appearance was in *The Young Philadelphians* (1959) for which he was nominated for an Academy Award for Best Supporting Actor and a Golden Globe Award for Best Supporting Actor – Motion Picture. He then appeared in Wichita Town (1959) with Joel McCrea. Next, he appeared as gunman Lee in *The Magnificent Seven* (1960), a role he essentially reprised twenty years later in *Battle Beyond the Stars* (1980), both films being adaptations of filmmaker Akira Kurosawa's 1954 Japanese samurai epic, *Seven Samurai*. Vaughn is the last surviving member of the seven actors who portrayed The Magnificent Seven. He played a different role, Judge Oren Travis, on the 1998-2000 syndicated TV series *The Magnificent Seven* and is the only surviving member of the title cast of the original 1960 film (although Rosenda Monteros, who played Petra, and Rico Alaniz, cast as Sotero, are still living).

In the 1963-1964 season, Vaughn appeared in *The Lieutenant* as Captain Raymond Rambridge alongside Gary Lockwood, the Marine second lieutenant at Camp Pendleton. His dissatisfaction with the somewhat diminished aspect of the character led him to request an expanded role. During the conference, his name came up in a telephone call and he ended up being offered a series of his own — as Napoleon Solo, title character in a series originally to be called *Solo*, but which became *The Man from U.N.C.L.E.* after the pilot was reshot with Leo G. Carroll in the role of Solo's boss. This was the part that would make Vaughn a household name even behind the Iron Curtain. Earlier, Vaughn had guest-starred on Lockwood's ABC series *Follow the Sun*. Also in 1963 he appeared in an episode of *The Dick Van Dyke Show* as Jim Darling, a successful businessman and an old flame of Laura Petrie in "It's A Shame She Married Me".

From 1964 to 1968, Vaughn played Solo with Scottish co-star David McCallum playing his fellow agent Illya Kuryakin. This production spawned a spinoff show, large amounts of merchandising, overseas theatrical movies of re-edited episodes, and a sequel *The Return of the Man from U.N.C.L.E. - The Fifteen-Year-Later Affair*. In the year the series ended, Vaughn landed a large role playing Chalmers, an ambitious California politician in the film *Bullitt* starring Steve McQueen; he was nominated for a BAFTA Award for Best Supporting Actor for this role.

In 1966, Vaughn appeared as a bachelor on the nighttime premiere of *The Dating Game*. He was picked for the date, which was a trip to London.

Vaughn continued to act, in television and in mostly B movies. He starred in two seasons of the British detective series *The Protectors* in the early 1970s. He won an Emmy for his portrayal of Frank Flaherty in "Washington: Behind Closed Doors" (ABC, 1977) and during the 1980's starred with friend George Peppard in the final season of *The A-Team*. According to Dirk Benedict, Vaughn was actually added to the cast of that show because of his friendship with Peppard. It was hoped Vaughn would help ease tensions between Mr. T and Peppard. In 1983 he starred as villainous multi millionaire Ross Webster in *Superman III*. In 1983-1984 he appeared as industrialist Harlan Adams in the short-lived CBS series Emerald Point N.A.S., replacing Patrick O'Neal. In 1989 Vaughn starred as an Army General in the low budget, cult zombie movie "Chud II".

In the mid 1990s, he made several cameo appearances on Late Night With Conan O'Brien as an audience member who berates the host and his guests beginning with, "You people sicken me..."

In 2004, after a string of guest roles on series such as *Law & Order*, in which he had a recurring role during season eight, Vaughn experienced a resurgence. He began co-starring in the British TV drama series *Hustle*, made for BBC One. The series was also broadcast in the United States on the cable network AMC. In the series, Vaughn plays elder-statesman American con artist Albert Stroller, a father figure to a group of younger grifters. In September 2006, he guest-starred in *Law & Order: Special Victims Unit*.

Since the mid-1990s, Vaughn has been a spokesman in a set of generic advertisements for various personal injury law firms around the U.S.A. and Canada, such as that of Connecticut and Massachusetts law firm Mark E. Salomone & Morelli, Georgia's Eichholz Law Firm and the Maine-based law offices of Joe Bornstein. The television commercial features Vaughn urging injured complainants to "tell the insurance companies you mean business."

Vaughn also appeared as himself narrating and being a character in a radio play broadcast by BBC Radio 4 in 2007 about making the film *The Bridge at Remagen* in Prague, Czechoslovakia, during the Russian invasion of 1968.

Frequent references are made to his playing Napoleon Solo and the character's great spying abilities.

In November 2011, it was announced that Vaughn would appear for three weeks in the British soap opera *Coronation Street*. His cameo as Milton in the long-running program lasted for three weeks, from January to February 2012.

Vaughn is a long-time member of the Democratic Party. His family was also Democratic and was involved in politics in Minneapolis, and early in his career, he was described as a "liberal Democrat".He was the chair of the California Democratic State Central Committee speakers bureau and actively campaigned for candidates in the 1960s.

Vaughn was the first popular American actor to take a public stand against the Vietnam war and was active in the Vietnam War-era peace group, Another Mother for Peace, and, with Dick Van Dyke and Carl Reiner, was a founder of Dissenting Democrats. Early in the 1968 presidential election, they supported the candidacy of Eugene McCarthy, mentioned for the Vice Presidency. The choice was prophetic, as McCarthy was not selected for the second position but did seek the Presidency in 1968. Vaughn was also reported to have political ambitions of his own, but in a 1973 interview, he denied having had any political aspirations.

In spite of being a registered Democrat, Vaughn does not support President Barack Obama, and described him as "not up to the job" in March 2009.

In his memoir, *A Fortunate Life*, Vaughn recalls watching his good friend Jack Nicholson stumble his way through a scene of *Bus Stop* in a mid-1950s acting class without the "confidence" to carry it off. "Nicholson declared, 'Vaughnie, I'm going to give myself two more years in this business. Then I'm going to look for another way to make a living.' 'Hang in there, Jack,' Vaughn told him. 'You're too young to quit.'

Vaughn married actress Linda Staab in 1974. They appeared together in a 1973 episode of *The Protectors*, called "It Could Be Practically Anywhere on the Island", in which Staab played a ditzy American whose dog was stolen; eventually Vaughn's character, Harry Rule, found the dog. They have adopted two children, Cassidy (born 1976) and Caitlin (born 1981). They reside in Ridgefield, Connecticut.

Herb Vigran

Herbert "Herb" Vigran was born June 5, 1910, in Fort Wayne, Indiana. He was a well-known American character actor in Hollywood from the 1930s to the 1980s. Over his 50-year career, he made over 350 television and film appearances.

He graduated with a law degree from Indiana University Law School but later chose to pursue acting.

After starting out on Broadway, he soon moved to Hollywood with no money and only a Broadway acting experience. In 1939, Vigran's agent helped him secure a lead in the radio drama *Silver Theatre*. The actor had a $5 recording made of the radio show and used it as a demo to get other jobs with his unique voice. He performed in radio shows with the likes of Jack Benny, Bob Hope, Lucille Ball, and Jimmy Durante.

He later had hundreds of film appearances on movies like *Pardon My Sarong* (1942), *It Ain't Hay* (1943), *The Noose Hangs High* (1948), all three with Abbott and Costello, *Texas, Brooklyn & Heaven* (1948) with Audie Murphy, *The Damned Don't Cry* (1950), *Abbott and Costello Meet the Invisible Man* (1951), *Bedtime for Bonzo* (1951), *The Star* (1952), *The Long, Long Trailer* (1953), *Dragnet* (1954), *White Christmas* (1954), *20,000 Leagues Under the Sea* (1954), *Hell on Frisco Bay* (1955) with Alan Ladd, *You Can't Run Away from It* (1956), *The Vampire* (1957), *Gunsight Ridge* (1957) with Joel McCrea, *The Gun Runners* (1958) again with Audie Murphy, *The Fugitive Kind* (1959), *Send Me No Flowers* (1964), *That Funny Feeling* (1965), *The Reluctant Astronaut* (1967), *The Love Bug* (1968), *Which Way to the Front?* (1970), *Support Your Local Gunfighter* (1971), *Cancel My Reservation* (1972), *Herbie Rides Again* (1974), *The Shaggy D.A.* (1976), *Every Girl Should Have One* (1978), *Airplane!* (1980), and *Amazon Women on the Moon* (1987).

In the rock and roll movie *Go, Johnny, Go* (1959), Vigran played an assistant to promoter Alan Freed and performed dialogue scenes with rock legend Chuck Berry.

He appeared in a number of *I Love Lucy* (1952-1954) episodes, and in the 1954 episode titled "Lucy Is Envious", Vigran is the promoter who hired Lucy and Ethel to dress up as "Women From Mars" for a publicity stunt.

With his bushy eyebrows and balding pate, he was easily cast in a wide variety of middle-aged "everyman" roles: cops, small-time crooks, judges, jurors, bartenders, repairmen, neighbors, shopkeepers, etc, in programs such as *Racket Squad* (1952), *I Married Joan* (1952-1953), *The Mickey Rooney Show* (1954), *Father Knows Best* (1955), *Tales of the Texas Rangers* (1955), *The Life and Legend of Wyatt Earp* (1956), *Blondie* (1957), *Richard Diamond, Private Detective* (1957-1958), *Adventures of Superman* (1952-1958), *Wanted: Dead or Alive* (1959), *Dragnet* (1952-1959), *Wichita Town* (1960) also with Joel McCrea, *Shirley Temple Theatre* (1961), *The Virginian* (1963), *The Fugitive* (1964), *I Dream of Jeannie* (1967), *Hawaii Five-O* (1969), *The Odd Couple* (1971), *Longstreet* (1972), *Hec Ramsey* (1972), *Kolchak: The Night Stalker* (1974), *Charlie's Angels* (1979), *Galactica 1980* (1980), *The Jeffersons* (1985), and *Remington Steele* (1985).

He also provided the voice of "Whitney's boss" on the Arrowhead bottled-water television (animated) and radio commercials in the 1960s.

In 1952, Vigran married the former Belle Pasternack. The couple had two sons.

Vigran was active up until his death from cancer on November 29, 1986 in Los Angeles. He was cremated.

Helen Vinson

Helen Vinson was born Helen Rulfs in Beaumont, Texas. September 17, 1907 and was an American film actress, who appeared in forty films between 1932 and 1945.

She was a tall and distinguished-looking woman with brown eyes and naturally curly hair. Miss Vinson's father was an oil man. Her personal life included a passion for horses she developed during her youth. She studied at the University of Texas at Austin.

In Austin, she met Mrs. March Culmore, director of the Houston, Texas Little Theater. Culmore took Helen as a pupil and soon the young woman was playing leads with The Little Theater Group. From Texas, she moved quickly to Broadway. Her first success in New York City was in a play called *Los Angeles*. A succession of performances followed and led to a contract with Warner Brothers. Later, she regretted her quick leap to Hollywood and motion pictures. She lamented, "If I'd stayed in New York longer, I'd be getting a much bigger salary out here now."

Vinson's screen career often featured her in roles in which she played the part of the other woman or (pre-Code) loose women with active romantic lives. Her first film role was *Jewel Robbery* (1932), which starred William Powell and Kay Francis. She appeared as Doris Delafield in *The Kennel Murder Case*, which starred Powell as Philo Vance. One of her memorable roles was in *The Wedding Night* (1935). She played the wife of Gary Cooper and the rival of Anna Sten, in a story about the Connecticut tobacco fields. Another performance was in the RKO film *In Name Only* (1939), in which she was cast as the treacherous friend of Carole Lombard, Kay Francis and Cary Grant.

Another stand-out role for Vinson was as an undercover federal agent posing as a femme fatale opposite Richard Cromwell in Universal Pictures's anti-Nazi action drama entitled, *Enemy Agent* (1940). She followed that role with the role of Helen Draque in *The Thin Man Goes Home*.

More of her roles included *The Captain Hates the Sea* (1934), *Private Worlds* (1935) with Joel McCrea, *King of the Damned* (1935), *Live, Love and Learn* (1937), and *The Lady and the Monster* (1944).

Vinson's film career ended in 1945. For her contribution to the motion picture industry, Vinson had a star on the Hollywood Walk of Fame at 1560 Vine Street.

Away from film-making and following her retirement, Vinson's activities made frequent trips to New York City to see Broadway shows, visited friends in her home state of Texas, and enjoyed the Mardi Gras in New Orleans. She was married to noted tennis player Fred Perry. She loved horses and had a private and personal mount named *Arrabella*.

Helen Vinson died in Chapel Hill, North Carolina in October 7, 1999, at age 92.

Arthur Vinton

Arthur Vinton was born Albert Hozel December 10, 1896 in Brooklyn, New York. He picked his stage name because it sounded good. He was married twice and had one daughter by the first marriage. But he disowned her when he found she had a mixed marriage. His second wife survived him for about a year and they had no children. His acting career began in NY with some noted leading roles including the notorious *The Constant Sinner* written by Mae West.

His Hollywood career spanned the 1930s, and he was a founding member of the Screen Actors Guild. After Hollywood he had a noted career in radio and was a regular on the show *The Shadow*. His resonant deep voice often cast him as the heavy in radio shows as *This is Your FBI*.

Some of his roles included *Man Against Woman* (1932), *Gambling Lady* (1934) with Joel McCrea, *Rendezvous at Midnight* (1935), and *Armstrong Circle Theatre* (1951).

He purchased a farm with a pre-revolutionary war house in NY State near Newburgh, and raised cattle for a while. He called the farm Brittany Hills. But after World War II he raised turkeys under the name "The Barefoot boy of Brittany Hills". Poultry was very profitable in that era and he was able to start a gourmet restaurant on Long Island. After his stroke he retired to the warmth of Guadlajara, Mexico. He even learned Spanish with a good accent, and was an effective fund-raiser for the Episcopal Church.

He was good at organizing events and was known for his ability to bring people into the Screen Actors Guild. His wife was a much better manager so she managed all of the finances of the successful farm. One of his hobbies was 3D photography.

He died February 26, 1963 at age 66 in Guadalajara, Mexico.

Joseph Vitale

Joseph Vitale was born September 6, 1901, in New York City, New York. He appeared in numerous films and television programs from 1934 to 1964.

Some of his appearances were in *Daredevil O'Dare* (1934), *Gildersleeve's Ghost* (1944), *Smash-Up: The Story of a Woman* (1947), *Yankee Buccaneer* (1952), *The Stranger Wore a Gun* (1953), *Rocky Jones, Space Ranger* (1954), *The Lone Ranger* (1955-1957), *Wagon Train* (1958), *Alias Jesse James* (1959), *Wichita Town* (1960) with Joel McCrea, *Empire* (1963), *Mister Ed* (1964), and his last film *Apache Rifles* (1964) with Audie Murphy.

He died June 5, 1994, at age 92 in Granada Hills, California.

Emmett Vogan

Emmett Vogan And Joel McCrea in *Adventure in Manhattan*

Emmett Vogan was born in Cleveland, Ohio September 27, 1893 and was an American actor with almost 500 film appearances from 1934–1957, making him, along with Bess Flowers one of the most prolific film actors of all time.

Some of his roles included *The Captain Hates the Sea* (1934), *Miss Pacific Fleet* (1935), *Adventure in Manhattan* (1936) with Joel McCrea, *Wells Fargo* (!937) again with Joel McCrea, *Youth Takes a Fling* (1938) a third with Joel McCrea, *They Shall Have Music* (1939) a fourth with Joel McCrea, *Espionage Agent* (1939) a fifth with Joel McCrea, *The Ghost Breakers* (1940), *Tarzan's New York Adventure* (1942), *The Yellow Rose of Texas* (1944), *The Bullfighters* (1945) with Laurel and Hardy, *The Naughty Nineties* (1945) with Abbott and Costello, *Superman* (1948), *Batman and Robin* (1949), *Carbine Williams* (1952), *Hopalong Cassidy* (1952), *The Abbott and Costello Show* (1953), *These Wilder Years* (1956), and *Cavalcade of America* (1957).

He died October 6, 1969 at age 76 in Woodland Hills, Los Angeles, California.

Theodore von Eltz

Theodore von Eltz was born in New Haven, Connecticut November 5, 1893 and was an American film actor. He appeared in more than 200 films between 1915 and 1957. Silent screen lead Theodore Von Eltz was the son of a Yale professor and educated at Hill School at Pottstown Pennsylvania. Originally prepped to become a doctor, he decided instead to pursue acting.

At age 19 he made his New York debut and soon was hitting the Broadway boards with performances in *Children of Earth* (1915), *Rio Grande* (1916) and *The Old Lady Shows Her Medals* (1917). Von Eltz evolved into a dark and dashingly handsome silent film actor. Well-dressed with a trimmed mustache, he romanced a number of the silent screen's most lovely stars in both comedy and drama, including Bebe Daniels in *The Speed Girl* (1921) and Viola Dana in *Fourteenth Lover* (1922), before moving into a pattern of disreputable second leads and support roles with *Tiger Rose* (1923), *The Sporting Chance* (1925), *The Red Kimona* (1925), *The Sea Wolf* (1926). He received lesser billing to a couple of animal heroes in *White Fang* (1925) and *No Man's Law* (1927).

By the advent of sound Von Eltz was firmly entrenched in character parts and was often relied upon to drum up sinister support such as his deceptive culprit in *The Arizona Kid* (1930); his gangster in *Red-Haired Alibi* (1932); the Shirley Temple vehicle *Bright Eyes* (1934), in which he played Jane Withers' annoyingly vexatious father; his henchman in *The Sun Never Sets* (1939); and, more notably, his minor role as the blackmailing pornographer whose actions ignite the classic film noir *The Big Sleep* (1946). On the other hand, he could also play benevolent doctors, lawyers, and servants and did so in a film career that nearly hit the 200 mark. By the late 1930's his billing had slipped considerably to the point he was frequently uncredited. A well-oiled player on radio, he voiced the part of Papa Barbour on the popular program *One Man's Family* from 1948-1949, but was later replaced.

More of his roles included *Great Mail Robbery* (1927), *The Arizona Kid* (1930), *The Eleventh Commandment* (1933), *Private Worlds* (1935) with Joel McCrea, Adventure in Manhattan (1936) again with Joel McCrea, *The Story of Vernon and Irene Castle* (1939), *The Great Man's Lady* (1942) a third with Joel McCrea, *Devil's Cargo* (1948), *Painting the Clouds with Sunshine* (1951), *The Abbott and Costello Show* (1953), *The Ford Television Theatre* (1954-1956), and *The Unholy Wife* (1957).

Von Eltz was married twice. First wife Peggy Prior was a screenwriter for Pathe Studios. They had two children, Teddy and Lori, the latter becoming the soap actress Lori March. Following their divorce and a bitter custody feud (which he lost), he married Elizabeth Lorimar in 1932. They remained together until his death October 6, 1964 at age 70. He passed away at the Motion Picture Country Home after an extended illness and was buried in Forest Lawn Memorial Park in Los Angeles.

Peter Votrian

Peter J. Votrian was born on June 12, 1942 in Chicago, Illinois. He is an actor, known for *Hans Christian Andersen* (1952), *Crime in the Streets* (1956), and *Fear Strikes Out* (1957).

More of his roles included *Adventures of Wild Bill Hickok* (1952), *Her Twelve Men* (1954), *The Gene Autry Show* (1954-1955), *Gunsmoke* (1955-1956), *The Oklahoman* (1957) with Joel McCrea, *Playhouse 90* (1957-1960), *Hawaiian Eye* (1962), and *Bob Hope Presents the Chrysler Theatre* (1963).

Murvyn Vye

Marvin Wesley Vye Jr. was born July 15, 1913 in Quincy, Massachusetts. He was a Yale-trained character actor and was associated for a time with the Theatre Guild in the 1940s.

Equipped with a tough-looking countenance and sturdy baritone, he was hired to originate the role of Jigger Craigin in the Guild's 1945 mounting of Rodgers and Hammerstein's *Carousel*, which also starred John Raitt and Jan Clayton. A spectacular success, this led to Hollywood offers and in 1947 he made an auspicious film debut (third billed) in *Golden Earrings* (1947) starring Marlene Dietrich and Ray Milland, playing Zoltan, a gypsy who sings the title tune.

Playing next a baddie in the Alan Ladd film *Whispering Smith* (1948) and Merlin in the Bing Crosby remake of *A Connecticut Yankee in King Arthur's Court* (1949), Vye returned to Broadway to co-star as the Kralahome in the musical *The King and I*. The musical, of course, went on to become a smash but without Vye for he quit the production during tryouts after his only song was cut. Unfortunately he would not recreate his Jigger role in the movie version of "Carousel" either. Cameron Mitchell took the honors.

Back in Hollywood, Vye became a standard fixture in mobster pics including *Al Capone* (1959) as Bugs Moran, *King of the Roaring 20's: The Story of Arnold Rothstein* (1961) with David Janssen, and *The George Raft Story* (1961).

With a homely, imposing mug made for adventure tales, he played everything from warrior chiefs to Blackbeard the Pirate. On TV he portrayed a number of corrupt characters on such shows as *77 Sunset Strip* (1959) and *The Untouchables* (1961-1962) and sometimes even played his tough guys for laughs. In between he appeared in musical productions of *Oklahoma!* and *South Pacific*, among others.

More of his roles included *Black Horse Canyon* (1954) with Joel McCrea, *The Best Things in Life Are Free* (1956), *Have Gun - Will Travel* (1957), *Maverick* (1957-1959), *Alcoa Presents: One Step Beyond* (1960), *Wagon Train* (1960-1962), *The Beverly Hillbillies* (1963), and *Gentle Ben* (1967).

Vye died August 17, 1976 at age 63 in Pompano Beach, Floridain at age 63.

Russell Wade

Russell Wade was born June 21, 1917, in Oklahoma City, Oklahoma, and was an American character actor. He moved to California in the late 1920s and attended Hollywood High School, appearing on stage before moving into films.

He appeared in over sixty WWII-era movies as various cadets and military rookie types, retiring in 1948 for a career in business and real estate in the Palm Springs area.

Some of those credits include *The Wrecker* (1933), *Ace Drummond* (1936), *Pick a Star* (1937) with Laurel and Hardy, *Topper* (1937), *The Goldwyn Follies* (1938) with Alan Ladd, *Three Blind Mice* (1938) with Joel McCrea, *Sorority House* (1939) with Veronica Lake, *You Can't Cheat an Honest Man* (1939), *One Night in the Tropics* (1940) with Abbott and Costello, *Keep 'Em Flying* (1941) again with Bud & Lou, *The Great Gildersleeve* (1942), *Tall in the Saddle* (1944), *The Body Snatcher* (1945), *The Bamboo Blonde* (1946), *Shoot to Kill* (1947), and his final film *Beyond Glory* (1948) with Alan Ladd and Audie Murphy.

He developed the El Dorado Country Club in the mid-1950s and was the chairman of the Palm Springs Golf Classic tournament, now called the Bob Hope Classic, there for numerous years.

Russell was awarded a Star on the Palm Springs Walk of Stars on Palm Canyon Drive and was the recipient of the Golden Plate Award from the American Academy of Achievement.

He and wife Janie had two children: Joanie, who predeceased him, and Jeff.

He died December 9, 2006, at age 89 in Riverside, California.

Charles Wagenheim

Charles Wagenheim and Joel McCrea in *Foreign Correspondent*

Charles Wagenhiem was born February 21, 1896. Initially drawn to an acting career to counterbalance an acute case of shyness, diminutive character actor Charles Wagenheim's career comprised hundreds upon hundreds of minor but atmospheric parts on stage, film, and television. Born in Newark, New Jersey, he was the son of immigrant parents. Enlisting in the military during World War I, he was compensated for an education by the government and chose to study dramatics at the American Academy of Dramatic Arts in New York, graduating in 1923.

After touring with a Shakespearean company, he appeared in a host of Broadway plays, several of them written, directed and/or produced by the prolific George Abbott, including *A Holy Terror* (1925), *Four Walls* (1927) and *Ringside* (1928). Following a stage part in *Schoolhouse on the Lot* (1938), the mustachioed Wagenheim turned to Hollywood for work. His dark, graveside manner, baggy-eyed scowl and lowlife countenance proved ideal for a number of genres, particularly crime thrillers and westerns.

In films from 1929, the character player scored well when Alfred Hitchcock chose him to play the assassin in *Foreign Correspondent* (1940) with Joel McCrea. He went on to enact a number of seedy, unappetizing roles (tramps, drunks, thieves) over the years but never found the one juicy part that could have put him at the top of the character ranks.

Usually billed tenth or lower, Wagenheim was more filler than anything else which his blue-collar gallery of cabbies, waiters, deputies, clerks, morgue attendants, junkmen, etc., will attest. Some of his better delineated roles came with *Two Girls on Broadway* (1940); *Charlie Chan at the Wax Museum* (1940); *Half Way to Shanghai* (1942); the cliffhangers *Don Winslow of the Navy* (1942) and *Raiders of Ghost City* (1944); *The House on 92nd Street* (1945); *A Lady Without Passport* (1950); *Beneath the 12-Mile Reef* (1953); and *Canyon Crossroads* (1956).

One of his more promising roles came as "The Runt" in *Meet Boston Blackie* (1941), which started Chester Morris off in the popular 1940s "B" series as the thief-cum-crime-fighter, but the sidekick role was subsequently taken over by George E. Stone.

More credits included *House of Horrors* (1946), *Joan of Arc* (1948), *Samson and Delilah* (1949), *Jim Thorpe, All-American* (1951), *Aladdin and His Lamp* (1952), *Boston Blackie* (1952-1953), *Blackjack Ketchum, Desperado* (1956), *The Toughest Gun in Tombstone* (1958), *One Foot in Hell* (1960), *Lonely Are the Brave* (1962), *The Addams Family* (1965), *Cat Ballou* (1965), *The Cincinnati Kid* (1965), *The Fugitive* (1966), *A Time for Dying* (1969) with

Audie Murphy, *Adam-12* (1970), *Harry O* (1975), *The Apple Dumpling Gang* (1975), *Baretta* (1975-1977), *James at 16* (1978), and *All in the Family* (1979).

Of his latter films it might be noted that Wagenheim was cast in the very small but pivotal role of the thief who breaks into the storefront in which the Frank family is hiding above in *The Diary of Anne Frank* (1959).

Wagenheim played the recurring role of Halligan on *Gunsmoke* (1967-1975).

On March 6, 1979, the 83-year-old Wagenheim was bludgeoned to death in his Hollywood apartment following a grocery shopping trip when he surprised a thief in his home. By sheer horrific coincidence, elderly character actor Victor Kilian, of *Mary Hartman, Mary Hartman* (1976) fame, was found beaten to death by burglars in his Los Angeles-area apartment just a few days later on March 11, 1979.

Gregory Walcott

Gregory Walcott was born Bernard Mattox in Wendell, North Carolina January 13, 1928 and is an American television and film actor. He is perhaps best known for having appeared in the 1959 Ed Wood film, the cult classic *Plan 9 from Outer Space*.

Walcott was raised in Wilson, North Carolina. While serving in the Army, he appeared as a drill instructor in the film *Battle Cry*, then as a military policeman in 1955's war-themed classic *Mister Roberts* with Henry Fonda, again as a military policeman in *The McConnell Story* (1955) with Alan Ladd, as the drill instructor with Tony Curtis in *The Outsider* (1961), and later *Midway* (1976) as Capt. Elliott Buckmaster.

He would appear in a number of western films, beginning with an uncredited role in *Red Skies of Montana* (1952) opposite Richard Widmark, then later more prominently as a gunslinger who tries to romance Claudette Colbert in 1955's *Texas Lady*.

Walcott had roles in many television series, including that of Stone Kenyon in two episodes of the NBC sitcom, *The People's Choice* with Jackie Cooper. He was frequently cast in westerns like *Bonanza* (seven times), *Maverick*, *Frontier Doctor*, *Wagon Train*, *The High Chaparral*, *26 Men*, *Sugarfoot* (with Will Hutchins and cast opposite another guest star, Joi Lansing, in the 1958 episode "Bullet Proof"), *Laramie*, *The Rifleman*, *The Tall Man*, *The Dakotas*, and in several episodes of CBS's *Rawhide*, through which he began a long collaboration with Clint Eastwood. Walcott had featured roles in Eastwood's films *Thunderbolt and Lightfoot*, *The Eiger Sanction*, *Joe Kidd*, and *Every Which Way But Loose*.

He appeared with Joel McCrea in *Wichita Town* (1960).

Walcott made a guest appearance on *Perry Mason* as Bill Johnson in the 1959 episode, "The Case of the Howling Dog." He also was one of the stars of a 1961–1962 NBC television series, *87th Precinct*, as Detective Roger Havilland. Walcott accepted guest roles on many popular television series, such as CBS's *Dennis the Menace*, with Jay North. He had recurring roles too in the original *Dallas*, *Murder, She Wrote*, and he appeared as Captain Diggs on the 1970s series *Land of the Lost*.

His other film work also includes the comedy *On the Double* alongside Danny Kaye, the violent drama *Prime Cut* with Lee Marvin, and in the chase film *The Sugarland Express* directed by a 24-year-old Steven Spielberg.

Walcott played a sheriff in the 1979 film *Norma Rae*, the film that won an Oscar for star Sally Field. He also agreeably made a cameo appearance in the 1994 *Ed Wood* bio-pic starring Johnny Depp, directed by Tim Burton.

Walcott long regretted having anything to do with *Plan 9*, but in a Sept. 10, 2000 *Los Angeles Times* interview, he said, "It's better to be remembered for something than for nothing, don't you think?"

Charlotte Walker

Charlotte Walker was born in Galveston, Texas December 29, 1876 and was a Broadway theater actress. She was the mother of character actress Sara Haden.

Walker made her stage debut as a teen. At nineteen she performed in London, England in a comedy called *The Mummy*. She performed with Richard Mansfield.

Walker appeared as June in *Trail of the Lonesome Pine*, in 1911. She would later reprise the role in Cecil B. DeMille's 1916 film *Trail of the Lonesome Pine*. David Belasco noticed her in *On Parole*. He signed her for starring roles in plays *The Warrens of Virginia, Just a Wife*, and *Call The Doctor*.

She continued to act on the Broadway stage. In 1923 she played with Ethel Barrymore in *The School For Scandal*. It was produced by the Player's Club.

Walker's motion picture career began in 1915 with *Kindling* and *Out of the Darkness*. *Sloth* (1917) is a five-reeler which features Walker. In the third reel of this film she plays a youthful Dutch maid who is about sixteen years old. The setting is an old Dutch settlement on Staten Island, New York. The theme stresses the perils of indolence to a nation of people. It cautions against permitting luxury to replace the simplistic life led by America's forebears. In her later silent film work Walker can be seen in *The Midnight Girl* (1925) starring alongside a pre-*Dracula* Bela Lugosi. *The Midnight Girl* is one of Walker's few silents that survive.

As a film actress Walker continued to perform in films into the early 1930s. Her later screen performances include roles in *Lightnin* (1930) with Joel McCrea, *Millie* (1931), *Salvation Nell* (1931), and *Hotel Variety* (1933).

Walker's first husband was physician Dr. John B. Haden. A daughter Sara Haden was born of this marriage and there may have been other children. After her divorce, she returned to the stage. Her second husband, Eugene Walter, was a playwright who adapted the novel *The Trail of the Lonesome Pine* for the Broadway stage. The second marriage also ended in divorce in 1930.

Charlotte Walker died in March 23, 1958 at a hospital in Kerrville, Texas at age 81. Her daughter Sara Haden became a well-known character actress.

Nella Walker

Nella Walker was born in Chicago, Illinois March 6, 1886 and was an American film actress and vaudeville performer of the 1920s through the 1950s.

In her teens she became half of the husband and wife vaudeville team "Mack and Walker", with her husband Wilbur Mack. By 1929 she had launched a film acting career, her first film role being in *Tanned Legs* alongside Sally Blane, Dorothy Revier, June Clyde, and Arthur Lake. She appeared in three films in 1929, and easily transitioned to "talking films", appearing in another four films in 1930, possibly making the smooth transition because she was never an established silent film actress.

In 1931 her film career took off, with her appearing in ten films that year, five of which were uncredited. Her marriage ended not long after her film career was on the rise, and from 1932 through 1933 she appeared in fifteen films, only five of which were uncredited. In 1935 her career only got better, and between that year and 1938 she had twenty three film appearances. Her biggest film during that period was in *Young Dr. Kildare* (1938) alongside Lionel Barrymore and Lew Ayres. Throughout the 1930s her career was strong, despite her never being a premier "star", she repeatedly had solid acting roles. She finished that decade strong in 1939 with nine film roles, only three of which were uncredited.

The 1940s mirrored her success of the previous decade in many ways, with her appearing in thirty seven films from 1940 to 1947. Now later in her career, and over 60 years of age, she slowed her career for a time, not having another role until 1950 when she appeared in *Nancy Goes to Rio* alongside Ann Sothern and Carmen Miranda. She appeared in another two films in 1952, then had her last film acting role in 1954, in the film *Sabrina* alongside Humphrey Bogart and Audrey Hepburn. She retired after that role, having appeared in one hundred and seventeen movies.

Other notable film roles over her career included *Indiscreet* (1931), *The Common Law* (1931) with Joel McCrea, *20,000 Years in Sing Sing* (1932), *Four Frightened People* (1934), *A Dog of Flanders* (1935), *The Saint Strikes Back* (1939), *Blame it on Love* (1940) with Alan Ladd, *Buck Privates* (1941) with Abbott and Costello, *Reaching for the Sun* (1941) again with Joel McCrea, *Air Raid Wardens* (1943) with Laurel and Hardy, and *Nancy Goes to Rio* (1950).

She settled in Los Angeles, where she was residing at the time of her death on March 22, 1971 at age 85.

Walter Walker

Walter Walker was born on March 13, 1864 in New York, New York. He was an actor, known for *Flying Down to Rio* (1933), *The Count of Monte Cristo* (1934), and *Dangerous* (1935).

More of his roles included *Her Excellency, the Governor* (1917), *So's Your Old Man* (1926), *The Common Law* (1931) with Joel McCrea, *From Hell to Heaven* (1933), *The Man Who Reclaimed His Head* (1934), *Topper* (1937), *Happily Buried* (1939), and *Smart Woman* (1948).

He died on December 4, 1947 in Honolulu, Hawaii. According to his NY Times obituary, his wife and a daughter (Mrs. L.H. Riley) survived him. He had been visiting his daughter and her husband, Lieut. Col. Riley, when he died.

Henry B. Walthall

Henry Brazeale Walthall was born on a cotton plantation in Shelby County, Alabama March 16, 1878 and was an American stage and film actor.

Walthall received his education from a private tutor. As a young man, he enlisted in the Spanish-American War, but was infected with malaria while his regiment was encamped in Jacksonville, Florida. Soon after his recovery, the regiment was discharged. He became ambitious for the stage and joined the Murray Hill Theater stock company, where he played small parts. Later he became affiliated with the American Theater stock company and soon afterward joined the Providence, Rhode Island, stock company.

Walthall began his career as a stage actor, appearing on Broadway in a supporting role in William Vaughn Moody's *The Great Divide* in 1906–1908. During his stage career, he appeared in *Winchester, Under Southern Skies* (1901) by Charlotte Blair Parker, *Pippa Passes, The Faith Healer, The Only Way* and other productions. For several seasons he was associated with Margaret Anglin and at the conclusion of that engagement, he joined the Biograph Company. His career in movies began in 1909 at Biograph Studios in New York with a leading role in the film *A Convict's Sacrifice*. This film also featured James Kirkwood, and was directed by D.W. Griffith, a director that played a huge part in Walthall's rise to stardom. As the industry grew in size and popularity, Griffith emerged as a director and Walthall found himself a mainstay of the Griffith company, frequently working alongside such Griffith regulars as Owen Moore, Kate Bruce, Lillian and Dorothy Gish, Mae Marsh, Bobby Harron and Jack and Mary Pickford. He followed Griffith's departure from New York's Biograph to California's Reliance-Majestic Studios in 1913. After a few months with Reliance, he joined Pathé for a short period.

He decided to go into the producing business and formed The Union Feature Film Company, the first to be devoted entirely to full-length films. The venture was not successful, however, and he again became associated with Griffith's company.

Given the relatively short length of films in the early years, Walthall frequently found himself cast in dozens of films each year. For those still unfamiliar with his face, however, he gained national attention in 1915 for his role as Colonel Ben Cameron in Griffith's highly influential and controversial epic *The Birth of a Nation*. Walthall's portrayal of a Confederate veteran rounding up the Ku Klux Klan won him large-scale fame, and Walthall was soon able to emerge as a leading actor in the years leading up to the 1920s, parting ways with Griffith.

He continued through the 1920s, appearing in *The Plastic Age* with Gilbert Roland and Clara Bow and a 1926 adaptation of *The Scarlet Letter* opposite Lillian Gish. Now in his 40s, he found his roles increasingly more of the "character" variety. Having experience as a stage actor, Walthall continued his career into the 1930s and, thanks to the Will Rogers film *Judge Priest* of 1934, was enjoying a late golden period of his career at the time of his death in 1936. He was supposed to play the part of Chang in *Shangri-la*, a role eventually taken on by H.B. Warner. Walthall's role as Marcel in *The Devil Doll* is not to be confused with Ernest Thesiger as Dr. Septimus Pretorius in *Bride of Frankenstein*. The roles they played as mad scientists mastered shrinking people and objects and even look alike.

More of his later roles included *Freedom of the Press* (1928) with Joel McCrea, *The Jazz Age* (1929) again with Joel McCrea, *Abraham Lincoln* (1930), *Ride Him, Cowboy* (1932), *The Murder in the Museum* (1934), *A Tale of Two Cities* (1935), and *China Clipper* (1936).

He has a star on the Hollywood Walk of Fame located at 6201 Hollywood Boulevard.

Walthall was married twice. His first marriage, to actress Isabel Fenton, ended in divorce after ten years in 1917. His second marriage, to actress Mary Charleson lasted from the following year until his death from influenza in June 17, 1936 at age 58.

George Wallace

George Wallace was born George Dewey Wallace June 8, 1917, in New York City, New York, and, at age thirteen, moved with his mom and her new husband to McMechen, West Virginia, a coal mining town where the boy began working in the mines.

He joined the Navy in 1936, got out in 1940, and then went right back in again when World War II started. A chief boatswain's mate, he ended up in Los Angeles after a total of eight years in the service.

Wallace supported himself with an array of odd jobs, from working for a meat packer ("knockin' steers in the head") to lumber-jacking in the High Sierras. A stint as a singing bartender attracted the attention of Hollywood columnist Jimmy Fidler, who helped him get his show-biz start.

Wallace enrolled in drama school in the late 1940s, while earning his living tending the greens at MGM. He soon began landing jobs in films and TV, most notably as Commando Cody in the Republic serial *Radar Men from the Moon* (1952).

He later made his Broadway debut in Richard Rodgers' *Pipe Dreams*, replaced John Raitt in *The Pajama Game* and was nominated for a Tony for his leading role in *New Girl in Town* with Gwen Verdon. Other stage roles have included *The Unsinkable Molly Brown* opposite Ginger Rogers, *Jennie* with Mary Martin, *Most Happy Fella* (during production, he met his wife, actress Jane A. Johnston), *Camelot* (as King Arthur), *Man of La Mancha, Company*, and more.

More film and television roles followed such as *The Lawless Breed* (1953), *Border River* (1954) with Joel McCrea, *Hopalong Cassidy* (1952-1954), *Drums Across the River* (1954) with Audie Murphy, *The Human Jungle* (1954), *Destry* (1954) again with Audie Murphy, *The Second Greatest Sex* (1955), *Forbidden Planet* (1956), and *The Tall Man* (1960).

In 1960, his career was stalled when a horse fell on him and broke his back during the making of an episode of TV's *Walt Disney's Wonderful World of Color* (1954) *Swamp Fox*. His painful recovery took seven months.

After he recovered he continued to get roles such as Frank McLowery in *The Life and Legend of Wyatt Earp* (1961), *Six Black Horses* (1962) a third appearance with Audie Murphy, *Texas Across the River* (1966), *Skin Game* (1971), *The Six Million Dollar Man* (1973), *Dusty's Trail* (1973), *The Towering Inferno* (1974), *The Bionic Woman* (1976), *The Private Files of J. Edgar Hoover* (1977), *Dallas* (1983), *Night Court* (1984), *Dynasty* (1986), *Chicken Soup* (1989), *Postcards from the Edge* (1990), *Sons and Daughters* (1991), *Star Trek: The Next Generation* (1992), *Walker, Texas Ranger* (1994), *JAG* (1997), *Bicentennial Man* (1999), *Buffy the Vampire Slayer* (2002), *Minority Report* (2002), and *Joan of Arcadia* (2004).

He sometimes billed himself George D. H. Wallace, to avoid confusion with comic George Wallace.

He died July 22, 2005, at age 88 in Los Angeles, California.

H.B. Warner

H. B. Warner was born Henry Byron Charles Stewart Warner-Lickfold in St John's Wood, London, England October 26, 1875 and was a British actor.

Warner was educated at Bedford School. His father, Charles Warner, was an actor, and, although young Henry had initially thought about studying medicine, he eventually followed in his father's footsteps and performed on the stage.

He began his film career in silent films in 1914, when he debuted in *The Lost Paradise*. He played lead roles, culminating in the role of Jesus Christ in Cecil B. DeMille's silent film epic, *The King of Kings* in 1927. Following that film, he was usually cast in dignified roles, in such films as the 1930 version of *Liliom* (as the Heavenly Magistrate), *Grand Canary* (1934, as Dr. Ismay), the 1935 version of *A Tale of Two Cities* (as Charles Darnay's servant), *Mr. Deeds Goes to Town* (1936) (as the judge), the original 1937 version of *Lost Horizon* (as Chang, for which he was nominated for the Academy Award for Best Supporting Actor), *You Can't Take It With You* (1938), *Mr. Smith Goes to Washington* (1939), *The Rains Came* (1939), and *The Corsican Brothers*. He also appeared in *The Divine Lady* (1929) with Joel McCrea.

In *It's a Wonderful Life* (1946) he played what was for him an atypical role, as the drunken druggist. He also appeared in *Sunset Boulevard* (1950) (in which he played himself), and *The Ten Commandments* (1956). Occasionally, Warner was seen in sinister roles, as in the 1941 film version of *The Devil and Daniel Webster*, in which he played the ghost of John Hathorne. Also that year he played the villainous role of Mr. Carrington in *Topper Returns*.

More of his roles included *Tom Brown of Culver* (1932) with Alan Ladd, *Supernatural* (1933), *Along Came Love* (1936), *The Man from Dakota* (1940), *Hitler's Children* (1943), *It's a Wonderful Life* (1946), *The Judge Steps Out* (1949), and *Here Comes the Groom* (1951).

Warner was married twice, to Rita Stanwood in 1919 and to F.R. Hamlin.

On December 21, 1958 Warner died in Los Angeles, California of a heart attack at age 83, and he is buried in the Chapel of the Pines Crematory in Los Angeles, California. Warner has a star on the Hollywood Walk of Fame, at 6600 Hollywood Blvd.

Robert Warwick

Robert Warwick was born Robert Taylor Bien October 9, 1878, and was an American stage, film and television actor with over 200 film appearances.

Handsome and with a booming voice, Warwick trained to be an operatic singer, but acting proved to be his greater calling. He made his Broadway debut in 1903 in the play *Glad of It*. One of his co-stars in this play was a young John Barrymore, also making his Broadway debut. Both men quickly became matinee idols.

For the next twenty years, Warwick appeared in such plays as *Anna Karenina* (1906), *Two Women* (1910), with Mrs. Leslie Carter, *The Kiss Waltz* (1911), *Miss Prince* (1912), in both of which he was able to display his opera-trained singing voice, *The Secret* (1913), *A Celebrated Case* (1915) and *Drifting* (1922) with Alice Brady, not to mention several other plays through the end of the 1920s.

Warwick started making silent films in 1914. He made numerous productions in the 1910s primarily in Fort Lee, New Jersey. Two films, *Alias Jimmy Valentine* (1951) and *A Girl's Folly* (1917), both directed by Maurice Tourneur have been preserved, and showcase Warwick as a silent actor, as well as Tourneur's directing talent, and both are available on home video.

From the 1920s on, Warwick alternated doing plays and silent films. He was fifty when sound films arrived, and now middle aged with his matinee idol looks fading, he found plenty of work in character roles in which his voice recorded well. This eventually necessitated his moving permanently to California to be near the film studios when they moved to Los Angeles.

Throughout the 1930s and 1940s, Warwick's dependable acting and resonant voice ensured that he was seldom out of work. His immense filmography includes such classics as *The Little Colonel* (1935) with Shirley Temple and *The Adventures of Robin Hood* (1938) with Errol Flynn.

He was one of a number of actors favored by director Preston Sturges and appeared in many of his films, among them *Meat and Romance* (1940) with Alan Ladd, *Sullivan's Travels* (1941) with Joel McCrea and Veronica Lake, *I Married a Witch* (1942) with Veronica Lake, *The Palm Beach Story* (1942) again with Joel McCrea, *Hail the Conquering Hero* (1944), and *Man from Frisco* (1944).

Other film credits include *The Three Musketeers* (1948), *Tarzan and the Slave Girl* (1950), *The Mississippi Gambler* (1953), *Chief Crazy Horse* (1955), *Walk the Proud Land* (1956) with Audie Murphy, *Night of the Quarter Moon* (1959), and *It Started with a Kiss* (1959).

Warwick made numerous appearances on television almost from its initial popularity in the late 1940s. In his seventies he was still hard at work and made appearances on every type of television show like *Biff Baker, U.S.A.* (1952), *Topper* (1954), *The Adventures of Rin Tin Tin* (1957-1959), *Twilight Zone* (1960), and *Dr. Kildare* (1962).

Warwick was married several times. Divorced from his first two wives, he survived his third, actress Stella Lattimore (1905–1960), before dying June 6, 1964 in Los Angeles at the age of 86. By his first wife he had one daughter, Rosalind, who bore him two grandchildren, and with his second wife another daughter, Betsey, who was a prominent published poet in Los Angeles and was buried next to her father at Holy Cross Cemetery in Los Angeles in 2007. His and his wife Stella's headstones are engraved "Beloved Father" and "Beloved Mother".

Ruth Warren

Ruth Warren is an actress, known for *Mr. Lemon of Orange* (1931), *The Guilty Generation* (1931), and Zoo in Budapest (1933).

More of her roles included *Lightnin'* (1930) with Joel McCrea, (1933), *The Gay Deception* (1935), *Our Relations* (1936), *Wells Fargo* (1937) again with Joel McCrea, *Union Pacific* (1939) a third with Joel McCrea, *The Man Who Wouldn't Die* (1942), *Sunday Dinner for a Soldier* (1944), *King of the Wild Horses* (1947), *Military Academy with That Tenth Avenue Gang* (1950), *House of Wax* (1953), *The Ford Television Theatre* (1952-1954), *The Phantom Stagecoach* (1957), *Lawman* (1959), and *Thriller* (1961).

Bryant Washburn

Bryant Washburn Franklin Bryant Washburn in Chicago, Illinois April 28, 1889 and was an American film actor. He appeared in 375 films between 1911 and 1947.

More of her roles included *The Burglarized Burglar* (1911), *The Gallantry of Jimmy Rodgers* (1915), *Ghost of the Rancho* (1918), *Burglar Proof* (1920), *Mary of the Movies* (1923), *That Girl Oklahoma* (1926), *Nothing to Wear* (1928), *Kept Husbands* (1931) with Joel McCrea, *When Strangers Meet* (1934), *The Amazing Exploits of the Clutching Hand* (1936), *Stagecoach* (1939), *Gangs, Inc.* (1941) with Alan Ladd, *War Dogs* (1942), *I Dood It* (1943), *The Master Race* (1944), *Two O'Clock Courage* (1945), and *Sweet Genevieve* (1947).

He died April 30, 1963 from a heart attack at age 74 in Hollywood. His interment was located in Culver City, California's Holy Cross Cemetery. His son, Bryant Washburn, Jr. (1915–1960), was also an actor, a major in the US Air Force Reserve, served during World War II and Korea, and predeceased him.

Mildred Washington

Mildred Washington was born March 16, 1905 in Houston, Texas. The name Mildred Washington isn't remembered but she appeared in twelve films in small parts but her presence, finesse, beauty and vivacious personality wasn't small. Mildred was a beautiful, curvaceous, popular Black actress and dancer in the 1920s and 1930s. She started on the stage appearing in musicals for many years and later conquered California nightclubs and theaters becoming a full-fledged, substantial, popular entertainer who was called the sensation of the West. She was headliner and dance director for many years at the legendary Sebastian's Cotton Club. Mildred was the ultimate performer; she was a skilled dancer who knew how to wow a crowd and amaze them with her great dance and lively stage presence as is seen in the Hollywood movies she appeared in. On the side she appeared in Hollywood films because it was her dream to be in movies. Her beauty and outgoing personality helped her into movies like many white females. Mildred had a magnetic charm that couldn't be overlooked on stage and screen. Mildred introduced a new image of Blacks, she wasn't the common homely, sad, blue, and unintelligible type, Mildred was gorgeous, fun-loving, spoke intelligently, had poise and though sexy she was quite dainty and winsome.

In Hollywood Mildred played the role of a maid in the pre-code era which meant Mildred wasn't forced to be demeaning or stereotyped. In the pre-code era, there were no rules, Blacks had more to do outside the stereotype and most importantly was apart of the films they appeared in not just a maid or servant thrown in. Mildred added her own winning personality, sense of humor and spark; she simply glowed on screen. She entertained her white employees when they were down and out, educated them on life, and lifted their spirits. Mildred was one of the few, very few, beautiful black women who played the maid roles, she wasn't overweight or homely but beautiful, engaging, and scintillating, often stealing attention in scenes from leading white stars because of her beauty, talent and sex appeal. Her persona was certainly in the same fashion as Clara Bow, Alice White, and Jean Harlow. Though, Mildred had little to do on screen in a few of her movies, she still took advantage of getting herself recognized. Her maid costumes was just that...a costume, it didn't define her or her talent and that's what the black community loved about her. Mildred got fan mail, requests for her autographed photo, and she was featured in many leading black publications and newspapers. Whether Hollywood wanted her to be a stereotype or not is not the question, she took it upon her own initiative to present herself the way she wanted and she took her roles seriously and presented them the best she thought would entertain the public. *Hearts in Dixie* was one of the first black cast films made in Hollywood where Mildred co-starred, Mildred was said to have gave an excellent performance, the reviews were in Mildred's favor but sadly the film is believed to be lost. Her best role was in *Torch Singer* starring Claudette Colbert, in which she played a maid/confidante to Colbert. In this particular film she showed her awesome versatility and sincerity, where she went from dramatic to comedic naturally in good timing and she did some hot dancing. She was just marvelous in her role that you would forget she was suppose to be a maid, sometimes Mildred forgot, because she made her roles significant by being an actress not a maid.

More of her roles included *Uncle Tom's Cabin* (1927), *The Shopworn Angel* (1928), *The Thoroughbred* (1930), *Blonde Venus* (1932), *Bed of Roses* (1933) with Joel McCrea, and *Only Yesterday* (1933).

Mildred was a highly educated and cultured woman. She graduated from Los Angeles High School where she was an honor graduate and valedictorian. She had two years at the University of California at Los Angeles and also studied at Columbia University. She could speak fluent Spanish and French. Mildred chose being an entertainer and actress as her career but her education was always there to fall back on. Off screen she lived well, she dabbled in real estate and one of the few black movie stars who made enough to own a big, beautiful home in which she had a maid working for her. Mildred was truly a Renaissance Black woman and a new kind of Black woman who didn't let anyone hold her back. Mildred was on her way to becoming a full-time actress and studio heads were very satisfied with her previous work and beauty but it was her untimely death in late 1933 that stalled her escalating screen career.

During a major earthquake in the spring of 1933, Mildred developed appendicitis when she fell running for cover from Graumans Chinese Theatre. Her death was caused by peritonitis following appendicitis; she died September 7, 1933 on a Thursday afternoon at the White Memorial Hospital during surgery. She was 28 years old. Her funeral was a star- studded one with many black and white stage and screen stars.

Pierre Watkin

Pierre Watkin was born in Sioux City, Iowa December 29, 1889 and was an American character actor in many films, serials, and television series from the 1930s through the 1950s, especially westerns. He is perhaps best remembered for his connection to the serial and television versions of *Superman*.

Watkin portrayed Perry White in both of the *Superman* serials of the late-1940s, which starred Kirk Alyn as the title character and Noel Neill as Lois Lane.

He played a couple of different characters in episodes of the television series, *Adventures of Superman*, in which John Hamilton had been cast as Perry White.

More of his roles included *If You Could Only Cook* (1935), *She's Dangerous* (1937), *Internes Can't Take Money* (1937) with Joel McCrea, *You Can't Take It with You* (1938), *The Mysterious Miss X* (1939) with Alan Ladd, *Rulers of the Sea* (1939) again with Alan Ladd, *Captain Caution* (1940) a third with Alan Ladd, *Petticoat Politics* (1941) a fourth with Alan Ladd, *Great Guns* (1941) a fifth with Alan Ladd, *It Ain't Hay* (1943) with Abbott and Costello, *Little Giant* (1946) again with Bud and Lou, *Two Years Before the Mast* (1946) a sixth with Alan Ladd, *Superman* (1948), *Knock on Any Door* (1949), *The Cisco Kid* (1950), *Canadian Mounties vs. Atomic Invaders* (1953), *Hopalong Cassidy* (1953), *The Lone Ranger* (1950-1955), *Shake, Rattle & Rock!* (1956), *Perry Mason* (1957-1958), *The Flying Fontaines* (1959), and *Wanted: Dead or Alive* (1960).

He was set to reprise his role as the editor of *The Daily Planet* in a revival of the series in 1959, as Hamilton had died in the interim since the cancelation of the original series. However, series star George Reeves also died in the summer of 1959, and those plans ended. Watkin himself died six months later.

He died February 3, 1960 in Hollywood, California at age 72.

Minor Watson

Minor Watson was born in Marianna, Arkansas December 22, 1889 and was a prominent character actor. He appeared in 111 movies made between 1913 and 1956.

His credits included *Dead End* (1937) with Joel McCrea, *Boys Town* (1938), *Yankee Doodle Dandy (1942)*, *Kings Row* (1942), *Guadalcanal Diary* (1943), *Bewitched* (1945), *The Virginian* (1946) again with Joel McCrea, and *The Jackie Robinson Story* (1950).

He died July 28, 1965 and is buried in Alton Cemetery in Alton, Illinois.

Patrick Wayne

Patrick Wayne was born Patrick John Morrison in Los Angeles, California July 15, 1939 and is an American actor, the second son of movie star John Wayne and his first wife, Josephine Alicia Saenz. He made over forty films in his career, including nine with his father. In addition Patrick Wayne held a role as the host of a 1990 revival of the television game show *Tic-Tac-Dough*, and hosted the short-lived *Monte Carlo Show* in 1980.

One of John Wayne's four children by his first wife, Patrick took his father's stage surname, Wayne. He made a total of nine movies with his father: *Rio Grande* (1950); *The Quiet Man* (1952); *The Searchers* (1956); *The Alamo* (1960); *The Comancheros* (1961); *Donovan's Reef* (1963); *McLintock!* (1963); *The Green Berets* (1968); *Big Jake* (1971).

Patrick made his film debut at age 11 in his father's *Rio Grande* (1950). He followed that with films directed by family friend and iconic director John Ford: *The Quiet Man* (1952), *The Sun Shines Bright* (1953), *The Long Gray Line* (1955), *Mister Roberts* (1955), and *The Searchers* (1956).

From 1957 to 1958, Wayne appeared as Walter on the CBS sitcom, *Mr. Adams and Eve*, starring Howard Duff and Ida Lupino as a fictitious acting couple living in Beverly Hills. Other television work included baseball teleplay *Rookie of the Year* (1955), directed by John Ford and starring John Wayne, and *Flashing Spikes* (1962), a baseball television anthology installment directed by John Ford and starring James Stewart, with John Wayne in an extended cameo role. Patrick Wayne played similar roles in both shows as baseball players.

Following high school Patrick attended Loyola Marymount University, where he was a member of Alpha Delta Gamma fraternity; he graduated in 1961. During this time he struck out on his own to star in his own film *The Young Land* (1959). Patrick enlisted in the United States Coast Guard in 1961. He supported his father in *The Alamo* (1960), *Donovan's Reef* (1963), *McLintock!* (also 1963), and *The Green Berets* (1968). Others included a role in Ford's sprawling epic *Cheyenne Autumn* (1964), a role as James Stewart's son in *Shenandoah* (1965), *An Eye for an Eye* (1966), *The Deserter* (1971) and a lead role in *The Bears And I* for Walt Disney (1974).

In 1966 at age 27, Wayne co-starred with Ron Hayes and Chill Wills in the seventeen-episode ABC comedy-western series *The Rounders*, based on the 1965 Glenn Ford and Henry Fonda film of the same name *The Rounders*.

He also appeared in *Mustang Country* (1976) with Joel McCrea.

Following work on his father's *Big Jake*, Patrick earned recognition in the sci-fi genre. His career peaked in the late 1970s in the popular matinée fantasy *Sinbad and the Eye of the Tiger* (1977), then *The People That Time Forgot* (1977). Wayne also screen tested for the title role of *Superman*. He was offered the role, but declined because of his father's cancer.

He co-starred as a romantic love interest to Shirley Jones in another brief TV series, *Shirley* (1979).

He had many appearances on popular TV shows of the 1970s and 1980s, including *Fantasy Island* (1978), *Murder, She Wrote* (1984), *Charlie's Angels* (1976), *Sledge Hammer!* (1986) and *The Love Boat* (1979-1986). Wayne appeared in the movie *Young Guns* (1988) as Pat Garrett. He also did a comic turn in the Western spoof *Rustler's Rhapsody* (1985) starring Tom Berenger.

He was married to Peggy Hunt from 1965 to 1978 and married Misha Anderson in 1999.

In 2003 Patrick became chairman of the John Wayne Cancer Institute.

Doodles Weaver

Doodles Weaver was born Winstead Sheffield Glenndenning Dixon Weaver May 11, 1911 in Los Angeles and was an American character actor, comedian, and musician.

Born into a wealthy West Coast family, Weaver began his career in radio. In the late 1930s, he performed on Rudy Vallée's radio programs and *Kraft Music Hall*. He later joined Spike Jones' City Slickers. In 1957, Weaver hosted his own variety show *The Doodles Weaver Show*, which aired on NBC. In addition to his radio work, he also recorded a number of comedy records, appeared in films, and guest starred on numerous television series from the 1950s through the 1970s. Weaver made his last onscreen appearance in 1981.

Weaver was one of four children born to Sylvester Laflin, a wealthy roofing contractor, and Annabel (née Dixon) Weaver. His older brother was Sylvester "Pat" Weaver who served as the President of NBC in the 1950s. Weaver's niece is actress Sigourney Weaver. He was of English, Scottish, and Ulster-Scots ancestry, including roots in New England. Weaver was given the nickname "Doodlebug" by his mother when he was a child because of his big ears and freckles.

He attended Los Angeles High School and Stanford University. At Stanford, Weaver was a contributor to the *Stanford Chaparral* humor magazine. He was also known to engage in numerous pranks and practical jokes and earned the nickname "The Mad Monk". He was reportedly suspended from Stanford in 1937 (the year he graduated) for pulling a prank on the train home from the Rose Bowl.

On radio during the late 1930s and early 1940s, he was heard as an occasional guest on Rudy Vallée's program and on the *Kraft Music Hall*.

In 1946, Weaver signed on as a member of Spike Jones's City Slickers band. Weaver was heard on Jones's 1947-1949 radio shows, where he introduced his comedic Professor Feetlebaum, a character who spoke in Spoonerisms. Part of the Professor's schtick was mixing up words and sentences in various songs and recitations as if he were suffering from myopia and/or dyslexia. Weaver toured the country with the Spike Jones Music Depreciation Revue until 1951. The radio programs were often broadcast from cities where the Revue was staged.

One of Weaver's most popular recordings is the Spike Jones parody of Rossini's "William Tell Overture". Weaver gives a close impression of the gravel-voiced sports announcer Clem McCarthy in a satire of a horse race announcer who forgets whether he's covering a horse race or a boxing match ("It's Girdle in the stretch! Locomotive is on the rail! Apartment House is second with plenty of room! It's Cabbage by a head!"). The race features a nag named Feetlebaum, who begins at long odds, runs the race a distant last—and yet suddenly emerges as the winner.

In 1966, Weaver recorded a novelty version of "Eleanor Rigby"—singing, mixing up the words, insulting, and interrupting, while playing the piano.

Weaver was a contributor to the early *Mad* Magazine, as described by *Time*'s Richard Corliss:

> Among the funny stuff: Doodles Weaver's strict copy editing of the Gettysburg Address, advising Lincoln to change "fourscore and seven" to eighty-seven ("Be specific"), noting that there are six "dedicates" ("Study your Roget"), wondering if "proposition" isn't misspelled and, finally exasperated, urging the writer to omit "of the people, by the people, and for the people" as "superfluous."

Weaver made his television debut on *The Colgate Comedy Hour* in 1951. He performed an Ajax cleanser commercial with a pig, and the audience reaction prompted the network to give him his own series. In 1951, *The Doodles Weaver Show* was NBC's summer replacement for Sid Caesar's *Your Show of Shows*; it was telecast from June to September with Weaver, his wife Lois, vocalist Marian Colby, and the comedy team of Dick Dana and Peanuts Mann. The show's premise involved Weaver dealing with an assignment to stage a no-budget television series using only the discarded costumes, sets, and props left behind by more popular network TV shows away for the summer. The series ended in July 1951.

Weaver went on to guest star on numerous television shows including *The Spike Jones Show*, *The Donna Reed Show*, *Dennis the Menace*, and *The Tab Hunter Show*. He also hosted several children's television shows. In 1965, he starred in A Day With Doodles, a series of six-minute shorts sold as alternative fare to cartoons for locally hosted kiddie television programs. Each episode featured Weaver in a first-person plural adventure (e.g., "Today we are a movie actor"), portraying himself and, behind false mustaches and costume hats, all the other characters in slapstick comedy situations with a voice over narration and minimal sets. The ending credits would invariably list "Doodles... Doodles Weaver" and "Everybody Else... Doodles Weaver."

He portrayed eccentric characters in guest appearances on such TV shows as *Batman* (where he played The Archer's henchman Crier Tuck), *Land of the Giants*, *Dragnet 1967*, and *The Monkees*.

He appeared in more than ninety films, including *Come and Get It* (1936) with Joel McCrea, *Swiss Miss* (1938) with Laurel and Hardy, *Li'l Abner* (1940), *Shine on Harvest Moon* (1944), *Superman* (1948), *Powder River* (1953), *The 30 Foot Bride of Candy Rock* (1959) with Lou Costello, *The Great Imposter* (1961), Alfred Hitchcock's *The Birds* (1963)(as the man helping Tippi Hedren's character with her rental boat), Jerry Lewis's *The Nutty Professor*

(1963), *Pocketful of Miracles* (1961) and, in a cameo, *It's a Mad, Mad, Mad, Mad World* (1963). He appeared in *Six Pack Annie* in 1975. His last movie was *Earthbound* in 1981.

Weaver was married four times and had three children. His first marriage was to Beverly Masterman in 1939. They had one child. They later divorced. His second marriage was to Evelyn Irene Paulsen from 1946 to 1949. In 1949, Weaver married for a third time to nightclub dancer Lois Frisell. Frisell had the marriage annulled in 1954.

Weaver's fourth and final marriage was to actress Reita Anne Green in October 1957. They had two children before divorcing in 1969.

On January 17, 1983, Weaver died at age 71 of two self-inflicted gunshot wounds to the chest. His death was ruled a suicide. Weaver's son later said that his father had been despondent over his failing health. His funeral was held on January 22 at Forest Lawn mortuary in the Hollywood Hills. He was buried in Avalon Cemetery in Santa Catalina Island, California. Weaver's memoirs, *Golden Spike*, remain unpublished.

Marjorie Weaver

Marjorie Weaver in Crossville, Tennessee March 2, 1913 and was an American film actress of the 1930s through the early 1950s.

She attended the University of Kentucky, and later the Indiana University, with interests in music. Weaver began her acting career as a stage actress in the early 1930s, and also worked as a model during that period, as well as a singer. She received her first film role, uncredited, in 1934. From 1936 through 1945 she would receive steady acting roles. She began receiving credited roles in larger productions, and starred opposite Ricardo Cortez in the 1937 film *The Californian*, and that same year she starred opposite Tyrone Power in *Second Honeymoon*.

From 1938 through 1945 she had twenty seven starring roles in films, some of which were B movies. The most notable film role was her role in *Young Mr. Lincoln* (1939), which also starred Henry Fonda and Alice Brady. Some of her more recognizable roles from that seven-year period included a role in the *Michael Shayne* mystery series opposite Lloyd Nolan, and her role in *Charlie Chan's Murder Cruise*.

More of her roles included *Here Comes Carter* (1936), *Ali Baba Goes to Town* (1937), *Three Blind Mice* (1938) with Joel McCrea, *Murder Over New York* (1940), *The Great Alaskan Mystery* (1944), and *We're Not Married!* (1952). She then retired from acting.

She had married businessman Don Briggs in 1943, with whom she would have a son and a daughter, Joel and Leigh. She and her husband opened a business in Los Angeles, which they operated until retirement, at which time they moved to Austin, Texas, where she died of a heart attack on October 1, 1994, at age 81.

Joan Weldon

Joel McCrea and Joan Weldon in *Gunsight Ridge*

Joan Weldon was born as Joan Louise Welton on August 5, 1930, San Francisco, California and is an American film and television actress. She began her career singing in the San Francisco Grand Opera Company chorus. Later she became a contract actress with Warner Bros. where she remained until her contract ended in 1954. Her most prominent film was the cult thriller *Them!* (1954).

Some of her other roles included *The Stranger Wore a Gun* (1953), *Riding Shotgun* (1954), *Gunsight Ridge* (1957) with Joel McCrea, *Day of the Badman* (1958), and *Home Before Dark* (1958).

Weldon had a brief television career in the 1950s. Her first appearance in 1955 was in an episode of *The Millionaire*, starring Marvin Miller. She made three appearances on *Lux Video Theater* in various roles. She also played Marian Keats in the title role of the *Perry Mason* episode, "The Case of the Angry Mourner" in 1957. Her final television appearance was in 1958 on *Shirley Temple Theater*.

She resumed her career as a singer in road company productions including *The Music Man* and *Oklahoma!*. Weldon retired in 1980.

Alan Wells

    Alan Wells was born George Alan Wells on March 23, 1926 in Benzonia, Michigan. He was an actor, known for *The Man Who Cheated Himself* (1950), *Beachhead* (1954), and *Cape Fear* (1962).

    More of his roles included *Apache Chief* (1949), *Hopalong Cassidy* (1953), *The Cisco Kid* (1955), *The Ten Commandments* (1956), *The Lone Ranger* (1953-1957), *Richard Diamond, Private Detective* (1958-1959), *Wichita Town* (1959) with Joel McCrea, and *Stagecoach West* (1961).

    First wed to Claudia Barrett in the early 1950s, he married Barbara Lang in 1956 in Ensenada, Mexico. He met her when she was a co-star with him on *Death Valley Days* (1955). The couple was estranged by March of 1957 and their marriage annulled in 1958 when Lang claimed that Welles' divorce from Barrett was finalized ten months after the date of their own wedding.

    He died on June 14, 2008 in Reno, Nevada at age 82.

James Westerfield

James Westerfield and Joel McCrea in *The Gunfight at Dodge City*

James A. Westerfield was born in Nashville, Tennessee March 22, 1913 and was an American actor of stage, film, and television.

Born to candy-maker Brasher Omier Westerfield and his wife Dora Elizabeth Bailey, he was raised in Detroit, Michigan. He became interested in theatre as a young man and in the 1930s joined Gilmor Brown's famed Pasadena Community Playhouse, appearing in dozens of plays. He played in numerous films following his debut in 1940, then went to New York and appeared on Broadway, winning two New York Drama Critics' Circle Awards for his supporting roles in *The Madwoman of Chaillot* and *Detective Story*. He then returned to Hollywood and made more than forty more films. Westerfield maintained an interest in the theatre. He directed more than fifty musicals in a summer-musical tent he owned in Danbury, Connecticut, and was the original stage director and producer for the Greek Theatre in Los Angeles. He directed three seasons of "Theatre Under the Stars" in Vancouver, British Columbia, and appeared in musical roles with the Detroit Civic Light Opera, the Los Angeles Civic Light Opera, and the San Francisco Civic Light Opera.

On film, Westerfield had roles in *The Howards of Virginia* (1940) with Alan Ladd, *The Magnificent Ambersons* (1942), *O.S.S.* (1946) again with Alan Ladd, *On The Waterfront* (1954), *Lucy Gallant* (1955), the 1957 Budd Boetticher-directed Western *Decision at Sundown* starring Randolph Scott, *Cowboy* (1958), *The Proud Rebel* (1958) a third with Alan Ladd, *The Gunfight at Dodge City* (1959) with Joel McCrea, a repeating role in *The Absent-Minded Professor* (1961) and its sequel *Son of Flubber* (1963), *Birdman of Alcatraz* (1962), *Man's Favorite Sport* (1964), *The Sons of Katie Elder* (1965), *Hang 'Em High* (1968) and *True Grit* (1969).

Westerfield had many roles on television, including seven episodes as John Murrel from 1963 to 1964 on ABC's *The Travels of Jaimie McPheeters*, starring child actor Kurt Russell in the title role. He made two guest appearances on *Perry Mason*, including the role of Sheriff Bert Elmore in the 1957 episode, "The Case of the Angry Mourner." He also appeared in a TV episode of The Lone Ranger in 1954 entitled "Texas Draw".

His other appearances were on such series as *Mike Hammer* (1958), *Richard Diamond, Private Detective* (1959), *Wanted: Dead or Alive* (1959), *Twilight Zone* (1961), *The Time Tunnel* (1966), *The Wild Wild West* (1969), *Gunsmoke* (1955-1969), *Bewitched* (1971), and *O'Hara, U.S. Treasury* (1971) with David Janssen.

Westerfield as a young man was a roommate of fellow Pasadena Playhouse actor George Reeves. The two remained close friends until Reeves's death in 1959.

Westerfield was married to Alice G. Fay (an actress under the name Fay Tracey), who, along with his mother, survived him. Westerfield died September 20, 1971) from a heart attack in Woodlands Hills, California, at the age of 58.

Helen Westley

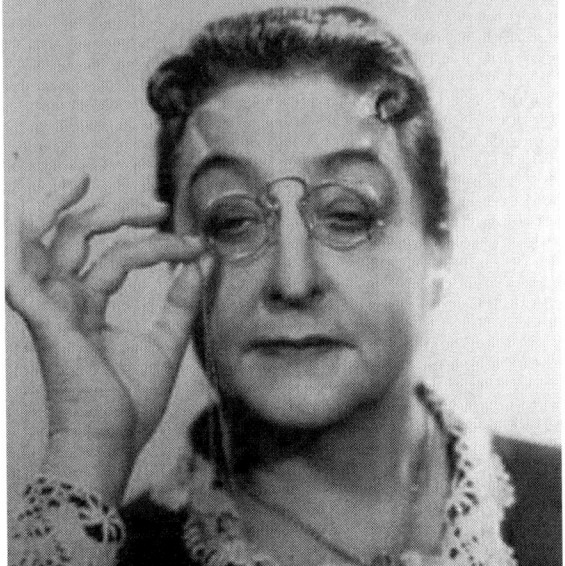

Helen Westley was born Henrietta Remsen Meserole Manney March 28, 1875 and was an American character actress.

Helen Westley was a member of the original board of the Theatre Guild, and appeared in many of their productions, among them *Peer Gynt*, and some of their productions of plays by George Bernard Shaw— *Caesar and Cleopatra, Pygmalion, Heartbreak House, Major Barbara, The Doctor's Dilemma* and *The Apple Cart*. She appeared in the original Broadway productions of two plays which, after her death, would be turned into classic Rodgers and Hammerstein musicals; they were *Green Grow The Lilacs*, which would become *Oklahoma!*, and *Liliom*, which became *Carousel*. Westley played Aunt Eller in the former, and Mrs. Muskat (who became Mrs. Mullin in *Carousel*) in the latter. She also appeared in the original Broadway production of Eugene O'Neill's *Strange Interlude*.

Westley played roles, both comic and dramatic, in many films. They included *Death Takes a Holiday, All This and Heaven Too*, four films opposite child star Shirley Temple (including *Dimples* and *Heidi*), the 1934 surprise hit *Anne of Green Gables*, the 1935 film version of *Roberta*, and the 1936 film version of *Show Boat*, in which she replaced Edna May Oliver, when Ms. Oliver declined to repeat her stage role as Parthy Ann Hawks. She also appeared in *Rebecca of Sunnybrook Farm* in 1938 with Shirley Temple and Randolph Scott as Aunt Miranda. In 1936 she played in *Banjo on My Knee* with Joel McCrea, Barbara Stanwyck, Walter Brennan and Buddy Ebsen.

Westley married John Westley, an actor on Broadway, on October 31, 1900. The couple separated in 1912. The marriage ended in divorce. The couple had one daughter, named Ethel.

She died December 12, 1942 at age 67 in Middlebush, New Jersey.

Cecil Weston

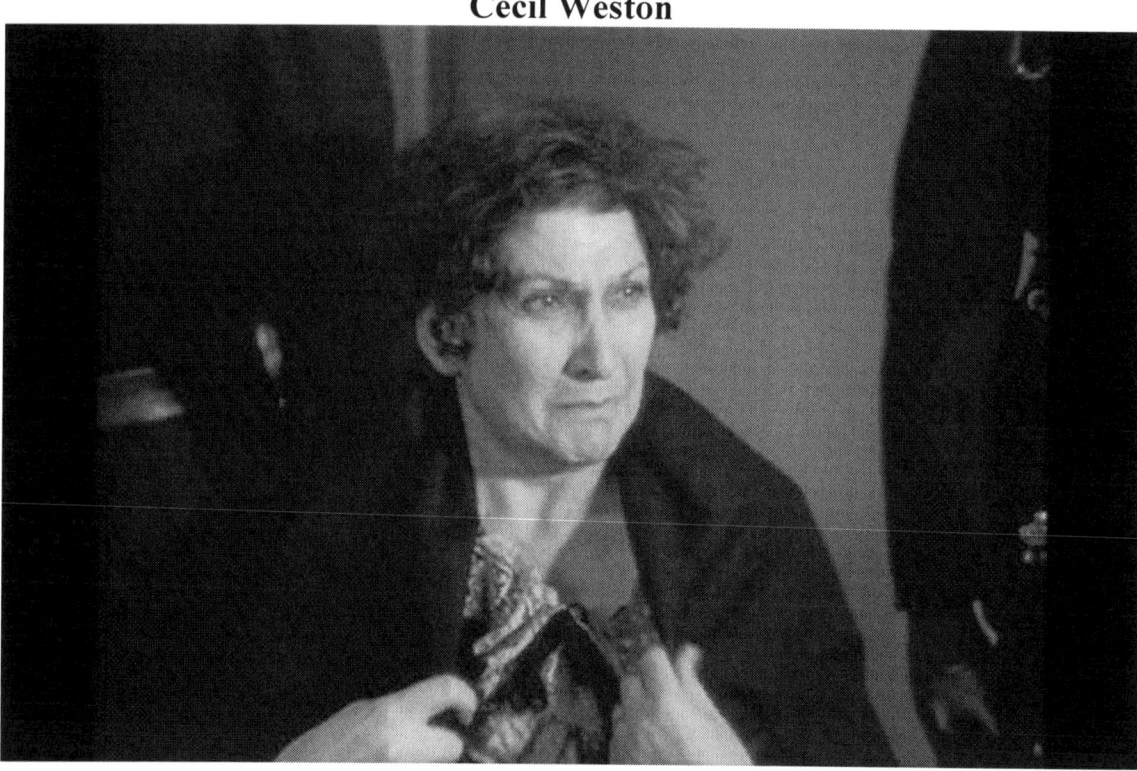

Cecil Weston was born on September 3, 1889 in Capetown, South Africa. She was an actress, known for *Banjo on My Knee* (1936) with Joel McCrea, *Money Madness* (1948), and Pride of the Blue Grass (1954).

More of her roles included *Dude Ranch* (1931), *Les Misérables* (1935), *Kidnapped* (1938), *Belle Starr* (1941), *Buffalo Bill* (1944) again with Joel McCrea, *The Walls of Jericho* (1948), *The Snows of Kilimanjaro* (1952), *You Can't Run Away from It* (1956), *Richard Diamond, Private Detective* (1959), *Noose for a Gunman* (1960), and *The Notorious Landlady* (1962).

She was married to Fred J. Balshofer. She died on August 7, 1976 in Hollywood, California at age 86.

Ruth Weston

Ruth Weston was born on August 31, 1906 in Boston, Massachusetts. She was an actress, known for *The Public Defender* (1931), *Smart Woman* (1931), and *Transgression* (1931).

More of her roles included *This Sporting Age* (1932), *Splendor* (1935) with Joel McCrea, *That Certain Age* (1938), and *Made for Each Other* (1939).

She died on November 5, 1955 in East Orange, New Jersey at age 49.

Yale Wexler

Yale Wexler was born on February 6, 1930 in Chicago, Illinois. He was an actor, known for *Time Limit* (1957), *Stakeout on Dope Street* (1958), and *Alfred Hitchcock Presents* (1959).

More of his roles included *Charlie Wild, Private Detective* (1951), *Stakeout on Dope Street* (1958), *Wichita Town* (1960) with Joel McCrea, and *Back Street* (1961).

He died on February 12, 1996 in Chicago, Illinois at age 66.

Arleen Whelan

Arleen Whelan was born in Salt Lake City, Utah September 1, 1914 and was an American film actress. She spent her early childhood in Pueblo, Colorado, where she attended High School. Her father was an electrician, who, upon opening his own electrical store in Los Angeles, moved the family westward. Arleen was enrolled in a beauty college and learned hairdressing and manicure, soon finding work for $18 a week in a salon on Hollywood Boulevard. There, she was 'discovered' by director H. Bruce Humberstone, who dropped in for a shave and ended up suggesting her name, as a likely candidate for movie stardom to Darryl F. Zanuck.

In May 1937, she was signed to a seven-year contract by 20th Century Fox, her salary now between $50 and $300 per week.She appeared in twenty-five films between 1937 and 1957,

After her screen test the studio cast Whelan as the female lead in a film version of Robert Louis Stevenson's *Kidnapped* (1938).

Some of her other credits included *Young Mr. Lincoln* (1939), *Young People* (1940), *Castle in the Desert* (1942), *Stage Door Canteen* (1943), *Ramrod* (1947) with Joel McCrea and Veronica Lake, *Dear Wife* (1949), *Passage West* (1951), *Flaming Feather* (1952), *Never Wave at a WAC* (1953), *Lux Video Theatre* (1953-1955), *The Women of Pitcairn Island* (1956), *The Badge of Marshal Brennan* (1957), and *General Electric Theater* (1962).

She was married to Alexander D'Arcy from 1940 to 1943, Hugh Owen from 1943 to 1953, and Dr. Warren O. Cagney from 1960 to 1961. All three marriages ended in divorce.

She died April 7, 1993 age 78 in Orange County, California.

Dan White

Dan White was born in Falmouth, Florida March 25, 1908 and was an American actor, well known for appearing in Western films and TV shows.

Dan White was born to George and Orpha White, one of twelve siblings. The Whites moved to Lakeland during World War I. By age 14, White was in show business. He left home to travel thousands of miles throughout the South in tent, minstrel, vaudeville and theater shows. His brother Willard joined him for nine years in a show in Tampa's Rialto Theater. Frances Langford worked with White during the time, and he convinced her to go to Hollywood. During this period, he met Tilda Spivey and proposed marriage on February 25, 1933. She had a 2-year-old child, Arthur Gifford, before her wedding. Dan left show business for financial reasons to work with the Civilian Conservation Corps. He still longed for a career in entertainment and took a cruise to Los Angeles. He and his family made extra stops at cities all over the country to earn money to continue the tour.

In January 1937, he stopped at Texarkana, Arkansas, where Tilda awaited the birth of their child. Her sister, Mary, who was in Texarkana, invited the Whites to stay there for a few months. The baby, June Larue White, was finally born, and the Whites continued toward California.

They arrived 16 days later and rented a house for 23 years, even film scripts were written in their own living room. Dan had a hard time finding a job and was in Panama working on the Pan American Highway. Although, upon return in 1938, he got work with the Republic Pictures Corporation, making six films in his first year. The first film was, *Prairie Moon*, with Gene Autry. White made $55 a week during that picture. He made about 300 films and 150 television cameos during his years in Hollywood. Around 70 percent were Westerns.

Among some of his well-known roles were *Shine On, Harvest Moon* (1938), *Destry Rides Again* (1939), *Gone with the Wind* (1939), *The Howards of Virginia* (1940) with Alan Ladd, *The Phantom* (1943), *The Invisible Man's Revenge* (1944), *Duel in the Sun* (1946), *Albuquerque* (1948), *Four Faces West* (1948) with Joel McCrea, *The Gunfighter* (1950), *Comin' Round the Mountain* (1951) with Abbott and Costello, *Lone Star* (1952), *The Lone Ranger* (1953), *Hopalong Cassidy* (1953), *Adventures of Wild Bill Hickok* (1952-1955), *Tales of the Texas Rangers* (1956), *The Ten Commandments* (1956), *Jailhouse Rock* (1957), *The Proud Rebel* (1958) again with Alan Ladd, *This Earth Is Mine* (1959), *Wanted: Dead or Alive* (1960), *Wichita Town* (1960) again with Joel McCrea, *Twilight Zone* (1961), *Have Gun - Will Travel* (1962), *Destry* (1964), *Jesse James Meets Frankenstein's Daughter* (1966), *The Cheyenne Social Club* (1970), *Adam-12* (1971), *Gunsmoke* (1960-1972), *Barnaby Jones* (1973), *Mannix* (1973), and *Beyond the Bermuda Triangle* (1975).

White and his wife had a third child, Donald Curtis White, born on November 9, 1941. He was offered the role of, "Sam the Bartender," in, *Gunsmoke*, but he didn't commit to the idea. He asked Glenn Strange to apply for the job.

Dan loved California for the almost 40 years he was there, but his true love was his old town in Florida. Upon retirement, he returned to Tampa and made appearances in Western Film Round-Ups and talk shows. He was often visited by his family until his death on July 7, 1980, in Tampa, Florida at age 72.

Huey White

Huey White was born on August 28, 1897 in Chicago, Illinois. He was an actor, known for *Female* (1933), *Gambling Lady* (1934) with Joel McCrea, and *Crash Donovan* (1936).

More of his roles included *The Mayor of Hell* (1933), *The Thin Man* (1934), *Bullets or Ballots* (1936), *The Last Gangster* (1937), and *Accidents Will Happen* (1938).

He died on June 23, 1938 in Los Angeles, California at age 40.

O.Z. Whitehead

Oothout Zabriskie Whitehead was born in New York City March 1, 1911 and was a stage and film character actor. He attended Harvard University. Called "O.Z." or "Zebby", he also authored several volumes of biographical sketches of early members of the Bahá'í Faith especially in the West after he moved to Dublin, Ireland in 1963.

Whitehead first appeared on Broadway in Martin Beck Theatre performing in *The Lake* (1933) in fifty-five performances from December 1933 to February 1934 which was Katharine Hepburn's first Broadway leading role and eleven other plays by 1939.

O. Z. Whitehead was one of the last surviving members of John Ford's "stock company" of character actors. Along with John Carradine, Donald Meek, Ward Bond, Ben Johnson, Harry Carey, Jr. et al., Whitehead was one of the many actors regularly employed by Ford to breathe life into even the smallest roles in his films. His best- known part was that of Al in Ford's 1940 adaptation of John Steinbeck's novel *The Grapes of Wrath*.

The Scoundrel (1935) by Ben Hecht, and Charles MacArthur which won a 1936 Oscar for Best Original Story was Whitehead's first film. Whitehead most famously played Al Joad (Henry Fonda's younger brother) in John Steinbeck's *Grapes of Wrath* (1940) which was nominated for and won several Oscars. Whitehead starred as Clarence in a stage production of *Life with Father* with Lillian Gish among a total of more than fifty films and TV series episodes performances. Whitehead's first TV episode was *The Arrow and the Bow* in *Cavalcade of America* in 1953 and continued in other shows like *Gunsmoke* (1958), *Bonanza* (1960), and two episodes of *Alfred Hitchcock Presents* (1960-1). In 1961 he made a guest appearance on *Perry Mason* as murderer Harry Beacom in "The Case of the Cowardly Lion." Shortly thereafter Whitehead moved to Ireland and participated in theatre arts there.

More of his roles included *Comin' Round the Mountain* (1951) with Abbott and Costello, *The San Francisco Story* (1952) with Joel McCrea, *I Spy* (1956), *The Horse Soldiers* (1959), *Two Rode Together* (1961), *The Lion in Winter* (1968), and *Hello Stranger* (1992).

In 1966 he won the Best Supporting Actor award at the Dublin Theatre Festival for his performance in Eugene O'Neill's *Hughie*, a part he was to reprise at the Peacock until 1989. In 1983 he played the role of American Ambassador David Gray in the RTÉ television drama *Caught in a Free State*, set in neutral Ireland during World War II. His final role was as the narrator/Voice in the Irish horror movie *Biological Maintenance Department* (1997).[1]

Whitehead died of cancer in Dublin, Ireland in July 29, 1998, at the age of 87.

James Whitmore

James Whitmore and Joel McCrea in *The Outriders*

James Allen Whitmore, Jr. in White Plains, New York, October 1, 1921 and was an American film, theatre and television actor. He won a Golden Globe Award and an Emmy Award, and was nominated for two Academy Awards.

Born to Florence Belle (née Crane) and James Allen Whitmore, Sr., a park commission official, Whitmore attended Amherst Central High School in Snyder, New York, before graduating from the Choate School in Wallingford, Connecticut.

He went on to study at Yale University, where he was a member of Skull and Bones, and had his first taste of radio drama as a member of the student-run WOCD-AM, later renamed WYBC-AM.

Whitmore was later commissioned as a second lieutenant and served in the United States Marine Corps in the Panama Canal Zone during World War II.

Following World War II, he appeared on Broadway in the role of the sergeant in *Command Decision*. Metro-Goldwyn-Mayer (MGM) gave Whitmore a contract, but his role in the film adaptation was played by Van Johnson. His first major picture for MGM was *Battleground*, in a role that was turned down by Spencer Tracy, to whom Whitmore bore a physical resemblance. He was nominated for the Academy Award for Best Supporting Actor for this role.

Other major films included *The Outriders* (1950) with Joel McCrea, *Angels in the Outfield* (1951)*The Asphalt Jungle* (1950), *The Next Voice You Hear* (1950), *Above and Beyond* (1952), *Kiss Me, Kate* (1953), *Them!* (1954), *The McConnell Story* (1955) with Alan Ladd, *Oklahoma!* (1955), *The Deep Six* (1958) again with Alan Ladd, *Black Like Me* (1964), *Guns of the Magnificent Seven* (1969), *Tora! Tora! Tora!* (1971), and *Give 'em Hell, Harry!* (1975), a one-man show for which he was nominated for the Academy Award for Best Actor for his portrayal of former U.S. President Harry S Truman. In the film *Tora! Tora! Tora!*, he played Admiral William F. "Bull" Halsey.

Whitmore appeared during the 1950s on many television anthology series. He was cast as Father Emil Kapaun in the 1955 episode "The Good Thief" in the ABC religion anthology series *Crossroads* (which can be viewed at archive.org). Other roles followed on *Jane Wyman Presents the Fireside Theater*, *Lux Video Theatre*, *Kraft Theatre*, *Studio One in Hollywood*, *Schlitz Playhouse*, *Matinee Theatre*, and the *Ford Television Theatre*. In 1958, he carried the lead in "The Gabe Carswell Story" of NBC's *Wagon Train*, with Ward Bond.

In the 1960-1961 television season, Whitmore starred in his own ABC crime drama, *The Law and Mr. Jones*, in the title role, with Conlan Carter as legal assistant C.E. Carruthers and Janet De Gore as Jones' secretary. The program ran in the 10:30 p.m. Eastern half-hour slot on Friday. It was cancelled after one year but returned in April 1962 for thirteen additional episodes on Thursday.

In 1963, Whitmore played Captain William Benteen in *The Twilight Zone* episode "On Thursday We Leave for Home". In 1965, Whitmore guest-starred as Col. Paul J. Hartley in "The Hero", of *Twelve O'Clock High*. In 1967, he guest starred as a security guard in *The Invaders* episode, "Quantity: Unknown". That same year, Whitmore appeared on an episode of ABC's *Custer* starring Wayne Maunder in the title role. In 1969, he played the leading character of Professor Woodruff in the TV series *My Friend Tony*, produced by NBC. Whitmore also made several memorable appearances on the classic ABC western *The Big Valley* starring Barbara Stanwyck and the classic NBC western *The Virginian* starring James Drury during the second half of the 1960s. From 1972-1973, Whitmore played Dr. Vincent Campanelli in the short-lived ABC medical sitcom *Temperatures Rising*. He also appeared in *Planet of the Apes*. Appeared in an episode of "Combat!" as a German officer masquerading as a Catholic priest.

Whitmore appeared as General Oliver O. Howard in the 1975 television film *I Will Fight No More Forever*, based on the 1877 conflict between the United States Army and the Nez Percé tribe, led by Chief Joseph. In 1979 Whitmore hosted a talk show of twenty-two episodes called simply *Comeback*. One of those segments focuses on the helicopter inventor Igor Sikorsky.

In 1986, Whitmore voiced Mark Twain in the first claymation film *The Adventures of Mark Twain*. Whitmore's had another major film role of that of librarian Brooks Hatlen in the critically acclaimed and Academy award-nominated 1994 Frank Darabont film starring Tim Robbins and Morgan Freeman, *The Shawshank Redemption*, based on the Stephen King novella *Rita Hayworth and the Shawshank Redemption*. Two years later, he co-starred in the 1996 horror/sci-fi film *The Relic*.

In 2002, Whitmore played a supporting role in *The Majestic*, a film that starred Jim Carrey. To a younger generation, he was probably best known, in addition to his role in *Shawshank*, as the commercial spokesman for Miracle-Gro plant food for many years.

In 2003, Whitmore appeared as Josh Brolin's father on the short-lived NBC drama series Mister Sterling.

One of the founding members of the Actors Studio, Whitmore did extensive theatre work. He won a Tony Award for Best Performance by a Newcomer in the Broadway production of *Command Decision* (1948). He later won the title "King of the One Man Show" after appearing in the solo vehicles *Will Rogers' USA* (1970) (repeating the role for TV in 1972), *Give 'em Hell, Harry!* (1975) (repeating the role in the film version, for which he was nominated for an Oscar) and as Theodore Roosevelt in *Bully* (1977) although the latter production did not repeat the success of the first two.

In 1999, he played Raymond Oz in two episodes of *The Practice*, earning an Emmy Award for Outstanding Guest Actor in a Drama Series. In 2002, Whitmore got the role of the Grandfather in the Disney Channel original film *A Ring of Endless Light*. Whitmore has a star on the Hollywood Walk of Fame at 6611 Hollywood Boulevard. In April 2007, he made his last screen appearance in a *C.S.I.* episode titled "Ending Happy" as Milton, an elderly man who provides a clue of dubious utility.

Whitmore was twice married to Nancy Mygatt, first in 1947. The couple had three sons before their divorce in 1971. One of those sons, James, III, found success as a television actor and director under the name James Whitmore, Jr. Another son, Steve Whitmore, became the public spokesman for the Los Angeles County Sheriff's Department. His youngest son, Daniel, was a Forest Service Snow Ranger and firefighter before he launched his own construction company.

Whitmore was married to actress Audra Lindley (died 1997) from 1972 until 1979. He later remarried Mygatt, but they divorced again after two years.

In 2001, he married actress and author Noreen Nash.

Whitmore is the grandfather of *Survivor: Gabon* contestant Matty Whitmore. In his later years, Whitmore spent most of his summers in Peterborough, New Hampshire, performing with the Peterborough Players.

Whitmore was diagnosed with lung cancer in November 2008, from which he died, at the age of 87 in February 2009, at his Malibu, California, home.

David Whorf

David Whorf was born July 24, 1934 in Syracuse, New York. Starting in the film industry as a child actor, Whorf first appeared in the film On Our Merry Way (1948) with an all-star cast including Jimmy Stewart, Henry Fonda, Paulette Goddard, Fred MacMurray and Burgess Meredith.

Summer Stock in New England at Marblehead, Ma. and Westport, Ct. punctuated his summers while attending Stanford University where he majored in Theatre Arts and Fine Arts. In 1953 Mr. Whorf was an apprentice at the Country Playhouse, Marblehead, Massachusetts. This was followed a few years later with a season at the Westport Country Playhouse. A theatre his father had played many years earlier. After a tour in the Army, he returned to film making, appearing in over fifty television shows and six feature films including a feature role in PT 109 (1963), the story of John Kennedy's experience in the South Pacific during the Second World War.

In 1961 he appeared with his father, Richard Whorf, in a pre-Broadway show One for the Dame. At this time, it was only the second time in recent Broadway history that father and son played father and son on stage. The show "closed out of town" due to financial problems after playing Ford's Theatre in Baltimore and at the Copley Theatre in Boston. In 1964 he wrote, produced and directed a short subject Another Way Home which received "Honorable Mention" at the Cork Ireland Film Festival.

Mr. Whorf spent two seasons in repertory theatre at Elitch Gardens in Denver, Colorado. Of the sixteen plays in which he appeared, he received accolades for Dark at the Top of the Stairs, Five Finger Exercise, and Little Mary Sunshine.

More acting roles included Gunsmoke (1958), Alcoa Presents: One Step Beyond (1959), Wichita Town (1960) with Joel McCrea, Bonanza (1962), Dr. Kildare (1963-1964), One Way Wahine (1965), and Christmas Every Day (1996).

In 1958 he became a member of the Director's Guild of America. As a first assistant director with director Larry Peerce, Mr Whorf worked on the Emmy Award winning mini-series A Woman Named Jackie (1991) filmed entirely in the Richmond, Virginia area. Other credits include Caddyshack (1980) and as Unit Manager on The Right Stuff (1983).

Mr. Whorf continues to work actively in the film industry in a multitude of capacities from Director to Unit Manager and Assistant Director. He has written three feature scripts; Deadly Intent has been optioned by a production company. In 1980, Mr. Whorf recognized the impact computers were to have on the film industry. He formed a software company with Rob Alger, Alnitak Computing Company, and created the first film production software package, "AD/80".

Frank Wilcox

Frank Reppy Wilcox was born March 13, 1907, in DeSoto, Missouri, and was an American character actor in scores of films after substantial stage experience. He was raised in Atchison, Kansas. The son of a railroad worker and law clerk, he wavered between various careers including oil exploration, but found his way after an introduction to the stage with the Atchison Civic Theatre and Kansas City Civic Theatre. He briefly attended the University of Kansas.

He moved from Kansas to California in 1930, where he lived with his grandparents and worked in the lemon groves near Pomona prior to opening a tire-repair shop in that city. He also helped found a theatre company in Pomona. He joined the Pasadena Community Playhouse, where he was spotted by a Warner Brothers talent scout looking for someone with a resemblance to Henry Clay, for the Warners short film *The Monroe Doctrine* (1939).

He signed with Warners as a contract player and was thereafter virtually never without work. He played in an enormous number of films over the next three decades, mostly in small supporting roles. He was equally adept at playing businessmen, attorneys, or historical figures, and was a familiar face on screen and on television for his entire career, though most people would have been unable to identify him by name.

Some of those credits include *Sergeant York* (1941), *Across the Pacific* (1942), *The Fighting Sullivans* (1944), *The Beginning or the End* (1947), *South of St. Louis* (1949) with Joel McCrea, as Pat Garrett in *The Kid from Texas* (1950) with Audie Murphy, *Go for Broke!* (1951), *The Greatest Show on Earth* (1952), *The Duel at Silver Creek* (1952) again with Audie Murphy, *Invaders from Mars* (1953), *Waterfront* (1954), *Abbott and Costello Meet the Keystone Kops* (1955), *Earth vs. the Flying Saucers* (1956), *Dance with Me, Henry* (1956) again with Bud & Lou, *Good Day for a Hanging* (1959), *Pete and Gladys* (1961-1962), *The Untouchables* (1959-1963), *Laredo* (1965), *Petticoat Junction* (1968-1969), *The Million Dollar Duck* (1971), and *Kung Fu* (1973).

Perhaps his greatest fame came in the TV role of oil company president John Brewster on *The Beverly Hillbillies* (1962-1966).

During the last years of his life, he was co-owner of a popular restaurant/bar in Encino, California, called The Oak Room. Wilcox died March 3, 1974, at age 66 in Granada Hills, California.

Robert Wilke

Robert Joseph Wilke was born May 18, 1914, in Cincinnati, Ohio. He was a prolific American character actor of primarily villainous roles. The son of German parents, Cincinnati feed-store manager August Wilke and his wife Rose, Robert Joseph Wilke grew up in Cincinnati. He worked as a lifeguard at a Miami, Florida, hotel, where he made contacts in the film business.

He was able to obtain work as a stuntman and continued as such until the mid-1940s, when he began getting actual roles in low-budget westerns and serials. A prominent appearance as one of the heavies in *High Noon* (1952) led to work in higher-quality films. He worked extensively in television as well as movies, and became an enormously familiar face, though a fairly anonymous one to the general public.

Some of his credits included *Buck Privates Come Home* (1947) with Abbott and Costello, *The Kid from Texas* (1950) with Audie Murphy, *The Abbott and Costello Show* (1952), *From Here to Eternity* (1953), *Wichita* (1955) with Joel McCrea, *Night Passage* (1957) again with Audie Murphy, *Never Steal Anything Small* (1959), *Wichita Town* (1959) again with Joel McCrea, *The Magnificent Seven* (1960), *The Hallelujah Trail* (1965), *The Fugitive* (1966), *A Gunfight* (1971), *The Boy Who Cried Werewolf* (1973), *How the West Was Won* (1978), *B.J. and the Bear* (1979-1981), and *Stripes* (1981).

His weathered visage made him a perfect western bad guy, but he occasionally played sympathetic parts as well, as in *Days of Heaven* (1978).

An expert golfer, he was said by his friend Claude Akins to have earned more money on the golf course than he ever did in movies.

He died March 28, 1989, at age 74 in Los Angeles, California.

Jean Willes

Jean Willes was born Jean Donohue in Los Angeles, California April 15, 1923 and was an American film and television actress. She appeared in approximately sixty-five films in her thirty-eight year career.

In 1947, she changed her billing to her married name, Jean Willes. Willes is familiar to modern viewers for her roles in several Three Stooges short subjects, such as *Monkey Businessmen* (1946), *A Snitch in Time* (1950), and *Gypped in the Penthouse* (1955). She was a favorite of director Edward Bernds, who cast her in many shorts and features.

Some of her other early roles included *So Proudly We Hail!* (1943) with Veronica Lake, *Salty O'Rourke* (1945) with Alan Ladd, *Blondie Knows Best* (1946) with Shemp Howard, *Slappily Married* (1946) with Joe DeRita, *The Winner's Circle* (1948), *Blonde Atom Bomb* (1951), *Son of Paleface* (1952), *Abbott and Costello Go to Mars* (1953), *Masterson of Kansas* (1954), *The Lieutenant Wore Skirts* (1956), *Invasion of the Body Snatchers* (1956), *No Time for Sergeants* (1958), *The FBI Story* (1959), *Ocean's Eleven* (1960), *McHale's Navy* (1964), *The Cheyenne Social Club* (1970), and *Bite the Bullet* (1975).

She was cast from an Air Force captain to prostitutes. She was one of the "four queens" pursuing Clark Gable in *The King and Four Queens* (1956).

Willes appeared on many television series in the 1950s, 1960s and 1970s, including *China Smith* (1952), *The Abbott and Costello Show* (1953), *The Adventures of Falcon* (1954-1955), *Tales of the Texas Rangers* (1955), *The Life and Legend of Wyatt Earp* (1956), *Tales of Wells Fargo* (1957), *Richard Diamond, Private Detective* (1958), *The Texan* (1959), *Wanted: Dead or Alive* (1958-1959), *Wichita Town* (1959) with Joel McCrea, *Hawaiian Eye* (1960), *Twilight Zone* (1961), *Cheyenne* (1962), *The Munsters* (1964), *Here's Lucy* (1970), *Kojak* (1975), and *The Blue Knight* (1976).

Willes's second husband was NFL football player Gerard Cowhig. The couple had one son, Gerry. January 3, 1989 at age 65 in Van Nuys, California.

Adam Williams

Adam Williams was born Adam Berg November 26, 1922, in Wall Lake, Iowa, and was an American film and television actor.

He was a veteran "bad guy" actor of 1950s film and TV who began his career after distinguished WWII military service as a U.S. Navy pilot, being awarded the Navy Cross.

Williams' notable roles included playing Larry, a car bomber, in *The Big Heat* (1953). In 1952, Williams played the lead role as Los Angeles woman killer in *Without Warning!*. Other roles included *The Yellow Tomahawk* (1954), *The Sea Chase* (1955), *The Oklahoman* (1957) with Joel McCrea, and *The Badlanders* (1958) with Alan Ladd.

He had a leading role in the 1958 science fiction movie *The Space Children*. Other notable roles include the psychiatrist in *Fear Strikes Out* (1957) and Valerian in *North by Northwest* (1959).

More roles continued in *The Badlanders* (1958), *Black Saddle* (1959-1960), *Twilight Zone* (1960), *Whispering Smith* (1961) with Audie Murphy, *Combat!* (1962), *Gunfight at Comanche Creek* (1963) again with Audie Murphy, *The Fugitive* (1965), *Custer* (1967), *The Horse in the Gray Flannel Suit* (1968), *Mannix* (1971), *Marcus Welby, M.D.* (1976), *Helter Skelter* (1976), *The Girl Called Hatter Fox* (1977), and *Sword of Justice* (1978).

An accomplished pilot, Williams also worked as an examiner for the FAA.

Adam Williams died from lymphoma in Los Angeles, California, December 4, 2006, at age 84.

Guinn Williams

Guinn "Big Boy" Williams was born in Decatur, Texas April 26, 1899 and was an American actor who appeared in memorable westerns such as *Dodge City* (1939), *Santa Fe Trail* (1940), and *The Comancheros* (1961). He was nicknamed "Big Boy" as he was 6' 2" and had a muscular build from years of working on ranches and playing semi-pro and professional baseball.

Williams made his screen debut in the 1919 comedy, *Almost A Husband*, with Will Rogers and Cullen Landis, and was featured in a large supporting role ten years later in Frank Borzage's *Lucky Star* with Janet Gaynor and Charles Farrell. Throughout the 1920s Williams would have a string of successful films, mostly westerns.

He then appeared in *The Great Meadow* alongside Johnny Mack Brown, which was Brown's breakout film. Throughout the 1930s, Williams acted in supporting roles, mostly in westerns, sports, or outdoor dramas. Although not the lead actor in any of them, he was always employed, and was successful as a supporting actor. He often played alongside Hoot Gibson and Harry Carey during that period. In 1941, he became one of many actors cast by Universal Pictures in their large film series, *Riders of Death Valley*. From the late 1930s to the mid-1940s, Williams appeared in supporting roles in a number of A-pictures, sometimes with high billing, such as *You Only Live Once*, and in Columbia's first Technicolour film *The Desperadoes* (1943).

More of his roles included *The Great Man's Lady* (1942) with Joel McCrea, *Song of Nevada* (1944), *She-Wolf of London* (1946), *Blaze of Noon* (1947), *My Friend Irma Goes West* (1950), *Castle in the Air* (1952), *The Bowery Boys Meet the Monsters* (1954), *Father Knows Best* (1957), *Wanted: Dead or Alive* (1958), *The Life and Legend of Wyatt Earp* (1955-1960), *It's a Mad, Mad, Mad, Mad World* (1963), *Hank* (1965-1966), and *Petticoat Junction* (1966).

His father, Guinn Williams Sr, represented the 13th Texas Congressional District in the United States House of Representatives from 1922 to 1932. Williams was frequently teamed with Alan Hale, Sr. as sidekicks to Errol Flynn in several of his pictures. In 1960, he was cast in the epic film *The Alamo* and in *Home from the Hill* with Robert Mitchum. His last role was opposite his close friend John Wayne and Stuart Whitman in *The Comancheros*.

He was married to three actresses, the first being silent film actress Kathleen Collins. For a time, he was married to B-movie actress Barbara Weeks. His last wife was Dorothy Peterson, whom he first met in the 1940s.

Williams died unexpectedly of uremic poisoning on June 6, 1962, at age 63.

Kathlyn Williams

Kathlyn Williams was born Kathleen Mabel Williams in Butte, Montana May 31, 1879 and was an American actress, known for her blonde beauty and daring antics, who performed on stage as well as in early silent film.

Kathlyn Williams was the only child born to Joseph Edwin"Frank" Williams, a boarding house proprietor, and Mary C. Boe (1846–1908) of Welsh and Norwegian descent. Williams displayed an early interest in becoming an actress in her youth which lead her to become a member of a community thespian group. She also joined the Woman's Relief Corps that allowed her to showcase her vocal prowess at local recitals. Although she was known for having an adequate singing voice, acting became Williams' main vocation. Williams attended Montana Wesleyan University (now Rocky Mountain College) in Helena during the late 1890s and graduated in 1901, where she excelled in elocution and voice, and her performances were highly praised. In May 1899, she recited "The Gypsy Flower Girl" at her university's annual competition. On May 29, 1900, Williams received a gold medal for her recitation of "Old Mother Goose" at Wesleyan's declamation contest. She lost her father around 1894 when she was a teenager, and her mother remarried a man by the name of Fred Lavoie in 1895. They divorced the next year.

In order to make ends meet, her mother made extra money by renting out homes in nearby Centerville. Her family was of limited means; therefore, Kathlyn had to rely on the charity of others to pay her way through school. Her acting aspiration also caught the attention of William A. Clark, a very wealthy Montana Senator, who helped finance her education and acting classes. Clark paid her tuition to the Sargent School of Acting which is more famously known as the American Academy of Dramatic Art in New York City. She was also given encouragement by Richard "Uncle Dick" Sutton, who owned several theaters in Butte, where Williams performed on stage early in her career. In 1900, her friends held a concert at Sutton's Theater for "Katie", as she was affectionately called, to gather funds to help pay her college tuition. By 1902, Williams joined a theater touring group called Norris & Hall and Company where she played the lead part of Phyllis Ericson in the popular play "When We Were Twenty One," mostly to good reviews. The play toured across the United States toward the end of 1903.

In the January 16, 1903 issue of the Dallas Morning News, an article in Amusements critiqued Williams' performance in "When We Were Twenty-One": "Miss Kathlyn Williams, who assumed the role of Phyllis, is an actress of rare ability, attractiveness, and grace of delivery".

Williams began her career with Selig Polyscope Company in Chicago, Illinois and made her first film in 1908 under the direction of Francis Boggs. By 1910, she was transferred to the company's Los Angeles film studio. Williams played "Cherry Malotte" in the first movie based upon Rex Beach's 1906 novel *The Spoilers* in 1914, a role portrayed in subsequent versions by Betty Compson (1930), Marlene Dietrich (1942), and Anne Baxter (1955). In 1916, she starred in the thirteen episode adventure film serial, *The Adventures of Kathlyn*. She was busy throughout the silent film era but age and the advent of talkies saw her make only five sound films, the last in 1935. Kathlyn evolved from a comedian and serial player in silents to portraying character roles in the early 1930s.

Some of her later roles included *The Single Standard* (1929) with Joel McCrea, *Road to Paradise* (1930), *Daddy Long Legs* (1931), *Unholy Love* (1932), *Blood Money* (1933), and *Rendezvous at Midnight* (1935).

Williams was married three times. Although many biographies erroneously cite her first husband as being Victor Kainer, he was in fact named Otto H. "Harry" Kainer (1876–1952), who ran an import and export business on Wall Street in New York City. They were wed on October 2, 1903, and their son, Victor Hugo, was born in 1905. The Kainers resided at 301 Nicholas Avenue in Manhattan. On May 8, 1905, she successfully sued her husband for $20,000 dollars for not paying her $10,000 on the day of their marriage and for every year of their marriage. The case made headlines in newspapers across the country, and made its way to the New York Supreme Court. They supposedly divorced over Kainer's disapproval of his wife having an acting career, and Williams subsequently obtained a divorce from Kainer in 1909 in Nevada. After the death of her Norwegian born mother in December 1908 and the failure of her marriage, Williams decided to revive her acting career. By 1910, Williams and her young son uprooted themselves to Los Angeles, California where she easily obtained acting jobs. On March 4, 1913, she married Frank R. Allen, also an actor, but the marriage was a failure from the start and lasted a little over a year. On June 30, 1914, she filed for divorce in Los Angeles and listed desertion as the reason as the failure of their marriage.

She later married Paramount Pictures executive Charles Eyton on June 2, 1916, in Riverside, California. The couple met approximately ten years earlier in Salt Lake City, Utah. Eyton went there to look over a new play. While there he met Kathlyn, who was a member of the Willard Mack stock company. Eyton and Williams were engaged earlier but a lover's quarrel broke them up. A second meeting in the movie camps of Los Angeles, California rekindled their love. Eyton was one of the owners of the Oliver Morosco Photoplay Company. On February 25, 1922, her beloved son, now called Victor Eyton, died suddenly at the age of 16 from complications from the influenza at Good Samaritan Hospital in Los Angeles, and his remains were cremated. Her son was previously enrolled at Harvard Military Academy before he became a student at Hollywood High School. In order to overcome her immense grief, the Eytons took an extended trip to Asia which lasted for four months. The Eytons eventually divorced in 1931.

On December 29, 1949, Williams was involved in a deadly automobile accident, which claimed the life of her friend, Mrs. Mary E. Rose, while they were returning home from a social engagement in Las Vegas. As a result of the accident, Williams lost her right leg. On April 8, 1950, Williams sued the estate of Rose for $136,615, citing negligence and claiming that the automobile had inefficient brakes. In June 1951, Williams accepted the offer of $6,500 dollars from the Rose estate.

Kathlyn Williams died of a heart attack in Hollywood, California September 23, 1960 at age 81. She was found dead in her bedroom at her 1428 North Crescent Heights apartment where she resided for nearly 30 years. Although it was widely reported that Williams became a wheelchair invalid since the loss of her leg, she still traveled and lead a productive life. She was cremated and her ashes were stored at the Chapel of the Pines Crematory in Los Angeles.

After her death, Williams bequeathed most of her monetary assets, which amounted to nearly $287,000, to charitable institutions such as The McKinley Industrial Home for Boys, the Motion Picture Relief Fund, and to an orthopedic and children's hospital. One of her last dying wishes was for a plaque to be placed at The McKinley Industrial Home for Boys to celebrate the memory of her long ago departed son.

For her contribution to the motion picture industry, Kathlyn Williams has a star on the Hollywood Walk of Fame at 7038 Hollywood Blvd.

Robert Williams

Robert Williams was September 15, 1894 in Morgantown, North Carolina. It's fair to say that if 'Frank Capra (I)' hadn't cast Robert "Bobby" Williams in his 1931 film *Platinum Blonde* (1931) the actor would be entirely forgotten today. When the movie was made available on video in the 1980s the promotional copy on the video box emphasized the names most buffs would recognize: actresses Jean Harlow and Loretta Young, and director Capra himself. But for many viewers there's no question about it, Williams steals the show, with his low-key flair for comedy and unique, sleepy-eyed charm. Viewers may well ask "Who is this guy, and why haven't I heard of him?" The reason is simple, and sad: he died of peritonitis in 1931 just as *Platinum Blonde* (1931) went into wide release, just when he was on the brink of stardom.

He was raised on a farm. The acting bug bit early: he ran away from home at age 11 to join a tent show. He endured a long, hard apprenticeship as an actor, performing on Mississippi river boats and in stock companies touring the Midwest before he reached New York as a young man. When Williams made his Broadway debut in the early 1920s, the New York stage had entered its richest era, when hundreds of shows opened each season. Williams' stage credits include *Eyes of Youth* opposite Marjorie Rambeau, *The Trial of Mary Dugan, Milgrim's Progress, Scarlet Pages,* and *Love, Honor and Betray with Alice Brady.* Several of these plays were made into silent movies but Bobby was not cast in the film versions, perhaps because he was based in New York. His best remembered Broadway role was that of Abie in the original production of *Abie's Irish Rose* (1922), an ethnic comedy considered old fashioned even when it opened. Critics hated it, but the show became the biggest success of its era, running for five years.

When Abie's Irish Rose opened, Bobby was married to singer Marion Harris, a vaudeville and recording artist who was far better known than he. Perhaps her greater fame was a source of tension, but for whatever reason the marriage did not last long. The couple had one daughter, also named Marion, who later became a singer in her own right under the name Marion Harris, Jr.

Even at the time of Williams' greatest Broadway success in *Abie's Irish Rose*, he seemed stalked by tragedy. Just a few days after the show opened, Bobby was driving from his home in Great Neck, Long Island, to the theater for a matinée performance. When he reached Corona, Queens, a 7 year-old boy named James Cali dashed into the street in front of his car. Williams was unable to stop or swerve, and the boy was knocked to the ground. The child died of a skull fracture hours later while Williams was held by the police for questioning. Character actor Wallace Ford, who had played the role of Abie during the show's pre-Broadway tour, stepped back into the role for the matinée and the next few performances while Williams recovered from shock. It appears that no charges were filed against him in the wake of the tragedy. Williams resumed the role of Abie but did not stay with the show much longer.

In the spring of 1924, Williams married actress Alice Lake, best known as leading lady in several film comedies made by 'Roscoe 'Fatty' Arbuckle' and Buster Keaton in the late 1910s. Once again, the marriage was brief. In February of 1925 the daily paper the New York Mirror detailed the couple's separation in an article with the headline: "Gay Life Parts Couple; Robert Williams, Juvenile Actor, Packs Trunk and Leaves His Wife, Alice Lake, Pal of Viola Dana." Without directly stating that either Lake or Dana were gay or bisexual, the article strongly implied that their relationship went beyond friendship, and was responsible for the breakup of Lake's marriage to Williams. The following day the newspaper allowed Dana a rebuttal in which she denied being a home wrecker and said she knew nothing of the Williams' marital problems. In any event, the couple divorced soon afterward.

For the next several years Williams remained busy with stage work. He also married actress Nina Penn, and at last seemed to find marital stability. In 1930 Williams was cast in the Broadway production of Donald Ogden Stewart's play *Rebound* which proved to be moderately successful, or at least successful enough to be purchased by RKO for filming. By this point the talkie revolution had hit Hollywood and the studios were snapping up plays, playwrights, and stage actors by the hundreds. Williams went to Hollywood and repeated his role of Johnnie Coles opposite Ina Claire in the film version of *Rebound*. In rapid succession he appeared in two other films for RKO, *The Common Law* (1931) with Constance Bennett and Joel McCrea, and *Devotion* (1931) with Ann Harding and Leslie Howard.

It was then that 'Frank Capra (I)' cast Bobby in *Platinum Blonde* (1931), for Columbia Pictures. Williams played down-to-earth reporter Stew Smith, who is drawn to socialite Anne Schuyler (Jean Harlow) despite their obvious differences in background. Stew marries Anne while his fellow reporter Gallagher, a gal accepted in the city room as "one of the boys," waits patiently for Stew to recognize that his marriage was a mistake and that she is in love with him. The role of Gallagher was assigned, rather bizarrely, to the luminously beautiful Loretta Young, who was then 18 years old and would never be anyone's idea of "one of the boys." For that matter, Harlow wasn't all that believable as a haughty socialite either, but for Williams the role of Stew Smith fit like a glove. This was the sort of role that within a few years would become the province of actors like Spencer Tracy, James Cagney, and occasionally Clark Gable: the man's man with attitude, macho without being obnoxious about it, a guy who is good at his work but has a faint air of insolence about him. Williams pulls it off beautifully and effortlessly steals the show from his miscast co-stars. One wants to see more of his work.

Unfortunately, his work was at an end, for this star-making performance turned out to be Williams' swan song. Bobby was rehearsing with Constance Bennett for his next RKO picture, *Lady with a Past* (1932), when he complained of stomach pains. After a day or two the pain worsened, and despite his protests Williams was rushed to a hospital for an appendicitis operation. Before the operation was completed his appendix burst. Days later, on November 3, 1931, Williams died of peritonitis. He was 34 years old. *Platinum Blonde* (1931) had been released just four days earlier, and the first reviews proclaimed that Hollywood had a new star. Instead, Robert Williams became one of Hollywood's great might-have-beens.

Rush Williams

Rush Williams was born Rush Pritchett Williams Jr. on February 6, 1924 in Texas City, Texas.

He is an actor, known for *Rocky Mountain* (1950), *Legion of the Doomed* (1958), and *Curse of the Undead* (1959).

More of his roles included *The Day the Earth Stood Still* (1951), *Beneath the 12-Mile Reef* (1953), *The Lone Ranger* (1956), *Trooper Hook* (1957) with Joel McCrea, *The Life and Legend of Wyatt Earp* (1959), *Hawaiian Eye* (1959-1962), *Destry* (1964), *Cool Hand Luke* (1967), and *Gunsmoke* (1968-1969).

Dave Willock

Dave Willock was born in Chicago, Illinois August 13, 1909 and was an American character actor. Willock appeared in 181 films and television series from 1939 to 1989. He is probably most familiar to modern audiences from his performance as Baby Jane Hudson's father in the opening scenes of the cult classic *What Ever Happened to Baby Jane?* (1962). He played seven different characters on CBS's *Green Acres* (1965-1970) with Eddie Albert and Eva Gabor, but mostly portrayed clerks or elevator operators.

He also teamed with actor Jack Carson on stage and radio, including a five-season run on CBS as Carson's nephew Tugwell on The Jack Carson Show from 1943-1949. Willock and Cliff Arquette had their own radio and television shows in the early 1950s. Both versions were called *Dave and Charley*; the radio version was heard circa 1950, but the television version of it was on the air for only three months in early 1952. He maintained a lifelong friendship with Arquette.

More of his roles included *Three Texas Steers* (1939), *Mr. Smith Goes to Washington* (1939), *Brother Rat and a Baby* (1940),with Alan Ladd, *Great Guns* (1941) again with Alan Ladd, *Yankee Doodle Dandy* (1942), *Lucky Jordan* (1942) a third with Alan Ladd, *Action in the North Atlantic* (1943), *Joe Palooka, Champ* (1946), *Chicago Deadline* (1949) a fourth with Alan Ladd, *The Lone Ranger* (1950), *It Came from Outer Space* (1953), *Revenge of the Creature* (1955), *The Buster Keaton Story* (1957), *Queen of Outer Space* (1958), *Richard Diamond, Private Detective* (1959), *Wichita Town* (1959-1960) with Joel McCrea, *Twilight Zone* (1960), *Wanted: Dead or Alive* (1959-1961), *4 for Texas* (1963) with The Three Stooges, *Gunsmoke* (1963-1964), *The Munsters* (1965), *Frankie and Johnny* (1966), *Adam-12* (1970), *The Roman Holidays* (1972), *Police Story* (1974), *The Streets of San Francisco* (1975), *Lou Grant* (1979), and *Sawyer and Finn* (1983).

He died of complications due to lung cancer on November 12, 1990 in Woodland Hills, Los Angeles, California at the age of 81. He is buried in Valhalla Memorial Park Cemetery. For his contribution to the television industry, Dave Willock has a star on the Hollywood Walk of Fame 6358 Hollywood Blvd.

Chill Wills

Chill Wills and Joel McCrea in *Cattle Drive*

Chill Wills was born Theodore Childress Wills in Seagoville, Texas, July 18, 1902, and was an American film actor, and a singer in the Avalon Boys Quartet.

He was a performer from early childhood, forming and leading the Avalon Boys singing group in the 1930s. After appearing with them in a few westerns, he disbanded the group in 1938 and struck out on a solo acting career.

He provided the deep voice for Stan Laurel's performance of "The Trail of the Lonesome Pine" in the 1937 movie *Way Out West*.

Other early roles included *Allegheny Uprising* (1939), *Sorority House* (1939) with Veronica Lake, *Belle Starr* (1941), *See Here, Private Hargrove* (1944), *Tulsa* (1949), *High Lonesome* (1950), *Rio Grande* (1950), *Cattle Drive* (1951) with Joel McCrea, *Tumbleweed* (1953) with Audie Murphy, and *Santiago* (1956) with Alan Ladd.

One of his more memorable roles was that of the distinctive voice of Francis the Mule in a series of popular films. Wills' deep, rough voice and Western twang were perfectly matched to the personality of the cynical, sardonic mule. As was customary at the time, Wills was given no billing for his vocal work, though he was featured prominently on-screen as blustery General Ben Kaye in the fourth entry, *Francis Joins the WACS* (1954).

Wills also appeared in numerous serious roles, including that of Uncle Bawley in *Giant*, a 1956 film starring Rock Hudson, Elizabeth Taylor, and James Dean.

Wills was nominated for Best Supporting Actor in 1960 for his role as Davy Crockett's companion "Beekeeper" in the film *The Alamo*.

From 1961–62, Wills starred in the short-run series *Frontier Circus* which aired for only one season on CBS.

He then appeared as Drago in *McLintock!* (1963).

In 1966, Wills was cast in the role of a shady Texas rancher, Jim Ed Love, in the short-lived ABC comedy/western series *The Rounders*, with co-stars Ron Hayes, Patrick Wayne, and Walker Edmiston.

Other roles continued in *Tarzan* (1968), *The Over-the-Hill Gang* (1969), *The Over-the-Hill Gang Rides Again* (1970), *Rod Serling's Night Gallery* (1970), *Alias Smith and Jones* (1972), *Pat Garrett & Billy the Kid* (1973), *Hec Ramsey* (1974), *Mr. Billion* (1977), and *Poco...Little Dog Lost* (1977).

Wills was a poker player and a close friend of Benny Binion, the founder of the World Series of Poker and former owner of the Binion's Horseshoe Casino in Las Vegas. Wills participated in the first World Series, held in 1970, and is seated in the center of the now famous picture with a number of legendary players.

His last role was in 1978 as a janitor in *Stubby Pringle's Christmas*.

Wills died in December 15, 1978, of cancer in Encino, California, at age 76. He is interred in the Grand View Memorial Park Cemetery in Glendale.

Henry Wills

Henry Wills was born on September 14, 1921 in Florence, Arizona and was an actor and stuntman known for his work on *One-Eyed Jacks* (1961), *The Greatest Story Ever Told* (1965), and *Pump Up the Volume* (1990). He was married to Gail and had four children. He died on September 15, 1994 in Los Angeles, California, USA.

He performed over 1400 horse falls on film and doubled for Dean Martin, Alan Ladd, Audie Murphy, Marlon Brando, Tony Curtis, Roy Rogers, Richard Widmark, Cameron Mitchell, and Robert Taylor.

Some of his acting roles included *The Frontiersmen* (1938), *Dark Command* (1940), *Adventures of Captain Marvel* (1941), *Tombstone: The Town Too Tough to Die* (1942), *Bar 20* (1943), *Great Stagecoach Robbery* (1945), *Joan of Arc* (1948), *Branded* (1950) with Alan Ladd, *Yankee Buccaneer* (1952), *Shane* (1953) again with Alan Ladd, *Saskatchewan* (1954) a third with Alan Ladd, *Black Horse Canyon* (1954) with Joel McCrea, *Wichita* (1955) again with Joel McCrea, *Gunfight at the O.K. Corral* (1957), *The Badlanders* (1958) a fourth with Alan Ladd, *Wanted: Dead or Alive* (1959-1960), *The Comancheros* (1961), *Nevada Smith* (1966), *Chisum* (1970), *Night of the Lepus* (1972), *The Soul of Nigger Charley* (1973), *Little House on the Prairie* (1977), *Coast to Coast* (1980) with Robert Blake, *The Legend of the Lone Ranger* (1981), *Kenny Rogers as The Gambler: The Adventure Continues* (1983), and *The Master* (1984).

He died September 15, 1994 at age 73 in Los Angeles, California.

Clarence Wilson

Clarence Wilson was born in Cincinnati, Ohio November 17, 1876 and was an American character actor with nearly 200 film appearances.

Wilson is fondly remembered today for his roles in several *Our Gang* films, most notably as Mr. Crutch in *Shrimps for a Day* and school board chairman Alonzo Pratt in *Come Back, Miss Pipps*, his final film.

More of his roles included *The First Born* (1921), *The Hunchback of Notre Dame* (1923), *Uncle Tom's Cabin* (1927), *Dangerous Paradise* (1930), *The Beast of the City* (1932), *The Sport Parade* (1932) with Joel McCrea, *The Son of Kong* (1933), *Hollywood Party* (1934), *One Frightened Night* (1935), *Rebecca of Sunnybrook Farm* (1938), *The Son of Frankenstein* (1939), *Haunted House* (1940), and *Angels with Broken Wings* (1941).

Wilson died at age 64 in Los Angeles, California on October 5, 1941, approximately three weeks before the release of *Come Back, Miss Pipps*.

Marie Windsor

Marie Windsor and Joel McCrea in *Frenchie*

Marie Windsor was born Emily Marie Bertelson in Marysvale, Piute County, Utah, December 11, 1919, and was an actress known as "The Queen of the Bs" because she appeared in so many B-movies and film noirs.

Windsor, a former Miss Utah, trained for the stage under Maria Ouspenskaya, and after several years as a telephone operator, a stage and radio actress, and a bit and extra player in films, such as *Joan of Paris* (1942) with Alan Ladd, she began playing feature and lead parts in 1947.

The 5'9" actress's first memorable role was opposite John Garfield in *Force of Evil* (1948) playing seductress Edna Tucker. Windsor also had large roles in film noirs including *The Sniper* (1952), *The Narrow Margin* (1952), *City That Never Sleeps* (1953), and Stanley Kubrick's heist movie *The Killing* (1956) playing Elisha Cook, Jr.'s scheming wife.

Other early roles included *Frenchie* (1950) with Joel McCrea, *The Eddie Cantor Story* (1953), *The Bounty Hunter* (1954), *Abbott and Costello Meet the Mummy* (1955), and *Swamp Women* (1956).

She continued to get juicy roles, appearing on such shows and films as *Maverick* (1957-1962), *Whispering Smith* (1961) with Audie Murphy, *The Day Mars Invaded Earth* (1963), *Destry* (1964), *Chamber of Horrors* (1966), *The Good Guys and the Bad Guys* (1969), *Support Your Local Gunfighter* (1971), *Hec Ramsey* (1972), *Cahill U.S. Marshal* (1973), *Adam-12* (1971-1973), *Freaky Friday* (1976), *Salem's Lot* (1979), *General Hospital* (1982), *Simon & Simon* (1983-1987), *New Adam 12* (1990), and *Murder, She Wrote* (1987-1991).

She was one of the 500 stars nominated to become one of the fifty greatest American screen legends as part of the American Film Institute's 100 years.

Windsor married twice, first briefly to bandleader Ted Steele, and later to Jack Hupp, a member of the 1936 U.S. Olympic basketball team. Hupp, with whom Windsor had a son, was posthumously inducted into the University of Southern California (USC) Athletic Hall of Fame in 2007.

After her acting career was over, Windsor became a painter and sculptor. She died December 10, 2000, of undisclosed causes on the day before her 81st birthday. She is interred with Hupp in Marysvale, Utah.

Charles Winninger

Charles J. Winninger was born in Athens, Wisconsin May 26, 1884 and was an American stage and film actor, most often cast in comedies or musicals, but equally at home in drama.

He began as a vaudeville actor. His most famous stage role was as Cap'n Andy Hawks in the original production of the Jerome Kern – Oscar Hammerstein II musical classic *Show Boat* in 1927, a role that he reprised – to great acclaim – in the 1932 stage revival and the 1936 film version of the show. He became so identified with the role, and with his "persona" as a riverboat captain, that he played several variations of the role, notably on the radio program *Maxwell House Show Boat*, which was clearly inspired by, but not actually based on, the Broadway musical.

After the 1936 *Show Boat*, Winninger largely abandoned the stage and stayed on in Hollywood, becoming one of its most beloved and most often seen character actors. He appeared in such classics as the 1937 *Nothing Sacred* (as the drunken doctor who misdiagnoses Carole Lombard), as B.J. Nolan in *Woman Chases Man* (1939) with Joel McCrea, the 1939 *Destry Rides Again* (as Wash, the sheriff who hires James Stewart as his deputy), as Deanna Durbin's father in the film *Three Smart Girls*, and as Abel Frake in the 1945 Rodgers and Hammerstein film musical *State Fair*. He played the protective Irish Grandfather in MGM's film version of George M. Cohan's *Little Nellie Kelly* (1940), and the father of a budding show-girl in *Ziegfeld Girl* (1941), both starring Judy Garland. In all of these films, Winninger was the very image of the kindly, lovable, chubby, grandfatherly figure, but in "Show Boat", especially, he showed that he could play a dramatic, emotional scene as well as any serious dramatic actor. He returned to Broadway only once more – for the 1951 revival of Kern and Hammerstein's *Music in the Air*.

Winninger had the lead role in only one film, 1953's *The Sun Shines Bright*, John Ford's companion piece to his own *Judge Priest*. Winninger played the role that Will Rogers had undertaken in 1934.

Winninger made a notable television appearance in 1954 in *I Love Lucy* as Barney Kurtz, the former Vaudevillian partner of Fred Mertz (played by William Frawley) in an episode titled "Mertz and Kurtz".

He died January 27, 1969 at age 84 and was buried at Forest Lawn Memorial Park in Hollywood Hills, Los Angeles.

Shelley Winters

Joel McCrea and Shelley Winters behind the scenes of *Frenchie*

Shelley Winters was born Shirley Schrift in St. Louis, Missouri August 18 and was an American actress who appeared in dozens of films, as well as on stage and television; her career spanned over fifty years until her death in 2006. Winters won Academy Awards for *The Diary of Anne Frank* and *A Patch of Blue*, and is also remembered for her roles in *A Place in the Sun* (Oscar-nominated for Best Actress), *The Big Knife*, *Lolita*, *The Night of the Hunter*, *Alfie*, and *The Poseidon Adventure* (Oscar-nominated for Best Supporting Actress).

Winters was the daughter of Rose (née Winter), a singer with The Muny, and Jonas Schrift, a designer of men's clothing. Her parents were Jewish; her father emigrated from Austria, and her mother had been born in St. Louis to Austrian immigrants. Her parents were third cousins. Her family moved to Brooklyn, New York when she was three years old. Her sister Blanche Schrift later married George Boroff, who ran The Circle Theatre (now named El Centro Theatre) in Los Angeles. Winters studied at The New School in New York City.

As the *New York Times* obituary noted, "A major movie presence for more than five decades, Shelley Winters turned herself into a widely-respected actress who won two Oscars." Winters originally broke into Hollywood as "the Blonde Bombshell", but quickly tired of the role's limitations. She washed off her makeup and played against type to set up Elizabeth Taylor's beauty in *A Place in the Sun*, still a landmark American film. As the Associated Press reported, the general public was unaware of how serious a craftswoman Winters was. "Although she was in demand as a character actress, Winters continued to study her craft. She attended Charles Laughton's Shakespeare classes and worked at the Actors Studio, both as student and teacher." She studied in the Hollywood Studio Club, and in the late 1940s she shared an apartment with another newcomer, Marilyn Monroe.

Her first movie was *What a Woman!* (1943). Working in films (in mostly bit roles) through the 1940s, Winters first achieved stardom with her breakout performance as the victim of insane actor Ronald Colman in George Cukor's *A Double Life*, in 1947. She quickly ascended in Hollywood with leading roles in *The Great Gatsby* (1949) with Alan Ladd, *Frenchie* (1950) with Joel McCrea, and *Winchester 73* (1950), opposite James Stewart. But it was her performance in *A Place in the Sun* (1951), a departure from the sexpot image that her studio, Universal Pictures, was building up for her at the time, that first brought Winters her acclaim, earning a nomination for the Academy Award for Best Actress.

Throughout the 1950s, Winters continued in films, including *Meet Danny Wilson* (1952) as Frank Sinatra's leading lady, again with Alan Ladd in *Saskatchewan,* most notably in Charles Laughton's 1955 *Night of the Hunter,* with Robert Mitchum and Lillian Gish, and the less successful *I Am A Camera* starring opposite Julie Harris and Laurence Harvey. She also returned to the stage on various occasions during this time, including a Broadway run in *A Hatful of Rain,* in 1955–1956, opposite future husband Anthony Franciosa. She won an Oscar for Best Supporting Actress for *The Diary of Anne Frank* in 1960, and another award, in the same category, for *A Patch of Blue* in 1966. She donated her Oscar for *The Diary of Anne Frank* to the Anne Frank House in Amsterdam.

Notable later roles included her lauded performance as the man-hungry Charlotte in Stanley Kubrick's *Lolita* (1962); starring opposite Michael Caine in *Alfie*; and as the once gorgeous, alcoholic former starlet "Fay Estabrook" whose emotional vulnerability the titular hero so cruelly exploits in *Harper* (both 1966); in *The Poseidon Adventure* (1972) as the ill-fated Belle Rosen (for which she received her final Oscar nomination); and in *Next Stop, Greenwich Village* (1976). She also returned to the stage during the 1960s and 1970s, most notably in Tennessee Williams' *Night of the Iguana*. She appeared in such cult films as 1968's *Wild in the Streets* and 1971's *Whoever Slew Auntie Roo?* She also provided the voice of 'Crystal' in *Frosty's Winter Wonderland* (1976) and *Rudolph and Frosty's Christmas in July* (1979). She appeared as one of the hijacked airplane's passengers in the Chuck Norris film *The Delta Force* (1986).

As the Associated Press reported, "During her 50 years as a widely known personality, Winters was rarely out of the news. Her stormy marriages, her romances with famous stars, her forays into politics and feminist causes kept her name before the public. She delighted in giving provocative interviews and seemed to have an opinion on everything." That led to a second career as a writer. Though not an overwhelming beauty, her acting, wit, and "chutzpah" gave her a love life to rival Monroe's. In late life, she recalled her conquests in her autobiographies. She wrote of a yearly rendezvous she kept with William Holden, as well as her affairs with Sean Connery, Burt Lancaster, Errol Flynn and Marlon Brando.

Winters had significant weight gain later in life, but lost much of the weight for (or before) an appearance at the 1998 Academy Awards telecast, which featured a tribute to Oscar winners past and present, at which a panoply of former winners, including Gregory Peck, Claire Trevor, Jennifer Jones, and Luise Rainer appeared.

Younger audiences knew her primarily for the autobiographies and for her television work, in which she played a humorous parody of her public persona. In a recurring role in the 1990s, Winters played the title character's grandmother on the ABC sitcom *Roseanne* (1991-1996).

Her final film roles were supporting ones: she played a restaurant owner and mother of an overweight cook in *Heavy* (1995), with Liv Tyler and Debbie Harry; *The Portrait of a Lady* (1996), starring Nicole Kidman and John Malkovich; and as an embittered nursing home administrator in 1999's *Gideon*.

Winters was married four times; her husbands were:

- Captain Mack Paul Mayer, whom she married on New Year's Day, 1942; they divorced in October 1948. Mayer was unable to deal with Shelley's "Hollywood lifestyle" and wanted a "traditional homemaker" for a wife. Winters wore his wedding ring up until her death, and kept their relationship very private.
- Vittorio Gassman, whom she married on April 28, 1952; they divorced on June 2, 1954. They had one child, Vittoria born February 14, 1953, a physician, who practices internal medicine at Norwalk Hospital in Norwalk, Connecticut. She was Winters' only child.
- Anthony Franciosa, whom she married on May 4, 1957; they divorced on November 18, 1960.
- Gerry DeFord, on January 14, 2006, hours before her death.

Hours before her death, Winters married long-time companion Gerry DeFord, with whom she had lived for 19 years. Though Winters' daughter objected to the marriage, the actress Sally Kirkland performed the wedding ceremony for the two at Winters' deathbed. Kirkland, a minister of the Movement of Spiritual Inner Awareness, also performed non-denominational last rites for Winters.

Winters also had a romance with Farley Granger that became a long-term friendship (according to her autobiography *Shelley Also Known As Shirley*). She starred with him in the 1951 film, *Behave Yourself!*, as well as in a 1957 television production of A. J. Cronin's novel, *Beyond This Place*.

She became friendly with rock singer Janis Joplin shortly before Joplin died in 1970. Winters invited Joplin to sit in on a class session at the Actors' Studio at its Los Angeles location. Joplin never did..

Winters died at the age of 85 on January 14, 2006, of heart failure at the Rehabilitation Centre of Beverly Hills; she had suffered a heart attack on October 14, 2005. Her third ex-husband Anthony Franciosa had a stroke on the day she died and, himself, died five days later.

Jane Wintin

Jane Wintin was born October 10, 1905 in Philadelphia, Pennsylvania. Statuesque, gorgeous Jane Winton was billed as the 'Green-eyed Goddess of Hollywood'. The former Ziegfeld Follies dancer appeared in a good number of films from 1925 - if not as the nominal star - then, at least, very high up the list of credits. Her aloof beauty was tailor-made for playing toffs or patrician socialites and she breezed through many such roles in both comedy and drama. Her most famous film, ironically, was as Donna Isobel in *Don Juan* (1926), not because of the acting involved (even though the star was John Barrymore), but because it first used the Vitaphone process to synchronize film and sound effects (though no dialogue), effectively making it a precursor to *The Jazz Singer* (1927), released a year later.

At Warner Brothers, Jane appeared back to back in the period drama *My Official Wife* (1926), and in one of the studio's most successful comedies of the year, as a seductive model in *Why Girls Go Back Home* (1926). She was also third-billed as the vamp rivalling Marion Davies for the affections of Johnny Mack Brown in *The Fair Co-Ed* (1927) with Joel McCrea and Lou Costello, and Davies's elder sister in her biggest hit, *The Patsy* (1928). She had smaller roles in two A-grade productions: *Sunrise* (1927) and the Howard Hughes-produced World War I flying drama *Hell's Angels* (1930). At the peak of her career, Jane, at her most glamorous, essayed a murder suspect in *The Furies* (1930), adapted for the screen by Zoe Akins.

Jane's star faded abruptly after 1930. She made a few more appearances in several 17-18 minute mystery 'featurettes', made at the Warner Brothers Vitaphone facilities in Brooklyn. In 1937, she left acting altogether. It is not entirely clear what, exactly, killed off her Hollywood career. One might logically surmise that it was the transition to sound pictures, and yet, the problem was not with her voice, or the lack of it. In fact, she became a soprano of international repute, one-time diva with the National Grand Opera Company in 1933, performing in *Pagliacci.* Some years later, she also sang on radio broadcasts in England.

In any event, Jane went globetrotting and devoting time to her various other talents. She was said to have been a decent painter and certainly played bridge rather well (a tribute to one of her three husbands, a grand master of the game, Michael T. Gottlieb). In the early 1950's, the multi-faceted Jane also wrote two novels: *Park Avenue Doctor*, and the period romance *Passion is the Gale,* a tale of "temptation and torment ", set in the Virgin Islands, featuring pirates, damsels in distress and other expected accoutrements of the genre.

She died September 22, 1959, at age 53.

Ian Wolfe

Ian Wolfe was born in Canton, Illinois November 4, 1896 and was an American actor whose films date from 1934 to 1990. Until 1934, he worked as a theatre actor. Wolfe mostly found work as a character actor, appearing in over 270 films.

Wolfe was also a veteran of World War I when he served as a volunteer medical specialist. His best-known role may have been in the 1946 movie *Bedlam*, in which he played a lawyer confined to an asylum.

Wolfe wrote and self-published two books of poetry *Forty-Four Scribbles and a Prayer: Lyrics and Ballads* and *Sixty Ballads and Lyrics In Search of Music*.

Some of is more notable roles included *The Barretts of Wimpole Street* (1934), *Mutiny on the Bounty* (1935), *Romeo and Juliet* (1936), *The Prince and the Pauper* (1937), *Blondie* (1938), *Allegheny Uprising* (1939), *Abe Lincoln in Illinois* (1940), *Foreign Correspondent* (1940) with Joel McCrea, *Sherlock Holmes in Washington* (1943), *The Scarlet Claw* (1944), *The Brighton Strangler* (1945), *Dressed to Kill* (1946), *Wild Harvest* (1947) with Alan Ladd, *Colorado Territory* (1949) again with Joel McCrea, *The Lone Ranger* (1949), *Hopalong Cassidy* (1952), *Seven Brides for Seven Brothers* (1954), *Rebel Without a Cause* (1955), *Cheyenne* (1956), "Mayerling" episode of *Producers' Showcase* (1957) with Audrey Hepburn, *Twilight Zone* (1963), *The Fugitive* (1963), *Gunsmoke* (1965), *Branded* (1965), *The Andy Griffith Show* (1966), *The Green Hornet* (1967), two episodes of the original *Star Trek* television series: "Bread and Circuses" (1968) as Septimus, and "All Our Yesterdays" (1969) as Mr. Atoz, *The Virginian* (1970), *Rod Serling's Night Gallery* (1972), *Hec Ramsey* (1973), *Adam-12* (1973), *Wonder Woman* (1975), *Hawaii Five-O* (1975), *The Frisco Kid* (1979), *Up the Academy* (1980), *WKRP in Cincinnati* (1981-1982), *Wizards and Warriors* (1983), *The Fall Guy* (1983-1985), *Amazing Stories* (1986), *Checking Out* (1989), and *Dick Tracy* (1990).

Wolfe, who worked until the last couple of years of his life, died January 23, 1992, at age 95, of natural causes in Los Angeles, California.

Louis Wolheim

Joel McCrea and Louis Wolheim in *The Silver Horde*

Louis Wolheim in New York City March 28, 1880 and was an American actor, of both stage and screen, whose rough physical appearance relegated him to roles mostly of thugs or villains in the movies, but whose talent allowed him to flourish on stage. His career was mostly contained during the silent era of the film industry, due to his untimely death at the age of 50 in 1931.

He attended Cornell University, where he graduated with a degree in engineering. After graduation he taught mathematics, including six years as an instructor at Cornell. Despite his rugged visage, Wolheim was intelligent and cultivated, speaking French, German, Spanish, and Yiddish. According to Wolheim, while at Cornell, he suffered an injury to his nose during a football game, and, after having the nose seen to by medical professionals, later that same day he got into a physical altercation (which he won), although his nose suffered more damage, ending up becoming almost a trademark for him. After the United States entrance into World War I, Wolheim joined the service, and was in Officer's training at Camp Zachary Taylor in Louisville, Kentucky when hostilities ended. Not wanting to remain in the service as a career, he asked for and was granted a discharge.

In 1914, on the advice of Lionel Barrymore and John Barrymore, Wolheim entered films. Both brothers also invited him to appear in the 1919 play *The Jest* in which the Barrymores co-starred. He would appear in at least three films with John Barrymore, *Dr Jekyll & Mr Hyde* (1920), *Sherlock Holmes* (1922), and *Tempest* (1928). Wolheim's fearsome visage almost immediately typecast him in roles as gangsters, executioners (as in D. W. Griffith's *Orphans of the Storm*) or prisoners. Towards the end of the 1920s he occasionally broke out of these stereotypes and played a comic Russian officer in *Tempest* and a rambunctious Sergeant in Howard Hughes's *Two Arabian Knights*. He also played a Chaneyesque gangster in Hughes's splendidly photographed *The Racket*.

Beginning with his appearance in the Barrymores' play, *The Jest*, Wolheim would appear in ten Broadway plays from 1919 through 1925. He received considerable acclaim as Yank in the original stage production of *The Hairy Ape* (1922) by Eugene O'Neill. His final play would be as the lead, Captain Flagg, in *What Price Glory?* in 1925. The play would be made into a film two years later, with Victor McLaglen in the role of Flagg. In 1922, with his fluent French, Wolheim translated Henri Bernstein's play, *The Claw*, into English, which his friend, Lionel Barrymore had a successful run on Broadway in.

Wolheim acted primarily in silent films, because of his sudden death at the close of the silent era, but he did appear several talkies, including *All Quiet on the Western Front*, *Danger Lights* and *The Silver Horde* with Joel McCrea (all in 1930) before he died. Wolheim was credited for a screenplay in addition to his acting career, for *The Greatest Power*, which starred none other than Ethel Barrymore. At the very end of his career, his final appearance was in *The Sin Ship*, which was also his only directing credit. The film was released in April 1931, after Wolheim's death, however after its completion Wolheim had decided that directing was not for him, and had stated he would only act from that point forward.

According to the biography included in the DVD version of *All Quiet on the Western Front*, Wolheim wanted, at one point in his career, to play romantic leads instead of tough "heavies." To that end, he sought to have plastic surgery performed on his broken nose. Executives at United Artists successfully obtained a restraining order against him from doing so, however.

Off-screen, Wolheim had a reputation as a genuinely caring individual, so much so that after his death, when flowers were usually sent to the funeral, his friends and co-workers instead took up a collection and gave the money, in Wolheim's name, to a fund to feed the hungry. James R. Quirk, editor and president of Photoplay Magazine, said of Wolheim, "This is no attempt to glorify an actor who has passed on. It is the truth, every word of it. Louis Wolheim was one of the finest and most generous souls I have ever known."

While preparing to appear in the film, *The Front Page*, Wolheim died suddenly on February 18, 1931, in Los Angeles at age 50. He had been losing drastic amounts of weight for the role, and news accounts from that time attributed his death to that weight loss. However, modern sources attribute his death to stomach cancer. He would be replaced *The Front Page's* cast by Adolphe Menjou.

Sheb Wooley

Shelby F. "Sheb" Wooley was born in Erick, Oklahoma April 10, 1921 and was a character actor and singer, best known for his 1958 novelty song "The Purple People Eater".He played Ben Miller, brother of Frank Miller in the film *High Noon*, played Travis Cobb in *The Outlaw Josey Wales*, and also had a co-starring role as scout Pete Nolan in the television program *Rawhide*.

Wooley was raised on a farm. He learned to ride horses at an early age and was a working cowboy and rodeo rider. He also played in a country-western band. Wooley tried to enlist during World War II, but was turned down for military service because of his rodeo injuries. Instead, he worked in the oil industry and as a welder. In 1946, he moved to Fort Worth, Texas, and became a country and western musician. He married Edna Ethel Bunt in Fort Worth and they moved to Hollywood in 1949. When they crossed the famous intersection of Hollywood and Vine on Christmas Day 1949, it was snowing.

Wooley appeared in dozens of western films from the 1950s through 1970s, most notably *High Noon*. In 1950 he appeared in Rocky Mountain with such veteran actors as Errol Flynn and Slim Pickens. In 1954, he played outlaw Jim Younger in the syndicated western series *Stories of the Century*. Wooley appeared four times in the syndicated western series, *The Range Rider*, starring Jock Mahoney and Dick Jones. He appeared in a 1953 episode of the *The Lone Ranger* entitled "Wake of War" and another episode entitled "Message to Fort Apache" in 1954. He appeared five times between 1951 and 1955 in another syndicated series, *The Adventures of Kit Carson*. He guest starred in *The Cisco Kid* in the role of Bill Bronson and as Harry Runyon in the episode "The Unmasking" of the CBS western *My Friend Flicka*. He played in *The Oklahoman* and *Trooper Hook* both in 1957 and with Joel McCrea. In 1958, he played Baxter in the movie *Terror in a Texas Town*. He appeared twice in the ABC western series, *The Life and Legend of Wyatt Earp*.

Wooley's big break came when he was cast as the drover Pete Nolan in the CBS western *Rawhide* (1959–1966) with Eric Fleming, Clint Eastwood, and Paul Brinegar. He also acted in the films *The Outlaw Josey Wales* and *Giant*.

In the 1940s, Wooley took an interest in his wife's young cousin, Roger Miller, who also grew up in Erick, Oklahoma. Wooley taught Miller how to play guitar chords and bought him a fiddle.

In the late 1950s, Wooley embarked on a recording career of his own with the song that made him famous, "The Purple People Eater". He followed with a series of lesser novelty hits. Wooley wrote the theme song for the long-running television show *Hee Haw*. In the UK he enjoyed a minor hit with the comedy single: "Luke the Spook" on the flip side was: "My Only Treasure" a ballad in the country and western tradition.

Wooley also had a string of country hits, his "That's My Pa" reaching No. 1 of Billboard magazine's Hot C&W Sides chart in March 1962. He was a regular on *Hee Haw* as the drunken country songwriter Ben Colder. He released music and performed as Ben Colder. Wooley also performed using his own name as well. Wooley had intended to record the song "Don't Go Near The Indians", but he was delayed by an acting job. Meanwhile, Rex Allen recorded the song and it was a hit. Wooley said he did not mind—he would do the sequel. His version was "Don't Go Near the Eskimos", about a boy in Alaska named Ben Colder (had never "been colder"). His song was so successful he continued using the name for forty years, one of his last recordings being "Shaky Breaky Car" (which parodied the song "Achy Breaky Heart").

His single "Hootenanny Hoot" was an Australian Top 10 hit in December, 1963.

Wooley is credited as the voice actor for the Wilhelm scream, having appeared on a memo as a voice extra for *Distant Drums* and later confirmed by his widow. This particular scream recording has been used by sound effects teams in over 200 films.

Wooley continued occasional television and film appearances through the 1990s, including an appearance as Cletus Summers, principal of Hickory High School in the 1986 film *Hoosiers*.

In 1996 he was diagnosed with leukemia. He died at the Skyline Medical Center in Nashville, Tennessee September 16, 2003 at age 82 and was buried in Hendersonville Memory Gardens in Hendersonville, Tennessee.

Wooley married his manager, Linda Dotson, and had two daughters named Christie and Shauna.

Douglas Wood

Douglas Wood was born on October 31, 1880 in New York City, New York. He was an actor, known for *Dangerous* (1935), *The Prisoner of Shark Island* (1936), and *Great Guy* (1936).

More of his roles included *Bottoms Up* (1934), *Dracula's Daughter* (1936), *Two in a Crowd* (1936) with Joel McCrea, *It Could Happen to You* (1939), *Buck Privates* (1941), *The More the Merrier* (1943) again with Joel McCrea, *Guest Wife* (1945), *Streets of San Francisco* (1949), *The Lone Ranger* (1950-1951), *Francis Covers the Big Town* (1953), *No Man's Woman* (!955), and *That Certain Feeling* (1956).

He died on January 13, 1966 in Woodland Hills, Los Angeles, California at age 85.

Judith Wood

Judith Wood was born Helen Johnson in New York City August 1, 1906 and was an American film actress from the end of the 1920s through the 1940s.

Wood moved to Hollywood, California to pursue an acting career in the late 1920s. Her first role was in the 1929 film *Gold Diggers of Broadway*. In that first film, as well as in the four she would star in during 1930, Wood would be credited under her birth name of "Helen Johnson".

Her first film of 1931 was *It Pays to Advertise*, which starred Carole Lombard. It would be the last film in which she would be billed under "Helen Johnson", and thereafter all of her film credits would be under the name "Judith Wood". In 1931, she was selected as one of thirteen girls to be "WAMPAS Baby Stars", along with actresses Marian Marsh, Karen Morley, Marion Shilling, and Barbara Weeks, among others.

Wood starred in six films in 1931, after which her career slowed to a crawl, and eventually faded out. She starred as Kitty Packard in the original Broadway production of *Dinner at Eight* but the film version went to Jean Harlow. She also appeared in *Girls About Town* (1931). In 1934 she only received three film roles, one of which was uncredited. In 1936 and 1937 she would have small but credited roles in two films, and then she would not receive another until 1941, which was uncredited. Her last film was in 1950, when she had an uncredited role in *The Asphalt Jungle* (1950).

Following that, she retired from acting, but remained in Los Angeles, California. She died there in April 6, 2002, of natural causes, at age 95.

Ward Wood

Ward Wood was born in Lewiston, Idaho April 8, 1924 and was an American actor and television writer.

Some of his credits included *Air Force* (1943), *Ramrod* (1947) with Joel McCrea and Veronica Lake, *Whispering Smith* (1948) with Alan Ladd, *Wake of the Red Witch* (1948), *Union Station* (1950), *The Cisco Kid* (1951), *Carbine Williams* (1952), *Space Patrol* (1951-1952), *Return from the Sea* (1954), *Broken Arrow* (1956), *Tales of the Texas Rangers* (1957), *Have Gun - Will Travel* (1959), *Ripcord* (1963), *Twilight Zone* (1964), *Get Smart* (1968), sixty-eight episodes as Lt. Art Malcolm
in *Mannix* (1968-1975), *Charlie's Angels* (1976), *Kojak* (1977), and *Dangerous Company* (1982).

He died November 3, 2001 at age 77 in Santa Monica, California.

Wilson Wood

Wilson Wood and Joel McCrea in *Stars in My Crown*

Wilson Wood was born Charles Woodrow Tolkien on February 11, 1915 in Huron, North Dakota. He was an actor, known for *The Barkleys of Broadway* (1949), *Zombies of the Stratosphere* (1952), and *Billy Rose's Jumbo* (1962).

More of his roles included *Two Sisters from Boston* (1946), *Command Decision* (1948), *Stars in My Crown* (1950) with Joel McCrea, *The Day the Earth Stood Still* (1951), *The Long, Long Trailer* (1953), *Three Brave Men* (1956), *Jailhouse Rock* (1957), *Please Don't Eat the Daisies* (1962), and *It Happened at the World's Fair* (1963).

He was married to Martha. He died on October 23, 2004 in Culver City, California, USA.

Harry Woods

Joel McCrea nd Harry Woods in *Colorado Territory*

Harry Woods was born in Cleveland, Ohio May 5, 1889 and was an American film actor, He appeared in nearly 250 films between 1923 and 1958. During his 35-year film career he acquired a reputation as a screen villain *par excellence*; his imposing size, powerful build, piercing eyes and snarling voice typed him as a bad guy to be reckoned with. He seldom played ordinary henchmen, usually cast as both the brains (the banker or saloon owner who secretly runs the bandit gang terrorizing the area) and the brawn behind the local villainy. Well respected by his peers—another prime screen villain, Roy Barcroft, once said of him, "Everything I know about being a bad guy I learned from Harry Woods".

Some of his roles included *Don Quickshot of the Rio Grande* (1923), *30 Below Zero* (1926), *The Lone Rider* (1930), *The Texas Ranger* (1931), *I Am a Fugitive from a Chain Gang* (1932), *The President Vanishes* (1934), *The Unknown Ranger* (1936), *The Last Train from Madrid* (1937) with Alan Ladd, *Wells Fargo* (1937) with Joel McCrea, *Block-Heads* (1938) with Laurel and Hardy, *Union Pacific* (1939) again with Joel McCrea, *Meet the Missus* (1940) again with Alan Ladd, *Sherlock Holmes and the Secret Weapon* (1942), *Marshal of Gunsmoke* (1944), *My Darling Clementine* (1946), *South of St. Louis* (1949) a third with Joel McCrea, *Colorado Territory* (1949) a fourth with Joel McCrea, *Best of the Badmen* (1951), *The Lone Ranger* (1953), *Stories of the Century* (1954-1955), *The Ten Commandments* (1956), *Gunsmoke* (1957-1960), and *Lawman* (1961).

He died 28 December 1968 in Los Angeles from uremia at age 79.

Morgan Woodward

Thomas Morgan Woodward was born September 16, 1925, in Fort Worth, Texas. He is probably best known for his recurring role in *Dallas* (1980-1987) as Marvin "Punk" Anderson. He also played the silent, sunglasses-wearing, "man with no eyes", Boss Godfrey (the Walking Boss) in *Cool Hand Luke* (1967) and holds the record for most Guest Appearances on the long-running Western TV series, *Gunsmoke* (1957-1974), with nineteen. He also appeared in the reunion movie *Gunsmoke: To the Last Man* (1992).

Woodward attended the University of Texas at Arlington, then Arlington State College in Arlington, Texas. He graduated from the University of Texas at Austin. Along with two of his four brothers, he has received recognition as a Distinguished Alumnus of the University. He is a member of the Pi Kappa Alpha Fraternity.

He went into active duty with the Air Force during the Korean War. He was sent to Korea and served with the Military Air Transport Command. After being demobilized, he did not return to law school but became an actor instead.

His brother, Lee Woodward, was the weatherman with a lion puppet named "King Lionel" on the television station KOTV in Tulsa, Oklahoma.

One of Woodward's longest TV roles was as the deputy/sidekick "Shotgun" Gibbs in 1955-1961 TV series *The Life and Legend of Wyatt Earp* starring Hugh O'Brian. On that series, Woodward played a tall, cantankerous, shotgun-toting backwoodsman who eventually became the trusted deputy of lawman Wyatt Earp in his days as a Kansas lawman. Though often overshadowed by the cool menace of Douglas Fowley's Doc Holliday, Woodward portrayed Gibbs as a solid, trustworthy, and more pragmatic partner to Earp, making Gibbs a character who, though ostensibly rough around the edges, would gradually come to share many of the qualities demonstrated over the years by another trusted TV deputy, Ken Curtis' world-weary Festus Haggen on *Gunsmoke* (1959-1975).

Some other credits include *Gunsight Ridge* (1957) with Joel McCrea, *Ride a Crooked Trail* (1958) with Audie Murphy, *The Gun Hawk* (1963), *The Sword of Ali Baba* (1965), *Gunpoint* (1966) again with Audie Murphy, *Firecreek* (1968), *Star Trek* (1966-1968), *Death of a Gunfighter* (1969), *Yuma* (1971), *Bonanza* (1960-1971), *Hec Ramsey* (1972), *Planet of the Apes* (1974), *Final Chapter: Walking Tall* (1977), *Logan's Run* (1977-1978), *Starsky and Hutch* (1978), *Centennial* (1978), *The Incredible Hulk* (1979), *The Misadventures of Sheriff Lobo* (1980), *Hill Street Blues* (1982), *The Dukes of Hazzard* (1980-1984), *Murder, She Wrote* (1989), *Renegade* (1993), *The Adventures of Brisco County Jr.* (1994), *The X-Files* (1995), and *Millennium* (1997).

Woodward was a familiar face on the hit television drama *Dallas* from 1980-1989. His recurring role of Marvin "Punk" Anderson, a friend of Jock Ewing's, and a member of the "cartel" of oil barons, became popular with viewers. As the series progressed Woodward's role became that of an advisor to the Ewing boys, and a voice of reason. His character's wife Mavis was played by character actress Alice Hirson. Hirson and Woodward were written out of the show during the 1989 season for budgetary reasons although the characters were mentioned in the following last two seasons of the show.

He appeared in the episode "The Assassin" of *T.J. Hooker* (1985) as Maj. Gen. Robert Selkirk who says in the episode about his efforts in the Korean War "I was a regular Audie Murphy".

In August 1988, he received the prestigious "Golden Boot Award" from the Hollywood Motion Picture and Television Fund.

In 1994, the Texas Arts Council presented Morgan with its Lifetime Achievement in the Arts Award in his hometown of Arlington, Texas. The city also named a prominent street "Morgan Woodward Way".

In 1997 Morgan celebrated fifty years in show business and was given the "International Star Award" in Los Angeles.

Woodward's chief hobby is restoring, rebuilding and flying antique airplanes. In aviation circles, he is recognized as an authority on Early American Aircraft and has received numerous awards for his restoration projects.

He has frequently appeared at Western film and television festivals around the country.

Hank Worden

Hank Worden was born Norton Earl Worden in Rolfe, Iowa July 23, 1901 and was an American cowboy-turned-character-actor who appeared in many Westerns.

He was raised on a cattle ranch near Glendive, Montana. He was educated at Stanford University and the University of Nevada as an engineer. He enlisted in the U.S. Army hoping to become an Army pilot, but washed out of flight school. An expert horseman, he toured the country in rodeos as a saddle bronc rider. During one ride, his horse landed atop him and broke his neck, but aside from a temporarily sore neck, Worden didn't know of the break until x-rayed twenty years later. While appearing in a rodeo at Madison Square Garden in New York, he and fellow cowboy Tex Ritter were chosen to appear in the Broadway play *Green Grow the Lilacs*, the play from which the musical *Oklahoma!* was later derived. Following the run of the play, he drove a cab in New York, then worked on dude ranches as a wrangler and as a guide on the Bright Angel trail of the Grand Canyon.

A chance encounter with actress Billie Burke at a dude ranch led her to recommend him to several movie producers. Worden made his film debut as an extra in Cecil B. DeMille's *The Plainsman* (1936), (though a few later films were released prior to *The Plainsman*). By this time, Tex Ritter had become a star, and Worden played sidekick roles in a number of Ritter's Westerns. A small part in Howard Hawks's *Come and Get It* (1936) with Joel McCrea led to a number of later appearances for that director, who also recommended him to director John Ford.

Worden eventually became a member of the John Ford Stock Company, and was directed by Ford twelve times in films and television. The connection with Ford led to an association with actor John Wayne, and Worden appeared in seventeen of Wayne's films. Foremost among his collaborations with Wayne and Ford is *The Searchers*, the 1956 classic Western in which Worden portrayed his most memorable role, that of "Mose Harper," the Shakespearean fool who only longed for "a roof over [his] head and a rocking chair by the fire."

Worden's best performances were given for demanding directors. He had a striking appearance: tall, thin, bald, his voice and mannerisms unforgettable to anyone who saw him. He worked steadily in television as well as films, long outliving Hawks, Ford, and Wayne, and achieving some late notice as the World's Most Decrepit Room-Service Waiter in David Lynch's *Twin Peaks* (1990-1991) TV series.

More of his roles included *Barbary Coast* (1935) with Joel McCrea, *Flaming Frontiers* (1938), *Brigham Young* (1940), *Cross-Country Romance* (1940) with Alan Ladd, *So Proudly We Hail!* (1943) with Veronica Lake, *The Great Moment* (1944) again with Joel McCrea, *Bud Abbott and Lou Costello in Hollywood* (1945), *The Bullfighters* (1945) with Laurel and Hardy, *Whispering Smith* (1948) with Alan Ladd, *Wagon Master* (1950), *Frenchie* (1950) a third with Joel McCrea, *Comin' Round the Mountain* (1951) again with Abbot and Costello, *Ma and Pa Kettle at Home* (1954), *The Lone Ranger* (1949-1957), *Rawhide* (1960), *Bonanza* (1960-1966), *Petticoat Junction* (1966-1968), *Rod Serling's Night Gallery* (1971), *Smokey and the Bandit* (1977), *Every Which Way But Loose* (1978), *Knight Rider* (1986), and *Almost an Angel* (1990).

In 1992, Worden hosted and co-produced with director Clyde Lucas an independent special shown on the Nostalgia Channel and some PBS stations entitled *Thank Ya, Thank Ya Kindly*. The special looked back on Worden's career and featured guests Clint Eastwood, Paul Hogan, Harry Carey Jr., Ben Johnson, Frankie Avalon, Burt Kennedy, and stuntman Dean Smith.

Widowed by his wife of 37 years (the former Emma Louise Caton) in 1977, he later shared his house for several years with actor Jim Beaver. In good health through his 91st year, he died peacefully during a nap at his home in Los Angeles on December 6, 1992. He was survived by his daughter Dawn Henry, whom he and his wife had adopted as an adult.

Fay Wray

Fay Wray and Joel McCrea in *The Most Dangerous Game*

Fay Wray was born Vina Fay Wray on a ranch near Cardston in the province of Alberta, Canada September 15, 1907 was a Canadian-American actress most noted for playing the female lead in *King Kong*. Through an acting career that spanned fifty-seven years, Wray attained international renown as an actress in horror movie roles. She was one of the first "scream queens".

After appearing in minor movie roles, Wray gained media attention being selected as one of the "WAMPAS Baby Stars". This led to Wray being contracted to Paramount Pictures as a teenager, where she made more than a dozen movies. After leaving Paramount, she signed deals with various film companies, being cast in her first horror film roles among many other types of roles, including in *The Bowery* (1933) and *Viva Villa* (1934), both huge productions starring Wallace Beery. For RKO Radio Pictures, Inc., she starred in the film with which she is most identified, *King Kong* (1933). After the success of *King Kong*, Wray appeared in many major movie roles and on television, finishing her acting career in 1980.

Wray was born to two Mormons, Elvina Marguerite Jones, who was from Salt Lake City, and Joseph Heber Wray, who was from Kingston upon Hull, England. She was one of six children. Her family returned to the United States a few years after she was born; they moved to Salt Lake City in 1912 and moved to Lark, Utah in 1914. In 1919, the Wrays returned to Salt Lake City again and then relocated to Hollywood, California, where Fay attended Hollywood High School.

In 1923, Wray appeared in her first film at the age of sixteen, when she landed a role in a short historical film sponsored by a local newspaper. In the 1920s, Wray landed a major role in the silent film *The Coast Patrol* (1925), as well as uncredited bit parts at the Hal Roach Studios.

In 1926, the Western Association of Motion Picture Advertisers, selected Wray as one of the "WAMPAS Baby Stars", a group of women who they believed to be on the threshold of movie stardom. She was at the time under contract to Universal Studios, mostly co-starring in low budget westerns opposite Buck Jones.

The following year in 1927, Wray was signed to a contract with Paramount Pictures In 1928, director Erich von Stroheim cast her as the main female lead in his film *The Wedding March*, released by Paramount. While the film was noted for its high budget and production values, it was a financial failure, but gave Wray her first lead role. Wray stayed with Paramount to make more than a dozen films and to make the transition from silent films to "talkie" films.

After leaving Paramount, Wray signed to various film companies. It was under these deals that Wray was cast in various horror films, including *Doctor X*. However, her greatest known films were produced under her deal with RKO Radio Pictures, Inc.. Her first film under RKO was *The Most Dangerous Game* (1932), co-starring Joel McCrea and shot at night on the same jungle sets that were being used for *King Kong* during the day, with the leads from both films, Wray and Robert Armstrong, appearing in both movies.

The Most Dangerous Game was followed by Wray's most memorable film, *King Kong*. According to Wray, Jean Harlow had been RKO's original choice, but because MGM put Harlow under exclusive contract during the pre-production phase of the film, she became unavailable and Wray was approached by director Merian C. Cooper to play the role of Ann Darrow, the blonde captive of King Kong. Wray was paid $10,000 dollars to play the role. The film was a commercial success. Wray was reportedly proud that the film saved RKO from bankruptcy. Wray's role would become the one with which she would be most associated.

She continued to star in various films, but by the early 1940s, her appearances became less frequent. She retired from acting in 1942, after her second marriage. However, due to financial exigencies she continued in her acting career, and over the next three decades, Wray appeared in certain film roles and also frequently on television.

Wray was cast in the 1953-1954 ABC situation comedy, *The Pride of the Family*, as Catherine Morrison. Paul Hartman played her husband, Albie Morrison. Natalie Wood and Robert Hyatt played their children, Ann and Junior Morrison, respectively.

Wray appeared in three episodes of CBS's courtroom drama, *Perry Mason*, the first of which was "The Case Of The Prodigal Parent" aired June 7, 1958. In 1959, she portrayed murder victim Lorna Thomas in "The Case of the Watery Witness". In 1965, she played voodoo practitioner Mignon Germaine in "The Case of the Fatal Fetish". In 1959, Wray was cast as Tula Marsh in the episode "The Second Happiest Day" of the CBS anthology series *Playhouse 90*. Another 1959 role was in the episode "The Morning After" of CBS's *Alfred Hitchcock Presents*. In 1960, she appeared as Clara in an episode of *77 Sunset Strip*, "Who Killed Cock Robin?". Another 1960 role was that of Mrs. Staunton, with Gigi Perreau as her daughter, in the episode "Flight from Terror" of the ABC adventure series, *The Islanders*.

Wray appeared in a 1961 episode of *The Real McCoys* titled "Theatre in the Barn". In 1963, she played Mrs. Brubaker in the episode "You're So Smart, Why Can't You Be Good?" episode of the NBC medical drama about psychiatry, *The Eleventh Hour*. She ended her acting career in the 1980 made-for-television film, *Gideon's Trumpet*.

In 1988, she published her autobiography, *On the Other Hand*. In her later years, Wray continued to make public appearances. In 1991, she was crowned Queen of the Beaux Arts Ball presiding with King Herbert Huncke.

She was approached by James Cameron to play the part of "Rose Dawson Calvert" for his 1997 blockbuster *Titanic* with Kate Winslet to play her younger self, but she turned down the role and the part of Rose was given to Gloria Stuart. She was a special guest at the 70th Academy Awards, where the show's host, Billy Crystal, introduced her as the "Beauty who charmed the Beast". She was the only 1920s Hollywood actress in attendance that evening. On October 3, 1998, she appeared at the Pine Bluff (Arkansas) Film Festival, which showed *The Wedding March* (with live orchestral accompaniment).

In January 2003, the 95-year old Wray appeared at the 2003 Palm Beach International Film Festival to celebrate the Rick McKay documentary film *Broadway: The Golden Age, by the Legends Who Were There*, where she was also honored with a "Legend in Film" award. In her later years, she also visited the Empire State Building frequently, once visiting in 1991 as a guest of honor at the building's 60th anniversary, and also in May 2004, which was among her last public appearances. Her final public appearance was at an after-party at the Sardi's restaurant in New York City, following the premiere of the documentary film *Broadway: The Golden Age, by the Legends Who Were There*.

Wray was married three times – to the writers John Monk Saunders and Robert Riskin and to the neurosurgeon, Dr. Sanford Rothenberg (January 28, 1919 – January 4, 1991).

She had three children: Susan Saunders, Victoria Riskin, and Robert Riskin, Jr. She became a naturalized citizen of the United States in 1933.

In her autobiography *On The Other Hand: A Life Story* she declares herself a Republican.

In 2004, Wray was approached by director Peter Jackson to appear in a small cameo for the 2005 remake of *King Kong*. She met with Naomi Watts, who was to play the role of Ann Darrow. She politely declined the cameo, and claimed the original "Kong" to be the true "King". Before filming of the remake commenced, Wray died in her sleep of natural causes on August 8, 2004, in her Manhattan apartment. Her friend Rick McKay said that "she just kind of drifted off quietly as if she was going to sleep... she just kind of gave out." She was 96 years old. Wray is interred at the Hollywood Forever Cemetery in Hollywood, California.

Two days after her death, the lights of the Empire State Building were extinguished for fifteen minutes in her memory.

In the 2005 film, Carl Denham (Jack Black) mentions he hired Ann Darrow (Naomi Watts) "because Fay was unavailable".

Lillian Yarbo

Lillian Yarbo was born in 1905 in Washington, D.C. She is an actress, known for *You Can't Take It with You* (1938), *Destry Rides Again* (1939), and *The Great Man's Lady* (1942) with Joel McCrea.

Some of her other roles included *Rainbow on the River* (1936), *Wives Under Suspicion* (1938), *There's That Woman Again* (1939), *The Return of Frank James* (1940), *Wild Bill Hickok Rides* (1942), *The Naughty Nineties* (1945) with Abbott and Costello, *My Brother Talks to Horses* (1947), and *Look for the Silver Lining* (1949).

Thomas Alan Yazloff

Thomas Alan Yazloff is an actor, known for his only role in *Buffalo Bill* (1944) with Joel McCrea. He played Kit Carson Cody.

Chick York

Chick York is an actor, known for his only five roles in *Domestic Bliss-ters* (1934), *How Am I Doing* (1935), *The Yearling* (1946), *Ramrod* (1947) with Joel McCrea, and *A Really Important Person* (1947).

Duke York

Duke York was born Charles Everest Sinsabaugh in Danby, New York October 17, 1908 and was an American film actor. He appeared in nearly 160 films between 1932 and 1952.

Modern viewers will remember York for his portrayals of grotesque monsters, ape men, or other scary goon-like characters in Three Stooges short films such as *Three Little Twirps* (1943), *Idle Roomers* (1943), *Shivering Sherlocks* (1948), and *Who Done It?* (1949). His most prominent non-monster role was as Kelly in *Higher Than a Kite*. York also played the role of King Kala in the serial Flash Gordon (1936).

More of his credits included *Island of Lost Souls* (1932) with Alan Ladd, *The Pursuit of Happiness* (1934), *Redheads on Parade* (1935), *Libeled Lady* (1936) with Jean Harlow, *They Gave Him a Gun* (1937), *Dick Tracy Returns* (1938), *Topper Takes a Trip* (1938), *You Can't Cheat an Honest Man* (1939), *Union Pacific* (1939) with Joel McCrea, *Destry Rides Again* (1939), *The Shadow* (1940), *Topper Returns* (1941), *Never Give a Sucker an Even Break* (1941), *Jackass Mail* (1942), *Who Done It?* (1942) with Abbott and Costello, *Arabian Nights* (1942) with Sabu, *Crazy House* (1943), *Lost in a Harem* (1944) again with Bud and Lou, *Road to Rio* (1947), *Isn't It Romantic?* (1948) with Veronica Lake, *Mississippi Rhythm* (1949), *Winchester '73* (1950), *The Lone Ranger* (1950-1951), *Adventures of Wild Bill Hickok* (1951), *The Range Rider* (1951-1952), *Carbine Williams* (1952), and *Trail Blazers* (1953).

York committed suicide in Hollywood, California January 24, 1952. He was 43.

Clara Kimball Young

Clara Kimball Young was born in Chicago, Illinois September 6, 1890 and was an American film actress, who was highly regarded and publicly popular in the early silent film era.

Clarisa Kimball was born to Edward M. and Pauline (née Maddern) Kimball, travelling stock actors. She made her stage debut at the age of three, and throughout her early childhood travelled with her parents and acted with their theater company. She attended St. Francis Xavier Academy, Chicago. Afterwards she was hired into a stock company and resumed her stage career, travelling extensively through the United States and playing various small town theaters.

Early in her career she met and married a fellow stock company and known Broadway actor named James Young. Young's previous wife had been the songwriter/lyricist Rida Johnson Young. After sending a photograph to Vitagraph Studios, Clara Kimball Young, as she was then known, and her husband were both offered yearly contracts in 1912.

In the new medium of motion pictures, and without much screen competition, Clara Kimball Young's star at Vitagraph rose quickly. Young was predominantly cast in one and two reel roles as the virtuous heroine. By 1913 she had become one of the most popular leading ladies at Vitagraph and placed at number seventeen in a public popularity poll. Unfortunately, many of Young's films from her early period with Vitagraph are now lost.

In 1914 Vitagraph released the drama *My Official Wife* which starred Young as a Russian revolutionary and was directed by her husband James Young and co-starred the popular leading man Earle Williams. The film, which is now lost, was an enormous success and launched Clara Kimball Young and Earle Williams into first place in the popularity polls and Young was immediately signed to a contract with legendary pioneering Hollywood mogul Lewis J. Selznick.

After a string of successful roles, Young was firmly established as one of the chief attractions of World Film Corporation and her husband James was now a much sought-after director. By 1915 Young's popularity was rivalling that of other early luminary actresses of the era: Mary Pickford, Dorothy and Lillian Gish, Pearl White, Edna Purviance, and Mabel Normand.

She became involved in a much publicized affair with Selznick, culminating in a 1916 divorce suit brought about by Young, charging his wife with alienation of affection. James Young finally obtained a final decree on April 8, 1919 on grounds of desertion.

Selznick quickly formed the Clara Kimball Young Film Corporation, installing himself as president, and formed Selznick Productions to distribute her films and those of some other independent producers. After only four films with Selznick however, the personal and business relationship began to sour and Kimball Young struggled to extricate herself from all business arrangements with Selznick, accusing him of defrauding her of her profits through a series of dummy corporations and by electing himself president of her company while not permitting her any input in her business affairs.

In 1917 Kimball Young became involved in an affair with Harry Garson, with whom she then teamed up with in a business venture. Garson had little experience in the motion picture business, and as a result Kimball Young's career began to sputter. Although she remained a popular actress into the early 1920s, Kimball Young suffered at the inexperience and alleged mismanagement and apathy of Garson.

She began suffering a series of press attacks for her business dealings and personal relationship with Garson. By 1925, her stardom began to fade and she made her last silent film *Lying Wives*. Kimball Young spent the remainder of the 1920s performing in vaudeville, and in 1928 quietly married Dr. Arthur Fauman. The advent of sound briefly revived her career, and she appeared in several featured talkie roles for RKO Radio Pictures and Tiffany Studios with only modest success, appearing only in bit parts including *Kept Husbands* (1931) with Joel McCrea, and a Three Stooges short *Ants in the Pantry* (1936), and extra roles in mostly lower budget pictures and having a stint on radio. One of her bigger roles is in the murder mystery *The Rogues Tavern* (1936) where she plays a sweet but fussy motherly woman who is hiding a very big secret.

She quietly retired from her acting career in 1941. Clara Kimball Young died of a stroke at the Motion Picture House on October 15, 1960, at age 70, in Woodland Hills, California and was interred at the Grand View Memorial Park Cemetery in Glendale, California.

For her contribution to the motion picture industry, Clara Kimball Young was given a star on the Hollywood Walk of Fame at 6513 Hollywood Blvd., in Hollywood, California.

Loretta Young

Joel McCrea and Loretta Young in *Three Blind Mice*

Loretta Young was born as Gretchen Young in Salt Lake City, Utah January 6, 1913 and was an American actress. Starting as a child actress, she had a long and varied career in film from 1917 to 1953. She won the 1948 best actress Academy Award for her role in the 1947 film *The Farmer's Daughter*, and received an Oscar nomination for her role in *Come to the Stable*, in 1949. Young moved to the relatively new medium of television, where she had a dramatic anthology series, *The Loretta Young Show*, from 1953 to 1961. The series earned three Emmy Awards, and reran successfully on daytime TV and later in syndication. In the 1980s Young returned to the small screen and won a Golden Globe in *Christmas Eve* in 1989. Young, a devout Roman Catholic, worked with various Catholic charities after her acting career.

She was the daughter of Gladys (Royal) and John Earle Young. At confirmation, she took the name Michaela. When she was two years old, her parents separated. She and her family moved to Hollywood when she was three years old. She and her sisters Polly Ann and Elizabeth Jane (screen name Sally Blane) worked as child actresses, but of the three, Loretta was the most successful.

Young's first role was at the age of three, in the silent film *The Primrose Ring*. During her high school years Young was educated at Ramona Convent Secondary School. She was signed to a contract by John McCormick (1893-1961), husband and manager of actress, Colleen Moore, who saw the young girl's potential. The name "Loretta" was given to her by Colleen, who later would explain that it was the name of her favorite doll.

Young was billed as Gretchen Young in the silent film, *Sirens of the Sea* (1917). It was not until 1928 that she was first billed as "Loretta Young" in *The Whip Woman*. That same year she co-starred with Lon Chaney in the MGM film *Laugh, Clown, Laugh*. The next year she was named one of the WAMPAS Baby Stars.

In 1930 when she was 17, she eloped with 26-year-old actor, Grant Withers; they were married in Yuma, Arizona. The marriage was annulled the next year, just as their second movie together (appropriately titled *Too Young to Marry*) was released.

In 1935, she co-starred with Clark Gable and Jack Oakie in the film version of Jack London's *The Call of the Wild*, directed by William Wellman.

She appeared in *Three Blind Mice* (1938) with Joel McCrea.

During World War II, Young made *Ladies Courageous* (1944; reissued as *Fury in the Sky*), the fictionalized story of the Women's Auxiliary Ferrying Squadron. It depicted a unit of female pilots during WWII who flew bomber planes from the factories to their final destinations. She also made *And Now Tomorrow* with Alan Ladd that same year.

Young made as many as eight movies a year. In 1947 she won an Oscar for her performance in *The Farmer's Daughter*. That same year she co-starred with Cary Grant and David Niven in *The Bishop's Wife*, a perennial favorite. In 1949 she received another Academy Award nomination for *Come to the Stable*. In 1953 she appeared in her last theatrical film, *It Happens Every Thursday*, a Universal comedy about a New York couple who move to California to take over a struggling weekly newspaper; her costar was John Forsythe.

Loretta Young hosted and starred in the well-received half-hour anthology series *The Loretta Young Show* (1953–1961). Her trademark was a dramatic entrance through a living room door in various high fashion evening gowns. She returned at the program's conclusion to offer a brief passage from the Bible or a famous quote that reflected upon the evening's story. (Young's introductions and conclusions to her television shows were not rerun on television because she legally stipulated that they not be, as she did not want the dresses she wore in those segments to "date" the program.) Her program ran in prime time on NBC for eight years, the longest-running prime-time network program hosted by a woman up to that time.

The program, which earned her three Emmys, was based on the premise that each drama was in answer to a question asked in her fan mail. The program's original title was *Letter to Loretta*. The title was changed to *The Loretta Young Show* during the first season (as of the February 14, 1954 episode), and the "letter" concept was dropped at the end of the second season. At this time, Young's hospitalization, due to overwork towards the end of the second season, required that there be a number of guest hosts and guest stars; her first appearance in the 1955–56 season was for the Christmas show. From then on, Young appeared in only about half of each season's shows as an actress, and served as the program's host for the remainder.

Minus Young's introductions and conclusions, the series was rerun as the *Loretta Young Theatre* in daytime by NBC from 1960 to 1964. It also appeared in syndication into the early 1970s, before being withdrawn.

In the 1962–1963 television season, Young appeared as Christine Massey, a free-lance magazine writer and mother of seven children, in CBS's *The New Loretta Young Show*. It fared poorly in the ratings on Monday evenings against ABC's *Ben Casey*. It was dropped after one season (26 episodes).

In the 1990s selected episodes from Young's personal collection, with the opening and closing segments (and original title) intact, were released on home video, and frequently were shown on cable television.

In 1988 she was awarded the Women in Film Crystal Award for outstanding women who, through their endurance and the excellence of their work, have helped to expand the role of women within the entertainment industry.

Young has two stars on the Hollywood Walk of Fame; one for motion pictures, at 6104 Hollywood Boulevard, and another for television, at 6141 Hollywood Boulevard. In 2011 a Golden Palm Star on the Palm Springs, California, Walk of Stars was dedicated to her.

Young was married to actor, Grant Withers, from 1930 to 1931. She married producer, Tom Lewis, in 1940 and they divorced very bitterly in the mid-1960s; Lewis died in 1988. They had two sons, Peter Lewis (of the San Francisco rock band Moby Grape), and Christopher Lewis, a film director. She married fashion designer Jean Louis in 1993. Louis died in 1997. Young was godmother to Marlo Thomas (daughter of TV star Danny Thomas).

In 1935 Young had an affair with a then-married Clark Gable while on location for *The Call of the Wild*. (Gable was married to Maria "Ria" Franklin Prentiss Lucas Langham.) During their affair Young became pregnant, but due to the moral codes placed on the film industry Young covered up her pregnancy in order to avoid damaging her career (as well as Gable's). When the pregnancy began to show, she went on a "vacation" to England, and several months later returned to California. Shortly before the birth, she gave an interview from her bed, covered in blankets, stating the reason for her long movie absence was because of a condition she'd had since childhood. Young gave birth to Judith Young on November 6, 1935, in a house she and her mother owned in Venice, California. Three weeks later she returned to movie-making. After several months of living in the house in Venice, Judy was transferred to St. Elizabeth's, an orphanage outside Los Angeles. When she was 19 months old, her grandmother picked her up and Young announced to gossip columnist Louella Parsons that she had adopted the infant. Few in Hollywood were fooled by the ruse and the child's true parentage was widely rumored in entertainment circles. Young refused to confirm or comment publicly on the rumors until 1999, when Joan Wester Anderson wrote Young's authorized biography. In her interviews with Anderson for the book, Young finally confessed that Judy was her biological child and the product of Young having had a brief affair with Gable. The child was raised as "Judy Lewis", taking the last name of Young's second husband, producer Tom Lewis.

According to her autobiography *Uncommon Knowledge*, some people made fun of Judy because of the prominent ears she inherited from her father. She states that at seven she had an operation to "pin back" her large ears and that her mother always had her wearing bonnets as a child. In 1958 Lewis' future husband, Joseph Tinney, told her "everybody" knew that Gable was her biological father. The only time Lewis remembered Gable visiting her was once at her home when she was a teenager; she had no idea he was her biological father. Several years later he appeared on *The Loretta Young Show* after Young had been in hospital for several months. Lewis was an assistant and was right behind her mother when she noticed Gable. They never had a relationship and she never saw him again. Several years later, after becoming a mother herself, Lewis finally confronted her mother, who privately admitted the truth, stating that Judy was "a walking mortal sin".

A scandal erupted in 1973, when Young's son, Christopher Lewis (then 29), was charged with child molestation, and filming and distributing child pornography, along with 13 other men whom the police labeled a "chicken flick ring". Lewis and the other men were indicted for soliciting boys ranging from age 6 to 17 to perform lewd acts in their movies. Pleading no contest to child molestation charges and potentially facing a significant term of imprisonment, Lewis was sentenced to probation and a $500 fine.

Young was a lifelong Republican. In 1952 she appeared in radio, print, and magazine ads in support of Dwight D. Eisenhower and was in attendance at his inauguration along with Anita Louise, Louella Parsons, Jane Russell, Dick Powell, June Allyson, and Lou Costello, among others. In both 1968 and 1980 she was a vocal supporter of Richard Nixon and Ronald Reagan. She was also an active member of the Hollywood Republican Committee with close friend Irene Dunne as well as Ginger Rogers, William Holden, George Murphy, Fred Astaire, and John Wayne.

From the time of Young's retirement in the 1960s, until not long before her death, she devoted herself to volunteer work for charities and churches with her friends of many years: Jane Wyman, Irene Dunne, and Rosalind Russell. She was a member of the Good Shepherd Parish and the Catholic Motion Picture Guild in Beverly Hills, California. Young did, however, briefly come out of retirement to star in two television films, *Christmas Eve* (1986), and *Lady in the Corner* (1989). Young won a Golden Globe Award for the former, and was nominated again for the latter.

In 1972, a jury in Los Angeles awarded Young $550,000 in her breach of contract suit against NBC. Filed in 1966, the suit contended that NBC had allowed foreign television outlets to rerun old episodes of *The Loretta Young Show* without excluding, as agreed by the parties, the opening segment where Young would make her entrance. Young testified that her image had been damaged by portraying her in "outdated gowns," and a jury agreed to less than the $1.9 million sought.

Young died on August 12, 2000, from ovarian cancer at age 87, at the Santa Monica, California, home of her half-sister, Georgiana Montalbán (the wife of actor Ricardo Montalban) and was interred in the family plot in the Holy Cross Cemetery in Culver City, California. Her ashes were buried in the grave of her mother, Gladys Belzer. Her daughter, Judy Lewis, also died of cancer, on November 25, 2011, at age 76.

Roland Young

Joel McCrea and Roland Young in *He Married His Wife*

Roland Young was born in London, England November 11, 1887 was an English actor. Young was educated at Sherborne School, Sherborne, Dorset and the University of London before being accepted into Royal Academy of Dramatic Art. He made his first stage appearance in London's West End in *Find the Woman* in 1908, and in 1912 he made his Broadway debut in *Hindle Wakes*. He appeared in two comedies written for him by Clare Kummer, *Good Gracious Annabelle!* (1916) and *A Successful Calamity* (1917) before he served with the US Army during World War I. He returned to New York when the war ended, and married Kummer's daughter, Frances. For the next few years he alternated between New York and London. He made his film debut in the 1922 silent film *Sherlock Holmes*, in which he played Watson opposite John Barrymore as Holmes.

He signed a contract with MGM and made his talkie debut in *The Unholy Night* (1929), directed by Lionel Barrymore. He was loaned to Warner Bros. to appear in *Her Private Life*, with Billie Dove and 20th Century Fox, winning critical approval for his comedic performance as Jeanette MacDonald's husband in *Don't Bet on a Woman*. He was again paired with MacDonald in the film version of *Good Gracious Annabelle!*, titled *Annabelle's Affairs*. He appeared in Cecil B. de Mille's *The Squaw Man*, and played opposite Alfred Lunt and Lynn Fontanne in *The Guardsman* (both 1931). He appeared with Evelyn Brent in Columbia's *The Pagan Lady* (1932) and Pola Negri in RKO's *A Woman Commands* (1932). His final film under his MGM contract was *Lovers Courageous* (1932), opposite Robert Montgomery.

Young began to work as a free-lance performer and found himself in constant demand. He appeared with Jeanette MacDonald, Genevieve Tobin and Maurice Chevalier in *One Hour With You* (1932) and with Kay Francis in *Street of Women* (1932). Alexander Korda invited him to return to England to make his British film debut in *Wedding Rehearsal* (1932). He returned to Hollywood and appeared in a diverse group of films that included comedies, murder mysteries and dramas, and also worked on Broadway. Among his films of this period, were *Ruggles of Red Gap* (1935), playing Uriah Heep in *David Copperfield* (1935) and H.G. Wells' fantasy, *The Man Who Could Work Miracles* (1936).

In 1937, he achieved one of the most important successes of his career, as the businessman Cosmo Topper, haunted by the ghosts of his clients played by Cary Grant and Constance Bennett. The film was one of the most successful films of the year, and for his comedy performance, Young received an Academy Award for Best Supporting Actor nomination. His wife was played by Billie Burke who wrote in her memoir that Young "was dry and always fun to work with". They also appeared together in *The Young in Heart* (1938), and the first of the *Topper* sequels, *Topper Takes a Trip* (1939). He continued to play supporting roles in comedies such as *Yes, My Darling Daughter*, with Fay Bainter and Priscilla Lane, but over the next few years the importance of his roles again decreased, but he achieved another success as Katharine Hepburn's uncle in *The Philadelphia Story* (1940). His last starring role was in the final installment of the *Topper* series, *Topper Returns* in 1941, with Billie Burke and Joan Blondell.

He continued working steadily through the 1940s, playing small roles opposite some of Hollywood's leading actors and actresses, such as Joel McCrea in *He Married His Wife* (1940), Joan Crawford, Marlene Dietrich, Paulette Goddard and Greta Garbo in her final film, *Two-Faced Woman* (1942). In 1945, he began his own radio show and appeared in the film adaption of Agatha Christie's *And Then There Were None*. By the end of the decade his film career had declined, and his final films, including *The Great Lover* (1949), in which he played a murderer opposite Bob Hope, and Fred Astaire's *Let's Dance* (1950), were not successful.

In the 1950s, Young appeared on several episodic television series, including *Lux Video Theatre*, *Studio One*, *Pulitzer Prize Playhouse* and *The Chevrolet Tele-Theatre*.

Young has two stars on the Hollywood Walk of Fame, one for film at 6523 Hollywood Blvd. and another for television at 6315 Hollywood Blvd.

Young was married twice, to Marjorie Krummer from 1921 until 1940, and to Patience DuCroz from 1948 until his death in New York City June 5, 1953 at age 65.

Wolfgang Zilzer

Wolfgang Zilzer was born in Cincinnati, Ohio January 20, 1901 and was a German-American stage and film actor.

Zilzer was born to German-Jewish emigrant Max Zilzer, who was engaged at the local theater. Zilzer's mother died soon after his birth and his father returned to Germany in 1905. Zilzer appeared at different stages in childrens roles and made his first movie appearance in the age of 14. Around 1930 he moved to the United States but had only small success as an actor. He returned to Germany, but after Adolf Hitler's seizure of power Zilzer fled to France, where he worked as dubbing voices at several French versions of Hollywood productions.

In 1935 Zilzer returned to Germany again, finally imigrating to the USA in 1937. Applying for a visa at the U.S. embassy, he first realized his already existing US citizenship. After his imigration he started to work with Ernst Lubitsch in several anti-Nazi movies, using pseudonyms to protect his father, who was still living in Berlin. With appearances in films from 1915 to 1986, Zilzer had one of the longest careers in cinema history.

Zilzer married the German-Jewish actress Lotte Palfi; both appeared in the 1942 movie *Casablanca*. After World War II Zilzer appeared at different stages in the United States and in Germany.

More of his roles included *Thou Shalt Not* (1928), *Espionage Agent* (1939) with Joel McCrea, *Confessions of a Nazi Spy* (1939), *Hitler - Beast of Berlin* (1939) with Alan Ladd, *Three Faces West* (1940), *The Devil with Hitler* (1942), *Hitler's Madman* (1943), *The Strange Death of Adolf Hitler* (1943), *Hotel Berlin* (1945), *Women in the Night* (1948), the episode "Beware This Woman" of *Lights Out* (1950) with Veronica Lake, *Singing in the Dark* (1956), *No Survivors, Please* (1964), *The Diary of Anne Frank* (1967), *Union City* (1980), *Lovesick* (1983), and *FDR: A One Man Show* (1987).

At the end of the 1980s Zilzer contracted Parkinson's disease and decided to return to Germany. His wife Lotte Palfi refused to do so and their marriage ended in divorce after almost 50 years.

Wofgang Zilzer died in Berlin June 26, 1991 at age 90 and is buried at the Waldfriedhof Zehlendorf.

Henry Zynda

Henry Zynda was born on May 9, 1904 in Liverpool, England. He was an actor, known for *The Great Waltz* (1938), *Hitler - Beast of Berlin* (1939) with Alan Ladd, and *Spy Smasher* (1942).

More of his roles included *Calling All Marines* (1939), *Espionage Agent* (1939) with Joel McCrea, *The Phantom Submarine* (1940), and *Invisible Agent* (1942).

He died on December 23, 1961 in Los Angeles, California at age 57.

Alphabetical Index of Co-Stars

I

Ince, John
Ince, Ralph
Infuhr, Teddy
Ingram, Jack
Inness, Jean
Irving, Ellis
Irving, George
Izay, Victor

J

Jackson, Jenie
Jackson, Selmer
Jamison, Bud
January, Lois
Jara, Maurice
Jarman, Claude, Jr.
Jaynes, Enid
Jeans, Isabel
Jenkins, Allen
Jenkins, Megs
Jenks, Frank
Joby, Hans
Johnson, Carmencita
Johnson, Chubby
Johnson, Kay
Johnson, Noble
Johnson, Tor
Jolly, I. Stanford
Jones, Gordon
Jones, L. Q.
Jones, Marcia Mae
Jordan, Bobby
Jordan, Dorothy
Jory, Victor

K

Kane, Eddie
Karloff, Boris
Keefer, Don
Keith, Ian
Kelley, Barry
Kelly, Kitty
Kelly, Nancy
Kelly, Paul
Kelly, Tommy
Kelton, Pert
Kemper, Charles
Kennedy, Adam
Kennedy, Douglas
Kennedy, Edgar
Kenny, Jack

Kent, Dorothea
Kerr, Donald
Kerr, Frederick
Kerrigan, J.M.
Keyes, Evelyn
Kilburn, Terry
Killian, Victor
Killmond, Frank
King, Wright
Kinsky, Leonid
Knight, Fuzzy
Kohner, Susan
Kolb, Clarence
Kolker, Henry
Kosleck, Martin
Kruger, Alma

L

Laffan, Patricia
Lake, Veronica
Lambert, Jack
Lanchester, Elsa
Landau, David
Lane, Charles
Lane, Richard
Larch, John
Largay, Raymond
Larsen, Keith
Lauter, Harry
Lawler, Anderson
Lawrence, Marc
Lawrence, Terry
Lawton, Frank
Le Clair, Blanche
Leeds, Andrea
Leigh, Nelson
Leslie, Nan
Leslie, William
Lessey, George
Lewis, George J,
Lewis, Mitchell
Lewis, Ralph
Linaker, Kay
Linden, Eric
Linder, Alfred
Lindgren, Orley
Linow, Ivan
Littlefield, Lucian
Lloyd, Norman
Lloyd, Rollo
Lloyd, Suzanne
Loft, Arthur
Logan, Ella
Lom, Herbert
Lomas, Jack
Love, Montagu
Lovejoy, Frank

Lukas, Paul
Lukats, Nick
Lummis, Dayton
Lyden, Pierce
Lyn, Dawn
Lynd, Helen
Lynn, Diana
Lynn, Jeffrey
Lynn, Sharon
Lyon, Richard

M

MacDonald, Ian
MacDonald, J. Farrell
Mack, Cactus
Mackaill, Dorothy
Macollum, Barry
Madison, Julian
Madison, Noel
Main, Marjorie
Malone, Dorothy
Mander, Miles
Mansfield, Rankin
Maricle, Leona
Marsh, Marian
Marshall, Brenda
Marshall, Herbert
Martin, Lewis
Martin, Tony
Mason, Louis
Maxey, Paul
Maxwell, Edwin
Maynard, Kermit
Mayo, Virginia
McCallin, Clement
McCarthy, Kevin
McCormac, Muriel
McCrea, Jody
McDaniel, Etta
McDonald, Francis
McDonald, George
McGlynn, Frank
McGregor, Malcolm
McGuire, Tom
McIntire, John
McIntyre, Leila
McIntosh, Burr
McNamara, Edward
McNaughton, Jack
McWade, Robert
Meek, Donald
Meeker, George
Melford, George
Mercer, Beryl
Messinger, Gertrude
Meyer, Emile

Meyer, Torben
Middleton, Robert
Mikler, Michael T.
Millan, Victor
Miles, Vera
Milford, John
Milland, Ray
Miller, Ivan
Miller, John 'Skins'
Mills, Mort
Mina, Nika
Miroslava
Mitchell, Ewing
Mitchell, Grant
Mitchell, James
Mitchell, Laurie
Mitchell, Rhea
Mitchell, Steve
Mitchell, Thomas
Mitchum, James
Mitchum, John
Moffett, Gregory
Mollison, Henry
Montenaro, Anthony C.
Montgomery, Goodee
Montgomery, Robert
Moore, Charles R.
Moore, Pauline
Moorhouse, Bert
Morales, Carmen
Moran, Frank
Moran, Polly
Moreno, Antonio
Morgan, Ralph
Morrison, Ann
Morrow, Jeff
Morrow, Vic
Mower, Jack

N

Nagel, Conrad
Naismith, Laurence
Nash, Mary
Negley, Howard
Neise, George N.
Nervick, Rick
Nesbitt, Cathleen
Nesmith, Ottola
Newlan, Paul
Nicol, Alex
Nigh, Jane
Niles, Denny
Nilsson, Anna Q.
Niven, David
Nixon, Marian
Nolan, Jeanette

Nolan, Lloyd
Norton, Edgar
Norton, Jack
Novak, Eva
Novarro, Ramon
Novello, Jay
Nugent, Elliott

O

Oates, Warren
Oberon, Merle
O'Brien, Pat
O'Brien-Moore, Erin
O'Connor, Robert Emmett
O'Donnell, Spec
O'Flynn, Damian
O'Hara, Maureen
Ollestad, Chase
Olsen, Moroni
O'Moore, Patrick
O'Neill, Henry
Orth, Frank
Osborne, Vivienne
O'Shea, Oscar
Osterloh, Robert
O'Sullivan, Maureen
Overman, Lynn
Owen, Reginald

P

Padden, Sarah
Page, Bradley
Paiva, Nester
Pallette, Eugene
Pangborn, Franklin
Paris, Jerry
Parker, Barnett
Parnell, Emory
Parsons, Milton
Pate, Michael
Patterson, Hank
Patterson, Kenneth
Peckinpah, Sam
Pendleton, Nat
Pendleton, Steve
Pepper, Barbara
Peterson, Dorothy
Petrie, Howard
Phelps, Buster
Phelps, Lee
Phillips, Carmen
Phillips, Phillip
Phipps William
Picerni, Paul
Pickard, John
Pickens, Slim
Pidgeon, Walter
Pine, Phillip

Pollard,, Snub
Potel, Victor
Powell, Richard
Powell, Russ
Pratt, Purnell
Prescott, Guy
Preston, Robert
Price, Sherwood
Prival, Lucien
Prouty, Jed
Puglia, Frank
Pukui, Napoleon
Punsly, Bernard
Pyle, Denver

Q

Quarry, Robert
Quartero, Nina
Quinn, Anthony

R

Raines, Steve
Rambeau, Marjorie
Rasumny, Mikail
Raven, John
Raymond, Cyril
Reed, Phillip
Reed, Ralph
Reeves, George
Reid, Carl Benton
Renno, Vincent
Reynolds, Adeline DeWalt
Reynolds, Gene
Rhodes, Erik
Richards, Addison
Ricketts, Tom
Ridgely, John
Ridges, Stanley
Ridgeway, Fritzi
Ridgeway, Suzanne
Ring, Cyril
Risdon, Elisabeth
Roach, Bert
Robards, Jason Sr.
Roberson, Chuck
Roberts, Florence
Roberts, Roy
Robertson, Willard
Robinson, Dewey
Robinson, Edward G.
Robson, May
Rogers, Gil
Rogers, Ginger
Rogers, Kasey
Rogers, Will
Romero, Carlos
Romero, Cesar
Rooney, Mickey

Rosenthal, Harry
Rosing, Bodil
Ross, Myrna
Ross, Peggy
Roth, Gene
Rouverol, Jean
Rudley, Herbert
Rudnick, Marcus
Rudolph, Oscar
Ruggles, Charles
Russell, Bing
Russell, Gail
Russell, John
Ruth, Mary
Ruysdael, Basil

S

Sande, Walter
Sanders, George
Sargent, Dick
Savage, Ann
Sawyer, Joe
Schallert, William
Schaefer, Billy Kent
Scott, Douglas
Scott, Randolph
Scott, Zackary
Seabrook, Gay
Sebastian, Dorothy
Seel, Charles
Shahan, Rocky
Sheffield, Reginald
Shepard, Jan
Sherman, Fred
Sherwood, Gale
Shilling, Marion
Shoemaker, Ann
Short, Gertrude
Shumway, Lee
Sidney, Sylvia
Siegel, Bernard
Siletti, Mario
Silva, David
Simpson, Ivan F.
Simpson, Russell
Simon, Robert F.
Sinclair, Betty
Skipworth, Alison
Smith Alexis
Smith, Art
Smith, C. Aubrey
Smith, John
Sofaer, Abraham
Space, Arthur
Sparks, Ned
Stanwyck, Barbara
Starr, Ron
Starr, Sally
Starrett, Jack
Stedman, Myrtle

Steele, Bob
Stellar, Carolyn
Stepanek, Karel
Stephenson, Henry
Stephenson, James
Stephenson, John
Stevens, K.T.
Stevens, Mark
Stevens, Naomi
Stevens, Onslow
Stevenson, Hayden
Stevenson, Houseley
Stewart, Eleanor
Stewart, Janet
Stewrat, Peggy
Stine, Jan
Stockwell, Dean
Stone, Lewis
Stone, Milburn
St. Polis, John
Stroheim, Erich von
Stubbs, Chuck
Sullivan, Barry
Sully, Frank
Sutton, Grady
Sweet, Blanche

T

Talbott, Gloria
Talbot, Lyle
Taliaferro, Hal
Tamiroff, Akim
Tannen, Julius
Tannen, William
Tashman, Lilyan
Taylor, Dub
Tead, Phil
Teal, Ray
Temple, Shirley
Tenant, Dorothy
Tessier, Robert
Tetley, Walter
Thomas, Frank M.
Thompson, Dee J.
Thorpe, Jim
Thundercloud, Chief
Tilbury, Zeffie
Toomey, Regis
Toones, Fred 'Snowflake'
Travers, Henry
Treacher, Arthur
Treaties, Chief Many
Treen, Mary
Trevor, Claire
Triesault, Ivan
Tucker, Forrest
Tucker, Wayne
Tufts, Sonny
Tully, Tom

Turich, Felipe
Tynan, Brandon

U

Urecal, Minerva
Unger, Charles

V

Vallee, Rudy
Vandergrift, Monte
Van Sickel, Dale
Varconi, Victor
Vassar, Queenie
Vaughn, Hilda
Vaughn, Robert
Vigran, Herb
Vinson, Helen
Vinton, Arthur
Vitale, Joseph
Vogan, Emmett
Von Eltz, Theodore
Votrian, Peter
Vye, Murvyn

W

Wade, Russell
Wagenheim, Charles
Walcott, Gregory
Walker, Charlotte
Walker, Nella
Walker, Walter
Wallace, George
Walthall, Henry B.
Warner, H.B.
Warwick, Robert
Warren, Ruth
Washburn, Bryant
Washington, Mildred
Watkin, Pierre
Watson, Minor
Wayne, Patrick
Weaver, Doodles
Weaver, Marjorie
Weldon, Joan
Wells, Alan
Westerfield, James
Westley, Helen
Weston, Cecil

Weston, Ruth
Wexler, Yale
Whelan, Arleen
White, Dan
White, Huey
Whitehead, O.Z.
Whitmore, James
Whorf, David
Wilcox, Frank
Wilke, Robert
Willes, Jean
Williams, Adam
Williams, Guinn
Williams, Kathlyn
Williams, Robert
Williams, Rush
Willock, Dave
Wills, Chill
Wills, Henry
Wilson, Clarence
Windsor, Marie
Winninger, Charles
Winters, Shelley
Winton, Jane
Wolfe, Ian
Wolheim, Louis
Wooley, Sheb

Wood, Douglas
Wood, Judith
Wood, Ward
Wood, Wilson
Woods, Harry
Woodward, Morgan
Worden, Hank
Wray, Fay

Y

Yarbo, Lillian
Yazloff, Thomas Alan
York, Chick
York, Duke
Young, Clara Kimball
Young, Loretta
Young, Roland

Z

Zilzer, Wolfgang
Zynda, Henry

Joel McCrea's Filmography

1. 1927 *The Fair Co-Ed*
2. 1927 *The Enemy*
3. 1928 *Dead Man's Curve*
4. 1928 *Freedom of the Press*
5. 1928 *The Five O'Clock Girl*
6. 1929 *The Jazz Age*
7. 1929 *The Divine Lady*
8. 1929 *The Single Standard*
9. 1929 *So This is College*
10. 1929 *Dynamite*
11. 1930 *The Silver Horde*
12. 1930 *Lightnin'*
13. 1931 *Once a Sinner*
14. 1931 *Kept Husbands*
15. 1931 *Born to Love*
16. 1931 *The Commom Law*
17. 1931 *Girls About Town*
18. 1932 *Business and Pleasure*
19. 1932 *The Lost Squadron*
20. 1932 *Bird of Paradise*
21. 1932 *The Most Dangerous Game*
22. 1932 *The Sport Parade*
23. 1932 *Rockabye*
24. 1933 *The Silver Cord*
25. 1933 *Bed of Roses*
26. 1933 *One Man's Journey*
27. 1933 *Chance at Heaven*
28. 1934 *Gambling Lady*
29. 1934 *Half a Sinner*
30. 1934 *The Richest Girl in the World*
31. 1935 *Private Worlds*
32. 1935 *Our Little Girl*
33. 1935 *Woman Wanted*
34. 1935 *Barbary Coast*
35. 1935 *Splendor*
36. 1936 *These Three*
37. 1936 *Two in a Crowd*
38. 1936 *Adventure in Manhattan*
39. 1936 *Come and Get It*
40. 1936 *Banjo on My Knee*
41. 1937 *Internes Can't Take Money*
42. 1937 *Woman Chases Man*
43. 1937 *Dead End*
44. 1937 *Wells Fargo*
45. 1938 *Three Blind Mice*
46. 1938 *Youth Takes a Fling*
47. 1939 *Union Pacific*
48. 1939 *They Shall Have Music*
49. 1939 *Espionage Agent*
50. 1940 *He Married His Wife*
51. 1940 *Primrose Path*
52. 1940 *Foreign Correspondant*
53. 1941 *Reaching For the Sun*
54. 1941 *Sullivan's Travels*
55. 1942 *The Great Man's Lady*
56. 1942 *The Palm Beach Story*
57. 1943 *The More the Merrier*
58. 1944 *Buffalo Bill*
59. 1944 *The Great Moment*
60. 1945 *The Unseen*
61. 1946 *The Virginian*
62. 1947 *Ramrod*
63. 1948 *Four Faces West*
64. 1949 *South of St. Louis*
65. 1949 *Colorado Territory*
66. 1950 *The Outriders*
67. 1950 *Stars in My Crown*
68. 1950 *Saddle Tramp*
69. 1950 *Frenchie*
70. 1951 *Cattle Drive*
71. 1952 *The San Francisco Story*

72. 1953 *The Lone Hand*
73. 1953 *Shoot First*
74. 1954 *Border River*
75. 1954 *Black Horse Canyon*
76. 1955 *Stranger on Horseback*
77. 1955 *Wichita*
78. 1956 *The First Texan*
79. 1957 *The Oklahoman*
80. 1957 *Trooper Hook*

81. 1957 *Gunsight Ridge*
82. 1957 *The Tall Stranger*
83. 1958 *Cattle Empire*
84. 1958 *Fort Massacre*
85. 1959 *The Gunfight at Dodge City*
86. 1962 *Ride the High Country*
87. 1970 *Cry Blood, Apache*
88. 1976 *Mustang Country*

Joel McCrea's Television Episodes

Wichita Town television series

Episodes

1.	The Night the Cowboys Roared	09-30-59
2.	Wyndham's Way	10-07-59
3.	Bullet for a Friend	10-14-59
4.	They Won't Hang Jimmy Relson	10-21-59
5.	Drifting	10-28-59
6.	Man on the Hill	11-04-59
7.	Day of Battle	11-18-59
8.	Compadre	11-25-59
9.	Passage to the Enemy	12-02-59
10.	Out of the Past	12-09-59
11.	Death Watch	12-16-59
12.	The Devil's Choice	12-23-59
13.	Biggest Man in Town	12-30-59
14.	Ruby Dawes	01-06-60
15.	Bought	01-13-60
16.	The Long Night	01-20-60
17.	Seed of Hate	01-27-60
18.	The Avengers	02-03-60
19.	Brothers of the Knife	02-10-60
20.	Afternoon in Town	02-17-60
21.	The Frontiersman	03-02-60
22.	The Hanging Judge	03-09-60
23.	Second Chance	03-16-60
24.	Paid in Full	03-23-60
25.	The Legend of Tom Horn	03-30-60
26.	Sidekicks	04-06-60

Joel McCrea French Photonovels

The First Texan 1956

Trooper Hook 1957

The Oklahoman 1957

The Oklahoman 1957

The Tall Stranger 1957   Fort Massacre 1958

Fort Massacre 1958

Joel McCrea Biographies

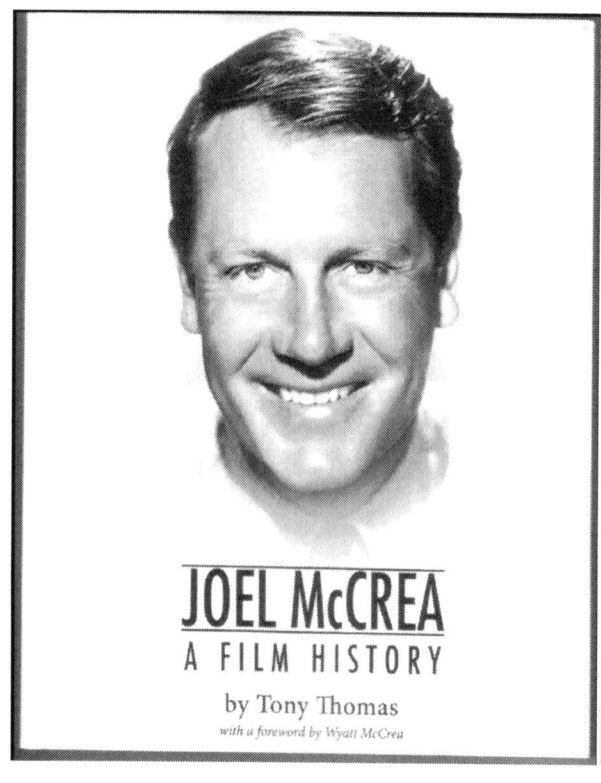

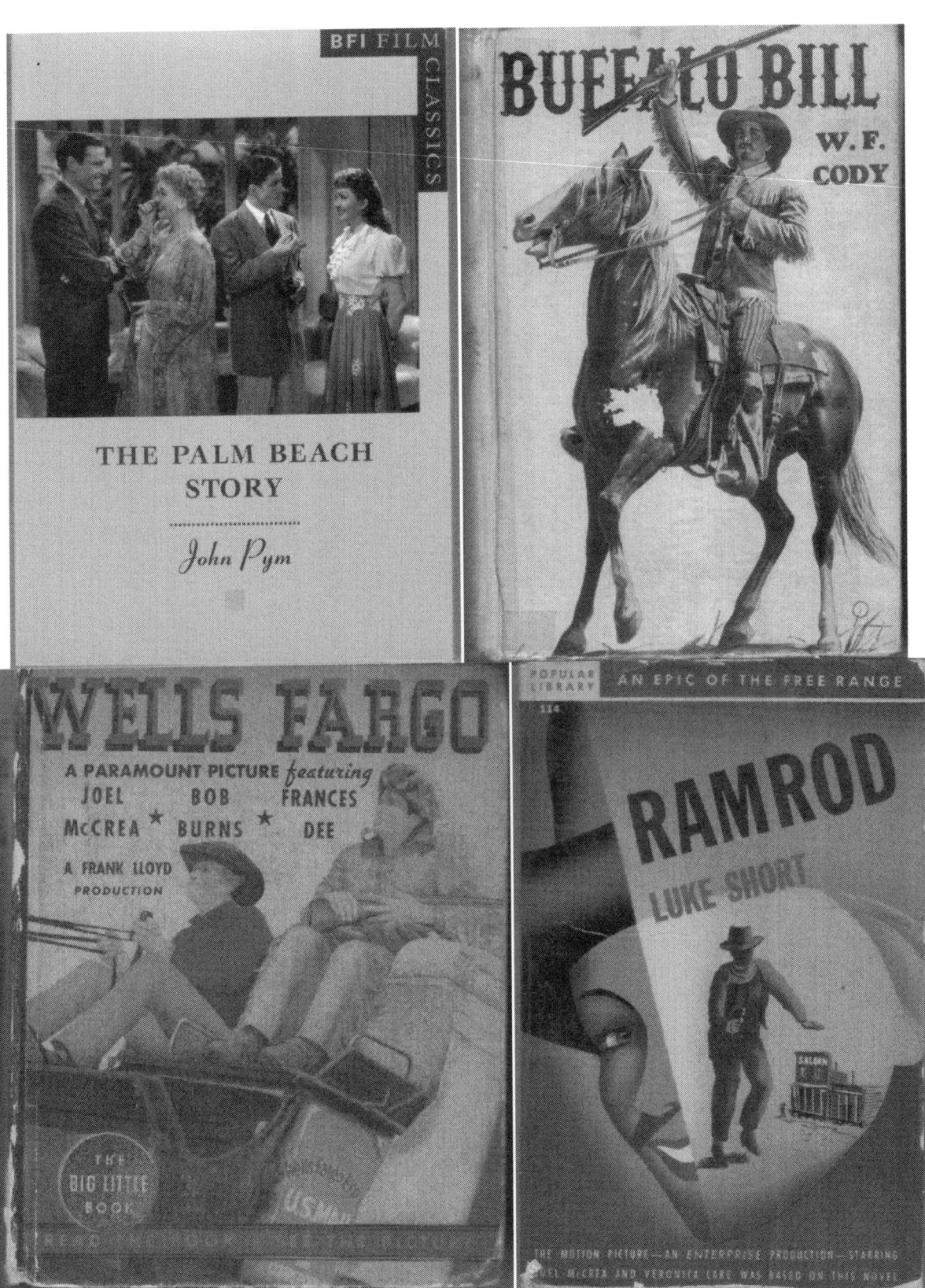

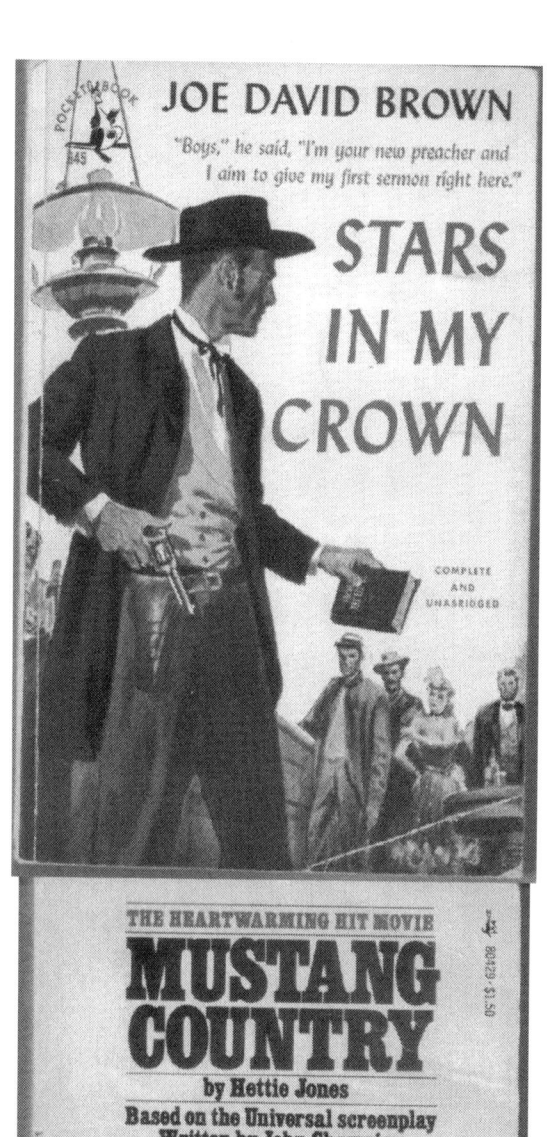

JOE DAVID BROWN

"Boys," he said, "I'm your new preacher and I aim to give my first sermon right here."

STARS IN MY CROWN

COMPLETE AND UNABRIDGED

THE HEARTWARMING HIT MOVIE

MUSTANG COUNTRY

by Hettie Jones

Based on the Universal screenplay Written by John Champion

Joel McCrea and Friends

(Not already in the book)

Joel McCrea with Audie Murphy

Joel McCrea with Gary Cooper

Joel McCrea with Katherine Hepburn

Joel McCrea with Dick Powell

Joel McCrea with John Wayne

About the Author

David Alan Williams was born in Iowa City and has traveled through thirty-four states and has lived in eleven of them, but currently lives with his wife of twenty-five years, four daughters, one grandchild, three cats, two dogs, and a Texas Loggerhead Snapping turtle in L.A. (Lower Arkansas). His wife Deborah is a math teacher at their local high school.

Printed in Great Britain
by Amazon.co.uk, Ltd.,
Marston Gate.